Andrew
With Best Regards

IRISH ARTS REVIEW

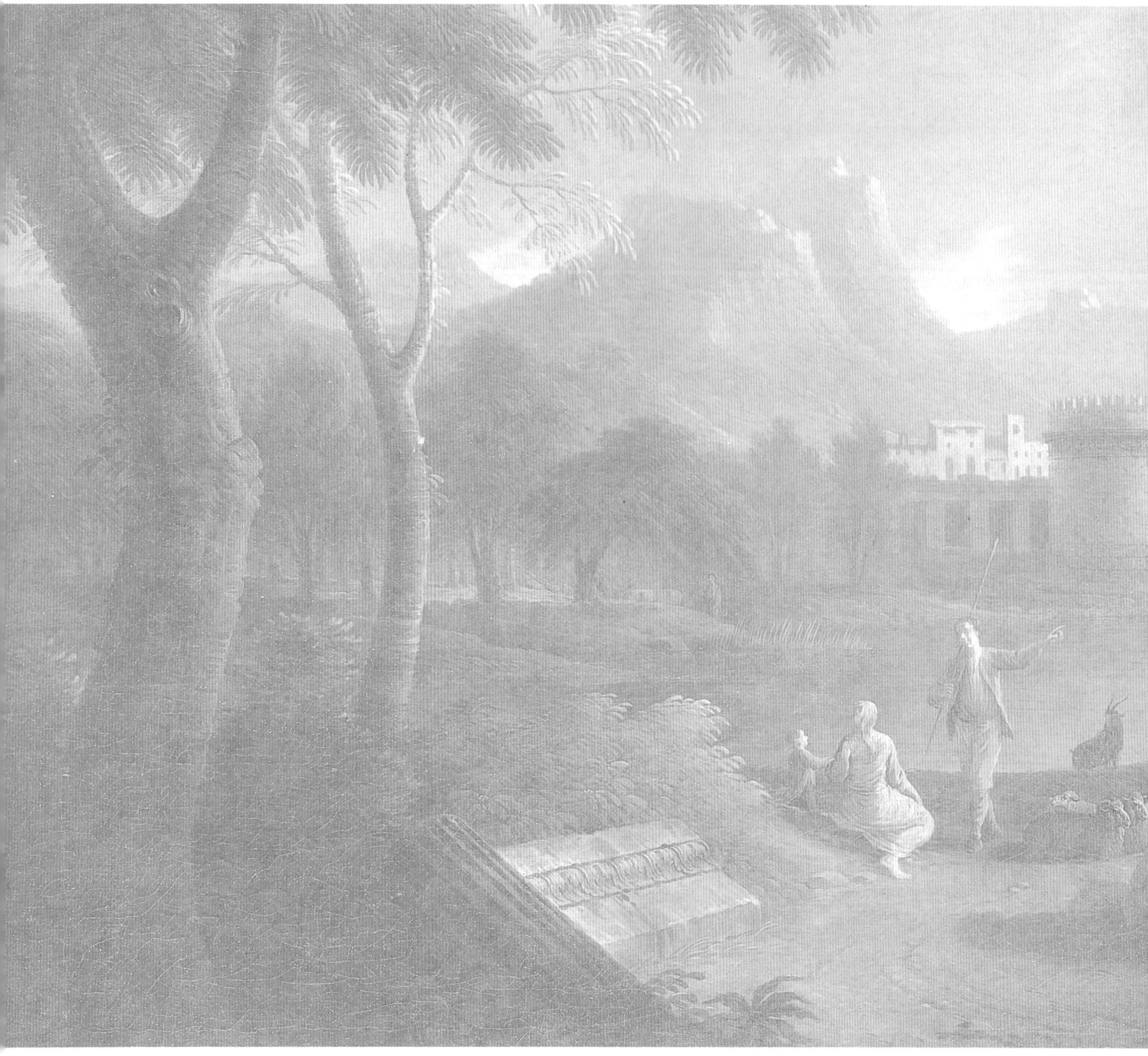

IRISH ARTS REVIEW

YEARBOOK 1994

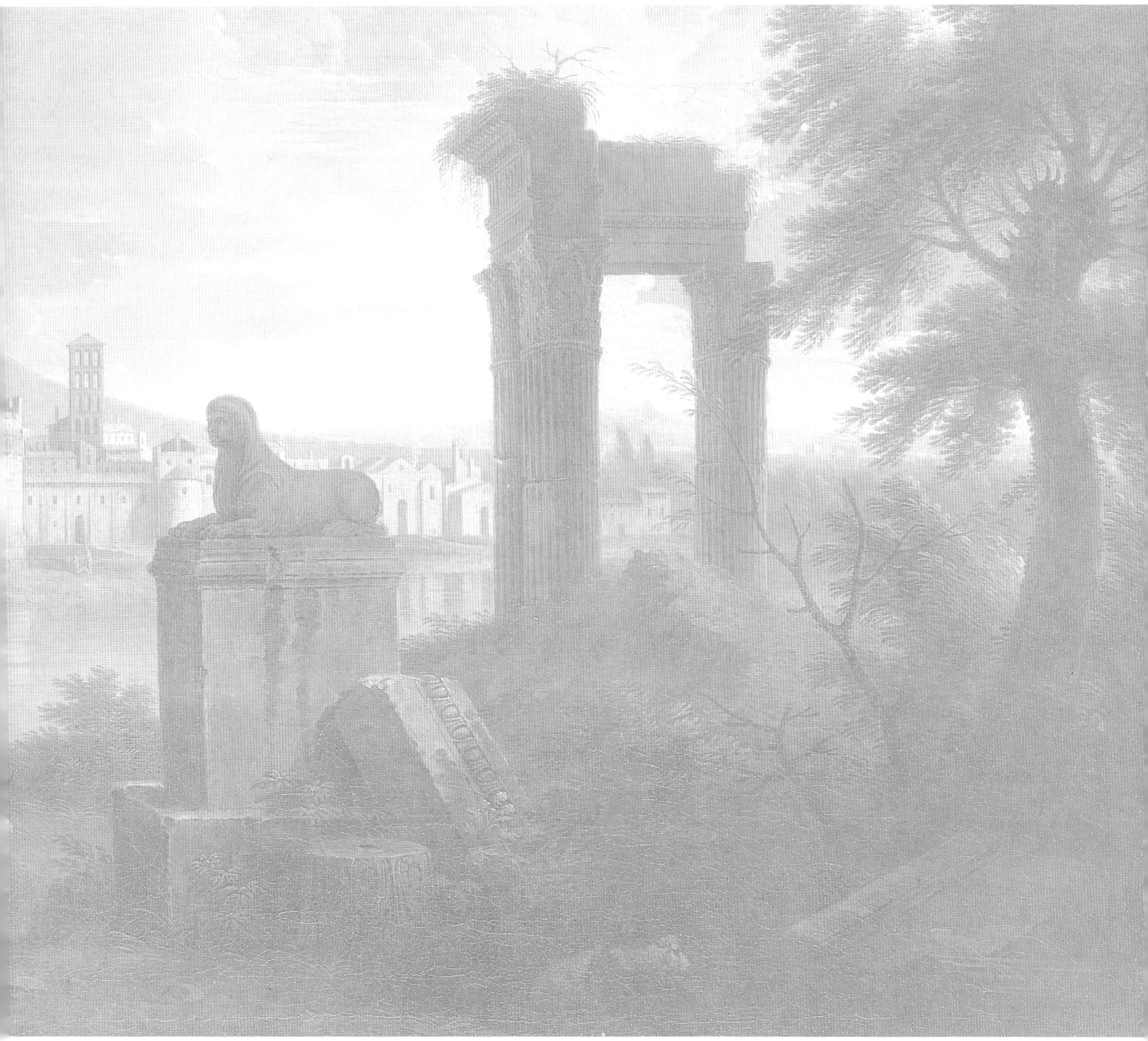

SPONSORED BY GPA

COVER ILLUSTRATION
Sean Scully, *Skerry*, 1992, oil on canvas, 91.4 x 76.2 cm.
Waddington Galleries, London.

TITLE PAGE ILLUSTRATION
Gabrielle Ricciardelli, *A Capriccio*. Oil on canvas laid on masonite, 100 x 134 cm.
Signed and dated 1757 (Christie's, New York).

Published for Ann Reihill by Eton Enterprises Limited, 22 Crofton Road, Dun Laoghaire, Co. Dublin, Ireland.

Irish Arts Review is sponsored by GPA Group plc, Shannon, Ireland.
The publishers also received a grant from the Arts Council of Northern Ireland, a grant from the Arts Council/An Chomhairle Ealaion and assistance from the Cultural Relations Committee of the Department of Foreign Affairs, Dublin.

ISBN0 – 9513722 – 8 – 9 (hardback) 0 – 9513722 – 9 – 7 (softback) ISSN 0791 – 3540

Editor: Alistair Smith. *Assistant Editor:* Elizabeth Mayes. *Managing Director:* Ann Reihill.
Advertising Manager: Vera Finnegan. *Administrator:* Anne Skelly.

Office: Irish Arts Review, 22 Crofton Road, Dun Laoghaire, Co. Dublin, Ireland.
Telephone 01-2808415, Fax 01-2808309.

Design: Q Design, 4 Strand Road, Sandymount, Dublin 4. Telephone 01-2839336

Typeset by Pat Brennan.

Printed in Singapore by C S Graphics Private Limited.

CONTENTS

IRISH ARTS REVIEW 1994 VOLUME 10

Foreword

GPA is happy to support the 1994 edition of Irish Arts Review and to continue an association dating back to 1986. The Review is firmly established as an authoritative and distinctive chronicle of events and trends in the visual arts in Ireland and the current edition maintains the high standards of content and presentation set by its predecessors.

This is the last edition of the Review to be published under the editorial guidance of Alistair Smith. We extend our compliments and our appreciation to him for his excellent contribution over the past four years. We wish Homan Potterton well as his successor and commend to him the objective of extending and deepening the already considerable influence of the Review.

T A Ryan
EXECUTIVE CHAIRMAN
GPA GROUP PLC

PREFACE

The *Irish Arts Review* celebrates its tenth anniversary this year. It began life in 1984 as a quarterly publication; the product of Brian de Breffny's enthusiasm for, and knowledge of, all things Irish. It has now defined and developed its character as the familiar *Yearbook*, and the fact that this has been achieved in years of financial stringency is tribute to its supporters. Primary among these is our major sponsor, GPA, but help received from the Arts Council of Northern Ireland, the Arts Council/An Chomhairle Ealaoin and the Department of Foreign Affairs is also crucial; the deep interest of these bodies in the *Yearbook* is as much a contribution to its well-being as the financial help which they give. Equally fundamental to the purpose of the *Yearbook* are those who form it – the authors, Editorial Board, staff, Managing Director, and all those friends and acquaintances who have drawn my attention to an artist worth featuring, a theme worth investigating, an exhibition or book to be reviewed. To all these, I am deeply grateful.

When I was first invited to involve myself with the *Review* in early 1989, I felt in need of a change of direction, a fresh challenge. Seeing Brian de Breffny's last edition through the press, and editing four successive years of the *Review* have certainly provided that. Being what is often described as 'non-Irish', I first undertook to assess objectively whether it might be wise to broaden the scope of the journal, concentrating more on the art of other countries and events abroad. It took only a little time or me to be convinced that the vigour of artistic practice and of the intensity of artistic debate in Ireland is such that the *Yearbook* could best serve its public by focussing ever more tightly on Ireland. Consequently, we have published articles on 'non-Irish' art only when it is interpreted by an Irish critic or scholar, as in this edition by Dorothy Walker, who reviews exhibitions of Matisse and Manessier, and David Scott who analyses Paul Delvaux.

In my view, this focussed policy has produced a journal which makes an increasingly significant contribution tothe dissemination of the Irish visual arts, both of the past and of the present.

If this editorial has a retrospective tone, there is a reason for it. This is my last year as Editor, and it is natural to cast an eye over the volumes on the shelf, and over the principal artistic events in Ireland during the past four or five years. They have been important years, with the creation of the Irish Museum of Modern Art, the continuing refurbishment and development of the National Gallery, and Dublin as Cultural Capital. Other, less public events which exemplify the strength of art-historical commitment, were the important Book of Kells conference (still reverberating, as Roger Stalley and Susanne McNab describe in this volume) and the location of the conference of the Association of Art Historians in Dublin. As we might expect, art itself has altered, the terms 'installation' and 'site-specific' now being household words; and the administration of the arts is changing its tone, with six new Directors in charge of the main Dublin institutions. They kindly agreed to be interviewed for this volume.

The *Yearbook* is now poised to move on to a different scale of ambition. To do this, it needs an Editor with a more detailed knowledge of Irish art and, more important, someone who will have sufficient time to devote to it. I am grateful to have been associated with a vital, developing publication and to be passing it on to the caring hands of my friend and former colleague, Homan Potterton, who I know will be welcomed by all those who have supported me in my years as Editor. In his hands, the *Review* will go from strength to strength. I wish him, and his colleagues, every success.

ALISTAIR SMITH
EDITOR

Arts Council

Awards to Visual Artists

Central to the role of the Arts Council is its strong commitment to the individual creative artist in Irish society. The awards described here are available to individuals in recognition of their achievements and to assist them in the pursuit of their art. A detailed brochure is available from the Arts Council outlining all the awards offered to individuals.

Bursaries *Closing Date: Friday 15th April 1994*

Bursaries from £1,000-£5,000 are made available for major work projects (limited number of post-graduate scholarships to colleges abroad).

Materials/Equipment/Documentation Grants *Closing Dates: Friday 11th March, 30th September 1994.*

Grants up to £500 are available for purchase of materials and production of basic catalogues about artist's work.

PS1 Studios, New York. *Closing date: Friday 4th March 1994.*

Together with the Arts Council of Northern Ireland and in association with the Ireland-America Arts Exchange, the Arts Council offers two annual fellowships - one to a resident or citizen of Northern Ireland and one to an artist born or resident in the Republic. A year's studio space is provided at the Institute for Art and Urban Resources at PS1, New York, along with accommodation and a monthly stipend. Final selection is made by a PS1 jury in New York in April. A detailed information sheet is available upon request.

Studio Grants to Groups/Co-operatives *Closing Date: Friday 11th March 1994*

A small budget will be made available in 1994 to groups who are establishing themselves in long-term studio spaces. Maximum grant available £500.

Travel Awards to Creative Artists *Closing Dates: 11th Feb, 13th May, 16th Sept, 11th Nov 1994*

Awards are granted to artists who wish to travel abroad to pursue their artistic careers: research projects and participation in exchanges and symposia are regularly funded (maximum value, £750).

The Macaulay Fellowship *Closing Date: 15th April 1994*

This award was established by W.B. Macaulay in honour of President Sean T. O'Kelly and is awarded on a rotating basis in visual arts, music and literature. Valued at £4,000 it is awarded to further the liberal education of young creative artists. Applicants must be under 30 years of age in the year of application (or 35 years of age in exceptional circumstances) and must have been born in Ireland. This award is offered in music in 1995 and literature in 1996.

George Campbell Memorial Travel Award *Closing Date: 1st April 1994*

This annual award of £1,000 instituted to celebrate the strong cultural contact which Irish artist George Campbell developed with Spain, is offered by the Arts Council/An Chomhairle Ealaíon, the Arts Council of Northern Ireland and the Spanish Cultural Institute. It is made specifically to allow for a period of work in Spain. The award is open to artists from the Republic in 1994.

Artflight - Arts Council/Aer Lingus Travel Awards

Creative and interpretative artists in all fields as well as administrators may apply for an award to fly return, ex-Ireland, to most destinations on the Aer Lingus network. In co-operation with the Arts Council of Northern Ireland, Artflight awards are also available to Northern Ireland residents. All letters of application, including c.v. and visual documentation should be made to the Arts Council/An Chomhairle Ealaíon. Full details are given on a special "Artflight" brochure.

For further information, contact: The Visual Arts Officer, The Arts Council, 70 Merrion Square, Dublin 2. Tel: (01) 661 1840 Fax: (01) 676 1302

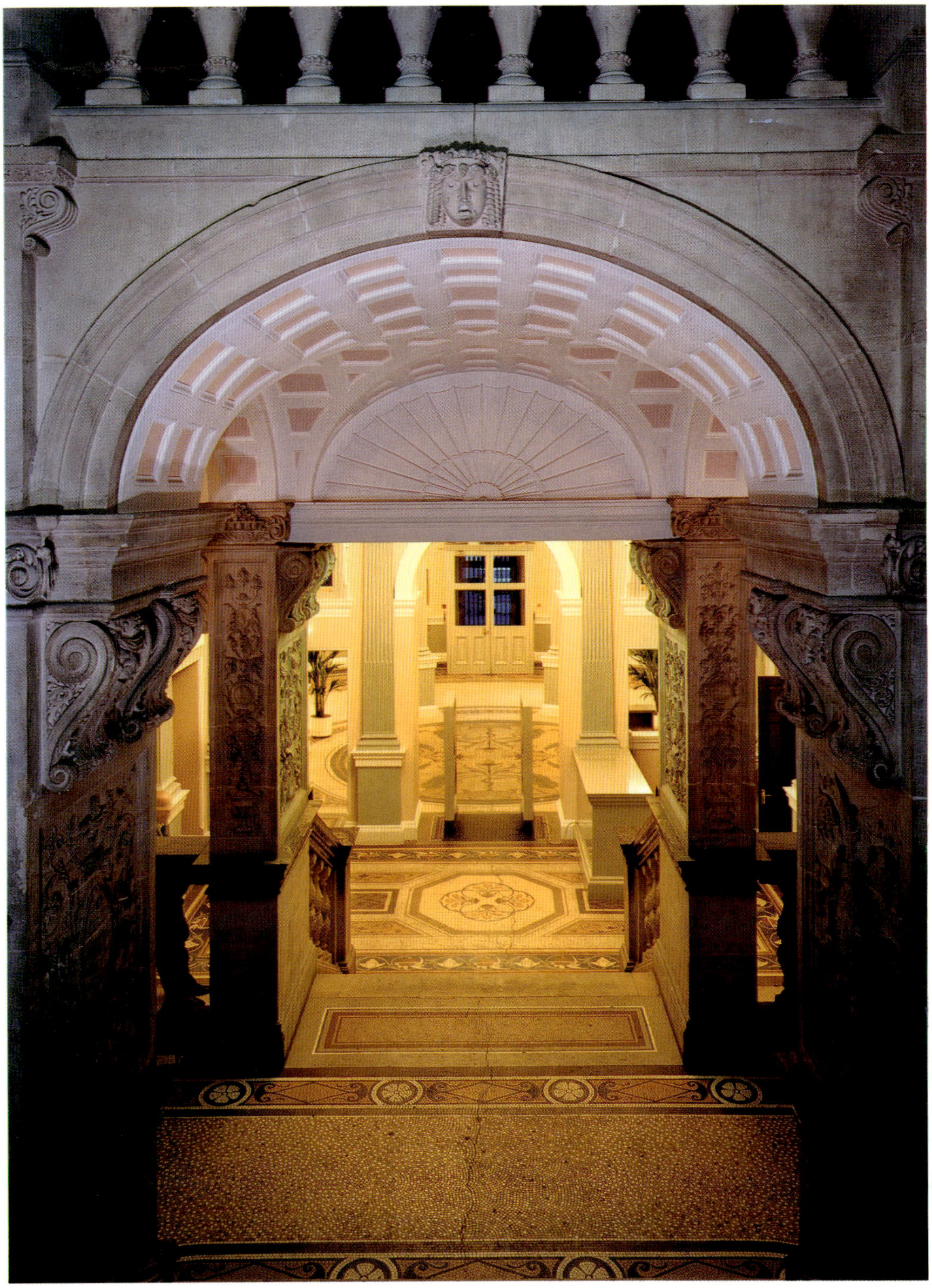

NATIONAL LIBRARY of IRELAND

National Library of Ireland

LEABHARLANN NÁISIÚNTA na hÉIREANN

KILDARE STREET,

DUBLIN 2.

Photo: Peter Moloney

Courtesy of: Norton Associates

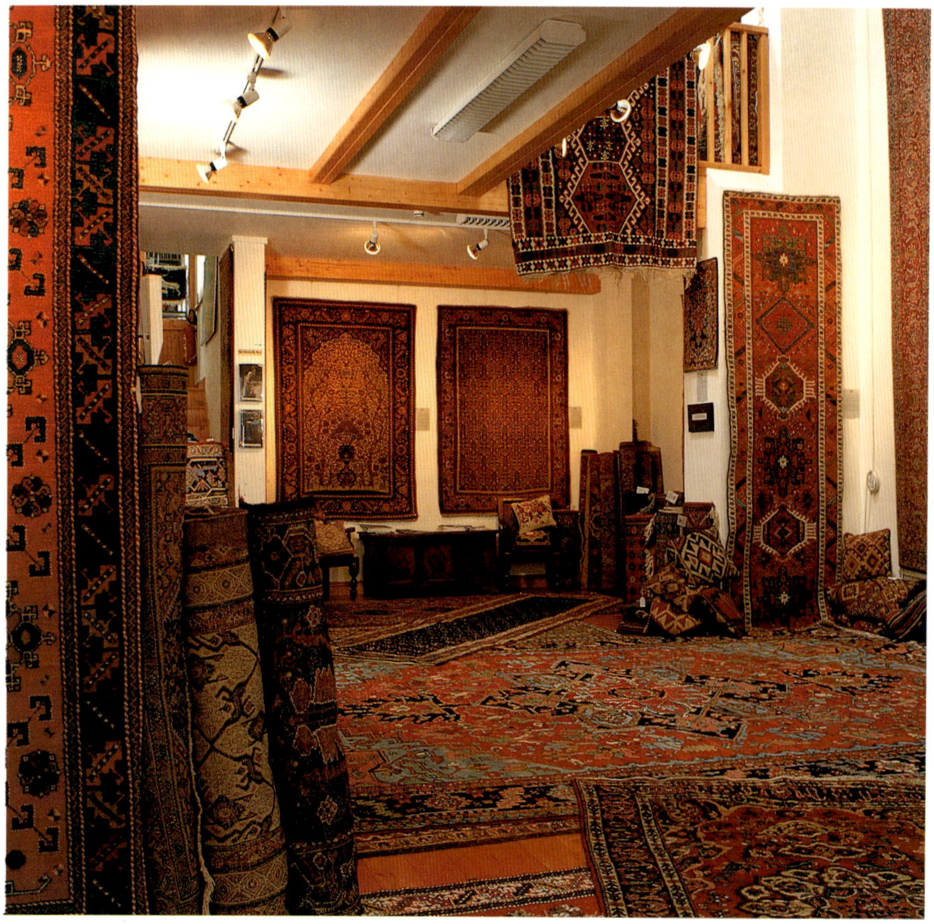

PETER LINDEN

IRELAND'S MAIN DEALER IN ANTIQUE & MODERN RUGS CARPETS, RUNNERS, KILIMS & TRIBAL WEAVINGS

NOW OPEN IN SPACIOUS NEW PREMISES

Open Monday-Saturday 10.00-5.30
or by appointment

15 GEORGE'S AVENUE
(OFF MAIN ST.)
BLACKROCK, CO. DUBLIN.
TELEPHONE 2885875.
FAX 2835616.

THE KIRK *Gallery*

CONTEMPORARY IRISH & EUROPEAN PAINTINGS, FINE PERIOD FURNITURE, RARE MAPS, PRINTS & THE APPLIED ARTS

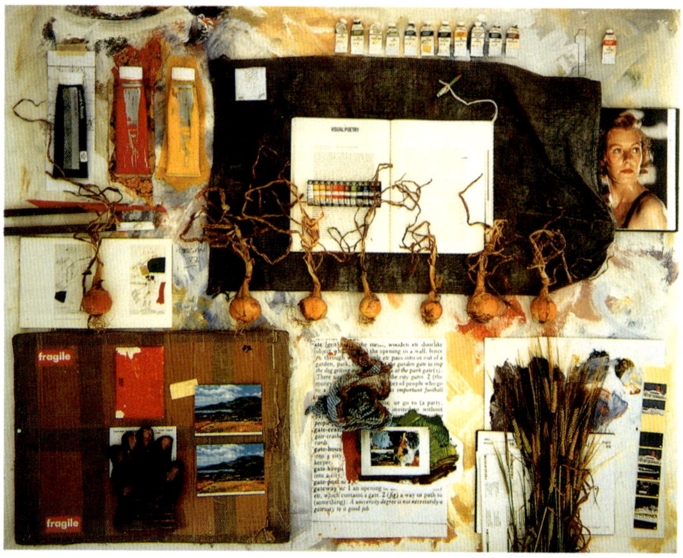

Thinking to some purpose. A dream must be a dream (Ciba Chrome) Peter Morgan

THE KIRK GALLERY, LR. CHARLES STREET, CASTLEBAR, CO. MAYO. TELEPHONE: 094-22452. FAX: 094-21127

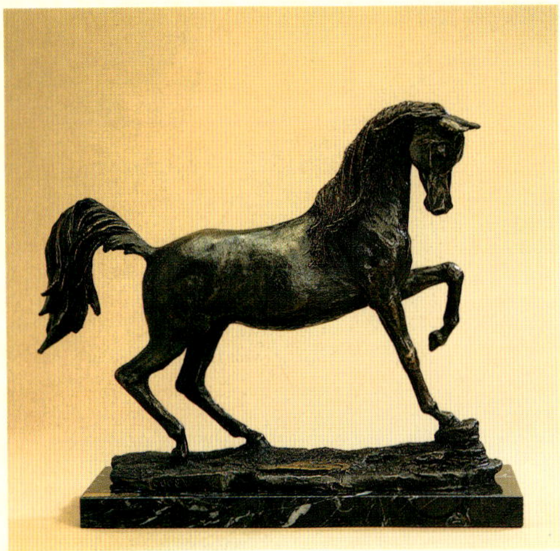

The Noble Steed
In beautifully patinated cold cast bronze, mounted on a black and white marble base, this horse is one of a range of four studies signed by the Spanish sculptor.
10"H x 11$^{1}/_{2}$"L. Price: £230.

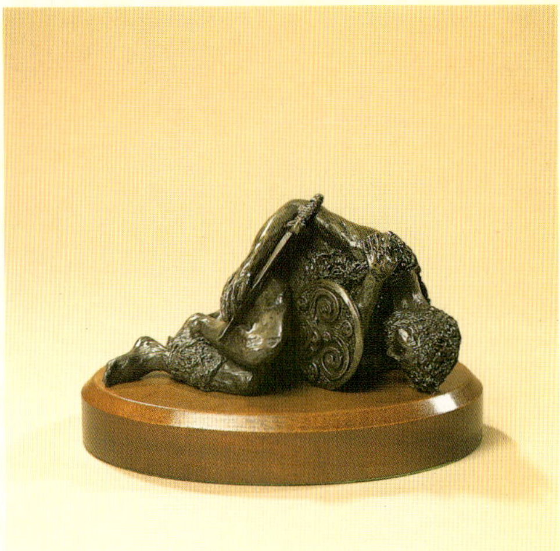

Hugh, King of Connacht
"All that we saw was his shadow under his shield" Mortally wounded, lying beneath his ornamented shield, his sword clasped under his arm, this poignant study portrays in death another great Irish legend. 4$^{3}/_{4}$"H x 8"L on polished mahogany. Price £150.

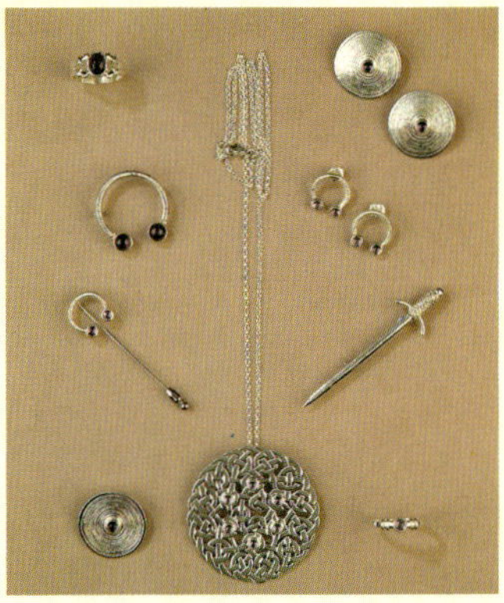

Traditional designs from old Irish manuscripts updated in Irish silver and decorated with amethysts or peridots.

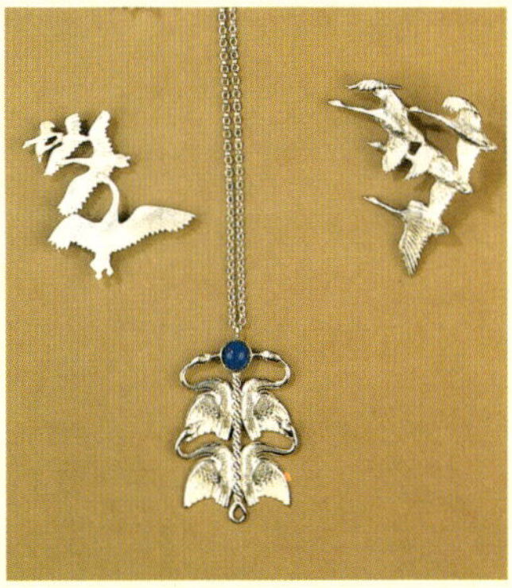

Children of Lir range of jewellery, consisting of two brooches, and one pendant, all are set in Irish silver. The pendant is set with a blue agate to represent the lakes in Ireland over which the swans flew.

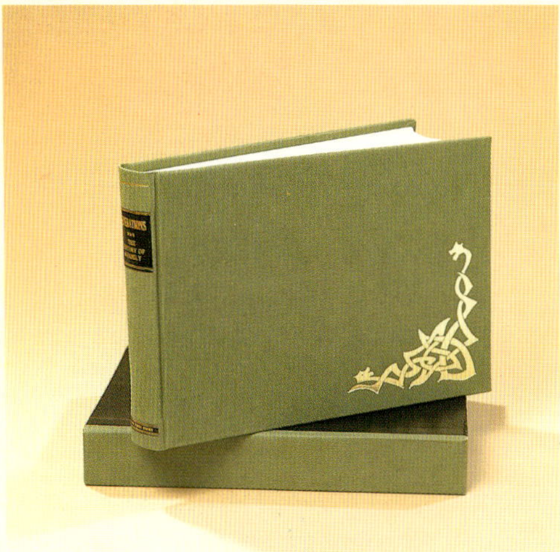

Generations: The History of a Family
This book answers the need for one place to record details of your own family history. Divided into sections with extra pages for a larger family, there is a section for special photographs and a pocket for small certificates. In hard cover, this book, size 9$^{1}/_{2}$" x 7" x 1$^{1}/_{2}$", has an olive green cloth binding with foil blocked gold celtic ornament, and comes in a black and olive green slip case. An Irish Times Book, price £35.

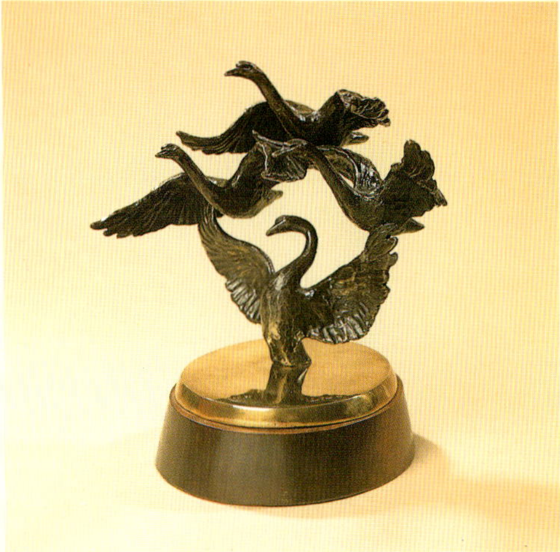

The Children of Lir
This pure bronze sculpture represents the best loved of Ireland's legends. The Children of King Lir, Aodh, Fiachra, Conn and Fionnuala were changed into swans to fly over the lakes of Moyle and Derravaragh until the coming of Christianity to Ireland. They retained the ability to speak and sing sweet music. This signed edition limited to 100 pieces is mounted on mahogany. 8"H x 4$^{1}/_{2}$"L. Price £250.

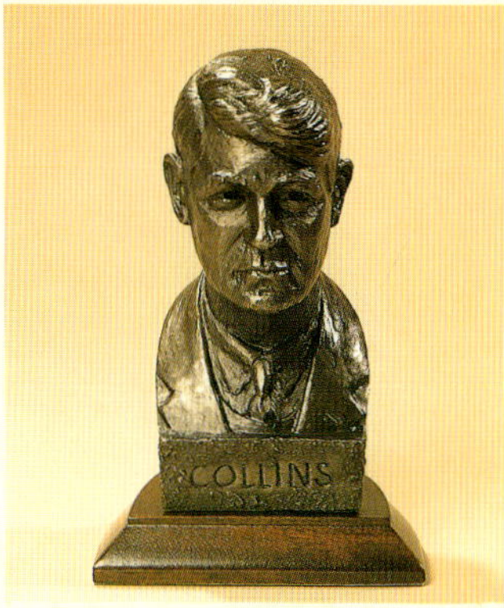

Michael Collins 1890 - 1922
To celebrate the life of Michael Collins this cold cast bronze has been taken from an original study commissioned from one of Ireland's leading portrait sculptors and offered under licence exclusively by The Irish Times Collection. 7$^{1}/_{2}$"H on a mahogany base. Price £85.

The Irish Times Collection specialises in portraying Irish legends in bronze and silver: political, historical and cultural figures in bronze; the horse, rugby, golf and sporting figures. Private and corporate commissions undertaken. Please write for details. 1993 colour catalogue now available.

THE IRISH TIMES

C·O·L·L·E·C·T·I·O·N **16 D'Olier Street Dublin 2 Ireland Tel: 01-6792022 Fax: 01-6797991**

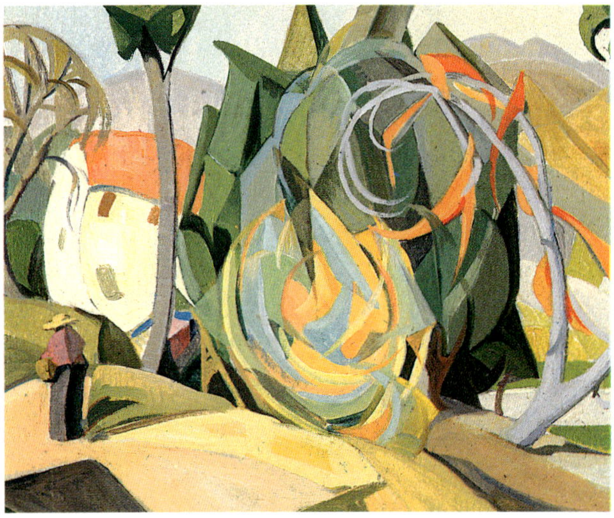

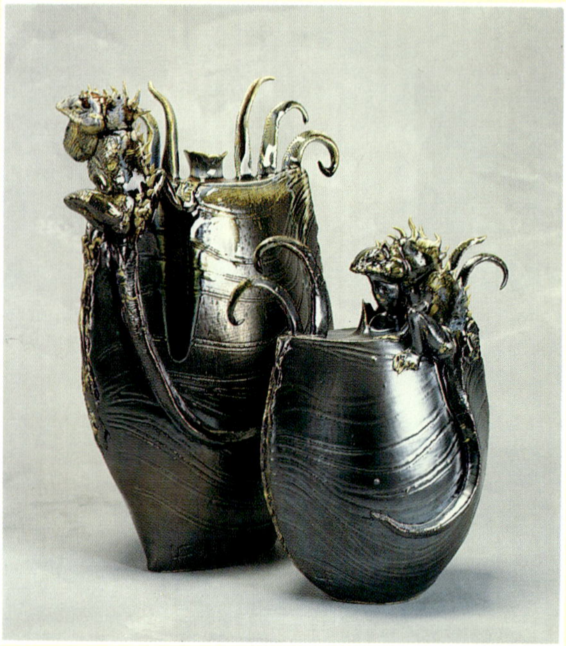

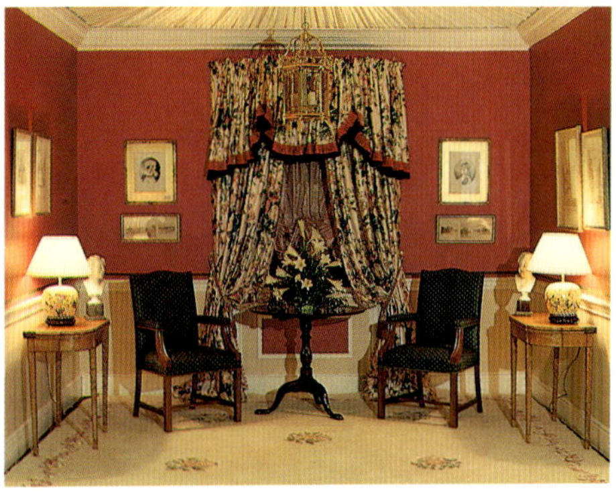

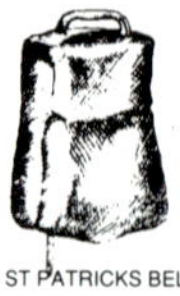

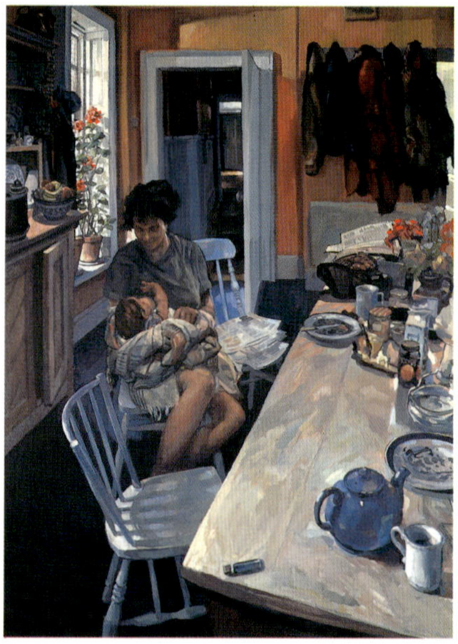

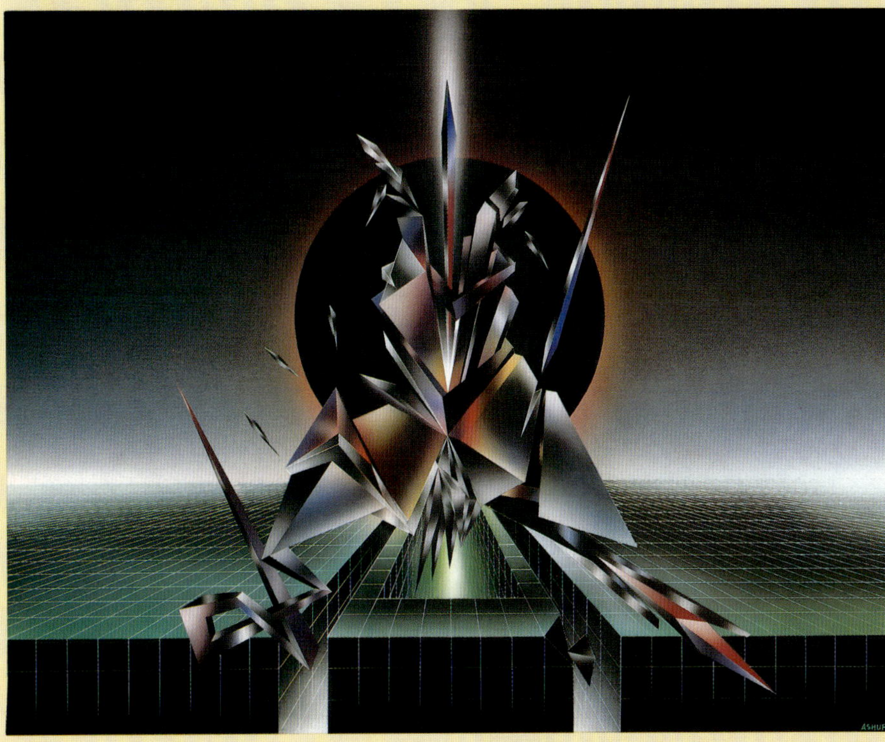
ASHUR

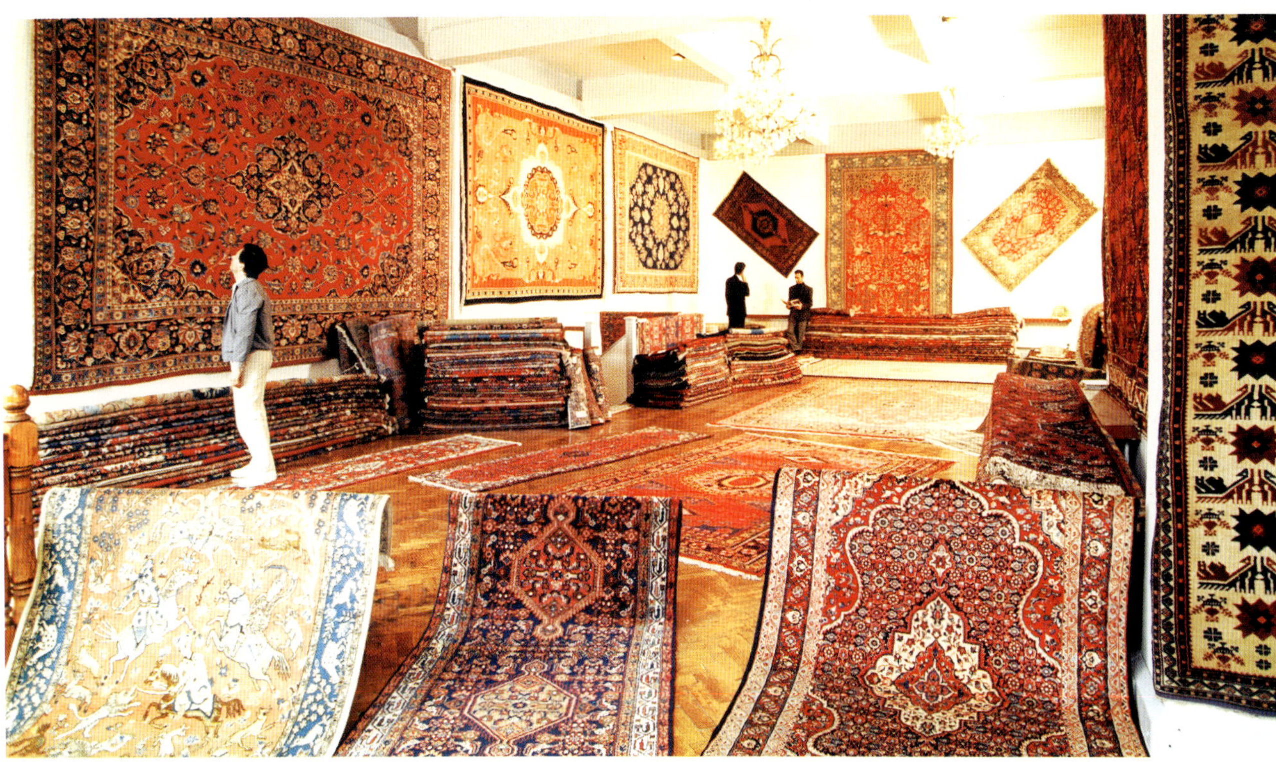

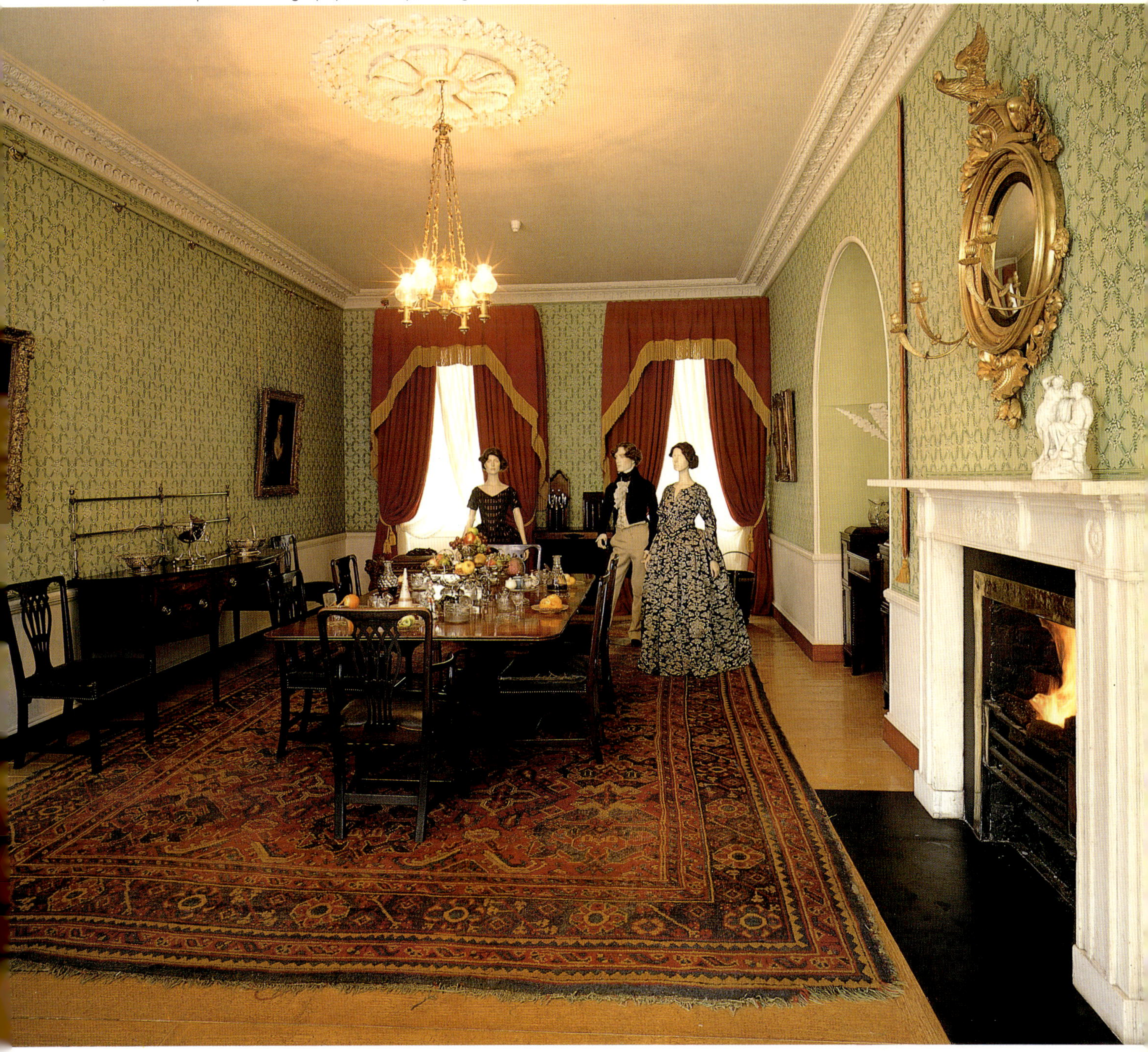

HUGH LANE MUNICIPAL GALLERY OF MODERN ART

Charlemont House, Parnell Square North, Dublin 1

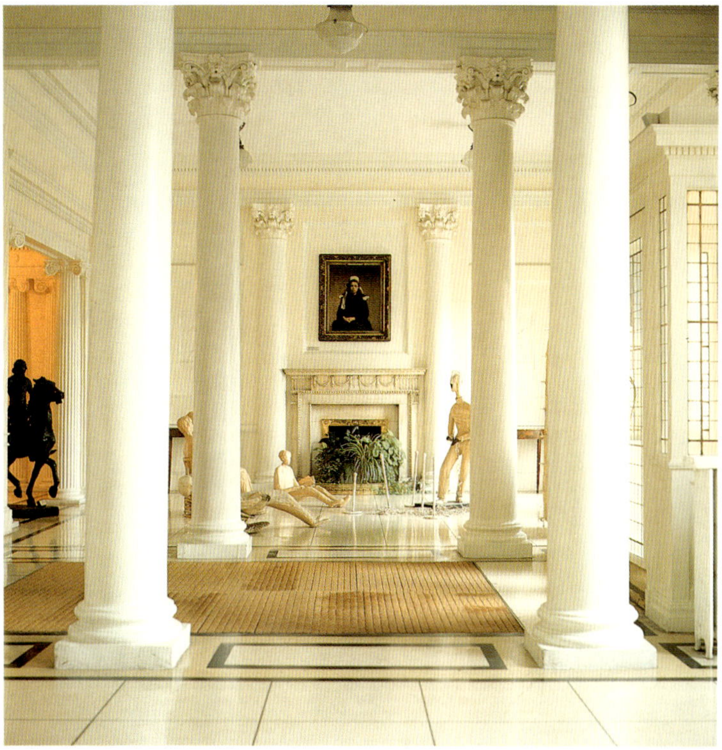

View of front hall with Breton girl by Roderic O'Conor and environment by Deborah Brown

Gallery Hours:
Tuesday to Friday 9.30-6pm
Saturday 9.30-5pm
Sunday 11.00-5pm

Forthcoming publication - November 1993
Hugh Lane Municipal Gallery of Modern Art
hardback and paperback with
over 100 colour illustrations

Concerts
Sundays at noon

Lectures:
Sundays at 2pm

Please check with reception for programme details
Self service restaurant and bookshop open within
Gallery Hours
Telephone: (01) 674 1903. Fax: (01) 672 2182
Admission free to all events

THE CRAWFORD MUNICIPAL ART GALLERY CORK

Located at Emmet Place, beside the Opera House, in the heart of the city.
Tel: 021 273377 Fax: 021 275680

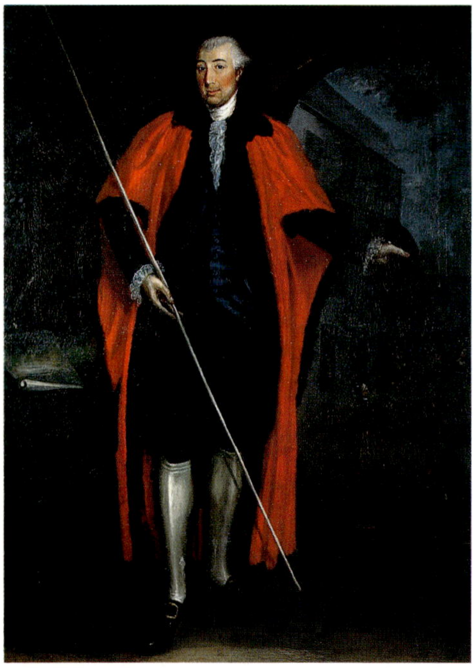

A recently restored portrait of Hugh Trayer Lawton, Mayor of Cork in 1776

Hugh Lawton was a prominent figure in 18th century Cork society, a partner in the trading and banking firm Calwell, Lawton and Carleton. He became sheriff of the city in 1767 and Mayor in 1776. During his mayoralty, the House of Industry in Cork was founded to rehabilitate those unfortunate enough to be reduced to begging in the streets. This portrait of Lawton, which hung for many years in the County Home (or workhouse) in Cork, shows the new House of Industry in the background, with inmates engaged in spinning and other productive pastimes. The Mayor holds a scroll, signed with his own name and dated 1776.

The restoration of this fine eighteenth century Irish portrait has been part-sponsored by the deputy Mayor of Bordeaux, Daniel Lawton, a descendant of Cork's mayor of 1776. Lawton Frères are prominent wine négociants in Bordeaux today and the Crawford Gallery is delighted to be able to highlight their historic connection with Ireland.

This important painting and many other fine works of art may be seen in the Crawford Municipal Art Gallery, located in the heart of Cork city adjacent to the Opera House and open to the public Monday through Saturday. The Gallery restaurant, run by Ballymaloe House, is excellent and, needless to say, can provide some fine Lawton Bordeaux wines.

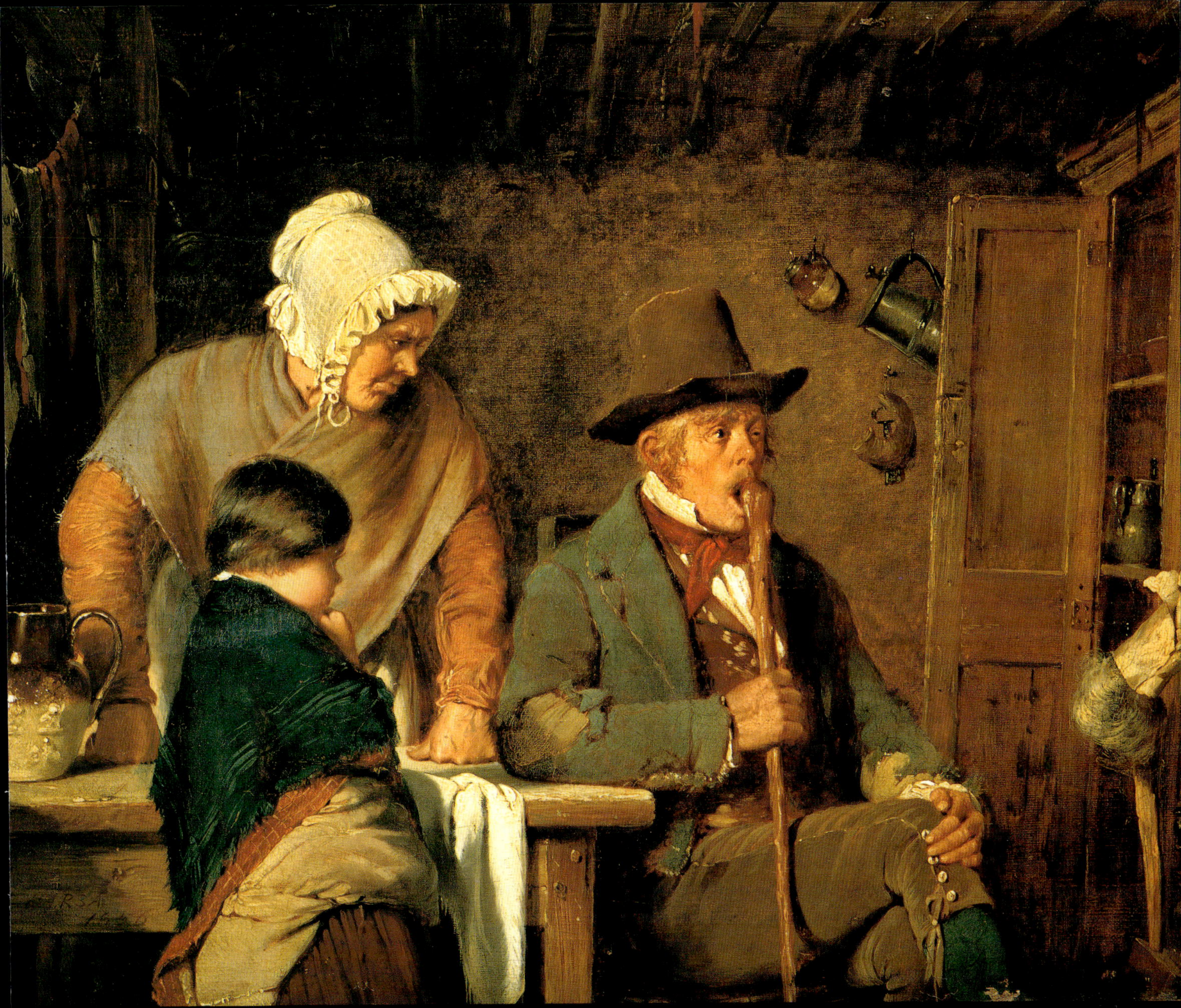

" A crow to pluck" Erskine Nicol (1825-1904)

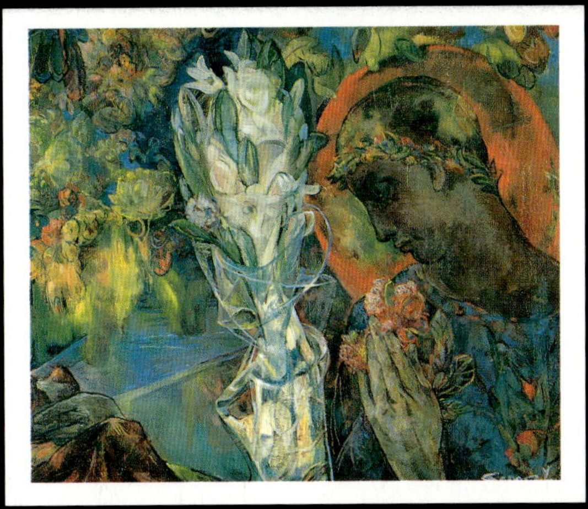

Allegorical Figure. Mary Swanzy (1882-1978)

NEWPORT HOUSE

NEWPORT • CO. MAYO • IRELAND

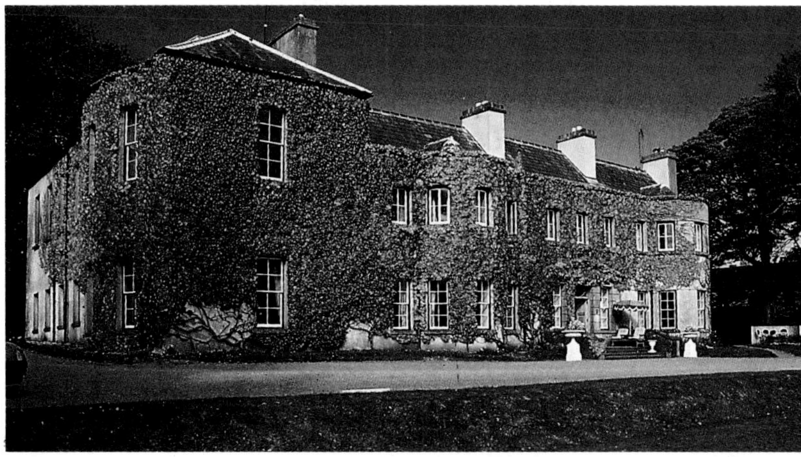

Famous as an angling centre, Newport House offers preserved salmon and sea trout fishing on the Newport River and Lough Beltra West. This historic house provides hospitality and comfort in an elegant setting, a cuisine based on fresh produce and a comprehensive wine cellar.

Member of the Relais & Chateaux and the I.C.H.R.A.

TELEPHONE (098) 41222 FAX (098) 41613

SLIGO ART GALLERY

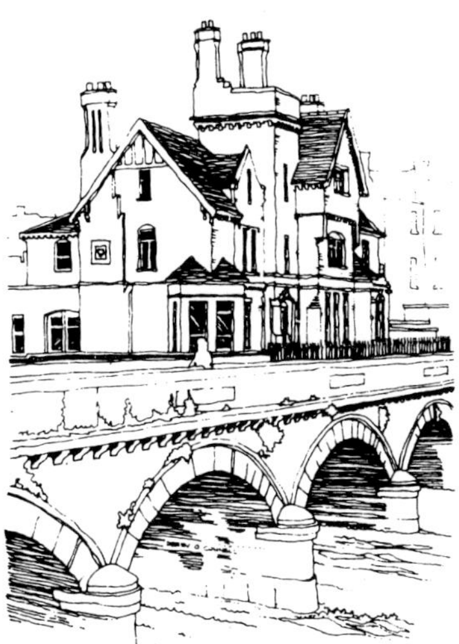

Organisers of Iontas Small Works Art Competition and Exhibition, in addition to a comprehensive programme of exhibitions and artistic events throughout the year.

Yeats Memorial Building
Hyde Bridge, Sligo
Telephone 071-45847
Fax 071-42780
Grant-aided by the Arts Council

THE GLEBE HOUSE AND GALLERY

Church Hill, Co. Donegal
The Derek Hill Collection

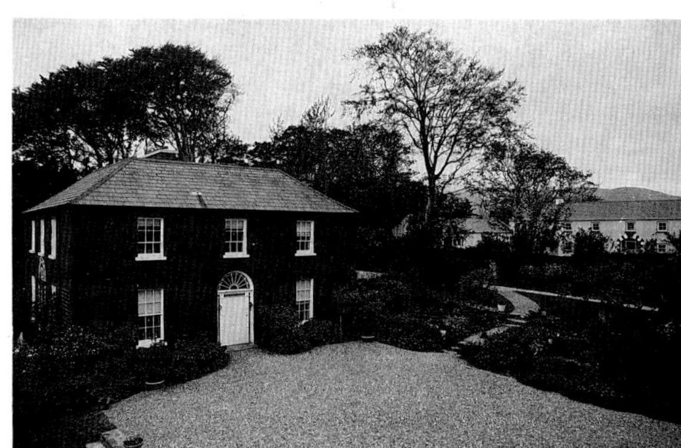

A beautifully located Regency house containing a magnificent collection of ceramics, glass, papers and textiles by William Morris, Islamic and Japanese art, and over 300 paintings and drawings by leading 20th century artists – Picasso, Kokoshka, Bonnard, Morandi,and Jack Yeats.

Open each year: Easter Saturday – following Sunday.
End of May – end of September.
Opening hours: Daily 11-6.30; Sun. 1-6.30; Closed Fri. Last tour of the House is at 5.30.

Telephone 074-37071

THE OFFICE OF PUBLIC WORKS

Connemara National Park
an experience not to be missed!

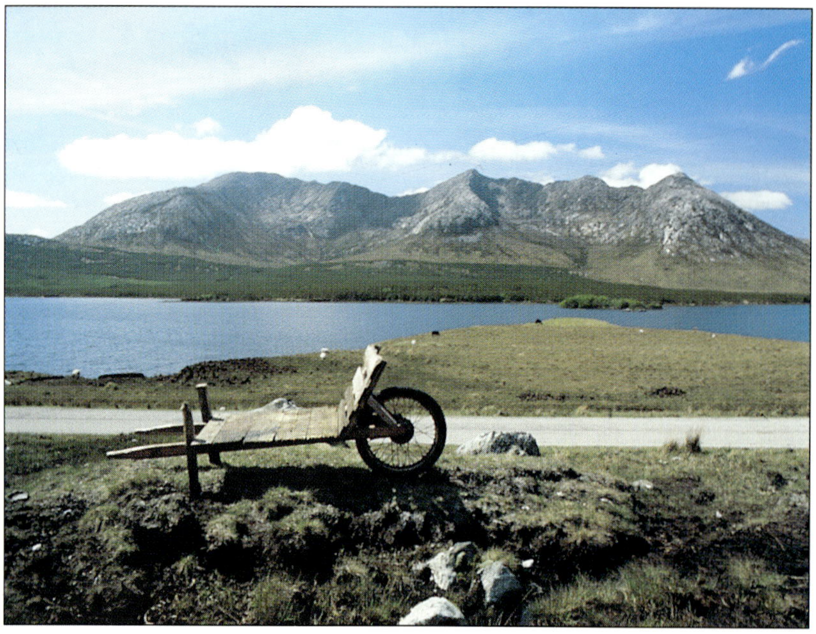

Two thousand hectares of ruggedly spectacular countryside ... the famous Twelve Bens mountain range ... huge expanses of grasslands and bogs ... rivers, waterfalls ... a myriad of flora and fauna ... Connemara National Park has it all!

A tour of the West simply wouldn't be complete without a visit to the Park. While you're there make sure you call in to the new Visitor Centre at Letterfrack, it will help you experience the Park to the full.

Connemara National Park is just one of the many areas around the country which are looked after by the Office of Public Works. It's all part of our work in protecting our national heritage - a heritage that is yours to experience and enjoy.

OPW

Oifig na nOibreacha Poiblí
The Office of Public Works

CLANCY CHANDELIERS

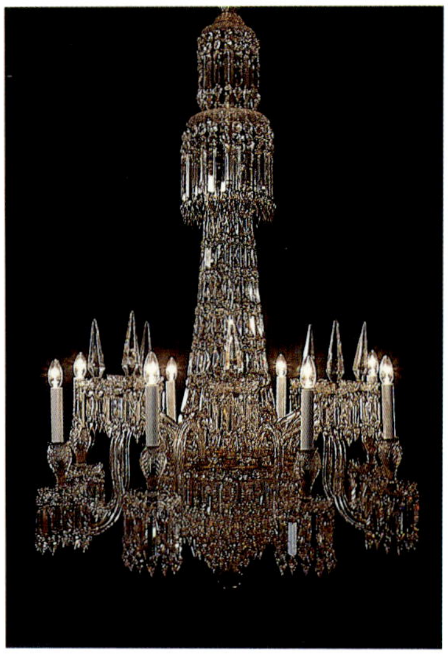

Original Irish Cut Glass Chandelier Circa 1830
Size 66 inches × 42 inches

Period and Reproduction Chandeliers
Bought and Sold

Professional Cleaning, Restoration
and Hanging Service

"VILLANOVA", BALLYWALTRIM, BRAY,
CO. WICKLOW
TELEPHONE 2863460

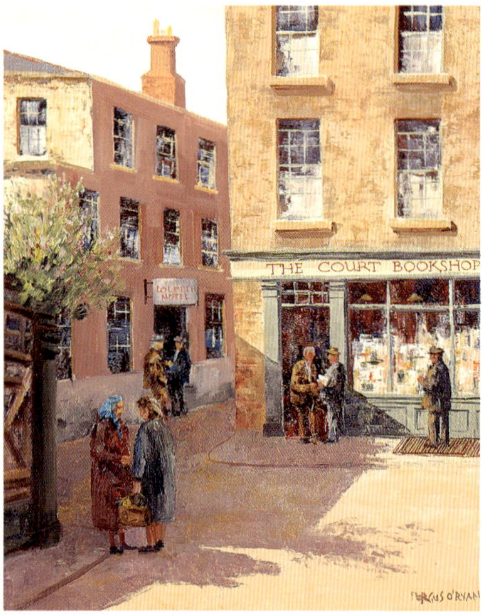

Crampton Court by Fergus O'Ryan RHA

COMBRIDGE FINE ARTS LTD

FINE ART
TRADE GUILD
Member of the
Fine Art Trade Guild

GAINSBORO HOUSE
24 SUFFOLK STREET
DUBLIN 2
Open 9.30-5.45 Mon to Sat
Telephone: 677 4652

Member of the
European Union of
Master Frame Makers

THE
IRISH
MUSEUM
OF
MODERN
ART

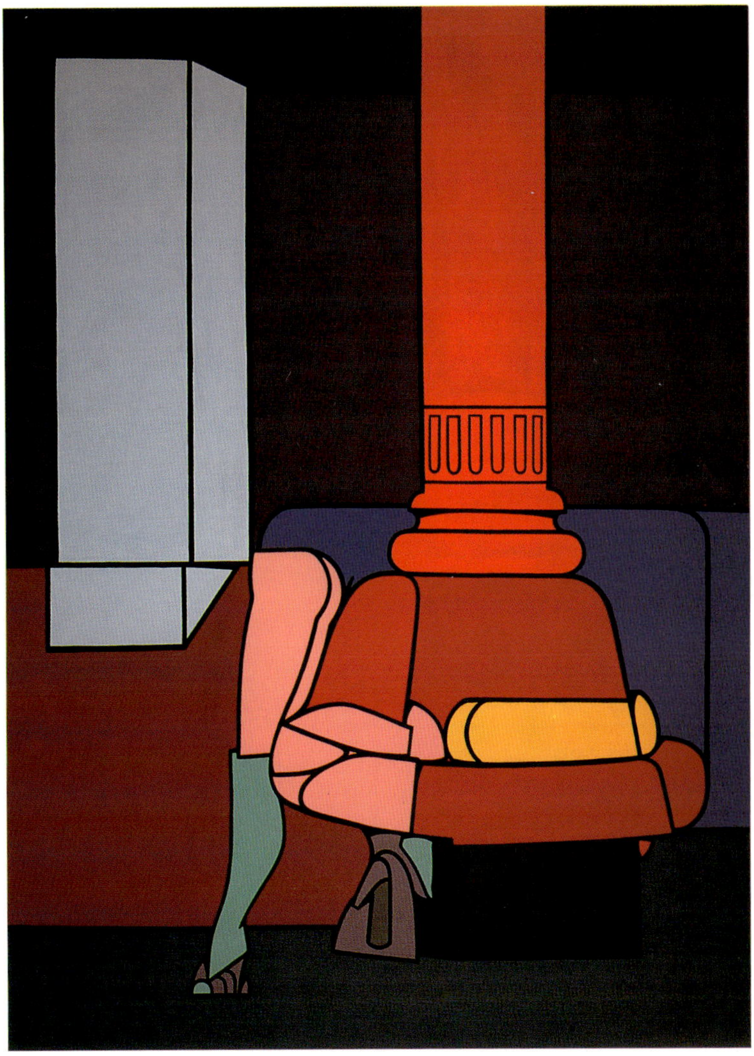

Valerio Adami *Beauty Parlour* 1970

a major work from the **Gordon Lambert Collection**
of Irish and international art donated to IMMA in 1992

Irish Museum of Modern Art
Royal Hospital Kilmainham
Dublin 8
Tel: 01 671 8666
Fax: 01 671 8695

Museum and bookshop open
Tue - Sat 10 - 5.30 Sun 12 - 5.30
Coffee shop open
Tue - Sat 11 - 4 Sun 12 - 5

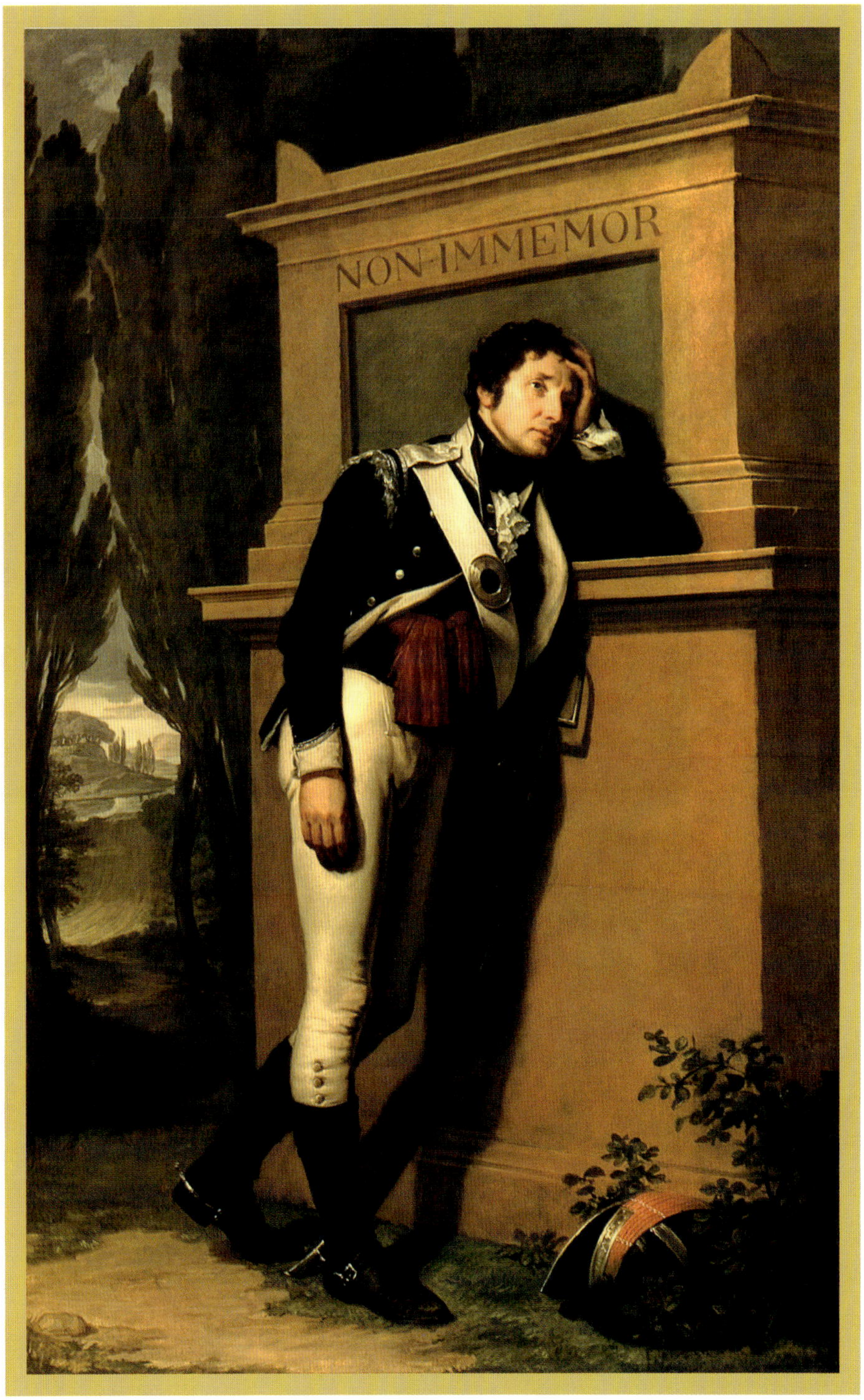

Lieutenant Richard St. George Mansergh St. George, c. 1756-1798 by Hugh Douglas Hamilton c.1739-1808

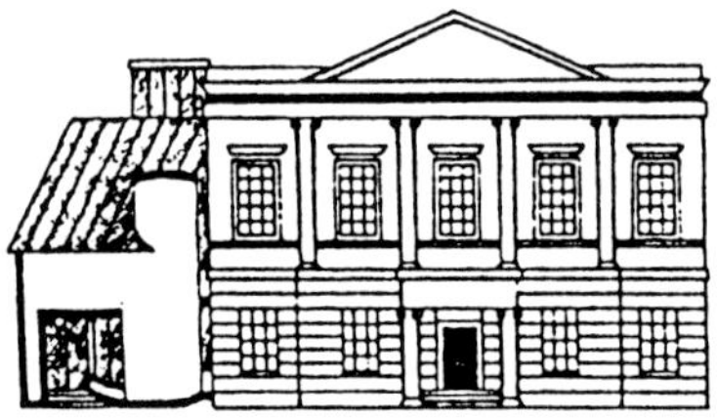

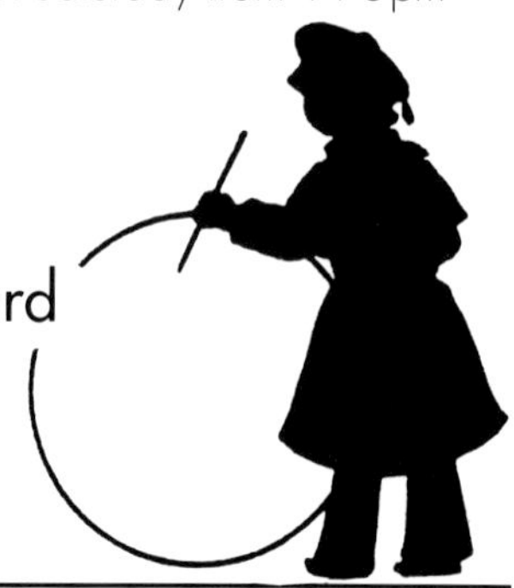

CALENDAR OF THE ART YEAR

A retrospective calendar of the visual arts in Ireland, events, exhibitions and publications, in the year from May 1992 until April 1993, compiled by **Elizabeth Mayes** with a commentary by **Robert O'Byrne**

May 1992

E V E N T S

13 Death of Banbridge-born sculptor **F E McWilliam.**

E X H I B I T I O N S

1 *Until 6 May*
Sean McSweeney. New Works. Narrow Water Gallery, Warrenpoint, Co Down.

1 *Until 9 May*
Roy Johnston. New Works. Fenderesky Gallery at Queen's, Belfast

1 *Until 18 May*
Alec Cobbe.Ib Jorgensen Gallery, Dublin

1 *Until 14 May*
Paul Kelly. Recent Paintings. Gorry Gallery, Dublin.

4 *Until 30 May*
Ulster Society of Women Artists. Central Library, Belfast.

5 *Until 15 May*
Ulster Watercolour Society.16th Annual Exhibition. Bell Gallery, Belfast.

5 *Until 22 May*
William Crozier – recent works. Sligo Art Gallery

6 *Until 16 May*
Royal Ulster Academy Association. Annual Exhibition. Malone House Gallery, Belfast.

7 *Until 23 May*
John Shinnors. Eighteen Paintings. Taylor Galleries, Dublin

8 *Until 26 May*
Doris Affeldt and **Sarah Iremonger**. New Paintings. Wyvern Gallery, Dublin

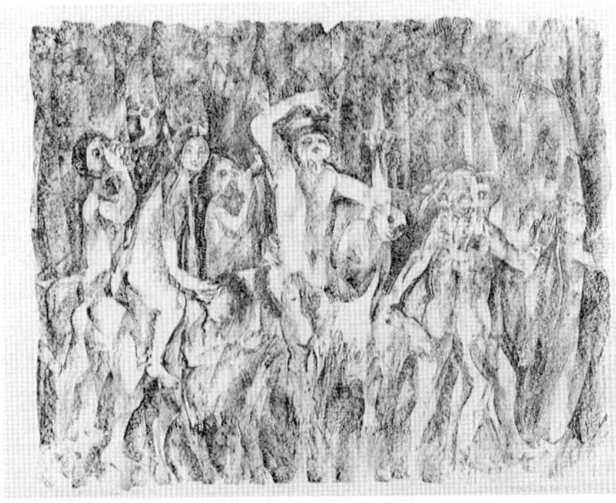

Louis Le Brocquy, *Children in a Wood II 1991.*

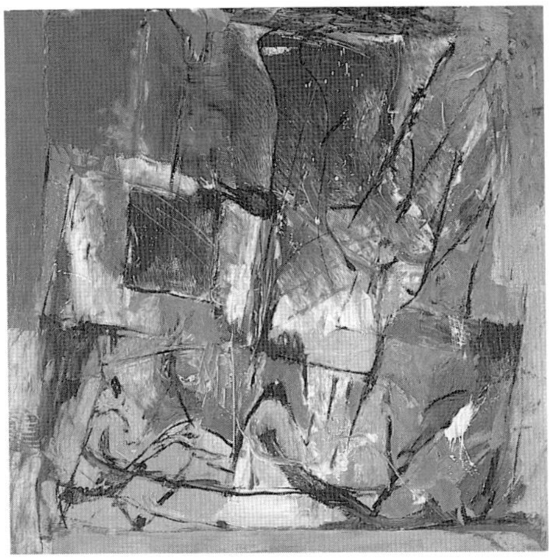

Richard Gorman, *Culdron, 1991.*

8 *Until 29 May*
Marion Miller – mixed media. Peacock Gallery, Craigavon.

8 *Until 5 June*
David Kinane, Sculpture. Project Arts Centre, Dublin

10 *Until May 30*
Eamon Coleman. Islands. Rubicon Gallery, Dublin

11 *Until 29 May*
Marion Miller. New Works. Peacock Gallery, Craigavon

12 *Until 30 May*
Gerry Sherry. New Works. Narrow Water Gallery, Warrenpoint.

14 *Until 30 May*
Louis Le Brocquy.Taylor Galleries, Dublin

15 *Until 6 June*
Moira McIver. **Men in Uniform**. Photographs and installation. Oliver Dowling Gallery Dublin

16 *Until 3 June*
Tim Goulding. Fire on the Mountain. New paintings in 'Night Fire' series. Jeffers Gallery Kinsale.

16 *Until 3 June*
Richard Gorman. Paintings done in Milan. Kerlin Gallery, Dublin.

16 *Until 13 June*
Colin McGookin. 'Scene from the Projection Box' New Paintings. Orchard Gallery, Derry.

18 *Until 30 May*
George Walsh – Oils. Cork Arts Society.

19 *Until 9 June*
Suzanne O'Driscoll. Paintings and Drawings. Solomon Gallery, Dublin

20 *Until 30 May*
Martin Meyler. **Private Lives** First Dublin solo show. Temple Bar Gallery.

May 1992

'Another opening, another show' runs the Cole Porter song, and certainly that was the abiding impression of May's many exhibitions, most of which had some merit, though few possessed enough to leave any substantial memory behind. Early in the month, *Alec Cobbe*, whose family used to live in Newbridge House outside Dublin and who now lives in the Robert Adam-designed Hatchlands Park in Surrey, which he restored for Britain's National Trust, held an exhibition of paintings at Dublin's Jorgensen Fine Art gallery. Called A *Painter's Journeys through Ireland and France*, perhaps in unconscious homage to Arthur Young's literary equivalent two centuries earlier, the show offered a mixture of landscapes and interiors treated in an equally lush impressionistic manner that gave all the modest-sized pictures an instantaneously seductive allure. The same comment could also be applied to Dubliner *Paul Kelly's* first solo show which opened at the Gorry Gallery across the street around the same time and, as an effective demonstration of its appeal, immediately sold every one of its sixty-two canvases. Undemanding landscapes and still-lifes fit to grace any drawing-room, these oils could most charitably be described as lacking any pretension. Somewhat more effort was required on the part of the viewer to appreciate *John Shinnors*' eighteen new paintings at the Taylor Gallery, looser and less monochromatic than hitherto but still offering enough of a challenge to a highly conservative market. Over at the Project Arts centre, sculptor *David Kinane*, in his debut one-man show, was yet more daring, with a fungus *Mycotos Dublinensis* designed to represent the capital's decay, constructed from more than two thousand recycled aluminium cans.

Louis Le Brocquy also demonstrated a rather surprising lyricism at the Taylor Gallery with six multicolour lithographs collectively entitled *Processions*, a small show of frieze-like figures owing a certain

CALENDAR OF THE ART YEAR

21 *Until 28 May*
Irish Art (O'Conor, O'Meara, Forbes, Henry, etc) Milmo-Penny Fine Art, Dublin

23 *Until 25 June*
Derek Hill :Paintings from a Private Collection 75th Birthday Exhibition. Glebe Gallery, Church Hill, Co Donegal.

23 *Until 28 June*
Outer Space. Eight artists, including **Willie Doherty,** at the forefront of new developments in photographic and videobased installations. Arnolfini, Bristol.

23 *Until 4 July*
Bobby Cox. Indian Journey.Tapestries and Photographs, Impact Gallery, Derry.

25 *Until 17 June*
Felicity Clear – prints & collages. Arts Council, Dublin

27 *Until 21 June*
Ciaran Lennon. Douglas Hyde Gallery, Dublin.

27 *Until 19 June*
Bernard McDonagh Retrospective. Sligo Art Gallery

28 *Until 21 June*
'On Y Va'. Touring exhibition – 14 young artists from Ireland, North and South. Hugh Lane Municipal Gallery, Dublin.

S A L E R O O M S

26 John Behan**, Flight of Birds**. Sold for £850. Maurice Wilks, **Cottages at Malin Head**. Sold for £2,400. Taylor de Veres, Dublin.

June 1992

E V E N T S

1 *Until 30 December*
Impact 92 – Derry. Festival programme of Arts Events

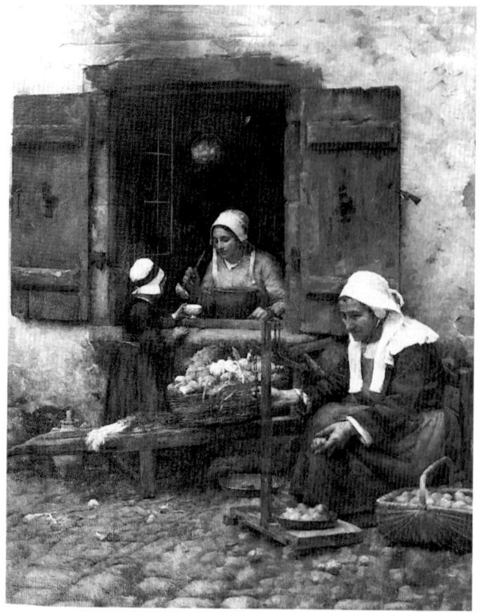

Stanhope Forbes, *Fair Measures: A shop in Quimperlé*. Milmo-Penny Fine Art.

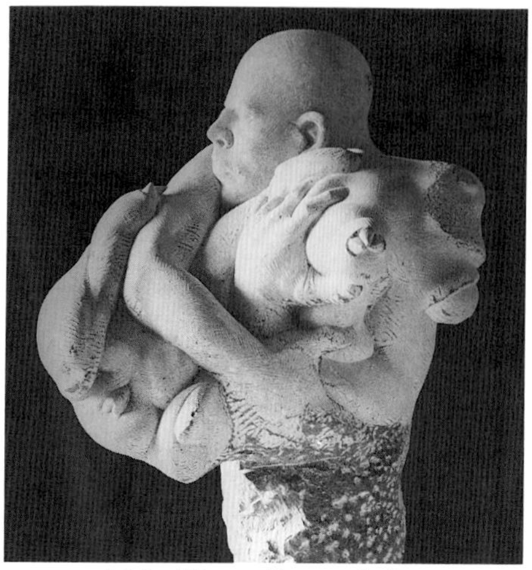

Michael Quane, *Figure and a Live Quadruped* 1992. On y Va.

3 Opening of **Bobby Dawson Gallery**, Dun Laoghaire, by Monica Barnes, TD. Group exhibition including works by Bobby Dawson, who died December 1991.

7 **In the Omnibus** (1860) watercolour by Honoré Daumier, stolen from Hugh Lane Municipal Gallery, Dublin.

9 *Until 19 June*
GPA Festival of Music in Great Irish Houses opened in Dunkathel House, Co Cork

12 *Until 14 June*
Seamus Heaney unveiled statue by **Conor Fallon** at Athenry, Co Galway in honour of his father, poet **Padraic Fallon** (d.1974). Three days of readings, lectures, folk music

16 Bloomsday. James Joyce's **Ulysses** celebrated in Dublin. Dublin artist **Gerald Davis** gave readings in Sydney

25 *Until 28 June*
People's Art Week. Display round St Stephen's Green. Also weekend displays on Merrion Square railings. Dublin Corporation.

E X H I B I T I O N S

1 *Until 13 June*
Carolyn Mulholland, sculpture. Ulster Arts Club Gallery, Belfast.

1 *Until 13 June*
Irene Wunderlich – Carved Wood. Cork Arts Society.

1 Until June 30
Barbara Allen, paintings and drawings. **Brian Magee**, ceramics. The Bay Tree, Holywood, Co Down.

1 *Until 20 June*
Small Happenings. Basil Blackshaw. Gordon Gallery, Londonderry.

5 *Until 25 June*
We must be mad? a question of conscience – oils by **Damien Morris**. Peacock Gallery, Craigavon

debt to cubism, though sufficient to negate the artist's own character. Over at the Kerlin Gallery, Dublin-born *Richard Gorman* showed more of his elegantly-painted abstracts produced in Milan, which managed to be both gritty in appearance and yet contemplative in manner. Meanwhile, in Derry's Orchard Gallery, *Colin McGookin* from Belfast offered *Scene from the Projection Box*, with a centre-piece of a triptych almost as long and luridly coloured as its seventeen-word title. The same gallery played host to a show of tapestries and photographs by English weaver *Bobbie Cox*, called *Indian Journey*. This has already been on tour around the sub-continent, which the artist first visited nearly twenty years ago and which clearly still acts as a primary source of inspiration. What can have inspired *Ciaran Lennon*'s dozen, dark and spare abstracts exhibited in semi-gloom at the Douglas Hyde Gallery? So spare, so cool were these pieces that they risked alienating viewers, even those who would normally have classified themselves as Lennon's admirers. No such fate awaited *On Y Va*, a show by fourteen young artists, seven from each side of the border who had all participated in an arts entrepreneurial course funded by the International Fund for Ireland Wider Horizons Programme and organised by Samco, a Cork-based sales and management consultancy. Having already been seen at Cork's Crawford Gallery, this arrived at the end of May to Dublin's Municipal Art Gallery before going on to the Old Museum in Belfast, in an exercise where logistics and good intentions were quite definitely given precedence over aesthetic judgement.

June 1992

The honourable intention of providing a permanent memorial to photographer *Bobby Dawson*, (one of the original members of the White Stag Group in the 1940s), who had died the previous December, was met with the establishment of a gallery bearing his name in Dun

CALENDAR OF THE ART YEAR

5 *Until 4 July*
Stephen McKenna. Kerlin Gallery, Dublin.

6 *Until 30 July*
Richard Livingstone & Robert Speers. Arts Council Gallery, Belfast.

6 *Until September*
Sculpture in Context 1992. Eighth year of site-specific exhibition. Fernhill Gardens, Sandyford, Co Dublin.

6 **Tony O'Malley – Work from the Sixties.** Butler Gallery,Kilkenny

9 *Until 26 July*
The Lake Isle of Innisfree – four artists from the Bernard Jacobson Gallery. Sligo Art Gallery.

11 *Until 3 July*
Strange Angels. Stained glass and paintings by **Peter Joseph Young**. Project Arts Centre, Dublin.

11 *Until 4 July*
Richard Gorman. New Prints. Graphic Studio Gallery Dublin

12 *Until 4 July*
Mary Fitzgerald. Orientation. Oliver Dowling Gallery Dublin

17 *Until 11 July*
Tom Matthews. Images from Lewis Carroll. Temple Bar Gallery, Dublin

17 *Until September*
Life Images of Ireland. Photographs by **Fr Francis Browne** SJ, spanning 60 years of Irish life in the early 20th cent.Sponsored by Ark Life Assurance. AIB Bankcentre Dublin

18 *Until 4 July*
Diarmuid Delargy, New Paintings and Prints. Taylor Galleries, Dublin.

19 *Until 10 July*
Nevill Johnson – 80th Birthday Exhibition. Tom Caldwell Gallery, Dublin.

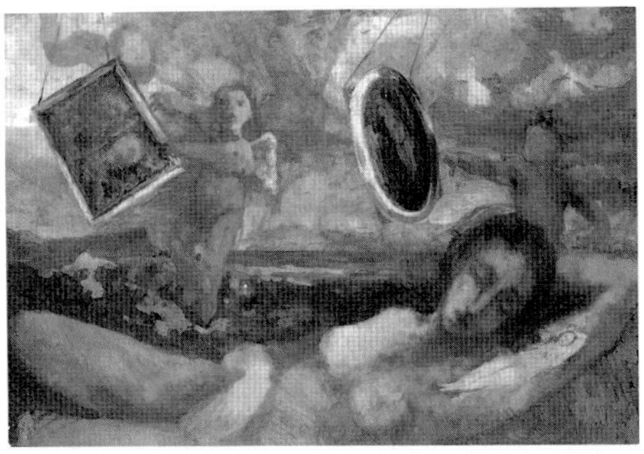
Diarmuid Delargy, *Venus in Northern Repose 1991.*

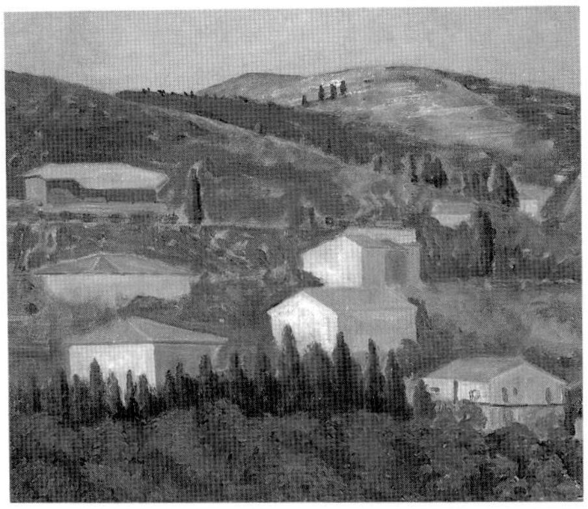
Stephen McKenna, *Landscape at Castiglioni, 1992.*

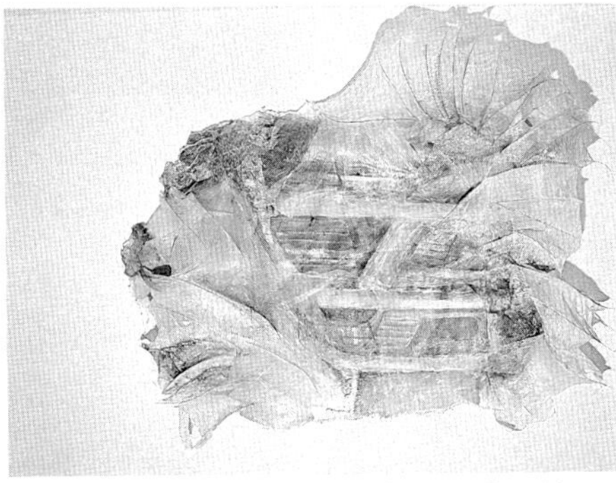
Larissa Gordon Watson, *L.W.R. 1991.* On y Va.

22 *Until 22 July*
Gavin Hogg, Arts Council, Dublin

23 *Until 11 October*
The O'Malley Collection. Works by Yeats, Hone, Jellett, Henry on permanent loan in memory of Ernie O'Malley. Irish Museum of Modern Art, Dublin.

24 *Until 30 June*
On Y Va. Touring exhibition from Hugh Lane Gallery. Old Museum Arts Centre, Belfast.

24 *Until 22 July*
John Keating. Pantheon Gallery, Dublin

29 *Until 11 July*
Sculpture by **Imogen Stuart**. The Square, Tallaght.

P U B L I C A T I O N S

18 **King's Inns Portraits** by Wanda Ryan-Smolin. The Honorable Society of King's Inns, Dublin, £14.95.

20 **Mildred Anne Butler** by Anne Crookshank; **Nathaniel Hone the Elder** by Adrian Le Harivel; **W J Leech** by Denise Ferran; **Roderic O'Conor** by Paula Murphy. *Lives of Irish Artists* series. Town House, Dublin £4.95 each hardback.

S A L E R O O M S

15 Richard Thomas Moynan RHA (1856-1906), **The Flower Seller**, signed and dated 1894. (lot 87) Sold for £18,000. Thomas P Adams, Main Street Blackrock.

17 George Russell AE, **Children in the Sand Dunes**. Signed with initials(lot 52) estimate £1,200/£1,800. Sold for £1,300. Richard Thomas Moynan RHA, **Study of a Young boy** (lot 53) £4,000 and **Portrait of the Artist's Daughter, Bridget, with her Doll,** (lot 92) £12,000. Sean Keating PRHA (1889-1978) **Connemara Woman** (lot 126) estimate £14,000/£18,000. Sold for £15,000. James Adam Salerooms, Dublin.

Laoghaire, opened by TD Monica Barnes at the start of June. A week later, poet *Padraic Fallon* was also the recipient of a posthumous tribute, with a whole week-end of festivities in his native town of Athenry, Co Galway which included the unveiling of a sculpture by his son *Conor* and the exhibition of a portrait series by his old friend, painter Tony O'Malley, called *Images in Recollection*. Mr O'Malley had a show of his own at the ever-innovative Butler Gallery in Kilkenny, albeit of work recollected from three decades earlier. Many of these pictures had never been publicly exhibited before and, for an audience accustomed to the more recent painting inspired by the Bahamas, the exhibition was something of a revelation, showing O'Malley during the period he spent in Cornwall to have been influenced, quite understandably, by the local St Ives school of abstraction.

Meanwhile in Dublin, English painter *Stephen McKenna*, who maintains a studio in Donegal, had another show which showed that Italy remained the main source of inspiration for his pictures, offering a form of fractured neo-classicism which all too often becomes over-burdened by its own erudition. Far more straightforward, both in execution and intent, was *Peter Joseph Young*'s exhibition *Strange Angels* at the Project Arts Centre, where painting and stained glass were shown with a romantically idealised approach towards nature predominating. At Oliver Dowling's Gallery, *Mary Fitzgerald*'s show, called *Orientations* revealed that her enthralment with a kind of abstract orientalism remained as strong as ever, but this time the form was a little more disjointed than before, thereby redeeming the work from any accusation of excessive orderliness. That objection could be made with more reason of *Richard Gorman*'s prints, following hard on his show of paintings, which were on view at Dublin's Graphic Studio. Beautiful and refined, they teetered perilously close to sterility, lacking even the immediate surface interest of his canvases. The figura-

CALENDAR OF THE ART YEAR

July 1992

EVENTS

1 Opening of refurbished **Dr Steevens' Hospital, Dublin 8**, as Eastern Health Board headquarters.

6 Appointment of **Fiach Mac Conghail** as Artistic Director of Project Arts Centre, in succession to Tim O'Neill

8 **Boyle Arts Festival**, Co Roscommon

8 Sale of **Gerald Kenyon**'s stock and private furnishings. Mealy's of Castlecomer and Town and Country Fine Art Ltd

15 *Until 26 July*
Galway Arts Festival

15 **George Moore Festival**, Mayo

15 *Until 16 July*
Sale of contents of **Humewood**, Co Wicklow. Hamilton Osborne King with Coonan of Maynooth.

19 *Until 8 August*
South Docks Festival. City Arts Centre, Dublin.

EXHIBITIONS

1 *Until 17 July*
Derek Hill 75th Birthday Exhibition, Crawford Gallery, Cork.

3 *Until 3 August*
'Iontas' – Fourth National Small Works Exhibition. Sligo Art Gallery.

4 *Until 25 July*
Simon Reilly. Arts Council Gallery, Belfast.

7 *Until 7 August*
Laura Venables 1965-1992. City Arts Centre, Dublin

7 **The Water and the Wild.** Landscape paintings by **Pat McKenna**. Frank Lewis Gallery, Killarney.

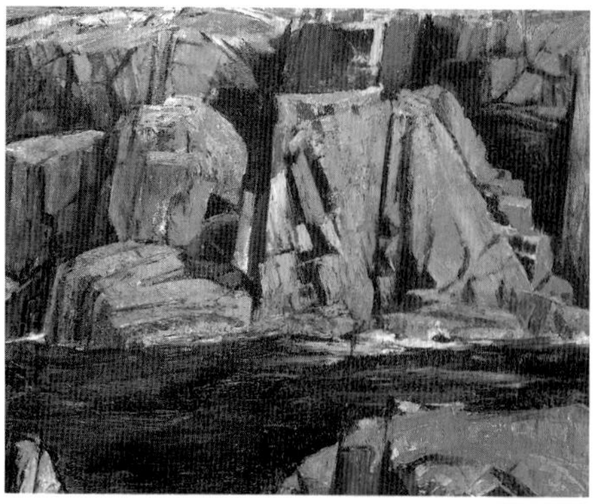

Derek Hill, *Greenport Rocks, Tory Island,* 1962.

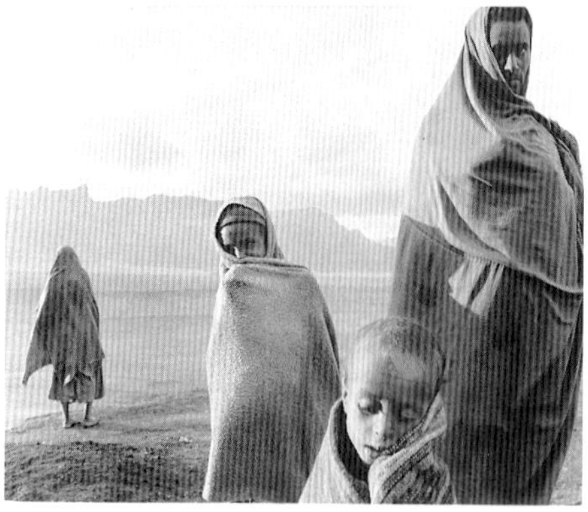

Sebastiao Salgado, *Ethiopia 1984*.

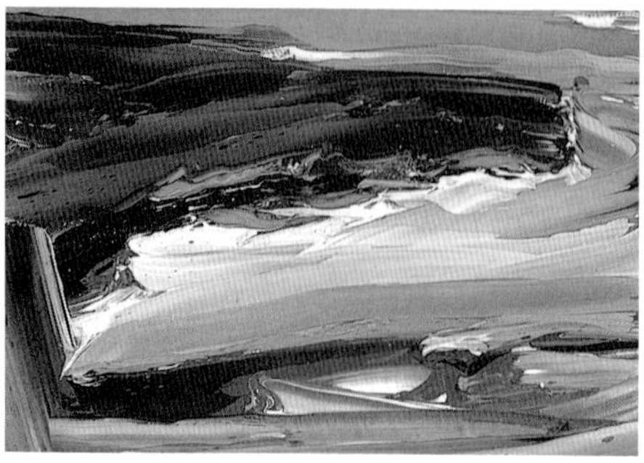

Seán McSweeney, *Inlet, Ballyconnell, Sligo,* 1992.

7 *Until 28 August*
Sebastiao Salgado. Photographs. Douglas Hyde Gallery, Dublin

8 *Until 28 August*
N I Arts Council Belfast **Print Workshop Exhibition**. Northern Ireland Business Centre, London.

9 *Until 25 July*
Inside and Outside. New Works by **Charles Brady**.Also **Shoreline and Bog,Sligo** by **Sean McSweeney**. Taylor Galleries, Dublin.

10 *Until 6 August*
Truss. Sculpture by **Eileen McDonagh**. Project Arts Centre, Dublin.

11 *Until 5 August*
Simon Ungers. Kerlin Gallery, Dublin.

15 *Until 30 August*
Portraits and Prospects. Watercolours from the Ulster Museum. National Gallery of Ireland, Dublin.

15 *Until 22 August*
Earth -Stone – Plant. Installation by **Cormac Boydell**. Temple Bar Gallery, Dublin.

20 *Until 8 August*
Derek Hill 75th Birthday Exhibition. City Gallery, Limerick.

22 *Until 19 August*
Icthys. Recent Work by **Valerie Joyce**. Pantheon Gallery, Dublin.

22 *Until 6 September*
The Gordon Lambert Collection. More than 100 works from one of the country's most important private collections, particularly rich in Op and Kinetic art and Conceptual art of the '60s and'70s, now the property of the Irish Museum of Modern Art. IMMA, Dublin.

22 *Until 27 September*
Chris Drury: Adharc. Site-specific sculptures. IMMA, Dublin.

tive tradition was vigorously defended during the same month by *Tom Matthews*, better known as a cartoonist for a number of national publications, who showed a series of drawings inspired by the work of Lewis Carroll at the Temple Bar Gallery. And at the Taylor Gallery, Northern artist *Diarmuid Delargy* showed paintings and prints which owed more than a passing debt to Titian and Delacroix, while the Pantheon Gallery showed that *John Keating* had still not rid himself of an all-absorbing interest in minutely reproducing the human form on paper and canvas. It was a relief, after such obsessive particularity, to turn to the exhibition which opened towards the end of June at the Irish Museum of Modern Art. The *O'Malley Collection*, assembled by American *Helen O'Malley-Roelofs*, who had lived in Ireland from the mid-1930s until 1950, offered an admirable representation, often on a modest scale, of that period's Irish art, with work by *Paul Henry, Evie Hone, Norah McGuinness, Cecil Salkeld, Patrick Scott, Nano Reid* and *Jack B Yeats* included. Eventually, these pictures may go to Turlough House near Castlebar, Co Mayo to become part of a larger O'Malley Collection, but for the few months, they were displayed in a series of groundfloor rooms that matched their size and aspirations quite perfectly.

July 1992

The Museum's neighbour, formerly *Dr Steevens' Hospital*, reopened its doors on 1 July as the Eastern Health Board's new Headquarters. Stripped of almost three centuries' accretions, the building, although built somewhat later than the Royal Hospital Kilmainham, looked to be the earlier of the two since its design, whilst undoubtedly similar, is far less sophisticated in detail; the architect responsible, *Thomas Burgh*, also designed St Werburgh's Church and Trinity College Library. At Trinity College itself, the Douglas Hyde Gallery's showing of work by Brazilian photographer *Sebastiao*

CALENDAR OF THE ART YEAR

23 *Until 26 July*
Ciaran Lennon. Works on Paper. Jerome O Drisceoil, Fine Art Agent, 58 Fitzwilliam Square, Dublin

23 *Until 13 August)*
Ciaran Lennon Retrospective. Limerick City Art Gallery.

27 *Until 19 August*
Drawings by **Kieran Carey**.One in a series of solo exhibitions by recent recipients of Arts Council grants. Arts Council, Dublin.

28 *Until 31 October*
Pearls before Wine. New work by **Joe McGill**. In association with Gutter Gallery, Restaurant Tosca, Suffolk Street, Dublin 2

31 *Until 28 August*
Anne Madden: Blue Paintings 1988-1990. Crawford Municipal Gallery , Cork.

31 *Until August*
Ecce Homo. Work by Marit Nyhuis, Fergal Fitzpatrick, Ivan Connolly and Edmund Leahy. Gutter Gallery, Fownes Street, Dublin.

August 1992

EVENTS

3 *Until 8 August*
27th Irish Antique Dealers' Fair. Mansion House, Dublin.

5 Government to acquire for the State **Castletown House**, Celbridge, Co Kildare, architecturally the most significant 18th century house in Ireland. Repairs estimated to cost £3 million.

15 *Until 23 August*
Kilkenny Arts Week. Opening by Baroness O Cathain, Kilkenny Castle.

21 University College Galway offers new **Diploma in Arts Administration**.

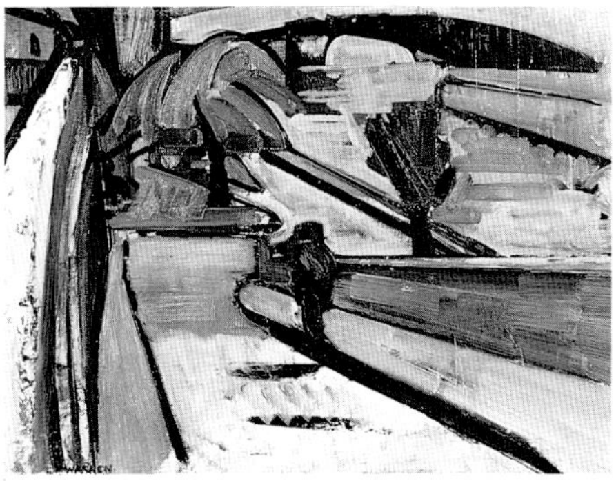

Barbara Warren, *Pont du Carrousel 1954*, Gordon Lambert Coll. IMMA.

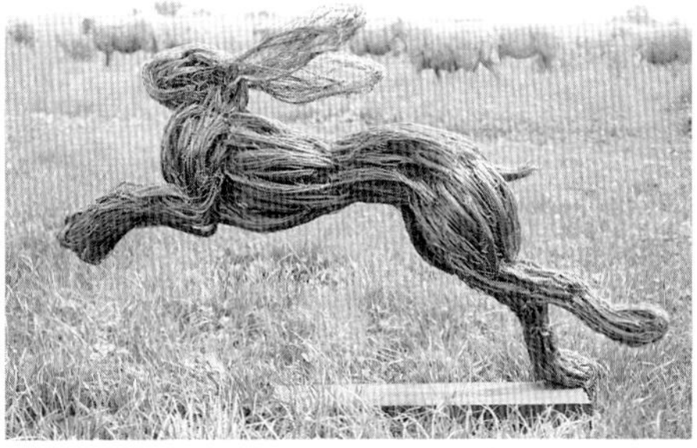

Sophie Ryder, *Hare, 1992*.

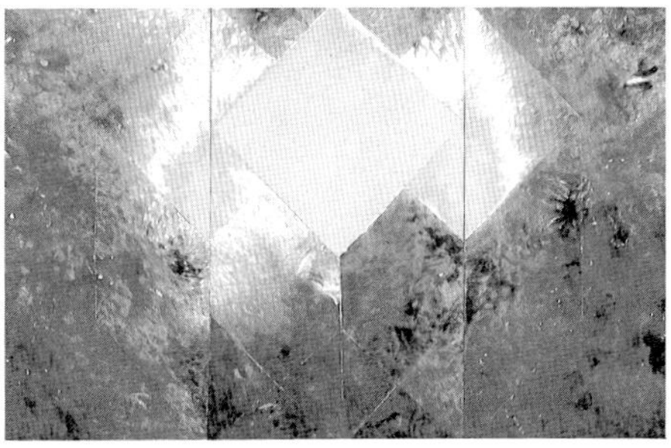

Anne Madden, *Sea Boxes, Vessels of Light I*.

29 Two paintings by **Harry Kernoff**, 'The Bridge on the Mall, Westport'and 'The Red Seat near Baggot Bridge' presented by the artist's cousin, Dr Leslie Kernoff, to the Hugh Lane Municipal Gallery, Dublin.

EXHIBITIONS

1 *Until August 15*
Structures of Stone. Pencil drawings by **Patricia Kelly**, Ardhowen Gallery, Enniskillen.

1 *Until 31 August*
Dar a Luz – Into the Light. Sculpture and Drawing by **Anne Wallace**. Orchard Gallery, Derry.

1 *Until 22 August*
Suburbanscapes by **Mary Burke**. Monaghan County Museum.

1 *Until 20 August*
Lividart by **Sean O'Flynn**. The Head Sculpture Gallery, 12 E. Essex St, Dublin.

3 *Until 27 August*
Pastel Society of Ireland. Flowerfield Arts Centre, Portstewart,Co Derry.

6 *Until 21 August*
100 Years of Irish Art from the Oriel Gallery.Sligo Art Gallery

6 *Until 29 August*
Actions of Thought. Recent works by **Michelle Keating** and **Sheila Richardson**. Belltable, Limerick

7 *Until 28 August*
New Work in Oils by **David Craig**. Peacock Gallery, Craigavon, N. Ireland.

8 *Until 9 September*
New work by Barrie Cooke, Dorothy Cross, Felim Egan, David Godbold, Richard Gorman, John Kindness, Elizabeth Magill, Stephen McKenna, Sean Shanahan. Kerlin Gallery, Dublin

Salgado attracted a record attendance for this venue. These pictures of exploitation and famine in Africa and South America were often already familiar from reproduction in myriad international publications, but still they managed to be extraordinarily moving, particularly since, gathered together in this fashion, they were able to make a powerful collective impact on the viewer. Set beside this show, other work, such as the charming collection of British and Irish watercolours and drawings from the Ulster Museum's collection, which went on show at the National Gallery, looked daintily lightweight stuff. At the Taylor Gallery, *Sean McSweeney* and *Charles Brady* both showed alluring landscapes, whilst at the Pantheon Gallery, *Valerie Joyce*'s exhibition *Icthys* could be simply summarised as a fishy notion in more than one sense of the word.

The Irish Museum of Modern Art offered *Adharc* by British artist *Chris Drury*, whose site-specific sculptures in wood, stone and turf were highly reminiscent of work created by his fellow countryman, *Richard Long*, and by Irish artists *Colm O Culain* and *James Scanlon*; like Drury, the latter had created a number of beehive-type structures, at Sneem, Co Kerry.

Also at the museum, a selection from one of the country's best-known private collections went on show, part of the 300-work donation made by *Gordon Lambert* which is particularly strong on Op, Kinetic and Conceptual art from the 1960s and '70s, with pieces by *Vasarely, Soto* and *Bridget Riley*, influenced no doubt by the tastes of the late *David Hendriks* with whom Lambert was closely associated. Even though many parts of the collection would not find favour just at the moment, they undoubtedly enrich the historical base of the museum's own holdings and, for this reason if no other, are worthy of note. Equally worth watching amongst the plethora of summer shows country-wide was the exhibition arranged by a handful of local collectors particularly *Fergus Ahern* for the annual Boyle Arts festival,

CALENDAR OF THE ART YEAR

15 *Until 23 August*
Paintings by **Liam Roberts**, Butler House; Drawings by **Sol LeWitt**, Butler Gallery; paintings by **Helena Gorey** and **Marie Caulfield**, photographs by **Carmel Cleary**, Technical School; sculpture by **Sophie Ryder**, Butler House Garden; ceramics by **Sonja Landweer**, Rudolf Heltzel Gallery; paintings by **Charlotte Wilcox**, Butler Gallery II. Kilkenny Arts Week.

15 *Until 12 September*
The Anatomy Theatre. Installation by Barbara Freeman. Orchard Gallery, Derry.

18 *Until 18 September*
Ciaran McClelland and **Paul Mosse**, City Arts Centre, Dublin.

18 *Until 29 August*
Derek Hill: Paintings from a Private Collection, RHA Gallagher Gallery, Dublin.

19 *Until 16 September*
Alchemy – new work by Annabel Koenig, Pat McGrath, Margaret Fitzgibbon and Barbara Dempsey. Pantheon Gallery, Dublin.

20 *Until 5 September*
Bow Bell Taylor Galleries, Dublin.

21 *Until 12 September*
Work by Basil Blackshaw, Felim Egan, Cherith McKinstry, Jane O'Malley, Tony O'Malley, Janet Pierce and Vivienne Roche. Model Arts Centre, Sligo

22 *Until 8 September*
Bridget Flannery. Rubicon Gallery, Dublin.

24 *Until 16 September*
Laura Venables. Arts Council, Dublin.

25 *Until 18 September*
Basil Blackshaw's Recent Paintings. Sligo Art Gallery.

26 *Until 12 August*
One That Always Remains. Bronzes, plasterwork and drawings by Margeret Fitzgibbon. Triskel Arts Centre, Cork.

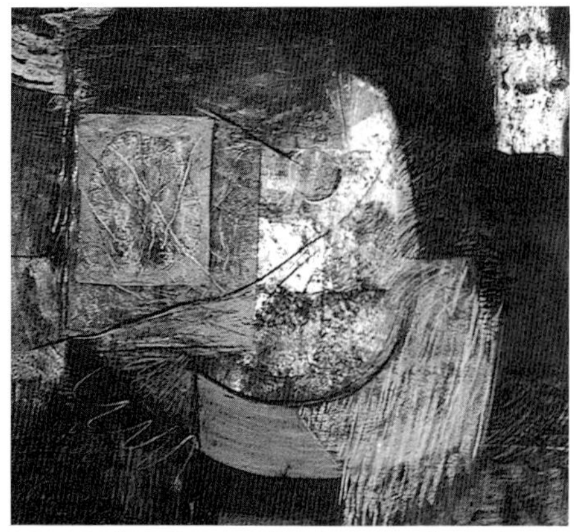

Barbara Freeman, *The Anatomy Theatre*.

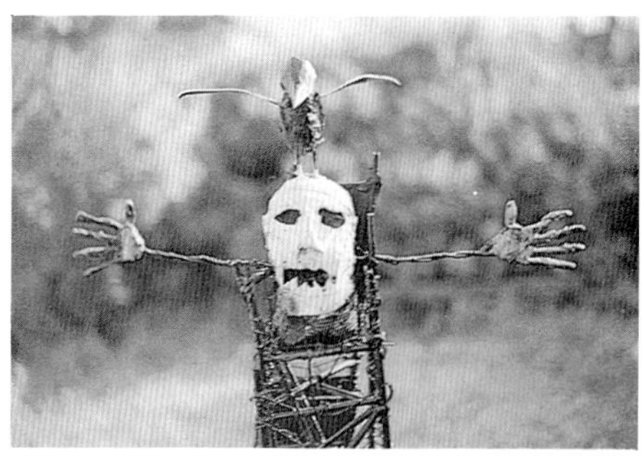

Margaret Fitzgibbon, *What appears to be yours*, 1992 from *Alchemy*.

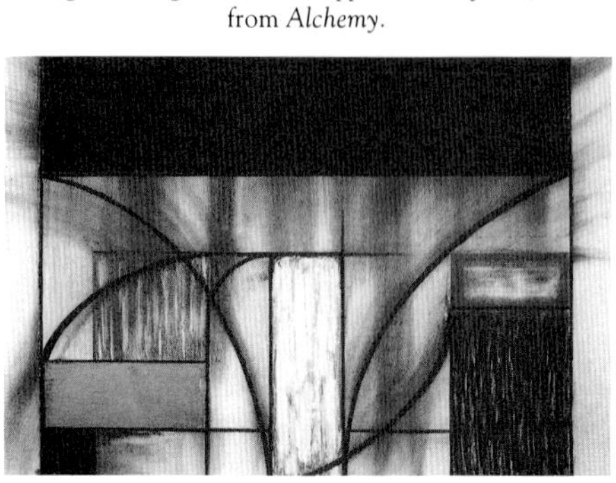

Brian Henderson, *Crescendo*.

27 *Until 16 September*
Donegal artist **Marie Barrett** and Belfast artist **Ronnie Hughes**, returned from New York. Arts Council Gallery, Belfast

27 *Until 13 September*
Aer Rianta Exhibition 1992. Sculpture and paintings by 20 artists including William Crozier, Conor Fallon, Vivienne Roche and Nancy Wynne-Jones. Cork Airport.

September 1992

EVENTS

4 *Until 14 September*
Dun Laoghaire Arts Week

6 *Until 9 September*
International Conference on The Book of Kells, Trinity College, Dublin (see report this issue)

13 **Heritage Day**, Office of Public Works. Free admission to cultural sites and exhibitions all over Dublin.

25 *Until 7 October*
Clifden Community Arts Week .

27 **Irish Film Centre** opened, Eustace Street , Dublin 2.

27 Opening of **Sculpture Trail**, Castlewellan Forest Park, Co Down.

30 *Until 28 October*
Free weekly lectures on 18th century artists, architects and patrons, Number Twenty Nine, Lower Fitzwilliam Street, Dublin 2.

EXHIBITIONS

1 *Until 29 September*
Almost Full Circle.Paintings by **Irene Uhlemann**, Temple Bar Gallery, Dublin.

3 *Until 19 September*
North, South, East, West. Recent drawings, **Brian Henderson**. Taylor Galleries, Dublin.

with a distinctive character which, whilst hardly at the cutting edge of contemporary Irish art, was not too excessively conservative either, taking in *Tony O'Malley, Charles Tyrell, Cecily Brennan, Barrie Cooke, Richard Gorman* and *Samuel Walsh* and so indicating a decided preference for richly-coloured abstraction. *Galway Arts Festival*'s visual arts contribution is always the weakest part of the programme, and this year was no exception, with yet another exhibition by the prolific *Brian Bourke* and a showing of lithographs and monotypes from Los Angeles' Cirrus Gallery and Gemini Print Studios being the highest points of a none-too-inspired offering.

August 1992

A much more impressive choice of shows was provided by the ever-reliable *Kilkenny Arts Festival*, opened in mid-August by Irish-born Baroness Detta O Cathain, who now runs London's Barbican Centre. Of course, there were low points here too – as before many of the fringe shows revealed their commercial motivation rather too blatantly – but on the other hand, the festival organisers managed to bring *Sol LeWitt* to Ireland for the first time, when he produced a series of site-specific wall drawings in the Castle's Butler Gallery.

The rough-grained surfaces of the rooms, seemingly, had caused initial problems, but these were overcome and the resulting work, colourfully decorative rather than anything more substantial, looked completely at home in the space available. Across at Butler House, *Liam Roberts*, originally from Wexford but now resident in New York, showed paintings of a predominantly, though not exclusively, Abstract-Expressionist nature. Outside, in the house's gardens, English sculptor *Sophie Ryder*, the festival's resident artist, created a greyhound and a hare from wirenetting, galvanised wire and scrap metal; these forms looked like the stripped-down skeletons of work by another English sculptor, *Barry Flanagan*. More

CALENDAR OF THE ART YEAR

5 *Until 29 September*
A Beginning – touring exhibition from Orchard Gallery of works made from bog materials by **Catherine Harper**. Belltable Arts Centre, Limerick.

5 *Until 10 November*
Sightlines – sculpture by **Vivienne Roche**. Crawford Gallery, Cork.

5 *Until 1 October*
New work by **Michael Flaherty**. Wellspring Gallery, Tralee, Co Kerry.

7 *Until 28 September*
Beyond Description. Touring exhibition from IMMA. St John's, Listowel, Co Kerry.

8 *Until 25 September*
'4 x 4'. 25th anniversary exhibition of recent work by the four artists in the first show in the Project Arts Centre , Temple Bar – **John Behan, Charlie Cullen, John Kelly, Michael Kane**.

8 *Until 10 October*
TCD Modern Art Collection: The Last Fifteen Years. Quatercentenary Exhibition. Douglas Hyde Gallery TCD.

11 *Until 26 September*
Origines. New works on paper by **Roy Johnson**. Oliver Dowling Gallery, Dublin.

11 *Until 26 September*
Paintings by **John Kingerlee**. Tom Caldwell Gallery, Dublin

12 *Until 3 October*
Paintings by **Poppy Melia**. Rubicon Gallery,Dublin.

12 *Until 7 October*
Howard Hodgkin – Hand-coloured prints 1986-1991. Kerlin Gallery, Dublin.

14 *Until 25 September*
Derek Hill 75th Birthday Exhibition. Christie's, London.

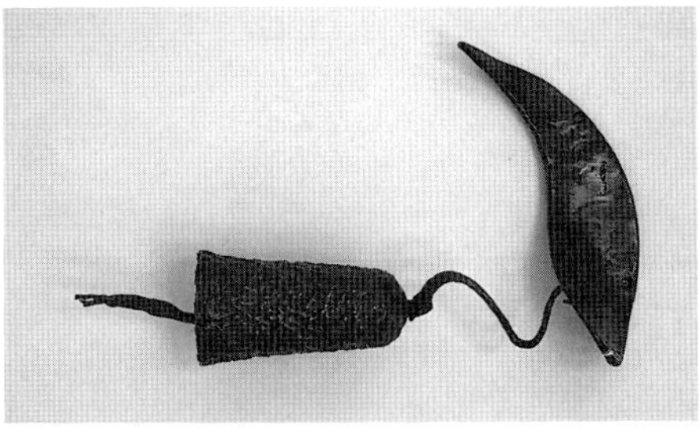

Vivienne Roche, *Olde Nes*.

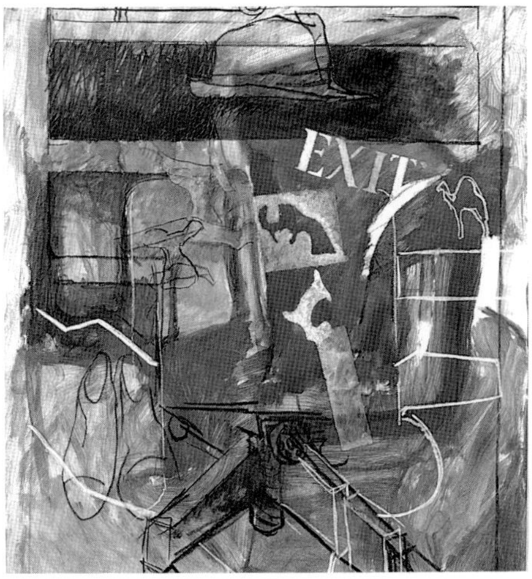

Charles Cullen, *Interior*.

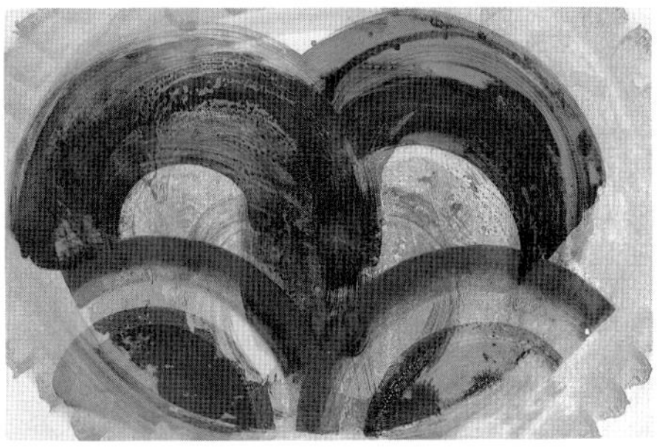

Howard Hodgkin, *Red Palm*, 1986-87.

14 *Until 26 September*
Quaker Tapestry Exhibition. Irish Life Centre, Dublin.

15 *Until 30 September*
George Walsh – stained glass and paintings. Also **Joseph Sloan**, sculpture and **Liam Treacy**, paintings. Kilcock Art Gallery,Kilcock, Co Kildare

15 *Until 26 September*
Oireachtas Art Exhibition, RHA Gallagher Gallery, Dublin. Prizewinners – Helen Bolger, Vincent Browne, sculpture and Michael O'Dea and John Kelly, painting.

16 *Until 17 October*
Marko Pognacik – Derry/Donegal Sculpture Project. Orchard Gallery, Derry.

16 *Until 11 November*
Sculpture by **Susanne Wolf**. Pantheon Gallery, Dublin.

17 *Until 1 November*
Alanna O'Kelly 'The Country Blooms ... A Garden and a Grave'. Multi-media installation on themes of the Great Famine. IMMA, Dublin.

18 *Until 31 January*
Portraits and Prospects. British and Irish Watercolours returned from tour of 14 venues in USA. Catalogue by Martyn Anglesea. Ulster Museum, Belfast.

21 *Until 16 October*
Paintings by **Sarah Durcan**. Arts Council, Dublin.

22 *Until 10 October*
Mainie Jellett rugs from original Cubist designs 1927-1935. European Modern Art Gallery, Dublin.

22 *Until 10 October*
Patterns of Survival. Site-specific installation by Una Walker. Arts Council Gallery, Belfast.

hard-edged pieces, though of a defiantly geometric abstract kind, were shown by *Francis Tansey*, as part of a group exhibition in the Kilkenny People Art Gallery before he had a solo show opening at the end of the month in Dublin's Solomon Gallery. After more than a decade of working in the same vein, Tansey now looks trapped into a repetitive pattern, defined by the same few shapes and lurid, primary-coloured palette. Still, at least this artist has a clear idea of what he wishes to do, unlike *Bridget Flannery*, whose solo show at the Rubicon Gallery revealed an exclusively tentative nature, producing pictures that hesitated between landscape and abstraction. No such doubts can ever have troubled *Derek Hill*, whose paintings from an unspecified private collection, were on tour for much of 1992, and reached the RHA Gallagher Gallery in Dublin during August, the show being opened then by the artist's old friend and chairman of Sotheby's *Lord Gowrie*. The exhibition, which subsequently went on to be shown in a rival auction house, Christie's, London headquarters, was a tribute marking Hill's seventy-fifth birthday, but the works were full of youthful dash, impetuosity and, above all the self-assurance that many much younger artists lack.

Kilkenny artist *Paul Mosse* has for long demonstrated a similar resolution, untroubled by critical response. At the City Arts Centre, almost twenty years of his output went on view, impressing visitors, above all else, with the original virtuosity and breathtaking proliferation of minute detail – definitely and defiantly an original.

Four artists who had been perceived as originals twenty-five years earlier but, it could be argued, failed subsequently to sustain that perception, had an anniversary show at the Project Arts Centre where they were the very first exhibitors in 1966. So much has changed during the intervening period, but not, sadly enough, the work of *John Behan, Charlie Cullen, John Kelly* and *Michael Kane*, once participants in an alternative arts movement,

CALENDAR OF THE ART YEAR

23 *Until 23 October*
Guilt by Association.Site-specific sculptures, texts and mixed-media works by five young Glasgow artists. IMMA, Dublin.

25 *Until 7 November*
Gilbert and George – The Cosmological Pictures. IMMA, Dublin.

25 *Until 10 October*
Private Deviations – multi-media exhibition Gutter Gallery, Dublin.

26 *Until 15 October*
Wetlands – landscape paintings by **Jacqueline Stanley**. Riverrun Gallery, Galway.

29 *Until 17 October*
Mary Lohan – Elements. Taylor Galleries, Dublin.

29 *Until 30 October*
Michael Hegarty – first solo show. City Arts Centre, Dublin.

29 **Shifting Angles** – sculpture, jewellery, pictures and weaving by **Carolyn Mulholland** and **Breon O'Casey**, Narrow Water Gallery, Warrenpoint.

P U B L I C A T I O N S

15 **Anne Crookshank,** 'In my View......The National Gallery of Ireland', **Apollo**, vol CXXXVI, no 367 (new series) September 1992. Professor Crookshank assesses recent developments at the NGI.

30 **Crawford Municipal Art Gallery, Cork, Summary Catalogue**, ed. Peter Murray. Launched by An Taoiseach. See review in this issue. Also *Masterpieces from the Crawford Art Gallery*.

S A L E R O O M S

?? William Sadler (1782-1839) **View of the Four Courts and Quays**, oil on panel, 46 x 61 cm. (lot 53) Sold for £5,000. Nathaniel Hone RHA (1831-1917), **St Doulough's Church, Raheny**, (lot 63) oil on board, sold for £1,700. Frank McKelvey RA(1895-1974) **Coastal Landscape**, oil, 37 x 50 cm., sold for £4,000 and **Marble Strand, Co Donegal** (lot 136) sold for £6,000. Flora Mitchell (1890-1973) **Watercolour views of Dublin** (lots 118-135) sold for between £700 and £1,800 each. James Adam Salerooms, Dublin.

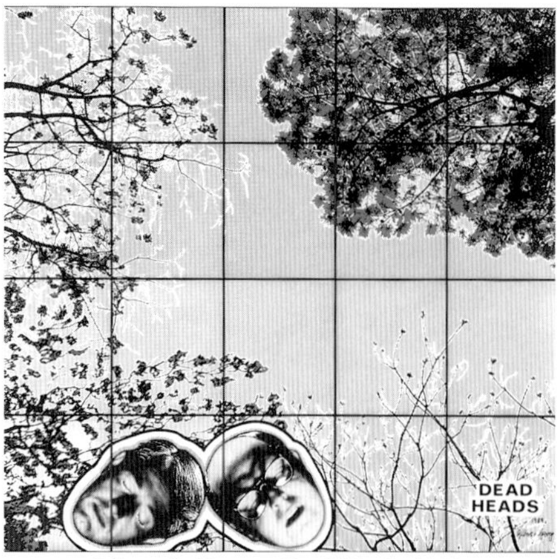

Gilbert & George, *Dead Heads, 1989.*

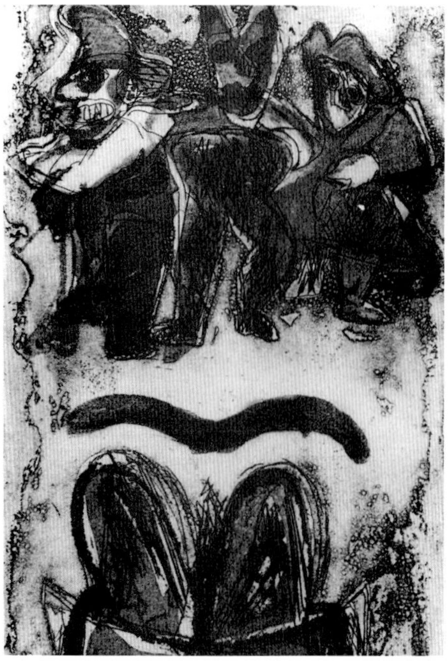
Alice Hanratty, *Garden Scene.*

October 1992

E V E N T S

4 Irish National Day at EXPO 92 Seville.An Taoiseach announces no more cuts in Arts Council grant for the coming year – 'the arts are underfunded.'

4 *Until 12 October*
37th Cork Film Festival.

5 *Until 17 October*
Dublin Theatre Festival. Principal sponsor – Irish Life.

15 Illustrated lecture by **Dorothy Walker on Documenta IX 1992**,in Kassel, the world's greatest modern art show. Goethe-Institut, Dublin.

16 Launch of **Association for the Visual Arts in Ireland** (AVAIL). Joint Chair: Elizabeth Kirwan (National Library of Ireland) and Olivia Fitzpatrick(Art and Design Faculty, University of Ulster, Belfast.)

20 Sale of contents of **Stackallen House**, Co Meath. Christie's and Hamilton Osborne King.

20 **Carey Clarke** elected President of the Royal Hibernian Academy, in succession to Thomas Ryan.

22 *Until 28 October*
41st Wexford Festival Opera.Opened by An Taoiseach.

28 **Mairead Dunlevy** appointed first Director of the Hunt Museum in Limerick.

and now looking out of step with the present currents.

September 1992

In many ways, Temple Bar Studios and Gallery have taken over the Project Arts Centre's mantle and the former, accordingly, was the venue for *Irene Uhlemann*'s *Almost Full Circle*, an exhibition of paintings which confronted with graphic rawness the aftermath of a car accident in which the artist was involved a year earlier. If Uhlemann's work appeared at times quite out of control, *Vivienne Roche*'s sculpture at the Crawford Gallery in her native Cork was an intensely-disciplined display of her mastery over steel and, in the smaller pieces, bronze. *Signlines* showed the undoubted influence of Scandinavia, where Roche had spent some time, and took the bell as a recurring motif, appropriately for a city in which that instrument strikes a familiar chord.

Much less familiar was the work of *Roy Johnston*, whose last show in Dublin had occurred in 1985 until Oliver Dowling's gallery played host to recent paintings during September. Johnston has been living in New York for the past six years but his loose, abstract style fitted with comfortable familiarity into the gallery's existing stable of artists. Just so, *Howard Hodgkin*'s hand-coloured prints found a natural home at the Kerlin Gallery, though their prices were somewhat greater than most Irish collectors are accustomed to paying, as the artist, who has since acquired a house in Co Cork, will no doubt quickly learn.

The usual jumble which is the Oireachtas art exhibition opened around the same time in the RHA Gallagher Gallery with few surprises amongst the innumerable exhibitors. What did surprise and, more importantly, disappoint, was *Alanna O'Kelly*'s installation at the Irish Museum of Modern Art. Called *The Country Blooms ... A Garden and A Grave*, it was intended to be an exploration of the Great Famine, though little in the orderly arrangement of

CALENDAR OF THE ART YEAR

EXHIBITIONS

1 *Until 16 October*
New work by **Norman Smyth**. Bell Gallery, Belfast.

1 *Until 24 October*
Prints by **Alice Hanratty**. Graphic Studio Dublin Gallery.

2 *Until 7 November*
Bronzes by **Alwyn Gillespie**, Tom Caldwell Gallery, Dublin.

1 *Until 15 November*
Beneath the Waves – assemblages by **Eoin Kelly.** Loafers' Bar, Cork.

3 *Until 31 October*
Monumental prints by Catalan artist **Antoni Tapies**. Butler Gallery, Kilkenny Castle.

3 Recent works by **James McConnell**. Gordon Gallery, Derry.

5 *Until 17 October*
Watercolours by **Rosemary McNamara**. Cork Arts Society Gallery, Lavitt's Quay, Cork.

5 Sculpture and drawings by **Margaret Fitzgibbon**. Limerick City Gallery.

6 *Until 3 January*
Touring exhibition of work of **Irish Professional Conservators' and Restorers' Association** (IPCRA). Ulster Museum, Belfast.

7 *Until 31 October*
New works by **Basil Blackshaw**, Tom Caldwell Gallery, Belfast.

7 *Until 24 October*
What does it mean? – mixed media collage by **Claudia Andrei**. Goethe-Institut, Dublin.

7 *Until 28 October*
Gwen O'Dowd – New Paintings. Kerlin Gallery, Dublin.

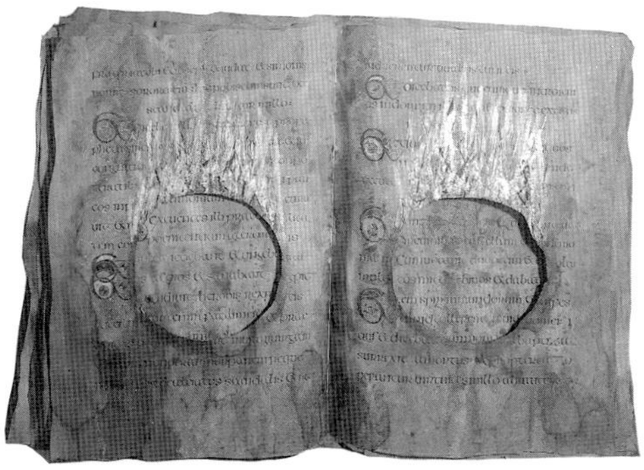

Denis Brown, *Kells Burning*

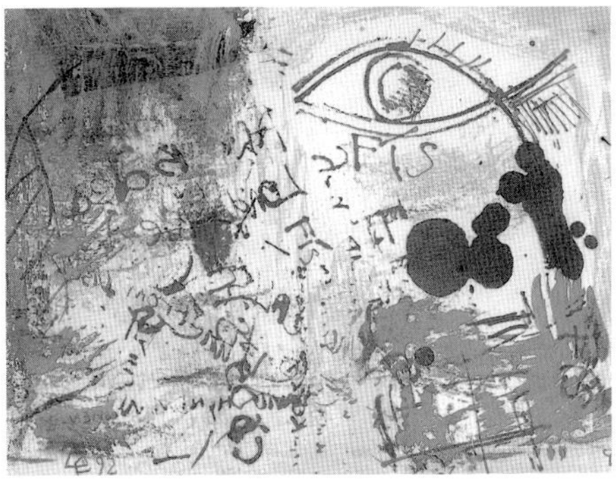

Tom Bevan, *Fís*.

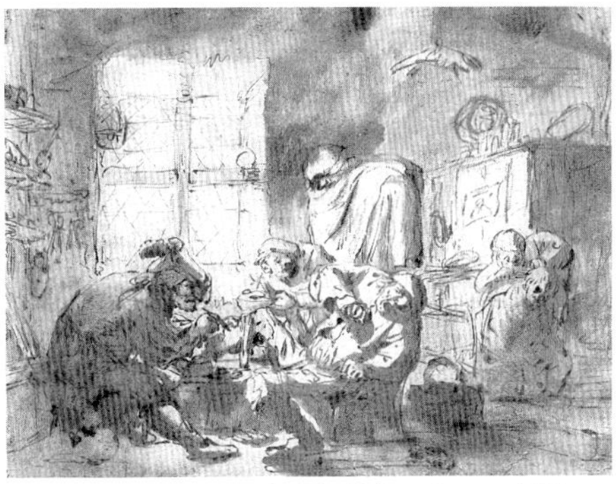

Adriaen van Ostade, *The Village Doctor*, NGI.

9 *Until 31 October*
New work by **Eithne Jordan**.Rubicon Gallery, Dublin.

9 *Until 30 October*
Beyond Description – works by eight well-known Irish artists from the permanent collection of the IMMA. First touring exhibition. Ennis Library, Co Clare.

11 *Until 23 October*
Inverse Alchemy, an exhibition of calligraphic works by **Denis Brown**, Riverrun Gallery, Dublin.

12 *Until 31 October*
Sculpture by **Alexandra Wejchert**. Solomon Gallery, Dublin.

13 *Until 28 October*
New work by **Trevor Geoghegan**. Kilcock Art Gallery.

14 *Until 31 October*
Studio porcelain by **Vivienne Foley**. European Modern Art, Dublin

14 *Until 6 November*
The Road to Basra – paintings by **Michelle Rogers**. Project Arts Centre,Dublin

14 *Until 7 November*
Multi-media 'contemporary Keltic Arts from Ulster' **Tom Bevan** and **Liam de Frinse**. Pantheon Gallery Dublin

17 *Until 4 November*
Twelve Stars – works from the European Parliament art collection. Arts Council Gallery,Belfast.

17 *Until 15 November*
Abstract paintings by Italian artist **Ugo Giletta**. Crawford Gallery, Cork.

18 *Until 29 November*
The Anatomy Lesson: Art and Medicine. National Gallery of Ireland, Dublin in association with the Royal College of Physicians of Ireland. Opening by HRH Princess Margriet of the Netherlands.

photographs and video presentations suggested this. September was not the best month for the Museum, as it also included *Guilt by Association,* from five Glasgow artists, a series of site-specific works which took eighteen months to prepare and yet managed to be entirely unmemorable. And the *Cosmological Pictures* from *Gilbert & George* looked merely arch in their religious devotion to what elsewhere long ago became tired symbols of kitsch – unless, or course, the entire show was intended to be a joke so private than no one other than the two artists could share it.

The private opening of the *Irish Film Centre* in Dublin's Temple Bar district at the end of September was almost as exclusive but much more entertaining, with a bevy of film and rock music performers imported to join the home-produced talent for the occasion. Formerly the Friends' Meeting House, the premises were transformed to accommodate two cinemas, a bookshop, bar, restaurant and large airy foyer which has subsequently been used as a venue for a number of sculpture exhibitions. And sculpture outdoors was offered on a new trail, the first ever in Northern Ireland, which was created in Castlewellan Forest Park to coincide with the British Presidency of the European Parliament; appropriately, the sculptors chosen included three from the province, three from the Republic and two from elsewhere in the European Community.

October 1992

From one of those member states, France, *Annette Messager* came *Telling Tales* to the Douglas Hyde Gallery, where her fantastical and elaborate creations explored the identity of women in society and art alike. The more modest concerns of the late James Sleator, a former President of the RHA, could be explored at the Gorry Gallery, where fifteen of his pictures, mostly portraits and still-lifes, were included in a large show which also offered eighteenth and nineteenth century art.

On the equally domestic scale, *Alwyn*

CALENDAR OF THE ART YEAR

22 *Until 30 October*
Exhibition of Irish Art, Milmo-Penny Fine Art Gallery, Dublin.

22 *Until 7 November*
Manumit – new paintings by **John Cronin**. Oliver Dowling Gallery, Dublin.

24 *Until 21 November*
Mickey Donnelly – new work. Orchard Gallery, Derry.

28 *Until 9 December*
Annette Messager – **Telling Tales**. Douglas Hyde Gallery, TCD.

28 **Catherine Kenny**. Temple Bar Gallery, Dublin.

29 *Until 14 February*
Richard Hamilton Retrospective. IMMA, Dublin (Tate Gallery 17 June-6 September)

29 *Until 14 November*
Nancy Wynne-Jones – new work. Taylor Galleries, Dublin.

30 *Until 18 November*
Richard Hamilton Print Retrospective 1979-1991. Kerlin Gallery, Dublin.

30 *Until 12 November*
Paintings by **James Sleator** PRHA (1885-1950) Gorry Gallery, Dublin.

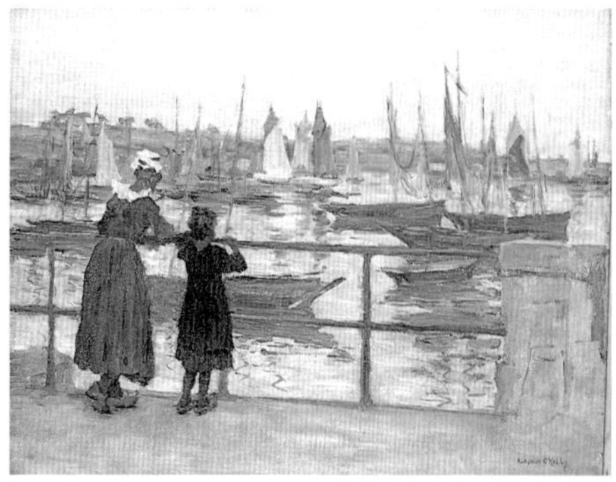

Aloysius O'Kelly, *Awaiting the Return, Concarneau*, Milmo-Penny Fine Art.

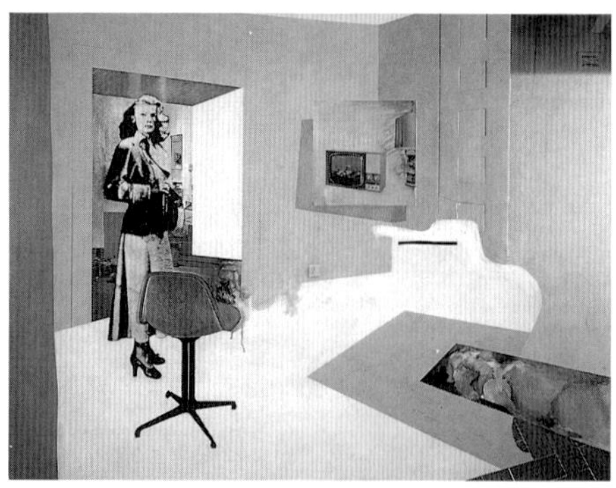

Richard Hamilton, *Interior II*, 1964.

PUBLICATIONS

20 Louis Le Brocquy, **The Irish Landscape**, (Gandon Books) £27.50 clothbound. Launched at Newman House, Dublin.

27 **Annual Report of Arts Council/ An Chomhairle Ealaion**. Total expenditure in 1991 was £10.8 million – £10m from State and £0.8m from other sources.

November 1992

EVENTS

5 **Irish Artists for Somalia**. Hundreds of Irish artists and collectors donated work for auction in aid of famine victims. Auctioned by John de Vere White in National Concert Hall Dublin. Raised over £50,000.

6 & 7 **Random Access**. Conference on site-specific, time-based and live art. Sculptors' Society, at Irish Museum of Modern Art.

9 **Irish Museum of Modern Art** announced grants totalling £34,000 from the Paul Hamlyn Foundation for the Education and Community Programme, and from the Henry Moore Sculpture Trust, for the Artists' Work Programme, for Irish and overseas artists.

9 Central Bank of Ireland issued new **£20 banknote**, designed by **Robert Ballagh**. First in a planned new series.

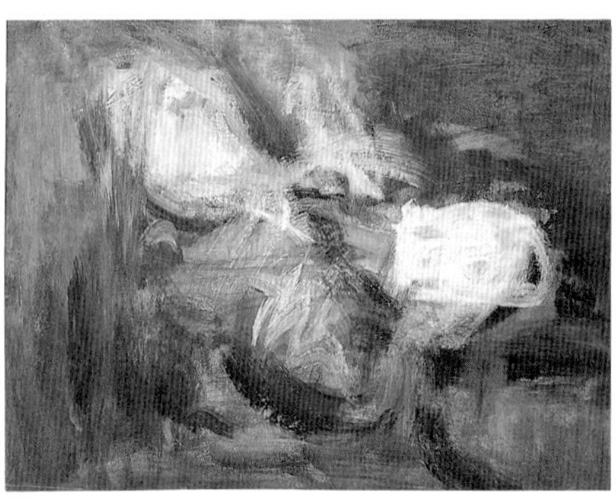

Nancy Wynne-Jones, *Waterlilies*, 1991.

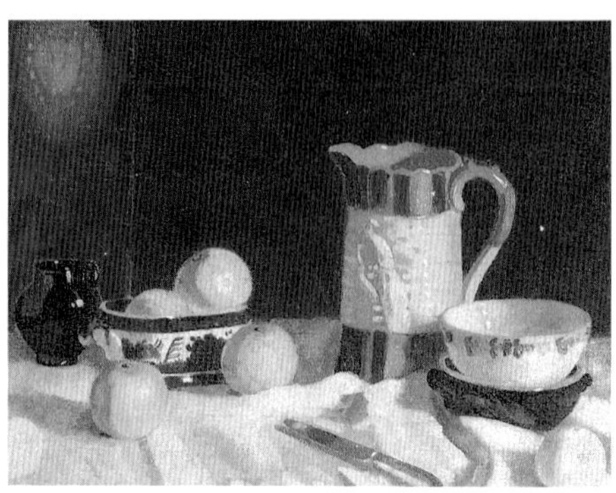

James Sleator, *Still Life with ceramic pots*, c.1920.

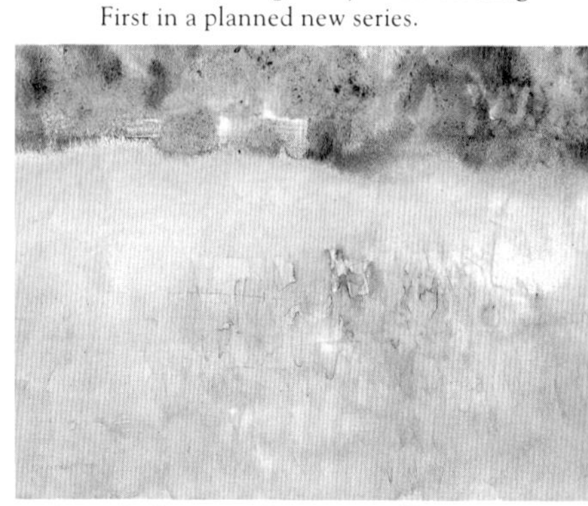

Louis Le Brocquy, *Goat in a Dublin Field*, 1991.

Gillespie had a show of bronzes at the Tom Caldwell Gallery in Dublin, while at the Graphic Studio, *Alice Hanratty*'s first solo show in more than a decade revealed a rather cool expressionist, unimpassioned but with a fine control of the medium. More prints, though this time on a monumental scale, arrived at Kilkenny's Butler Gallery as one stop of a European tour. Catalan artist *Antonio Tapies*, obviously much better known here as a painter, this time produced etchings, achieving maximum effect with minimal means, aided by scale but also by his own authority. *Gwen O'Dowd*, who enjoyed an equal success in the same gallery two years earlier, offered her latest work at the Kerlin Gallery, once again with the sea as a motif, although now it was not the Welsh coast but the West of Ireland and the Aran Islands which provided the inspiration. O'Dowd's contemporary, *Eithne Jordan*, showed at the same time in the Rubicon Gallery, her expressionist paintings brighter and less burdened by dark shadows than hitherto, and a similar light freshness could be found amongst *Alexandra Wejchert*'s sculptures at the Solomon Gallery. Nothing especially new here, nor in the book *The Irish Landscape* by *Louis Le Brocquy* which was issued around the same time by Gandon Books.

The sense of *déja-vu* was even more palpable at the Museum of Modern Art where British artist *Richard Hamilton*'s retrospective, organised in association with the Tate Gallery, arrived at the end of the month. Running all the way from a series of very early oils dated 1940 which had never been shown before in public right up to a painting of 1992, the exhibition as a whole revealed that Hamilton's reputation was hindered rather than enhanced by his excessive association with pop art, since his concerns were so much wider and more fascinating than this one movement could ever be. Another side of Hamilton was also available for inspection in the print retrospective mounted simultaneously at the Kerlin Gallery, which included illustrations to Joyce's *Ulysses* and reflection

CALENDAR OF THE ART YEAR

11 **Second Brian de Breffny Memorial Lecture** by Brian May. Heritage Centre, Carrick on Suir, Co Waterford.

14 **New Model Arts Centre** opened in Sligo with Barrie Cooke Retrospective.

19 **President Mary Robinson**, patron of **Cothu**, presented **1992 Arts Sponsor of the Year Awards**.Best Sponsor, Irish Life Assurance, for Dublin Theatre Festival; Best Single Sponsorship, Aer Rianta , for Kremlin Gold Exhibition, IMMA; Best First Time Arts Sponsor, Kingscourt Bricks, for Kingscourt Sculpture Symposium, Co Cavan; Best Community Arts Sponsorship, Northern Telecom, Galway, for theatre in Galway Arts Festival; Special Award for Heritage, Gallaher(Dublin), for restoration of Newman House(see article in this issue); Cothu/Irish Permanent Award, Pavee Point Trust/James Crean for National Traveller Arts Festival. In association with The Sunday Business Post .

21 **Florence in the Age of Lorenzo De' Medici**. Seminar in the National Gallery of Ireland.

26 **Waterford Crystal** presented two chandeliers to Hugh Lane Municipal Gallery following its recent extensive refurbishment by Dublin Corporation.

27 Death of Irish-born painter, **Sir Sidney Nolan**.

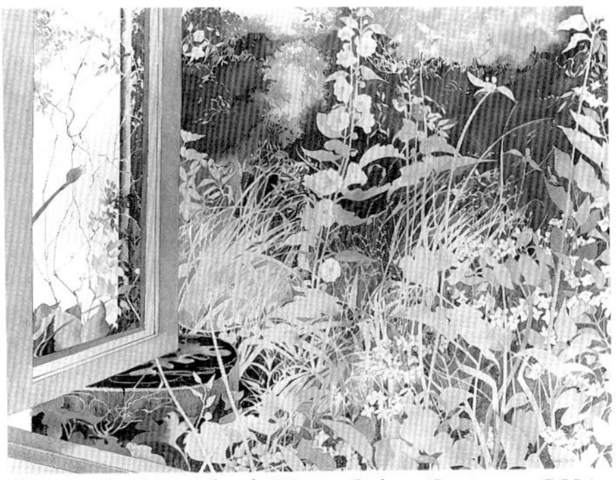
Kay Doyle, *Heir Island*. Water Colour Society at RHA.

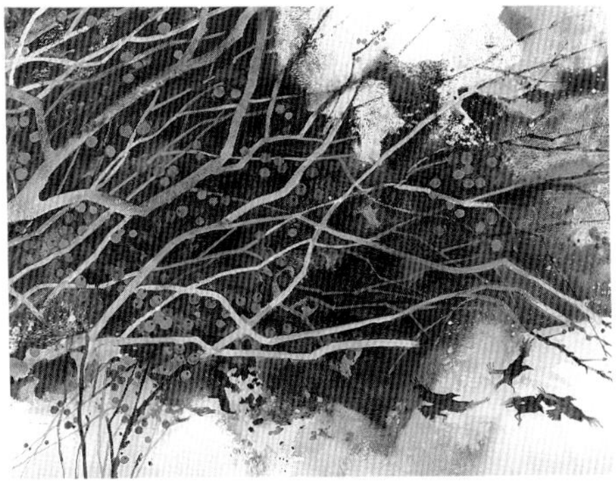
John Skelton, *The Haw Lanterns*, Water Colour Society at RHA.

EXHIBITIONS

2 *Until 13 November*
Martin Mooney & Roy Petley. Bell Gallery, Belfast

2 *Until 14 November*
John Behan ARHA – Sculpture. Cork Arts Society.

2 *Until 17 November*
138th Annual Exhibition of the Water Colour Society of Ireland. RHA Gallagher Gallery, Dublin.

2 *Until 26 November*
Sculpture by **Tom Bevan**, Flowerfield Arts Centre, Portstewart, Co Derry.

3 *Until 18 November*
Graham Gingles – Mid Life Retrospective Exhibition. Narrow Water Gallery, Warrenpoint, Co Down.

3 *Until 25 November*
Jack B Yeats, Waddington Gallery, London.

4 *Until 28 November*
Felim Egan – new paintings. Fenderesky Gallery, Belfast.

4 *Until 23 December*
Sean Scully, Waddington Gallery, London.

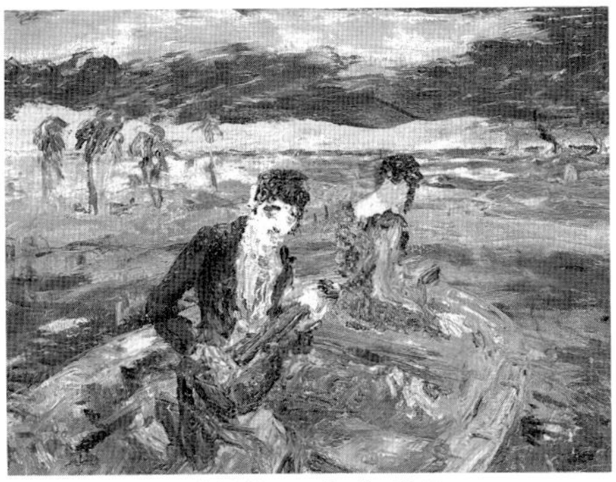
Jack B Yeats, *Drift*, 1941.

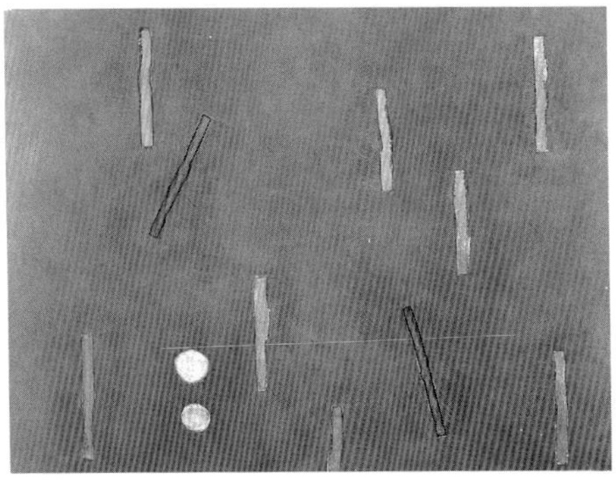
Felim Egan, *Pool, 1992.*

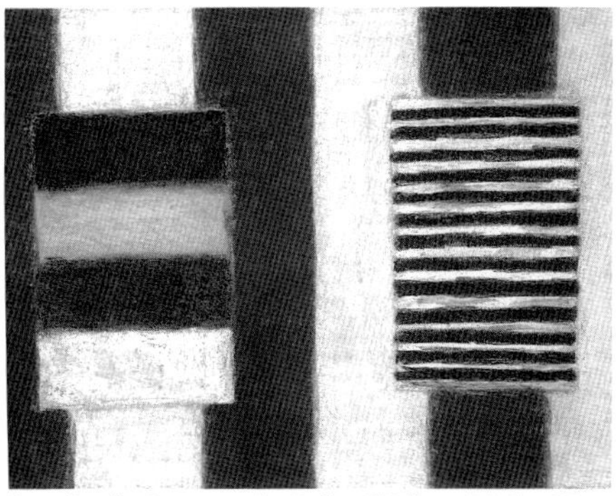
Sean Scully, Drawing for Robin Walker, 7 July 1991.

on the political problems of Northern Ireland. Anticipating another major retrospective, the Taylor Gallery showed recent work by *Nancy Wynne-Jones* towards the close of October, and then early the following month, an exhibition spanning thirty-five years of her career was presented at the RHA Gallagher Gallery, having already toured venues around the rest of the country.

Married to sculptor *Conor Fallon* and resident in Ireland for the past twenty years, Wynne-Jones – like *Tony O'Malley* whose early work had been seen some months previously – lived and worked for some time in St Ives and the influence of that place and period lingers on in her later paintings. Her lyrical landscapes retain a freshness even when produced more than thirty years ago, making this one of the most delightful shows of 1992.

November 1992

As at the RHA Gallagher Gallery, the *Water Colour Society of Ireland* held its annual exhibition, in which landscapes, though all too often of a rather more insipid character, again predominated. The rumbustious landscapes of *Jack B Yeats* were shown in an exhibition of paintings, drawings and watercolours by this artist held a week later at the Taylor Galleries to celebrate the launch of *Hilary Pyle*'s authoritative *catalogue raisonné* of Yeats' oil paintings – massive, three-volume publication limited to only 1,000 copies and therefore almost certain to become every bit as collectable as the pictures they document.

Had November been deemed the month for landscape? So it appeared, as the same theme provided an inspiration for *Ross Wilson*'s new paintings at the Kerlin Gallery, though these pictures verged close to outright abstraction. And at the same time, in the Hugh Lane Gallery, President Robinson opened an exhibition of work by the late *Ernest Hayes* in which landscape once again predominated. If this show was intended to enhance Hayes' rep-

CALENDAR OF THE ART YEAR

4 *Until 29 November*
Nancy Wynne-Jones Retrospective 1957-1990. RHA Gallagher Gallery, Dublin.

5 *Until 1 December*
Michael Evans & Vivienne St Clair-Collins. Wellspring Gallery, Tralee.

10 *Until 27 November*
Petals & Stems – coloured etchings by **Grainne Cuffe**. European Modern Art , Dublin.

10 *Until 18 November*
The Blues is a Feeling. Photographs by **James Frayer**, City Arts Centre, Dublin.

10 *Until 28 November*
Adrian Hall, NSW Australia- paintings created during a residency in Derry. Arts Council Gallery, Belfast

11 *Until 5 December*
Recent works by **Betty Maguire**.Pantheon Gallery, Dublin.

11 *Until 29 November*
Paintings by **Oliver Whelan**. RHA Gallagher Gallery.

11 *Until 31 January*
Craigie Horsfield – Photographic Works. Irish Museum of Modern Art.

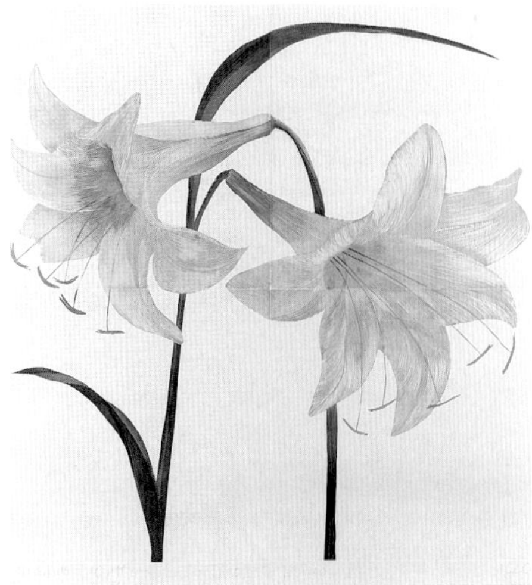

Grainne Cuffe, *Two Lovely Lilies*.

11 *Until 11 January*
Neil Shawcross. Northern Ireland Business Centre, London. Arts Council of Northern Ireland.

12 *Until 6 December*
Fresh Maumratta Hares and Other Paintings from The Periphery – paintings by **Dermot Seymour**. Project Arts Centre, Dublin.

12 *Until 28 November*
Paintings by **Fergus Martin**. Oliver Dowling Gallery, Dublin.

16 *Until 28 November*
James Scanlon – Stained Glass and Mixed Media. Cork Arts Society

19 *Until 5 December*
Screenprints by **Tim Mara**. Graphic Studio Dublin Gallery.

19 *Until 5 December*
Martin Gale – Still-life paintings. Taylor Galleries, Dublin.

20 *Until 9 December*
New paintings by **Ross Wilson**. Kerlin Gallery, Dublin.

21 *Until 10 January*
Photomontages by German artist **John Heartfield** (1891-1968). IMMA, Dublin.

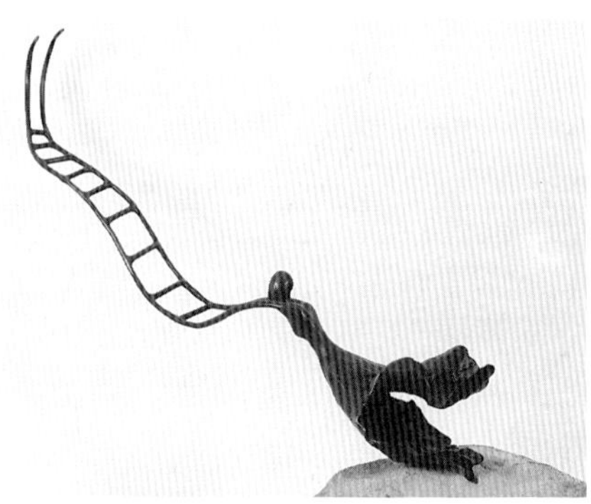

Betty Maguire, *Unfold*, 1992.

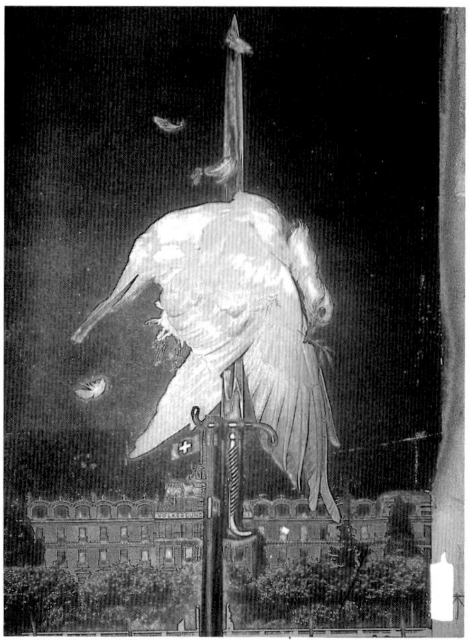

John Heartfield, *The Spirit of Geneva* 1992.

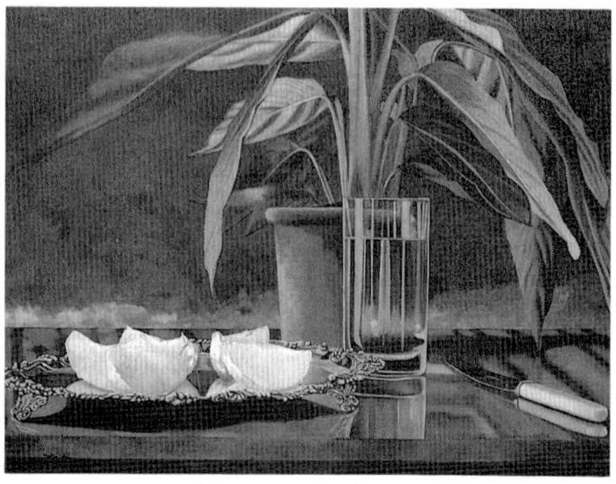

Martin Gale, *Oasis*.

utation, then it most definitely must be judged a failure since, whatever about their individual charms, collected together, the paintings revealed an artist of limited abilities, much-too-much given to repeating stated formulae in the worst academic manner.

How refreshing, therefore, to turn to *Fergus Martin*'s cool, minimalist abstracts at the Oliver Dowling Gallery, which made no concessions to the viewer but, precisely because of their uncompromising stance, merited and received attention. Similarly, the Museum of Modern Art offered two artists this month, both of whose work impressed by its rigid discipline. *Craigie Horsfield*'s large-scale black and white photographs, created in London and Poland, had a harsh spare quality every bit as affecting as *John Heartfield*'s photomontages which, during the 1920s and '30s, waged war against the rise of German fascism. That Heartfield was ultimately unsuccessful, both in his personal crusade and as an artist in his later life, made the work from this earlier period all the more poignant. At the end of November two young entrepreneurs, *Karen Reihill* and *David Britton*, undertook a new gallery venture in Dublin which ought to meet with greater success than Heartfield achieved. During the same period, *Jerome O Drisceoil*, who had opened his own premises in the Spring, unveiled *Artfolio*, a collection of limited edition prints by five Irish artists. And the same month saw the publication of a tribute to another, in this instance deceased, Irish artist, *Roderic O'Conor*, written by *Jonathan Benington*, which should serve further to enhance the reputation of this painter.

December 1992

Scottish-born, but now Irish-resident, painter *William Crozier* was the subject of a film tribute, given a private screening at the Taylor Galleries in early December before being shown on RTE in the new year. And, since retrospectives and tributes seemed to be in favour, for the first

CALENDAR OF THE ART YEAR

24 *Until 31 January*
Unspoken Truths – works by 32 Dublin women. Opened by President Robinson. IMMA, Dublin.

26 *Until 3 December*
Artfolio – limited edition prints . Jerome O Drisceoil, 58 Fitzwilliam Square, Dublin.

28 *Until 24 December*
New work by **Fergus Delargy**. Orchard Gallery, Derry.

28 *Until 24 January*
Ernest Hayes RHA. Hugh Lane Municipal Gallery, Dublin. Opened by President Robinson.

PUBLICATIONS

10 Hilary Pyle, **Jack B Yeats: a Catalogue Raisonné of the Oil Paintings**. 3 vols.1856 pp. 1822 ills. £450. (Andre Deutsch, London, 1993).Launched at Taylor Galleries, Dublin, with concurrent exhibition.

18 Jonathan Benington, **Roderic O'Conor: a biography, with a catalogue of his work**. 248pp.inc 88pp. full colour. £29.95. (Irish Academic Press, Dublin, 1993). Launched in the National Gallery of Ireland by Mr Nicholas Robinson. In association with Co-operation North. Reception sponsored by Glen Dimplex.(See review in this issue.)

20 Paul Larmour, **The Arts & Crafts Movement in Ireland**. (Friar's Bush Press, Belfast,1993) (See review in this issue.)

25 **Annual Report of the Arts Council of Northern Ireland**. (Arts Council, Belfast.)

December 1992

EVENTS

9 Private screening in the Taylor Galleries, Dublin, of Cian O hEigeartaigh's film on the Scottish-born painter **William Crozier**.

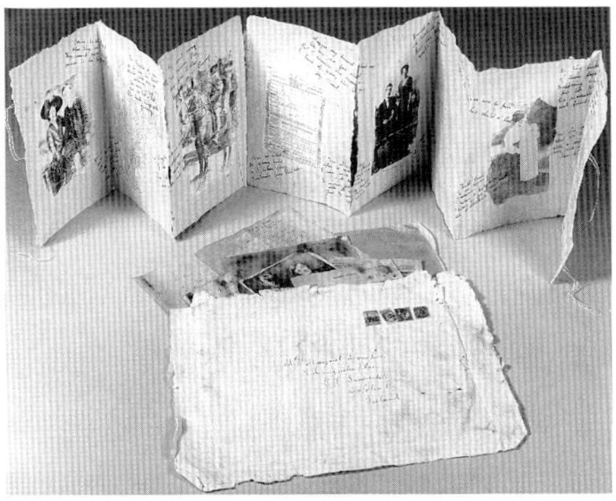

Mary McCann, *Letters Unfolding* from *Unspoken Truths*

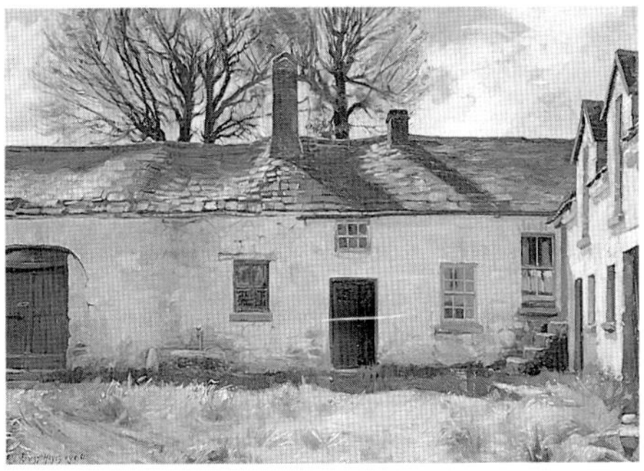

Ernest Hayes RHA, *Sunlit Roofs, 1961.*

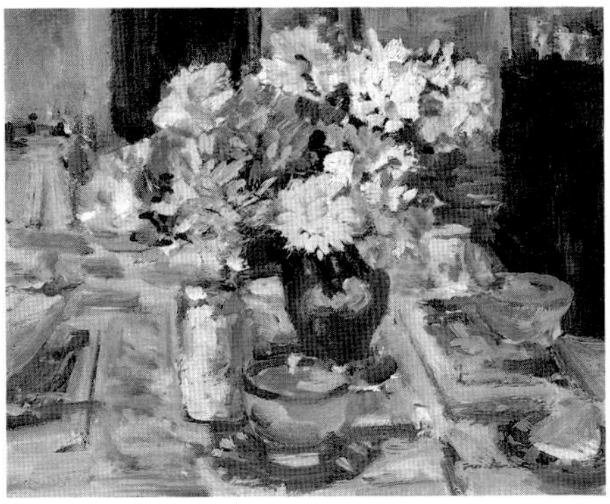

James O'Halloran, *Summer Flowers.*

9 Dinner in honour of **Gordon Lambert**, recently retired chairman of Contemporary Irish Arts Society.

10 Dublin City Council, on the casting vote of the acting chairman, voted to approve the design by **Scott Tallon Walker** for the second phase of the civic offices at Wood Quay.

11 Three Irish architectural heritage projects received **EC awards in Brussels** – the restoration of Dr Steevens' Hospital in Dublin and two projects in Limerick, the late 18th-century Crescent and the Milk Market.

11 **An Taoiseach,Albert Reynolds**, informed the **Arts Council** that he proposed increasing their annual grant in 1993 to £11.5million

17 National Gallery of Ireland acquired Portrait of **Richard St George Mansergh St George** by Hugh Douglas Hamilton(c.1739-1808). Now on public display in the Irish Rooms.

EXHIBITIONS

1 *Until 19 December*
Radu Dragomirescu. Narrow Water Gallery, Warrenpoint.

1 *Until 31 December*
Treasured Objects Restored & Conserved. The Work of the Irish Professional Conservators' & Restorers' Association. Travelling Exhibition(see IAR 1992 pp.139-143). Ulster Museum, Belfast.

4 *Until 20 December*
Art for Africa. Exhibition inspired by President Robinson's visit to Somalia. Contributions from over 70 Irish artists. Crawford Municipal Art Gallery, Cork.

4 *Until 23 December*
Requiem – new paintings and drawings by **Samuel Walsh**. Oliver Dowling Gallery, Dublin

4 *Until 17 December*
Lights and Reflections. Paintings by James O'Halloran. Gorry Gallery, Dublin.

time in thirty years, the Ulster Museum brought together its collection of pictures by *Sir John Lavery*, one painter who never seems to have fallen from grace even if the publicity for this show called him 'the painter of an era.' Very much an artist of the present, at least in his use of computer technology, *Charlie Whisker*, who spends much of his time in Los Angeles working on pop videos, had a show of paintings at the Kerlin Gallery. By comparison, *Geraldine O'Reilly*'s selection of drawings at the Project Arts Centre, employing only conté, chalk and watercolour, seemed defiantly old-fashioned, as did *John Moore*'s paintings on show at Restaurant Tosca, owned by *Norman Hewson*, brother of well-known collector and occasional musician *Bono*.

Samuel Walsh showed more of his geometric abstracts at the Oliver Dowling Gallery; his previous exhibition had been bought in its entirety by the Irish Museum of Modern Art where British mechanical artist *John White* presented his latest installation. Given the rapidly approaching Christmas festivities, this had the apposite title of *Party Piece.*

January 1993

The anti-climactic flatness that inevitably follows those seasonal parties was relieved in mid-January by the news that *Michael D Higgins* had been appointed the first-ever *Minister for Arts, Culture and the Gaeltacht* in the coalition government just then formed. A well-known poet, Mr Higgins soon proved to be as generous with words in speech as he was in print and, during the first few months in office, he clearly relished every opportunity to talk at length about his ambitions; it remains to be seen whether his language is matched by equally lavish deeds. A more subdued appointment was that of *William Gallagher*, hitherto curator of *Derek Hill's Glebe Gallery* in Co Donegal to the post of Visual Arts Co-Ordinator at the *Boole Library, UCC* which, by coincidence had just been vacated by his wife, *Hilary*

CALENDAR OF THE ART YEAR

4 *Until 28 March*
Sir John Lavery. Ulster Museum.

5 *Until 00 January*
Silent Stones – photographic works by **Allen Kennedy & John P Coyle**. Orchard Gallery, Derry.

11 *Until 6 January*
Di die in diem – new paintings by **Charlie Whisker**. Kerlin Gallery, Dublin.

11 *Until 15 January*
Rites – drawings by **Geraldine O'Reilly**. Project Arts Centre, Dublin.

14 *Until 27 January*
Elke Thonnes – paintings. Arts Council, Dublin.

15 Until 23 December
Party Piece – installation by **John White**. IMMA,Dublin.

16 *Until 31 December*
Clay and Stone – new works by **Sonja Landweer**. Taylor Galleries, Dublin.

17 *Until 31 December*
Paul Wilson, new paintings. One Oxford Street, Belfast.

P U B L I C A T I O N S

5 **Decantations: A Tribute to Maurice Craig**. (Lilliput Press in association with Penguin Books.)

8 Helen Coburn, **The Joy of Collecting**. £15.99 (Wolfhound , Dublin)

S A L E R O O M S

8 Sarah Purser, **Summer Flowers**, £9,500. Mary Swanzy, **Kerry Cow**, £2,500. Taylor de Veres, Dublin.

16 Tony O'Malley HRHA, **Summer Sea, Sunset**, £900. Jack B Yeats, **Up the Canal**, £10,000. James Adam Salerooms, Dublin

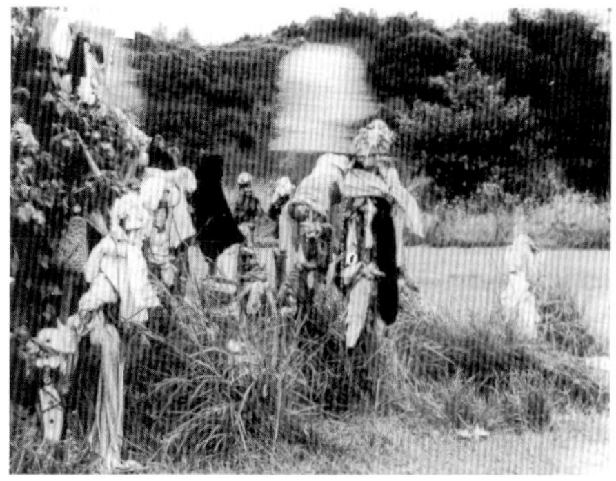

Pilgrims, Doonwell, from *Silent Stones*, Orchard Gallery.

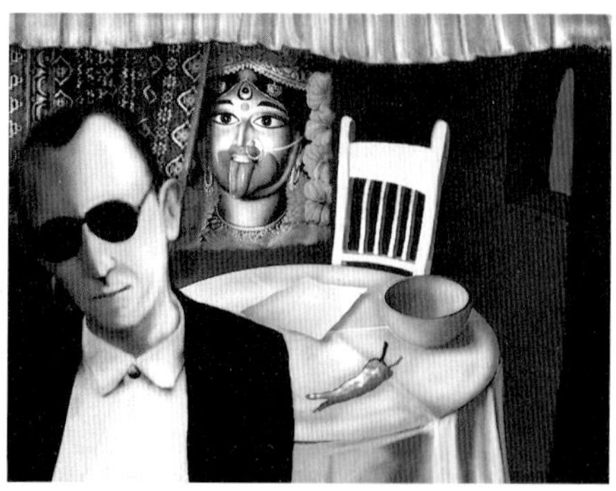

Charlie Whisker, *Perhapsless Mystery of an Unwritten Smile* 1992.

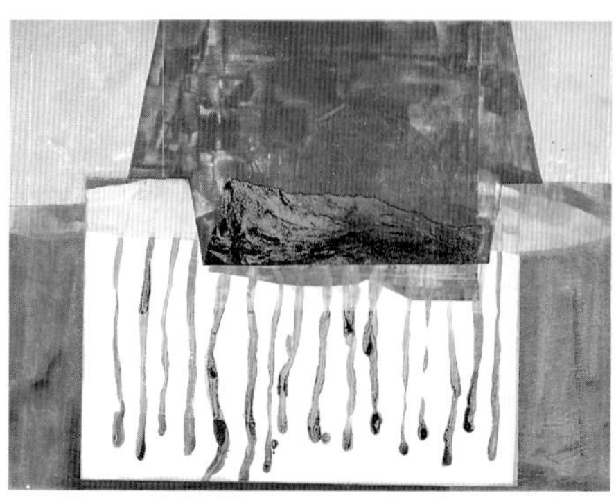

Fionnuala Ní Chiosain, *mixed media on wood.*

January 1993

E V E N T S

12 **Michael D Higgins** appointed first **Minister for Arts, Culture and the Gaeltacht**.

12 *and 14 January*
Dr Marian Burleigh-Motley (Metropolitan Museum of Art, New York) lectured in Ulster Museum, Belfast on Picasso and on George Russell.

13 Launch of **Irish Museum of Modern Art** programme of events and activities for 1993.

14 Belfast-born artist **Shirley MacWilliam** began six-month residency as Tate Gallery, Liverpool's fifth Momart Fellow

15 **William Gallagher**, formerly of the Glebe Gallery, Co Donegal, appointed Visual Arts Co-ordinator at the Boole Library, University College, Cork in succession to **Hilary O'Kelly**.

18 Islamic art expert **David James**, former curator for twenty years in Chester Beatty Library, Dublin, jailed for five years for larceny of manuscripts and Koran pages.

29 Lecture by **Philip Napier**, sculptor, on his British School at Rome Scholarship. Arts Council Gallery, Belfast.

E X H I B I T I O N S

6 *Until 6 February*
David Godbold. Douglas Hyde Gallery, TCD.

8 *Until 27 January*
Fionnuala Ni Chiosain – new paintings. Kerlin Gallery, Dublin.

9 *Until 30 January*
Mark Pepper – Past Present Past. Orchard Gallery, Derry.

O'Kelly, organiser of the previous year's *Nancy Wynne-Jones* retrospective. Looking forward rather than backwards, the exhibition *On the Balcony of the Nation* which had been on tour for more than two years in the USA, returned to Northern Ireland to be seen at the Arts Council Gallery in Belfast. The work by five artists was predominantly figurative as was that of *David Godbold* who was given a kind of mid-term retrospective at the Douglas Hyde Gallery with a catalogue essay of determined earnestness by *Caoimhin MacGiolla Leith* which seemed almost at odds with the artist's jokey work. The references to religion in Godbold's pictures, whilst increasingly overt, remain distinctly ironic with a steady dependence on twentieth century cartoon icons to undermine the borrowed iconography of earlier eras. Just as entertaining, *Peter O'Kennedy* held a show called *Bambino* at the Project Arts Centre which was filled with five Fiat 126s transformed into such amusing novelties as a giant pink cupcake and a metal hedgehog. The sixth vehicle, intended to be an aquarium on wheels, unfortunately had to be removed from the premises on the day of the opening when it was discovered to suffer from serious leakage. In Belfast, the Ulster Museum held an exhibition of *Tom Phillips'* work which had come from the Royal Academy in London, whilst in Dublin, the Museum of Modern Art took the show of *Tony O'Malley's 1960s paintings* originated by Kilkenny's Butler Gallery. O'Malley was one of the plethora of artists included in the *Vincent and Noeleen Ferguson Collection of Contemporary Art* on display at the RHA Gallagher Gallery, where he kept company with the likes of *Basil Blackshaw, Charlie Brady* and *Paddy Collins*. But the range and quality of pictures was so diverse that only a judicious hanging saved this show from looking like a complete hotch-potch. The coherence one exhibition lacked was provided by another, dedicated to Finnish architect *Alvar Aalto's* work at the RIAI's headquarters in Merrion Square, the start of anexciting 1993 programme in this venue.

CALENDAR OF THE ART YEAR

12 *Until 12 February*
Ken Hardy – Customs & Excise. City Arts Centre, Dublin.

13 *Until 6 December*
Sculpture by **James McKenna – Prairie Pretensions.** Pantheon Gallery, Dublin.

14 *Until 7 March*
Tom Phillips RA. Ulster Museum, Belfast.

14 *Until 10 February*
Cracow-Cork Exhibition. Crawford Gallery, Cork.

18 *Until 29 January*
Bambino – Exhibition of Fiat 126s interfered with by **Peter O'Kennedy**. Project Arts Centre, Dublin.

21 *Until 21 March*
Tony O'Malley – Work from the 60s. IMMA, Dublin.

23 *Until 13 February*
Sculpture by **Damien Coyle, Vernon Carter, Don Prince**. Arts Council Gallery, Belfast.

25 *Until mid March*
Vincent and Noeleen Ferguson Collection of Contemporary Art. RHA Gallagher Gallery, Dublin.

27 *Until 12 February*
The Mystery of Form – exhibition of the work of the Finnish architect **Alvar Aalto** (died 1976) .Royal Institute of Architects, Ireland, 8 Merrion Square, Dublin.

27 *Until 28 February*
Civic Offices, Wood Quay, Dublin, architectural competition. Exhibition of model of winning design by **Scott, Tallon, Walker** and drawings of all eight entries. City Hall, Dublin.

P U B L I C A T I O N S

4 David Oldfield, **Later Flemish Paintings in the National Gallery of Ireland: The Seventeenth to Nineteenth Centuries**. (National Gallery of Ireland). Sixth in series of comprehensive illustrated descriptive catalogues of the Gallery's collection. £30 pb. (See review in this issue.).

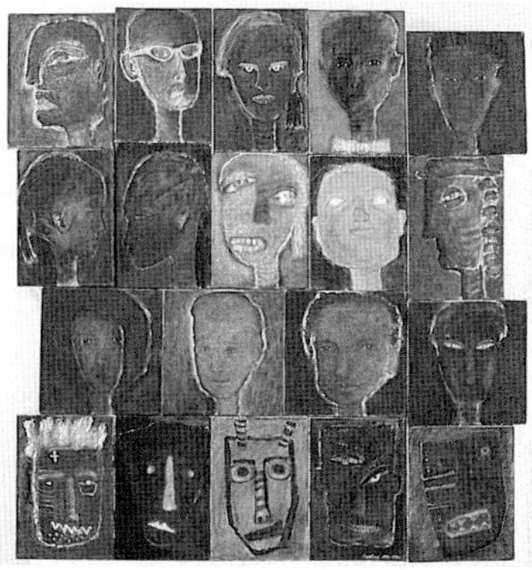

Dorota Martini, *Men, where do we go?* from *Cork-Cracow* at the Crawford.

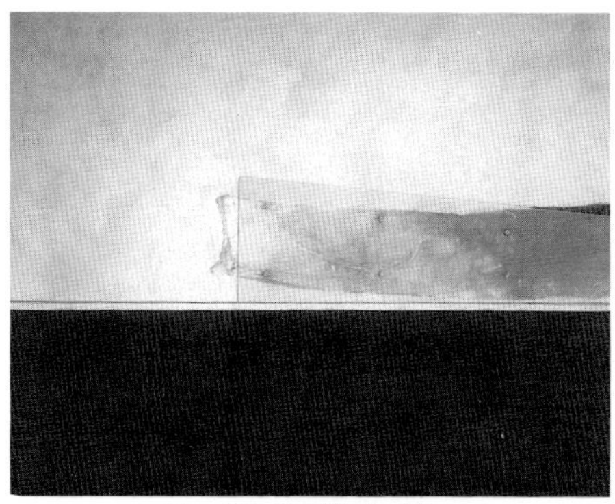

Mary FitzGerald, *Equilibrium*.

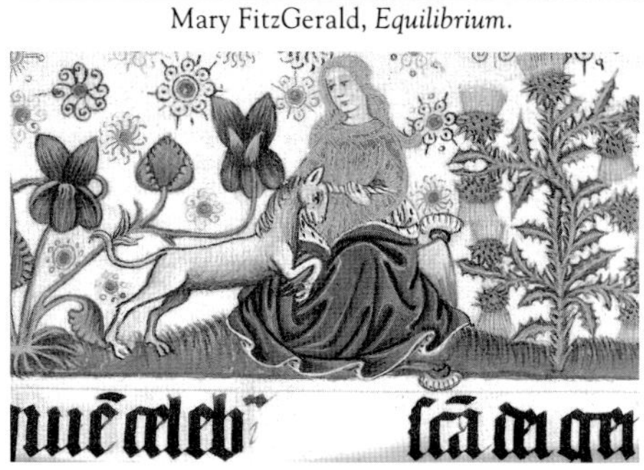

The Virgin and the Unicorn (TCD MS 81 fol22Ov) in *Birds and Beasts from the Bible to the Beagle and Beyond.*

February 1993

E V E N T S

3 Dublin architects **de Blacam and Meagher** won Architectural Association of Ireland Downes medal for excellence for **Beckett Theatre** in Trinity College Dublin.

4 Dublin Corporation announced appointment of **Arts Officer**, to begin work in March, as recommended in 1992 Dublin Arts Report

23 **Louis Le Brocquy** and author **Mary Lavin** awarded by Aosdana the rank of Saoi, its highest honour, 'in recognition of creative work which has made an outstanding contribution to the arts in Ireland'. Arts Council, Dublin.

24 **Irish Heritage Properties conference** on the future of the Irish Country House. Merrion Square, Dublin.

25 Opening by President Mary Robinson of **National Library of Ireland**'s new exhibition room with 'Room for Books' – watercolours of Irish Library Interiors by **Alison, Countess of Rosse**.

E X H I B I T I O N S

2 *Until 20 February*
Mary Fitzgerald – Continuum. First solo exhibition in New York comprising work specially made for the space. Catalogue by Declan McGonagle. Jain Marunouchi Gallery, Broadway, New York.

2 *Until 2 December*
Birds & Beasts from the Bible to the Beagle and Beyond. Manuscripts, fossils, early Egyptian sculpture, costumes from travels of Captain Cook. The Colonnades, Trinity College , Dublin.

February 1993

Contemporary Irish architecture was under scrutiny in early February, when the Architectural Association of Ireland presented its annual awards, with the Downes Medal for excellence going to the *de Blacam and Meagher* practice for its stunning new *Beckett Theatre building in Trinity College, Dublin.* Although making almost no impact on the streetscape, the structure's tiered internal facade of wood is highly reminiscent of Elizabethan theatres and gives the location a presentiment of the drama inside. Elsewhere in TCD, the Old Library's Colonnades exhibition area reopened for the season with a delightful show called *Birds and Beasts* which examined man's attitude towards other animals through manuscripts and early printed books as well as fossils, ancient Egyptian sculpture and costume from the travels of Captain Cook loaned by the National Museum. The building's upper Long Room was just one of the Irish libraries painted by *Alison, Countess of Rosse* for a collection of watercolours, *Room for Books,* which inaugurated the National Library's new exhibition space. The day after this show was opened by the President Mrs Robinson, the Taoiseach Albert Reynolds was the first speaker at a conference on the future of Irish country houses such as the Rosse's own home, *Birr Castle.*

The future of the arts in Cork city was under discussion in February, following the release of the Arts Development Committee's *Report on the State of the Arts in Cork.* Still, the visual arts certainly seemed to be healthy enough with the *Cork Arts Society* holding its thirtieth anniversary exhibition the same month and, a fortnight after this event, the Crawford Art Gallery hosting a show of paintings and graphic works by Swiss artist *Théophile-Alexandre Steinlen,* whose best work captures the spirit of *fin-de-siècle* Paris.

What will yet come to be seen as best representing Dublin at the end of the present century? Well, Dublin painter *Mary*

CALENDAR OF THE ART YEAR

3 *Until December*
Illuminated manuscripts from the Western Collection. Chester Beatty Library, Dublin

4 *Until 26 February*
Catherine Harper – Sculpture and Drawing. Project Arts Centre, Dublin.

5 *Until 6 March*
Rebecca Peart – Paintings and Drawings . Pantheon Gallery, Dublin

5 *Until 28 February*
Leaving Fragments Behind – work from 1988-1993 by **Helen Bradbury**. Peacock Gallery, Craigavon, N I

8 *Until 20 February*
Cork Arts Society 30th anniversary exhibition opened by President Mary Robinson. Lavitt's Quay, Cork

9 *Until 6 March*
Searching for a Place – Paintings by **Mike Harris**. Pantheon Gallery, Dublin.Opened by Michael D Higgins, Minister for Arts,Culture and the Gaeltacht.

9 *Until 18 April*
Marie Foley – Sculpture. IMMA, Dublin.

11 *Until 26 February*
The Kirk Gallery Artists' Agency Premier Group Show. Opened by Minister for the Arts Michael D Higgins. Irish Life Exhibition Centre, Dublin.

13 *Until 13 March*
Jeff Dennis. Orchard Gallery, Derry.

16 *Until 18 March*
Jerome Connor- Irish American Sculptor (1874-1943). National Gallery of Ireland, Dublin. Opened by Michael D Higgins, Minister for Arts.

17 *Until 10 March*
Installation by **Susan Francis**. Arts Council Gallery, Belfast.

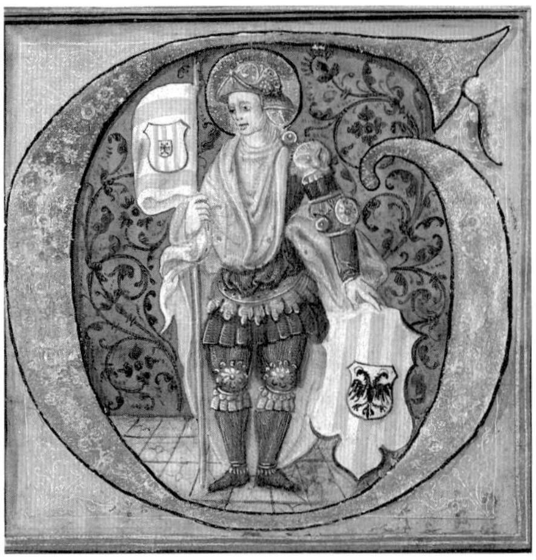

Illuminated initial 'G', Italian ms. c.1500. Chester Beatty Library.

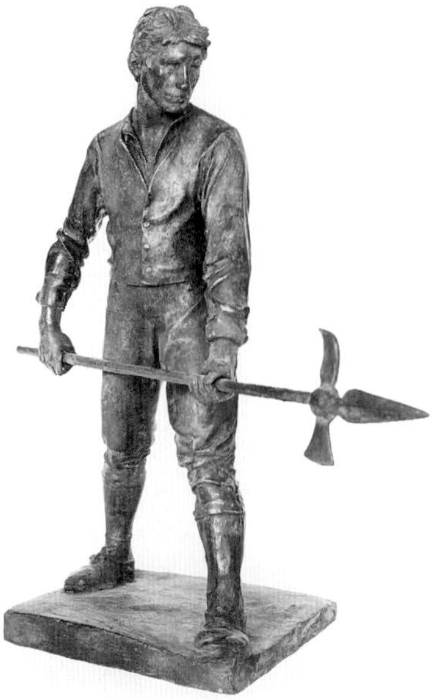

Jerome Connor, *Pikeman.*

18 *Until 6 March*
Gatherings – new work by **Pauline Flynn**. Oliver Dowling Gallery, Dublin.

19 *Until 25 March*
Paintings and graphic works by **Théophile-Alexandre Steinlen** (1859-1923). Crawford Gallery, Cork.

19 *Until 19 March*
Dorothy Cross – John Kindness – Kathy Prendergast. Sculpture. Kerlin Gallery, Dublin.

22 *Until 20 March*
Avis Newman – Vicious Circle. Douglas Hyde Gallery, Dublin.

24 *Until 13 March*
Thurloe Connolly paintings from the 1940s and 1950s. Also ceramic sculpture by **Yvonne Boydell**. European Modern Art, Dublin.

26 *Until 28 February*
Paintings by **Denise Ferran** & **Hilary Bryson**.Cavehill Gallery, Belfast.

31 *Until 8 April*
Paintings by Wicklow artist **Stanley Pettigrew**. Milmo-Penny Fine Art, Dublin.

PUBLICATIONS

1 **Rosemarie Mulcahy**, 'The meeting of Jacob and Rachel: Murillo's 'Jacob' cycle complete', **The Burlington Magazine**, vol.CXXXV, no.1079(February 1993). Dr Mulcahy attributes this painting , given anonymously to the National Gallery of Ireland in 1987, to the Spanish artist **Murillo**, c. 1660-65.

18 **Cork Arts Development Committee's Report** on the State of the Arts in Cork. Launched by the Lord Mayor of Cork, Ald Michael Martin TD , Crawford Gallery, Cork.

Fitzgerald, whose oriental influences echo those acknowledged by artists 100 years earlier, had her first one woman exhibition in New York during February, while back in Ireland *Mike Fitzharris,* his pictures somewhat indebted to *Tony O'Malley's* Bahamian work, had a show at the Pantheon Gallery called *Searching for a Place.* Maybe the place being sought was in Ireland's eventual cultural history, such as that finally allocated to sculptor *Jerome Connor* who, half a century after his impoverished demise, was given a major retrospective at the National Gallery. By no means an original talent, Connor still seems to have suffered during his lifetime from the stifling conservatism which dominated this country during the first decades after independence. What might he have made of the very different sculpture on show at the Kerlin Gallery during February? Work by *John Kindness, Dorothy Cross* and *Kathy Prendergast,* the exhibition's only unifying feature was a common audaciousness, as seen in Kindness' *Romulus and Seamus* where an enormous pink mosaic pig suckled two infants and Cross's *Amazon* – a tailor's dummy covered in cowhide with a single metal nipple.

Altogether more dainty sculpture could be found at IMMA, where Cork-born *Marie Foley* showed sixteen of her pieces. As before, these fragile constructions were made from porcelain, wood and polished slate, imbued with a deeply spiritual sensibility as though totems from a lost world's rituals. A similar mysticism permeated the exhibition by English artist *Avis Newman* which was installed in the Douglas Hyde Gallery at this time. Extremely severe in their minimalism, the paintings were accompanied by perspex boxes in which rested white books each with a single black motif. The gallery organisers' fondness for this form of cool austerity, manifested over a considerable period of time, now led to a vigorous exchange of letters in the press between its supporters and those who objected on the grounds that the work shown was not only not to their taste, but all too frequently by non-Irish

CALENDAR OF THE ART YEAR

March 1993

EVENTS

1 Irish artists **Dorothy Cross** and **Willie Doherty** selected for Venice Biennale June – October 1993.

1 Minister for the Arts , Culture & the Gaeltacht, **Michael D Higgins**, announced in Tralee that the **National Museum** is to be given autonomy under an independent board of management.

1 Demolition of **95 Capel Street**, listed Georgian (1730s) building.

12 Opening of **The Kirk Gallery**, Lower Charles Street, Castlebar, Co Mayo by **Charles Haughey**.

29 Launch by **Mr Nicholas Robinson** of the Friends of the Hunt Museum, University of Limerick, to promote interest in Irish antiquities and European decorative and fine arts.

EXHIBITION

1 *Until 13 March*
Franziskus Wendels, Belfast. Series of Paintings. Fenderesky Gallery at Queen's, Belfast.

2 *Until 26 March*
Cork-Cracow – Polish Art. City Centre, Dublin

2 *Until 30 May*
Aspects of Irish Painting : 1960 to 1990 from the IMMA Collection and a selection from the P J Carroll Collection. Irish Museum of Modern Art, Dublin

4 *Until 25 April*
Frank McKelvey RUA RHA (1895-1974).Ulster Museum, Belfast.

4 *Until 24 March*
Contemporary Tyrolean Art. RHA Gallagher Gallery, Dublin.

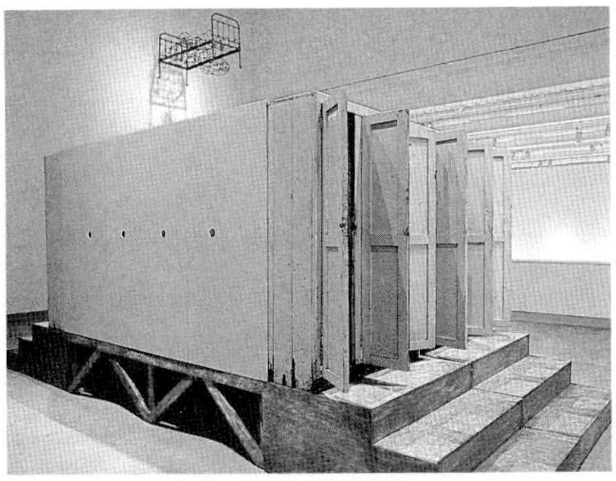

Sculpture by Dorothy Cross

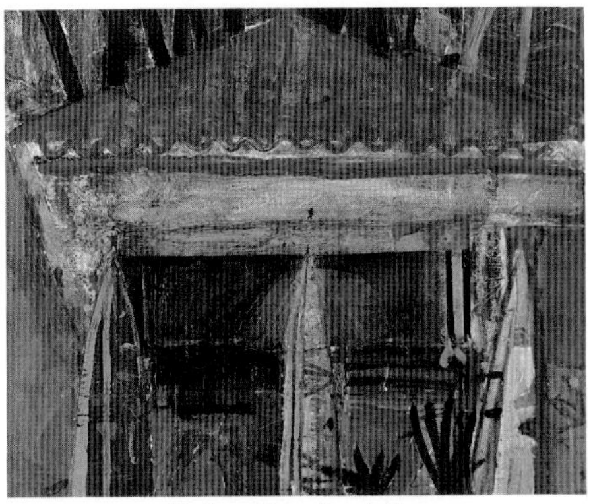

Barbara Rae, *Beach Hut*.

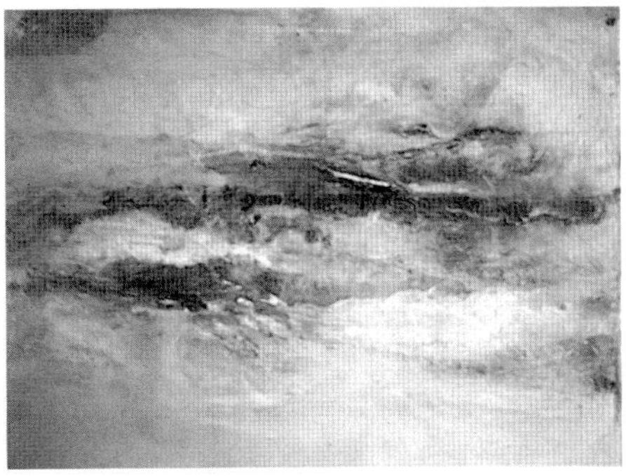

Janet Pierce, *Wave Surge*.

5 *Until 26 March*
Dogs of the Road – panels and murals by **Kieran Behan**. Project Arts Centre, Dublin.

5 *Until 27 March*
John Breakey. The Gordon Gallery, Derry

11 *Until 16 April*
Paintings and collages by Scottish **Barbara Rae**. Jorgensen Fine Art, Dublin

12 *Until 30 March*
Paintings by **Guggi** (ex-Virgin Prunes). Kerlin Gallery, Dublin.

12 *Until 27 March*
Watersong – paintings by **Janet Pierce**. Taylor Galleries, Dublin.

12 *Until 24 April*
E V + A, adjudicated by Catalan gallery director, **Gloria Moure**. Limerick City Gallery.

16 *Until 3 April*
Mark Ainsworth and **Brian Fielding**. Arts Council Gallery, Belfast

18 *Until 30 April*
Tribal Images by **Ray Gillespie**. N I Business Centre,Berkeley Street, London.

20 *Until 30 April*
Ida Applebroog. Orchard Gallery, Derry

23 *Until 1 April*
Contemporary Textiles by young N.Ireland artists **Karen Fleming, Angela Ginn** and **Elaine Megahey**. Flowerfield Arts Centre, Portstewart, Co Derry

23 *Until 31 March*
From Killyleagh to Cairo, The Work of Dr Edward Hincks, Ulster Assyriologist and Egyptologist. Ulster Museum, Belfast

28 *Until 18 April*
Gouaches by **Pieter Sluis**. European Modern Art, Dublin.

---

artists. Just when it appeared that art was no longer capable of creating controversy, this debate demonstrated that passions could still be stirred by an artist, to quote Ruskin, 'throwing a pot of paint in the face of the public.' On this occasion, though, no litigation was threatened. Fifty years ago, similar arguments raged over the merits of the *White Stag Group*, one member of which, *Thurloe Connolly* was given a retrospective at the European Modern Art Gallery in late February. Mr Connolly did not care to come back to Ireland for the opening, having departed this country for the South of France in the early 1950s, but his first wife, *Yvonne Boydell*, sister of composer *Brian Boydell* – another White Stag member in his youth – did make the journey from her home in England and the evening took on the character of a joyful reunion of old friends from an earlier period of rebellion.

March 1993

Members of a later generation of artists were included in a show called *Aspects of Irish Paintings 1960-90* at the Museum of Modern Art, which included fifteen works drawn from the *PJ Carroll Collection* by such well-known names as *Le Brocquy, Madden, Souter* and *Farrell*. One of their most recent successors, *Kieran Behan*, had his first solo exhibition at the Project Arts Centre *Dogs of the Road*. It featured a serious of murals of striking low-relief wall panels made entirely of brick which would not have looked out of place in ancient Egypt or Babylon. Work of a highly static nature was also shown by ex-Virgin Prune *Guggi* in his second one-man exhibition at the Kerlin Gallery, the opening of which attracted three out of four members of *U2* as well as a large percentage of the capital's rock management. All very different from the more sedate crowd at *Janet Pierce's* show, her first for far too long, which was unveiled on the same night at the Taylor Galleries. A meditative response to landscape, *Watersong* took an altogether more subdued approach to

29 *Until 21 April*
Bernadette Kiely. Arts Council, Merrion Square, Dublin.

30 *Until 9 May*
J J Tissot: Prints from the Gotlieb Collection. National Gallery of Ireland Dublin.

30 *Until June*
Paintings by **Ivan Connolly**. Restaurant Tosca, in association with the Gutter Gallery, Dublin.

PUBLICATIONS

15 Peter Harbison, Homan Potterton and Jeanne Sheehy, **Irish Art and Architecture from Prehistory to the Present**. (Thames & Hudson, London , £14.95paperback). Very welcome reprint of this authoritative survey, out of print since 1989.

25 S B Kennedy,**Frank McKelvey – A Painter in his Time**.(Irish Academic Press, Dublin £29.95) To coincide with McKelvey exhibition in the Ulster Museum.

26 **Martello – 10th anniversary issue**. Articles on Salkeld, Keating, Knuttel, Le Jeune, Post-Modernism. (Duke Press, 17 Duke Street, Dublin 2.) £6.00.

29 Patrick Doran, **Fifty Treasures from the Hunt Collection**. (Treaty Press, Limerick.) £35 – proceeds in aid of the Hunt Museum to be established in the Custom House, Limerick.

April 1993

EVENTS

2 Unveiling of stained glass window by **James Scanlon** commissioned by the Friends of the Crawford, Crawford Art Gallery, Cork

15 Announcement in the Irish Times by the National Gallery of Ireland that the painting **The Taking of Christ**, lent to them by the Jesuits, from their house in Lr Leeson Street, Dublin, may be an original work by the Italian master **Caravaggio** (1571-1610)

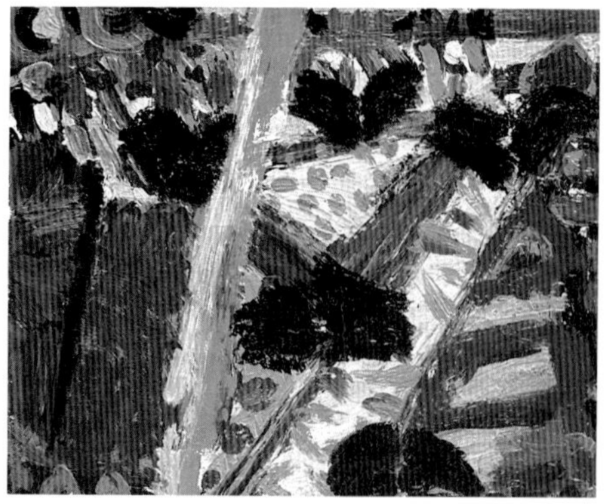

Bernadette Kiely, *Weir No 9*.

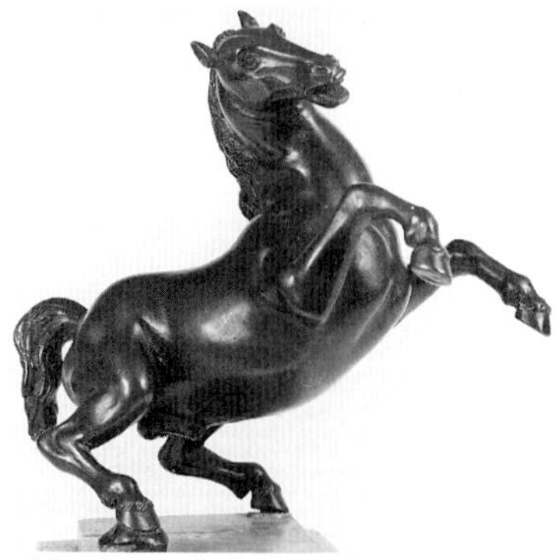

After Leonardo da Vinci, *Rearing Horse* (16th cent) The Hunt Collection, Limerick.

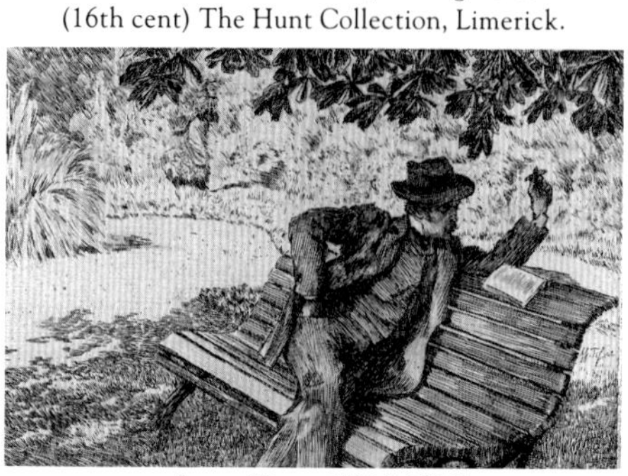

James Tissot (1836-1902)
Renee Maupern Denoisel reading in his garden.

26 Opening of final stage of the National Gallery of Ireland's **European Old Masters US tour** (after San Francisco, Chicago & Boston), IBM Gallery of Art and Science, New York, and renovation of Ireland House in New York University as focus of Irish culture. Both attended by An Taoiseach, Albert Reynolds.

27 Inauguration of **Programme of Exhibitions for 1993** by the Minister for Arts, Culture and the Gaeltacht, Michael D Higgins. Chester Beatty Library, Dublin.

28 Two men arrested in London following the recovery of 13 of the 16 artefacts stolen in a break-in at the **Chester Beatty Library** on 27 June 1991.

EXHIBITIONS

1 *Until 29 April*
Photographs by **Bryan Wharton**. Dublin Writers' Museum.

1 *Until 30 July*
The Art of Surimono – privately published Japanese woodblock prints. Chester Beatty Library, Dublin

2 *Until 30 April*
Paintings by **Patrick Viale**. Andrews Lane Theatre Gallery. One of many cultural events in Dublin in association with Festa Italiana throughout April 1993.

2 *Until 30 April*
Paintings by **Austin McQuinn**. Project Arts Centre, Dublin.

2 *Until 27 April*
Paintings by **Sean Shanahan**. Kerlin Gallery, in association with Festa Italiana.

3 *Until 17 May*
Recent paintings by **Pat Crowley**. Gordon Gallery, Derry

4 *Until 29 May*
Marcantonio Raimondi – Renaissance prints. Chester Beatty Library, Dublin

colour than Scottish painter *Barbara Rae's* brilliantly finished canvases at Ib Jorgensen's gallery around the corner. And Limerick's ever-colourful annual open-submission exhibition *EV+A* opened once again, with an eclectic selection made by Catalan adjudicator *Gloria Moure* which sprawled across the city but was then gathered together in a catalogue which imaginatively consisted of a postcard collection of all the work included. For those looking for a more traditional approach, the Ulster Museum provided a retrospective of Ulster painter *Frank McKelvey*, whose landscapes fetched increasingly high prices at auction during the late 1980s, but then rather fell from fashion again. This show, and its accompanying monograph by SB Kennedy, ought to help restore the artist's fortunes – not to mention those of the collectors who had invested in him lately.

April 1993

Helping to restore the National Gallery's fortunes, an announcement came in mid-April that the painting entitled *The Taking of Christ*, on loan to the institution from the Jesuit order who had long believed it to be by the Flemish master Gerrit Van Honthorst, could actually be a lost *Caravaggio*. Only two months earlier, in the Burlington Magazine, *Dr Rosemarie Mulcahy* had confirmed the attribution of another National Gallery painting, *The Meeting of Jacob and Rachel* donated anonymously in 1987, to seventeenth century Spanish artist *Bartolomé Estaban Murillo*. Neither of these canvases, of course, was included in the *National Gallery's European Old Masters Tour around the USA* which reached its last destination, the IBM Gallery in New York, having already been seen by more than 300,000 visitors at earlier venues. Back in Ireland, Dublin played host to a *Festa Italiana* almost as shambolic as Italian politics during the same period. Amongst the visual arts programme's more successful exhibitions were a show at the Kerlin Gallery of cool, geometric abstracts by

CALENDAR OF THE ART YEAR

5 *Until 30 April*
Watercolour landscapes by **James Flack**. Kenny's Bookshop and Art Gallery, Galway.

5 *Until 30 April*
New Paintings by **Rita Duffy**. Newry & Mourne Arts Centre, Newry.

5 *Until 30 April*
New works on paper – **Geraldine Ormonde**. Peacock Gallery, Craigavon, N Ireland.

6 *Until 16 May*
Theophile-Alexandre Steinlen – paintings and graphic works. Hugh Lane Municipal Gallery, Dublin.

6 **Patricia Hurl & Therry Rudin** – Call and Response. Also prints by **Linda Condon**. City Arts Centre, Dublin

8 *Until 29 August*
Lee Jaffe: Cordially Yours. Multi-media works, first showing in Ireland. IMMA, Dublin.

8 *Until 1 May*
Prints from **Giorgio Upiglio's Grafico Uno** print workshop in Milan. Graphic Studio Gallery, Dublin, in association with Festa Italiana.

8 *Until 1 May*
Dante's Paradiso by **Pamela Hardesty**. Pantheon Gallery, Dublin; opening by Michael Longley, Writer-in- Residence at Trinity College, Dublin.

8 *Until 28 April*
Tom Bevan – mixed-media assemblages . Arts Council Gallery, Belfast.

8 *Until 22 August*
Paintings from the **Haverty Trust** in the Ulster Museum, Belfast. Fifty important Irish 20th century paintings, donated by Trustees under the terms of the will of Thomas Haverty(c.1825-1916).

8 *Until 28 May*
New sculptural work by **Henry Pim**. Ulster Museum

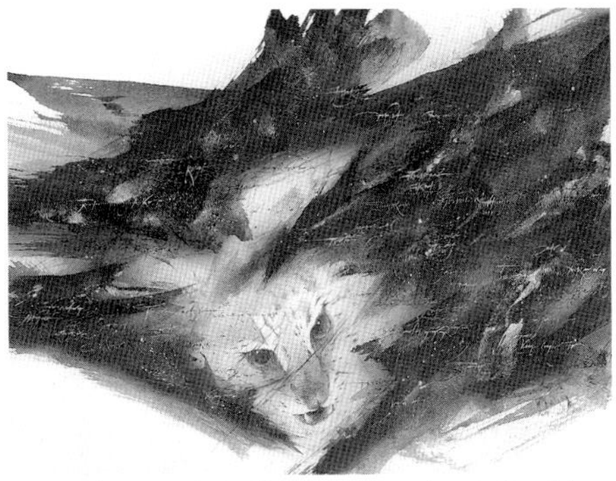

David McGrail, *And Tonight Everything is Possible.* RHA Annual Exhibition.

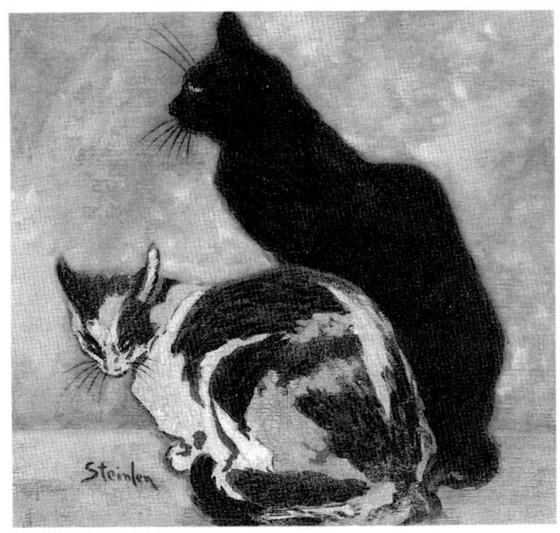

Théophile-Alexandre Steinlen, *Les Chats.*

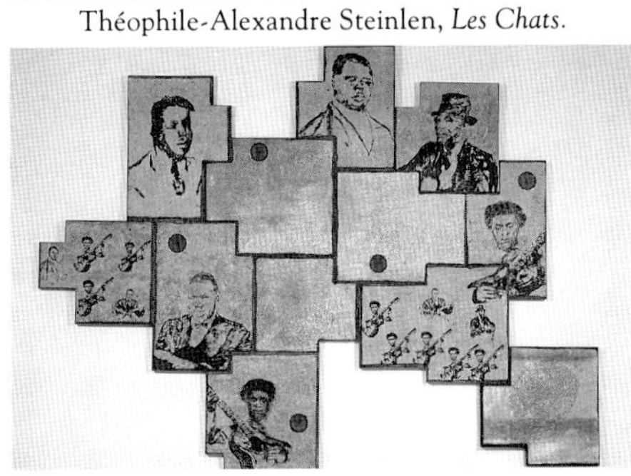

Lee Jaffe, *If Luck Don't Change, 1990.*

15 *Until 7 May*
Finola Jones & Eileen McDonagh.Green on Red Gallery, 58 Fitzwilliam Square, Dublin.

19 *Until 1 May*
Josef Keys – mixed media. Cork Arts Society.

20 **Mary McGinty – Telling Tales**. The Square, Tallaght.

22 *Until 30 April*
Cecil Maguire RUA. Bell Gallery, Belfast

22 *Until 22 May*
Texture and Light – Ceramics and Drawings by **Anthony O'Brien**. European Modern Art, Dublin.

23 *Until 8 May*
In the Mountains – Watercolours by **Catherine Flanagan**.Ulster Arts Gallery, Belfast

26 **Six feet Under** – works by **Marin Grant**. Garter Lane Arts Centre, Waterford

27 *Until 22 May*
Royal Academy of Arts 163rd Exhibition, RHA Gallery, Dublin.

27 *Until 19 May*
Patricia Looby. Arts Council, Dublin

29 *Until 22 August*
Home Rule – new photoworks and sculptures by New York artist **Elaine Reichek**. IMMA, Dublin

29 *Until 5 June*
Cabbages and Kings – monotypes by **Ruth O'Donnell** & **Stephen Lawlor**. Opening by Eilis Dillon. Pantheon Gallery, Dublin

30 *Until 25 May*
New paintings by **Barrie Cooke**. Kerlin Gallery, Dublin

The Retrospective Calendar of the Art Year is compiled by the Assistant Editor, Elizabeth Mayes, to whom should be sent information and photographs for possible inclusion.

Sean Shanahan, an Irish artist who, like *Richard Gorman,* has settled in Milan. And from that city, master printer *Giorgio Upiglio* brought over to the Graphic Studio a representative cross-section of his work, including examples by *Mimmo Paladino, Enrico Baj* and his wife, *Rita Galle.* The Chester Beatty Library offered Renaissance prints by *Marcantonio Raimondi,* while the Pantheon Gallery proposed *Dante's Paradiso* as interpreted by *Pamela Hardesty.* The Museum of Modern Art appeared to have by-passed this particular event altogether, celebrating instead the work of two American artists, *Lee Jaffe* and *Elaine Reichek;* in both cases, polemic was the *leitmotif,* with the causes and effects of racism examined to an extent well beyond the necessities of consciousness-raising. Similarly, at the City Arts Centre, *Linda Condon* reflected on violence within families, whilst *Patricia Hurl* and *Therry Rudin* explored the complexities of family relationships. It was a relief to turn from these dark broodings to the collection of Irish painting from the *Haverty Trust* on show at the Ulster Museum, which included pictures by such artists as *Leo Whelan, Maurice MacGonigal, George Campbell* and *Gerard Dillon.* The same venue hosted a show of ceramics by *Henry Pim* and this medium was also used by *Anthony O'Brien* for his exhibition at European Modern Art in late April. This show was opened by *Ciaran MacGonigal,* director of the RHA Gallagher Gallery, where on the previous evening, the *163rd annual RHA exhibition* opened in the presence of two presidents, seventeen ambassadors and more than two thousand mere mortals. Another opening, another show it might have been, but with sufficient allure to mean that before the end of that first night, over a hundred works had been sold. Would that all other exhibitions during the previous twelve months had been so successful.

Robert O'Byrne

Robert O'Byrne is a writer and critic.

THE NEW DIRECTORS

In the past four years, six of the major arts institutions in Dublin have acquired new Directors. Earlier this year, Alistair Smith interviewed them:

Barbara Dawson
HUGH LANE MUNICIPAL GALLERY, PARNELL SQUARE

Declan McGonagle
IRISH MUSEUM OF MODERN ART, KILMAINHAM

Raymond Keaveney
NATIONAL GALLERY OF IRELAND, MERRION SQUARE

John Hutchinson
DOUGLAS HYDE GALLERY, TRINITY COLLEGE

Michael Ryan
CHESTER BEATTY LIBRARY AND GALLERY OF ORIENTAL ART, SHREWSBURY ROAD

Ciarán MacGonigal
RHA GALLAGHER GALLERY, ELY PLACE.

After a period at the National Gallery of Ireland, Barbara Dawson became Director of the Hugh Lane Gallery, in Parnell Square, Dublin, in 1991 at the age of 34. The Gallery is funded by Dublin Corporation which grants approximately £600,000 per annum for running expenses. The Director reports to the City Manager via the City and County Librarian. Traditionally, an Arts Advisory Committee meets four times a year.

A very long time ago I had a friend who confided in me that she coveted the Directorship of the Hugh Lane Gallery. One of the reasons for her enthusiasm was the beautiful flat occupied by the Director.

You are sitting in part of it; and as you can see it's no longer a flat, but an office, if rather a grand one.

Well, that has certainly changed over the years. I imagine that you have all sorts of other changes in mind.

I think I'd rather say developments: thinking first about the collection – the Gallery has a very fine collection of art works, over 2,000 in all, with a strong French influence, a representative collection from the English School and, of course, a large twentieth century collection of Irish art. Bearing in mind the history of the collection, which was established by Hugh Lane and his supporters as a Municipal Gallery of Modern Art in 1908, I would like to see the collection improved by the addition of significant works which would directly link to and ensure the continuity of those schools of paintings already represented. As it is a Gallery of Modern Art, those artists represented have, over the years, challenged art theory and critical criteria of previous generations. Our purchasing grant is small and so most of the international artists which I feel should be included in a Modern Art Gallery, such as ours, for the benefit of emerging artists and the general public, are, alas, out of reach.

So what have you bought since you've been in situ?

Well, a Dorothy Cross sculpture, *Shark Lady in a Ballgown* – it's on exhibition in Room One. A Tony O'Malley painting from the 1970s – his Bahamian period. I've also bought an early May Guinness, an Irish artist who's not very popular at the moment, and so that wasn't too expensive. Not much research has been carried out on her to date and while she is already represented in the collection, *Umbrella Pines in a Landscape* is an important addition and will present the student with an opportunity of a more in-depth understanding of her style and technique. In theory it is our policy, in certain cases, to collection more than one work by an artist so as to increase our comprehension and appreciation of their artistic development.

The May Guinness must be from the time when the collection is at its strongest, the early part of the century, which seems to be very popular with the public.

Yes, I'm sure it's true that people take time to grow into art. At the end of this century, I think they'll be really enjoying the 1970s. But our strong holding of early twentieth century Irish and Continental art, with works by Monet, Bonnard, Manet, Yeats, Nathaniel Hone, Osborne and others, is surely responsible for the fact that we have had over 253,000 visitors last year.

That's astonishing, given the population. More than the Irish Museum of Modern Art at Kilmainham I think. By the way, do you worry about your policy overlapping with Kilmainham, or the National Gallery or the Douglas Hyde's?

No, for instance, the Douglas Hyde does not have a permanent collection and so the policy, I understand, is structured around its strong programme of temporary exhibitions. The National Gallery of Ireland and the Irish Museum of Modern Art evolved from different circumstances. Each of the institutions mentioned has an individual personality with certain strong attractions and so offers an even greater variety of art to our public and overseas visitors. It's rather like, although a lot smaller than, the situation in Paris, where you have the Louvre, the Musée d'Orsay, and the Musée d'Art Moderne de la Ville de Paris.

What about collecting? Isn't there an overlap there?

Yes, somewhat. But that can be an advantage, particularly with regard to Irish art. It allows for the possibility of an Irish artist to be represented in more than one institution thus presenting an increased opportunity to view their work. The history of the Municipal Collection is such that its Irish collection, for example, begins at the turn of the century and any purchasing policy must take an overall view of the collection. By continuing to purchase contemporary art, we are continuing a strong tradition established in 1908, when the collection was first opened to the public, of representing an independent school of Irish art. It is my aim to present a large representative collection of twentieth century Irish art beginning with John B Yeats and Nathaniel Hone and continuing down to the present day. With this on view to the public, one can evaluate visually as well as academically the development of the Irish school. Should finances allow, our policy would support the inclusion of keyworks by those international artists who have had such an influence on the development of art. Just as we have paintings by Monet, Degas, Corot and others, it would be desirable to have other major artists, such as Dali, Georges Braque, Raoul Dufy, Rothko and even Baselitz.

But surely there must be an anxiety about the fact that it's quite possible, as things stand, for the owner of a Jack Yeats painting – let's say he or she is getting on and wants to settle what is going to happen to it when the time comes – could legitimately negotiate with yourself, IMMA or the NGI. Is this worrying?

Well I think you'll find that people identify with different galleries. By the time an owner gets to the stage of endowing a painting to any institution, he's likely to have developed an allegiance to one for a

THE NEW DIRECTORS

number of reasons. We are Dublin's Municipal collection, that, to some, would be the primary reason for bestowing a gift or bequest. The public perception of the Gallery and its support for the Gallery is underlined by the number of donations and bequests received since its foundation. Fortunately this continues and, recently, Mrs Eyre-Maunsall, through the Friends of the National Collections of Ireland, presented us with a very interesting portrait of *Sarah Purser on the Steps of Mespil House* by Mary Swanzy.

The Municipal Gallery qualifies as a national collection?

Yes, we do. The Friends of the National Collections of Ireland was founded by Sarah Purser in 1924 and the Friends have been very supportive of the Gallery ever since then. Indeed, Sarah Purser herself was instrumental in the acquiring of Charlemont House for the Municipal Collection.

How else do you see the collection developing?

I see it expanding in relation to what is here already. Certain art forms, such as video works, should now be accommodated and as we have some superb stained glass, I would see this Gallery as the natural centre for its display and for the preservation of archive material relating to it.

Like all other Gallery Directors, you must have building plans.

Well, the fact is that our collection comprises about 2,100 works, including watercolours and drawings, and the building can only show about fifteen per cent of that at any one time. So there is an obvious need for more space. It's also sad that the building just isn't suitable for the display of our excellent collection of Irish stained glass, so the public can't really have any real access to our holdings of important work by Harry Clarke and Wilhelmina Geddes, for example.

Yes, that is a pity. The tradition of stained glass in Ireland is so strong, it's a great pity that there's no real display of it available. I suppose you could begin by making slides available.

I would like to see us making some proper progress towards informing the public about the collection in many different ways. For this a lecture theatre is essential. You will notice we have no lecture theatre at present. It seems to me to be essential to have a lecture theatre in a Gallery so that when we aren't able to display our stained glass, for instance, we can at least give public lectures with slides gaining access in that manner.

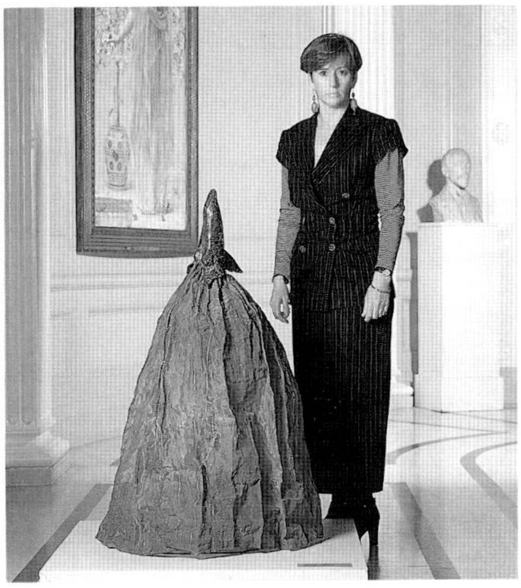

Barbara Dawson and Shark Lady in a Ballgown *by Dorothy Cross.*

Yes, I'm sure that would be really popular. I was astonished to see so many people here for a concert.

Yes, we have had a great response from the public for our concerts at noon on Sundays; more than five hundred people came to hear the first performance of Michael Holohan's *Solstice,* and 1,700 people for our Christmas Concert. There's something a little bit magical about music played among paintings, and that's greatly appreciated. The London *Independent*, in a review of Dublin's concert programme, lately described our programme at the Gallery as the most innovative in the city.

Obviously, in addition to these entertaining events, we would want to develop more educational activities and hope to build on our fledgling educational policy which lays special emphasis on community based projects. The Gallery is smack in the middle of one of Dublin's less well off areas, where the local community isn't necessarily traditionally thought of as 'gallery-goers'. It's a challenge to me to have them enter that William Chambers hall of their own accord.

I suppose the real problem is deciding on your priorities.

Yes, one is to the public and another is to the collection.

Is funding another?

Well, I think we are sympathetically treated as far as funding goes. Of course, you can always have more but Dublin Corporation provides approximately £600,000 a year in funding. The real problem is the staff structure.

No one is going to believe what you're now going to say.

Well, I'm afraid it's true. The only qualified curatorial person on the staff is me.

I can't think of any other Gallery with an important collection and a lively temporary exhibition programme that has so few staff. How do you cope?

We are able to hire the appropriate curatorial input for our various exhibitions, otherwise they just couldn't happen. But this policy doesn't alleviate the problem of lack of curatorial continuity desired to promote both the permanent collection and our temporary exhibition programmes. We have a backlog of work to overcome in terms of documentation, photography and publications. We receive help from volunteers for specific events, but we simply can't approach certain areas like the archives, for example, until we have enough qualified help to allow us put in hand a systematic policy.

One of the possessions I prize is my copy of the reprinted catalogue of 1908.

That was done in 1984. And, thankfully we are about to embark on a new policy of publications. I have started on a volume of selected masterpieces or highlights from the collection which is due to be published this autumn. We plan to have over a hundred works reproduced in colour and approximately sixty of them Irish artists, many of which will be contemporary.

How do you find the time?

I don't. I promised myself a study day a week, but that's gone by the board, but I'm hoping to get a little study time each fortnight to push this on a bit. I am very fortunate with the team I have working with me on this book.

And after Masterpieces?

I'm hoping to compile a complete inventory of the collection. The work on the masterpieces will, of course, be of assistance in that.

THE NEW DIRECTORS

You say you're not badly off in terms of money to run the Gallery on a day-to-day basis, yet you promote sponsorship quite actively.

Yes. The Corporation funding covers the daily costs of maintenance and staffing, but extra money is always required for exhibitions and publications. Telecom sponsored for our Ernest Hayes exhibition and ABN-AMRO Bank has given us funding for the forthcoming book. We have been fortunate to have managed to raise about £80k in the last fourteen months.

About as much as your salary, I imagine.

Ah: Much more!

Declan McGonagle

In 1991, Ireland's own Irish Museum of Modern Art opened at the Royal Hospital, Kilmainham, Dublin. In this interview, its Director, Declan McGonagle, outlines his policy for its future development.

The foundation in 1991 of the Irish Museum of Modern Art at Kilmainham is the great success story of Ireland's cultural development over the past few years. Is it right to assume that funds of European origin were used?

No. But the fact that Dublin was European cultural capital in 1991 made it, tactically, a good year to open the museum. The sequence of events leading up to it was this. There was a general debate in the mid-eighties about the Royal Hospital at Kilmainham. Then the GPA exhibition which Dorothy Walker selected was shown here in 1986 and it looked very well. The Arts Council collection was shown here in '87 and looked very well, and it was recommended to the Taoiseach that this building would be ideal for a museum of contemporary and modern art. You remember Rosc was here in 1988 and it was agreed by many of the people who saw it, that it was the better part of the two sections of the Rosc exhibition of that year. It had the Costakis collection and contemporary projects, and it was able to deal with both of them fairly comfortably. So in fact the decision was made in 1988 that it would be the museum of modern art; and they set up a committee to advise on what it would take to establish such a museum.

So it was just a question of timing.

It was timing. So 1991 was not a funding mechanism for the museum because we didn't draw any money from that budget at all. It was a programming mechanism. In fact I remember when the board was appointed in late '89 or early '90 they issued an advertisement which I originally didn't see but by April 1990 I was appointed as the Director Designate. But for a variety of reasons I couldn't start until October. I remember discussing whether we could open in 1991 and my instinctive reaction was we should open as soon as possible, that we should hit the ground running, that we should make use of the head of steam that the City of Culture would give us, that if you like, government were hot about the project and should be kept hot. If we had strung out the development phase for two years, I think we would have lost momentum. Some people were describing to me as problematic the building, the nature of its architecture, its structure, its distance from the city centre, the fact that we wouldn't have much money to start a collection – all those so-called problems never registered with me anyway. We had to come up with new practices, new ways of working. We couldn't go shopping for a collection, we therefore had to develop critical relationships with artists and persuade artists that this was an interesting place to be and to work; we had to build upon relationships with other institutions in order to borrow work, and prove that we could do so within a critical framework in which that work could be shown. So I actually believe, although some people might find this difficult to understand, that it would have been more difficult to create an interesting institution if we *had* had twenty million pounds.

I think this is the brilliant thing; you have actually reconceived the image of the modern art gallery by this process of toing and froing with artists, toing and froing with the general public, which is at the centre of what you are doing and on top of that, you've got, you know, the beginnings of your acquisition policy.

I remember saying 'I know the opening is taking place on the 25th May 1991, but that's not the real opening, the opening is our first three years. So it'll take us at least three years, to map out the territory that we're going to inhabit, and we may even build the walls of the house in that time but you won't have a finished house in that time.'

This seems to me to be very wise in retrospect. If you look at Stuttgart, in the first year it was open, it had a huge audience then a fall; and similarly the new Courtauld Galleries, in London, in their first year had two hundred and fifty thousand people, then an immediate fall-off, last year one hundred. You painted a corner of the picture and are gradually filling it in.

I thought it was a necessity that was due in the context of museums, because I think that one of the problems museums have is the idea that they are finished institutions, that a museum is a terminus.

That there's an art history that's finished.

That there's an art history that's finished, and is by definition over and its meaning is fixed. I keep thinking of this image of the train coming into the station and stopping. What we have the potential to do here, which I believe is required in this context at this time is what may allow us contribute to a wider debate. We can be a porous institution. Because we don't have huge modernist spaces, we have to work in a different way.It means that we are forced to rethink relationships with artists. I think we can articulate an artist's idea on the scale that it needs to be articulated.

You know the kind of international exhibition that goes from one rather anonymous space in one country, the Hilton Hotel of art galleries in one country to the Hilton Hotel of art galleries in another. People like yourself who've seen the same shows in different counties see that nothing happens to them; they are prepackaged and not informed by the different galleries or their public, whereas it's different in a tricky building like this. It was very interesting to see the Richard Hamilton exhibition at the Tate, which has a building which can be manipulated, and then see it here where the smaller rooms actually worked terribly well.

It had to be remade, rethought; in situations where we are collaborating with ten other museums, or one other museum or whatever, or taking a show like the Hamilton Show from the Tate, this building requires it to be remade, so what you get is a new exhibition, a new statement by the artist; and that was one of the reasons Richard was very interested in working here. He had the chance to reconsider and make a new exhibition. Equally the Gilbert and George – one of the keys to Gilbert and George's work is the confrontational aspect, and you just couldn't avoid that in our spaces, because the viewer was completely encased in these huge, powerful, frontal works.

So in fact, even where you show the same work, it has to be reconsidered in terms of its orientation. The very thing that people said could have been problematic becomes part of our subject and therefore becomes a major advantage. I am often on the receiving end of 'we're doing this show, do you want it next April?' and my first answer is 'no, but maybe the artist could come over and we'll see'. And I react the same way to offers of acquisitions, I say come in, have a look, and if you still feel that that's the work to represent you best, then we'll talk about it; and the possibility to be particular and local without being parochial, is a thing I think artists find very attractive.

It's marvellous because it actually is creating what I'd call a new job description for the curator or director, but since I'm in that world, I understand how time consuming that whole business is. How many staff have you got to support you?

The overall staff is about fourty-four, that includes twenty-four security attendants, but they're called mediators because part of their function is to engage people rather than protect the object and there's then the administrative staff. Curatorially, we have two curators, one in charge of Education and Community, the other is Head of Exhibitions. And we have had money recently from the Hamlyn Foundation to find an educational assistant and we have two curatorial assistants for exhibitions. There is a PR person, there are three people working on finances, and others on general administration.

So that conventional type of post, the person who curates collection ...

That's one of the curatorial assistants, she is responsible for collections management.

Have you any vision of what the collection will be like in, say, ten years time?

No, I don't, it's open. I'm often asked what's to be the quota of Irish artists and national artists. We don't have a quota.

I don't think that idea does a service to Irish artists. But the fact is that the majority of works that we have bought for the collection so far are by Irish artists. In the first few months after I was appointed we had debates within the Board about, what the collection would do, how it would be formed, what it would be for, and we laid down a number of basic points. One was that we would buy from this point onwards, and that we would accept donations or loans of works from the early part of the twentieth century up to the present. It was clear that the collection and our function in general, would be Irish and international without making any false claims for Irish artists, or indeed for international artists. We wouldn't have an Irish ghetto; the thing that Irish artists need more than anything else is to have their works tested in the world and I think international artists maybe like to have their own work tested here. So, while I'm aware of the political realities, the programming logic seeks not to make those distinctions either through buying work, commissioning exhibitions or commissioning new works for the collection. I also wanted to include right from the beginning a sense that, as much as buying objects, we will commission ideas, even if we couldn't realise some of those projects – we have a project for the chapel, we have an Audio Arts project for the meadow which we may not realise for a while. So I think we should collect ideas which may or may not be capable of being articulated in finished form immediately, and plan into the future how these may be developed in the building, in rooms, on walls, on floors, in the meadow, in the grounds – whatever way.

Are you anxious about becoming too active as a conceptual force, I mean, too proactive in a conceptual way – you have all these ideas which you implant. Is it the case of the institution becoming the commissar?

I would not be worried about that. If the context expands, it will need more input from more people.

Well, you are a very influential person and the more this museum takes on its character, which you are very open about, the more every piece of it is you.

Yes, well, I have very strong opinions about things and I make no apologies about that – this may sound arrogant but if we can do better I see no reason why we shouldn't do better. It doesn't require the earth to work with given artists and equally it doesn't require any reduction in standards to include the community – if it is a question of setting up models of excellence then those are the minimum standards we should be operating under. That should be in the forefront of my mind, I can't be anything other than I am (and I say *I* in terms of the institution).

I think we suffer from a nineteenth century inheritance about the status of the object which has got in the way – despite the last thirty years when the object has been dematerialised and then materialised again. I hope I am not sounding as if we should close down all museums and do away with the object as such. What I am saying is that in Dublin there is a Museum of Modern Art, there's a National Gallery, there's a Municipal Gallery, there's a Douglas Hyde, there's a RHA – we should all complement each other and we should be talking about how value can be added by each institution, not competing with one another.

There is still a point of competition though: isn't there? What happens when someone with his or her Jack B Yeats over the fireplace is going to decide where to bequeath it in Ireland. Now he can still give it to the National Gallery, the Municipal Gallery or to you. Have you made your peace with the so called 'monolithic treasure houses' in that way?

We haven't got to that yet. That has been mentioned quite a lot in the public discussion about IMMA's birth and what it would mean for other institutions. But what we have started is a process whereby the directors of the institutions meet and talk. I have confidence in the people involved that it will lead towards a set of circumstances where we don't compete with each other. Now what that actually means in relation to individual holdings of Yeats or early twentieth century up to the 1940s I am not quite sure. We are beginning a process actually going to be very important: IMMA aims to have a major retrospective every two to three years, researched, documented and catalogued. And we would want to articulate a point of view about that work – how it came about, the context that produced it, why it's important, etc. On a ongoing basis we are now going to see that research is carried out on individual artists of the twentieth century (a) to build up an archive and

THE NEW DIRECTORS

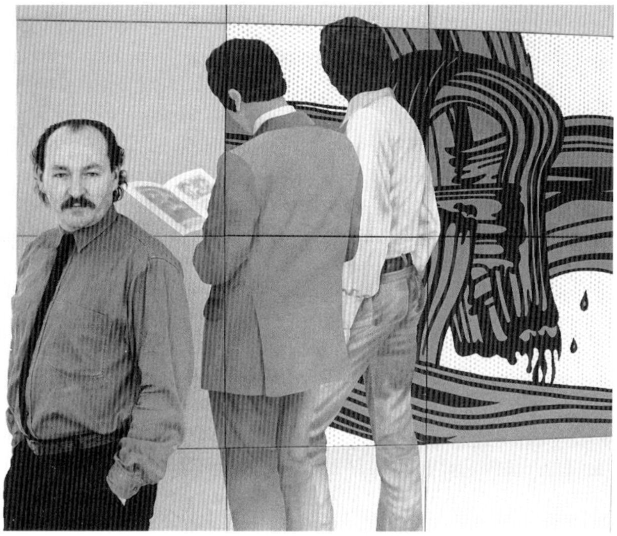

Declan McGonagle, IMMA.

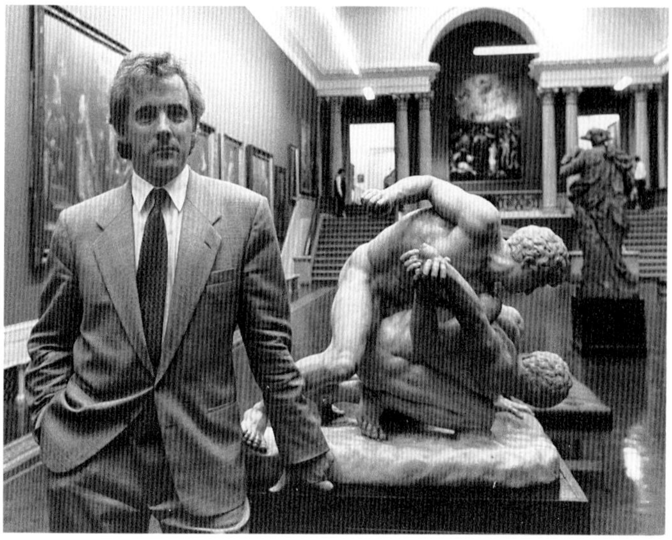

Raymond Keaveney, National Gallery of Ireland.

(b) to create those small polemical exhibitions based on individual bodies of work by those artists. So we could show someone like Nano Reid, for instance, with a group of works or whatever. But what we want in our programme is always to have a window from the present into the historical.

Yes. I constantly find myself quoting T S Eliot's Tradition and the Individual Talent, *written about 1928, I think, but it seems to me to be not out of date – what it says is that the artist or the poet influences the past as much as he or she is formed by it.*

Yes, one of the problems that artists have had to suffer in Ireland over that historical period is the lack of a superstructure which would provide a critical background. I was going to use the word 'amnesia' but it's the wrong word because memory didn't exist. It just wasn't there. It didn't exist for my generation. When I was at college Mainie Jellett wasn't a figure. She wasn't present in any way as a historical reference.

I don't know what it's like in Ireland at present – but in Britain there are some artists, the generation of painters who emerged in the 1960s, who just are not being shown now. This has got to do with swings of fashion, but it means that art college students just don't know about them. And perhaps it is the role of the institution to do what's not being done elsewhere.

And it doesn't always require the major retrospective exhibition to do that. Another thing, I believe that, at whatever date in history a work of art was called into existence, it is nevertheless contemporary, because we read it with contemporary eyes. And we can do this now with the necessary lack of innocence because the last ten or fifteen years has proved that the previous system of classification was unreliable. The old system – the life of the artist, cause and effect etc., has been called into question. Since the Renaissance, the assumption has been that we have been engaged in cultural progress. I think many people would look around today and say 'Progress? What progress?' Ireland never had a complete modern period, and therefore, by definition, it can't have a post-modern period. But aspects of premodern, modern and postmodern are visible.

Yes, that emerged really clearly from the Mainie Jellett Exhibition, and the commentaries on it, that the conventions of European modernism had never become cemented here.

Yes, we are very different from the large metropolitan centres of art. In them a museum can be seen to be a finished entity, a place where finished things go. You feel that the train pulls into the station and it stays there, and you can walk all over it while its in the station but its not going anywhere.

To turn to the present arrangements, rather than the future ... What are your funding sources?

Directly from government. IMMA is managed by a Board of Directors because we have been set up as a company. These Directors are nominated by government, appointed by the Taoiseach basically.

Sponsorship?

We have been very active, and fortunate.

Museum charges?

No. The museum's free. But special exhibitions require an entry charge where extra costs have been incurred.

I see that gifts and bequests are coming in all the time.

Yes.

De-accession?

Naturally, this hasn't arisen yet, but we accept donations unconditionally so, theoretically, it could happen in the future.

Visiting public? Do you have your figures to hand?

Yes. In the first eight months in 1991, about 200,000. Now that was bumped up by the Kremlin Gold Exhibition which was a City of Culture Exhibition. In our first full year, 1992, we had about 200,000.

Well, that's very good, starting from scratch, and considering that people have to find their way from the City Centre, something that isn't too easy for tourists. I suppose it might be a good idea for a special bus to run from say, Dawson Street.

THE NEW DIRECTORS

Well, there is the advantage. Our research shows that when people come they spend much longer here. It's like an excursion.

To the McGonagle Estate? Are you going to tell me how much money you get per annum.

Yes, it's IR£1,000,000. £900,000 running costs, £100,000 acquisition.

That's excellent. If you weigh it out that's about £4.50 per head for each visitor. Good value.

Raymond Keaveney

Formerly Assistant Director of the National Gallery of Ireland in Merrion Square, Dublin, Raymond Keaveney became its Director four years ago. Here he discusses recent developments at the Gallery and his plans for the future.

A great deal seems to have happened to the Gallery since you became Director. Suddenly money seems no problem. Where were the funds found?

Money, as you well know, is always a problem, but there has been improvement. The funds to finance the various developments have come from the Exchequer, the National Lottery, the Shaw Bequest and the monies generated by various programmes, including exhibitions to the USA and Japan.

What have they been principally devoted to?

These funds have been applied principally to the upgrading of the existing buildings which were in very poor repair and which were beginning to expose the collection to the risk of damage. Other funding has been devoted to the acquisition of a site on Clare Street adjacent to the Gallery for the construction of a new wing to the Gallery. The overall plan is to consolidate and make more efficient use of the existing fabric and complement this by providing new accommodation for what cannot be managed within the present building complex.

What plans are in hand for the future development of the buildings?

More specifically this means refitting the existing gallery spaces, reclaiming lost gallery space, which had been adapted for administrative offices and other uses, and the upgrading of services to the public. It also involves improvements in fireproofing and the installation of an addressable fire alarm system.It means the introduction of state-of-the-art security systems. It will mean not just a radical redesign of the exhibition spaces which were refurbished in 1968 but also the installation of full air-conditioning there.

The possibility of constructing a new extension on Clare Street has permitted a review of the accommodation of a number of departments and services currently housed in the historic building. The old lecture theatre will be ceded to the library for use as bookstacks, and a new lecture theatre, with raked seating will be housed in the Clare Street extension. The temporary exhibition facility currently housed in room 14 will be relocated to Clare Street, where it will occupy the prime display location. Additional display space for the permanent collection will also be provided in the Clare Street extension allowing the Gallery to double its hanging space for Irish paintings and provide for the display of the National Portrait Collection which has been off view since the early 1970s. Extended facilities for children and students will also be provided, as well as a restaurant and bookshop. The Clare Street extension will provide the Gallery with more than 33% additional space overall.

Where precisely are the funds coming from?

The funding for the project will come from three different sources. Initial funding is being provided by the Gallery itself through monies received from the Shaw Bequest and funds generated by various Gallery programmes. A critical element of the funding is to be sought from the European Regional Development Programme. Finally, the Gallery plans to win support for the project from the private sector.

Who is going to manage the design?

The Gallery has an open mind with respect to the design of the new extension and is considering a range of options.

In the past the Office of Public Works has come in for a lot of criticism.

Over the past four years, since my appointment as Director, I have worked with the OPW on a number of major projects at the Gallery, including the refurbishment of the 1864 wing and the Milltown wing, both of which tasks were accomplished with efficiency and sensitivity. Currently they are working on the 1968 extension, a job which will involve not only the complete redesign of the interior spaces but also the introduction of sophisticated technical services. In all these instances I have found their approach to be professional and competent. It is a great benefit to someone like me to have the services of a body such as OPW at my disposal, as I can confidently rely on their experience and expertise. That is not to say there cannot be some areas of difference. Sometimes there are differing views on priorities. Also, there is always the thorny problem of allocating the financial resources. Tact and patience on both sides is called for in overcoming these problems.

Which of your current initiatives do you consider to be particularly significant?

In the past year we have toured a major exhibition from the collection across the United States, where it went on view at the Art Institute of Chicago, the Fine Arts Museum of San Francisco, the Museum of Fine Arts in Boston and at the IBM Gallery in New York. This event, apart from attracting generous sponsorship from IBM, promoted the merits of the collection to an American audience, who for the most part would never have suspected that Dublin had such fine pictures.

In August of this year we opened a similar show in Japan. It will visit five venues over a nine-month period. Again this show will educate its Japanese audience as to the range and quality of our collection in Dublin. This show has been arranged in association with *The Tokyo Shimbun*, which has financed the tour.

In October we open an exhibition of Irish Watercolours and Drawings at Boston College. This show will be the inaugural event in the new Gallery attached to the university. This exhibition will later travel to New York.

With respect to our domestic programme, following Jerome Connor, James Jacques Tissot, and the return of our IBM show, the main element in our exhibition schedule this year will be *The Master Revealed*, a show dedicated to the presentation of our new Caravaggio. This is the painting which was discovered by Sergio Benedetti of our Conservation Department, in the Jesuit house in Leeson Street, just five minutes from the Gallery. The

THE NEW DIRECTORS

picture had rested unrecognised in the house for well on seventy years. When we approached the Jesuit fathers about the possibility of bringing the picture into the Gallery for examination they were very positively disposed and they have since stated that the picture will remain on long term loan at the Gallery where it can be enjoyed by the public.

The Master Revealed will be the Gallery's last exhibition for fifteen months, as all our energies over the next few years will be devoted to getting the Gallery ready for the reopening of the refurbished 1968 wing in March 1995. Prior to the reopening we will need to commission the new airconditioning equipment and rehang the entire collection. We will also be working on a series of new publications to complement the new presentation of the collection, which will include a reappraisal of the Irish pictures and the establishment of a new Yeats Gallery. This will almost certainly involve the closure of the collection to the public for a brief period, from about Christmas 1994 to March 1995.

Am I right in thinking that you started up the Friends of the National Gallery?

As part of the Gallery's policy to generate interest and support from the public in the Gallery the Friends of the National Gallery was established in 1990 Operating out of number 90 Merrion Square, a Georgian house acquired and restored by the Gallery in the late 1980s, the Friends membership programme has grown to almost 1,500. Through its programmes, the organisation introduces the public to the collection and educates them on various aspects of its history and importance. It organises lectures and tours and special events. In many respects it complements the energetic programme organised by our Education Department which last year, among other things, provided guided tours for over 30,000 visitors. Apart from facilitating members of the public to become more closely involved with the Gallery, the Friends, through their membership subscriptions have assisted in the enrichment of the collection through contributing to the purchase of works for the collection including works by Yeats and Latham. The information desk at the entrance to the Gallery is manned by volunteers drawn from the Friends.

There has been an amazing upsurge in visitor figures.

Since 1988, attendance figures have grown from 480,000 visitors per annum, to over one million per annum, a figure that puts the gallery on a par with the Rijksmuseum and the Uffizi. This is tremendously satisfying, as it indicates that the tremendous range and quality of the collection, which is truly worldclass is at last being recognised.

Are you wary about having areas of overlap with other galleries?

Essentially, we do not see any difficulties of overlap with other galleries. We have a specific brief to collect Old Masters, historic Irish pictures and Irish portraits. The new Irish Museum of Modern Art collects the work of living Irish artists, as does the Hugh Lane Municipal Gallery of Irish Art, though both these institutions to a greater or lesser degree have also an interest in late nineteenth and early twentieth century work.

Recently we have been very fortunate to acquire a major portrait by Hugh Douglas Hamilton representing Richard Mansergh St. George grieving at the tomb of his dead spouse. When I say fortunate, let me explain. The painting went for sale at Sotheby's, who put a reserve of £100,000 to £150,000 on it. We knew that if the picture, which we admired greatly, achieved the price indicated by the auction house, then it would be beyond our means, as our total annual grant for the acquisition of pictures is just £100,000. In the event the picture was bought in and we negotiated its purchase for just over £70,000.

Do you feel that the law is making it easier for public collections to acquire works of art?

A recent amendment in the new Finance Act makes it attractive for a private collector to lend to a public collection for a period. This can be done on the understanding that, for five years, if he then sells the work, he wouldn't be liable for Capital Gains Tax. I think that this was originally added to the Statute Book to promote IMMA which, of course, has to create a collection from scratch. But naturally it may benefit us and other collections too.

How would you like to see this improved?

The ideal situation would make it possible for individuals to donate works in lieu of tax. That would help us enormously, although, of course, we have benefited from generous gifts and bequests from public spirited individuals. Think of the Besit Collection, for example, and the collection given by Maire NcNeill Sweeney. Not everyone can afford to give without receiving some benefit, however.

Do you feel you're well funded in general?

We get a direct government grant. It currently stands at just over IR£1 million, which is very modest indeed. From this we have to make acquisitions. And I think the public get good value. It means that we are given about IR£1 per visitor. I think pound for pound we probably give the best value of any gallery anywhere.

In terms of sponsorship you've done tremendously well over the past two or three years, haven't you?

We have. Our exhibitions programme is, like our publications programme, totally self-financing. We consider there will be a need for increased sponsorship in the future if we are to realize the kind of exhibition schedule we are currently considering.

Could you describe the composition of your Board?

The responsibility for the management of the Gallery is vested in the Board of Governors and Guardians. This Board is made up of seventeen members, ten of whom are appointed by the Government and seven of whom are ex-officio. Those nominated by the Government are appointed for five year terms, which may be renewed.

I had the impression that the present Chairman, W D Finlay, had been in place for quite a time.

The chairman is appointed by the Board, who elect a candidate every three years. Obviously, they are very happy with the current incumbent who has expertly guided the Gallery through some very difficult times and has made an important contribution to the promotion of a number of significant developments.

Personally, do you miss the old days when you could pursue art-historical research?

Yes. The burden of administration does severely limit your opportunity to pursue research. It is something you miss quite a lot. After all, your whole motivation in getting involved in museum life was your interest in paintings and your desire to learn more about them. But it is imperative that you acknowledge that as Director, the administration of the collection is your most important responsibility. Research is tremendously important, but it should only be undertaken when you are confident that the administrative concerns are taken care of.

There has been some criticism of some of your innovations, particularly in an article in Apollo.

One has to accept that it is impossible to please all of the public. One has to look at and identify shortcomings. Then you have to list your priorities and set about improving the situation.

When I took over as Director, staff had been reduced to thirty-five, the fabric of the building was causing concern and attendance figures were falling. One cannot deny that there was genuine cause for complaint. Over the past four years we have worked hard to make improvements. But we appreciate that we still have some way to go. We have mapped out a programme which will, over a period of time take care of the most serious complaints. Having said that, there are areas of operation where success is as much a factor of taste or opinion as anything else. In those areas it will be impossible to achieve a unanimity with respect to our achievement or lack of it.

John Hutchinson

John Hutchinson became Director of the Douglas Hyde Gallery in 1991. In this interview he discusses his policies and the controversies about recent exhibitions.

For the benefit of those who aren't familiar with the Douglas Hyde Gallery, would you give an account of its character and history?

The Douglas Hyde Gallery is situated in Trinity College, at the Nassau Street entrance to the Arts Block. I think of its position as particularly appropriate for us, as it is on a border between the closed world of the university and the busy city outside.

Briefly, the Douglas Hyde, as we now know it, was established in 1978, when the Arts Block was opened. Its creation was due, in no small measure, to the energy and enthusiasm of Professor George Dawson, who negotiated an arrangement with the Arts Council, whereby the

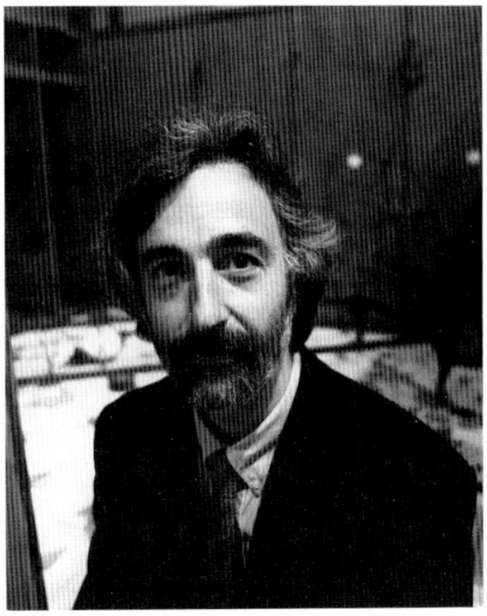

John Hutchinson, Douglas Hyde Gallery.

College agreed to provide the space, basic running costs, and security staff, while the Council promised to grant-aid the exhibition programme and other staff salaries. That arrangement still stands, although we also raise other revenue by means of sponsorship, collaborations, patronage schemes, and bookshop sales.

The Gallery is now an independent charitable organisation, with a Board of Directors, of whom half are appointed by the College, and half by the Arts Council. I'm responsible for the running of the Gallery, and I formulate an exhibition programme which is discussed and agreed with the Board. We have a full-time Administrator, Danae Kindness, and three part-time staff – Janet Pierce, the Education Officer; Sheila Gorman, the Administrative Assistant; and Pat O'Rourke, the Exhibitions Assistant. We also draw on the help of a team of students, most of whom are History of Art undergraduates.

Has this always been so?

The staff structure has been fairly stable over the last few years, but in its early days the Gallery was run by a Curator, who had less autonomy and less assistance. When Pat Murphy became Director in 1984, after the Gallery became a limited company, the organisation quickly grew to its present stature. I made a few adjustments when I came, but no substantial changes. By Irish standards we are generously provided for, but compared with similar institutions abroad we have limited resources. Many visiting curators express surprise at what we are able to achieve.

Would you like to tell me exactly how much you have to spend in a year?

We get about £130,000 from the Arts Council, which accounts for most of our spending money. Trinity College gives us about £25,000 in benefits-in-kind.

Do you have a permanent collection?

No. There is a permanent collection of modern art in Trinity, but it now has nothing to do with us. The Douglas Hyde is a public, university-based, gallery for temporary exhibitions.

And what is the Gallery's exhibition policy?

It has gradually evolved since the Gallery was founded. Initially the programme was very eclectic – it ranged from curious historical shows to important exhibitions of contemporary art and had no particular focus. But Pat Murphy had a clear view of what he wanted to achieve, and by the time he left, in 1990, the Douglas Hyde had found a specific niche for itself. It concentrated on contemporary art, with about half of the shows being Irish, and the rest international. As far as I know, the board, and especially our Chairman, Professor David Spearman, was most supportive of Pat's shift in direction.

In effect, the Douglas Hyde became the country's leading contemporary art gallery and was soon recognised as such both at home and abroad. The Douglas Hyde was also the first Irish contemporary art gallery to produce a series of first-rate exhibition catalogues. By the end of the decade, a show at the Douglas Hyde was considered a real achievement for an Irish painter or sculptor and an attractive proposition for most international artists.

Has this situation changed now that there are other major and active galleries in Dublin?

Inevitably. Several other galleries now produce serious contemporary exhibitions and good catalogues, so a show at the Douglas Hyde isn't quite as crucial to a practising Irish artist as it was a few years ago. But the development of the Douglas Hyde coincided with a remarkable increase in activity on the Irish art scene, and naturally the art world infrastructure has expanded to reflect that growth. It was no coincidence that The Irish Museum of

THE NEW DIRECTORS

Modern Art came into being at the turn of the decade.

In what ways has the advent of IMMA affected the Douglas Hyde Gallery?

Well, we're no longer the senior contemporary art gallery in the country. IMMA, given its current focus, has taken over that role. This means, for instance, that a famous international artist like Anselm Kiefer, who showed at the Douglas Hyde in 1990, would probably choose to exhibit at IMMA rather than here, were he invited to do so. A national institution, by definition, has real status. But this doesn't mean that I automatically defer to IMMA's seniority: if I felt that the work of a celebrated artist was particularly relevant to our exhibition programme, I would try to convince him or her that the Douglas Hyde was the right place in which to show. We do have certain advantages, after all: the Douglas Hyde has a history and an established reputation, and we have a central location in the middle of town. Although our attendance figures have been affected, to some extent, by the existence of IMMA and the development of the other galleries, there is still substantial interest in our programme. And we're very easy to reach.

How would you define the Gallery's public?

Broadly speaking it consists of the art world and young people. I suppose you could say that the majority are between eighteen and thirty years of age. A fair proportion of our visitors simply come in out of general interest, but they don't form the core of our public. I should emphasise, though, that we do have a very successful education programme, which operates on many levels. I'm conscious of the need to provide access to the exhibitions, which can be intimidating to the uninitiated.

What are your attendance figures?

They are fairly consistent throughout the year at between 180 and 260 a day.

Hasn't there been some recent correspondence in the newspapers about the Douglas Hyde's exhibition programme?

Yes – it developed momentum after a controversial exhibition we held in April. Detractors feel that our programme is too modish and conceptual; our supporters argue that the programme's current focus is a sign of the Gallery's energy and perspicacity!

But isn't it true that the Douglas Hyde's exhibitions are increasingly difficult and elitist?

Well, they're certainly intended to be challenging. Oddly enough, though, most of our 'difficult' shows are as well attended as others that might appear to be more accessible. And I'll certainly admit that most of the art we're showing at the Douglas Hyde demands thought. In my view the main function of art is to deepen our understanding of life, in all its complexity, and, after all, life does not just revolve around the accepted values of the *status quo*. I have great affection for classical art – I worked in the National Gallery for almost ten years, so it would be surprising if I didn't – but I do believe that the most challenging art being made today usually comes in unconventional forms. Not all of it will stand the test of time, but I think that it falls to galleries like the Douglas Hyde to bring such work to the public's attention.

Is IMMA not covering similar ground?

Yes, but our programme has a very specific slant. We're showing art that explores one or other of two themes: 'identity' and 'spirituality'. The idea is that a kind of dialectic is set up between those themes, which, broadly speaking, are on opposite sides of the ideological spectrum, and that the programme will have a cumulative effect. I've also asked most of the artists we're working with to respond to the gallery space, which some would describe as an awkward concrete cube. The result is that many of our exhibitions are site-specific.

In any case, I'm not convinced that IMMA will be able to continue to place such emphasis on contemporary exhibitions. While I agree with most of Declan MacGonagle's ideas about the 'deconstruction' of received notions regarding the role of art museums, I don't think that you can ignore the need for cultural stability and permanence. In other words, sooner or later IMMA will have to concentrate on historical shows and on its collection. And, in an ideal world, I'd like to see the Hugh Lane Gallery focus on the Lane collection, which could be contextualised in any number of interesting ways. The Gallagher Gallery, in due course, should become a leading showcase for more conventional contemporary art, which would be appropriate for an institution that is run by the Royal Hibernian Academy. In short, I think that our various roles could be more sharply differentiated. But we all get together on a regular and friendly basis to discuss what we're doing, so at least we're aware of each other's plans and intentions. And although there's a degree of healthy competition between us, it's tempered by genuine mutual support.

Michael Ryan

I've always been amazed that this treasure-house of middle-Eastern and oriental art, which enjoys a vast international reputation, is located in a suburban garden in Dublin. How does it come to be here, after all Chester Beatty was American wasn't he?

Yes, he was but he had some Irish ancestors and so this made him look to Ireland when he was thinking of a home for his collections.

When did he come to Ireland?

In the late 1940s. After the war his main residence was in London. There was a Labour landslide in 1945. Well, he couldn't see himself getting on with a Labour government, so he looked to Ireland. He took a house on the corner of Ailesbury Road and bought a nearby site in Shrewsbury Road;he built his library on it, plus the house that we're in now, as a residence for his librarian. The second Gallery on the far end of the site was added later, and was completely remodelled and extended in 1973.

Who was responsible for the design of the first building?

An architect was employed, of course, but Chester Beatty must have been the real designer. He was thinking of posterity, and was being quite carefully wooed by the Irish government. They granted him honorary Irish citizenship and encouraged him to settle. Eventually, it came to be understood, before his death in 1968, that the library would be left in trust in Ireland.

When did that actually happen?

September 1968. Chester Beatty died in January of that year. This will put in place a Board of up to twelve Trustees; one is appointed by the President and one by the Taoiseach; one the Director of the National Library *ex officio*.

What did the government put into the pot?

Well, originally there seems to have been

THE NEW DIRECTORS

a gentleman's agreement to the effect that the government would contribute the running costs, but there was no endowment, either from government or Chester Beatty.

And that persists? The impression, perhaps because of the richness of the collections, is that you have lots of money.

That impression is wrong, although the grant-in-aid continues; at present it is £345,000 per annum. Actually we are very poor. We have few other resources (although we have been generously supported by Telecom Eireann, to mount our Hiroshige exhibition). We are currently carrying a deficit of £125,000, which is a major drag on our ability to do things.

How do you go about reducing something like that?

Well, we have devised a plan of retrenchment, and have taken pretty swift action. One unusual thing, for an institution run from the public purse, is that we get our grant paid up front – which minimises bank charges.

Do you find that the administrative structure, with your twelve Trustees, works well?

Yes. I enjoy working with the Board and they bring a wealth of contacts and tremendous body of experience to the library. We've obviously been dealing with "first aid" matters this year; there's been an element of crisis management because of the theft.

Legally, was the theft from the Trustees?

Yes. The Trustees of the Library are different from those of public bodies. For a start, this is a charitable trust and the Trustees themselves carry a very high liability, and they must maintain, for example, public liability insurance. So they're not like government nominees. That's a point that's not often understood. As Trustees, they're legally obliged to do all they can to recover the items stolen from the Trust.

Is recovery a possibility?

Well the success rate has been very, very good. I don't want to sound overconfident, but the police have done a magnificent job, and we've got back about 660 folios of Korans, and a number of Indian miniatures and pieces of calligraphy. The New York Public Library, which bought material through Sotheby's has returned it to Sotheby's; the David Samling in Copenhagen has returned material. A number of people in the trade in Islamic antiquities have behaved very honorably.

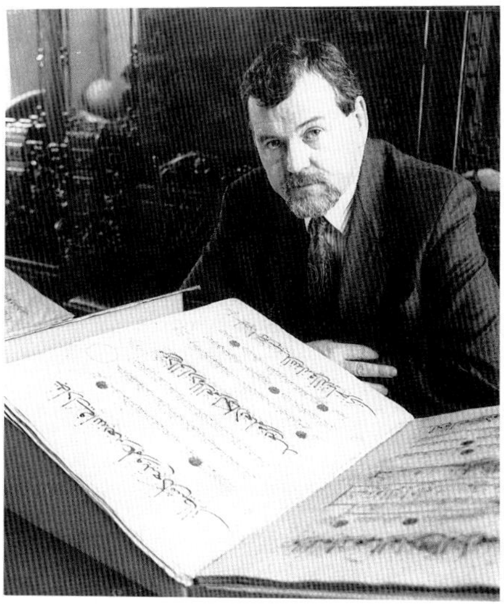

Michael Ryan, Chester Beatty Library.

Do you feel the Library's reputation will have become tarnished through the thefts?

It certainly has been painful for my colleagues who were here when the thefts came to light. They feel betrayed, quite rightly. Now the trial is over we can turn the corner and remind people of the more positive aspects of our work.

What's first on the agenda?

As long ago as last summer we started looking around for a new site, and since last autumn we've had a great deal of interest and support from the Department of the Taoiseach and the Office of Public Works, and now the new Department of Arts, Culture and the Gaeltacht. So, we have identified a particularly desirable site at Dublin Castle, but at this moment, I just don't know if we're going to get it. It's a free-standing office block to the rear of the state apartments, along the side of the old Vice-regal gardens.

So that would put you right in the centre of things.

Yes. Yes. That building – it's eighteenth century – has to be restored, and there are plans to extend it. It would be easy for that extension to be developed for museum/-gallery-type purposes, giving us a two-fold building, with the older part being used for offices and study-rooms and the new extension being given over to exhibition areas. It wouldn't be huge – about 20,000 sq. ft. – but more than adequate for our purposes.

It would put you on the tourist route.

I think that's important, but we also want to be in one single building where it would be easier to manage the collections and make them secure. We want better facilities – study rooms, facilities for visiting scholars, a restaurant, commercial and schools facilities, proper access for the disabled.

And education?

Obviously. But you're talking about an institution with a very, very small staff. We have two full-time and one part-time curators, plus me, plus Vera Greiff who effectively runs the administration, and security staff. We don't have dedicated shop staff or education staff. We have a tremendously supportive group of volunteer guides, provided by our Friends. They also organise regular series of lectures and other events.

Is there a demand from students?

Yes. We have recently had a great number, particularly from the College of Art, and the Trinity students have been particularly interested in the Raimondi/Dürer Exhibition. We also have a constant stream of research scholars coming to visit, from language students to high-powered Armenian scholars.

The visit of Japanese conservators was particularly important.

Oh, yes. They worked here on some of our Japanese literary scrolls. Since then Dr Hirayama, the President of Tokyo University of Art and a very distinguished painter, has been in discussion with us. His foundation exists solely for the conservation of important Japanese collections outside Japan. Our Japanese scroll collection is one of the best small collections in the world. We hope to have some of them conserved in Japan. Have you seen the Surimono exhibition we're showing now?

Those are so beautiful. You don't need to be an orientalist to appreciate just how special they are. This is just one of a fairly vigorous programme of exhibitions?

Yes. We plan a regular programme through-

THE NEW DIRECTORS

out the year. They are small scale, but choice. Most notably, we are to show an exhibition devoted to Hiroshige at the RHA Gallery in the summer.

Now that hasn't been done before.

Not since the 1950s when Chester Beatty showed at The National Gallery and at Trinity. Basically we want the whole of Ireland to know what we've got. I have a feeling that our western collections have been somewhat overlooked. Our western curator, Charles Horton, is systematically planning exhibitions of our major western print holdings. For instance, after his Raimondi/Dürer selection, we will show Goya's *Disasters of War*.

Charles Horton must have a lot to do – if he curates the whole of the western collections.

Not only that, but he doubles as Reference Librarian. No one person could do both jobs. So you can see how grave the staffing problem is. Also, we need a replacement in the Islamic/Arabic area. Our Indian collection is wonderful as will be understood when the catalogue comes out this year.

Is there any hope of adding to the staff?

Well, we are competing for funding now in an effort, not only to add to the curatorial staff, but also to increase the essential support staff. First of all, we need to keep our buildings open longer to the public, and to make them more user-friendly. And we need to beef up the administration and our commercial and educational undertakings. All this ought to be in place before we move. Unfortunately, I can't promise anything – funding isn't easy to come by at the moment.

Since your collections are mainly oriental and middle-eastern. There's no way that you compete for acquisitions with other Irish institutions?

Well, only in the area of European prints, since the National Gallery has a large collection. Ours is bigger, probably the second largest in the island, but, in terms of quality, I think it has to be recognised as the best collection of Old Master prints.

Chester Beatty obviously felt very deeply about the objects he collected. Did he have a command of the languages of the countries whose art he collected?

Well, not many people would have competence in them all – or even have a detailed knowledge of their history and art. But Chester Beatty was open to them, and he employed the very best scholarly help to guide his acquisitions. He also hired the internationally-reputed scholars of the day to catalogue the collections.

Is the work still continuing?

Well acquisition isn't a top priority any more. Naturally, we are able to accept donations and bequests, in a discriminating way, but we don't have the resources to compete at the top of the international market. Judicious buying of, say, European prints, Japanese prints and certain categories of Oriental manuscripts might become possible again once we reduce the deficit. Then we might make over an annual sum for acquisition. But the present areas of priority are conservation, administration, exhibitions and so on. We are continuing to publish the collection – last year a catalogue of our Dürer prints was published to accompany a joint exhibition with the Kunsthalle in Bremen. The catalogue *Tales of Japan* was prepared by Mrs Ushioda, our Japanese curator, to accompany an exhibition of our Japanese scrolls. A full survey of our Japanese works will shortly be published by the Kordansha publishing house, and a survey of our literary texts is about to appear in Japan and, we hope, in Europe also. The library catalogues prepared over the years are standard references in their field and we hope to continue this.

Do you acquire for the research library?

Now this is an area where development is more possible. We need to develop policies in concert with other bodies. To achieve a decent research library in some of the areas covered by the collection we will have to enter into agreements with other libraries so that the total book-buying fund for specialist research in Ireland is not dissipated by duplication. It has been estimated that we would need £250,000 to bring our library of Islamic and other reference material up to scratch. At present, we are pursuing a policy of active co-operation with relevant university departments. Of course, in order to be active in all the areas of development which we have in mind, we need about £450,000 a year and no debts.

But your top priority is to make the collections more public.

Well, I don't want, by implication, to seem to be belittling my predecessors. The fact is that since the library became a charitable trust, exhibitions have been mounted constantly, some of great importance. The drag has always been the location – there has never been any lack of imagination in our programming, nor any lack of effort in publicising our endeavours. I think people have begun to recognise that we have collections of international significance – Persian, Indian, Turkish, Armenian, Japanese, Russian icons, coins – one could go on for ever. But they don't realise that you don't have to be an expert to gain great enjoyment and inspiration from these collections. Or I should say, an increasing number does realise this – attendance figures are going up beyond the annual seven thousand average. But it's still difficult getting people out here.

Ciarán MacGonigal

I've never been sure of the precise relationship between the Gallagher Gallery and the Royal Hibernian Academy.

Well, the links are institutional and architectural. First, the RHA holds all its council meetings and so on in the building.. The building is the physical home of the Academy. Then, the Gallery is within the RHA building. The whole structure is really quite recent with construction beginning only in 1972. There was then a long period of inactivity; then in 1986 a group of interested persons decided to complete the project. They formed a trust and then Charles Gallagher made a considerable contribution to get the building started again. As a whole, the building is still unfinished, but the Gallery itself was completed.

So the Gallery is actually owned by the RHA?

It is leased from the RHA and a Board administers it. The Gallagher family are represented on that Board by Charles Gallagher and Mrs Marese Gallagher. When Mr Gallagher can't attend, Mrs Evelyn Healy deputises for him.

I presume the Academy is also represented on the Board.

Oh, yes. The President of the RHA sits on it and one other Academician. The RHA also nominates a representative from outside the Academy.

THE NEW DIRECTORS

How is the policy of the Gallery generated?

There is an Exhibitions Sub-Committee chaired by the President. That committee includes a nominee from the Arts Council. And it's with that committee that I, as Director, work. Our recommendations then return to the main Board for confirmation.

You say the Arts Council has a representative on the Board. Does that mean that the Council funds you?

Yes. We have an annual grant which at present stands at £50,000. The rest of our funding is formed from donations and covenants, and through self-generated income. The total amounts to about £200,000 per annum.

How many staff do you have?

In addition to myself, we have an administrator and an Exhibitions Officer. Then other functions are carried out by part-time staff. It's all pretty skeletal.

My impression is that you have very large exhibition galleries, and only a small permanent collection. With such a small staff, there must be considerable problems in keeping those galleries constantly in service, constantly filled with interesting exhibits.

Yes,devoting part of the galleries to the permanent collection would be rather difficult, since it is really quite small. It's made up of diploma work and also donations and bequests. It doesn't really represent a specific view of the history of art. You could say, however, that it adds to the systematic collections of Irish art held elsewhere in the country. It amplifies the known history.

The main event of the exhibition year appears to be the annual RHA exhibition.

Yes. It always creates a great deal of interest. In fact, the Gallery in effect pays part of its lease to the Academy by allowing the Academy to have its exhibition here. My involvement is minimal. About 1,800 works were submitted this year. The exhibition is made up of works by Academicians and Associates, and a few invitees – there are thirty Academicians and ten Associates (they're sort of 'junior ranks'), and there can be an unlimited number of honorary members. So that accounts for the core of the exhibition. The rest is made up of a selection from the send-in.

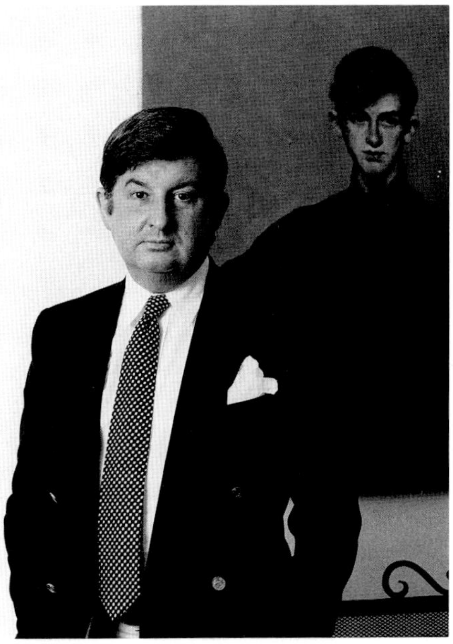

Ciarán MacGonigal, RHA Gallery.

Are you in the selection committee?

Well, first of all, the work of the members is included – no selection involved. Then, the submissions are selected, and I'm thankful that I'm *not* on that Committee, which is made up of members of the Academy.

How do you view the exhibition, and indeed the nature of the RHA itself?

Well, I often say to young artists who might be critical of the RHA – 'look, you are an academy as well; you are setting a standard; you are setting up an aesthetic and you too are erecting inclusion and exclusion zones'.

Beyond the RHA exhibition, how do you see the exhibitions policy?

Obviously because of the physique of our galleries, we are in a position to show work on a scale that the Irish Museum of Modern Art can't cope with, and, clearly, artists and organisers who are aware of that make themselves known to us. And of course I'm in constant touch with Declan McGonagle, and not just because we get each other's letters! It's all too easy to be driven by circumstances, to be driven by the need to provide a constant diet bread and circuses. My own taste is towards interactive shows. For example, last Christmas we had the Armagh Rhymers here. They're a folk dance group and the event was a combination of the exhibition and of folk dance and singing. We did two shows a day for children, and they were *entranced.* We also had Rubato Ballet who did a show in a set designed by van Oost, and artists came in and painted and sculpted upstairs in response to the performance, and it grew. I like this notion of joint art practice.

And it must expand the profile of your audience.

Yes. We had musicians in who were both young composers themselves, and involved in the dance group. I also try to make the social element of it important. I want to increase the number of events we have here. Where appropriate, we arrange dinners. It's a way of attracting different people they attract a lot of corporate people – who might otherwise never come here, who might otherwise give their energies to golf or ballet. Just before I came they had a big dinner for Cooperation North and the whole place was given over to the great and the rich – well, the rich anyway – and there were people have who have never set foot in a gallery before. This is also crucial to us since we have to raise our own funds.

Yes. How else would you get them into the Gallery?

The biggest step is the one across the threshold. That's the theory of supermarket selling. You've noticed how they continue the paving of the shopping mall right into the supermarket, so that you just keep walking right in.

So clearly we can look forward to shows of very wide appeal.

I'd like to do a large theatre design show, and a major fashion exhibition, again looking to an expanded public. And, in terms of the visual arts, a Giacommetti sculpture exhibition. And we are planning exhibitions of Anthony Wishaw, David Hockney and Bert Irvine.

Well, the galleries are virtually made for Albert Irvine.

And I'd really like to organise some big group of the best work of the Academicians, and a major showing of interesting portraits, with the emphasis very much on *interesting.*

The last twenty years has seen the British

THE NEW DIRECTORS

Royal Academy develop from a proudly retrograde institution into a major international exhibition centre. What would you say to the criticism that the RHA is still behind the times?

I'm never sure what that phrase means. At any given time a gallery responds to demands from pre-existing situations – artists who are already in practice, for example. The revolving nature of taste and museological practice means that you are either *in advance* of the times or *ahead* of it.

But there can be no doubt that the RA in London was at one time anti-modernist. Then, when they consciously moved out of that phase, making contact with artists working in more up to date modes, it helped them to make an important step to becoming more broadly representative – which is clearly your intention.

Yes. I'd *adore* to be able to show more and younger artists in order to prepare the next set of constituents as to what it's like to work with a gallery. I'd also like some artist-in-residence schemes.

Do you have the space for artists-in-residence?

I'll show you round behind the scenes here in a moment. There are whole areas of this building which are ripe for development.

So you have plans to develop the building as a whole?

Oh, yes. That's very high on the agenda. Given our location and public expectation, we need to develop a restaurant and a bookshop. As can be seen from the example of the National Gallery, these would immediately increase our visitor numbers.

What are your attendance figures at present?

About 100,000 a year. I'd like that to increase, and the building is part of the answer to that. We're just finishing our Sculpture Court now, which will have the effect of providing an enhanced entrance, much more fitting to an institution of status. The next thing is to start on the rest of the building.

You must spend a lot of time writing begging letters.

I do, but of course the recession has affected people's ability to help. But it's easing a bit.

Not so long ago, one was very much aware of the great personal interest in the arts of the then Taoiseach, Mr Haughey. And he used his power to great effect, as I discovered. Is there still the same sense of commitment on the part of the new Minister?

Certainly, but at any time the Taoiseach will always have more power than any Minister.

Have you got Friends?

Sometimes I wonder. Oh, you mean with a capital? We don't, and I don't believe this is an option at the moment, since we haven't got enough to offer them. Having been Secretary to the Friends of the National Collections for many years, I'm aware that these things can reach a plateau and then tail off. And, at times, the provision of space for Friends is really less necessary than space for the collection itself.

Nevertheless, a Friends situation, a Restaurant and a Bookshop would be of intense interest to me as a not-too-far-away stage to be achieved. And this can be incorporated in the present building, as could a Members' Common Room and Members' Library.

What else would you like to see in the developed building?

Well, this is outside my jurisdiction, but I would like to see the RHA once again actively involved in the education of artists. I believe that it should re-open its Diploma Schools for postgraduate work. At the moment, post graduate study has to be undertaken substantially abroad. This doesn't suit everybody, and it creates a drain on our artistic resources.

And I understand that there is space in the top of the building for a number of studios.

Yes indeed.

In terms of ideas like that, can I assume that someone somewhere has an overview of gallery developments?

Now this is important. You've been talking to my colleagues in other galleries and you realise that there are areas of overlap. In my view, there is a case for a kind of Director-General whose brief would be to rationalise processes and spaces. The fear, of course, is that 'rationalisation' might mean 'cutting down', but you might well be cut anyway, in a totally unsystematic way.

I look at it this way. Ireland has a population of three and a half million, with one million in Dublin. We have, relatively, quite a lot of museums and galleries. There is bound to be an overlap both in terms of administration and acquisitions. At some point I would not be surprised if the Ministry said: 'look, we want to look at this again. We have complex structures to administer each museum and just in terms of ordinary staff this quintuplication need not take place.' And the budgets may need to be looked at.

I also think that each museum area will need to make up its mind about which objects should never leave Ireland under any circumstances. And there should be a clear idea about which public collection should get these objects, or which public collection should administer these objects should they be left *in situ* in a country house, or whatever.

My impression is that there has been an enormous expansion in terms of art education in Ireland, but it hasn't filtered through to those who haven't followed courses of study. To me, there is still a feeling in the general public, that art is not for them. They see it as a preoccupation of the elite.

When I used to lecture at the National Gallery, I used to say to people after a tour of the collection – 'If you liked one or two of the pictures you've seen, I believe you. If you've liked three or four, I still believe you. If you've liked more than five, I begin to wonder, and if you've liked around ten I just think you've got no discrimination at all.' There was always a sense of shock, but I think there is an assumption that all pictures throughout the span of history are good, with some better than others. I walk through a gallery and I don't stop at a picture unless it puts its hand out and says stop.

What kind of pictures do that for you?

Well there are distinct periods I like. The period around Duccio, for example and some British eighteenth-century paintings.

I like the Barbizon School, certain things by Monet and Toulouse-Lautrec. But, as for big experiences, when I went to Chicago and saw that painting of Van Gogh's bedroom I was actually moved to tears. And it's that fundamental experience that drives me in my work here.

Alistair Smith

Alistair Smith is Director of the Whitworth Art Gallery, University of Manchester.

SEAN SCULLY

In anticipation of the forthcoming exhibition in IMMA, **Alistair Smith** discusses the artist Sean Scully and his recent paintings.

Sean Scully is, arguably, today's most important Irish-born contemporary painter. Although he left Dublin, the town of his birth, at the age of four, and has not lived in Ireland since, he has maintained Irish connections and a commitment to the Irish art community. With paintings in important museums throughout Europe, Australia, the USA and Ireland itself, he enjoys an international reputation as heir to the pioneering first generation of Abstract Expressionists and as the upholder of abstract painting through the 1970s and 1980s when figurative art commandeered the attention of the art world.

This essay is provoked by three circumstances. One – a respect for and enjoyment of Scully's work. Two – the publication in 1990 of a monograph on the artist. Three – the forthcoming retrospective exhibition at the Irish Museum of Modern Art, which will surely bear an analytic relationship to that monograph.

The book I refer to is Maurice Poirier's *Sean Scully* published by Hudson Hills Press of New York. Since Scully's work displays both the extroversion of his American forerunners and, at times, an oriental predilection for contemplation, it is fitting that the monograph was written and designed in the USA and beautifully manufactured in Japan. Hudson Hills Press includes in its publications list books on Ellsworth Kelly and Mark Rothko, both of whom can be identified as source material for Scully. Indeed, Scully combines in his art the materiality of Kelly (the way his paintings are, first and foremost, *physical*) with the transcendentalism of Rothko's incorporeal fields of colour.

The paintings occupy the main part of Poirier's book in the form of 135 full-page colour illustrations, arranged chronologically into six sections. Each section is preceded by a shortish text which incorporates already published material, and provides a critical assessment of Scully's development up to the time of his magisterial travelling exhibition which originated at the Whitechapel Art Gallery (London) in 1989. It has to be said that Poirier could not hope to be aware either of the detail of post-war working-class life in London or of the precise nature of the British art college culture which Scully experienced. Consequently, the account which he presents of the early years is Scully's own, and the text, in general, has the virtue of being an interpretation of the artist's own view of himself. This constitutes a valuable approach to an artist whose work is so overwhelmingly autobiographical, but it leaves the way open for a precisely-researched historical assessment.

In his first paragraph, Poirier introduces the contrasts '... on the one hand, he is Scully the lyric poet ... on the other hand, he is Scully the fighter.' Throughout his childhood and teenage years, playground fights and then gang brawls form a *leitmotif* against which to set Scully's discovery of Picasso's *Child holding a Dove* and Van Gogh's *Chair*. Of the latter, Scully has said, 'It was as if the world had just stopped. It had a kind of nobility, an honesty about it'. To the good fortune of the art public, it was the artist rather that the street-fighter who gained the upper hand, took evening classes, and then trained at Croydon and Newcastle University from 1968 to 1972. At that time, as a consequence of Richard Hamilton's period as Professor there, the Newcastle art department could claim to be the most lively and innovative in the UK. The emphasis was not, however, to Scully's taste '... anything that was a kick in the pants for abstraction and high art was okay ...' since by that time he had recognised in himself a deep response to Rothko and had painted a number of pieces in homage to his '*simplicity and unpretentiousness*'.

While at Newcastle, Scully declared his allegiance, not to the prevalent 'conceptual/pop', but to the form of art which he has consistently practised and refined ever since. His not-so-solemn oath took the form of a painting (no longer extant) entitled *Newcastle Boogie-Woogie*. While its title exemplifies his wit, it also makes reference to a famous painting from Mondrian's last years – and constitutes an act of homage to the century's first, transcendental, abstract painter. *Broadway Boogie-Woogie* is one of Mondrian's most animated paintings, but Scully's paeon to the energy of Newcastle exceeded by far Mondrian's measured effect with an array of impenetrable overlapping vertical and horizontal bars. This was to be an example of what can now be discerned as Scully's 'grid period'.

Looking at these pictures now, one recognises in them an almost antiquarian sense of period; they summarise much that was current in the early seventies. With deferential bows in the direction of both op art and serial painting, Scully made use of all the techniques in vogue at the time – acrylic, spray-gun, masking tape and shaped canvases among them. Yet the results were emphatically personal, vibrant and extroverted, not to say *macho*.

The 'grid' paintings display a busy, often frenetic, overlap of straight lines (or bars), either diagonal or at rightangles to one another. Some of the bars seem to jump forward from the painting into 'real life' space; they also seem ready to project beyond the confining edges of the canvas – however large the painting, and some of them measure as much as eight feet, they have the feel of a detail cut from a much larger whole, whose energy might well fill the world. Scully has talked of his early liking for the 'wall of sound' which was the hallmark of pop music record-producer Phil Spector. The grid paintings can be construed as Spector's visual equivalent.

It was this form of painting which won Scully both his prize at Liverpool's John Moores Exhibition, his first fellowhip in the USA, and which was featured in his first one-man show at the Rowan Gallery in London. The exhibition sold out and attracted a good critical response. Contrariwise, Scully immediately undertook to remake his art in the manner of 'serious high-minded abstraction', his mind very much on American precedents.

The results of this avowal are immediately visible in the paintings which Scully made in the years 1974 and 1975, when he decisively abandoned the explosive effects of the grid years for a cooler, more poised re-assessment of Mondrian. Instead of attacking the spectator, the paintings seek to reason. Just how radically different from the grid paintings they were, is attested by the fact that this 1973 'grid' show sold out, while his cooler 1975 show failed to sell one painting.

Scully's next five years, when he took up residence in New York, are described by Poirier as a period of 'abnegation and solitary retreat'. The work produced was the least colourful, least gestural, most stoical of the artist's career. The majority of the paintings were made up of narrow stripes in the tradition of minimalist formal abstraction, the influence of other 'stripe' painters – Agnes Martin, François Morellet, Brigid Riley, early Frank Stella –

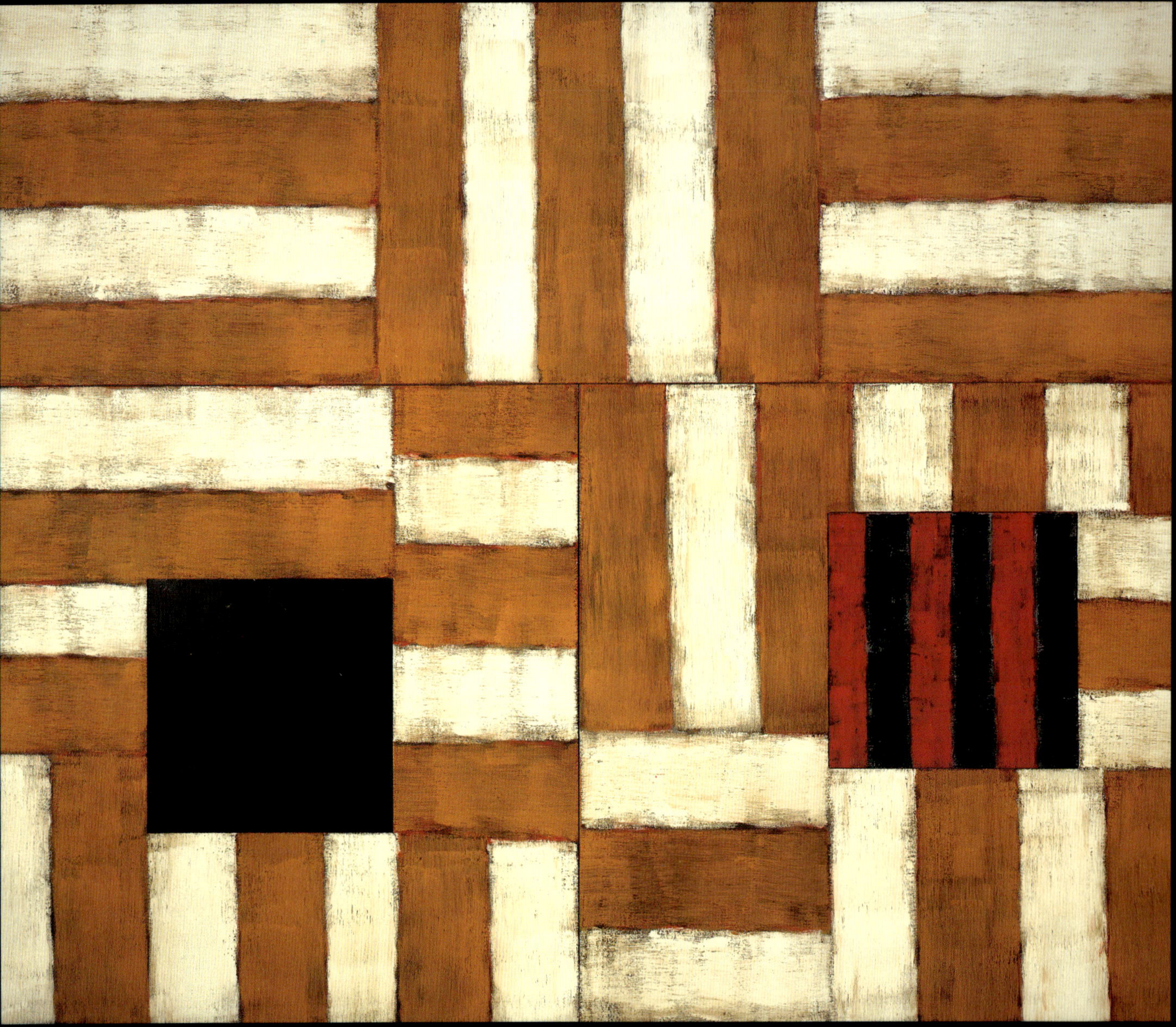

Sean Scully, Why and What (Yellow) 1988. *Oil on canvas with steel panel. A: 92.1 x 304.8cm. B and C: 152.7 x 152.7cm. Hirshorn Museum and Sculpture Garden, Smithsonian Institution. Holenia Purchase Fund, 1989.*

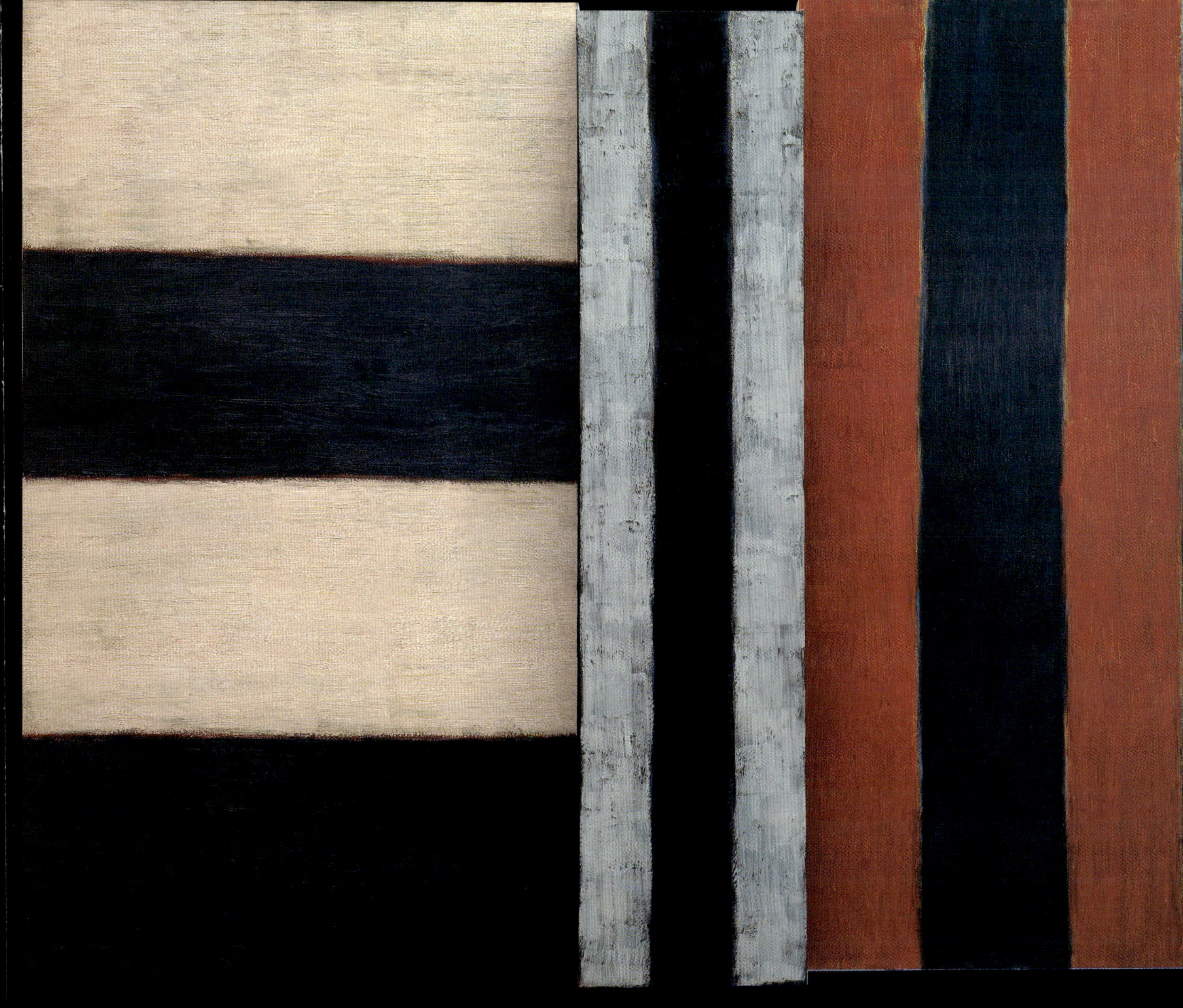

Sean Scully, Paul. *Oil on canvas, 259 x 320 x 240, Tate Gallery, London.*

often being quoted. The psychological distance of the paintings, and their aura of self-sufficency and self-contemplation, made public 'entry' into them difficult and it is perhaps as a result of this that Scully's support at the time came principally from one or two committed individuals who were able to relish the courageous abandonment of his natural ebullience. Despite this sudden change from major to minor key, however, the work was still autobiographical, making due obeisance to what Poirier describes as 'a Zen-inspired philosophy of life'. In a sense, Scully went into retreat in order to reconsider the very basis of his painting, examining scale, line, medium, colour, gesture, brushstroke. Through this process of self-analysis there emerged a disciplined, rational procedure and a philosophical form of painting. The art parallels the life – the street brawls had been translated into the punishing self-discipline of karate (in which Scully holds a black belt).

It is interesting to compare Scully's work of the years 1975-80 with contemporaneous work in Western Europe, where the extravagances of neo-expressionism were seizing the public eye. If Scully approached his unconscious through meditative self-analysis, the 'Junge Wilden' of Düsseldorf and Cologne hoped to express the abandon and indiscipline of their inner lives through a liberated revision of figurative art . Nothing could be less like Scully.

In this era, there was constant debate over the 'relevance' of figurative art as opposed to non-figurative (abstract) painting. This was often carried out in rather simplistic terms, whereby figuration was recognised as relevant to people (even 'the people') and a carrier of humanist messages, capable of furthering social change, class struggle, feminist liberation *et al.* And abstract art was not.

Confidence pervades the picture with which Scully recorded his rejection of neo-expressionist figuration. Painted in 1984, three years after his emergence, from the years of the narrow stripes he called it *No Neo.* It and others of the time like *Paul* and *Why and What (Yellow)* are products of Scully's mature style, which he has sustained today. They attest the humanist significance of non-figurative art, demonstrating its ability to communicate to the public a whole gamut of thought and emotion.

Despite their spiritual basis, their physique has become more pronounced over the years. *Paul,* for example, contains a section in relief. In a work like *Maestà,* this element of carpentry refers to the elaborate framing and panelling of an Italian Renaissance altarpiece, as does the title (which is shorthand for *The Virgin and Child in Majesty,* the subject of a famous altarpiece by Duccio).

More important, the paintings convey in contemporary language the emotional qualities of the devotional pieces to which they aspire.

The range of expression is formidable, and is founded on Scully's colouring, which has developed steadily since he abandoned acrylic for oil in 1979. Added to this is his effective use of insets – small paintings (on separate boards or canvases) which are interjected into the large compositions, sometimes with classical inevitability, sometimes with with delightful throwaway arbitrariness.

In a recent large triptych *Spirit,* shown at the Waddington Galleries in 1992, these implants assume a large proportion of the composition, comprising the two left-hand barred rectangles of oil paint. In *Why and What (Yellow)* of 1988 he had chosen to insert a small steel panel into a painting composed of several separately-stretched units. In *Spirit* the steel area has expanded to form the background fields to the two left-hand panels; despite its associations with large-scale construction (ship-plates and the like) the steel areas give the effect of being worked as tenderly as any oil painting.

Although Scully creates square and vertical paintings, somehow I think of them as being mainly of horizontal disposition. They read, therefore, rather like staves of musical notation, or as stanzas of verse. While all are proudly abstract, they are replete with associations. I think it is important, however, to insist that while we should be aware of these associations, the meaning of the paintings does not depend upon them.

A primary method of creating reference is through titles. These may refer to authors like Joseph Conrad (*Heart of Darkness*), Samuel Beckett (*How It Is*), Joyce (*Araby*) or Nabokov (*Pale Fire*), or to the kind of spiritual atmosphere which the painting evokes – *Adoration, Empty Heart.* Visual associations are perhaps less obvious but are probably more fundamental, having been subsumed at an early stage in Scully's development. His experience of wooden plank fences and huts in his London childhood was consolidated later by Mexico where he photographed tumble-down shacks (also wooden). Scully took his photographs from directly in front of the huts, and they bear a direct relationship to both his recent work in woodcut and to the sense of worn planking that his brushstrokes can evoke.

Scully's paintings are normally very large. This, and their often forceful demeanour might make it difficult for us to realise their refinement, a quality which is always easier to appreciate on a small scale. Yet they are complex in their formation and, as a result, have a sophisticated range of effects. Each stripe is the result of a layering of colours, some of which shine through the top layer – a contemporary derivation of traditional 'Old Master' oil technique. The edges of the stripes meet in a range of ways, from soft, loving blurs to hard-edge confrontation, particularly sharp at the edges of the 'implants'. And contrasts and correspondences are set up between the shapes of the various rectangles and stripes, all of which are treated with a great variety of brushstrokes, albeit dedicated to maintaining the direction and character of the stripe.

Scully's most basic allegiance is to the stripe and to evocative colour. Both can be detected in his memories of a visit to Morocco as early as 1969, where he saw long strips of dyed wool being hung out side-by-side by carpet-makers '... maybe six inches by eight foot long'. This experience has obviously been enlarged through contact with Navajo blankets and Kelims. There is always a feeling that his paintings create something of the atmosphere of exotic places.

None of these comparisons, however, go very far in explaining the art. The identikit picture, composed of highly-coloured stripes, wooden planking and American Abstract Expressionism, serves only to emphasise the achievement, which is finally a question of character. Scully has evolved with enormous commitment a method of conveying to us his subjectivity. The method is quite deliberately disciplined in form, yet admits of endlesss variation. As I write, I can barely wait to see the forthcoming exhibition at Kilmainham. Scully has not always been kindly treated by every part of the Irish art establishment, but I am confident that he will now be embraced by the Irish public.

Alistair Smith

THE LIGHT OF NOON

Dorothy Walker
comments on 20th century French Catholic art, and its relation to Irish artists, in her review of two major exhibitions: *Henri Matisse* (Museum of Modern Art, New York, Sept 1992-Jan 1993) and *Alfred Manessier* (Grand Palais, Paris, Oct 1992-Jan 1993).

Having seen, within a few weeks of each other, the retrospective exhibition of Alfred Manessier at the Grand Palais in Paris, and of Henri Matisse at the Museum of Modern Art in New York, it struck me that the link between these great but very different French painters is in fact a religious one. Were it not for the chapel at Vence, one would not immediately think of Matisse as a religious artist; rather the contrary: his strong sensual vision always seems firmly based in humanity and the delights of this world. Yet that is precisely what he brought to the chapel at Vence and which makes it such a hymn to the glory of God: the wonderful French joy of living, dedicated to the creator of life.

The full-size maquettes of the stained glass windows for the chapel, shown in New York, with their abstract designs in early-summer colours of blue, yellow and green, and their rising movement held in stillness, are a perfect vehicle of expression of the soul aspiring to God, an incredible mysticism in the clear light of day.

Manessier's palette is darker, more Spanish, and more consistently abstract. He is more directly concerned with the gospels, with the life of Christ, and indeed with the political implications of Christ's message to humanity. The French, however, are convinced anti-clericals, and there is no doubt in my mind that Manessier's reputation has not achieved the degree of greatness that it deserves because of his preoccupation with religion, even though, or perhaps because, this preoccupation took an abstract form. He also suffered from the timing of a powerful *Zeitgeist* in that the tidal wave of American Abstract Expressionism swept the world at the exact period when Manessier's work was making a lone stand in France, and so his work lost attention to the new Americans.

But his commanding large-scale abstractions such as *The Trial at Burgos*, undeniably Spanish in its passion, its dark red and black colours, and, indeed, its subject, or *The Ninth Hour*, a painting of awe and despair with a sense of catastrophic space in the picture planes, complement Matisse's bright noon light with a corresponding dark, a John of the Cross 'aunque sea noche', comparable to Heaney's beautiful *Station Island* poem. It is curious how Manessier has this Spanish shadow in his painting, since he is just as French in his background and upbringing as Matisse. Matisse absolutely embodies 'la lumière de l'Île de France', and even more so, 'la lumière du Midi', seen through so many window paintings, openings to light, to vision, to inspiration, a seizure of light like that of the Marian cathedrals, streaming through painted glass in the mediaeval builders' ambition to construct temples of pure glass, uninterrupted light, almost achieved in the Sainte-Chapelle in Paris.

Manessier, also, worked with stained glass all his artistic life; a major exhibition of his stained glass work ran parallel to the Grand Palais exhibition in the Centre International du Vitrail in Chartres. His stained glass also takes an abstract form, relying on colour to express the religious experience.

His most complete work in this medium is the church at Abbeville in Picardy completed this year, a complementary work in stained glass to his forty-year series of abstract painting on the Passion of Christ. These windows are very much in the French tradition of the great cathedrals with their superb use of blue, in particular, but generally in the fusion of rich, sonorous colour, deployed in figurative narrative in the mediaeval windows, although used for a spiritual narrative of emotion in Manessier's windows. While I have not seen the church, the artist has shown me the maquettes and colour studies in his studio in Clamart, and has explained his ideas on the sequence of colour in relation to the Passion.

The Spanish light in the paintings is different, dependent on the shadows, as in Goya, where things are always going on in the shadows. These shadows are different again from the northern dark which is more a sense of winter, of things buried in the dark, seeds which will need the light to germinate; so while there is one natural light, one source of daylight and sunlight, there are different kinds of natural dark, the darkness of night, and darkness of things buried or hidden in the earth. Rouault had more affinity with the dark, with suffering and despair, whereas Messiaen in his music was concerned with the mystical sublime. A philosopher like Teilhard de Chardin could combine the harmonies of Taoism with the mysticism of Christianity, fused, again, by the French *joie-de-vivre*. Gabriel Marcel, the Christian Existentialist, now almost forgotten, was in fact a very definite voice and force in my Existentialist youth in Paris after the Second World War, a time of inspired activity in Catholic art. The Dominican priest Père Couturier was influential in having artists like Matisse, Rouault and Manessier involved in church art; the great architect Le Corbusier designed his church at Ronchamp and the Dominican monastery at La Tourette. It was a period full of hope, inspiration, and real art, and it is interesting that the Papal Nuncio in Paris at the time was Cardinal Roncalli, later the great Pope John XXIII.

There is no comparable concern for aesthetics now and it is my own belief that the vulgarity of the current liturgy is a major contributing factor to the wholesale defection of young people from the Catholic Church, apart from the reactionary and unacceptable attitudes of the Vatican to issues like homosexuality or the role of women. Novelists and playwrights like Mauriac, Claudel, and Montherlant were at that time in full vigour (much to the disgust of one Samuel Beckett, I may add). Conor Cruise O'Brien's book *Maria Cross* discusses French Catholic writers of the time in detail.

It seems as if that supremely fruitful period came to an end with the publication of Pope Paul VI's encyclical *Humanae Vitae*, which in terms of science was like the silencing of Galileo, denying the validity of scientific development in relation to human reproduction, an attitude just as silly as denying that the earth goes around the sun.

Matisse in relation to Irish art of his time

The most fascinating parallel between Matisse and an Irish artist lies in the work of Roderic O'Conor. O'Conor's land and seascapes of 1892/93, when he lived at Pont-Aven in Brittany, are extraordinarily similar to the Matisse of 1905 at Collioure in the Midi. For example, *Seascape with Pink Foam* (1892), *Field of Corn, Pont-Aven* (1892), *The Foaming Sea* (1892) and

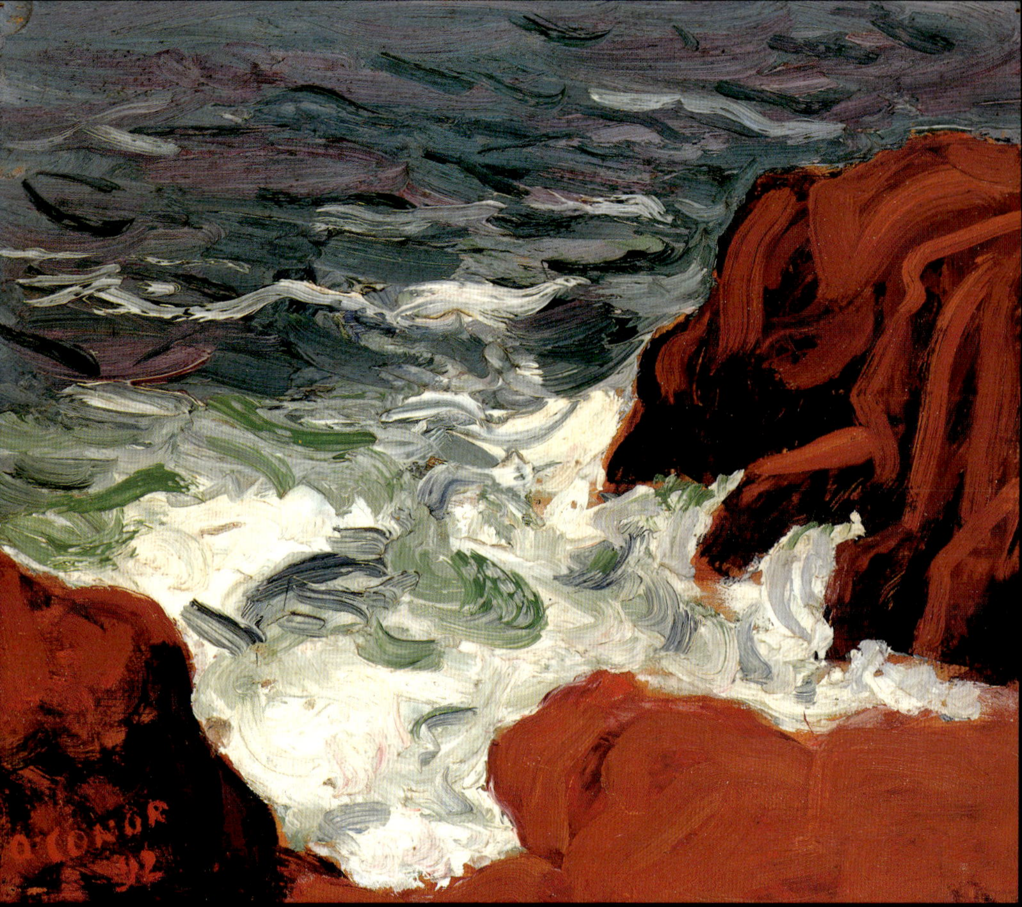

Roderic O'Conor(1860-1940), The Foaming Sea. *Pyms Gallery, London.*

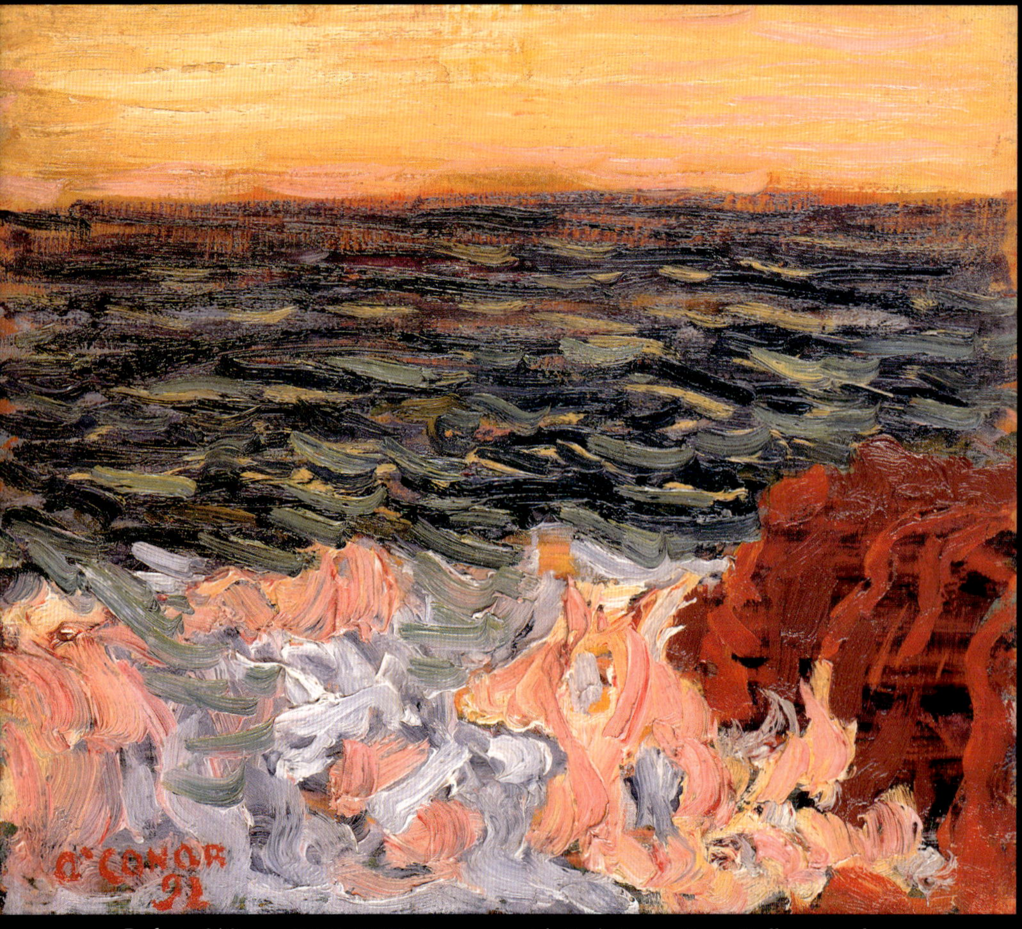

Roderic O'Conor (1860-1940), Seascape with Pink Foam. *Pyms Gallery, London.*

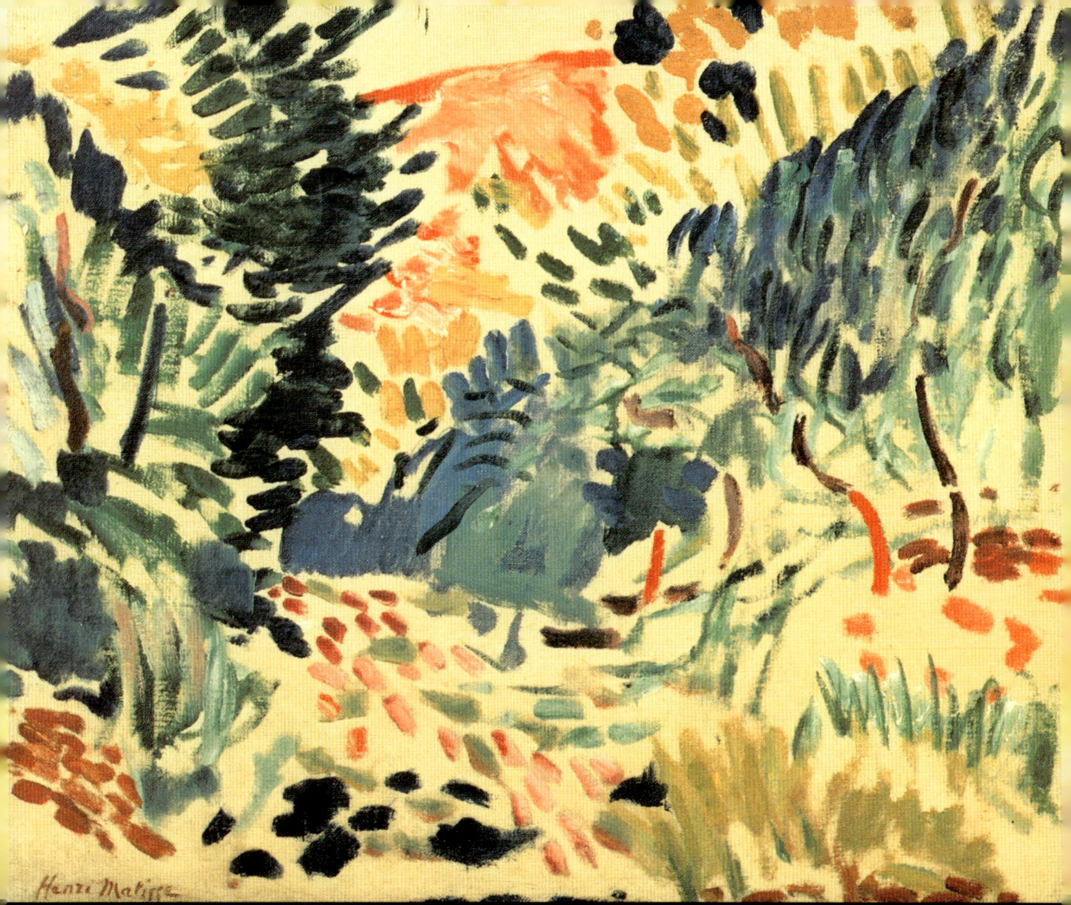

Henri Matisse, Landscape at Collioure,1905. *Oil on canvas, 39 x 46.2 cm.*
The Museum of Modern Art , New York. Fractional gift of Mrs Bertram Smith

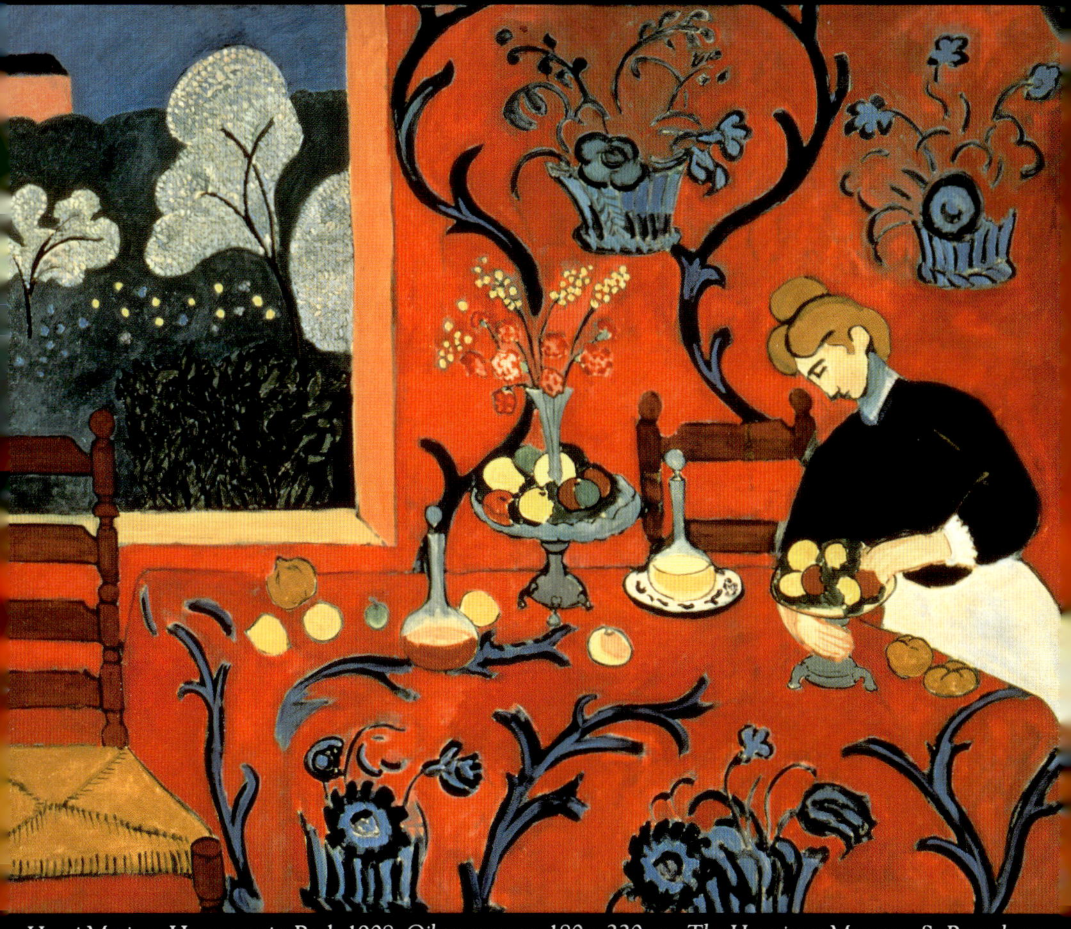

Henri Matisse, Harmony in Red, 1908. *Oil on canvas, 180 x 220 cm. The Hermitage Museum, St Petersburg*

THE LIGHT OF NOON

some later works of 1898 – *Orange Rocks and Sea, Promontory, Brittany* – share a very similar vision, colour sense, scale, and indeed method of painting. Matisse's paintings of Collioure in 1905 are considered to be the first 'Fauve' paintings; Derain was with him in Collioure for the summer and their paintings, along with others by Vlaminck, Manguin, and Marquet, caused a sensation at the Salon d'Automne of the following autumn, causing them to be christened 'les fauves', the wild beasts. O'Conor was so reticent about his work, and he has been so thoroughly neglected for most of this century that his original breaking of the Fauvist ground over a decade before Matisse, has not been acknowledged.

The interesting thing about Matisse's visit to Brittany in 1896 and his subsequent paintings is that, far from being full of light and colour like O'Conor's earlier works, they in fact quite resemble Patrick Collins's grey, misty paintings of Irish landscape, particularly *Large Grey Seascape* (1896), and *Seascape at Goulphar* (1896).

One of the most significant paintings for Matisse's own development was *The Open Window*, painted at Collioure in 1905, not his first window painting but his first opening onto the Mediterranean light which was to flood his work for a greater part of his life. The difference in the Collioure paintings from all of his previous work is truly remarkable, as if an electric light had been switched on in a shuttered room. The colours sing at full pitch with an ecstatic exuberance, and in a work such as *Interior at Collioure – the Siesta* the painting is baked in heat, in hot greens which also continued throughout his life, in cool orange, recalling Louis le Brocquy's experience on his first visit to Spain in 1956 when he discovered that the strong sunlight had the curious effect of making normally cool colours, like blue and green, seem hot, and normally hot colours like red or orange, cool. This is certainly borne out in Matisse with his consistently 'hot' green, that brilliant emerald which reappeared most noticeably in the Moroccan paintings of 1913, the great *Standing Riffian* from St Petersburg, *On the Terrace*, and again the dry, hot blue of *The Casbah Gate*. The light of the Midi opened his eyes, opened his palette to colour; it is the most exciting phase of all his paintings, this opening of the new century with the vision of a great artist.

There also seems to have been an actual change in his eyesight, possibly new spectacles? Quite suddenly, in 1906, a whole range of paintings are in much closer focus, and they also come indoors: *Still Life with a Red Rug; Marguerite; Marguerite Reading*, to name a few.

His painting, from his earliest days as a student, was paralleled with works of sculpture in bronze, many of them portrait heads like that of the model Jeannette, who looks so French that one can almost hear her voice. These heads of Jeannette, III, IV and V, from 1910, were prophetic of Picasso's much later monumental heads of women in 1931.

Both in sculpture and in painting, Matisse is a most interesting portraitist. The delightful portrait of his son Pierre as a young boy (1909) harks back again to the O'Conor striped paintings of 1893, such as the superb *Peasant Woman Knitting* shown

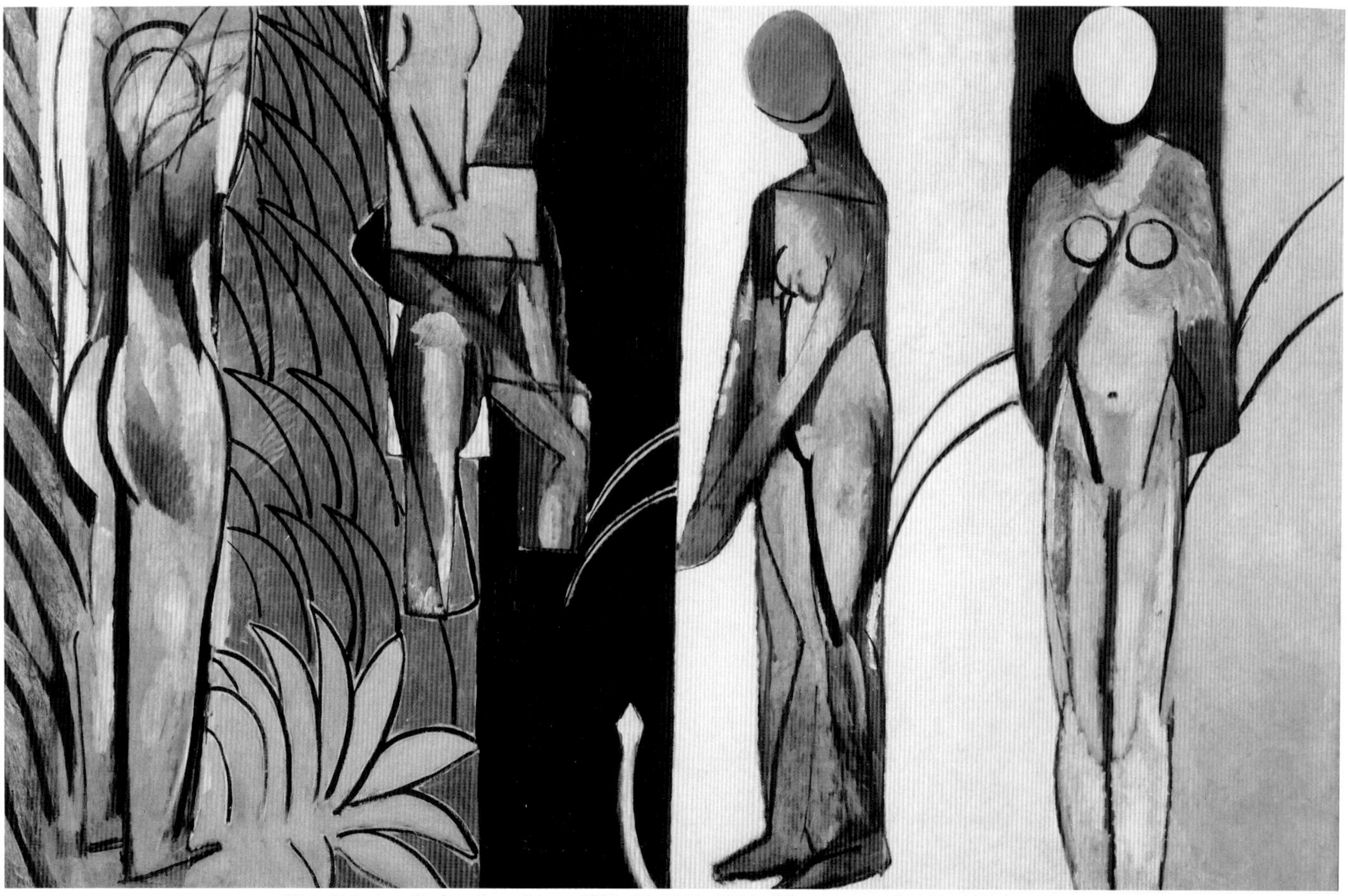

Henri Matisse, Bathers by a River, *1909-10, 1913, 1916. Oil on canvas, 261.8 x 391.4 cm. The Art Institute of Chicago. Charles H and Mary F S Worcester Collection.*

THE LIGHT OF NOON

in the Cork Rosc exhibition of 1971.

But Matisse himself foreshadows German Expressionist painters like Max Beckmann in his simplified schematic portraits such as that of Olga Merson (who closely resembles the art dealer Annely Juda), or Jeanne Valerin, and the *Spanish Woman* and *Algerian Woman* (1909). He then reverts to French charm with *The Girl with Green Eyes* and the wonderful portrait of Greta Moll, which has the same arabesque background that appears in many lovely paintings of this time including *Harmony in Red* (the superb red dining-room), and *Still Life with Blue Tablecloth*. Her smile, so broadly and directly painted, is yet as subtle as any Leonardo.

Even more direct portraits, like that of Auguste Pellerin (1917) and Michael Stein (1916) are reminiscent of the frontal Byzantine steadiness of Edward McGuire, with subtlety again imbued into the broad direct style of painting. It is hard not to be reminded time and again of familiar artists echoed in the work of Matisse, the echo necessarily being in reverse: William Scott in *Gourds* (1916), Norah McGuinness in the general rhythm of her work, and in the subject matter of luxurious vegetation and gardens. The young painter Elizabeth Cope continues this tradition.

Anne Madden has said that all her window paintings stem from the *French Window at Collioure* of 1914 which is directly related to her concerns of an opening into the darkness of the mind. Patrick Ireland has acknowledged his debt to Matisse's *Red Studio* in his *Red Room* rope drawing at Kansas University, used as the venue for the University's memorial service on the death of Jean-Paul Sartre: Matisse's great decorative set-pieces throughout his life obviously had a profound influence on the short-lived 'pattern painting' movement of the late 1970s, including the American-Irish artist Timothy Hennessy, and Matisse's example reinforced the natural instincts of a complex artist like the very interesting printmaker Tim Mara, who has taken almost as

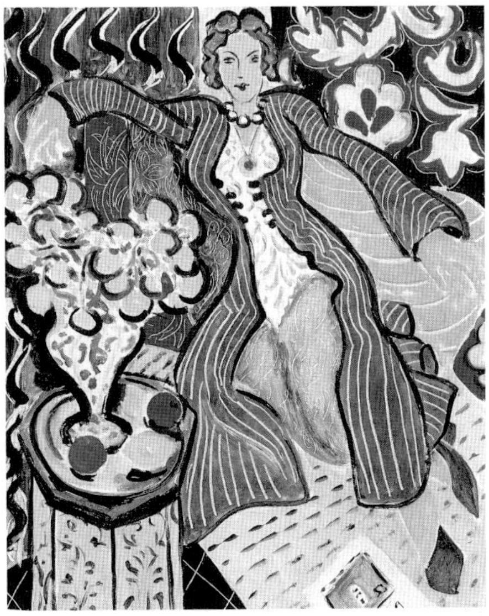

Henri Matisse, Woman in a Purple Robe, *1937. Oil on canvas, 81 x 65 cm. The Museum of Fine Arts, Houston. The John A and Audrey Jones Beck Collection.*

daring leaps as Matisse in putting multiple textures and patterns together in a single image. Paintings like *Woman in a Purple Robe* would be nightmares of conflicting patterns without the authoritative synthesis of Matisse and his philosophical conviction of the richness and diversity of human life.

One of the advantages of a big exhibition is that it is possible to include less successful works, to see where the master's hand in fact slipped, so that one has a much more acute perception of how finely balanced the successful works are, to see how that ease which characterizes all great art is so hard won. In general, Matisse's painting of the Great War period 1914-1918, has a slightly forced air, as if he were trying to gainsay his natural bent for the decorative and the curvilinear to attempt work of a more angular abstraction, like the *View of Notre-Dame* (1914). While this is interesting in the light of later painting by, for example, the American painter Diebenkorn, it is reassuring to see Matisse returning to his own graceful mode in *Sculpture and Vase of Ivy* (1917). I think the most successful of the 'abstract' paintings is *Bathers by a River* which he worked on from 1909 to 1916 (Art Institute of Chicago). The very stylised figures are set against vertical panels of black, white and grey, as austere as anything by Barnett Newman, relieved on the left-hand side of the painting by two panels of his customary leafy vegetation. The scale of this painting is also remarkable for the period, measuring 8ft 7ins by 12ft 10ins, having originally been conceived as the third section of the Shchukin commission for *La Danse* and *La Musique*.

War years, both wars of 1914 and 1939, brought about a change of colour. Matisse, the supreme master of vibrant colour, reverted to black backgrounds, particularly in the Great War of 1914, less consistently so in the 1940s.

No such sombre mood seems to have affected him at the thought of his own approaching death. The work of his final years when he could no longer paint but devised a whole new *oeuvre* by means of painted paper cut-outs, is one of the most sublime achievements of the human spirit in the last years of life, the indomitable courage of a crippled artist who to the very end maintained his *joie-de-vivre*, his *art-de-vivre*, enjoying the images of graceful female nudes swimming on the walls of his dining-room while he worked on the perennial images of Christianity for the Chapel of the Rosary: the Madonna and Child, a model saint, the Way of the Cross, illuminated by his beatific windows. Simultaneously he was illustrating a large wall-panel of *The Thousand and One Nights* which bears the text 'Elle vit apparaître le matin. Elle se tut discrètement.' (She saw the light of day appear. She became discreetly silent.) In 1952, il vit apparaître la mort. Il se tût discrètement.

Dorothy Walker

Dorothy Walker is a leading Irish art critic.

INVESTIGATING THE BOOK OF KELLS

The Commentary Volume published in association with the recent facsimile of the Book of Kells is reviewed by **Roger Stalley**

The Book of Kells has been described on several occasions as the Irish equivalent of the Sistine Chapel ceiling, a comparison that is not quite as bizarre as it might first appear. Both are works of great religious profundity, where the manual execution of the painting seems to verge on the miraculous. As national icons, both are now submerged by the weight of the tourist trade and the banalities that accompany it. Within Ireland, however, the Book of Kells tends to be regarded as a curiosity, rather than the country's outstanding work of art (a point exposed at the wonderfully instructive conference in September 1992 by the complete absence of the so-called 'art' correspondents of the national media). (See Conference Report in this issue).

Illuminated manuscripts by their very nature are exclusive objects, and, with only four folios on view at any one time, it is difficult for the public to grasp the richness of the Book – the constant humour and vitality of the ornament, the freshness of the pigments, the unwavering beauty of the script and the haunting ambiguity of the religious imagery. Gone are the days when distinguished visitors to Trinity College could leaf through the pages for themselves, but the new facsimile produced by Faksimile Verlag Luzern does at least allow more people to grasp the totality of the work. Those who purchase the facsimile (current price $18,000) also receive a substantial commentary volume, designed to provide 'a picture of the current state of scholarship'. Edited by Peter Fox, Librarian of the College, it includes chapters by a number of distinguished scholars, representing an important landmark in the study of the manuscript.

The text opens with an intriguing foreword by Umberto Eco. Given what follows, this seems a little out of place, the publishing equivalent of getting an international soccer star to open a local supermarket. The editor's introduction then provides a survey of previous publications of the manuscript and explains how the present facsimile came about (the initial overtures to Trinity College were made as far back as 1979). Gearoid Mac Niocaill outlines the history of the monasteries at Iona and Kells, and this is followed by the real meat of the book, an analysis of the text by Patrick McGurk. Gospel texts varied considerably during the early middle ages and a great deal can be learnt from the hundreds of minor variations in the choice of

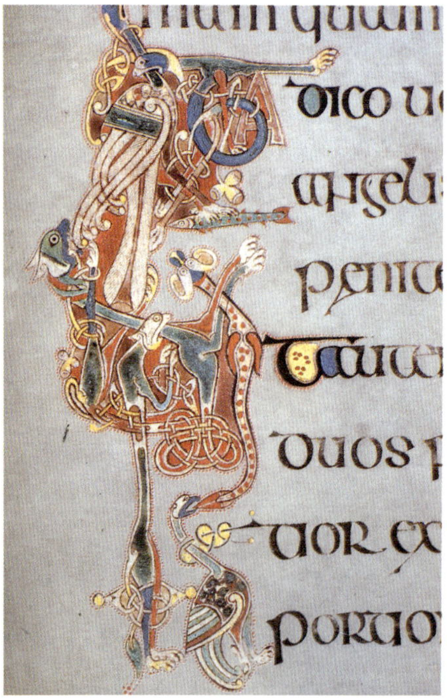

Book of Kells, fol.250v. Fighting birds and animals forming the letters I T A (2nd line.) And below, the letters A I of the word 'ait'. St Luke 15 ,vs 10-11.

words and phrases. The Book of Kells contains a mixed Irish text, combining old Latin readings with those from the Vulgate (the version produced by St Jerome in the later fourth century). McGurk also examines the Canon Tables, the lists of concordances or parallel passages in the different Gospels. The issues are complex but the author explains them with unerring clarity. There is a fascinating account of the numerous spelling mistakes and errors to which the labouring monks succumbed, including the well known repetition of a whole page (folio 218v, repeated on 219r). McGurk concludes that 'to the textual scholar, the quality of the Gospel text of the Book of Kells, does not match its artistic exuberance and virtuosity'. Eighty one pages are then devoted to an appendix listing all those Gospel readings that vary from the Stuttgart edition of the Vulgate. This is highly technical material, useful to have in print, but valuable for only a handful of scholars. Gearoid Mac Niocaill returns with a section on the Irish charters, the latter containing records of land transactions at Kells inserted on blank pages of the book in the twelfth century. These were not the only additions to the manuscript, which has quite a range of odd scribbles and signatures. In the sixteenth century a certain Gerald Plunket of Dublin annotated it copiously with English translations, inserting his own signature and initials whenever he felt like it (there is incidentally no truth in the story that Queen Victoria and Prince Albert signed the medieval vellum: they added their names to a flyleaf, which has since been removed).

Bernard Meehan, Keeper of Manuscripts at Trinity College, and Tony Cains, Head of the Conservation Laboratory in the Library, provide a comprehensive physical description of the manuscript, a section of the book that makes fascinating reading for art historians. It includes an analysis of the vellum, the way it was processed, and an estimate of the number of calves required (approximately 185). Tony Cains argues that the tiny holes in some of the folios, traditionally thought to have been caused by warble flies burrowing into the calves, were in fact caused by over rapid putrescence during the preparation of the skins. The manuscript has been rebound at least five times, the most horrendous being in 1821 when the Dublin binder, George Mullen, decided to soak some of the pages to get them flat and then compounded his crime by cropping up to half an inch off the folios, removing some of the illumination in the process. After this the College was understandably nervous whenever the question of rebinding arose. Not many people will be aware of the tense negotiations that took place in 1952-3, before the last rebinding by Roger Powell, when, for conservation reasons, the manuscript was bound into four separate volumes.

The colours employed by the scribes of Kells are far more diverse than those found in equivalent books of the time and the identification of the pigments remains an important issue. For self-evident reasons, only non-destructive methods of analysis are possible, leaving identification open to doubt in some instances. Tony Cains discusses the problems against the background of comments made by Werner and Roosen Runge in the companion vol-

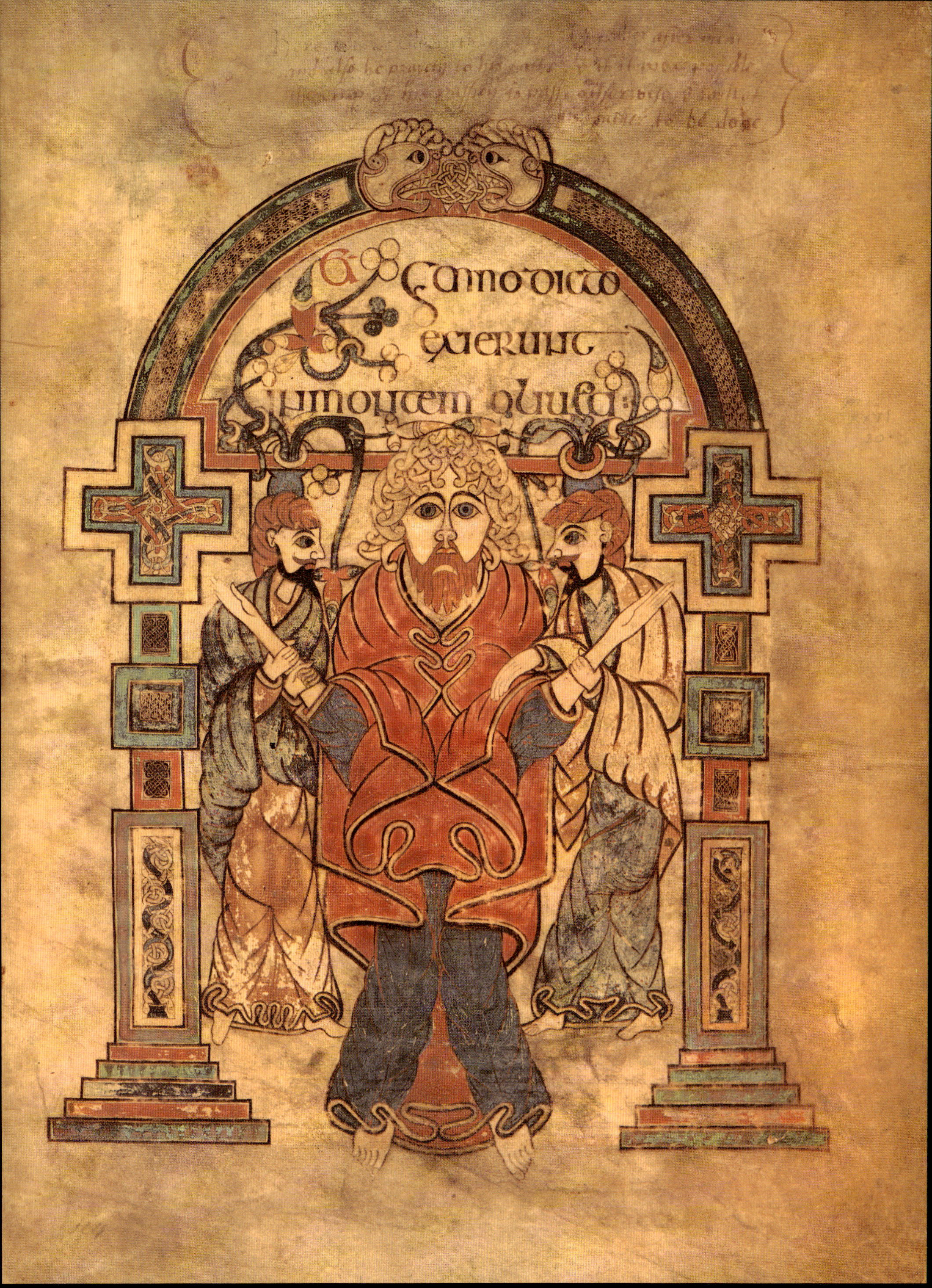

Book of Kells, fol. 114r. The so-called 'Arrest' of Christ.

INVESTIGATING THE BOOK OF KELLS

ume to the Lindisfarne facsimile. He points out that some of the colour changes previously ascribed to a lack of skill by the artists are in fact the result of chemical changes over a long period of time. The main pigments used are clear enough – orpiment, vermilion, verdigris, ultramarine, indigo and folium, the latter producing the many shades of mauve and purple. More problematical is the script, or rather the number of scribes involved in producing it. Some years ago the late Julian Brown argued that the text was the work of a single great master, but Bernard Meehan confirms Francoise Henry's impression that several scribes collaborated on the work. The evidence is unquestionable, although one needs the facsimile to follow the arguments. Francoise Henry believed there were three main scribes, but Dr Meehan convincingly demonstrates that Henry's hand 'C' contains so many variations and inconsistencies that at least one extra scribe must have been involved. Dr Meehan discusses many other aspects of the palaeography and layout of the pages, and he has much of interest to say about the relationship between script and decoration. This leads to an important chapter on the illumination itself by Jonathan Alexander of the Institute of Fine Arts in New York.

Professor Alexander is a world authority on medieval illuminated books and he gives a lucid summary of the existing literature, explaining the art-historical issues encountered in the more elaborate pages. He discusses the type of models the artists may have had in front of them and considers the extent to which the animal ornament may have conveyed religious meaning. Comparing the situation to that found in later Romanesque art, he concludes judiciously that 'even if they sometimes had either a more general or occasionally a more specific significance, it is impossible to believe this was always the case'. Elsewhere he shows how the imagery provides a mysterious, miraculous background for the Gospel text, inducing a sense of awe and encouraging meditation. With some reticence, Professor Alexander also gives us his views on the date and provenance of the manuscript.

Finally, there is a fascinating chapter by Bernard Meehan on the history of the manuscript, explaining the circumstances of its arrival in Trinity College and how it has been looked after since. It was not until the middle years of the nineteenth century that the general public were allowed into the library to see it and many a visitor has been turned away, sometimes for the good of the manuscript. In 1919 the then Librarian was approached at Front Gate by an irate priest, armed with tracing paper, who tried (unsuccessfully) to insist on his right to trace the folios! In 1853, when 'strangers' were first admitted to the library, 18,675 people signed the register. In 1992, close to 300,000 visitors paid to see the Book.

Although the Commentary tackles a wide range of issues, it forms a rather unbalanced volume. Only 65 of the 382 pages deal directly with the painted decoration and many of the art-historical issues deserve more thorough treatment. The editorial committee may have felt constrained by Francoise Henry's well-rounded study of 1974,[2] deciding not to cover the same ground. The basic repertoire of ornament, such as animal interlace, contorted human figures, the so-called Celtic or ultimate '*La Tene*' motifs is barely mentioned, let alone analysed at length. The Celtic elements in the Book, the fantastic spirals within the *Chi Rho* initial for example, are based on centuries of experience, being handled with unprecedented fluency and ingenuity. The animal and bird interlace also has a fascinating pedigree, which urgently needs reassessment in the light of recent studies in metalwork. Even more neglected is the background of the Kells figure style, which everyone knows so well from countless reproductions and postcards. The distinctive human profile – with a powerful chin, large nose, 'frontal' eye, and hair ending in a curl at the nape of the neck – is found in both Irish and Pictish stone carving, but its ultimate origin remains a mystery. Many years ago OK Werckmeister argued that it was derived from Visigothic art in Spain,[3] but recently scholars have pointed to remarkable parallels in Celtic metalwork on the Continent. Most of these figures are found in the hundreds of ornate initials that enliven the book, initials that deserve to be studied as a subject in their own right. Also neglected are the geometrical processes used to lay out the more elaborate pages. This type of work has been done for the Lindisfarne Gospels and other Insular manuscripts; it is long overdue for the Book of Kells. A more curious omission is the neglect of the physical layout of Iona, where the book was almost certainly made. While the Commentary volume obviously could not cover everything, it would have been useful to have a modern account of the island monastery, particularly in the light of recent archaeological investigations.

A number of inconsistencies between the chapters gives the impression that the authors did not read one another's contributions before publication. Professor Alexander, for example, takes it for granted that 'there never were, nor were there intended to be, portraits of St Mark and St Luke', a puzzling comment, given Dr Meehan's contrary assumption that such portraits did once exist. As many of the more ornate pages in the manuscript were painted on single leaves, it is not unreasonable to suppose that some have been detached and lost in the course of time. Professor Alexander's conclusions about the provenance of the book also seem unnecessarily tentative in the light of recent historical opinion: '... the evidence is confused, and there is still no consensus after over a hundred years of scholarly study as to date or place of production'. This is misleading, because there *is* a growing consensus among scholars that the book was prepared, not at Kells, but on the island of Iona, almost certainly before 802/6, and that it was made to honour the memory of Saint Colum Cille (or Columba). The principal argument regarding provenance rests on the type of historical evidence provided by Gearoid Mac Niocaill. There are no indications that the monastery at Kells (founded in 807 from Iona) had the wealth, resources or expertise necessary to embark on such an ambitious undertaking for at least half a century after its foundation. In contrast, Iona at this time was over two hundred years old, with a wealth of tradition and accumulated resources. The community is known to have included 'eminent scribes' and, until it was savagely attacked by the Vikings in 802 and 806, maintained an active scriptorium. Moreover it is important to remember that from an early date the Book of Kells was known as 'the great gospel book of Colum Cille'; it was Colum Cille who had founded the monastery at Iona back in the sixth century.

An equally fundamental question is the relationship between script and decoration. In some places the scribe left a space for initials to be filled in later, but there are dozens of cases where text and ornament are so intimately linked that they must have been carried out by the same person. Dr Meehan cites one case where a

INVESTIGATING THE BOOK OF KELLS

serif was ingeniously extended to form the tonsure of a monk, and another where a word is broken in two to allow the paw of a cat to descend from an initial above. There are even cases where the script intrudes on the pigment, showing that the painting was not invariably carried out later. Some years ago Carl Nordenfalk concluded that in many instances the initials 'were completed before the following text had been written, so that we may imagine the calligrapher switching back and forth as he worked, from pen and ink to brush and colour'. Alexander rightly has doubts about this, observing that it is unlikely that paints were mixed for tiny areas at a time. But the initials were first outlined in ink (some remain unfinished), and it seems probable that the drawing, if not the painting, was done as the text was being written. In his discussion of the illumination, Alexander still seems to speak in terms of collaboration between scribes and illuminators, as if they had separate responsibilities. While such divisions of labour became common in later periods, it seems an artificial (and anachronistic) distinction to make in the era of the Book of Kells. Much of the ornament has a consistency of method, which compares closely with the work of the calligrapher. Animal heads and human faces, for example, follow similar formulae throughout the book, as if the artists were using a familiar alphabet. In the eighth century the differences been writing and drawing were not as great as they might seem today.

The issue of scribe and artist is one of several that seem to fall between the contributions of the different authors. Another is the purpose of the manuscript.

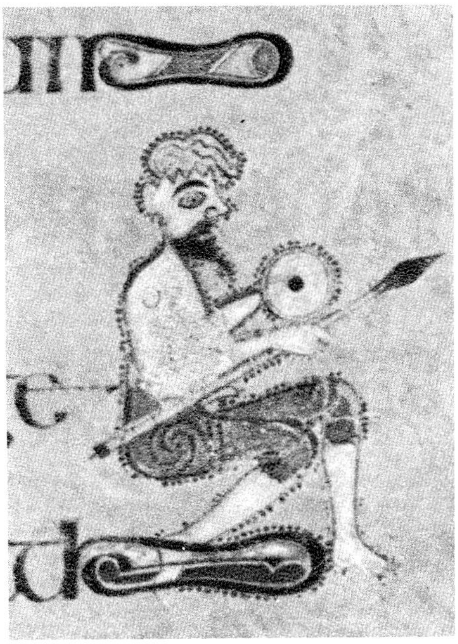

Book of Kells, fol.200r. Warrior with a typical 'Kells' profile, decorating St Luke's version of the genealogy of Christ.

Although the Book of Kells must rate as one of the most extravagant and sumptuous gospel books ever made, its function is, surprisingly, mentioned only by Patrick McGurk in his throw away comment that 'the book was not made to be read or studied' but was designed 'presumably for a particular sacred purpose'. We shall probably never know the exact circumstances which lead to the making of the book, but, as several scholars have suggested, it may be associated with the enshrining of Colum Cille's relics during the second half of the eighth century. The number of uncorrected errors in the gospel text shows that it was not suitable for the Gospel reading during mass and its true purpose should perhaps be seen in symbolic rather than utilitarian terms. Exotic decoration was a way of adding mystery and authority to the divine word, a means too of enhancing the status of the monastery and honouring its founding saint.

Despite its limited scope, the Commentary volume is packed with important information and observations, raising all sorts of interesting issues. It is not, however, the last word on the Book of Kells. Many questions were taken further in the 1992 conference, the proceedings of which will serve as a crucial adjunct. In the meantime it will be a tragedy, not least for the authors, if the Commentary volume is not given wider circulation. At the time of writing it can only be purchased in conjunction with the facsimile. It is clear that few people have seen it, let alone read it.

Roger Stalley

Roger Stalley is Professor of History of Art in Trinity College Dublin.

NOTES

1. *Evangeliorum quattuor codex Lindisfarnensis* edited by T.D. Kendrick and others, 2 vols (Olten, Lausanne, 1956-60)
2. *The Book of Kells: reproductions from the manuscript in Trinity College Dublin. With a study of the manuscript by Francoise Henry* (London, 1974).
3. O.K.Werckmeister, 'Three problems of tradition in pre-Carolingian figure style: from Visigothic to insular illumination', *Proceedings of the Royal Irish Academy*. 63C (1963), pp 167-89.

THE BOOK OF KELLS CONFERENCE

Susanne McNab reviews the Book of Kells Conference, held in Trinity College Dublin, September 1992.

The Book of Kells is full of secrets that, in spite of the renewed efforts of learned enquiry, it continues to refuse to yield. Where was it written? When? By how many scribes? Why was it written? What is the meaning of its decoration? These are some of the deceptively simple-sounding questions that even to this day no-one has been able to answer conclusively although many ingenious attempts are made. The incomparable beauty of the manuscript, its complex, stunning decoration, make the enigma of its creation all the more fascinating. The recent conference, held in Trinity College Dublin from the 6th to the 9th of September was centred and closely focussed on a 'state of the art' examination of current theories concerning the Book of Kells. It attracted a gathering of international scholars of the greatest eminence in the field of early Christian Irish art. Three public lectures were given but it was largely organised so that a large number of short papers provided the opportunity to hear the widest possible range of specialist responses from archaeological, historical, paleographical, liturgical, iconographic and technical points of view. There is no need to apologise for not being able to mention more than a few of the individual contributions because the Proceedings of the conference, edited by Felicity O'Mahony, are due to be published by the Scolar Press. The quality and diversity of the conference papers ensure that this will be an important reference resource for all who have an interest in the subject.

The intractability of the puzzle as to when and where the book was made did not deter a large number of the contributors from courting the options. Sometimes this remained the sub-text of a discussion on stylistic links between illumination and other media such as stone-carving or metalwork. It will be interesting to see how innuendo becomes fixed into the unyielding medium of language in the published papers. A bizarre and amusing symptom of this compulsion to confront the unsayable, perhaps even the unknowable, was provided by Dr Peter Harbison in his closing address. He pounced on his battle-weary audience to demand a show of hands in favour of firstly, either an Iona or a Kells provenance and secondly, an eighth or ninth century date for the manufacture of the book. It is hard to convey the unease disguised in hilarity that this sudden public exposure induced in the audience. But a serious conference is never marred by its lighter moments and there were several of these over the days of careful reflection and intense exchange of conflicting views.

Some areas of enquiry which are now being recognised anew to be of profound importance were re-examined and were well represented at the conference. Examination of the social, political and ecclesiastical background to Ireland in the Early Christian period helps to indicate a more clearly delineated cultural context for the book. In this regard Professor Donnchadh O'Corrain gave a compelling inaugural public lecture telling of a very complex cultural structure which benefited from the powerful resources of bishops and abbots. Renewed contact with Rome and interaction with Visigothic Spain gave rise to a 'celebration of the technology of literature.' Understanding and relating aspects

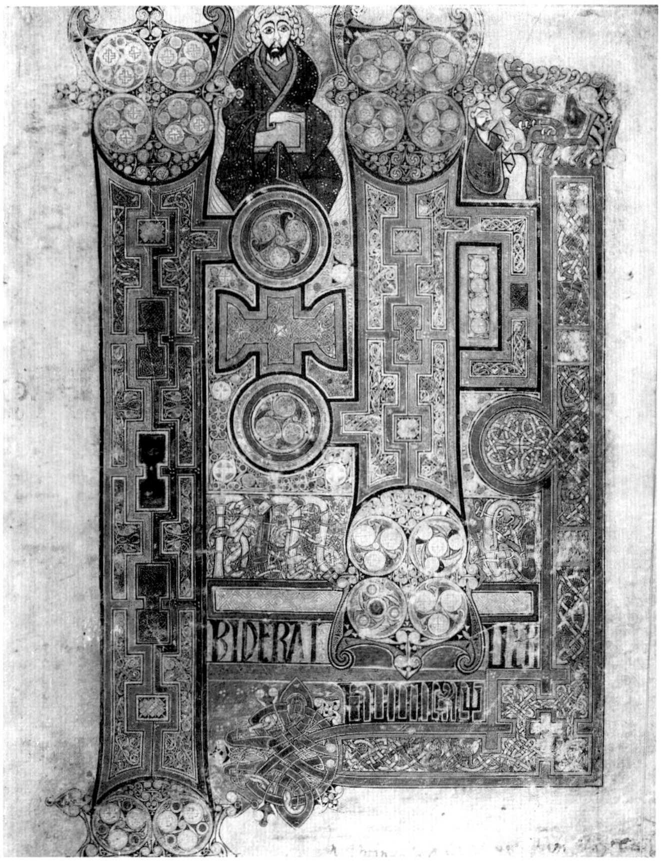

Book of Kells, fol.292r. Opening words of John's Gospel

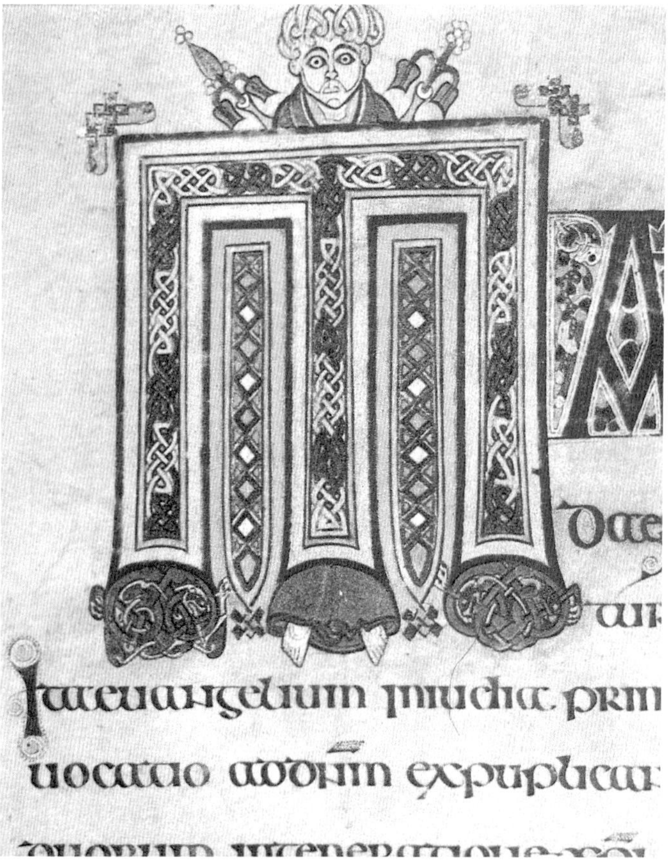

Book of Kells, fol.12r. The beginning of the 'argumentum' of Matthew's Gospel.

THE BOOK OF KELLS CONFERENCE

of coeval liturgical practices to the precise ceremonial function of the Gospel books, and the significance of both figurative and abstract decoration opens the way for a new understanding of iconography and regional influences.

This is an area which Professor Eamon O Carragain has explored in relation to the high crosses of Ruthwell and Bewcastle and, more recently, Muiredach's Cross in Monasterboice. It was intriguing to hear him apply similar methods to investigating the possible role a lavish manuscript, such as the Book of Kells, might have played in the ceremonies associated with the Easter Vigil in the early Irish church.

A number of papers paralleled this kind of discussion. Professor Martin Werner continued to build on his previous research in which the minutiae of ornament is linked with liturgical practices, and ingenious relationships were proposed between closely-observed detail and a textual diagram of the Holy City in Adamnan's *De Locis Sanctis*. These types of argument are, of necessity, severely abbreviated for delivery at conferences and their fine tuning can only be fully appreciated in written form.

Perhaps the conference was a little out of balance with several relentlessly-detailed iconographical explorations often centred on the same illuminated page.

Several speakers discussed the scientific examination of the physical properties of the manuscript: the materials which are used in the book and the process of its making. Microscopic analysis of technical methods do not prove to be ends in themselves but offer the future potential of resolving the problems of date and provenance. This is provided that there is mobility of ideas between experts in different fields; so that, for instance, experts in certain specialist areas, such as pigment analysis, are sufficiently aware of the discourse which surrounds the object of their investigations, that they know what questions need to be asked of it.

Some of the most vivid conjuring of the monastic ambience out of which the book may have been produced was dealt with in archaeological accounts of the monastic sites of Iona and Kells, but entirely without *hocus pocus*. Ian Fisher's delineation of the expansion of the monastery of Iona in the eighth century, indicated in overlapping lines of earthworks, convincingly recreated that far distant time. Excavated debris of holly and hawthorn gave rise to the suggestion that holly may have been cultivated for its green dye which could be used by the scribes in their manuscripts and, more unexpectedly, that perhaps hawthorn hedges served as protective barriers between the monks and dangerous ground as they went about their business in the black, island night-time. Leather shoes were found with tongues rising up to the heel, as illustrated worn by St Matthew in the Book of Durrow. Leo Swan's discussion of the monastery at Kells, assisted by aerial photographs, gave a similarly worldly archaeological account of the development of the site, stressing a level of continuity in its form which has been maintained to the present day; unlike Iona, he remarked, which 'died in the ninth century.' Both papers demonstrated the value of a methodology which reclaims the past in real sense and this does not devalue but rather enhances its mystery.

Stylistic and iconographical links which may or may not transcend different media and which may hold implications for assessing the effects of patronage or the regional production of artworks were raised in several papers. Michelle Brown, who is always interesting in what she has to say and in the way that she says it, drew attention to some exuberant qualities of the lacertine display script in the southern English Tiberius group of insular manuscripts and hinted that these may be echoed in the Book of Kells. Professor Roger Stalley compared aspects of the iconography of the sculpted high crosses at Kells with that found in manuscript illumination. His pragmatic view that the two media may reflect the very different functions of the crosses and manuscripts, public and private respectively, and that the iconography is therefore drawn from different sources, opens the way for more consideration in the future. Dr Michael Ryan's discussion of the Book of Kells in relation to contemporary metalwork suggested that there is little direct stylistic comparative evidence to show that the makers of the book worked alongside metalworkers. This cautions against any assumption that the Book of Kells was necessarily produced within a metalworking milieu.

The conference was run at a cracking pace with faultless efficiency. The only off-key note was felt by participants who were not staying on campus as they were refused permission to park their cars in Trinity. This was more than a little inconvenient for obvious reasons and as this was prior to the beginning of term it was considered rather severe, if not discourteous. There were many humorous moments, delivered with great panache, such as Professor Etienne Rynne's speculations on the significance of the drolleries. In the end the same questions remained about the Book of Kells with the same divergence of views. This was clear during the final session of questions and comments when views were expressed about whether the book was ever intended to be actually read, was intimately concerned with expressing the theological controversies of the time, or whether it was practically functionless, unusable – the ultimate coffee table book, the expression of a megalomaniac desire to be the best in the world. Professor Jonathan Alexander, whose definitive published work on insular manuscripts established a clear working basis for much of the subsequent explorations into this labyrinthine subject, took an unexpected turn into areas more usually associated with contemporary issues; perhaps this was because he of all people can see when solid research becomes stretched into inventive speculation. He touched on current questioning of truth, meaning and the semiotics of visual language. He suggested that we should reconsider the psychoanalytical aspects of the fantastic imagery in the Book of Kells and its potential for carrying emotional charges such as terror or ecstasy. This should be related to the slippage engendered in communication between instigator and receiver across any given time. However, spending four days within range of the object of all this attention showed us all that the instability inherent in this awareness can only be wryly offset against the experience of coming into contact with the Book of Kells itself. The sight in the Long Room of Trinity College Dublin of queues of late twentieth-century individuals, some of whom may be wearing ankle boots with tongues rising up the heel, daily waiting to set eyes on the open pages of the real, the actual book, is in itself fascinating and oddly reassuring.

Susanne McNab

Susanne McNab is a graduate of Trinity College Dublin where she also completed her Ph D on Twelfth Century Irish Figure Sculpture. She is a lecturer in History of Art at the National College of Art and Design where she specialises in medieval and twentieth century Irish art.

THE REDEMPTION OF MEANING

The Chapel of Reconciliation at Knock, designed by de Blacam and Meagher, represented Ireland at the Venice Biennale (Dec 1992-Jan 1993). **John Olley** appraises this refreshingly modern building, with its traditional symbolism.

In the 1980s, meaning in architecture was a topic for earnest discussion. Practice responded with conscious attempts to reintroduce the claimed missing dimension. Fuelled by the rhetoric of a theory dependent upon semiotics, building aligned itself with what Peter Fuller called the 'mega-visual tradition' borrowing images from mass media and advertising. Alternatively the shapes of the past could be pillaged and pastiched in the hope that the result would be meaningful. But, in all this, one is left with an uneasy feeling that architecture has either fallen prey to a formalism which made it no more than a branch of graphic art, or succumbed to a new addiction to witty and far-fetched imagery, reducing language to fetishism. The 'nineties are set to follow suit. This contrasts with the belief of Gottfried Semper and his twentieth-century echoes, that culture and its meanings are subject to a process of evolution rather than invention. Are the images and forms of post-modernism, then, no more than a reflection of paranoia generated by society's fear of meaninglessness?

However, there remains an institution and building type, the church, where representation and meaning ought not to be a problem. Even if the layman can no longer decipher the complexity of symbolism and allusion locked up within the plan, form and details of a Gothic cathedral and its gloss of figurative art in stone or glass, much remains intelligible for ecclesiastical use. Over centuries religious signs and symbols have been constantly renewed and refreshed, like language itself. Continuity and change have been ensured by the exercise of exegesis and the urge to make the scriptures comprehensible and contemporary, a process recorded in the physical fact of sacred buildings and their landscapes.

The remarkable work of Le Corbusier at Ronchamps and La Tourette, and the haunting designs of Asplund and Lewerentz, attempted to revitalise the Christian mysteries through building. They shrouded traditional symbols in an architectural experience which matched the intellectual with the sensuous. Alas, the norm in the twentieth century has been a resort to spatial and sculptural conceits, often with soaring and swooping shapes shouting for attention on the rural or urban horizon. With these forms, the resulting vessels seem unable to sustain or accommodate a sense of wonder in the celestial and terrestrial intelligence or to accrue layers of meaning.

The same vacuity was promised by the majority of entries for the 1988 architectural competition for the design of a Chapel of Reconciliation for the shrine at Knock in the West of Ireland. Some rehearsed a post-modern litany of borrowed and processed shapes and images, while others created formal confections of great complexity confusing the scale of the intended building. The only mitigating circumstance was the unprecedented requirement of the brief for the provision of sixty confessionals and associated waiting space for three hundred in addition to the chapel for five hundred. The winning submission, designed and now completed by the Dublin practice of de Blacam and Meagher, was distinguished for its elegant simplicity of form and plan which rendered both brief and site manageable and inevitable.

Knock is located in the unpromising topography and climate of east Co Mayo. Almost as if ordained to compensate for this aberration in divine creation, it was there in 1879 that an apparition was seen on the south gable of the parish church. This has assured an importance for the location beyond expectations of geography or political moment. A million and a quarter pilgrims are received each year, a count equal to a third of Ireland's population. In response Knock has been developed to exploit the devout, both spiritually and economically. Expansion reached its zenith in the 1980s with the construction of an airport, the ambition of the late

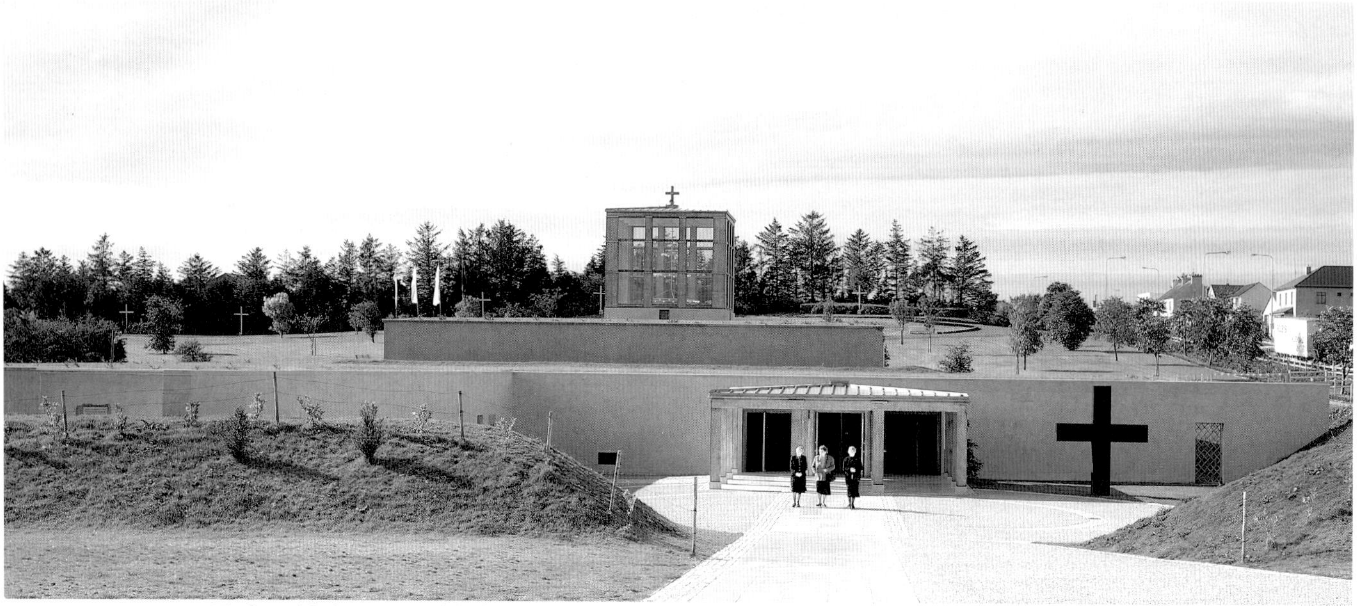

The line of the limestone path leads down to the portico of the chapel of reconciliation beneath a turf covered roof, and behind its lantern rises the re-creation of Calvary.

THE REDEMPTION OF MEANING

Monsignor Horan.

The spirit of the place has been distressed. Hard against the sacred site, the main street of the village has been stretched by commercial pressure, as cafés, fast food and souvenir shops jostle for position. From without sanctity and dignity are assailed, but within chaos looms from the menagerie of ecclesiastical buildings scattered in the holy precinct. The real challenge of the competition was to establish a physical rationale in the religious enclosure and to restore a spiritual tranquillity. The allotted position for the new chapel occupies a gentle fold in the land between the shrine and a recreation of Calvary, which rises to the south. The completed building creates a landscape, linking shrine to Calvary and introduces an ordering intelligence to the overall complex.

A sequence of simple geometric figures lead us from the site of the apparition to the view of Calvary. The line is interrupted but not obscured by the cube of the beacon-like lantern set on the sunken, squat, turf-covered stepped mound that is the chapel. A surrounding earth bailey opens to greet the descent from the shrine, and forms a court edged by planar ashlar walls as if quarried from the building itself. Over the line of the limestone pavement which led the way downhill is inscribed two circles of sets, marking out the gravelled court and gathering the enclosure towards the hypostyle portico, a narthex for the chapel. To the right, contrasted against the cream limestone wall is the black bulk of the carbonised oak cross executed by the sculptor Michael Warren. Inside another figure appears - from within a cage of columns the square sanctuary glows with soft, reflected light. The hovering lantern washes the robust reredos, a triptych of bleached oak with central inlaid gold cross whose arms stretch out to embrace wings on which the word is written in white calligraphic script. Confronting the altar is the primitive cross form of the stout steel 'T' which lifts the turf covered roof. The surrounding oak colonnade supports a steel channel whose strengthening shear webs combine with the detail of the metal caps to mark each column-head with the sign of the Cross. The surrounding quadrate ambulatory is itself enclosed by bays attendant on the confessionals. In each space for reconciliation, whether cubicle or tiny room, a low window frames a small verdant square of the berm with its projected parapet of hawthorn. After confession, the warm flood of light returns attention towards the altar, and on leaving the chapel, the view through the narthex and the geometry of the courtyard leads the eye up the slope towards the site of the original theophany.

On addressing issues of detail and structure, the competition design matured and improved. The original submission had a certain resonance with the work of Asplund, but the development leaned heavily upon Lewerentz. The lantern and its position on the body of the church points to an adaptation of the 1931 chapel at Enköping. Inside, the seating in the chapel nods to the informal layout in the Saint Peter's, Klippan, as its rigid concentric semicircles with radial aisles eased to a scatter of variable arcs. Also from Klippan comes the central structural element, the stout column and short cross-beam - a logical structure loaded with symbolic weight. The primitive force of the original is subdued as it loses its central position and fades from its dramatic exposure to light. The rawness of the cross of Saint Peter's has been tamed and presented out of context, thereby relieving it of most of its emotional charge as it rises to support, not a billowing vault of brick jack-arches, but the blandness of flat concrete slabs. At Knock, Lewerentz is made polite, as he provides a digest of forms rather than an inspiration digested.

Beyond the enclosing square of columns, the spatial clarity fades as the idea of an ambulatory is lost through lack of definition and articulation, neither the manipulation of light, colour, shape, nor material is brought to bear on this broad stretch of space. In attendance outside each confessional cubicle, delicately designed and detailed furniture is no match for this wide unfocused space. The result, a confusing filigree of carpentry which rattles untidily in this expanse. Although beautiful in itself, the furniture cannot control the fearsome numbers to be organised and subdued before the confessional. With the architects' attention to detail well demon-

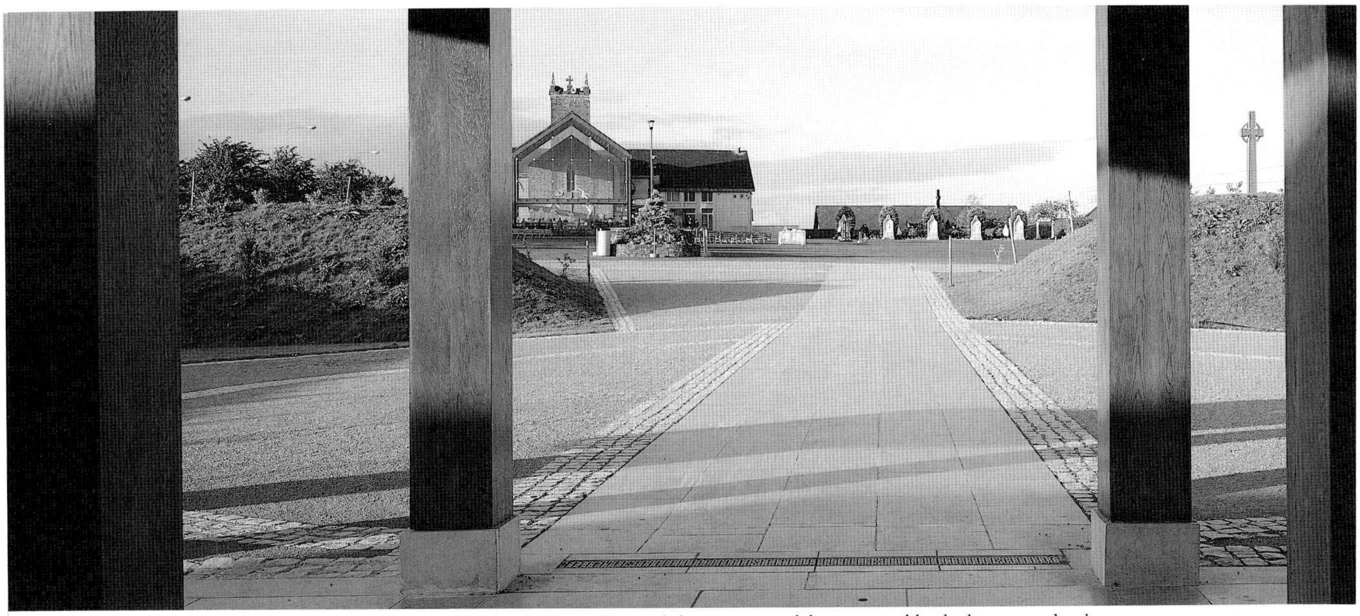

On leaving the chapel, the view through the narthex and the geometry of the courtyard leads the eye up the slope to the gable of the parish church, the site of the 1879 apparition.

THE REDEMPTION OF MEANING

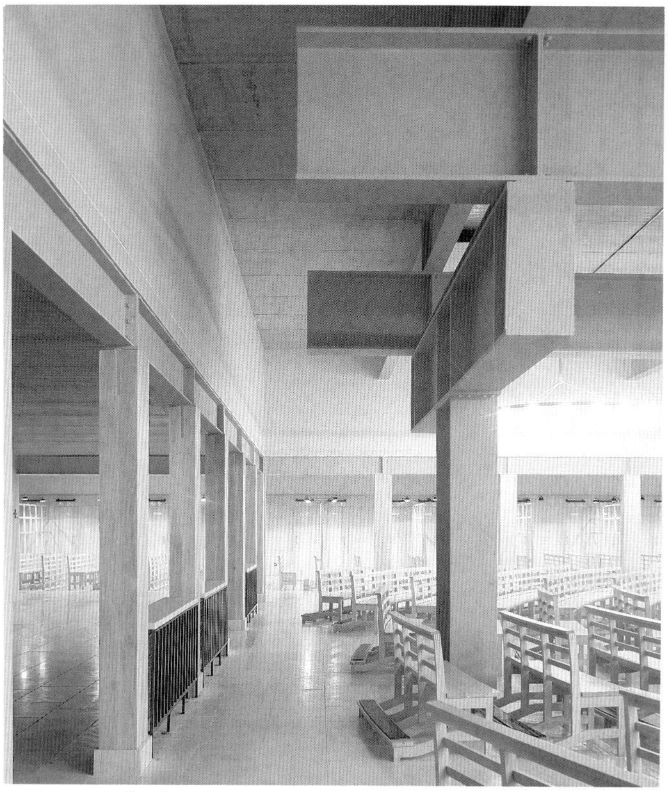

Opposite the altar the stout steel column and short cross beam form the sign of the primitive Cross to become both structure and symbol. Behind is the cage of columns which defines the edge of the square nave and marks off the confessional cells and their attendant waiting spaces.

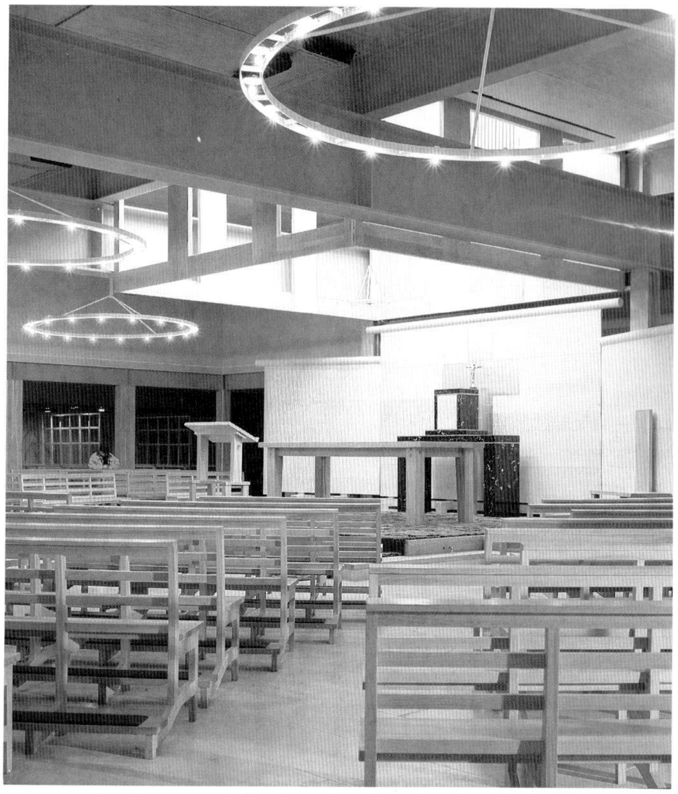

Looking towards the altar where the soft reflected light from the lantern illuminates the Irish and English prayers written on the oak reredos in white calligraphic script.

strated elsewhere, the ambulatory and its relationship to the nave should have sung.

Colin St John Wilson writes of the structural 'T' in Lewerentz' church of Saint Peter's:... 'at one stroke this technical device of column and cross-beam thrusts into the centre of the church a form that irresistibly recalls the central symbol of both the New and the Old Testament'.[1] Here the fusing of symbols of the Tree of Life and the Cross invokes an established tradition. In the church of San Clemente in Rome, the apsidal mosaic reveals against its glowing background of gold tesseræ the symbiosis of Tree and Cross. From its base flow the four rivers of Eden and beneath this, in a lower register, the Lamb of God, all combine to make the whole a concordance between Paradise and the Celestial City. Also, the monastic cloister garden with its quadrate form and fountain or central tree, shares some of this metaphoric reading. Around this medieval representation of Paradise an ambulatory is provided for devotion and contemplation. To confirm this imagery, the bible describes Heavenly Jerusalem: 'The city lieth four square... and I saw no temple therein: for the Lord God Almighty and the Lamb are the temple of it. ... the glory of God did lighten it, and the Lamb is the light thereof... In the midst of the street of it, and on either side of the river, was the tree of life'.[2] In the chapel at Knock, an ambulatory surrounds the square of the nave which glows with the light of the lantern as it washes the words written on the reredos, and standing in its midst is the support for the building, the primitive form of the 'T', both Cross and Tree of Life. Unlike the decorative mosaic in San Clemente, this representation *is* the building, its very structure, plan and function.

The act of reconciliation is seen as a spiritual rebirth, a symbolic entry into the Celestial City. It is a counterpart to the central event of the Christian dogma, the crucifixion and resurrection which itself is no more that an apotheosis of an archaic rite, a celebration of renewal, of death and rebirth. The great Neolithic cairns of the Irish landscape, Newgrange, Knowth and others were the sites of burial but also served some of the functions of a temple. At Newgrange, a passage leads beneath the mound to a central vaulted space, the womb of Mother Earth to which the dead are returned, and where the annual rebirth of nature is celebrated as rays of the winter solstice sunrise penetrate the chamber.

The geometric tumulus and gathering forecourt of the Chapel at Knock resonates typologically, symbolically and functionally with the court cairns of the Irish landscape. With its double crown of hawthorn, and its relationship to the replica of the Hill of Calvary, it is the Holy Sepulchre. On entry this re-creation of the terrestrial Jerusalem becomes Celestial. The Chapel at Knock, through its very form and construction, whether intended or not, is charged with symbolic potential. Is this the path to redemption for meaning in architecture?

John Olley

Dr John Olley is Lecturer in the School of Architecture, University College, Dublin.

NOTES

1. Colin St John Wilson, 'Sigmund Lewerentz and the Dilemma of the Classical', *Perspecta*, 24, 198, p.67.
2. *Revelations*, XXI, 16, 23, & XXII, 2.

THE IRISH PAVILION AT EXPO '92.

The Irish Pavilion at the World's Fair EXPO 1992 in Seville attracted much admiration. **Kate Robinson** describes how Ireland's achievements were presented to the international visitors.

The overnight train to Seville is not the most comfortable though it was the only available way to travel. The journey ended in a huge, modern railway terminal, very different from the old days. The great city, even in October, is still blanched by heat of thirty degrees centigrade, under a white fireball. Since this is by no means to everyone's taste, making it tolerable for the visitor was the biggest challenge to be met by all who participated in the great World's Fair, EXPO, of 1992.

This was sited on a rough wasteland, the 'island' of La Cartuja, where the Rio Guadalquivir divides and later reunites. Christopher Columbus probably stayed here in the monastery of Santa Maria de las Cuevas, while awaiting Isabella's decision whether to finance his daring adventure, after refusals by other powerful European monarchs. Reclaimed, the island became a new world for the last great International Fair of the twentieth century, converted initially by the imagination of the Spaniards and then by the technocrats of the participating nations, who met and overcame unusual challenges. The most important of those was the heat. Spread out flat under the burning sun, the site was like an open grill.

The Spanish designers planned avenues bordered with acacia trees, planted several years before Spain was confirmed as the host country. When the trees developed, rustic arches were placed along the paths.

The foliage, laid over these, created shady 'acacia walks,' pleasantly cool, decorative pathways, which contrasted a gentle softness against the strong, high-tech angles of much of the ultra-modern architecture.

Water used as ornament, both aural and visual, delights the visitor to Spain. It is also a natural cooler and was lavishly used at EXPO. A new lagoon was created on the island and this, with the ring of the river as well as sprinkler systems, sprays and other amenities did much to cool the torrid temperature. It was an integral part of the design of the Irish Pavilion, both inside and out. Living as we do on an island, our story is as much about water as it is about land, about rock as it is about sea. The exterior of the Pavilion very cleverly reminded us of the nature of our environment.

In 1988 the EXPO Committee issued its invitation to the world to take part in 'L'Esposizione Universale Sevilla 1992,' giving possible participants four years to make up their minds and decide how to take part. The theme was 'Discovery,' in celebration of the 500th anniversary of Columbus's discovery of the New World. It could be given various interpretations: geographic, scientific, artistic, spiritual, intellectual.

About a year before the opening date, the Irish Government invited a group of architectural consultants to submit plans for a Pavilion.

Ironically, Arthur Gibney and Partners (Architects) were not among the invitees. But the grapevine in Dublin is extremely efficient and, just in time, that firm, in association with Billy Wilson and Associates (Architects) in Cork and with MF Kent as contractors, requested and received approval to compete from the Department of the Taoiseach, which was running the competition. The group won and were appointed to develop the project.

The site allotted to Ireland was quite small compared with those of many others, but it was in a central location on the main walk, clearly visible from the monorail which passed a few yards away as it travelled around the periphery. The EC pavilions formed one block; those of Luxembourg and the Netherlands were next to the Irish, while opposite was the marvellous Cathedral of Water by Nicholas Grimshaw.

The Pavilion consisted of two elements, a rotunda or drum intersecting an octagonal form set on a rocky shoreline. It was linked to the land by a bridge shaded by large sails. The drum was an evocation of features from the landscape, unmistakably recalling the ancient mound of Newgrange, the Round Towers of the monks and the Martello towers of the Napoleonic age. The octagonal form, partly glazed, rose like a cliff from the surrounding rocks as they were washed by the water below. It was a harmonious and vivid reminder to the Spanish and their guests of our island state. The sails had a double function, one obvious, the other to provide shade for the visitors queueing to enter. The water also had another role to play: it kept the Pavilion cool.

It was essential, first, for the interior designers to place Ireland geographically in relation to Spain and the rest of Europe, since it is so often confused with Holland or Iceland or even located in mid-Atlantic. It is now thought that Ireland was first colonised by the Milesians or other early settlers coming from Northern Spain, a theory also supported by Evans and O'Riordan.[1] It is said that their boats, if pointed north and left to drift, would have been carried by the currents to the Irish coast.

The interior space was small despite being on two levels, so in order to maximise it, great ingenuity was used in its design. Maps were used to clarify locations. Three video screens and three slide-projection screens were placed at intervals within the pavilion to provide the necessary continuity between large set screens and dioramas.

Teaspaint, a consortium of design teams specially brought together for the project, was responsible for the interior design. Working in close collaboration with Eigse, the Heritage group from Trinity College, Dublin, they created a sequential display of Ireland's historical relationship with Europe, particularly Spain, and the Americas, and the remarkable achievements of her people. 'The venture became a great national effort,' according to Ronnie Petrie, chief of the team. The theme for the Irish pavilion mirrored that for EXPO, 'Discovery.'

A logo is an identification: the Irish logo achieved star quality. Timing is all, and Tom Meenaghan, just before he designed it with more than a stroke of genius, had a lucky opening.

Working on another project, he had shortly before seen the 'Broighter Hoard' in the National Museum, a group of gold objects from the first century BC. Among them was a gold model boat, nine inches long, with mast and oars. Meenaghan seized on this to design a graphic, a boat with oars and a mast, adding five Miróesque heads. It became one of the most famous images from EXPO, was used extravagantly even in cartoon comments and won the prize for the best logo. A commemorative pin of it was made, which was to become a prized possession.

THE IRISH PAVILION AT EXPO '92.

From earliest times the Irish talent for astronomy has found expression. It is the principal feature of the tumulus at Newgrange, where the alignment of the sun's rays with the central chamber at dawn during the winter solstice remains a mysterious feat achieved a thousand years before the Great Pyramid of Egypt was built. 'Our working hypothesis is that Newgrange is the deepest expression of the Boyne Culture's quest for attunement with divine-cosmic reality.'[2]

In 1845 William Parsons, 3rd Earl of Rosse, invented the largest telescope on earth, casting the great mirror himself. For seventy years it remained unchallenged, seminal in the investigation of space. Much more advanced studies continue at various Irish universities and the School of Cosmic Physics, with contributions being made to space programmes in Europe, the United States and Russia. A photographic image of the giant telescope was one of those televised. To learn more about it one pressed a button and information and further images followed.

Close in achievement to the building of the telescope was the first splitting of the atom at the Cavendish Laboratory, Cambridge, where he then worked, by Professor of Physics Ernest Walton. With Sir John Cockcroft, he won the Nobel Prize in 1932.

The influence of the Irish monks on the Christian faith is widely known in the story of their journeyings to restore civilisation to the European mainland after the Dark Ages. Teachers, saints and martyrs, they left Ireland to live a nomadic existence, not for aggrandisement, but for God, building monasteries and schools of renown, from Ireland to Kiev, odysseys shown in vivid imagery, by plan, map and diorama. Saint Brendan and his famous 'Navigatio,' known throughout the Continent in the Middle Ages, is illustrated with a kneeling monk beside a boat obviously preparing to put to sea. Tim Severin's recent voyage in a currach similar to that described in the narrative, proved that the claim that Brendan had discovered America in the sixth century was certainly possible. From many accounts 'We see the curraghs (sic), when intended for long voyages, were made large and strong, furnished with masts and solid decks and seats, and having the hides tanned.'[3]

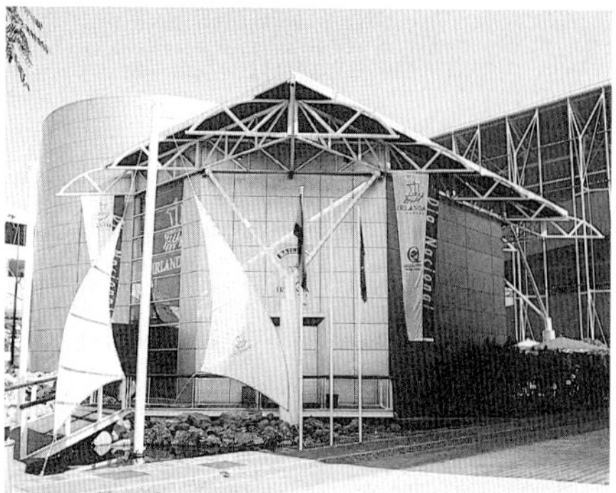

The gangway to the entrance can be seen here. The National Day(4 October 1992) flag is in place. The sails , with the famous logo, affording shelter from the sun, are also a reminder of the island nature of Ireland.

The National Museum illuminated these early centuries with reproductions of the recently discovered Derrynaflan paten and chalice (eighth-century). The Shrines of the Book of Dimma (twelfth century) and of St Patrick's Bell (1100 AD) were also represented, as was the Stowe Missal. A copy of the distinguished Swiss facsimile of the Book of Kells (eighth-century) was exhibited.

As well as triumph there was tragedy, illustrated in the great historical catastrophes. A seventeenth-century Catholic student at the University of Salamanca was forced to study there because under Penal Law No. 5, all education was barred to Catholics. An eighteenth-century Irish soldier, in full dress, of the Mahoney Regiment in the Royal Spanish Army, was a casualty of the flight from Ireland of the leaders and chiefs, one of those 'leaving all that is most dear in life for a strange land in which they will have to endure much,'[4] to serve in armies that knew little of their people. Students as well as soldiers wore uniforms. Éigse authenticated both.

Photography was lavishly used to illustrate aspects of history. It became a popular art-form from its inception in the nineteenth century with some famous innovations in Ireland, including the production of the first colour photograph. Emigration was a central theme, with imperishable images of the pathetic fugitives from the Ireland of the famine and the landlord recalling that terrible, artificial disaster that became a hiatus in modern Irish history.

The Director of the Pavilion, Mr Denis Rafter, crowned the technical achievement with a cultural programme that was

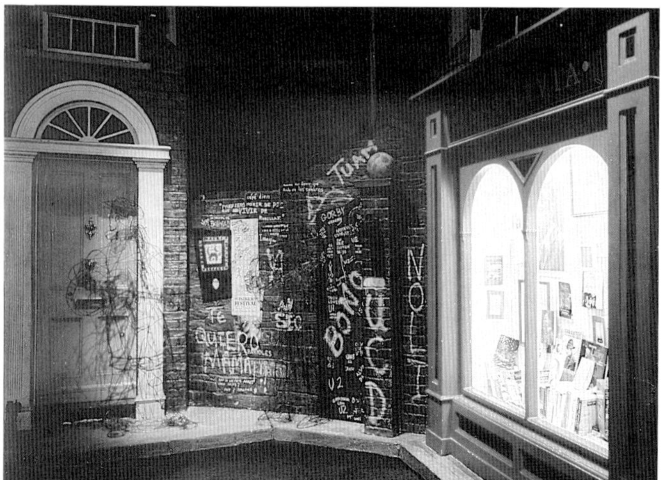

Shown in this area were a Georgian doorway, symbol of Ireland's capital city, graffiti of artists and stars , and portraits and accounts of the lives and works of the greatest Irish writers.

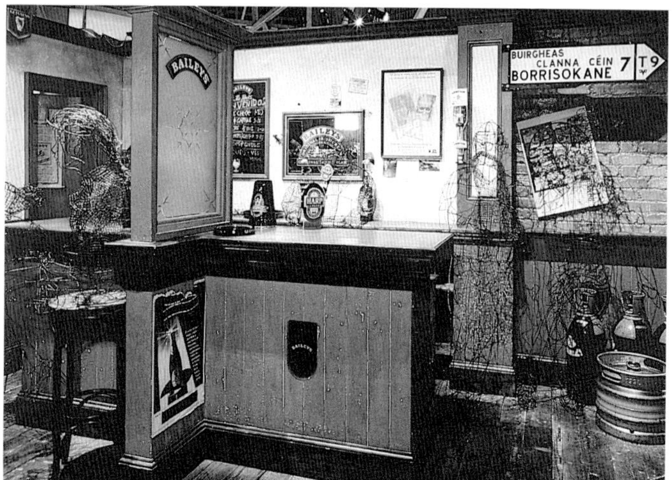

The classic 'pub with no beer'. Bill Fallover's wire figures can be seen occupying the bar stools. This entire design has been retained in Seville to represent Ireland in a commemorative museum of scenes typical of every participating country.

THE IRISH PAVILION AT EXPO '92.

widely acclaimed and that testified to the continuing originality of the people.

June was literature month: Beckett's portrait on a television screen invited investigation, and at the push of a button Barry McGovern was babbling Lucky's conundrums to the desert. Eamonn Morrissey performed his one-man show *Joycemen*, based on the characters from *Ulysses*, and Seamus Heaney gave a poetry reading.

Macnas Street Entertainment brought the giant 'Gulliver, the tallest visitor to EXPO' and floated him on the Guadalquivir. It seems to represent much that was fancied about Ireland, the hilarity, the imagination, in matters of comedy larger than life.

The satirist in Swift would have delighted in its huge success as it pleased both the literati and the children.

'Irlanda: It has more than compensated for the modesty of its pavilion with its hospitality and a huge number of artists.'[5] The Director told me that the presentation had achieved a merit rate of four in a scale of five.

Literature, poetry, music, street entertainment, the visual arts, all were given ample representation. The most important of the events was the *Seville Suite*, specially composed by Bill Whelan and played by the RTE Concert Orchestra and soloists under the baton of Proinnsias O Duinn to celebrate 'Ireland Day' at EXPO. It commemorates the disastrous Battle of Kinsale in which the Irish/Spanish Alliance was routed by the English with the resultant destruction of the ancient Gaelic order.

The Flight of the Earls after 1601 is encapsulated in the story of 'Red' Hugh O'Donnell, Earl of Tyrconnell, one of the greatest and most romantic of the Irish Princes. The music describes the event: the bitter defeat at Kinsale and O'Donnell's lament for his slain comrades. In a storm-tossed sequence all the emotional anguish of humiliation, loss and hopeless departure from his beloved land are expressed. But hope of a return is renewed with the vision of the warmth and grandeur of the Spanish landscape and in the magnificence of the Earl of Caracena's welcome to Galicia in the great hall of his castle.

A brilliant piece of choreography celebrated the intertwining of Spanish and

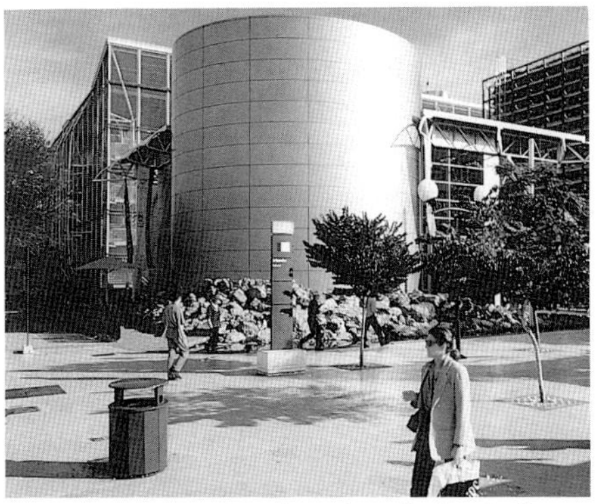

The exterior, taken from the right-hand side, showing the round tower as it rises from the rocks, hinting at the Irish shoreline. (All the photographs were taken the day after the EXPO closed; because of the crowds, it would otherwise have been impossible to do so.)

Irish culture. Father Pat Aherne of Siamsa created an ensemble in which Flamenco dancing meshed with the Irish hornpipe, emphasising both the similarities and the differences between the two styles.

It was performed by Michael Murphy and Maria Pages, reputedly 'one of the most sensual of all Flamenco dancers.' Clothed in glorious colour and glamorous robes, the subtleties of the Spaniard's physical movements were contrasted with the formal patterns of the Irish hornpipe as danced by the Irishman clothed in the tweedy masculine gear of the West of Ireland. An analysis of the music established a remarkable relationship between Spanish and Irish measures and harmonies.

John O'Conor gave a piano recital in Seville and Gerard Gillen played the organ in the largest Gothic cathedral in the world, a magnificent sound. The Chieftains, their music and their stage presence, captivated the audiences at Seville as they had done from the Americas to China. Popular modern sounds were heard from Sharon Shannon, De Danann; and the St Lawrence O'Toole Pipe Band had a mighty following.

Unlike many other pavilions where ethnic food and drink was provided in the large areas available to them, the Irish could only provide a well fitted-out bar, but without drink. The bar in Ireland is the social meeting place where chat, comment, wit, criticism and frequently inspiration provide vital entertainment. Figures lounged at the bar, ingeniously composed from wire by Bill Fallover, whose work in this medium has been seen at the Aer Rianta Exhibitions at Dublin Airport. The area was covered with photographs of literary figures juxtaposed with literary graffiti. The tone was both elegant and sharp.

Paintings by Peter Collis and Sean Fingleton hung inside the pavilion. Maurice McDonagh's prize-winning sculpture, *The Wall*, will remain permanently, representing Ireland, among the works of other nations in the Sculpture Park commemorating EXPO '92, in the garden of La Cartuja.

When finally the Pavilion was complete, the organisers dared to hope that they would manage to attract half-a-million visitors, that after all this effort they would, at least, not be ignored. At the end of the six months of EXPO, one and-a-half million visitors had been received, a remarkable achievement on a shoestring of less than £3.5 million. It was a tribute to the organisers, to the ingenuity of the Director and to the dedication of what was generally acknowledged to be his 'charming staff.'

Kate Robinson

Kate Robinson is an art historian, critic and curator. She is a Guide at the Chester Beatty Library and Gallery of Oriental Art.

ACKNOWLEDGEMENTS

My sincere thanks are due to the Director of the Irish Pavilion, Mr Denis Rafter, and his staff in Seville; to Mr James O'Connor, Architect; to Mr Finbarr Wall of the OPW; Mr Ronnie Petrie of MDA and Mr Keith Nolan of Pan-AV and to Ms Barbara Galavan of McGuinness Whelan, Music Publishers.

NOTES

1. Estyn Evans, *Prehistoric and Early Christian Ireland. A Guide*. London, 1966, p.5. Sean P. Ó Riordan and Glyn Daniel, *New Grange*. London, 1966, p.133.
2. Brendan Purcell, 'In search of Newgrange: Long Night's Journey Into Day.' *The Irish Mind*, ed. Richard Kearney. Dublin, 1985, p. 319, n8.
3. P W Joyce, *A Social History of Ancient Ireland*. Dublin, 1913, 425, vol. 2.
4. Maurice N Hennessy, *The Wild Geese*, London, Sidgwick & Jackson, 1973. Epigraph, Chapter 1, p. 15: Patrick Sarsfield after the defeat in 1691.
5. Analysis of the various pavilions at the conclusion of EXPO '92 by the journal A.B.C., one of the three most prestigious newspapers in Spain.

IMAGINING AN IRISH PAST: THE CELTIC REVIVAL 1840-1940

Nicola Gordon Bowe reviews the catalogue of the exhibition *Imagining an Irish past: the Celtic Revival 1840-1940* held at the Smart Museum of Art, University of Chicago, 5 February-16 June 1992.

This exhibition celebrated the University of Chicago's centenary by focussing on its little-known collection of nearly two hundred exquisite 'Facsimiles of Irish Antiquities', made specifically for the 1893 Chicago World's Columbian Exposition. The Dublin silver- and goldsmith and jeweller, Edmond Johnson, took exact plaster casts from the best of the recently-excavated rich store of early Irish metalwork for his astonishingly accurate, scale replicas. These range from very small Early Bronze Age gold lunule, Late Bronze Age ribbon torques, gold penanular rings, dress fasteners and collars and Iron Age bronze fibule (all BC) to Early Christian penanular brooches, hair, bronze and ring pins, and a number of specifically-documented shrines and croziers. Treasures like the twelfth century Processional Cross of Cong, the Shrine of St Patrick's Bell, the 'Tara' brooch and Ardagh Chalice, nationally acclaimed (and ubiquitously plagiarised), were exactly reproduced, except for the preciousness of the originals' materials. They attest to the technical skills of their creators and their painstaking copyist.

Johnson's metal paraphrases of the ancient Irish wooden drinking love-cup, or 'mether,' approach the spirit of modern interpretation which was apparent in certain pieces shown at the inaugural (1895) exhibition of the Arts and Crafts Society of Ireland. But, in the 1890s, what was principally admired by Irish romantic nationalists and an avid market alike was faithful reproduction. Such was the success of Johnson's displays in the two Irish villages erected in Chicago that examples of his replicas were soon on sale at Marshall Field's and Tiffany's, smart department stores in Chicago and New York, and he sold his 'spectacular group' of facsimiles to the Columbian Museum (now the Field Museum of Natural History) in Chicago. They remained there until 1941, when they were transferred to the University of Chicago and in 1967, as a teaching collection, to the Smart Museum.

The exhibition and its small but generally well-illustrated and informative catalogue were carefully arranged to emphasise the context in which this collection should be seen. Many of the 284 items exhibited were drawn from Chicago (University and otherwise) collections, amplified by loans from the National Museum in Dublin and the Ulster Museum in Belfast.

Thus, the exhibition opened with a small section on *The Discovery of the Celtic Past*, featuring key mid-nineteenth-century texts illustrating Celtic ornament (eg John Obadiah Westwood's *Palaeographia sacra pictoria* (1843-5), the illustrated Catalogue of the Great Exhibition of 1851 and Owen Jones' *The Grammar of Ornament* (1856)), or antiquarian findings (published by Henry O'Neill and Samuel Ferguson) beside later interpretations, including Johnson's facsimile of the emblematic 'Tara' Brooch. Section Two, *The Dissemination of the Celtic Revival: Ireland, England, Scotland, and the United States 1840-1940*, no less, opened with an earlier 1869 (Joseph) Johnson dish, based on the foot of the Ardagh Chalice, whose later facsimile made by his kinsman, Edmond Johnson, is the star in a section of artefacts made between 1850 and 1912; their common factor is their decoration in Celtic interlace. It included the fine 1903 version of his *St Patrick* triptych that the English Arts and Crafts enamellist Alexander Fisher made for the National Museum of Ireland's study collection, an undocumented silver book, bracelet and bog-oak hair tidy, a weak piece of Frederick Vodrey pottery, a Della Robbia Ware vase remarkable only for its zoomorphic *entrelac* pattern and its use of Irish clay, and some good earlier West & Son commercial silverware. Scotland was represented, surprisingly summarily, by an elaborate quaich (or drinking cup) by William Mackie of around 1876. A sizeable selection of Liberty's not always obviously Celtic-inspired Cymric and Tudric ranges of decorative metalwork represented England, mostly through Alexander Knox; Celtic was extended to include Manx. This digression, which does not refer to Liberty's enthusiasm for and exhibition of Irish-made Donegal carpets or Mary Watts' well-known essays in Celtic ornament in ceramics and textiles, was pursued in a catalogue essay. It was a pity this did not address Knox's successful assimilation of ancient forms and decoration into lively contemporary design, for example in the pewter champagne bucket exhibition; this, coupled with Liberty's achievement of a viably commercial process finds no parallel in early twentieth century Ireland – a fact much lamented by progressive critics of the Arts and Crafts movement. American representation (Chicago excluded) got short shrift with a gilded bronze Celtic Desk Set and a glass Tyg(?) with a questionable date made in the Tiffany Studios at Corona, New York.

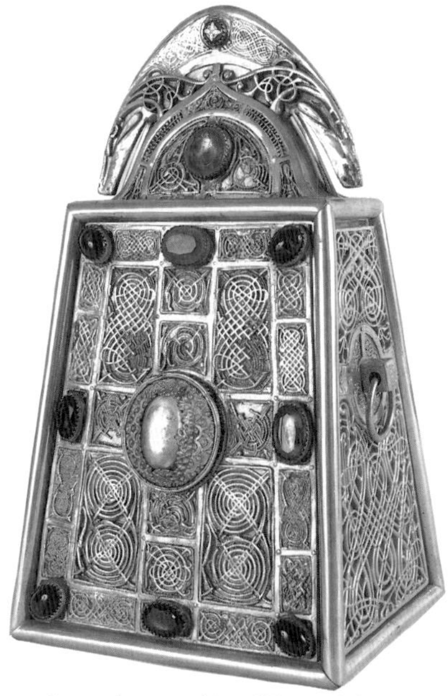

Shrine of St Patrick's Bell by Cudulig Ua Inmainen, c. 1100. Metal, ht. 26 cm. Facsimile by Edmond Johnson. David and Alfred Smart Museum of Art , University of Chicago, gift of the Field Museum of Natural History.

The third section, *Irish Nationalism and the Celtic Revival* began with figurative work of a sentimental or symbolic nature, favouring fanciful notions of native materials, superior souvenirs of an imagined past. The firm of Edmond Johnson appeared again with a fairly standard Freedom Box of 1904 beside a 1919 Belfast-made three-handled cup, a presentation box containing the new 1928 Saorstat Eireann coinage by Percy Metcalf (sic), and three Dun Emer Guild items, backed up by an extended passage in the catalogue. The Guild's embroidered royal blue poplin dress of unflattering cut, with neo-Celtic devices and accoutrements of *brat* and headband, made for the romantic nationalist wife of the first Chief Justice of the Irish Free State, probably best illustrated the exhibition's fundamental concept; this was expounded in the introduction by the catalogue's editor and the Smart Museum's then Director, Teri J Edelstein.

IMAGINING AN IRISH PAST: THE CELTIC REVIVAL 1840-1940

Next followed the bulk of the Johnson Chicago exhibit in the section misleadingly referred to as *Edmond Johnson and the Irish Pavilion of the World's Columbian Exposition*, since Ireland was represented at the Fair by two rival Irish villages, Lady Aberdeen's for the Irish Industries Association, and Mrs Ernest Hart's for the Donegal Industrial Fund. A contextual account of the nature of the Exposition, describing details and the significance of Ireland's contribution, was however, ably recounted by Neil Harris in the catalogue essay *Selling National Culture*, although he did seem unaware of comparatively recent Irish scholarship in the field, bar the deservedly ubiquitous references to Jeanne Sheehy's seminal *The Rediscovery of Ireland's Past: The Celtic Revival 1830-1930* (1980). His essay was followed by Cheryl Washer's on *The Work of Edmond Johnson: Archaeology and Commerce*. She constructed a useful historical account of the Johnson family of jewellers, goldsmiths and silversmiths, availing of the few surviving archives and other primary sources. She has also recorded Edmond Johnson's relationship with and technical approach to the original antiquities, mostly in the collection of the Royal Irish Academy, after the Academy's antiquarian vice-president, the third Earl of Dunraven, had engaged him to 'clean, repair, and study' the craftsmanship of the newly discovered Ardagh Chalice. She suggests his consequent enthusiasm, application and informed expertise may well have led to his representation in Chicago in the Manufacturers' Building, as well as in the two Irish villages – and certainly established a ready market for his work, thus disseminating the Celtic style in America.

Fittingly, the exhibition concluded with a small section on *The Celtic Revival in Chicago*, although the inclusion of the architectural firm of Louis Sullivan and his partner Dankmar Adler on the grounds of his eclectic synthesis of Owen Jones' pan-cultural sources (including Celtic), and his own idiosyncratic, nature-based stylisation, seems anomalous. However, quite justifiably included is exemplary Celtic-inspired Arts and Crafts metalwork from the lesser known Carence Crafters with their attractive small silver accessories and the renowned Chicago hobbyist turned metalsmith, Robert R Jarvie; also a poster and a panel of deceptively conventional-looking stained glass decorated with Celtic interlace and symbol by the eccentric Missouri-born Thomas A O'Shaughnessy, a former graphic student of the celebrated Czech artist Alphonse Mucha (at the Chicago Art Institute's School of Design). His conversion to Celtic ornament after a 1900 study visit to the Book of Kells in Dublin led to an eleven-year quest, resulting in windows conceptually more interesting than their execution, and currently the subject of some interest. This section also includes two decorative volumes recording traditional Irish music by the Chicago policeman, Francis O'Neill, and elaborately Celtic-ornamented desk-top furniture produced in the 1920s by Marshall Field's in-house Craft Shop.

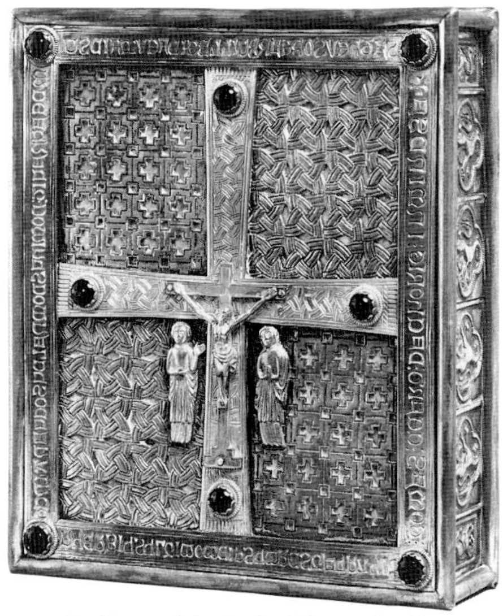

The Shrine of the Book of Dimma (back). Mid 12th cent., altered in 15th and 19th cents.. Metal, 17.4 x 20.3 cm. Facsimile by Edmond Johnson. David and Alfred Smart Museum of Art, University of Chicago, gift of the Field Museum of Natural History.

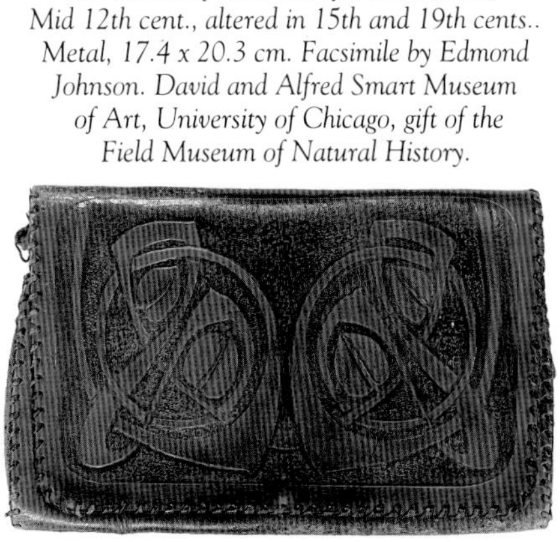

Liberty & Co, London, Archibald Knox (designer). Handbag. Metal, leather impressed front and back with Celtic entrelac patterns in colour, 30.5 x 20.3 cm.

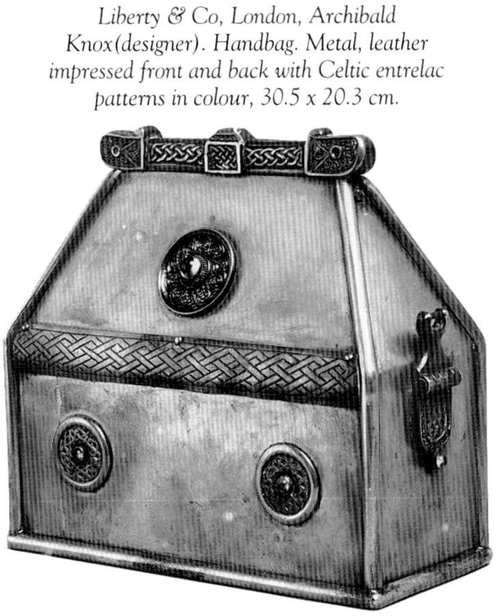

Lough Erne Shrine, c. 7th or 8th cent., metal, ht. 15.9 cm. Facsimile by Edmond Johnson. David and Alfred Smart Museum of Art, University of Chicago, gift of the Field Museum of Natural History.

There were a number of notable omissions and questionable inclusions in both exhibition and catalogue, not least a vacuous, wasteful essay on *Celtic Revivals and Women's Work* in the latter, which ignored and failed to assess any work past or present on the subject. The lack of specific tabulation in the catalogue proper to items illustrated makes reference laborious and the checklist texts seem arbitrary, unsourced, and of no particular value. Clearly-referenced biographical entries and some information in the catalogue entries could have been achieved with guest contributors or a reasonable amount of research, using existing documentation. Some close-up details, sharper black-and-white photographs and more contemporary images would have illustrated the technical points made in Washer's essay on Johnson and taken advantage of the local historical sources in which Chicago is so rich. Their omission constituted a wasted opportunity. Nevertheless, by attempting to present Johnson's work in some sort of historical, ideological and national (both Irish and American) context, this exhibition achieved a worthy goal in an accessible, attractive format.

Nicola Gordon Bowe

Dr Nicola Gordon Bowe is a lecturer in History of Art and Design at the National College of Art and Design, Dublin. She has published and lectured widely on early twentieth-century decorative arts, especially the stained glass and Arts and Crafts revivals early this century in Ireland. She held a Steele Scott Fellowship at the Huntington Library, California 1991-92 and is editor of Reviving Dreams: Vernacular Expression in Turn of the Century Design *(Irish Academic Press 1993).*

A MONUMENT BY GRINLING GIBBONS

A monument in St Patrick's Cathedral Dublin is the most important surviving work by Grinling Gibbons in Ireland. Its history is outlined by **Edward McParland.**

At the eastern end of the south wall of the south transept of St Patrick's Cathedral, Dublin, is a monument to Archbishop Narcissus Marsh[1]. It closely resembles Grinling Gibbons's monument to Sir Cloudesley Shovell of 1708 in Westminster Abbey. Letters among the Wicklow papers in the National Library of Ireland show that the Marsh monument too is by Grinling Gibbons. It is thus his most important surviving work in Ireland.[2]

The monument and its inscription are noted in the *Journal for the Year 1906* of the Association for the Preservation of the Memorials of the Dead, Ireland, vol. VI, no. 3 – part 1, Dublin, 1906, pp. 524-25, and in Victor Jackson, *The Monuments in St. Patrick's Cathedral Dublin,* Dublin, 1987, pp. 70-71. Both sources transcribe the inscription recording Marsh's career: Provost of Trinity College, Dublin, Bishop of Ferns and Leighlin, Archbishop successively of Cashel, Dublin and Armagh, Primate of All Ireland, and frequently a Lord Justice of the kingdom. He founded, built and endowed Marsh's Library in Dublin, the first public library in Ireland.[3] He died in 1713.

His monument was first erected out of doors in St Patrick's churchyard, by the west wall of his library. In 1728 it was moved into the cathedral to stand in one of the arches of the southern nave arcade.[4] It was moved to its present position later in the nineteenth century.

Apart from Marsh himself, and Gibbons, the other people involved in the erection of the monument include Benjamin Huson, Hugh Howard and his brother Robert, and Marmaduke Coghill.

The monument is inscribed 'Monumentum posuit Benjamin Huson'. Notwithstanding such prominence, Huson is obscure. In 1705 a Benjamin Huson proceeded to his BA in Trinity College Dublin 'on recommendation of the Primate', i.e. Marsh.[5] Further patronage from Marsh followed when Huson (or Hughson, Hewson or Hewetson) became precentor of Armagh in 1709.[6] Huson witnessed, along with Robert Howard, the will Marsh made on 22 February 1712 (new style) of which a copy is in Marsh's Library. Dying in 1720, he was buried in Marsh's vault.[7]

With Robert and Hugh Howard, sons of Ralph Howard of Shelton in Co Wicklow, the interest quickens. Not only does their correspondence allow the attribution of the Marsh monument to Gibbons, but it throws light, too, on Anglo-Irish contacts with artistic circles in London in the early eighteenth century. Hugh made his career in London. He was Keeper of State Papers, and Paymaster of the Works.[8] An intimate of Sir Thomas Hewett the surveyor-general, he entertained hopes of succeeding Vanbrugh as Comptroller of the Works. He was, too, a painter and connoisseur, he is the suggested author of the portraits of Marsh in Trinity College Dublin and in Marsh's Library,[9] while Vertue records Captain Marcellus Laroon the Younger's reference to '... the Great great. Sr. Hu <Mr. Howard> Director & privy Councellor to Noblemen & Gentlemen that

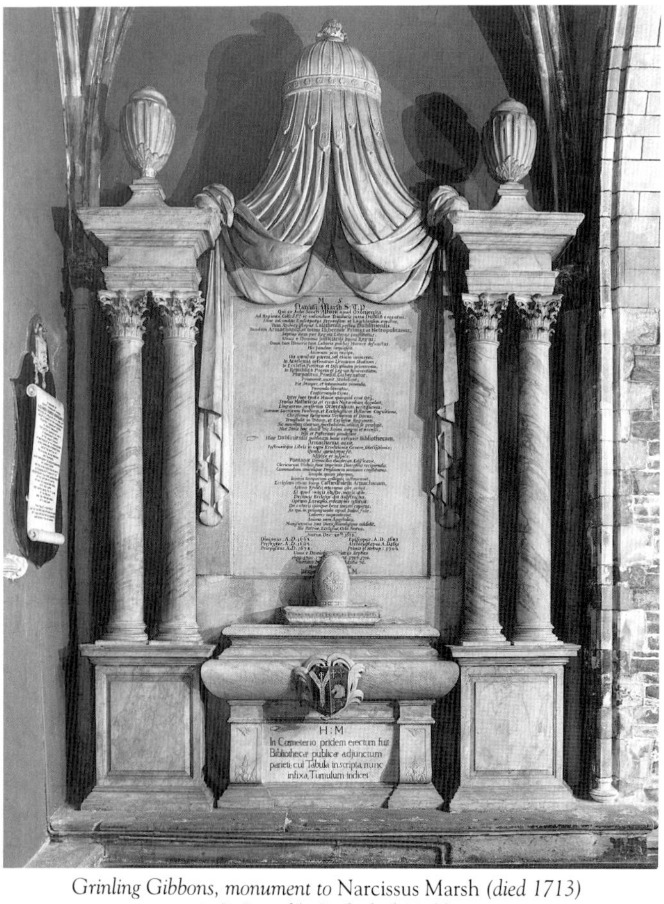

Grinling Gibbons, monument to Narcissus Marsh *(died 1713) in St Patrick's Cathedral, Dublin*

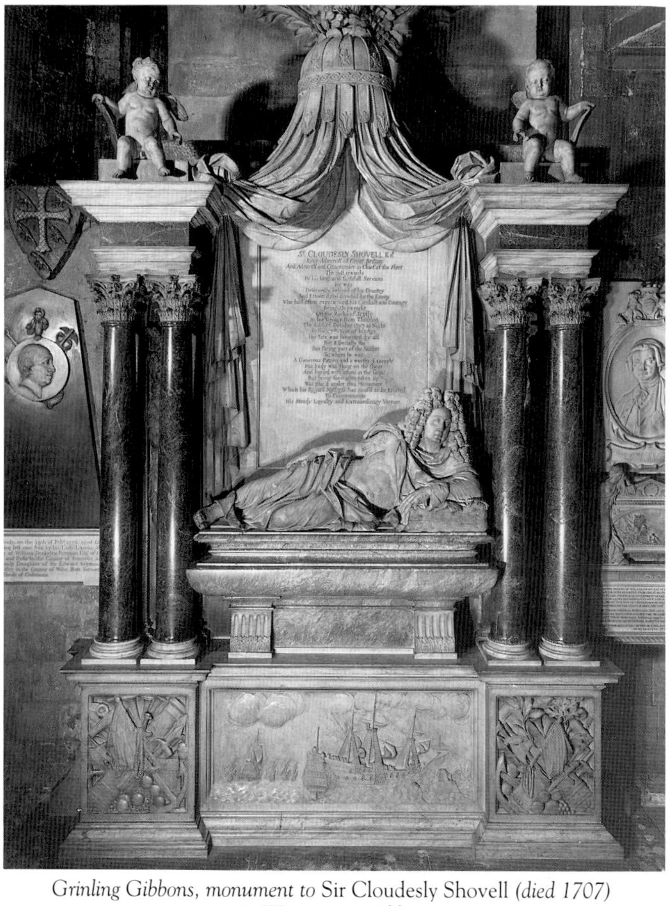

Grinling Gibbons, monument to Sir Cloudesly Shovell *(died 1707) in Westminster Abbey*

A MONUMENT BY GRINLING GIBBONS

purchase Pictures …'[10] Hugh's letters from London show him arranging for the dispatch to his friends in Ireland of paintings, medals and books. Among the correspondents for whom he negotiates is his brother Robert, a trusted friend of Marsh and successively Bishop of Killala and Elphin, and Marmaduke Coghill, Chancellor of the Irish Exchequer and executor of Marsh's will.[11] On 8 September 1716 Hugh Howard writes from Bath to Robert[12]

> *I writ to you at Mr. Gbbons [sic] request, by the person who is to set up the Primates Monumnt. that he may be furnish'd with w[ha]t mony he may have ocasion for in that work, by the Executors; which wil be allowd in the payment that is to be made when the work is finish'd, it was near done when I left London, and I took al the care I coud about the Inscription.*

The letter is directed to Dublin and must therefore refer to an Irish monument. Hugh Howard was well placed to act as go-between in this affair. He was not only, according to Vertue, 'vers'd <& well skilld> by observations on the works of painters sculptors &c', but also he would have been acquainted with Gibbons through the Society of Virtuosi of St Luke of which Howard was steward in 1707 as was Gibbons in 1709.[13] As we have seen, his brother and correspondent, Robert, was a witness to Marsh's will of 22 February 1712, and to its codicil of 28 April 1713.[14]

This letter of 1716 throws light on a postscript to a later letter from Hugh Howard to his brother in the same collection.[15] On 14 November 1717 he writes, this time from London 'I long since sent Mr Gibbon's recept in ful to Dr Coghil, but dont know if he receiv'd it'. This letter contains other references to questions of siting in Dublin 'the Statue of ye King', presumably that of George I then in contemplation by the Corporation as a successor to Gibbons's *William III* of 1700-1701. That Gibbons's 'recept' refers to the Marsh monument, however, is suggested by the fact that Dr. Marmaduke Coghill was one of the executors of Marsh's will (and Dublin's *George I* is traditionally attributed to John Van Nost the elder).

The Marsh monument enlarges Gibbons's documented *oeuvre,* but adds little to his reputation. Contemporary with his last known work, the Chandos monument at Whitchurch, Middlesex, the design is repeated from the Shovell monument of 1708, without the rich polychromy and without any figure sculpture. As Beard points out, the *baldacchino* and drapery link the Shovell monument (and now the Marsh one) to the monuments to George Stepney (died 1707, Westminster Abbey, attributed to Gibbons), to Archbishop Sharp (died 1714, York Minster, attributed to Francis Bird), and to Sir William Boughton (died 1716, Newbold-on-Avon, Warwickshire, by John Hunt).[16]

The design also reappears in William Kidwell's celebrated monument to Sir Donat O'Brien (died 1717) in Kilnasoolagh, Co. Clare,[17] which, with its polychromy and effigy, is closer to Shovell's monument than to Marsh's. If Kidwell, as seems certain, was taking Gibbons as a model for the O'Brien commission – 'the most obviously baroque monument in the entire country'[18] – what a pity that he did not learn from Gibbons at St Patrick's how to manage correctly the architectural details at Kilnasoolagh!

Edward McParland

Dr Edward McParland is a Lecturer in the History of Art Department in Trinity College, Dublin, and Secretary of the Irish Architectural Archive.

NOTES

1. I am grateful to the Director and staff of the National Library of Ireland, to Mrs Muriel McCarthy of Marsh's Library, Dublin, and to Mr Philip McEvansoneya for much assistance in the preparation of this article.
2. For Gibbons's *William III* in Dublin (destroyed), and his two Southwell monuments in Kinsale, see Geoffrey Beard, *The work of Grinling Gibbons,* London, 1989, and Rolf Loeber, 'Arnold Quellin's and Grinling Gibbons's monuments for Anglo-Irish patrons', *Studies* (Dublin), LXXII, no. 285 (Spring 1983), pp.84-101.
3. Muriel McCarthy, *All graduates and gentlemen, Marsh's Library,* Dublin, 1980, p.26.
4. Marsh's Library, Dublin, 'A Book Prepared and given by Narcissus Lord Arch: Bishop of Armagh; In Which is to be entered … The Act of Parliament For settling and preserving a Publick Library for ever …', ms, record of the visitation to the library on 9 October 1729.
5. George Burtchaell and Thomas Sadleir, *Alumni Dublinenses,* Dublin, 1935, p.421.
6. Rev James B Leslie, *Armagh clergy and parishes,* Dundalk, 1911, p.34, who adds that Huson was related to Marsh.
7. Marsh's Library, Dublin, 'Register Book of St Patrick[s] May ye 25th 1687 [to] July ye 13th 1798', ms.
8. J Mordaunt Crook, 'The Office of Works, 1719-1782', in H M Colvin (general ed.), *The history of the King's Works,* V, London, 1976, pp.79-80.
9. Michael Wynne, 'Hugh Howard, Irish portrait painter', *Apollo,* XC (October 1969), pp.314-17, and Anne Crookshank and David Webb, *Paintings and sculptures in Trinity College Dublin,* Dublin, 1990, p.97.
10. *The twenty-second volume of the Walpole Society 1933-1934, Vertue note books volume III,* Oxford, 1934, p.40.
11. Marsh's Library Dublin, miscellaneous Marsh manuscripts relating to property, single sheet entitled 'A Schedule of Writeings delivered by the Right Reverend Father in God John [Stearne] Lord Bishop of Dromore and Marmaduke Coghill Doctr of Laws Executors of the last Will and Testament of the most Reverend Father in God Narcissus late Lord Archbishop of Armagh …' The document is undated but Stearne was Bishop of Dromore from 1713 to 1717.
12. National Library of Ireland, unsorted Wicklow papers, PC 227, folder dated 1717-1722.
13. Ilaria Bignamini, 'George Vertue, art historian and art institutions in London, 1689-1768: a study of clubs and academies', *Walpole Society,* LIV (1988), pp.1-148, and William T. Whitley, *Artists and their friends in England 1700-1799.* London, 1928, II, p.243.
14. Marsh's Library Dublin, miscellaneous Marsh manuscripts relating to property; this will deals with the disposition of only part of Marsh's estate.
15. See note 12 above.
16. Geoffrey Beard, *The work of Grinling Gibbons,* London, 1989, p.79.
17. Rupert Gunnis, 'Some Irish memorials', *Quarterly Bulletin of the Irish Georgian Society,* IV, no. 1 (January-March 1961), pp.1-3; Homan Potterton, 'William Kidwell, sculptor, c1644-1736', *Quarterly Bulletin of the Irish Georgian Society,* XV, nos. 3 and 4 (July-December 1972), pp.80-124.
18. Homan Potterton, 'William Kidwell, sculptor, c1664-1736', *Quarterly Bulletin of the Irish Georgian Society,* XV, nos.3 and 4 (July-December 1972) pp.81-83.

WORD AND IMAGE

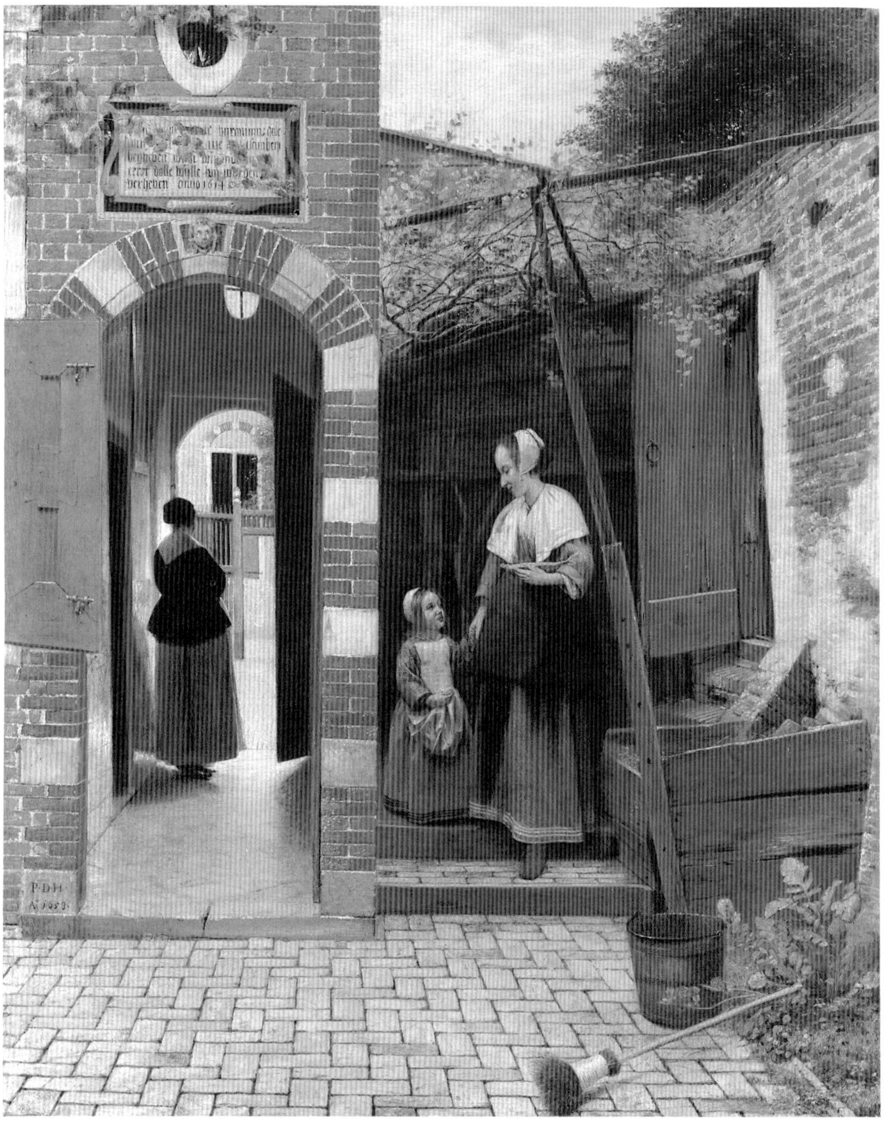

Pieter de Hooch, Courtyards in Delft. *1659, National Gallery, London.*

for Gordon Woods

Oblique light on the trite, on brick and tile –
Immaculate masonry, and everywhere that
Water tap, that broom and wooden pail
To keep it so, House-proud, the wives
Of artisans pursue their thrifty lives
Among scrubbed yards, modest but adequate.
Foliage is sparse, and clings. No breeze
Ruffles the trim composure of those trees.

No spinet-playing emblematic of
The harmonies and disharmonies of love;
No lewd fish, no fruit, no wide-eyed bird
About to fly its cage while a virgin
Listens to her seducer, mars the chaste
Precision of the thing and the thing made.
Nothing is random, nothing goes to waste:
We miss the dirty dog, the fiery gin.

That girl with her back to us who waits
For her man to come home for his tea
Will wait till the paint disintegrates
And ruined dykes admit the esurient sea;
Yet this is life too, and the cracked
Out-house door a verifiable fact
As vividly mnemonic as the sunlit
Railings that front the houses opposite.

I lived there as a boy and know the coal
Glittering in its shed, late-afternoon
Lambency informing the deal table,
The ceiling cradled in a radiant spoon.
I must be lying low in a room there,
A strange child with a taste for verse,
While my hard-nosed companions dream of war
On parched veldt and fields of rain-swept gorse;

For the pale light of that provincial town
Will spread itself, like ink or oil,
Over the not yet accurate linen
Map of the world which occupies one wall
And punish nature in the name of God.
If only, now, the Maenads, as of right,
Came smashing crockery, with fire and sword,
We could sleep easier in our beds at night.

Derek Mahon

THE RESTORATION OF NEWMAN HOUSE

Newman House, University College, Dublin, has recently been splendidly restored. **Christine Casey** reveals new information on the history and conservation of this elegant Georgian house.

Numbers 85 and 86 St Stephen's Green are two of the best and most original Georgian townhouses in Dublin, one a sumptuous residence of 1738, the other a later Georgian house of 1765. By good fortune this important pair of buildings were united in common ownership in the mid-nineteenth century. Their combination offers a unique opportunity to view in one property the development of Dublin domestic architecture during the course of the eighteenth century and illustrates particularly well the dramatic stylistic evolution of Irish plasterwork during the period. Since 1989 these houses have undergone extensive restoration which has revealed much about their original appearance and about their development during the course of two centuries.

History

A fresh look at the documentary sources for the history of Newman House has added to and significantly amended the traditional account of their construction and ownership. Number 85, the smaller and earlier of the two buildings, was formerly believed to have been built to the designs of Richard Castle for Hugh Montgomery of Derrygonnelly, County Fermanagh.[1]

A closer inspection of the title deeds for Number 85 St Stephen's Green and related properties suggests that the builder of this house and Mr Montgomery of Fermanagh were two separate individuals.[2] Captain Hugh Montgomery who began building Number 85 in 1738 and who died in 1741 was the only son of Sir Thomas Montgomery, a lawyer of the Middle Temple who received a knighthood in 1686.[3] In 1702 Sir Thomas Montgomery owned extensive lands in the town of Drogheda where he was then resident.[4]

By 1725 Hugh Montgomery had inherited his father's County Louth properties and held a commission as a captain in Colonel Hayes' regiment of foot.[5]

In March of 1738 Hugh Montgomery leased from Abel Ram 'a piece or parcell of ground lying on the southside of St Stephen's Green in Dublin adjoining the house then lately built by Capt Corneille containing in the front to said Green sixty-one feet or thereabouts'.[6] The plot was number 12 in the original Corporation allotment of 1664 when it had been set to one Arthur Eccles 'gentleman'.[7] Bounded on the north by the Green and on the south by Leeson's Fields, it was adjoined on the east by the house of John Corneille, second engineer of the Kings Works in Ireland, and on the west by a vacant plot also owned by Abel Ram. On 8 February 1741, the site 'together with the messuage lately built thereon by Hugh Montgomerie' was sold to Mr George Johnston by John Lyons and Charles Caldwell, executors of the 'last will and testament of Hugh Montgomerie late of the said city'.[8] Captain Montgomery, 'a gentleman of great honour and veracity' had died on 29 April 1741 from 'a deep decay' and 'after a lingering illness'.[9] He was survived by a sister Dorothea, whose husband John Lyons was one of the executors of the will. Dorothea's second son Hugh Lyons later assumed the name Montgomery and inherited his uncle's estate.[10]

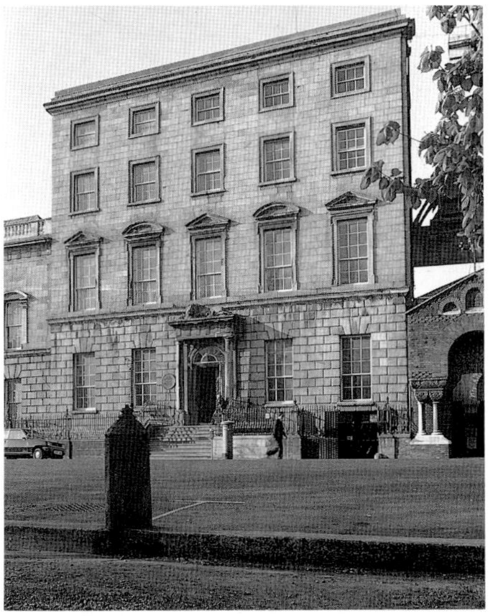

Newman House, 85-86 St. Stephen's Green

Hugh Montgomery's elusive career and untimely death are rendered all the more intriguing by the great quality of Number 85 St Stephen's Green. By comparison Number 84, the house of Captain John Corneille, has simple wainscoted interiors and modest room cornices which serve to highlight the grandiose plan and opulent interior decoration of his neighbour's house. While there is no documentary evidence for the attribution of Number 85 to Richard Castle, the character and distinction of the building would suggest the involvement of an accomplished designer. The use of a spiral service stair is seen elsewhere in Castle's work as is much of the decorative detail in Number 85. With the Castlehume link no longer tenable, evidence for Castle's authorship is necessary in order to sustain this attribution.

Whatever the identity of its designer, the grandeur of Number 85 is undisputed. The house is a miniature Palladian *palazzo* of two stories and an attic over a basement with an impressive stone frontage to St Stephen's Green. Approximately forty feet wide, the house is compact in plan with four principal rooms on the ground floor and three on the *piano nobile*. The entrance hall is the largest interior on the ground floor and is simply wainscoted with plaster panels above, and a black and white flagged marble floor. Off the hall is the Apollo Room, an diminutive interior with a remarkable figurative plasterwork scheme by the Lafranchini brothers depicting Apollo and the nine muses. The principal stair of Number 85 is an early instance of the use of mahogany in a Dublin house and is carved with Tuscan balusters and ornamental tread-ends.

The grandest and most consciously architectural interior in the house is the Saloon on the first floor, which at 35'x20' fills the entire breadth of the building. Grandeur of scale and proportion are here combined with rich interior articulation and ornament. A pair of Corinthian doorcases on the inner wall lead to the stairhall and an ante-chamber, statue niches articulate the end walls of the room and the elevation to St Stephen's Green is richly expressed by a Corinthian order raised on pedestals framing a central Venetian window and sash windows on each side. The coved ceiling is decorated with an ambitious figurative scheme by the Lafranchini.

In 1755 the house was purchased from George Johnston by Richard Chapel Whaley who also acquired the adjoining site, and in 1765 began building Number 86 St Stephen's Green, a much larger and more grandiose house.[11] Evidently inspired by Charlemont House, the designer of Number 86 is unknown, though the involvement of Robert West is likely. Very large and very grand, the house contains elaborate rococo plasterwork and joinery. The hall is flagged in limestone and

THE RESTORATION OF NEWMAN HOUSE

Portland stone and, though much altered in the nineteenth century, retains two Doric doorcases on the inner wall, an enriched Doric cornice and a hybrid foliate frieze. The former dining-room was the principal ground-floor reception room of the Whaley house, and was modelled upon the 'French room' of Charlemont house.[12] Its walls are decorated in Louis XV fashion with large rectangular panels flanked by tall thin panels and oval medallions, and foliate ornament inside and around the panel frames. The stairhall is among the most impressive domestic interiors of its date in Dublin richly ornamented with panels of varied size and profile containing in and around them a wealth of rococo ornament including strapwork pendants, cornucopiae, musical instruments and the famous birds of the Dublin school. The first floor of Number 86 was designed for entertaining purposes and contains three large reception rooms with splendid rococo ceilings which are attributed to the school of Robert West.

Though united in joint ownership during the lifetime of Richard Chapel Whaley, the houses were later separated when Number 85 was sold, and it was not until 1865 that the properties were again joined. In 1854 the newly-established Catholic University of Ireland received its first students in Number 86 and in 1865 it acquired Number 85 from the family of the late Judge Nicholas Ball. University Church was built under the direction of John Henry Newman, the first rector of the new University and the Aula Maxima was begun in 1876 to the designs of J J McCarthy. During the course of the nineteenth century Number 85 was considerably altered by successive occupants of the house. The early nineteenth-century remodellings may be attributed to George La Touche who purchased the house in 1818 and to Judge Nicholas Ball who lived here from 1830 to his death in 1865. Further alterations were made to the house by the Catholic University in conjunction with the building of the Aula Maxima from 1876 to 1878 and later in a refurbishment of 1939-40.

These combined buildings, which were later to become known as Newman House, served during the nineteenth century as the premises of the Catholic University, and, later, of its successor University College. In 1912 the construction of a new purpose-built university building at Earlsfort Terrace removed the St Stephen's

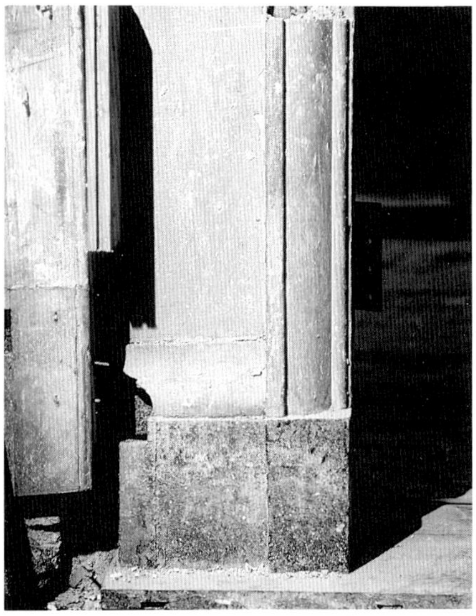

Section of original architrave discovered during restoration.

Green buildings from the centre of College life and during the 1920s and 1930s they steadily declined. A rehabilitation programme of 1939 cleverly adapted the building for the social activities of the University and remodelled the basement as a restaurant annex to Earlsfort Terrace. The purpose of the 1939 building project was to consolidate the fabric of the houses and ensure their continued use by the University. It was characterised by utilitarian measures such as the removal of original joinery, replacement of floors, pouring of cement throughout the basement and insertion of new concrete and metal stairs.

moved to a new campus at Belfield, Newman House was again underused and sorely in need of rehabilitation. At that time, despite an increasing appreciation of Irish Georgian architecture, no eighteenth-century house in the city had yet been restored or opened to public view. Conscious of the great quality of Numbers 85 and 86 and of the building's important literary and historical associations, the College decided that a role within heritage-based tourism would be the most appropriate new use for Newman House. In 1989 a programme of restoration was initiated whose aim was to restore the building's eighteenth-century interiors while preserving something of the spirit of the University during the days of Newman, Hopkins and Joyce. The restoration programme was jointly devised by Alistair Rowan, former Professor of the History of Art at University College Dublin and David Sheehan of Sheehan and Barry, Architects, under the direction of Sean Brennan, UCD's Buildings' Officer. Valuable help and advice have been received from David Griffin of the Irish Architectural Archive, Dr Edward McParland of Trinity College Dublin and Desmond Fitzgerald, the Knight of Glin.

Restoration

Current approaches to architectural conservation range from extreme reluctance to remove or modify any historical accretions to a building to a thorough-going enthusiasm for period reconstruction based on historical and stylistic principles. Minimal intervention, though admirable in its aim to retain the rich organic potential of many buildings, can fail in some cases by disregarding the aesthetic potential of a building. For instance, an ugly Victorian draught-lobby in a handsome early Georgian entrance hall may reflect the usage of the building in the nineteenth century, but this value must be weighed against its negative impact on a rare eighteenth-century panelled interior. Period restoration also has its pitfalls and can result in the complete removal of the historical patina of a building. The restoration of Newman House has endeavoured to follow a path between these approaches. While many of the utilitarian alterations of the nineteenth and twentieth centuries have been redressed, restoration has relied heavily on clear physical and historical evidence discovered during the course of conservation.

The Apollo Room of Number 85 clearly illustrates this approach. One of the finest stucco interiors of its date in Ireland, the Apollo Room has suffered a radical nineteenth-century remodelling. Evidently considered too small for contemporary entertaining purposes, the room had been joined to the inner parlour of Number 85 by opening a broad elliptical archway in its rear wall, thereby destroying the Lafranchini decorative scheme. Two of the room's nine muses, masks, garlands and a group of playing putti were removed in order to accommodate the new open plan. Happily the plaster figures and ornaments were not discarded but were removed and reinstated in haphazard fashion on the walls of the inner parlour. At a later stage the University filled in the archway with a door and stud-partition, thus reinstating the original room plan but abandoning the

THE RESTORATION OF NEWMAN HOUSE

plaster muses in the inner room, which, by then, had become little more than a large vestibule connecting Numbers 85 and 86.

In recognition of the great quality of the Apollo Room plasterwork, a decision was made to reconstruct the rear wall and to reinstate the displaced plaster figures. As no drawings of the Apollo Room had survived from the eighteenth century, the design of the missing wall was a conjectural restoration based upon the evidence of the discarded plaster figures and the surviving scheme in the Apollo Room. Initially a symmetrical arrangement was presumed with the door in the centre and the muses on each side. When the archway and floor coverings were removed, however, it was found that the original pine floorboards of the Apollo Room ran beyond the wall line on the left-hand side, thus clearly indicating an asymmetrical design. A new doorcase and wainscoting were made upon the model of existing joinery and paint-scrapes were taken to determine the original colour-scheme.

An altogether more difficult problem was encountered in the stairhall of Number 85, which had been even more dramatically remodelled during the nineteenth century. Initially the space had been altered by opening an archway in the wall at the top of the stair, designed to introduce light from the stairhall into an inner parlour whose windows had been blocked up by an extension to the rear of the house. Later, even more radical remodelling was due to the building of the new Aula Maxima, a large assembly and examination hall which was built against the eastern end of the house. Its initial effect was to block up the Venetian window which formerly lit the stairhall of the house. Rather more intrusive was the insertion of a flight of stairs from the first floor landing of Number 85 to a suite of new classrooms above the Aula Maxima. This necessitated the removal of the eighteenth-century ceiling and the insertion of a new stair across the original entrance to the Saloon of the house. The stair as it ascended also cut awkwardly into the blind arcading of the upper stairhall. The results of these remodellings were most unattractive, destroying not only the spatial character of the original stairhall but also the sense of procession up the principal stair to the Saloon. The nineteenth-century archway and stair were consequently removed; the eighteenth-century ceiling level was replaced upon the evidence of surviving timbers; and the original entrance to the Saloon was reinstated.

During the course of investigation in the stairhall, a number of very interesting discoveries were made. The most surprising of these is an elliptical window placed directly above the Venetian window which had evidently been bricked-up and plastered over when the Aula Maxima stair was inserted. From a design perspective, the effect is odd and ungainly and further investigation is required in order to determine whether the lunette is original or a later insertion. Other less perplexing discoveries include a fragment of architrave to the original door of the Saloon which was found embedded behind the nineteenth-century stair. This has provided the model for new joinery.

Outlines of the original plaster decoration on the walls of the stairhall have been uncovered from beneath a modern plaster skim. Prior to the commencement of restoration the only surviving ornaments in the hall were an armorial cartouche above the Venetian window, and a pair of swags or garlands of oak leaves, fruit and flowers flanking a second cartouche on the wall at the head of the staircase. Removal of modern plaster in other areas has revealed that the swags continued around the entire stairhall with a large pendant drop between each pair. Using

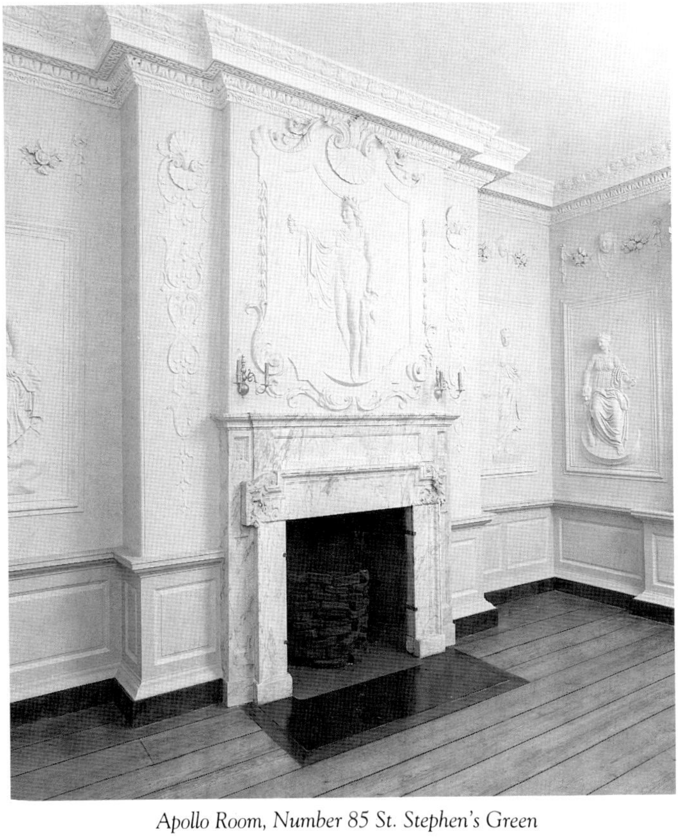

Apollo Room, Number 85 St. Stephen's Green

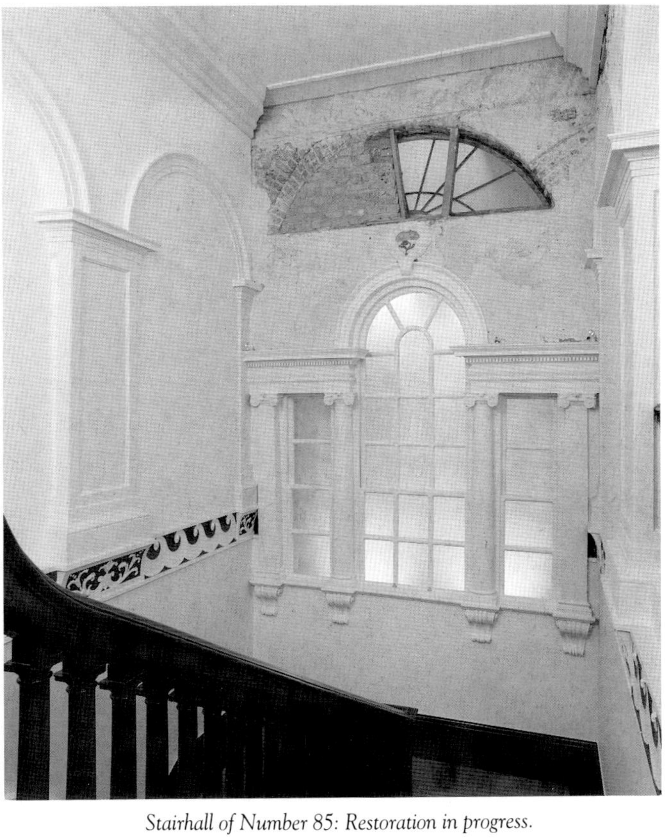

Stairhall of Number 85: Restoration in progress.

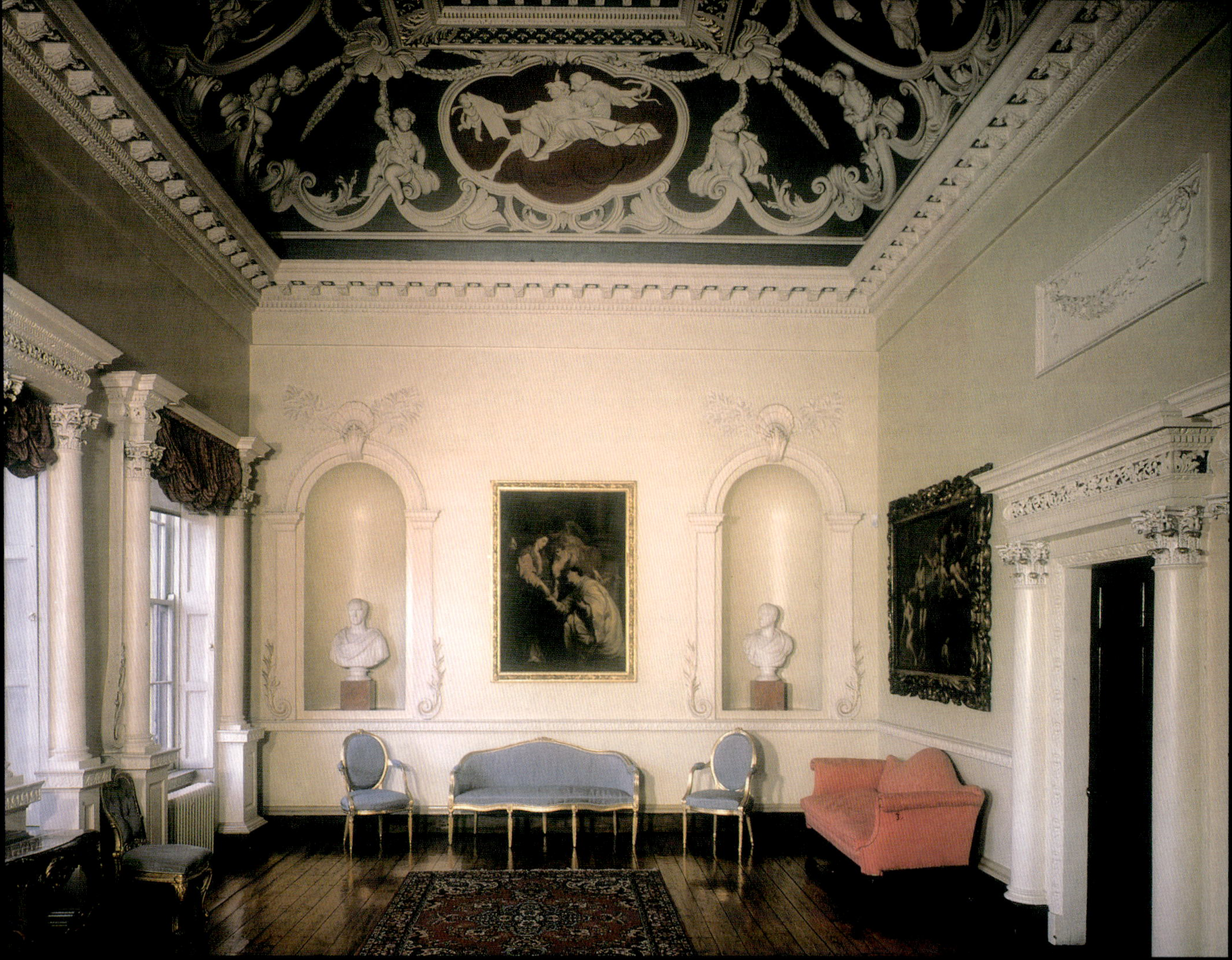

The Saloon, Number 85 St Stephen's Green.

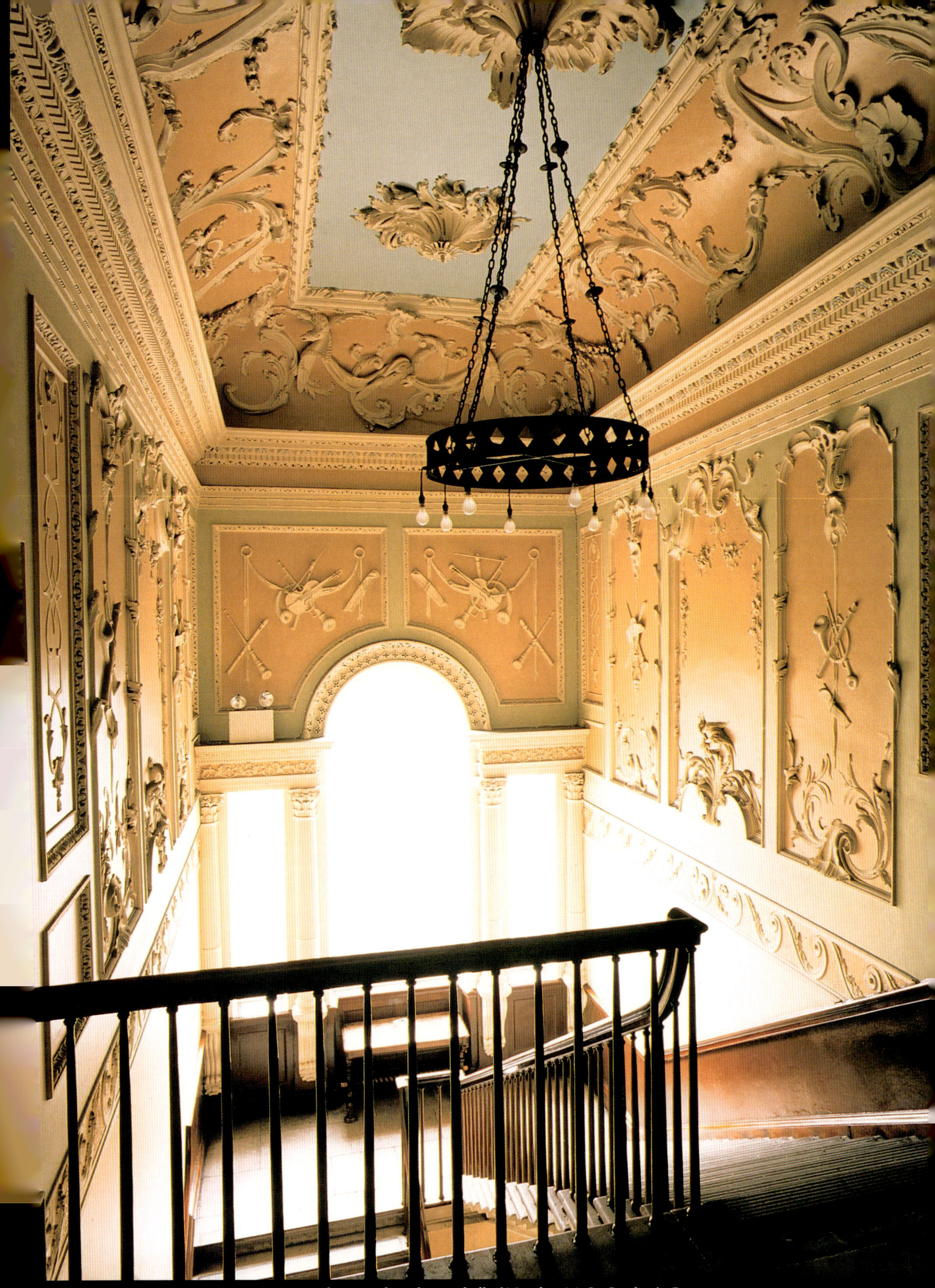

THE RESTORATION OF NEWMAN HOUSE

impressions from the surviving swags, it will be possible to recreate this decorative scheme. Difficulty arises on the window wall where the relationship of the swags and the lunette window are somewhat unclear.

In tandem with the restoration of the stairhall, work has begun on the grandest interior of Number 85, the Saloon. At some stage during the nineteenth century, contemporary taste for brightly-illuminated interiors prompted the occupants of Number 85 to lower significantly the cills of the Saloon windows, and to splay the jambs of the side windows. Cutting back the cills has resulted in a thoroughly disjointed elevation to St Stephen's Green where the base of the Corinthian order framing the windows stand almost a foot above the modern cill level.

Other alterations to the Saloon largely date to the 1939 refurbishment when the original floor, wainscoting and skirting were removed. At that time the niches at each end of the room were remade, and the frieze was reduced to a plain and ungainly projection at the base of the entablature. The ceiling was painted in strong greys, reds and white, a scheme which does little to compliment the Lafranchini stucco. At an unknown date the original chimneypiece was removed from the Saloon and replaced by an early nineteenth-century chimneypiece. Evidence for the original design has been provided by the Irish Georgian Society Records of 1910, and by a surviving marble fragment of the chimneypiece.

The studious approach to period restoration seen in Number 85 stems from a recognition of the building's rarity and exceptional quality. While Dublin still retains an impressive complement of later eighteenth-century houses, early townhouses with ambitious plasterwork interiors are few and far between. While there were undoubtedly other houses of this calibre in the city during the mid-eighteenth century, these are now gone, and Hugh Montgomery's house is therefore a most precious remnant of Dublin's Georgian past.

* * *

Number 86 St Stephen's Green was the first of these houses to be purchased by the University and has, as a result, strong associations with John Henry Newman and the origins of the Catholic University. One of the principal first-floor reception rooms was appropriated in 1851 as the committee room of the Catholic University, and has been known since then as the Bishops's Room. A small room on the second floor of the the house was the study and bedroom of the poet Gerard Manley Hopkins, who came to the University as Professor of Classics in 1884 and who died here in 1889. James Joyce, who was a student here from 1899 to 1902, records in his early writings glimpses of the building in its role as a small Jesuit-run University. The strength and evocative power of these associations dictated a rather different approach to the restoration of Number 86. Rather than return the Bishops' Room to a drawing room of 1765, the interior is shown in its mid-nineteenth-century form. A fragment of early flock wallpaper discovered behind a doorcase provided enough evidence to recreate a paper for the room. Similarly in the Hopkins room, fragments of a nineteenth-century rag paper were uncovered and matched by blocks from a contemporary London firm.

In a period of restraint for all sectors of the economy, support for the Newman House restoration had been generous and enthusiastic. Bord Failte and Dublin Tourism, who provided initial European Regional Development Fund funding of £100,000, were attracted by the potential of the building as a centre of focus for Georgian art and architecture, and as a place of considerable literary and historical interest. What could not perhaps have been anticipated was the enormous public interest which emerged in the task of restoration itself. The revival of traditional crafts, the painstaking cleaning, conservation and repair of plasterwork and joinery, and the sheer excitement of discovering a building's inner secrets have met with wholehearted enthusiasm from the thousands of visitors who have seen Newman House during the course of the past three years. Convinced of the value of this activity and of its importance for the preservation of Georgian Dublin, Gallaher (Dublin) Ltd, committed a further £400,000 to enable the restoration of the stairhall and Saloon of Number 85 St Stephen's Green. By the time these words are printed that task will be complete and a new episode in the history and restoration of Newman House will have begun.

Christine Casey

Dr Christine Casey is curator of Newman House. University College Dublin, and joint author with Alistair Rowan of North-Leinster, *volume two in the* Buildings of Ireland *series, to be published September 1993.*

NOTES

1. C P Curran, *Newman House And University Church*, Dublin 1953 p6. The second son of a captain in William III's army, Montgomery was a substantial landowner and a neighbour of Sir Gustavus Hume, Richard Castle's first private patron in Ireland. Upon his marriage to Elizabeth Armar, Montgomery inherited the estate of Blessingburne, and his son Hugh later acquired the estate of Castlehume.
2. Registry of Deeds. 95/351/66772. 109/221/75651. 89/299/63294.
3. W A Shaw, *The Knights of England*. London, 1906. vol II, p262. No direct connection between Thomas Montgomery and the Fermanagh Montgomerys has as yet been established.
4. NLI. D16, 386. D16, 259L.
5. NLI. D16, 386. Military records established that his first commission as Lieutenant was granted on January 29th 1722. During the 1720s and 1730s our only knowledge of Montgomery's activities are extensions to leases of his properties in Drogheda, in which he is referred to as being of that town and on one occasion of 'Ballymaladdy, County Down', Registry of Deeds 89/299/632294. *A list of the Colonels, Lieutenant Colonels, Majors, Captains, Lieutenants & Ensigns of his Majesty's Forces* ... London, 1740 p66.
6. Registry of Deeds 95/351/66772.
7. J T Gilbert, *Calendar of Ancient Records of the City of Dublin*. Dublin, 1894, vol. iv, p305.
8. Registry of Deeds 109/221/75651.
9. *The Dublin Journal*, Tuesday 5 May – Saturday 9 May 1741.
10. Genealogical Office. ms 107, 184-85.
11. Registry of Deeds 169/455/114565.
12. Ex. info. David Griffin. Irish Architectural Archive.

'CALL DOWN THE HAWK'

The recent work of Anne Yeats displays technical originality and distinctive images of solitariness. **Hilary Pyle** discusses the painting *Tribute to W B Yeats* in the context of the artist's development.

Early in the Spring of 1992 Professor George Dawson of Trinity College asked Anne Yeats to paint a tribute to her father, W B Yeats, for the vestibule of the new Beckett Centre for the Performing Arts in Trinity College, Dublin. His scheme was an original one, asserting the interdependence of the arts with theatre at the centre.[1] His idea was to fill the vestibule with responses by Irish artists to certain prominent Irish men of the theatre, both past and present. John Kelly was asked for a tribute to Dion Boucicault, Brian Bourke to honour Brendan Kennelly, and Michael O'Dea was invited to paint a portrait of Derek Chapman. Patrick Collins, agreeing to pay tribute to John Millington Synge, told Professor Dawson that *Riders to the Sea* had recently been constantly in his mind.

Dawson's proposal to Anne Yeats had its element of irony. Here at the height of her career was the opportunity to confront once again the national genius who had dominated her creative persona since she was born. In *A Prayer for my Daughter*, written at the time of her birth, the artist's father had walked and prayed that 'she become a flourishing hidden tree', living

like some green laurel
Rooted in one dear perpetual place.

His dramas were among those for which she planned sets when starting out as a theatrical designer. She spent the greater part of four months contemplating what the subject of her *Tribute* should be and then executing it.

Her approach was practical; her aim to find an image which would convey the spirit of her father's ceaseless searching and his isolation, as well as the ruthlessness of his genius. She explored his plays and his poetry for such an image, rejecting her father's declared symbol of the Tower as 'too phallic', and 'too indulgent to the tourist'. Inevitably she toyed with birds, which invade her recent paintings as regularly as his late poetry, considering 'the rook delighting heaven', 'the sudden thunder of the mounting swan' and an eagle image, filling her sketchbook with preliminary drawings. Minnaloushe creeps through the pages among the other sketches. But she kept coming back in 'the mind's eye' to the theatrical image posed by Yeats in his play *At the Hawk's Well*; and she eventually took her theme from his poem, 'The Hawk', published in *The Wild Swans at Coole*, in 1919, the year she was born.

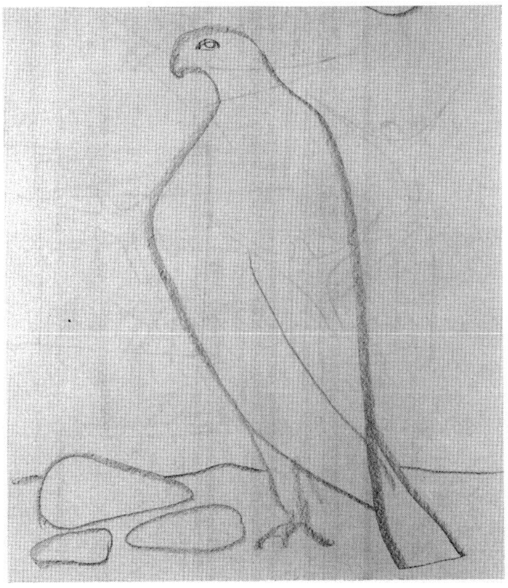

An example of Anne Yeats' preliminary drawings (1992) for Tribute to W.B. Yeats. *The artist's collection.*

The commission was a challenge to Anne Yeats not only for the point of view of subject-matter but because she was required to paint a canvas measuring three feet by three feet for the first time – larger than her normal canvas. She had also to adjust to 'thinking square'. Having found her subject, she painted rapidly, not at first satisfied with the result, but in the end coming up with a vivid and arresting image of the free arrogant being from 'The Hawk':

I will not be clapped in a hood,
Nor a cage, nor alight upon wrist,
Now I have learned to be proud
Hovering over the wood
In the broken mist
Or tumbling cloud.[2]

On to a background of dark tumbling blues, composed of oil pigment squeezed out of the tube onto canvas, and spread around and profounded with rags, she glazed her drawing of a hawk. She outlined it in white, at first painting the eye in cadmium red as a focus for the painting. Rereading the poem next day, she was reminded of the 'yellow-eyed hawk of the mind' and painted the eye chrome, through which the red is seen to shine. Pale forms glowing vaguely at the base of the picture may be the stones at the hawk's well, or eggs in the hawk's nest – she intends an ambiguity.

Superimposed on the blue, like a rigid mask hovering in unknown celestial depths, the hawk symbol recalls the anvil on which Yeats wished his final bodily form to be contrived, 'such a form as Grecian goldsmiths make ... set upon a golden bough to sing'.[3] Jane Lindskold has referred to the hawk as one of Yeats's personal magical symbols,[4] and this visual image made by his daughter has its magic and mystery. It is seductive, yet at the same time it is coldly austere. The painting has drawn as much out of the artist as of the poet, the artist confronted in her task of paying tribute to the great with admitting the common origins of their dynasties.

Since she completed the work, the picture has – fruitfully – been succeeded by some further paintings, identical in size, in which Anne Yeats has had room for more personal expression. *Curlews in a Storm* is a recognisable landscape, with the vague green of waves or grass under a midnight-blue tangle of clouds, partially blotted out by a descending black drench. Nine white birds, stylised like the hawk to resemble paper cut-outs, fly over the storm, detached from its natural intensity. In *Bird Over Water*, which is a swirl of midnight blue colouring, tossed with impasto unlike *Curlews* which is smooth, a stylised seagull is centred in a vortex of cloud and moving air. The spectator is strongly aware of the loneness of being, the theme which the artist has taken most closely to herself. The image might have been the moon, she will say,[5] but it became a tiny bird. Alone in artifice, alone in nature, the solitary symbol floats.

The hawk is a rarity in Anne Yeats, called 'down from the air', as in her father's poem, for her *Tribute* painting. Her general practice, she admits, is to paint what is around her. Since she went to live in Dalkey some years ago, she has been intrigued by the succession of colour contrasts in the garden which surrounds her house and studio. She is repeatedly aware of sea- and song-birds, conscious of the cat stalking across the grass. When she lived in Dublin in Mount Street, and before that in Exchequer Street, it was the people she painted. A woman sited on one of the bridges would offer a bunch of dying tulips for sale, and on one occasion a bunch of dying rhubarb! She was struck by the physicality of her presence, at the same time as observing how withdrawn her spirit was. She painted an old man with many coats, string trailing out of his pockets.

* * *

Born into the inspirational background of father, mother, uncle, aunts, and grandfather, all pioneers in the various imaginative modes, it was almost inevitable that Anne Yeats would choose some artistic pattern for her own life. She left school at thirteen to study in the Royal Hibernian Academy Schools, drawing from the antique five hours a day for three years under the tutelage of Maurice MacGonigal. The more retiring Henry Tisdall 'would take your drawing and cover it with doodles of feathery lines'. She worked hard, excelling at the instant poses the students were required to draw in their last life-class each day.

She went to Spain before being invited into the Abbey Theatre in 1936 as assistant to the stage designer, Tanya Moseiwitch. The following year, aged eighteen, she went to Paris to study at the Paul Collin School of Theatre Design, a visit which was satisfactory from the point of view of introductions, and the opportunity to go to the theatre nightly – 'twice on Sundays', but which made her too aware of what loneliness was. She returned to the Abbey, soon to become chief stage-designer, a post which she held until 1940. Disillusioned by the limits set on her at the Abbey, she worked freelance, for Illsley and McCabe productions, for the Lyric Theatre Company for many years, and, in Cork, for the Opera House.

Her sets and costumes are generally strong in line and colour. During the ten and more years in which she worked in the theatre, she produced designs for *The Land of Heart's Desire, The Death of Cuchulain* and *The Only Jealousy of Emer*, by her father, and many plays by Austin Clarke, Lady Gregory, and Shaw, designing also for her uncle Jack Yeats's first production in the Abbey Experimental Theatre, *Harlequin's Positions*. She also made backcloths for opera and ballet. Much of the material she worked with in the Abbey, however, was stock scenery, to be adapted for each successive play. A pair of ram's horns recurs in her designs! The Abbey, she says, had no interest in design as such but simply regarded it as a background for words; and she remembers producing sev-

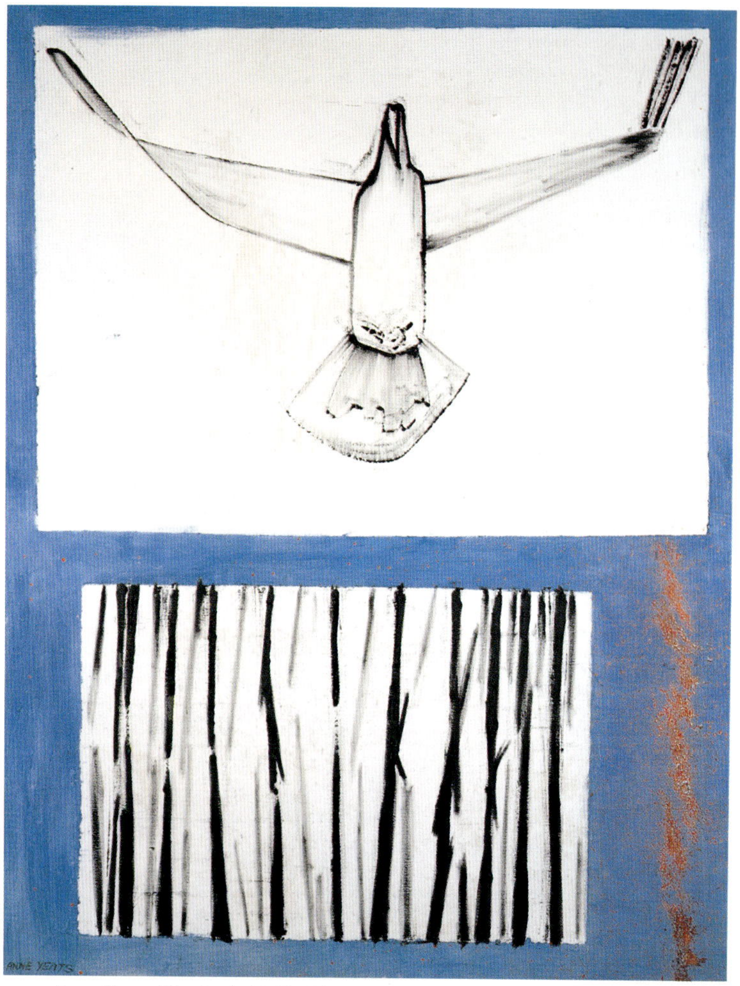

Anne Yeats, The Bird, *1965. Oil on canvas, 91 x 61 cm. The artist's collection.*

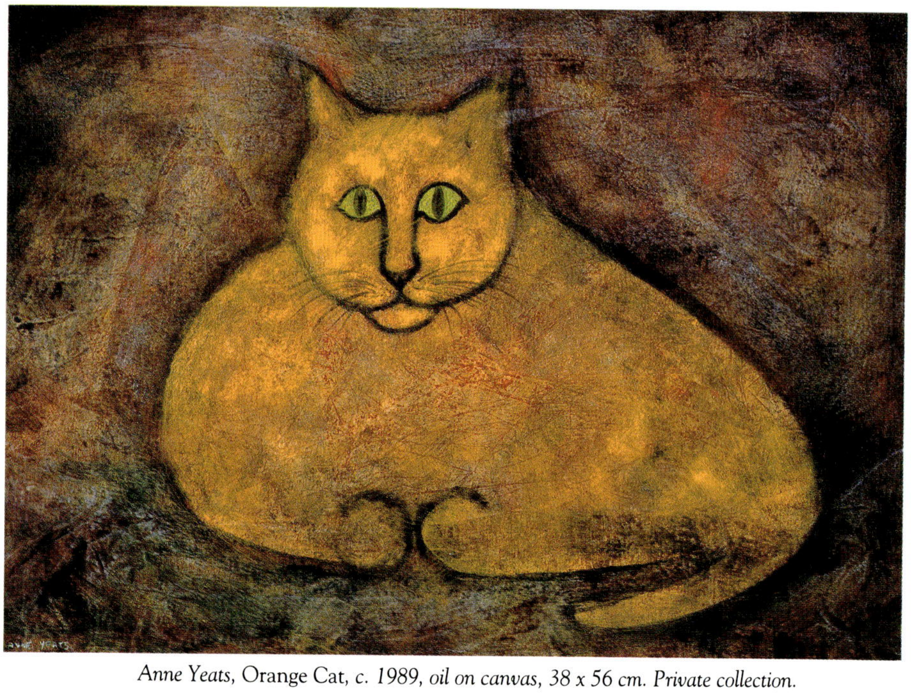

Anne Yeats, Orange Cat, *c. 1989, oil on canvas, 38 x 56 cm. Private collection.*

'CALL DOWN THE HAWK'

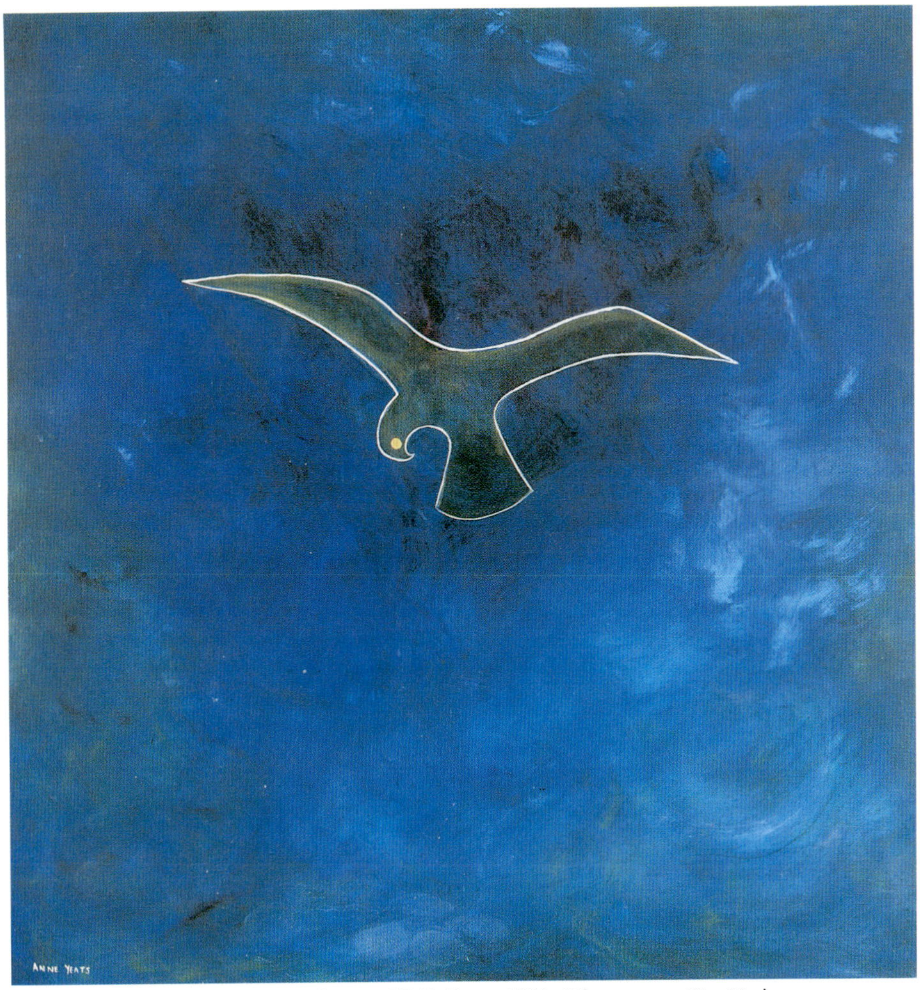

Anne Yeats, Tribute to W. B. Yeats, *1992. Oil on canvas, 92 x 92 cm. Beckett Theatre, Trinity College, Dublin.*

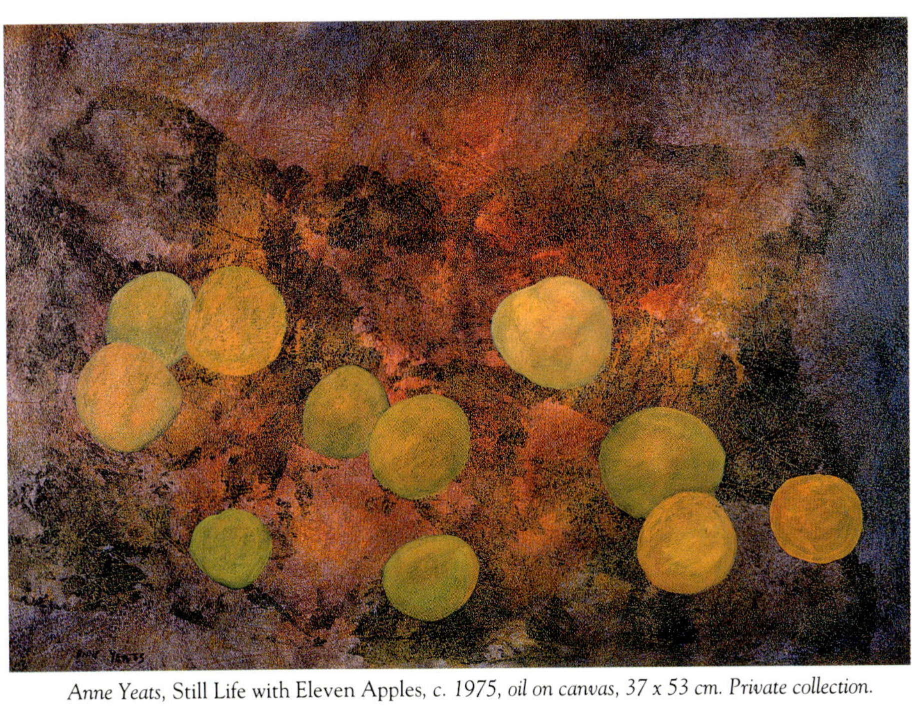

Anne Yeats, Still Life with Eleven Apples, *c. 1975, oil on canvas, 37 x 53 cm. Private collection.*

enty costumes and the sets for *The Story Brought by Brigid*, by Lady Gregory, for ten shillings (the 50p of the time), most of which was invested in a magnificent costume composed of yards of white towelling for Bob Mooney in the part of Christ.

At first she found that her work in the theatre related to her first childish enjoyment of her uncle's juvenile stage characters, and to the model theatre which she owned when she was eleven, when she acted out all the parts in *Hamlet* on her own. However she now knew that theatre design – dependent on and curtailed by the many people involved – did not suit her.

By the time that she left the Abbey Theatre, she had realised that she wanted to paint, and she attended the School of Art under Keating to refresh her hand at drawing. It was a period which she describes as 'depressing' – her attempts at anatomy and perspective were only successful when she 'faked' or copied, she says; so she left.

Looking around for lessons from a live artist, she wrote to her uncle, Jack B Yeats. He replied that he couldn't teach her because he didn't know how. He had had to teach himself. Her next call was on Mainie Jellett, who was soon to die, but who gave her a piece of advice she had never forgotten, warning her to be careful about placing a curve near the straight edge of a picture.

Her experience in stage design, Jellett's pervading modernist influence and that of the *Living Art* artists with whom she was to exhibit for years, assisted in the formation of a personal style. But even more powerful was the influence of the reproductions she studied. Since there was no modern painting to be seen in Dublin during the war, Anne Yeats had found the work of Picasso, Matisse and Braque, to her excitement, reproduced in *Studio Art Magazine*, and here was the source of many of her modern mannerisms. She worked first in watercolour, following the example of John Butler Yeats, her grandfather and Jack Yeats, and had her first picture, *Saeta* ('Mourning'), accepted for the inaugural exhibition of the *Irish Exhibition of Living Art* in 1943. This Spanish figurine, full of an angst inspired by music, was unlike the studies of down-and-outs and hungry children which she was doing at the time, and she feels it expressed something solely of herself. *Snack Counter*, another small work of this period, now in the Crawford Art

'CALL DOWN THE HAWK'

Gallery in Cork, is an example of the humour with which she looked at modern life around her – which she still exercises. It was bought by the playwright Lennox Robinson.

During the 1940s, she was experimenting ceaselessly with watercolour and ink, drawing 'shawlies', street musicians, which she coloured delicately, and fashioning more robustly the still-lifes which later became a regular subject. With ink she combined wax, letting the colour run down into the hollows of rough watercolour paper. She began to look seriously at Irish painting, studying her uncle's late work (which she had not yet taken to). She tells a story of how she seated herself before *Low Tide* in the Dublin Municipal Gallery looking intently for a duration of twenty minutes. Suddenly before her eyes the images fell into place.

In 1947, her second visit to Paris introduced her to real modern painting, and, for the first time, to Monet 'in the flesh', rather than in monochrome reproduction. What she remembers is the revelation of colour. She cycled down through France. Returning to the continent in 1956, Sicily was for her 'an explosion of excitement'. She kept a detailed diary from which she worked when she came back. Discovering that it was impossible to capture the totality of a new experience when sketching, she has developed the practice of noting down in words what she sees, and this capacity to visualise through the medium of words has stayed with her all her life. Her preliminary studies for the *Tribute* are scattered with words and ideas.

Anne Yeats's first oil painting to be shown in public was *Lark Hill*, accepted in 1944 for the *Living Art* exhibition. She was elected to the Living Art Committee not long afterwards, and served on it for many years, becoming identified with the pioneering spirit of the period, and showing in the company of Le Brocquy, Hanlon, Hone, McGuinness and Collins. But she did not paint consistently in oil until the 1950s, working first on board primed with gesso, and later on canvas. Her first paintings featuring women alone date from this time, and show an advance in emotional breadth. It was about now that Nevill Johnson[6] persuaded her away from colour into 'putty' toned pictures, affecting her style for a long period. the grey tones enhanced the subject-matter, and individualised a style which still proclaimed a School of Paris influence.

Woman in a Red Hat is a typical example of Anne Yeats's studies of solitariness dating from the 1960s, a figure painted on canvas, sitting by the door thinking beneath the moon. The abstract lines of the chair contrast poignantly with the actuality of her presence. *Bird*, painted the same year, in 1965, is a large single form, escaping from a cage. The dots of red paint might be interpreted as blood, the image even as a form of resurrection, though the artist regards the picture more abstractly, as 'growing out of thoughts'. The solitary women – or men – she says, are 'probably me'. She likes to study people singly. Even in groups she feels they seem alone. This sensitivity to solitariness can lead to misunderstanding. *Women Walking at Night*, when shown at the *Irish Exhibition of Living Art*, was denounced by President O'Kelly as 'a disgrace to Irish womanhood'; while *The Scarecrow* painted about the same time, offended some viewers who thought it was a crucifixion.

While images of the solitary have always been a preoccupation, technique has been equally important. She soon turned from putty tones back to colour, and to perfecting a way of working in oil which parallels her earlier watercolour wax technique. This new manner involved working with butter muslin, and she has continued the practice up to the present. The muslin is soaked in thin oil pigment, after which the cloth is transferred to the canvas, and removed after a while, leaving an imprint. She may use several colours, and when the surface satisfies, it becomes a background for still-life or for some other striking image. In *Still Life with Eleven Apples* (a motif that has been repeated both in oil and in print), green and yellow fruit lie side by side against a mist of autumny colour. *Orange Cat*, a primitive beast as enigmatic as the creatures on the cross at Monasterboice, glows and gazes out of a ground which gives an impression of collage. The veiled colours throw up all kinds of counter-images, not purposefully fabricated by the artist, but developing unexpectedly out of her cloth technique. As in the early Paris-derived period, when she would allow an image to develop its own shape, she likes the relationship of the natural and the artificial to grow gradually into a form of enigma. Her colours and forms, however, are now stronger and more conclusive, filling out the canvas. In her solo exhibition in Sligo in 1989, three tiny pictures of seagulls presaged the majestic hawk of her current *Tribute*, being among the first birds she painted using this cloth technique.

Anne Yeats is detached about her origins. She took up the use of her second and family name, 'Butler', only at the time of her father's centenary. Otherwise she has always been simply 'Anne Yeats'. But, in common with the rest of her family, there has always been the instinctive urge to fuse word and paint in her work. Many Irish writers have related to her as an illustrator, Bryan Guinness asking her to illustrate *The Animal's Breakfast* in 1950, and, more recently, Denis Devlin choosing one of her drawings to illustrate his poem *St Malo*.[7] In the Beckett Theatre, Trinity College, for the first time she has been obliged to associate her own paintings with her father's writing. Calling down the hawk, in response to a father who prayed when she was born that her linnet thoughts should

have no business but dispensing round
Their magnaminities of sound,

is perhaps a measure of her independence of mind, and the integrity with which she approaches her subject-matter. *Tribute to WB Yeats* is among her best work, a strong individual picture, which unites her technical originality with an image of solitariness so specifically her own.

Hilary Pyle

Hilary Pyle is an author and critic. Among her recent publications is Jack B Yeats: A Catalogue Raisonné of the Oil Paintings *(London 1992)*

NOTES

1. Professor George Dawson in conversation with the author, October 1992.
2. WB Yeats, *Collected Poems*, London 1965, pp. 167-68.
3. WB Yeats, 'Sailing to Byzantium'. *Collected Poems*, p.218.
4. Jane Lindskold, 'The autobiographical occult in Yeats's "The Second Coming",' *Eire-Ireland*, Geimhreadh 1991, p. 49 et seq.
5. The artist in conversation with the author, October 9, 1992.
6. See Cyril Barrett, *Irish Art, 1943-1973* (Rosc Chorcai, 1980), p. 35.
7. Denis Devlin, *The Heavenly Foreigner* (1967), 17-18.

SINCLAIR'S DREAM: THE WATERFORD ART MUSEUM

In a space formerly occupied by ruins, Sinclair discovered a little circular Art Gallery ... He paid sixpence to go in, but was informed that there were several free periods in the week and arrangements for groups of school children to see the pictures free of charge ... it was a well chosen collection of paintings and sculpture, mainly by Irish artists, but with a considerable representation of the art of other countries as well. He noticed that local artists took quite an important place there.

V D Farrington, 'Waterford as it should be' *The Waterford News*, 29 July 1938.

In 1939 Waterford Art Museum was opened by the artist Paul Henry. The development of the present collection is outlined by **Peter Jordan.**

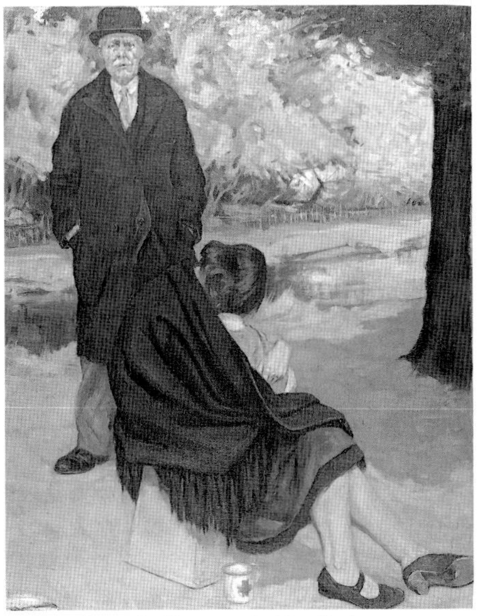

Louis Le Brocquy, Belfast Refugees at Mespil Road, *Dublin, 1941, oil on shantung silk mounted on board, 65 x 51cm, Waterford Municipal Art Collection.*

Farrington's futuristic whimsy reflects in many ways the aspirations of a number of like-minded people, who about this time were lobbying for the establishment of an art gallery, or more precisely art museum, in the city. They were aware that Dublin, Cork, Belfast and, most recently, Limerick already possessed art galleries, and that the time was now right for Waterford to play a role 'in the reconstruction of the cultural life of the nation'.[1] Farrington voices their concern: that such a municipal art collection should be accessible to all, irrespective of financial status; that it would serve a didactic purpose for school children and others interested in art, and that as well as providing a representative selection of Irish and international art; it should feature the work of local artists in a prominent way.

By the mid 1930s, a growing interest in the visual arts was discernible in Waterford. This may seem surprising in view of the fact that it was well known that the government, in the person of An Taoiseach, Eamon de Valera, viewed the fine arts as a luxury which the country could ill afford. Tainted with the traditions of a deposed gentry, the fine arts were not perceived as 'part of native Irish tradition'.[2] However, as early as January 1934, an article appeared in *The Waterford News* entitled, 'Waterford and Art', which described the foundation of a School of Art in Waterford in 1852.[3] It also referred to two highly successful art exhibitions which had taken place in the city during the nineteenth century, and ended with the plea. 'Is it expecting too much to hope that in the near future this city of ours could repeat the experiment of the years 1857 and 1879'?

The response came just over a year later, when in March 1935, the paper reported a 'Remarkable Exhibition of Paintings' at Newtown School, Waterford, together with a suggestion by the Headmaster, Arnold Marsh (husband of the painter, Hilda Roberts)[4] that a permanent municipal gallery should be set up in Waterford.[5] Thus the first of the annual *Waterford Art Exhibitions* was held in the gymnasium of a local school. It consisted of reproductions of Old Master works loaned from the Medici Society in London, and according to Mr Marsh, attracted a great number of enthusiastic visitors, many of whom 'I saw for the first time in my life'.[6]

The exhibition was deemed a great success, and the ensuing euphoria prompted a letter to *The Waterford News* reiterating the need for a local permanent art collection, with the added proviso, that, as well as reproductions of great European works, it should include examples by 'some of the foremost Irish artists of today'.[7] In keeping with the prevalent mood of post-Independence nationalism, the writer proposed that the Corporation should sell off a number of paintings of English kings which were in their possession, as a means of funding the project. These canvases, which reportedly included a portrait of George I by Kneller, had earlier been removed from the civic Council Chamber, and were now languishing in the lumber room of the City Hall.[8]

Later that same year, a second exhibition was staged at Newtown School. It had originally been intended to hold a 'follow up' exhibition of more Medici prints, this time of the Modern schools of painting, but for reasons unclear, they failed to arrive. Thus, fortuitously for the cause of local art, it became necessary 'to use whatever examples of modern painting could be obtained at short notice'.[9] Apart from a number of nineteenth and twentieth century prints, there were forty pictures by Hilda Roberts, including 'some fine portraits of Achill Island children'.[10] Already noted for her portraits, two of which are presently in the Municipal Collection, Roberts had exhibited in Dublin since 1928, and was a prizewinner at the Aonach Tailteann Exhibition of 1932.

Added stimulus to the event was provided by the visit of Mainie Jellett, who gave a lecture on modern art. Apart from her considerable contribution to Irish Art as a painter, Jellett was an active teacher and proselytiser of Modernism.[11] The exhibition was proclaimed a further great success, and speaking again on the prospect of a municipal art collection, Arnold Marsh suggested that the best way to start it off would be to buy some reproductions, and in this way create the nucleus of a collection at no great expense.[12] It is interesting to note their differing perspectives; Marsh looking backwards to an earlier European tradition, one continued in Ireland by the conservative RHA, Jellett forwards to the development of modern Irish art, which she further progressed by co-founding the *Irish Exhibition of Living Art* in 1943.

In March of the following year, 1936, the gymnasium at Newtown was again commandeered, and this time filled to capacity with an exhibition of 150 works.[13] For the first time in the city, an exhibition was held of contemporary Irish art by such eminent practitioners as Sir William Orpen and the President of the RHA, Dermod O'Brien. A passionate advocate of the need to promote art consciousness in Ireland[14], O'Brien proved to be a great supporter of the movement to found a municipal collection in Waterford, and subsequently donated three works towards it. A special feature of the exhibition, which occasioned excited comment, was a separate section devoted to the work of Munster artists including Hilda Roberts and the noted Waterford-born critic, con-

SINCLAIR'S DREAM: THE WATERFORD ART MUSEUM

noisseur and painter Arthur Power. [15]

This success was repeated again in 1937, when the exhibition appears to have been rather more of a mixed bag, though still very much an *Irish* one. This time 160 works were shown, classified as either, *Dublin, Irish* (general) or *Local.* Notable Irish painters such as Seán Keating, Mainie Jellett and Jack B Yeats were represented, but just as in Sinclair's little circular Art Gallery, 'local artists took quite an important place there'.[16] In this and subsequent years it became the practice to engage a well-known artist to officiate at the exhibition's opening. On this occasion it was Paul Henry who did the honours, and when asked to comment on the exhibition, he replied generously and gratifyingly, that it was 'very good indeed, and especially the local stuff'.[17]

Henry, whose essential vision of rural Ireland had featured as the frontispiece of *The Official Free State Handbook* in 1932, was probably the most popular artist in the country at the time. He had contributed several works to the 1937 exhibition, but was noticeably unrepresented the following year, having 'recently sold practically all his pictures'.[18] The reason for this appears to have been an upsurge in the national art market, or put the other way, the market for *National* art, resulting in what *The Waterford News* described as, a veritable 'epidemic' of picture buying. Despite this omission, the 1938 exhibition, offered the viewer according to Hilda Roberts, 'a splendid array of modern Irish work'.[19] Just as in Sinclair's 'little circular Art Gallery', there was a week-day admission charge of 6d, the price of a bottle of stout at the time, but it was arranged that Sundays should be free, 'so that no lover of art need miss a visit'.[20]

The 1938 exhibition was opened by the 'distinguished Dublin man', Jack B Yeats. A review in *The Waterford News* about a week later, commenting on the mounting sales of pictures, noted that, a few years ago 'lovers of pictures and painting in Waterford were a small body'. Today however, 'their numbers are rapidly growing, and amongst all classes, public appreciation is on the increase'.[21] There was certainly increased reportage in the local press of the activities of artists with Waterford connections. These are at times tinged with extravagance, as in the following report featured in *The Waterford News* of 26 May 1939. Under the heading, 'World Famous Waterford Artist', the

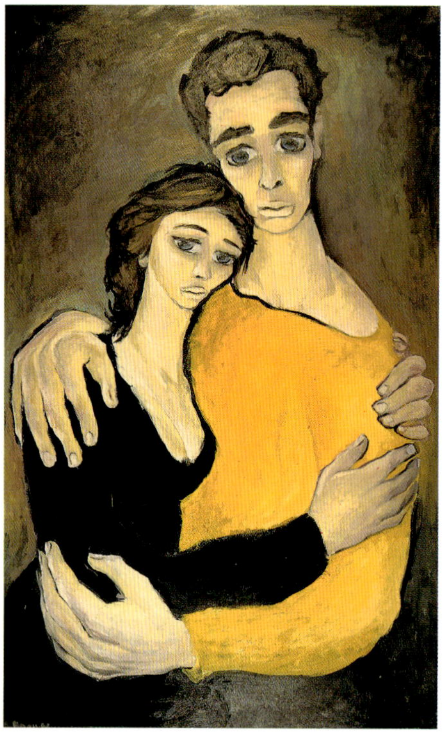

Dany Lartigue, Les Retrouvés, *1944, oil on canvas, 129 x 79.5cm, Waterford Municipal Art Collection.*

writer describes some etchings by Mr Power O'Malley, a native of Ring, County Waterford, as being favourably compared by an expert to those of Rembrandt.

In the light of such burgeoning confidence and enthusiasm, it can have come as little surprise to the editor of *The Waterford News*, when in July 1938, the following circular arrived on his desk. 'In view of the interest in art which has been awakened by the recent exhibitions of pictures in Waterford, we feel that the time has come to establish a permanent collection here'.[22] The letter goes on to cite the example of the city of Limerick as recently succeeding in raising sufficient funds to found an art gallery, and appeals to the public of Waterford for support in a similar undertaking.[23]

During October of that year, a deputation from the city visited the Department of Education in Dublin. Officials there were sympathetic to the venture, and offered support, provided that 'substantial and enthusiastic local demand' could be demonstrated. In a report on the visit, *The Waterford News,* which also voiced full support for the initiative, pointed out that the project offered an important addition to the cultural life of the city, 'not alone for those whose occupation or chief hobby is concerned with art, but for the public in general also'.[24] This egalitarian argument for support is much to the fore of press comment at the time. Remarking on the gratifying response to the public appeal, *The Waterford News* proposed to publish the list of subscribers, in order to demonstrate publicly the 'width and depth' of the support.[25] It is interesting to note however, that the subscribers came largely from the ranks of the Protestant/Anglo-Irish ascendancy[26], though the enthusiasm shown reflects a new confidence in an emergent post-Independence culture.

On 12 May 1939, *The Waterford News* was able to announce that the City Art Gallery was an accomplished fact, and that the official opening was soon to follow. A generous response to the public appeal had enabled the Organising Committee to buy a number of 'pictures of merit' (see below), which together with donated works, would be sufficient to form the nucleus of a collection.[27] The City Commissioner offered the use of a room in the Municipal Library, and this was readily accepted, although with some reservations as to the long-term suitability of the premises.

Commenting at the time on the need for more adequate display facilities for the collection, the Waterford-born artist, critic and statesman, Edward A McGuire, suggested that a grant from public funds should be made available, to secure 'an old and dignified house' for the purpose.[28] He clearly had in mind the example of the old Harcourt Street house in Dublin, which had until recently at that time, held and displayed the Lane pictures, in an 'intimate and friendly atmosphere'.[29] However no such grant proved to be forthcoming, and the search for Sinclair's 'little circular Art Gallery' was to continue.This negative response is scarcely surprising, in view of the economic stringencies of the period, when even a scheme for a series of gramophone records in Irish which would have cost £200, had been cut by the Department of Finance.[30]

At its inauguration, the embryo collection comprised some seventeen works of art, mostly by well-known contemporary Irish artists. While cost and availability may have determined choice to some degree, it also clearly reflects the desire on the part of the organisers to assert a distinctly *National* identity for the collection.[31] Six paintings had been bought by the founding committee, including a

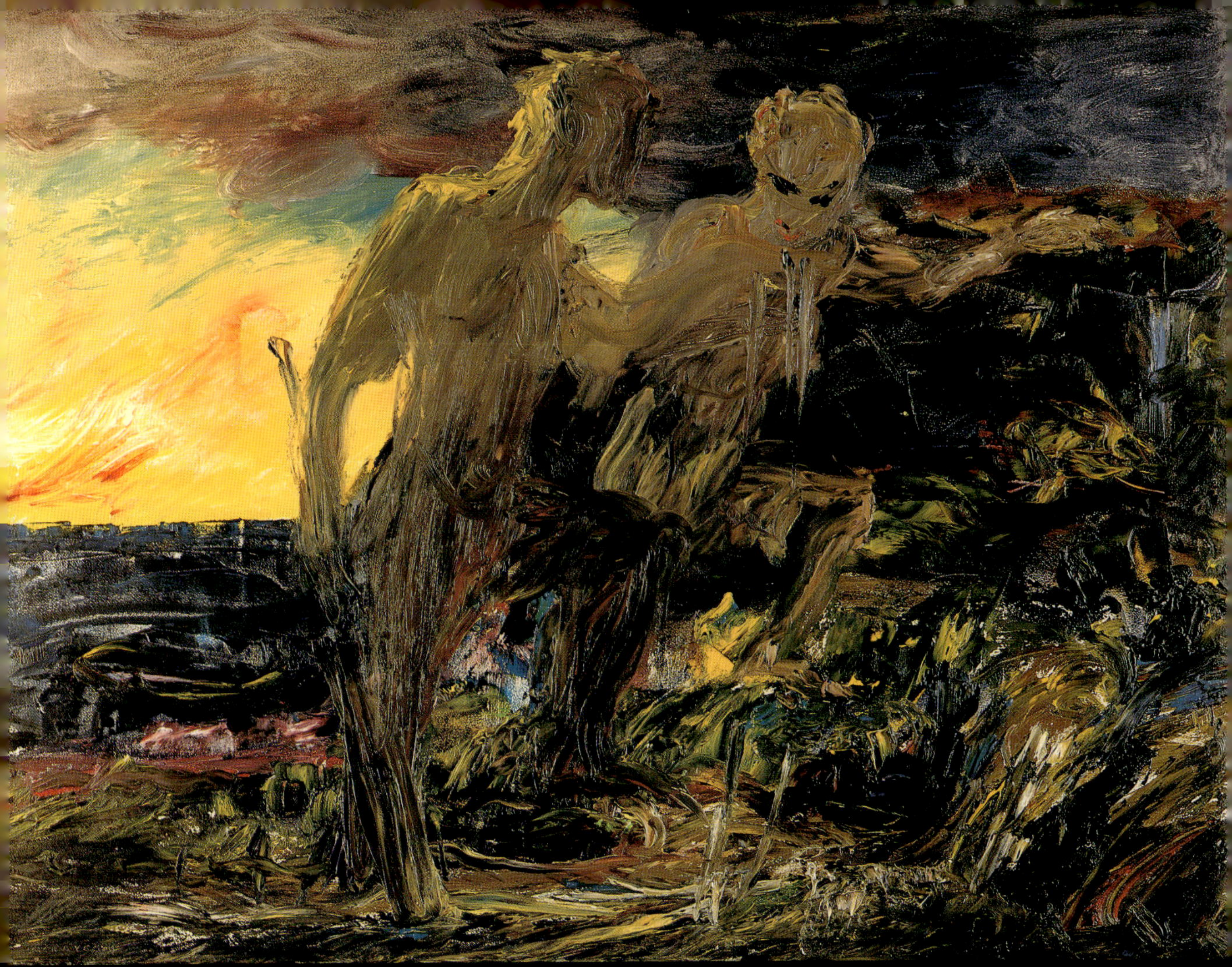

Jack B Yeats, 'While Grass Grows…', 1945, *oil on canvas*, *74 x 61cm*,
Waterford Municipal Art Collection

SINCLAIR'S DREAM: THE WATERFORD ART MUSEUM

pietistic study by Charles Lamb, entitled. *Breton Peasants at Prayer*, and fashionable West of Ireland landscapes by Seán Keating, Frank McKelvey and Maurice MacGonigal.[32] Donated works included landscapes by James Humbert Craig and Harry Kernoff, portraits by Seán Keating and Hilda Roberts, and a marble bust by the nineteenth-century sculptor, John Hogan. Together with these came a mezzotint copy of a self-portrait of Jan Steen, by one Eugene Tilly and an Irish Chippendale chair.[33]

The inclusion of the chair in the collection is an important reminder that the original intention of the founders was not to establish an art gallery *per se*, but an 'Art Museum'. This distinction seems to have been an important one at the time, arising perhaps out of a desire to demonstrate, in a time of austerity, the practical application of artistic principles to the design of useful objects. A year or so earlier, Edward A McGuire, writing in the periodical *Ireland To-day*, and echoing the thoughts of his contemporary, Herbert Read, had called for just such an application of art to industry.[34]

The matter of title is discussed in a short article entitled 'The Waterford Municipal Art Museum' in *The Waterford News* by William Glynn, a teacher at Newtown School.[35] Glynn states that the term 'Art Museum' was consciously chosen to emphasise the educational purpose and wider scope of the proposed institution. '... in addition to painting and sculpture, an Art Museum will find room for furniture, porcelain and in particular, anything representing local craftsmanship at its best – at least one fine case containing representative pieces of Waterford glass'. Again, Glynn like Sinclair, wishes to see 'local art' taking 'quite an important place there'.

In part of a series printed in *The Waterford News*, entitled, 'Under Ireland's Eye', Edward A McGuire discusses Waterford's new picture collection in the context of a national art revival.[36] He states that the fostering of Fine Art is an obligation on the Irish nation builders of the day, if they are to preserve and create a culture. 'There is no reason why we cannot make our people aware of the art of painting by bringing pictures to them in every town in Ireland. The man in the street must be made to know that these picture collections are for him'. To the sceptic who sees art as only for the 'high-

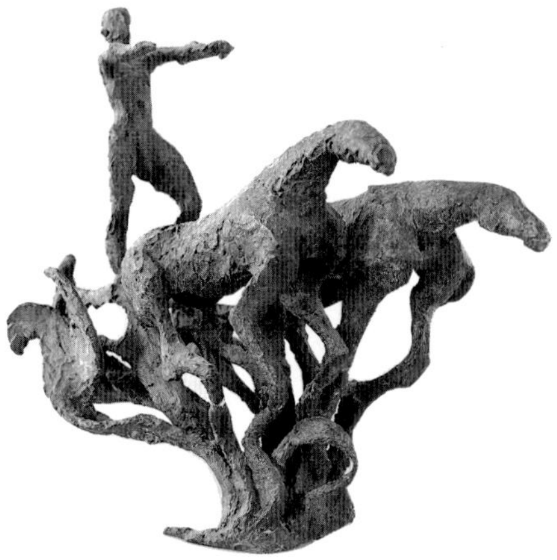

Oisin Kelly, Chariot of Fire, acquired in 1977, bronze, 58 x 72 x 30 cm, Waterford Municipal Collection.

brow', he recommends a visit to the Dublin galleries on a Sunday afternoon, when 'crowds of humble folk are to be seen thronging the halls'. In fact attendance figures at the National Gallery had declined markedly during the late 1930s.[37] Such crusading Arnoldian idealism seems now tainted with condescension, but was in line with the aspirations of the times, whatever the reality.[38]

In Waterford at least, one of McGuire's desires came to fruition, when on 14 July 1939, just fifteen months since the inception of the idea, and in the presence of a large and 'representative' gathering, the Músaem Ealadhan Chathair Phortláirge (Waterford Municipal Art Museum) was formally opened by the artist Paul Henry. After praising the faith and vision of the organisers, Henry welcomed the advent of the Museum as providing a stimulant for students and scholars in Waterford; as providing a source of pleasure and profit to the citizens and as 'a very great asset to the city of Waterford'.[39]

The inception of the Municipal Art Museum, occasioned a certain amount of civic pride, and J K in *The Waterford News* commenting on the event, noted that Waterford could now take its place with its sister cities as a centre to which art students might come to study and learn. He admitted however that, 'the gallery as yet is small compared with those of Dublin and Cork'.[40] In fact the collection as a whole at this point amounted to no more than sixty works, one third of which were on loan from Arthur Power. These included a Delacroix, a Corot and two drawings by Modigliani;[41] so for a brief period, the collection boasted an important European dimension. By 1941 however, Power's temporary loan had been reclaimed, and it was nearly a decade later before the collection gained any more 'art from other countries'. This included a portrait bust of the British composer Ralph Vaughan-Williams, by Jacob Epstein, and a striking image of two embracing wartime refugees, entitled *Les Retrouvés* by the French artist Dany Lartigue.

During the 1940s the collection was steadily augmented by additions from a new source, the charitable trust.[42] As Brian Kennedy has pointed out, during the twenties and thirties Ireland had begun to experience an upsurge in private patronage, aimed at the acquisition of art works for public collections.[43] In 1941, representatives of the committee visited an exhibition of works on offer to Irish galleries by the Thomas Haverty Trust, and obtained five paintings 'of the first rank' for the collection[44] including the mysterious, poetic and stridently coloured, *While Grass Grows* ... by Jack B Yeats. The Trust was to prove a rich vein, providing quality acquisitions on a number of subsequent occasions, such as the fascinating early Le Brocquy, *Belfast Refugees at Mespil Road, Dublin*, 1941, presented in 1945.

Expansion continued throughout the 1950s, 60s and 70s, under the capable guidance of 'The Waterford Art Advisory Committee'[45], a body which evolved from the founding committee, until the collection reached its present size of over two hundred works.[46] An annual grant made available for the acquisition of new works by Waterford Corporation, and later the Arts Council Joint Purchase Scheme, enabled the committee to acquire such pieces as the fine heroic bronze, entitled *Chariot of Fire*, by Oisin Kelly.

It is difficult to gauge the extent of public appreciation of the new museum. In an article in *The Waterford News*, dated 14 February 1941, welcoming the addition of the Yeats painting to the collection, the writer observes that the committee had been 'much gratified by the number of visitors since the gallery was opened, and by the interest shown in unexpected quarters'. However, in another feature dated later that same year, the writer states, 'Though opened nearly two years ago, the gallery is not at all sufficiently known to the people of Waterford'.[47] This conflict of evidence suggests a further gap between aspiration and reality, and the need for qualified acceptance of newspaper reports referring to the collection's 'wide appeal'.

SINCLAIR'S DREAM: THE WATERFORD ART MUSEUM

Whatever the situation with regard to public response, there is constant reference in the newspapers of the time to the shortage of exhibition space, and the quest for a more suitable permanent home for the collection. In the article referred to above, the author looks forward to further expansion of the collection, 'if more adequate premises should become available'. Later that same year, 1941, at the opening of the annual Waterford Art Exhibition at Newtown School, the Mayor Alderman James Aylward, aware of the problem, expressed the wish to see that the splendid art treasures in the possession of Waterford Corporation would be properly housed in the council chamber of the City Hall.[48]

After half a century of troubled and unsatisfactory location,[49] it looks as if Sinclair's dream will at last materialise. Waterford Corporation recently agreed to offer a permanent home to this valuable aspect of the city's cultural heritage. Not in the 'little circular Art Gallery' however, but in the newly refurbished Council Chamber of the City Hall as proposed by Alderman Aylward.[50]

Peter Jordan

Peter Jordan is an art historian and critic who lectures at Waterford RTC. In 1987 he compiled a catalogue of the Waterford Municipal Art Collection. He is currently writing a PhD thesis on the subject of Irish Municipal Art Collections, under the auspices of the Institute of Irish Studies, The Queen's University, Belfast.

NOTES

1. See *The Waterford News*, 15 March 1935, p.5, letter signed, 'An Fweelaun'. A sense of provincial civic rivalry at this time is indicated in an article in *The Waterford News*, 10 December 1937, which refers to Waterford's recent progress in art matters, 'before ever Limerick moved'.
2. See Brian P Kennedy, *Dreams and Responsibilities: the State of the Arts in Independent Ireland*, The Arts Council, Dublin, 1990, p.30.
3. See *The Waterford News*, 12 January 1934, p.9.
4. For a brief biography of Hilda Roberts, see entry by Nicola Gordon Bowe, *Irish Women Artists, From Eighteenth Century to the Present Day*, Exhibition Catalogue (IWA Cat.), The National Gallery of Ireland and The Douglas Hyde Gallery, Dublin, 1987, p.184.
5. See *The Waterford News*, 1 March 1935, p.10.
6. See *The Waterford News*, 8 March 1935, p.10.
7. See letter, signed 'An Fweelaun', ibid.
8. See *The Waterford News*, 25 July 1947, p.4., letter signed 'E.N.', which states that, 'In 1920 when the Sinn Fein organisation captured the Corporation we decided to sell the portraits of three kings believing that they would realise a few thousand pounds ... We engaged Dr Strickland, a Director of the National Gallery, Dublin, to value the pictures. Dr Strickland examined the portraits and declared them worthless'. They were subsequently removed to storage and allowed to dilapidate.
9. See *The Waterford News*, 29 November 1935, p.8.
10. 'When she exhibited in 1932 in a group show of Dublin painters, Hilda Roberts' work was singled out as unique in its promise of genius ...]her collection of child portraits was easily the most outstanding', Nicola Gordon Bowe, IWA Cat., 1987, p.142. No.129.
11. See S B Kennedy, *Irish Art and Modernism, 1880-1950*, The Institute of Irish Studies, QUB, Belfast, 1991, pp.48-49, for a discussion of Jellett's contribution to the Modern Movement in Ireland.
12. See *The Waterford News*, 29 November 1935, p.8.
13. See *The Waterford News*, 13 March 1936, p.7.
14. See *The Waterford News*, 16 February 1940, p.7, for report of a speech on this theme by Dermod O'Brien at the opening of the 1940 Waterford Art Exhibition.
15. A highly respected figure in the city, and occasional contributor of articles on art matters to the local press. See for example, *The Waterford News*, 6 April 1937, p.3, 'Surrealism' and 'Why pictures fetch big money'.
16. See *The Waterford News*, 26 February 1937, p.7.
17. *ibid.*
18. See *The Waterford News*, 4 March 1938, p.5.
19. *ibid.*
20. See *The Waterford News*, 25 February 1938, p.7.
21. See *The Waterford News*, 11 March 1938, p.5. The claim of art's appeal to 'people of all classes', is reiterated by Arnold Marsh.
22. See *The Waterford News*, 8 July 1938, p.7.
23. See *The Waterford News*, 22 October 1937, p.3., and 15 July 1938, p.7. for examples of other letters citing the Limerick precedent.
24. See *The Waterford News*, 28 October 1938, p.9.
25. *ibid.* The list was eventually published in *The Waterford News*, 7 July 1939.
26. R F Foster, *Modern Ireland 1600-1972*, Penguin, London, 1988, p.534 notes that after Independence. 'A modest unofficial form of "Ascendancy" lingered on'.
27. See *The Waterford News*, 12 May 1939.
28. See *The Waterford News*, 16 June 1939, for an article by McGuire entitled, 'Waterford's New Picture Collection'.
29. *ibid.*
30. See J J Lee, *Ireland 1912-1985, Politics and Society*, Cambridge, 1989, p.225.
31. See *The Waterford News*, 26 June 1936, p.9. A pamphlet circulated to the newspaper by W J Jacob, honorary treasurer of The Academy of Christian Art (founded 1929), 'shows that a study and knowledge of art is of great service to Catholics'.
32. See S B Kennedy, *op. cit.* pp.176-79, for a brief analysis of this School.
33. See *The Waterford News*, 7 July 1939, for a full list of donations.
34. See Brian P Kennedy, *op. cit.*, p.37.
35. See *The Waterford News*, 14 July 1939, p.5, article signed, 'W.M.G.'.
36. See *The Waterford News*, 16 June 1939.
37. A Kelly; *Cultural Policy in Ireland*, The Irish Museums Trust, Dublin, 1989, p.38, notes that, 'Gallery attendance figures in 1936 were 39,336, a figure which fell to 24,723 in 1941'.
38. See J J Lee, *op. cit.*, p.129. He cites the example of Eoin McNeill who 'told the Dail in 1923 that Ireland's destiny was to be a teaching nation'.
39. See *The Waterford News*, 21 July 1939, p.8.
40. *ibid.*
41. See *The Waterford News*, 14 July 1939, p.5. The Modigliani drawings in the Gallery at this time are also referred to by Power in his biographical account, *From the Old Waterford House*, The Carthage Press, Waterford and Dublin, 1940, p.59.
42. See *The Waterford News*, 16 June 1939. This method of acquisition is recommended to the organisers in an article by E A McGuire.
43. See S B Kennedy, *op. cit.* pp.84-89, for an account of this phenomenon.
44. See *The Waterford News*, 7 February 1941, p.3., for a full list of acquisitions.
45. A memo dated, 13 May 1949, in the Corporation archives, states that the AAC was constituted on 3 November 1949, as a semi-official committee of Waterford Corporation. See Brian P Kennedy, *op. cit.*, p.102 for an account of the establishment of such committees nationwide.
46. For a full listing of items in the present collection, See Peter Jordan, *Waterford Municipal Art Collection*, Arts Council/Waterford Corporation, 1987.
47. See *The Waterford News*, 30 May 1941, p.6, 'Waterford's Municipal Art Museum'.
48. See *The Waterford News*, 13 June 1941, p.6.
49. Various possible locations were suggested at different times including: one of 'the handsome new (cattle) sheds on the Quay', by Hilda Roberts in 1938, and the recently renovated 'Bishop's Palace' in the early 1970s. The collection remained however an adjunct to the Municipal Library, until the advent of the Garter Lane Arts Centre in 1984. The bulk of it was subsequently removed to a store-room in the City Hall for security reasons.
50. Proposed by the City Manager in his Estimates Report to the City Council, December, 1992.

ART NEEDLEWORK IN IRELAND

Anthony Symondson SJ discusses magnificent altar frontals in Dublin and Kildare, designed by the architect Sir Ninian Comper and executed by the Royal Irish School of Art Needlework (1894-1915) at the height of its achievement under Lady Mayo's patronage.

In 1894 two significant developments in the applied arts took place in Dublin. The first was the founding of the Arts and Crafts Society of Ireland by Dermot Robert Wyndham Bourke, seventh earl of Mayo. The second, the re-founding of the Royal Irish School of Art Needlework by his wife, Geraldine Ponsonby.[1] Both ventures were linked by associations wider than the mutual enthusiasm of their founders. The Arts and Crafts Society and the Irish School were strongly influenced by Lord Mayo's friend, William Morris. They forged links with major English Arts and Crafts designers and they shared analogous intentions. The Irish School played a conspicuous part in the four exhibitions mounted by the Arts and Crafts Society in Dublin between 1895 and 1910 and its work was often isolated for praise.[2]

Little these days is known of the Royal Irish School of Art Needlework, mainly because it suddenly came to an end in 1915, leaving no records, but also because the greater part of its work was domestic or confined to costume, thus perishable and easily discarded or forgotten.[3] It would now be almost impossible to create any firm impression of the Irish School's achievement but for the survival in Kildare Cathedral and St Patrick's Cathedral, Dublin, of three of a series of five richly embroidered altar frontals designed by the Scottish church architect, Sir Ninian Comper (1864-1960),[4] executed by the School between 1897 and 1902. These cast light on the exceptionally high standards achieved by the School's ecclesiastical work. The identification of these frontals was made possible by the survival of Comper's designs, kept in the Drawings Collection of the British Architectural Library, London.[5]

The Irish School was founded in 1882 by the Vicereine, Katrine, Countess Cowper, who was so impressed by the skill in embroidery of certain Irish ladies on the borders of her circle that she brought them together under a committee which superintended the financial and business arrangements necessary for the sale of their work. The manageress and artistic director was the Baroness Pauline Prochazka. Lady Cowper's intention was primarily to relieve poor gentlewomen. She was following the same pattern as the English Royal School of Art Needlework, South Kensington, which was also partly founded in 1872 to supply suitable employment for indigent gentlewomen. In 1901

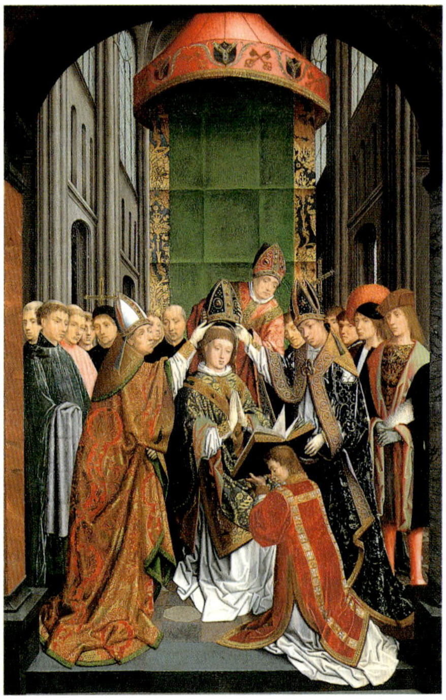

Master of the Youth of St Romold, The Enthronement of St Romold as Bishop of Dublin, c. 1490. *Oil on oak panel, 114.5 x 71.3 cm. (NGI cat. no. 1380). This panel exemplifies Comper's aesthetic and liturgical ideals expressed in his early work.*

Lady Mayo published an account of its origins in which she suggested that the failure of Lady Cowper's venture was not so much the result of lack of money or patronage, as of cumbersome management, 'the difficulty of freeing taste from the quagmire of ignorance' and the charitable basis of employment which contributed an 'eleemosynary element fatal to success'.[6]

She kept the School in its existing premises, 23 Clare Street, Dublin, but reorganised the whole system, placed it on a sounder commercial basis, made it less exclusively genteel, and re-opened it under a new executive committee with a paid manageress and fourteen workers. Fee-paying pupils were admitted and lessons were given in all branches of art embroidery, including church work. Among the pupils were women who wished to make a trade of their embroidery, members of religious orders and girls from convent schools.[7] In this way the School entered the Irish industries movement.

In 1899 the Irish School moved to newly-built premises, 20 Lincoln Place, which it shared with the Royal Institute of Architects of Ireland, next door to the Irish Industries Association, where it remained for sixteen years. By 1901 the number of workers had increased to twenty-three and Lady Mayo was able to claim that 'the embroidery that is sent from our house will prove to future generations that the women of the nineteenth century are not behind those of previous times in the artistic and skilful use of their needle'.[8]

Lady Mayo was a woman of broad culture and accomplishments. Thomas Sadleir described her rare qualities soon after her death in 1944:

> *From her youth she had united a gracious personality with a wide range of culture and a keen love of outdoor amusements, a combination seldom found. As a girl she was fond of music, her enthusiasm inducing her to make a collection of historical instruments. Later she became a keen collector of many forms of art, furniture, china, mezzotints, needlework, of which she acquired specimens in several European countries. Poultry, gardening and the mysteries of the still-room also occupied her attention. But though a discerning connoisseur of the arts and a real lover of the countryside by inclination, she was, above all, a kindly woman, of most high purpose. Her charity was not merely the cash down bazaar type; it was that untranslatable* caritas *of the Romans of old, that could and did extend pity even to one's enemies ... During the many years she and her household lived at Palmerstown, they made it a real centre of hospitality, where sportsmen, artists and bibliophiles, rubbing shoulders with English politicians and authors, were constantly entertained.*[9]

She was the prime mover behind Lord Mayo's founding of the Arts and Crafts Society and his own burgeoning interest in the applied arts.

Lady Mayo was dedicated to making art needlework in Ireland take its place in the front rank of art. She was herself an accomplished embroideress and designer and had great enthusiasm for the craft:

> *I love those beautiful designs – those delicate traceries which adorn the wonderfully-wrought vestments, the quilts and the*

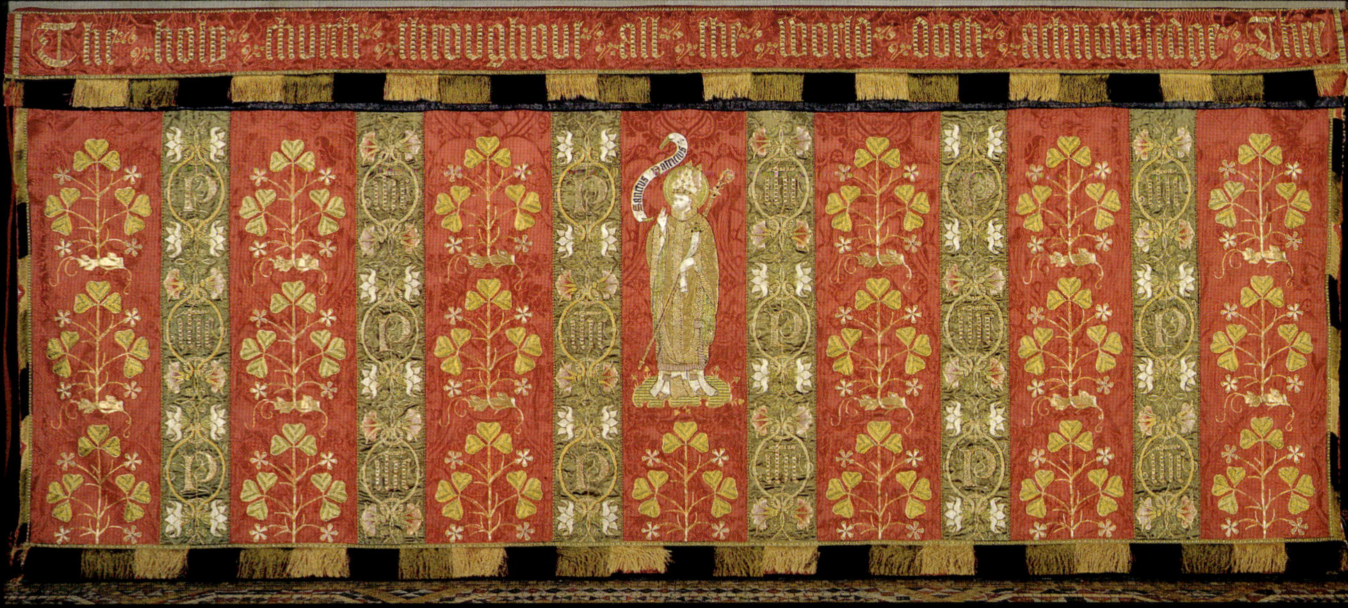

Crimson frontal for the high altar, St Patrick's Cathedral, Dublin, 1899-1900, 280 x 150 cm.

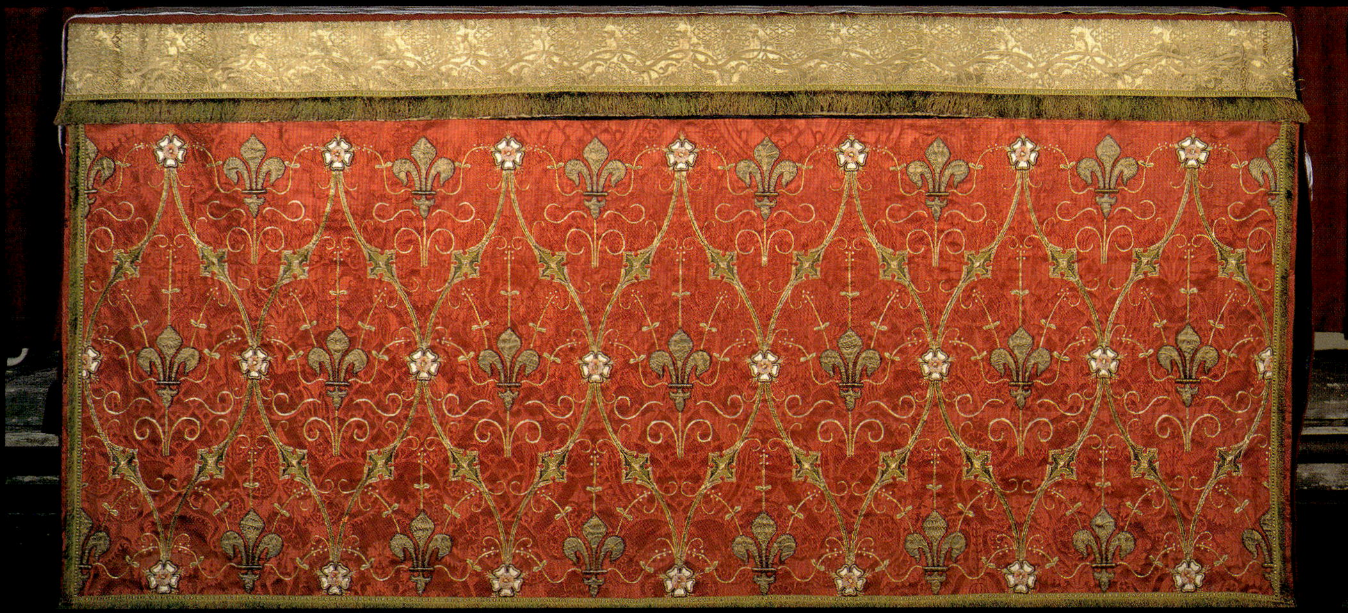

Rose-red frontal for the lady chapel, St Patrick's Cathedral, Dublin, 1900-01, 213 x 110 cm.

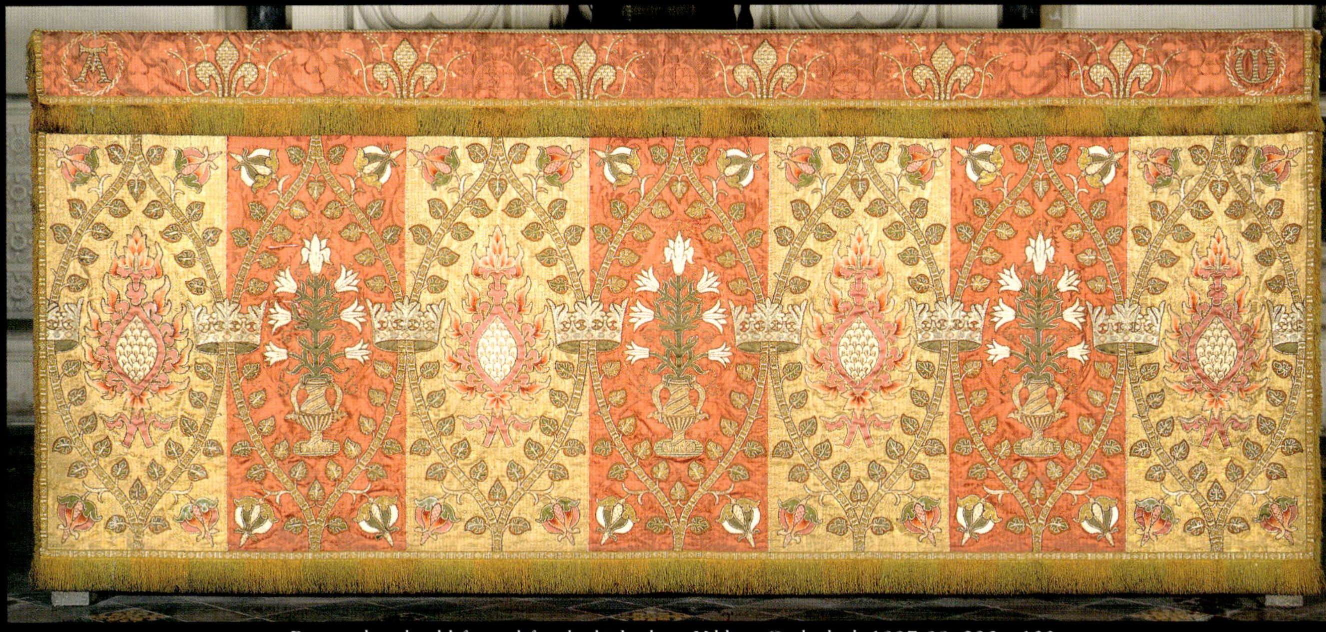

Rose-red and gold frontal for the high altar, Kildare Cathedral, 1897-98, 230 x 100 cm.

ART NEEDLEWORK IN IRELAND

> *screens, to execute which (with marvellous and complicated stitches introduced) formed the principal occupation of the lady of olden times. Her frame was her close and intimate companion, and these elaborate art pieces filled the long hours of solitude imposed upon her by her household tyrant. Who can say whether she was a whit less happy than we in our advanced freedom?*[10]

In the first exhibition of the Arts and Crafts Society, in 1895, Lady Mayo showed an embroidered linen cushion cover, adapted from a drawing by the English church architect, John Dando Sedding, which was praised for the decorative effect it achieved by simple means.

In 1897 Alan Cole, the Official Examiner in Art, of the Department of Science and Art, South Kensington, visited Irish lace-making and embroidery schools in order to help them raise their standards of design. He included the Irish School and made a distinction between it and other schools he had visited:

> *I should perhaps say that the Institution is hardly a school in the stricter sense of the word: the greater amount of work is done by ladies, who are glad of the occupation and of its remuneration; when called upon, the school provides instruction to beginners and learners.*

There he met Lady Mayo and Miss Harriet Beresford, the Manageress. Cole discussed some of the revisions he thought might be adopted in the ornamentation of the embroideries with Miss Beresford and Mrs Swan, the School's designer and draughtswoman, who was also employed to look after patterns and signs. When he was shown specimens of the different kinds of embroidery that were being done he noticed their similarity to the work of the Royal School of Art Needlework, South Kensington. Later, at Palmerstown, he showed Lady Mayo photographs of work which he thought would provide better exemplars. In his report Cole wrote, 'Lady Mayo was much interested in them and thought important suggestions could be derived from them fot the improvement of embroideries done at her school'.[11]

Lady Mayo's major innovation was in the design of the work produced by the Irish School. Baroness Prochazka was described by Mrs Ernest Hart as having 'a happy genius for designing' but from descriptions of her work it was heavily dependent upon copying old patterns. For artistic direction Lady Mayo turned to England. She was in correspondence with

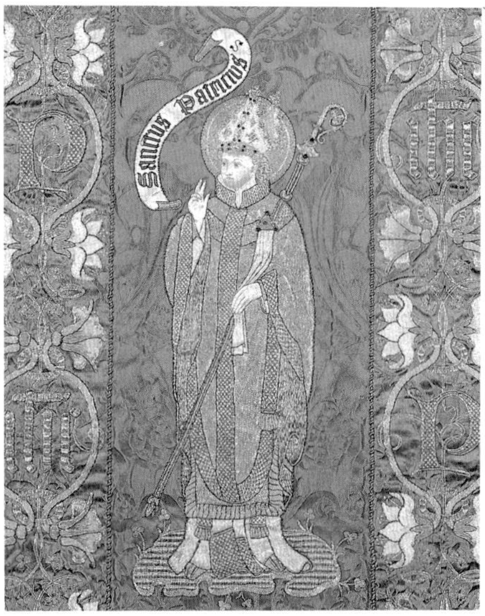

Detail of St Patrick, central panel, frontal for the high altar, St Patrick's Cathdral, Dublin, 1899-1900.

some of the 'best designers of the day'.[12] The catalogues of the exhibitions of the Arts and Crafts Society are instructive in identifying some of them. They included Walter Crane and Kate Greenaway[13] (both of whom designed book-covers); work was made up from designs supplied by Morris & Co. A surprising choice was the Revd Ernest Geldart, an English clerical architect who had been a pupil of Alfred Waterhouse and who was the author of *The Art of Garnishing Churches* (1882) and the *Manual of Church Decoration and Symbolism* (1899). Geldart's work was influenced more by the Aesthetic Movement of the 1880s than the new directions initiated by the Arts and Crafts Movement. John Ninian Comper's association with the Irish School was established early in Lady Mayo's reformation and was occasioned by a commission for an altar frontal for Kildare Cathedral. It should not, however, be thought that the Irish School was exclusively bound to England. Celtic design, inspired by the Book of Kells, was sometimes applied, especially in some of the magnificent embroidered dresses which became a principal feature of the School's work.[14]

Comper was a pupil of the church architect, George Frederick Bodley. In 1888 he had established an ecclesiastical practice in partnership with William Bucknall, a pupil of the architect Edward Robert Robson. Comper became the most influential church architect practising in England during the first half of the twentieth century. At this time he was lodging with Father George Hollings SSJE, a Cowley Father who was chaplain of the Society of the Sisters of Bethany, an Anglican religious order, in Lloyd Street, Clerkenwell.[15] Like many Anglican convents, the order had an embroidery room, but not then one of noticeable distinction. In 1886 Comper, at the age of twenty-two, had been invited to design a mitre for their sacristy.[16] Soon after, the School of Embroidery of the Sisters of Bethany was founded under Comper's direction. Its object was 'to follow as closely as possible upon the lines of the old English work in its best days'. These were understood to have been the fourteenth and fifteenth centuries.[17]

In this way Comper moved from the influences of the Aesthetic Movement which he had imbibed from Bodley. He declined to follow the free expression of the Arts and Crafts but established an independent line of his own, basing his work on late-medieval precedent. The Bethany School came to produce the finest church embroidery in the British Isles, higher than the standards of other Anglican convent embroidery rooms. In time the school achieved work of matchless quality which was the most accomplished at that time to be found in Northern Europe.

In 1896 Comper completed the chapel of St Sepulchre in the crypt of St Mary Magdalene's, Paddington. Comper's design was inspired by English medieval miniatures and Flemish panel paintings. It is a living fusion of both influences. It was directly influenced by the fifteenth-century chapel of St Mary Undercroft in Canterbury Cathedral. But as an expression of the late-medieval Gothic of Northern Europe, in which Flemish mingled with English influences, it demonstrated Comper's magical power of resurrecting Gothic. The chapel and its furniture made a powerful impact upon ecclesiastical taste.[18]

Integral to the chapel's iconography is an altar frontal of yellow velvet embroidered with two tiers of seraphim divided into five panels by thin orphreys of gold embroidered with the monogram of St Mary Magdalene.

In 1897 Comper met Mrs Percy Wyndham when she was brought to see the chapel by Father Philip Waggett SSJE.[19] Madeline Wyndham is today best known for being the châteleine of Clouds,

ART NEEDLEWORK IN IRELAND

a country house at East Knoyle in Wiltshire, designed by Philip Webb. She was the mother of George Wyndham[20] the politician; her three daughters were dramatically painted by John Singer Sargent. Her children were members of an exclusive aristocratic group known as the Souls, all of whom were in polite revolt against the Victorianism of the older generation. Mrs Wyndham was also a London hostess with a house at 44 Belgrave Square. An admirer of the Pre-Raphaelites, she was a friend and patron of William Morris and Sir Edward Burne-Jones and was painted by George Frederick Watts. An enamellist, she was a pupil and patron of Alexander Fisher, an Arts and Crafts silversmith and enamellist, whose work she actively encouraged.[21]

What most impressed her in St Sepulchre's chapel was the altar frontal. At the time she met Comper, she had long been closely involved in the Royal School of Art Needlework, South Kensington. Her experience had been sought by her friend Geraldine Mayo in her own revival of the Irish School in Dublin. Mrs Wyndham tried to persuade Comper to become the South Kensington School's artistic director but he declined. When Lady Mayo sought advice on a suitable designer for an altar frontal she recommended Comper without reserve.[22]

From the moment of their introduction by Mrs Wyndham, Lady Mayo and Comper established an instinctive sympathy. They were contemporaries and remained friends for the rest of her life.[23] Quite apart from their interest in church embroidery and the applied arts, they shared the same religious convictions. Anglo-Catholicism was the guiding spiritual force in Lord and Lady Mayo's English circle. Many of the Mayos' friends became Comper's patrons. When they were in London they both formed part of the congregation of St Cyprian's, Clarence Gate, from its completion in 1903; it was Comper's early masterpiece. Lady Mayo regarded it as the most beautiful church in London.[24]

Kildare Cathedral was re-opened in 1896 by the Archbishop of Canterbury, Edward White Benson, after a long and surprisingly restrained restoration by GE Street. Its rescue, after lying roofless for three hundred years, was greeted with enthusiasm by the ecclesiastically-minded members of the Church of Ireland in Co Kildare. There was, for example, Mrs Wakefield of Carnalway Lodge. Since her widowhood in 1888 she had given her energies and fortune to relieving the local Catholic poor, to whom she was devoted, and re-building St Patrick's, Carnalway, in the Hiberno-Romanesque style under the direction of James Franklin Fuller.[25] She offered the Dean an altar frontal and turned to the Irish School for its execution.

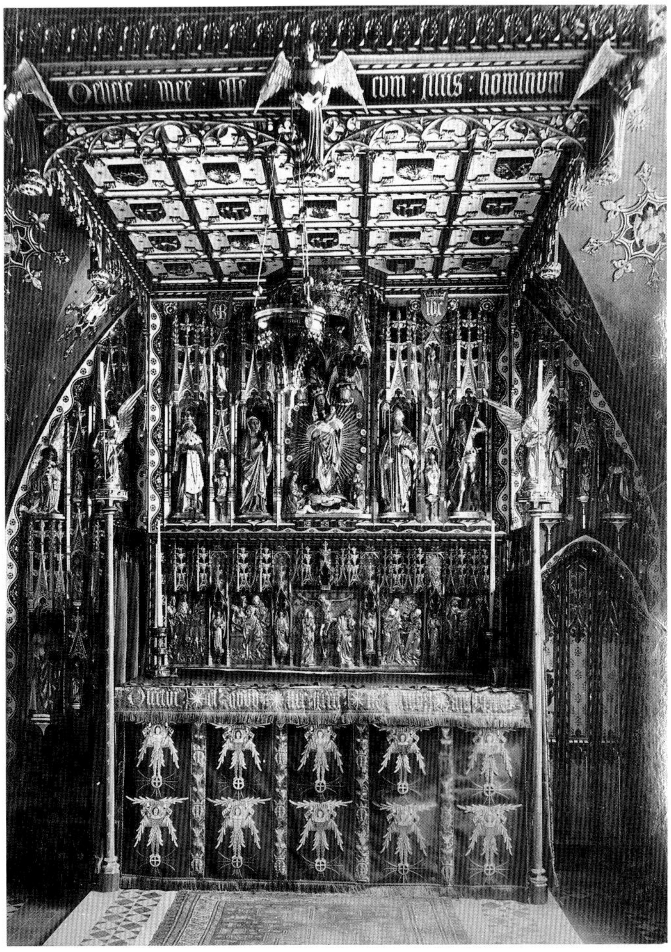

Chapel of St Sepulchre, St Mary Magdalene, Paddington, London, 1895-96. The altar frontal led to Lady Mayo's introduction to Comper by Mrs Percy Wyndham.

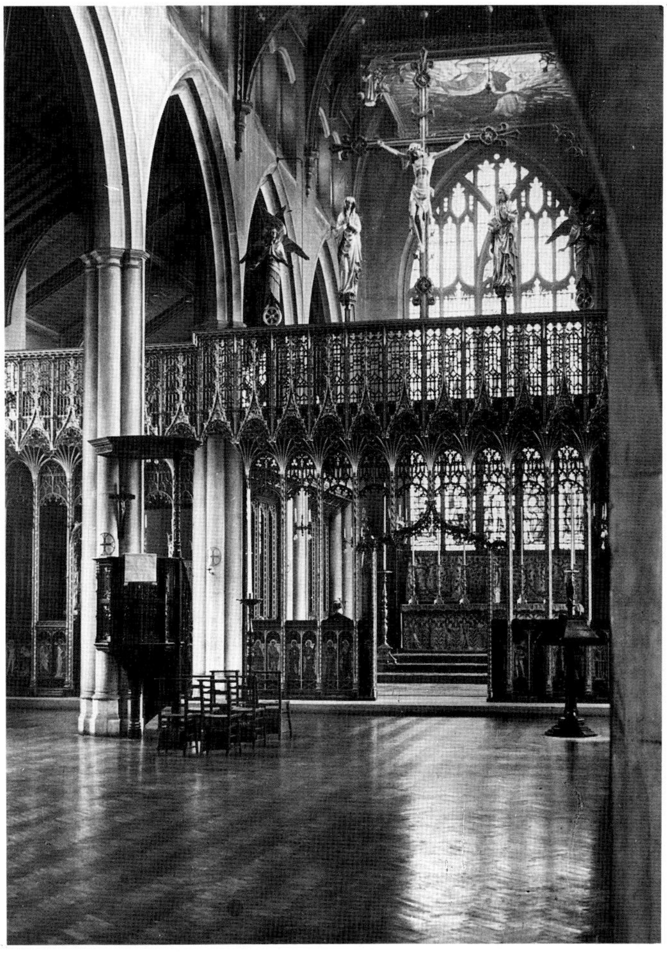

St Cyprian, Clarence Gate, London, 1902-03. Lady Mayo considered it to be the most beautiful church in London and was a member of the congregation. The rose briar patterns on the altar hangings are similar to those first designed by Comper for the frontal at Windsor Castle.

ART NEEDLEWORK IN IRELAND

Lady Mayo found it difficult to fulfil her Anglo-Catholic convictions in the puritanical bareness and coldness of the Church of Ireland. The opportunity of providing an altar frontal for Kildare Cathedral designed by such an artist as Comper was eagerly seized. Not only would it enhance the reputation and standard of the Irish School but, indirectly, would contribute to a better standard of churchmanship.

Comper did not like to design windows, furniture or embroidery for churches without knowing who was the patron saint and the date of the building. He wanted to establish his work in local tradition and make it an integral part of its architectural context.[26] At Kildare, pictorial iconography was forbidden under a severe application of the Church of Ireland's canons; but the legend of St Brigid inspired the frontal's symbolism.

Elaborately embroidered in alternate panels of cloth of gold and crimson silk damask, a row of vesica-shaped branches, executed in metallic braid with leaves of gold thread, contain alternate centres representing pineapples in couched gold thread, alive with St Brigid's eternal flame, executed in rose-red and pink floss; and lilies in green and white floss, heavily outlined, standing in vases of couched gold thread, symbolizing her virginity. Linking the alternating panels are crowns of silver thread, symbolizing her heavenly reward. The spandrels formed by the points of the vesicas are embroidered with formalised pomegranates, in silk floss, completed by a fringe of parti-coloured silk in two shades of green. The super-frontal is worked with a row of six *fleurs de-lys* in gold basket stitch on a crimson ground, with the Alpha and Omega enclosed in plaited circles at each extremity, and has a matching parti-coloured fringe.

Comper's design is not a replica of fifteenth-century work, even though it exhibits the mentality of a Flemish panel painter. It is a fusion of his own personal elements, precedent and naturalism. For instance, the vases of lilies are taken from the outer panels of the Annunciation in van Eyck's painting of *The Adoration of the Mystic Lamb*, in Ghent, translated into embroidery. The flowers and fruit are directly modelled from nature. Although they make a formalised pattern, they retain their freshness and were executed to look as though they had been newly laid on the surface of the frontal. The disposition of these elements is conceived in late-medieval terms but in a way entirely personal to Comper himself.

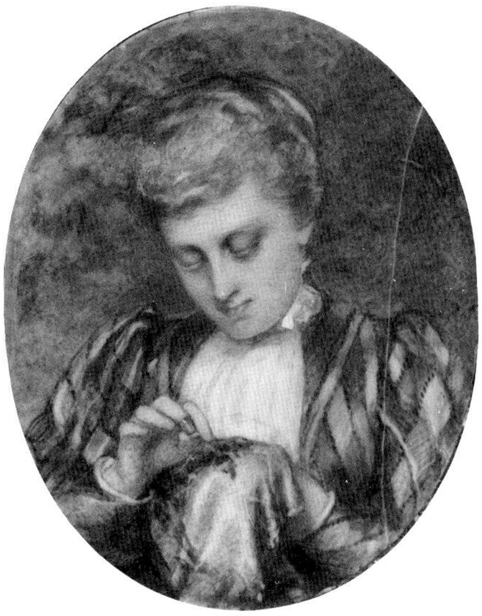

Geraldine, Countess of Mayo (1863-1944), *portrait miniature showing her at her embroidery frame. Private Collection.*

For the Irish School, the Kildare frontal represented a *tour de force*, demonstrating the standards it had begun to achieve under Comper's influence. When it was finished Lady Mayo declared: 'I think I may say, without fear of contradiction, that it is about as good a specimen of artistic needlework as the present day can produce'.[27]

Mrs Wakefield was equally pleased. She commissioned Comper in 1898 to design the east window of Carnalway church. It is a striking window, representing an idealistic depiction of *The Transfiguration*. The *Irish Ecclesiastical Gazette* praised it, describing it as 'not only beautiful but elevating, the best quality of glass, unique, uncommon and luminous'; but the window's late-Perpendicular Gothic style and the ruby-coloured robes of the angels were considered to be out of character with the Hiberno-Romanesque character of the church.[28] Later still, in 1902, Mrs Wakefield commissioned a small gilded reredos, representing *Christ at Emmaus*.[29]

The success of the Kildare frontal led to further commissions. The national cathedral of St Patrick, Dublin, was an obvious setting for the work of the Irish School. Lady Mayo had, however, been anticipated in 1891 by the Dean's daughter, Miss Minna Jellett, who had initiated an ambitious scheme for a sequence of heavily embroidered altar frontals for the high altar and lady chapel. Most were executed by the embroidery school of the Anglican community of St Mary the Virgin, Wantage. Miss Jellett died in 1898, and for the continuation of the scheme the Dean turned to Lady Mayo.[30] Internal tradition suggests that Lady Mayo's involvement might have been controversial; there are no references to the frontals commissioned by Dean Jellett in the cathedral muniments, nor are they referred to in the *Irish Ecclesiastical Gazette*.

The frontal for the high altar was designed as a national statement. A figure of St Patrick occupies the centre of seven panels on a softly-patterned ground of crimson silk. He is represented vested, croziered and mitred, in the act of blessing, standing on a green shamrock-powdered sward. The figure is executed in gold and green silk appliqué, embroidered in couched gold thread and white floss, with small jewels in the crocketted mitre. The six flanking panels are embroidered with conventionalised sprigs of shamrock and gold daisies divided by six orphreys of yellow green silk, embroidered in gold couched work with the monogram IHS alternating with St Patrick's own monogram, unified by borders of white crown imperial lilies and roses in white and rose floss silk. It has a crimson super-frontal inscribed 'The Holy Church throughout all the world doth acknowledge Thee', (from the *Te Deum*), in black-letter, executed in green, black and gold thread, divided by small sprigs of shamrock. The frontal is a work of delicacy and refinement, demonstrating the finish, faultless and exquisite, achieved by the Irish School at what had become the best period of its life.

In 1900 Queen Victoria made her last state visit to Dublin. She was the President of the Irish School and while she was in Dublin she was shown examples of the School's work which greatly impressed her. She gave two commissions, of which the first was for an altar frontal for the lady chapel of St Patrick's. Comper was chosen as the designer for both of them. The lady chapel frontal is simpler than the frontal for the high altar. The design is composed of an overall pattern of cusped and linked vesicas in gold thread, unified by formalised powderings of dog roses in white floss and *fleurs-de-lys* in cloth-of-gold appliqué on a rose-red ground. It has a plain super-frontal of cloth of gold with a fringe of yellow green. There is a distinction in the colour of the frontal, rose-red

ART NEEDLEWORK IN IRELAND

rather than the crimson of the frontal for the high altar. The adoption of this tone had serious implications for the future of Comper's work, of sufficient significance to justify a digression.

Purity of colour was an essential element of Comper's aesthetic quest. It was for this reason that, in 1893, he had begun to design his own ecclesiastical textiles which were woven by a long established firm of Spitalfields silk weavers, M Perkins & Son, of 25-27 Curtain Road, Shoreditch.[31] Under the influence of Bodley, the fashion had set in in church work for muted half-tones, olive green, brownish or scarlet reds.[32] Comper saw that they were not true to the colours he had seen in medieval textiles and embroidery, nor to the luminous purity of colour found in Flemish panel paintings and illuminated manuscripts. His early attempts to achieve the old traditional red are found in the Kildare frontal and the frontal for the high altar of St Patrick's. What he sought even more ardently was the pure rose colour seen, not only in Flemish paintings,[33] but surviving in the rose-red hangings of Central and Southern Italian churches.

In the early summer of 1900 Comper had made his first visit to Rome. What impressed him, and influenced his evolution as an artist, were the compartments of bright, deep-coloured blue set in the solidly gilded coffered ceilings of St John Lateran, juxtaposed with the basilica's rose-red hangings. They prepared the ground, and sowed the seed, of an aesthetic revision that would take Comper from his exclusive Northern European Gothic ideals to others of diverse and far-ranging influence.[34]

Fresh from Rome and under the influence of what he had seen of Mediterranean colour, these royal commissions led to a significant development in his design for embroidery and evolution of colour in his search for the desired rose-red in which Lady Mayo played a decisive part.

She introduced him to Sir Thomas Wardle, of Leek, in Staffordshire, whose experiments in vegetable and oriental dyeing and art printing on silk, cotton and wool had made him the foremost dyer of his time. Wardle was a friend of the Pre-Raphaelites. He had taught William Morris all he knew about dyeing. Comper told him that he wanted to use the pure traditional dyes in his experiments, dyes that Morris and Bodley avoided, substituting recipes of their own. Comper had

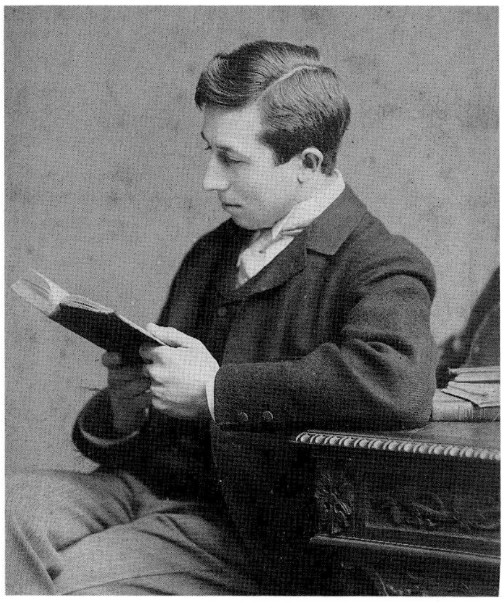

Sir Ninian Comper (1864-1960).

secured a piece of Italian rose-red silk which had been brought back from Sicily by his friend Mrs Edmund McClure.[35] Wardle was able to reproduce it, and other colours, with greater scientific accuracy than the original and also to secure its fastness.[36] The result was first used in the altar frontal for the lady chapel of St Patrick's.

Both altar frontals appear to have excited muted antagonism, despite their beauty and standard of execution. The frontal for the lady chapel, for instance, was not used after the formation of the Irish Free State in 1922 because the *fleurs-de-lys* and roses were considered to be royalist symbols. The colour for the frontal for the high altar was objected to on the ground that St Patrick was not a martyr, while the absence of pentecostal symbolism made it unsuitable for use at Whitsun. The choice of colour was made by Comper because red was the most frequently used liturgical colour in Northern European medieval sequences. He was antagonistic at this period of his life to the modern Roman colour sequence which was followed by other frontals in St Patrick's. He believed that it contravened the ornaments rubric of the Book of Common Prayer which stipulated that what had prevailed in the chancels of English churches in the second year of the reign of King Edward VI 1548-49, was the standard which should apply to all Anglican churches and cathedrals.

But quite apart from these objections I suspect that there was an instinctive prejudice against work that was so single-mindedly medieval, in which St Patrick was represented with such meticulous pontifical fidelity. Dean Jellett appeared to have given Lady Mayo and Comper a free hand. The occasional use, until recently, of these frontals has led to their immaculate condition, as fresh as the day they were made.[37]

Comper only once visited Ireland, spending two days, 14 and 15 May 1902, in connection with his work for the Irish School and for Mrs Wakefield at Carnalway, staying a night there and meeting Lady Mayo in Dublin next day. He loved it. In a letter to his mother, written in pencil on board the *Anglia* leaving Dublin, he tells how he took a night train from Euston to Holyhead and then the early morning mail packet to Kingstown:

> *I had a long day yesterday, arriving in Dublin about 7.30 and at Carnalway at about 10.30. It was about 3am when we approached Holyhead. A wild moon with two rifts in the morning sky; then a red lighthouse and a long line of white surf; and in fear I climbed up into my bed on board and awaited the tossing that never came! In the morning the sunshine was beautiful on Dublin bay, and all along to Harristown, my last station, the Wicklow mountains were beautiful and blue behind a foreground of pale English green, so different from the pines at Braemar.*
>
> *In the afternoon I drove through the great military camp to Kildare and saw the small cathedral church, and my altar frontal (as also my altar frontal at St Patrick's today). At Carnalway I saw the glass which we painted for the east window about 2 years ago, and arranged for a reredos.*
>
> *My hostess, Mrs Wakefield, was full of praise of the Irish Catholics, and I am almost surprised to find how much I have felt in this respect, as if I had crossed over to France or Belgium. So far as two days in a small area can give one an impression of Ireland, I am much pleased with it; what strikes me most of all is that it seems a godly place. I have been wandering about Dublin quite at random all this evening.*[38]

The second commission given by Queen Victoria to the Irish School was for an altar frontal of white silk for the Queen's private chapel, Windsor Castle. Comper recognised that the frontal was of determinant importance as much for the Irish School as for his own artistic development; but it gave him a great deal of trouble. He strongly believed in the medieval practice of applying heraldry as ornament. A royal commission for a

ART NEEDLEWORK IN IRELAND

chapel in Windsor Castle, adjacent to St George's Hall with its integral associations with medieval chivalry and the Order of the Garter, made the application of heraldry altogether suitable. Comper's design placed a figure of St George slaying the dragon in the centre between shields of Queen Victoria and the Prince Consort, both encircled by the garter, on a ground of Tudor rose briars.

The Queen was approaching the end of her reign. When Comper's drawing was submitted for approval it got no further than Princess Beatrice who objected to heraldry and sent an amendment for a sacred monogram for the centre. By the time the second design was ready, the Queen was dead; but on re-submission King Edward VII accepted the original.[39]

Writing in 1907, in an article on art embroidery in Ireland, published in association with the Irish International Exhibition, Miss Beresford, the Irish School's manageress, writing under her married name of Mrs Domvile, isolated the Windsor frontal for description when she referred to ecclesiastical embroidery and stated that: 'This specimen of Irish industries had been much admired'.[40] But unaccountably she wrote that the frontal was made for St George's Chapel, Windsor, whereas Comper's drawings, and his subsequent reminiscences, show that it was made for the private chapel at Windsor Castle.

Regrettably, the altar frontal is no longer to be found at Windsor, nor in the Royal Collection, and no references to it survive in the Royal Archives. In addition to its value as a work of art, it is significant not only in Comper's development as a designer but in demonstrating how he used precedent.

The precedent for the Tudor rose briars in the Windsor frontal came from a cope of gold tissue belonging to Stonyhurst College, Lancashire, which formed part of the vestments bequeathed by King Henry VII to Westminster Abbey in 1509. The structure of the woven design is in the form of sinuous branches of rose briars enclosing the Tudor badge and portcullises.[41]

Comper did not see this cope until his first visit to Stonyhurst in 1924. In 1886, the year he had established his association with the Sisters of Bethany, Lady Marion Alford published her monumental volume, *Needlework as Art*, a work of immense influence upon the evolution of art embroidery, dedicated to Queen Victoria.

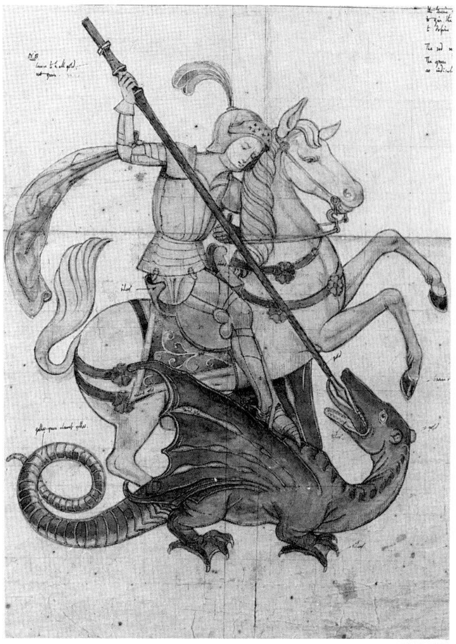

Sir Ninian Comper, Design for centre of altar frontal for the King's private chapel, Windsor, 1901, *Pencil, pen, and wash on paper, 72 x 48 cm. (Drawings Collection, British Architectural Library, RIBA, London).*

Comper knew this work and read it at an impressionable period of his life.[42] It would also have been known to Lady Mayo. Many of its sentiments are echoed in her own account of her enthusiasm for embroidery and her aesthetic ideals.

Lady Alford isolated for praise and emulation English late-medieval embroidery and the embroidery and textiles of Flanders:

> *All the most beautiful and picturesque needlework that we possess of the truly ecclesiastical Gothic type, and which belongs to the perfect flowering of the art, is of the fourteenth and fifteenth centuries, just before the spirit of the Renaissance crept northward over Europe, preceding the reformation and its iconoclastic effacements. ... The perfection of the embroideries of Flanders of that period has never been exceeded, and it continues still to produce the most splendidly executed compositions in gold and silken needlework, of every variety of stitches.*[43]

She illustrated the Stonyhurst cope, proposing it as a fruitful precedent;

> *I should advise the young ecclesiastical designer to study the principles which guided the designers of some of the finest Gothic examples which remain to use, such as the great Stonyhurst cope, and the palls of the different London companies. All these have their brilliant and effective treatment; they are intended to be glorious, and either represent massive jeweller's work or tissues of wrought gold.*[44]

Those winding briars in the Stonyhurst cope formed, from their first application in the Windsor frontal, a conspicuous feature in Comper's subsequent design for embroidery. He translated them into painted decoration, sculpture and painted glass as well as embroidery, to the point of almost wearisome repetition. But it is unlikely that he would have developed this theme so consistently if he had not first recognised its suitability for a royal commission analogous to King Henry VII's bequest.

A result of Comper's visit to Ireland in 1902 was a commission from the new Vicereine, Rachel, Countess of Dudley, for an altar frontal for the private chapel of the Viceregal Lodge, Phoenix Park. A preliminary pencil sketch shows a design similar to the smaller frontal in St Patrick's Cathedral, but it is too rudimentary to be able to identify its details.[45] No photographs of the private chapel at this period exist. Like its companion at Windsor, the frontal appears to be lost.

Comper's association with the Irish School lasted for its best and most productive years. There is no doubt that his tutelage significantly contributed to the exceptional standards that were attained. Those years were superintended by Miss Beresford, manageress from 1894 to 1906.[46] It is not unjustifiable to deduce that the stability and continuity of her long association, in combination with Lady Mayo, facilitated the achievement of such standards. Between 1906 and 1915 she was followed by three manageresses.[47] Although the Irish School was a major contributor to the Arts and Crafts Exhibition in 1910, subsequent infrequency of references to it suggest a gradual decline, concluded by the Great War.[48]

When I discovered Comper's drawings for the Irish School I was inclined to place them in the context of his early work, executed by the School of Embroidery of the Sisters of Bethany, and see them as marginal to his development. I was wrong. If Comper had not been invited by Lady Mayo to design for the School it is unlikely that he would have met Sir Thomas Wardle, a meeting which led to such decisive experiments in his evolution as a colourist. Rose-red became inseparably associated with his work, to an extent that, for those who know and admire it, it is an immediately identifiable constituent. Nor is it likely that he would have re-

ART NEEDLEWORK IN IRELAND

ceived the Windsor commission that led to such formative developments in his decorative design. But equally, if Comper had not become associated with the Irish School it is doubtful if it would have achieved such a high standard of execution in ecclesiastical work. Comper's involvement brought the School into the mainstream of British design, as Lady Mayo herself intended when she forged strong links with English designers.

Comper's involvement with the Irish School also casts a different light on an Arts and Crafts enterprise. Linda Parry has expressed the difficulties of closely defining this term, 'I have never been happy to use the expression "Arts and Crafts" as a descriptive term as there is no one historic style that matches such an all-embracing yet nebulous title'.[49] Yet an influential body of art historians has tended to isolate the Arts and Crafts Movement, placing it within doctrinaire and exclusive boundaries, founded upon the supremacy of William Morris from whom it has been understood evolved a spinal column of stylistic development culminating in the Modern Movement. Artists whose work was analogous but faithful to precedent, without being slavishly derivative or pure copyists, have frequently been ignored, their work dismissed as *pastiche* and therefore valueless as an expression of contemporary art.

What emerges so strongly in the work of the Irish School and the patronage of the Earl and Countess of Mayo, whose commitment to the ideals of the Arts and Crafts Movement was unswerving, is their admiration for work directly inspired by the past and their inclusion of it in the work of the School and the Arts and Crafts Society. Independently from applying Comper's refined and perfected medievalism, the Irish School produced much domestic and church work founded on sixteenth-century precedent, as well as inspiration drawn from Celtic sources, suggesting little independence of interpretation.

Lady Mayo made a point of writing: 'We can copy or originate according to the wishes of our patrons'.[50] The same relaxed attitude was also found in the work of the Royal School of Art Needlework in London, where design inspired by Pre-Raphaelite and Arts and Crafts principles and historic precedent was freely applied. In a wider context the same duality of choice was to be found in the Art-Workers Guild, an influential English society

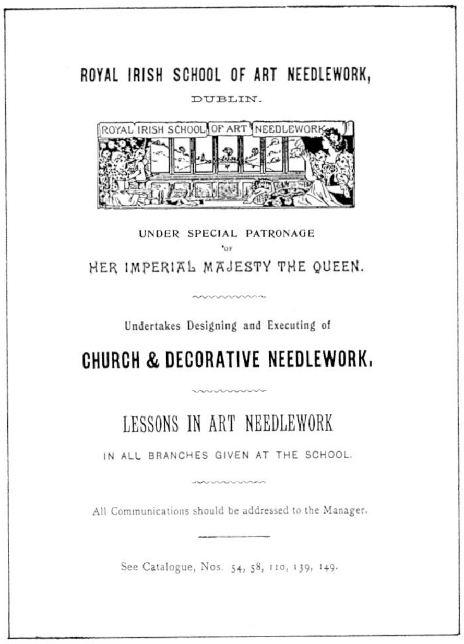

Advertisement for the Royal Irish School of Art Needlework, catalogue of the Arts and Crafts Society of Ireland, fourth exhibition, 1910. Decoration by Richard Orpen.

founded in 1884 to unite the arts and crafts within an architectural context.

In Lady Mayo's work for the Irish School she applied shining idealism and elevated intentions in an endeavour which fulfilled her piety, her own considerable artistic gifts, her natural love of beauty and her reason. Her intentions were as much altruistic and practical as aesthetic, demonstrated by her commitment to the Irish industries movement. She moved the Irish School from a small and ineffectual setting to one in which were provided opportunities of skilled training under the best available direction, thus enabling women to make an independent living. She did not limit the School's wider appeal by confining its work to Celtic interlace and runic symbolism, like Mrs Hart and the Donegal Industrial Fund, but opened it to widely diverse styles and less provincial influences. Her direct response to beauty was not governed by narrow principles or relative theories of design but was free and spontaneous:

I would put forward one more motive for giving support to such efforts as we are engaged upon. It is well known that nothing lowers the tone of the mind more than a low tone in the surroundings; and it will be remembered that it was the rule in Greek domestic life that no object in daily use, however lowly it might be, should be fashioned after a low or sordid type. In the poorest households the child's eye grew accustomed to forms of beauty and art, fashioned out of the rudest materials. So let it be with us![51]

If this article has done nothing else, I hope it will have opened a fuller investigation into the work of the Royal Irish School of Art Needlework and lead to further discoveries of its work in whatever medium, style or context. The School achieved a standard of excellence unequalled by any similar Irish enterprise.[52]

Anthony Symondson SJ

Anthony Symondson is a Jesuit scholastic studying theology at the Milltown Institute, Dublin. In 1988 he mounted an exhibition, Sir Ninian Comper: The Last Gothic Revivalist, *at the Royal Institute of British Architects, Heinz Gallery, Portman Square, London.*

ACKNOWLEDGEMENTS

I am deeply grateful to the following who have given me information and help with this article: Her Majesty Queen Elizabeth, the Queen Mother, for initiating a search for Comper's altar frontal at Windsor, and Sir Alexander Aird and the Very Revd Patrick Mitchell, Dean of Windsor, for undertaking it. Miss Pamela Clark, Deputy Registrar of the Royal Archives, for seeking references to the Windsor frontal. The Earl of Mayo, the Hon Charles Bourke and Mr Mark Bence-Jones for seeking a portrait of Geraldine, Countess of Mayo. Dr Nicola Gordon Bowe has been of invaluable help not only in generously sharing her knowledge of the Arts and Crafts Movement in Ireland and lending books and articles but in organising expeditions to find Comper's altar frontals, and reading this article. I must also thank the Very Revd M E Stewart, Dean of St Patrick's Cathedral, Dublin, for showing Dr Gordon Bowe and me the altar frontals, for reading this article and granting access to the cathedral's muniments, to his secretary Mrs Hampton and to Canon Bradley. The Very Revd M. Byrne, Dean of Kildare, also generously gave time to Dr Gordon Bowe and me when he showed us his cathedral's frontals. Dr R Refaussé, librarian of the Representative Church Body Library, gave me access to otherwise inaccessible books and periodicals. Mr John Holohan read this article, lent books and made valuable suggestions for further research. Finally, I have to thank the Rector of my community, the Revd Fergus O'Donaghue SJ, the Revd Diarmuid O Laoghaire SJ and, most of all, the Revd Joseph Veale SJ, who spent much time editing my typescript and who organised a memorable expedition to Carnalway.

NOTES OVERLEAF

ART NEEDLEWORK IN IRELAND

NOTES

1. *Journal & Proceedings of the Arts and Crafts Society of Ireland,* Vol 1, 1, Dublin 1896. Evidence given by Lady Mayo to the Department of Agriculture and Technical Instruction for Ireland, published in *Ireland: Industrial and Agricultural,* 1901, pp. 272-73. I am grateful to Dr Nicola Gordon Bowe for drawing my attention to Lady Mayo's evidence. Nicola Gordon Bowe, 'The Irish Arts and Crafts Movement (1886-1925)', *Irish Arts Review Year Book,* 1990-91, pp. 172-88; Gordon Bowe, 'The Arts and Crafts Movement in Ireland', *Antiques,* December 1992, pp. 864-75; Paul Larmour, *The Arts and Crafts Movement in Ireland,* Belfast 1992, pp. 12-14, 56-63.
2. One of the principal exhibits in the first exhibition in 1895 was 408, a four-post bed of carved walnut, designed by M. Morahan and executed by him and P. Lynch. It was lent by Lord Houghton. The bed had hangings and a quilt executed, under the supervision of the manageress, Miss Harriet Beresford, by thirteen embroideresses from the Irish School. In the second exhibition in 1899 Lord Mayo lent a casket in inlaid wood (215), designed by R Anning Bell and inlaid by P Lynch.
3. Mayo op cit 'Any work that can be done by the needle we undertake to do, and in the best manner. Books embroidered on parchment or satin are a speciality, also church embroidery of all descriptions.'
4. Anthony Symondson, *Sir Ninian Comper: The Last Gothic Revivalist,* London, Royal Institute of British Architects, 1988. Comper was born in Scotland of English parentage. His Scottish nationality was nominal. Though he never lost his love of Scotland, nor repudiated his membership of the Scottish Episcopal Church, he lived and worked in England from 1882 until his death. Dr Larmour, op cit p13, refers to the altar frontals at Kildare and in St Patrick's but he does not identify the designer as Comper.
5. These drawings have, with two exceptions, indefinitely been deposited in store and are currently inaccessible.
6. Mayo op cit.
7. Mrs Domvile, 'Art Needlework in Ireland', *Irish Rural Life and Industry,* Irish International Exhibition 1907, p.227. I am grateful to Dr Nicola Gordon Bowe for drawing this article to my attention.
8. Mayo op cit.
9. Thomas Sadleir, 'Geraldine, Countess of Mayo', *Journal of the Co Kildare Archaeological Society,* vol XII, 8, 1944 and 1945, pp.lxv-vj. I am grateful to Mr Henry McDowell for referring me to Lady Mayo's obituary.
10. Mayo op cit.
11. Barbara Morris, *Victorian Embroidery,* London 1962, p.215.
12. Ibid. Larmour op cit pp.12-13. Dr Larmour gives valuable information on the early life of the Irish School but he does not recognise the implications of Lady Mayo's involvement with British designers and the consequences for the standards achieved by the School.
13. Lady Mayo possessed family portraits of her nieces Joan, Mabel and Eileen Ponsonby by Kate Greenaway. Will, 29 June 1937.
14. Domvile op cit. A full account of this feature of the School's work is given in Mrs Domvile's article.
15. Symondson op cit pp. 13-14.
16. The mitre still exists in the possession of the Sisters of Bethany; it was exhibited in the Comper exhibition 1988.
17. Prospectus of the School of Embroidery of the Sisters of Bethany.
18. Symondson op cit pp13-14.
19. This meeting took place on 8 March 1897; Comper's diary.
20. For George Wyndham's influence on Comper see Symondson op cit p. 18 and J N Comper, *Further Thoughts on the English Altar, or Practical Considerations on the Planning of a Modern Church,* Cambridge 1933, p.33. In 1913 Comper designed the east window of the church at East Knoyle, erected as a memorial to Wyndham by his widow, Sibell, Countess of Grosvenor, and both Houses of Parliament. When Lady Grosvenor saw the finished window in 1916 in Comper's study she wrote: 'The heavenly transparent Vision of yesterday, will ever shine in my heart – it was a lovely Candlemas joy ... I knew the glass would be beautiful – but every bit is a jewel.' After the window had been erected it inspired further rhapsodies: 'I could find no words yesterday to thank you for the beauty and holiness of the window. I could only feel you had put a special inspiration of glow & Glory into the beautiful work of your hands ... I loved seeing it yesterday, on Our Lady's Eve & my very old Birthday – I felt George & Percy were in the shining of it, loving it too.' (Letters 3 February; Lady Day, 25 March 1916; Comper's private papers).
21. Jane Abdy and Charlotte Gere, *The Souls,* London 1984, pp. 82-101 and passim; Jane Ridley and Clayre Percy, *The Letters of Arthur Balfour & Lady Elcho,* London 1992, passim.
22. J N Comper, 'Some Later Works of Restoration & Additions to Ancient Buildings', unpublished ms; Comper's private papers. Comper occasionally designed for the Royal School of Art Needlework until after the Second World War, but he did not have a controlling influence on it. Mrs Wyndham persuaded Alexander Fisher to design embroidery for the School, *Catalogue of an Exhibition of Victorian and Edwardian Decorative Arts,* Victoria and Albert Museum 1952. p118.
23. No early letters between Lady Mayo (1863-1944) and Comper survive covering their association in the Irish School; they were destroyed, with much early correspondence, when Comper's study was severely damaged by enemy action in 1944. Surviving correspondence begins in 1913 and continues intermittently until 1938. Her admiration for Comper's work was boundless. For instance, her reaction to his major church, St Mary's, Wellingborough, Northamptonshire (1904-31): 'This requires no answer! only I have to write & tell you how *beautiful* I think St Mary's, Wellingboro' is. I went there on Friday last & had two lovely hours in the church between trains. First the ironstone pillars & their beautiful capitals are so splendid & then the statues, & the windows gave me such a feeling of beauty that I can't express in words what I think. The outside too is magnificent & a delightful stonemason told me a lot about where the stone came from etc.
I felt inclined to search for a house & go & live there, so as to be near & able to go in continually but, anyhow, I shall go again when the tower etc. is finished.
Please don't be bored with me for writing but I simply *had* to tell you how wonderfully beautiful I think it.' (Letter 15 June 1931; Comper's private papers).
24. 'I always think that St Cyprian's is the most beautiful church I know – anywhere – & I always say a thanksgiving prayer for you when I go there.' (Letter 28 December 1936; Comper's private papers). During her lifetime Lady Mayo had paid an annual premium of £12.18s.0d (£12.90p) for repairs and restoration of St Cyprian's. In her will (op cit) she endowed a policy to operate for forty years after her death, concluded in 1984. When in Ireland Lord and Lady Mayo frequently worshipped at St Bartholomew's, Dublin. After Lord Mayo's death in 1927 she presented a leather bound memorial book to St Bartholomew's in his memory.
25. Mrs Wakefield, née Hewitt, was a member of Viscount Lifford's family; she died in 1909: information from Mr Henry McDowell. C M L Clements and Gertrude Jeffers, *St Patrick's Church, Carnalway, Centenary Celebrations 1891-1991,* pp. 3-4. I am grateful to Col Clements and the Ven W B Heney, Archdeacon of Kildare, for giving me a copy of the parish history and for showing me the church.
26. These requirements were stipulated in the Sisters of Bethany's prospectus.
27. Mayo op cit; the Kildare frontal was illustrated as evidence of the Irish School's work.
28. *Irish Ecclesiastical Gazette,* 1901, p. 981.
29. Letter from Comper to Mrs John Comper, 15 May 1902; Comper's private papers.
30. The muniments of St Patrick's Cathedral contain Miss Jellett's account book for her embroidery scheme and a set of receipts from St Mary's Embroidery School, Wantage, continuing to 1901. There are no references to Comper's altar frontals. In 1902 Dean Bernard was appointed and the *St Patrick's Cathedral Gift Book* was started. He continued the connection with Wantage but his daughter also worked a green and a red burse and chalice veil. More significantly, an entry for a frontal appears in January 1907: 'Altar Frontal (Green) for the Choir, worked by the Misses Whitty, presented by Miss Callwell.' Dr Larmour illustrates this frontal on p. 25 of his book attributing its execution to the Irish School. Though Miss Daphne Whitty was manageress of the School for a year in 1907, there is no evidence in St Patrick's that it had anything to do with the frontal. Miss Whitty's frontal cost £56. An earlier green frontal for the high altar had been made up from old needlework by the Irish School in 1903; it was superseded by Miss Whitty's frontal and no longer exists. Between 1909 and 1915 several small commissions, mainly for burses, chalice veils, bookmarkers and

ART NEEDLEWORK IN IRELAND

altar linen, were given to the Irish School by Dean Bernard and his successor, Dean Ovendon, all of which are recorded.

31. Symondson op cit p30. Correspondence file, 1893-1929, M Perkins & Son Ltd. The firm was founded in 1913 and remained in Shoreditch until 1943 when incendiary bombs destroyed the building.
32. In 1874 G F Bodley, his partner Thomas Garner and Gilbert Scott the Younger founded a firm, Watts & Co, Baker Street, for the sale of church fabrics, wallpapers, furniture, metalwork and decorative materials made to the partners' designs. It had immense influence on ecclesiastical taste and colouring. Anthony Symondson, 'Wallpapers from Watts & Co', *The Connoisseur,* 204, no 820, June 1980, pp. 114-121.
33. The tone Comper was seeking may be seen in the fifteenth-century Flemish paintings of St Romold, by the Master of the Youth of St Romold, in the National Gallery of Ireland (cat. nos. 1380, 1381). The panel depicting the enthronement of St Romold as Bishop of Dublin exemplifies the ideals which Comper was seeking in his own work. At one time in the collection of the Duke of Devonshire, Chatsworth, it would have been seen by Comper in 1892 in an *Exhibition of Pictures by masters of the Netherlandish and allied schools of the XV and XVI centuries,* mounted at the Burlington Fine Arts Club, London.Christiaan Vogelaar, *Netherlandish Fifteenth and Sixteenth Century Paintings in the National Gallery of Ireland,* Dublin 1987, p. 54. I am grateful to Miss Paula Hicks for giving me an extract about this painting from this work.
34. Comper was in Rome 7-25 May 1900; Comper's diary. A further step in his aesthetic development took place when he visited the National Museum on his last day and noticed 'the same mouldings of architecture, the same turn of fold sin the draperies of statues and the identical lines of decoration as in East Anglia.' Comper, *Further Thoughts ...* op cit, p33. This development continued on a second visit to Rome, and a first to Sicily on the same journey, in1905, and to Greece in 1906.
35. Comper, 'Some Further Works ...' op cit. Linda Parry, *Textiles of the Arts and Crafts Movement,* London 1988, passim.
36. From 1900, until the Second World War, Comper used no other firm of dyers than Wardle & Co.
37. The smaller frontal is now permanently on the altar of St Peter's chapel, in the north quire aisle.
38. Letter from Comper to his mother op cit.
39. Comper, 'Some Further Works ...' op cit. In 1901, Comper was commissioned at short notice by Viscount Halifax to design a medieval catafalque for a Solemn Requiem Mass for Queen Victoria at St Matthew's, Westminster. Lady Mayo possessed a watercolour of it painted by her father, the Hon Gerald Ponsonby, a younger son of the fourth Earl of Bessborough. The catafalque, or 'herse' as Comper preferred to call it, is described in a letter from Comper to his mother which also mentions the Windsor frontal: 'Strange! My frontal design got no further than the Princess Beatrice who objected to heraldry. Ere the second design was ready the Queen was dead. The enclosed is from Lady Mayo about them. It is deplorable about the heraldry as shown in that incident ...' Lady Mayo's letter has disappeared. (Letter 31 January 1901; Comper's private papers).
40. Domvile op cit, p. 228. Mrs Domvile mentions that regimental colours and naval flags were also a feature of the Irish School's work: 'Amongst those may be mentioned the Irish Guards, the Coldstream Guards, the Seaforth Highlanders etc. Old Colours have also been repaired and restored, and Flags of Historical interest thus preserved.' She resigned from being manageress of the Irish School in 1906.
41. I am grateful to the Rector of Stonyhurst, the Very Revd Michael O'Halloran SJ, for giving me much valuable information on the Stonyhurst cope.
42. In Comper's sketchbook 'VIII East Anglia, Belgium etc '94 '96', f1 is a pencilled note, 'Needlework. Lady Marion Alford.' Comper's private papers.
43. Lady Alford, *Needlework as Art,* London 1886, p. 329.
44. Ibid p. 348.
45. The drawing is inscribed: 'Altar for private chapel at the Viceregal Lodge, Dublin. Her Excellency Lady Dudley.' The second Earl of Dudley was Viceroy of Ireland 1902-05.
46. Harriet Sarah Beresford (d 1931), eldest daughter of the Revd William Montgomery Beresford, Rector of Lower Badoney, Co Tyrone; married, as his third wife, Major Herbert Winnington Domvile, of Loughlinstown House, Co Dublin, 3 November 1906. *Burke's Irish Family Records,* 1976. Dr Larmour (op cit) consistently gives Miss Beresford the Christian name Susan.
47. The manageresses were as follows: 1907 Miss Whitty; 1908-11 Miss Persse; 1912-14 Miss Ruby Lyon. On Miss Lyon's resignation no manageress was appointed to succeed her.
48. The last frontal designed by Comper for the Irish School is elusively referred to in the catalogue of the Arts and Crafts Society's exhibition in 1910. Exhibit 112 is simply described as an 'Altar frontal, embroidered. Designed by J N Comper. Executed by Miss Boyd.' It had no provenance and was entered for sale for £40. I am grateful to Dr Nicola Gordon Bowe for showing me this catalogue entry.
49. Parry op cit, p7.
50. Mayo op cit.
51. ibid.
52. The disbandment of the Irish School did not mean the end of Comper's work in Ireland. He went on to design a series of painted glass windows, mainly memorials to the fallen in the Great War. Comper's glass is to be found at Kilbride, Co Wicklow; Kilternan, Co Dublin; and All Saints, Blackrock, Co Dublin. In 1928 he designed a rich white altar frontal for Kilkenny Cathedral, presented by Lady Constance Butler, in which, for the last time, he used the Stonyhurst briars. It was executed between 1929-31 by the Sisters of Bethany and cost £416.10s.0d (£416.50p). Lady Constance's commission was the most ambitious he received for embroidery between the two World Wars, on a scale equal to his early work. In 1938 he designed a simpler white frontal for St Fin Barre's Cathedral, Cork, made by the Church of Ireland order, the Sisters of St John the Evangelist, Sandymount, Dublin. (Letter from Mother Catherine Margaret CSJE, 27 November 1992). Comper's last Irish work was the tombstone of Basil, fourth Marquess of Dufferin and Ava, at Clandeboye, Co Down. The commission was obtained for him by the poet, John Betjeman, in 1946. (Letter from Comper to Betjeman, 3 December 1946, Betjeman papers; Anthony Symondson, 'John Betjeman and the Cult of J N Comper', *Journal of the Thirties Society,* vol. 7, (1991), pp. 3-13, 52).

CONTINENTAL EUROPEAN SOURCES FOR GEORGE BARRET

Michael Wynne uncovers some definite continental sources for the landscapes of George Barret (1728/32-84).

Students of Irish eighteenth-century landscape painting have had for a long time to rely on the hypothesis that aspiring painters depended largely on prints and drawings by continental masters for the skill shown in their mature works.

While some landscape painters left Ireland after their basic training, chiefly to visit Italy, especially Rome and its diverse surrounding countryside, none of them developed skills, in oil on canvas, comparable to those who remained at home, or merely crossed the Irish Sea to Great Britain.

A landscape painter like Forrester, for example, who did some beautiful drawings, produced paintings which seem to compete with each other for darkness of tone, and dullness of execution. In only one case has the writer seen a Forrester with a low glow from a setting sun.

The failure of the Irish landscape artists in Italy is all the more pointed when one thinks of history painters like James Barry or portrait and subject painters such as Hugh Douglas Hamilton, who are truly of international standing. The hypothesis presented in the opening paragraph is valid, and hopefully will be proven correct as more evidence emerges. In the meantime, I wish to draw attention to some very direct sources for George Barret.

Joseph Leeson, subsequently 1st Earl of Milltown, was in Rome in the 1740s, while his magnificent house, Russborough in County Wicklow, was being built. Among his acquisitions there were eight small gouaches by Giovanni Battista Busiri (1698-1757), a man of very modest talent, when one considers the standard of view painting at the time.

Nonetheless, it is clear that Leeson asked Barret to use at least three of these views in order to provide him with larger paintings on canvas. *The Roman Forum* (Fig 1) by Busiri is the basis for Barret's view of the same area (Fig 2). The differences are minimal, a few less figures in the middle ground, the slightly altered position of some stones. One might presume that Leeson bought his four very beautiful Paninis on the same visit to Rome, since they are dated 1740. One of these depicts *The Roman Forum* (Fig 3) and it is perplexing that he did not ask Barret to use this as the basis for his painting, which is in fact larger than the Panini. Adopting the later date for Barret's birth, one must therefore query the date of Leeson's Panini purchase.

Another of the Busiri gouaches depicts *The Colosseum* at Rome (Fig 4). This, too, was the basis for a view of the same subject by Barret on a large scale (Fig 5). The basic composition is virtually identical, minor changes occurring in the tree at the left hand side. Very small changes are to be found in the bottom right hand corner, where Busiri's damaged signature is to be found. Leeson owned a very fine Panini of the Colosseum, a much more detailed painting (Fig 6). Again one must ask why the Busiri was used as the basis for Barret's large oil. The possibility is that Leeson bought the Busiris in 1744, and then bought the Paninis on his second visit to Rome in 1752, having commissioned Barret to execute the Russborough decorations in the intervening years.

Yet a third Busiri was used by Barret. It shows a *View of Tivoli with the Temple of Vesta* (Fig 7). It is handled with more agility, probably because the artist could be freer with his gouache technique while painting a landscape and an abundantly cascading waterfall. Yet again, Barret has produced a large oil of the very same view; the profile of the town of Tivoli silhouetted against the sky is alike; so, too, the two men in the bottom right foreground. Barret fails here in translating the gouache waterfall into oils. There is, however, absolutely no doubt about his use of the Busiri as a prototype (Fig. 8).[1]

Can one be absolutely certain that the three unusual large views are by George Barret? In the fields of, say, pure science or mathematics one would have to say, 'No'. Even in art history one must be cautious, since the earliest list of paintings at Russborough is that given in Neale's *Views of Seats of Noblemen and Gentlemen* published in 1826. By today's standards of cataloguing, Neale's two pages appear trifling. I have had to refer regularly to these very pages, again and again, over a period of some twenty years. The attributions of eighteenth-century paintings are all correct; a remarkable number of seventeenth-century pictures are given to their correct masters, including some Florentine ones not commonly found in Great Britain or Ireland. Copies are noted as such, and certain paintings are admirably left without an author. Yes, there are mistakes; would that all the Poussins were correct!

Thus, Neale is remarkably useful. He

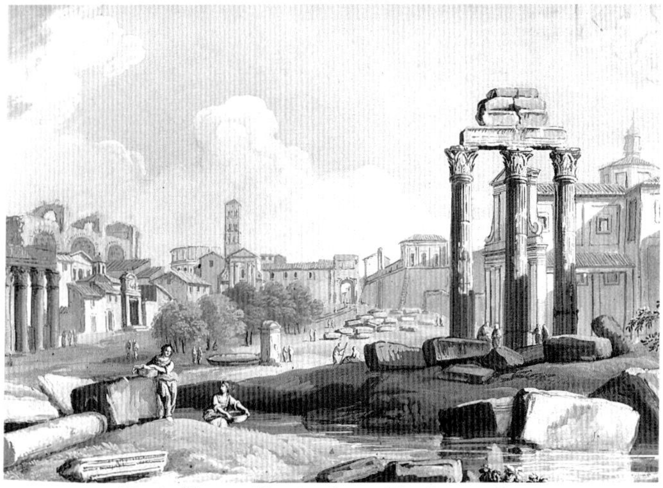

Fig. 1, Giovanni Battista Busiri, The Roman Forum.
Gouache on paper, 22.9 x 34.6cm
National Gallery of Ireland, cat. no. 7406

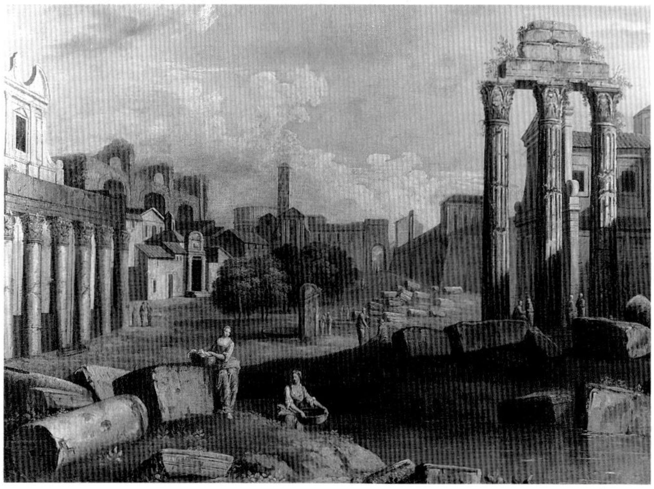

Fig. 2, George Barret, The Roman Forum.
Oil on canvas, 98 x 151cm.
National Gallery of Ireland, cat. no. 1632

CONTINENTAL EUROPEAN SOURCES FOR GEORGE BARRET

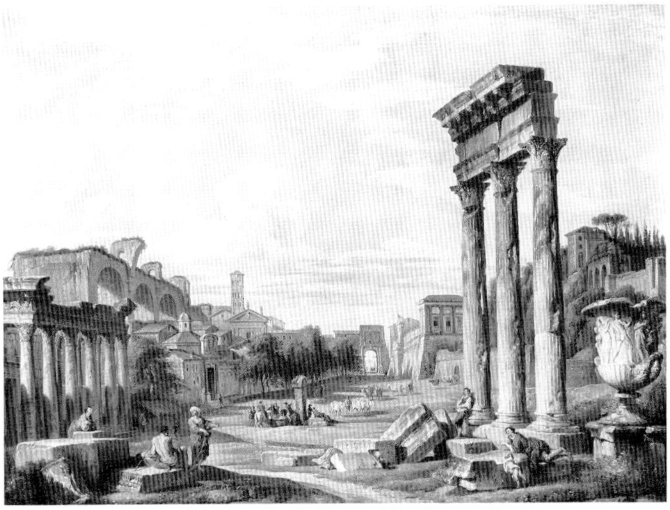

Fig. 3, Giovanni Paolo Panini, The Roman Forum.
Oil on canvas, 73 x 99cm
National Gallery of Ireland, cat. no. 726

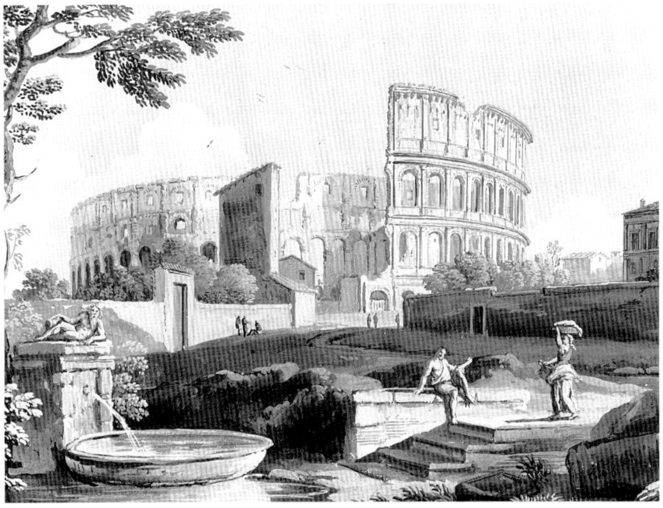

Fig. 4, Giovanni Battista Busiri, The Colosseum.
Gouache on paper, 22.6 x 34.5 cm.
National Gallery of Ireland, cat. no. 7405

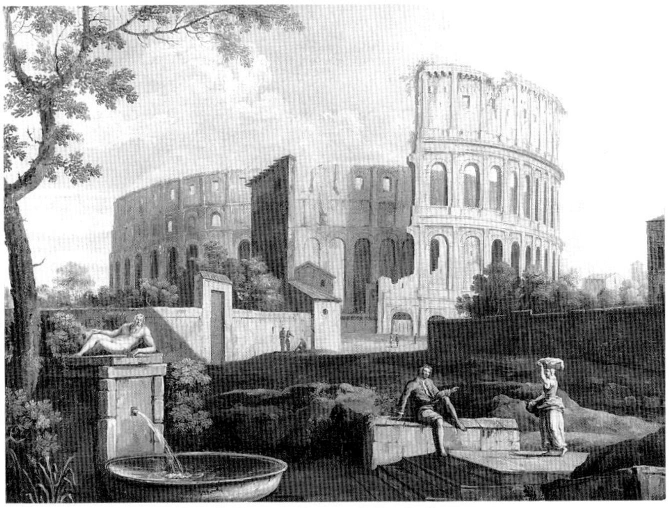

Fig. 5, George Barret, The Colosseum.
Oil on canvas, 98 x 151cm.
National Gallery of Ireland, cat. no. 1633

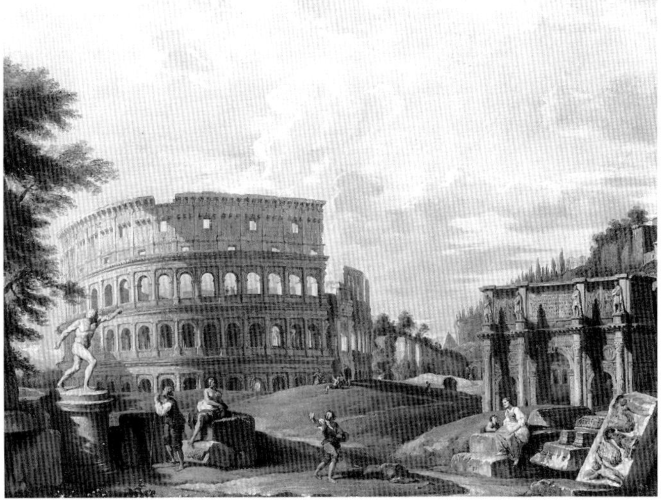

Fig. 6, Giovanni Paolo Panini, The Colosseum.
Oil on canvas, 73 x 99cm.
National Gallery of Ireland, cat. no. 725

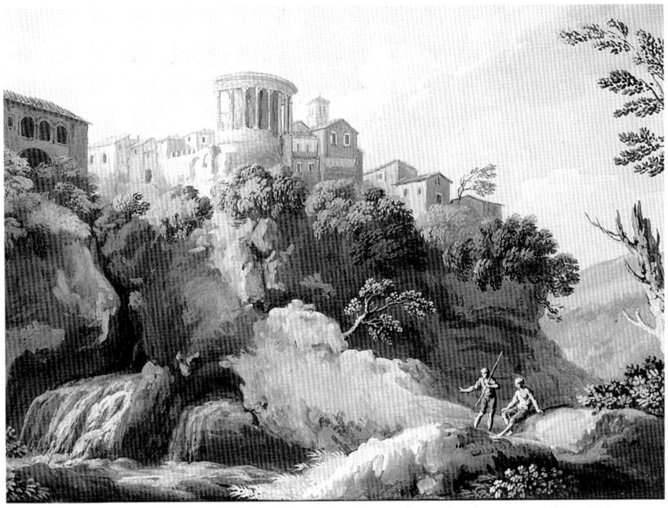

Fig. 7, Giovanni Battista Busiri, View of Tivoli with the Temple of Vesta.
Gouache on paper, 22.9 x 34.4 cm
National Gallery of Ireland, cat no. 7404

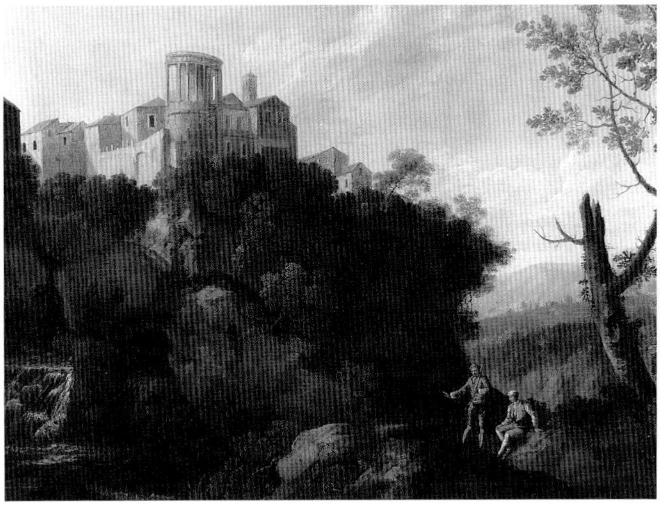

Fig. 8, George Barret, View of Tivoli with the Temple of Vesta.
Oil on canvas, 99 x 150cm
National Gallery of Ireland, cat. no. 1635

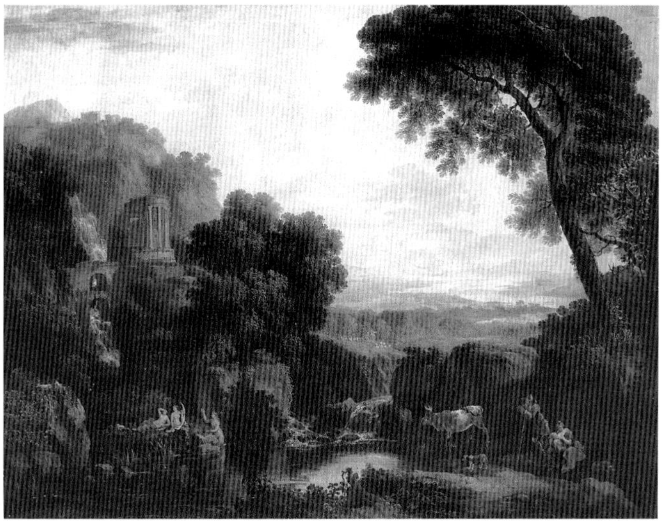

Fig. 9, George Barret, An Italianate Landscape with a Capriccio View of Tivoli. *Oil on canvas, 104.1 x 138.4 cm. Christie's, 12 July 1991, lot 68A*

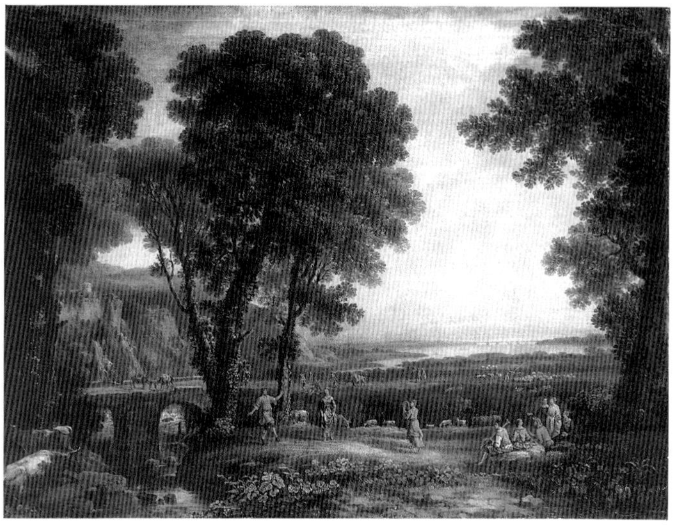

Fig. 10, George Barret, An Italianate Landscape with a Shepherd dancing. *Oil on canvas, 104.1 x 138.4cm Christie's, 12 July 1991, lot 68B*

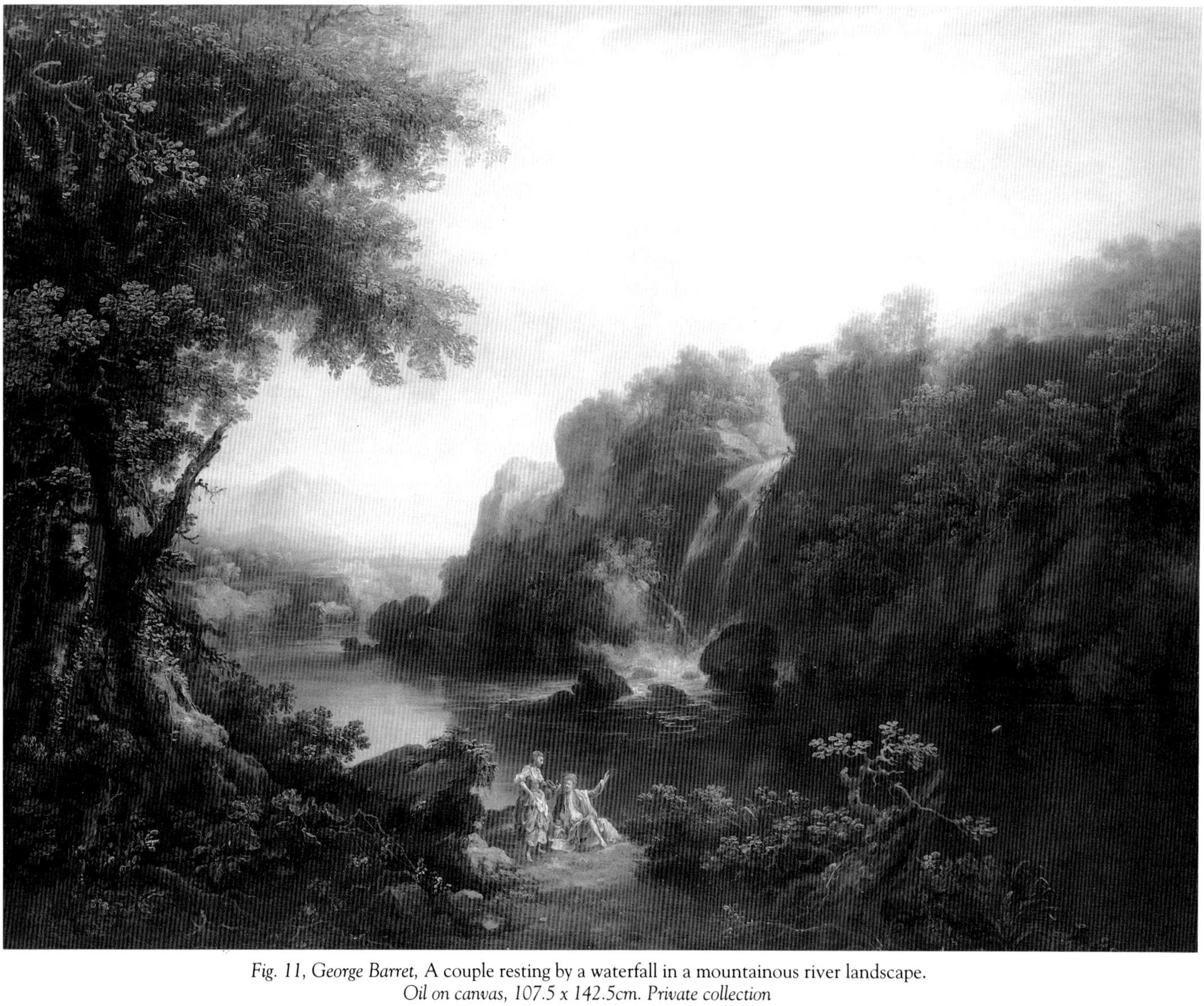

Fig. 11, George Barret, A couple resting by a waterfall in a mountainous river landscape. *Oil on canvas, 107.5 x 142.5cm. Private collection*

records that the Library contained eleven Barrets, hung at a height to permit seven foot bookcases to sit comfortably below them. The three landscapes under discussion found their place in the company of what are clearly typical Barrets.[2]

Amidst the other eight Barrets the three large views, taking their tone from the Busiri gouaches, look rather blanched. Hopefully, one day it will be possible to see those eleven Barrets hung again in that Library (the present Dining Room). Extant photographs show how appropriate was that particularly high chimneypiece, and where could the pictures have been shown more appropriately, than in a room dedicated to academe?

Recently there appeared at Christie's two large paintings, extremely well painted, copies by Barret of works by Claude Lorrain, consigned by an anonymous vendor, but with the fascinating provenance 'Almost certainly in the collection of the Rev. Samuel Madden (1686-1765),[3] and thence by descent'. One, *An Italianate Landscape with a Capriccio View of Tivoli*, measuring 104.1 x 138.4 cm, is a copy of Claude's *Landscape with Argus guarding Io*, a painting now at Holkham Hall in Norfolk,[4] but accessible to Barret through J Wood's engraving of 1746, when the picture belonged to Humphrey Edwin. Lot no 68A in Christie's sale, 12 July 1991, in a typical Irish shouldered frame, the Barret is of such a size that it must have been commissioned (Fig. 9). What artist would have undertaken such a work in the hope that a client might appear?

This hypothesis is reinforced by the fact that there was a pendant to this picture, namely lot 68B in the same sale (Fig 10).

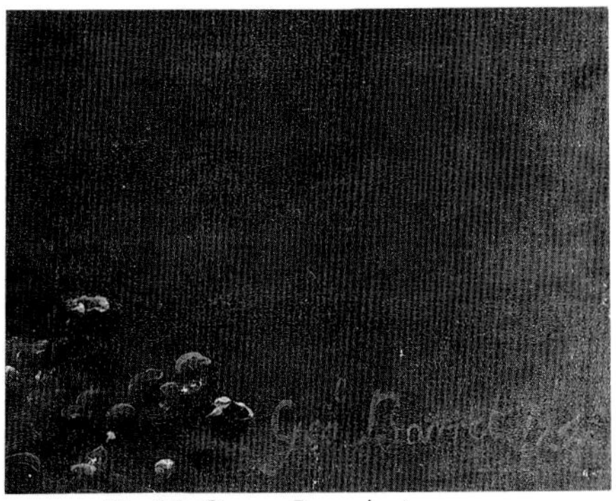

Fig. 12, George Barret's signature on A couple resting by a waterfall in a mountainous river landscape.

Described as *An Italianate Landscape with a Shepherd Dancing*, it is a copy of Claude's *Landscape with Rural Dance*, whose location in these islands is unknown until recorded as being with Agar in 1784, the year in which it was engraved by Lowry, and the year in which Barret died. An earlier engraving must have been made, and known to Barret. The painting is exactly the same size as its pendant.

Both pictures are painted with relish, with lots of *impasto*, and without any hint of the boredom involved in being obliged to make copies. To make copies at this scale was indeed a challenge. Internally there is an element which supports the hypothesis of a commission from a Madden. One of the family's properties was Castle Watter, close to the southern end of Upper Lough Erne in County Fermanagh, in a very scenic area. Here Lough Erne is very narrow, dotted with small islands; as one moves in a north-westerly direction the lake widens, but of course does not reach its full size until Lower Lough Erne, beyond the town of Enniskillen. These Barret copies after Claude have delightful meandering watery vistas, utterly reminiscent of the scenery of Upper Lough Erne.

It is worth noting another Barret, which was on the London market a few years ago, even though it is not known to be a copy. A large painting (Fig 11), it is a complex composition, handled with great skill, and probably more French than Italian in inspiration. The group of figures is superbly treated, and overall is a clarion of competence. This painting reiterates the fact that Barret was a major landscape painter before he went to England; it is signed and dated (Fig 12), in the 1750s; unfortunately the last digit is missing but the vital third one is there.

The adage 'It is a bad workman who blames his tools' cannot be always used. The 'tools' available to the young George Barret, and indeed to many other young Irish painters of the eighteenth-century, were meagre indeed, but they certainly used them to great effect. From our scant knowledge of Irish private collections in the early part of the eighteenth century, a few young painters might have seen some Dutch seventeenth century landscapes of quality. The best Irish collections, especially with an Italian and French emphasis, began to be formed only from the middle of the eighteenth-century. Hopefully more copies, precise or free, will emerge to show painters' indebtedness to continental masters, as in the case of Irish stuccodores.

Michael Wynne

Dr Michael Wynne is the Keeper of the National Gallery of Ireland.

NOTES

1. From the known documentation about the Leeson (Milltown) collection, which unfortunately only begins (scantily) in 1826, there is no mention of a Panini of this ancient town and its famous waterfalls.
2. Cf the illustrations in *Country Life* for January 1937. The Milltown Library was the room used by the Turtons, the Dalys and most recently the Beits as the Dining Room.
3. The Madden family, with properties in both Counties Fermanagh and Monaghan, was well established by the beginning of the seventeenth century, contributing notably to the fields of agriculture, culture and the arts. The Reverend Samuel Madden, a Trinity College don, was one of the founders of the Dublin Society (subsequently, and to this day the Royal Dublin Society). This gentleman instituted a series of premiums for outstanding performance under different headings, and to this day is referred to as 'Premium' Madden. 'Premium' bequeathed to Trinity College, Dublin, an eclectic collection of seventeenth and eighteenth century paintings, some of high quality.
4. Marcel Rothlisberger, *Claude Lorrain: the paintings. Critical catalogue*. vol.1 (1961) pp.240-42. no.86.

BORRIS LACE

Rare and beautiful lace made in Borris, Co Carlow is described by **Nellie O'Cleirigh.**

Borris Lace owes its name to the small, pretty village of Borris in County Carlow. Like so many other Irish laces, its establishment was an effort by a landlord family to provide much needed employment. The village of Borris formed part of the estate of the McMorrough-Kavanagh family, who could trace their ancestry back a thousand years and could claim descent from the Kings of Leinster.

Borris is a 'Tape Lace' similar to the laces called Princess, Renaissance or Battenberg in America and on the continent. In the beginning the tape was handmade but later a machine-made tape was used, which was bought in quantity by the Kavanagh family from SA Sands and Co, Lace and Net Manufacturers, 26 Stoney St, Nottingham. Family tradition holds that Lady Harriet Kavanagh, while visiting the island of Corfu in the Mediterranean with her son Arthur, shortly before the Great Famine, was so impressed by specimens of old Greek lace that she bought some pieces. She intended having them copied in Borris by the local women thus enabling them to add to the meagre earnings of their menfolk. Lady Harriet also brought from Venice and Milan specimens of Genoa Tape lace.[1]

Lace was fashionable in Victorian England, and the advent of the crinoline gave the industry a great boost as it required quantities of lace to trim each garment. Consequently, because of the destitution caused by the Great Famine, philanthropic ladies – reverend mothers in convents, clergymen's wives, ladies of means and landlord's families – sponsored several of the Irish laces.

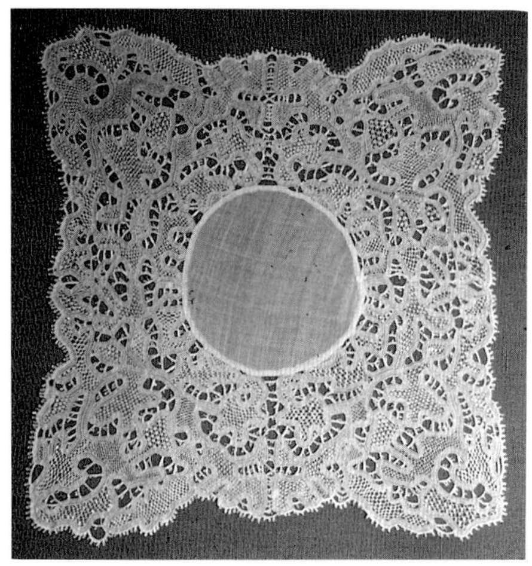

Handkerchief of Borris Lace, also from the collection in the National Museum of Ireland.

Lady Harriet was followed in the control of this lace industry in 1855 by her daughter-in-law, Frances Mary Forde Leathley, who had married her cousin, Arthur, Harriet's youngest son.

The lace-making industry was expanded by Frances Kavanagh. Each week a class was held, at first in the Protestant school and later in the cottages. At the class, materials were distributed with directions for work; beginners started by making small squares; they graduated on to narrow borders. Mrs Arthur Kavanagh's standards were very high, and it was remembered even years later that, if she was not satisfied, she would put her scissors through a piece. She was also reputed to have drawn all the designs herself. Like her mother-in-law, Harriet, Frances was widely travelled and had seen examples of a wide variety of European laces.

In addition to the Kavanagh family, there was always a 'work-mistress' who was paid. Mrs Poole, who was in charge in 1872, was paid the princely sum of £12 per year, but she also got one penny in the shilling as commission, her total earnings for a year being £32 to £36. Mrs Poole was succeeded by Miss Rebecca Devine and then a Mrs Purdy. The last instructress was Miss Jacob, who was the grand-daughter of the Estate Agent.[2] Apart from the paid supervisor, the Kavanagh family women were principally remembered as promoting the lace-making, and Arthur McMorrough Kavanagh was reputed to have been particularly interested, as he was in any enterprise for the improvement of the lot of the estate tenants. When a committee was set up in 1884 to improve the quality of Irish lace, Mrs Arthur Kavanagh was one of its members, subscribing £2, the same figure as other patrons of small industries. Money prizes were offered for the production of designs for the various classes of work, including braid and cord lace. We do not know whether Borris lace ever won a prize but there are no samples of it included in the book published by the committee.[3]

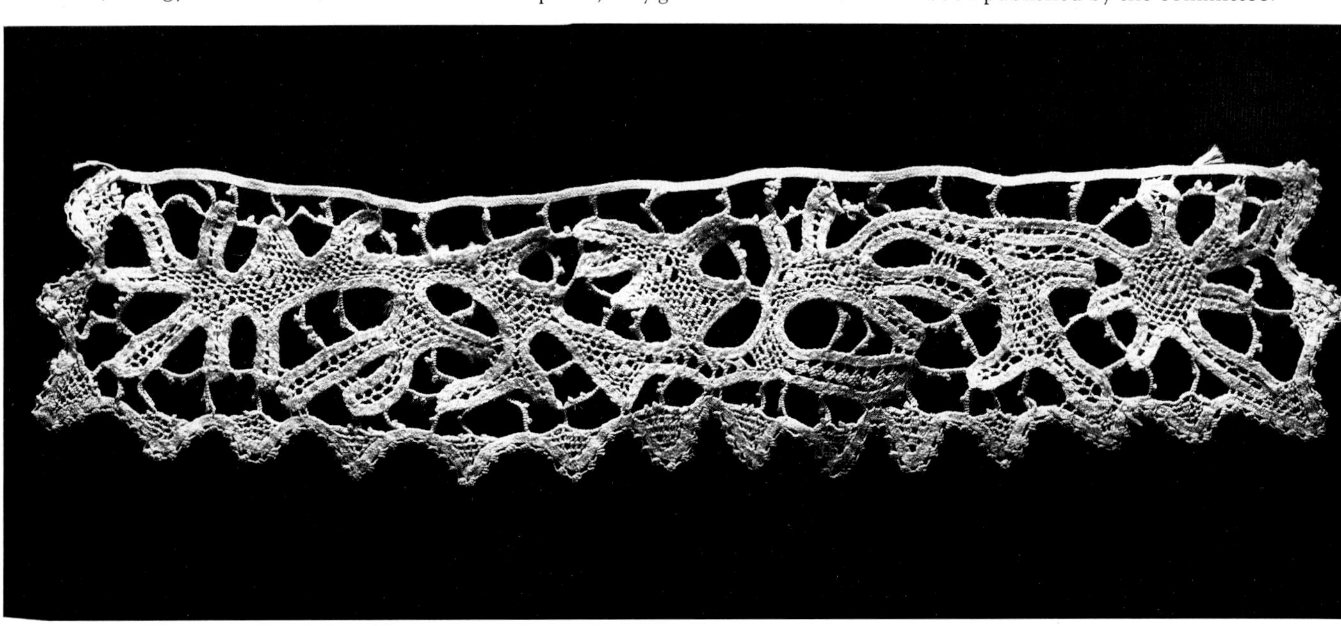

Section of cuff of Borris Lace (1868), showing hand made tape. National Museum of Ireland.

BORRIS LACE

The First World War saw a decline in demand for Borris Lace as it did for all European laces. Later, in the 1930s, the local parish priest, a Father Murphy, tried to revive the craft and held displays in the large Dublin hotels. An altar-cloth made by Mrs King at this period won a prize in a competition organised by the Country Women's Association, but by 1960 there were only three lace-makers left in the village and most of the work was exported to America.

Where was the lace sold? We do not know much about the early sales but the Kavanagh family in Borris House have some records of the industry dating from 1912 to 1927. During that period, the largest customer was the Irish Linen Stores in New Bond Street in London, who bought edgings, collars, cushions, lace for nighties, doyleys and motifs. The entire sales for the year to this firm were about £200, varying from £3.10.0 to £30.0.0 per month. There were also other sales of edgings, insertions and squares as well as cloth surrounds. Table mats with centre pieces were 28/- per set. There were orders for camiknickers and 'shamrock mats' which were more expensive than other kinds. In the 1930s they sold a pomegranate pattern. There were a number of private sales, mostly to friends – titled customers with Irish connections. Many of these buyers would have been related to the family, most of the Irish titled families being in some way related to one another. Hayward's of Old Bond Street in London were another customer. Goods were often sent on approval, particularly tea-cloths and 'sofa spreads'. Private customers were not always quick to pay and there are several entries in the account book of reminders being sent out. At Borris House, there are no surviving copies of the instructions used, but a number of simple drawings remain. These would appear to have been redrawn and reused, the border being particularly amateurish. A cuff, in the collection in the National Museum, shows that the standard of design and drawing was higher in the earlier years.

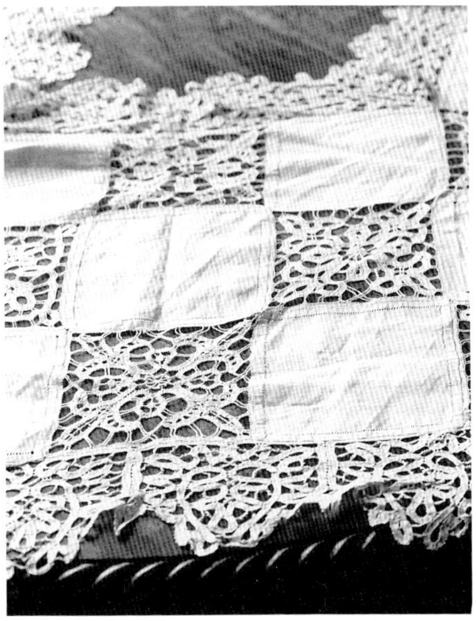

Table cloth with square cut out of centre. Several different designs in the squares. Borris House collection.

The McMorrough-Kavanagh family own a number of pieces, presumably unsold when the business finally closed. These are mostly table mats of varying designs and using different thicknesses of tape. There is also a large cloth with a square cut from its centre. A deep border of lace is sewn all round the square and arranged at the corners as if intended to stand up. There also exist a number of simple designs and bundles of linen thread, as well as samples of the tapes used.

How was the lace made? The drawings were traced on a light-coloured paper; this was then gummed to a piece of holland to make it firm. Commencing at the left of the pattern, the cord or braid was run on the lines of the pattern. In turning the ovals and rounds, the tape was pressed on the pattern until the edges were perfectly flat and easy; at the angles both the edges were pressed to the pattern. Then the tape was folded over to form the point. The filling stitches used to hold the tape together are those used in needlepoint.

Tape lace was made in other areas in Ireland; it was also the style of lace enjoyed by the amateur. The embroidery and lace manuals published in London from the 1840s by Eleonore Riego de la Branchardière include designs for collars and borders which are much more elaborate than the Borris work extant. *Needlecraft,* a journal published by the Manchester School of Embroidery in the early 1900s, offered patterns for edgings, tea cosies, sleeves, insertions, table-covers, collarettes, table-centres, and fans. The *Needlecraft* books also included pho-

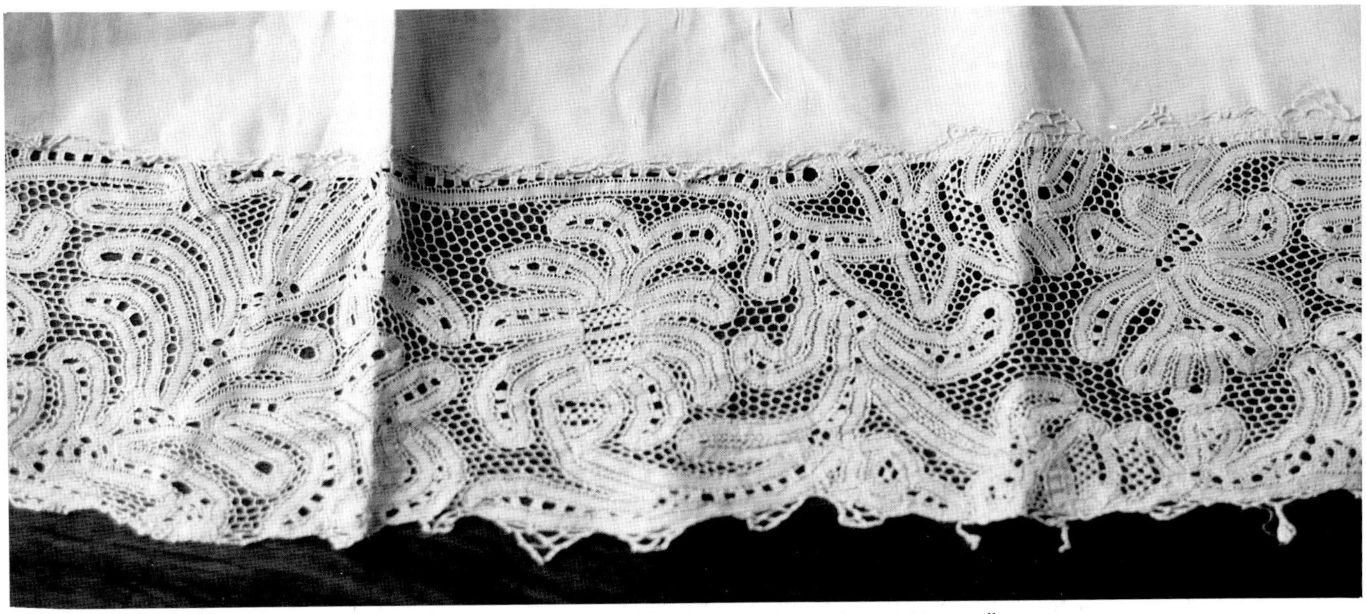

Edging of cloth using coarse tape and with hexagonal ground. Borris House collection.

BORRIS LACE

tographs of the various braids or tapes then available and a selection of the needlepoint stitches to be used in joining the braids.

Examples of the early lace made in Borris are very rare. The National Museum of Ireland has one sample of a cuff in a trailing 'coral' pattern laid down in a needlepoint braid. The outer sides of the pattern are connected by picot bars, technically known as 'brides' but in Borris called 'crags'. The centres of the design are ornamented with needlepoint stitches, further enriched by minute knots called 'picots'. The cuff was finished off by a picot edging.

After some years, the Kavanaghs changed to making 'Tape Guipure', where ready-made, bought tape replaced the handmade fabric. Most of the surviving pieces are in a coarse tape with the fillings in heavy thread. In Borris House there are also samples of table-mats where the entire background is worked in a hexagonal ground.

How big was the industry? Borris lace-making was never a very large undertaking. 'About twenty elderly widows who were in special need of financial help' are quoted as making the lace, in the earlier period and, in 1907, the report of the Home Industries Section of the Irish International Exhibition held in Dublin claimed that there were fourteen workers and a 'ready market, but no more labour available'.

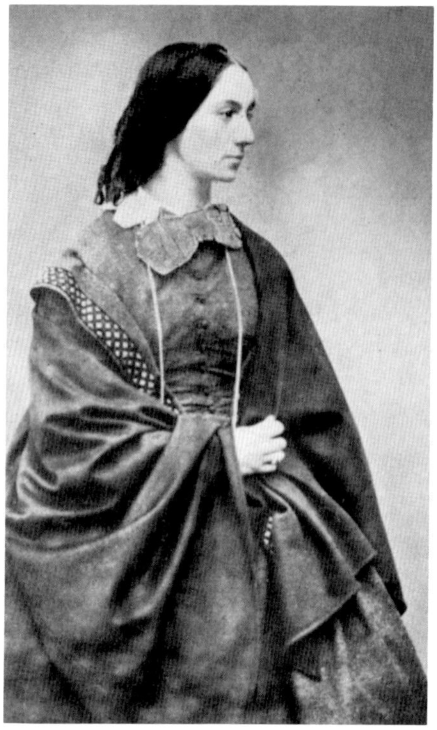

Frances Kavanagh.

Perhaps the most interesting person associated with Borris lace was Arthur Kavanagh, the son of the founder, Harriet. He was known as 'the cripple Kavanagh' because he was born with only stumps of arms and legs. He was born in 1831, the youngest child of his father's second marriage. He conquered his disadvantages, learning to ride, draw and later write, holding the brush or pen in his mouth. In later life he travelled in Persia and India. He learned to shoot, and even had his own yacht in which he sailed from Borris, down the Barrow, and from Waterford to London. When his older brothers died unexpectedly as adults, he became heir to the estate and was elected a Member of Parliament. He is credited with achieving outlets for Borris lace when he attended Parliament in London.

The Kavanagh collection at Borris House includes some European lace which was the personal property of the family. The lace can be seen by groups who make a previous appointment with Mrs Kavanagh and a tour of the house can also be arranged.

Nellie O'Cleirigh

Nellie O'Cleirigh, author of Carrickmacross Lace *(Dolmen Press 1988), writes and lectures widely on Irish lace and crafts.*

NOTES

1. I M MacLeod, 'Borris Lace 1875 to 1960', *Carloviana*, No 9 (1960) pp27-30.
2. Information supplied by the Kavanagh family.
3. 'A Renascence of the Irish Art of Lace-Making' with introductory notes and descriptions by ASC (Alan S Cole). Published London, Chapman & Hall Ltd., 1888. Facsimile edition published by Ulster Folk & Transport Museum in 1988.

THOMAS ROBERTS, 1748-1778

Michael Wynne presents a new assessment of the work of the Irish 18th century landscape artist, Thomas Roberts, and traces his journeys around Donegal and Dublin

Eighteenth-century Waterford produced one very fine architect, John Roberts (1714-96) who designed both cathedrals in the city, as well as some fine mansions in the south-east of the island. By his wife, Mary Susannah Sautelle, he had a large family, one of whom, Thomas Roberts became one of Ireland's foremost landscape artists.

The baptismal records of Waterford Cathedral show that Thomas was baptised on 22 May 1748. After basic education in his native city, Thomas came to Dublin to study at the Dublin Society's Schools, under the landscape painter James Mannin. In his first year, 1763, he won a prize at the Schools.

Following his training there, he became apprenticed to George Mullins who was active from 1763 to 1775. The young Roberts undoubtedly lived with Mullins, over the ale house *The Horseshoe and Magpie,* which actually belonged to Mullins's wife, and was located in the heart of Dublin, in the Temple Bar area.

In order to study the work of Thomas Roberts, it is necessary to consider seriously that of Mullins. Signed and dated 1768 is a set of four ideal landscapes of generous proportions, which the Earl of Charlemont had commissioned for his house at Marino, a few miles north east of the city, overlooking Dublin Bay.[1] The four sizeable canvases are uneven in quality (perhaps due to the intervention of an injudicious restorer) and depict the four times of the day. The two finest are indeed of high quality. Did Thomas Roberts, still living in Mullins's house, participate in the execution of these pictures? There may never be an answer to this question.[2]

That George Mullins was an accomplished painter in his own right may perhaps be best illustrated by *The Fishing Party,* an elegant picture, signed and dated 1772, in the Ashmolean Museum, Oxford.[3] Roberts had moved out of his own address at least three years previously. In the Oxford work one observes Mullins's complete competence in handling a group of figures seated on the ground.

In 1978 the writer gave two medium-sized ovals to Roberts: *Ideal Landscape with Ladies Bathing* and *Ideal Landscape,* then in the collection of Major John Madden, a descendant of one of the founding fathers of the Dublin Society.[4] Following constructive conversations with both Crookshank and Glin, an attribution to Mullins is much more likely. The bathing ladies are handled in a manner close to the group in the painting in the Ashmolean Museum.

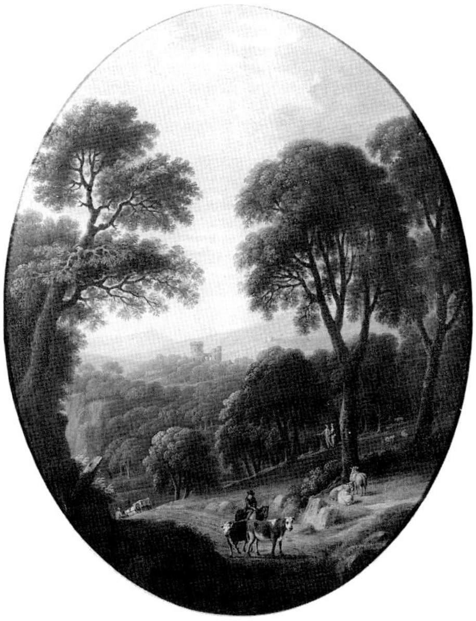

George Mullins, Ideal Landscape.
Oil on canvas 76 x 60.5 cm.
Private Collection.

A picture which should be reaffirmed as by Roberts is *View of Bray with Bathers.*[5] It is the general facture, both of the buildings and the background, which suggests this. Rather than the County Wicklow town, however, the scene is almost certainly the river Dodder with the bridge at Clonskeagh, about four miles south from the centre of Dublin, and a little inland.

Just because a picture has a finely-wrought group of figures does not make it a Mullins rather than a Roberts, where one is searching for the correct attribution. As will be seen, Roberts was no mean figure painter.

In 1769 Thomas Roberts obtained his own address, and exhibited from it at the Society of Artists in Ireland (SAI). The range of his subjects, apart from specific views, is quite remarkable; it suggests that in his six years of study and apprenticeship he must have closely examined drawings and engravings, mainly at the Dublin Society.

His *Ideal Landscape* is an exceptionally competent eighteenth-century interpretation of a seventeenth-century Claudian model; its fluidity matches any of his topographical works. In the same collection is *A Sea Storm,* possibly exhibited as number 46 at the SAI in 1771. Were this painting covered with a thick layer of darkened varnish, one would be forgiven for attributing it to Vernet.

A Land Storm is a rather unusual title which Roberts used on a number of occasions. In a private collection is a picture to which it could be applied. An awesome sky, menacing rock, stormswept trees and turbulent water give great power to this work.

Horses play an interesting role in Roberts' output. *Portrait of Bold Sir William (a Barb) an East Indian Black, and French Dog, in the possession of Gerald Fitzgerald Esq,* exhibited at the SAI 1772, (no 69) indicates by its very title that the horse is the principal focus of attention. However, in many other works, where horses are more incidental, the artist shows a fine competence in drawing them.

Thomas Roberts is rightly renowned for his topographical paintings. Viewpainting is a term originally applied to the work of Italian artists, and other continental counterparts, who accurately depicted scenes in and around towns and cities. Prime examples are Canaletto's paintings of Venice and the Veneto, and London, Bellotto's of cities in Italy, followed by Dresden, Vienna, Munich and Warsaw, and Panini's, above all, of Rome. Because of the realism shown in his depiction of towns and their environs, of houses and their demesnes, it is surely correct to extend the term *vedutista* or viewpainter to Thomas Roberts.

It would be very interesting to know Thomas Roberts' method of work in developing his landscape views. At present one may only hypothesise. John Turpin has done exhaustive work in tracing the development of painting schools in Dublin, from the earliest recorded times down to the present day. Despite combing the earliest sources, he has been unable to add to the received knowledge of the early tuition at the Dublin Society's Schools.

At these, which Roberts frequented, prior to becoming an apprentice to Mullins, he had teaching from the 'Frenchman', James Mannin, not one of whose works is known today; he had access to a collection of engravings and some original drawings; he undoubtedly

THOMAS ROBERTS, 1748-1778

worked in the medium of chalks, the undisputed technique of the figurative side of the Society's schools. It is not known whether aspiring artists were even taught the rudiments of oil technique; Roberts would have learned or perfected this during his apprenticeship with George Mullins.

What equipment did Roberts bring with him on his journey through counties Meath, Monaghan, Cavan, Fermanagh and finally Donegal? The only honest answer is 'We do not know'! In the view from Castle Watter, there is in the foreground, an artist seated in front of an easel on which is a substantial canvas; a youngster holds a parasol to protect the artist, while a tall man looks over the artist's right hand shoulder. A good sized Roberts landscape measures between ninety centimetres and one metre wide; the canvas on the easel in this painting could easily be in this category.

The device of putting an artist's self-portrait, at work, into the foreground of a painting has a long tradition. Since not one pencil sketch, or not one watercolour, by Thomas Roberts is known at present, one can only conjecture that Roberts endeavoured to paint in oils on canvas out of doors.

This last hypothesis receives further credence when one looks at the view of the Casino at Marino, County Dublin, which belongs to the Whitworth Art Gallery, University of Manchester.[6] In the close foreground of this is an artist, shown in profile, standing in front of a canvas about a metre wide; the stretched canvas sits on an easel, and the artist has no attendant or observer near by; when shown at Colnaghi's in 1988, it was fully attributed to William Ashford.

It would appear, therefore, that Roberts, where possible, liked to paint the finished canvas on site; some of the larger imaginary landscapes, and the great views in the park at Carton, County Kildare, undoubtedly were finished indoors. With the interest in Roberts generated, at least from the time of the small bi-centenary exhibition in 1978, held in the National Gallery of Ireland, any scrap of paper by him would surely have been noted.

Because one is dealing with a maximum period of ten years, and on account of the places visited, it appears appropriate to describe the view painting aspect of the painter's work under two headings: 'The Road to Donegal' and 'Around Dublin'.

The Road to Donegal

Whether or not Roberts reached the Atlantic at Ballyshannon as the result of one or more expeditions, it is fascinating to follow him on his progress north and west of Dublin through paintings which survive and which in some cases show relatively minor places.

The first known location is Beau Parc, County Meath, the home of the Lambart family, (now extinct in the main line). This lovely house is perched above the river Boyne on the south bank, immediately opposite Slane Castle. In the exquisite view taken from the Slane Castle side of the Boyne, only a small portion of the Palladian house can be seen. A boat and fishermen lend scale and further interest to this beautiful tract of water. The painting is extremely well preserved, and was the basis of one of Milton's lovely aquatints.[7]

There are some other, not very spectacular, views of this stretch of the Boyne. Now, unfortunately, lost is a fine sweep of the river showing Slane Castle from the south east, proudly standing on its prominent hill, and prior to the alterations made to the designs of Francis Johnston.[8]

Moving northwards, Roberts visited Dawson's Grove (later known as Dartrey), a substantial red brick house which had been recently built for Viscount Cremorne. Four views survive, two of which show very little of the buildings, while the other two give a clear idea of the house and of the parish church nearby. Because of its proximity, one of Ireland's most beautiful red brick houses, Bellamont Forest, can be glimpsed.

Approximately about the same latitude, but some fifteen miles to the west, is the small town of Belturbet, today a dim relic of the once thriving borough, situated at the top of Upper Lough Erne, in County Cavan. The Roberts view of Belturbet was a rediscovery, shown at the exhibition early in 1992 by the Cynthia O'Connor Gallery, Dublin. Apart from its historical value in showing what Belturbet was over two hundred years ago, this is one of the paintings which demonstrates the artist's ability to paint figures. The foreground shows a group of people engaged in fishing operations, some of them straining as they pull on ropes.

Moving northwards into County Fermanagh, but still very much in the typical landscape of Upper Lough Erne, is a view from Castle Watter, the seat of Colonel Madden. A small painting, it includes a little figure of the artist sketching, with an umbrella to protect him from the sun. This is probably the picture exhibited at the SAI in 1771, (no 43). This was where the Reverend Dr Samuel

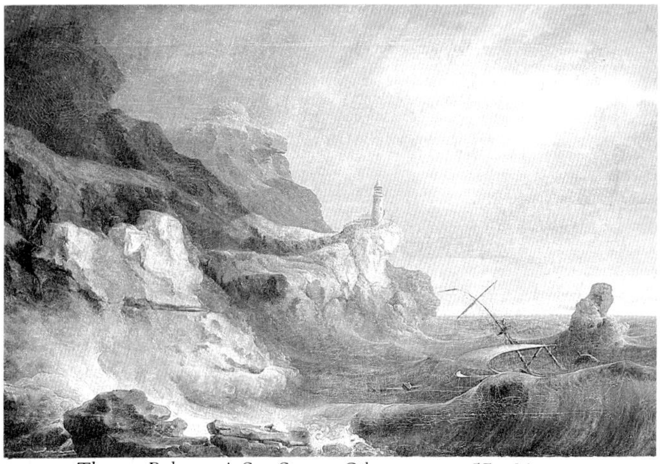

Thomas Roberts, A Sea Storm. *Oil on canvas. 57 x 91 cm. Private collection.*

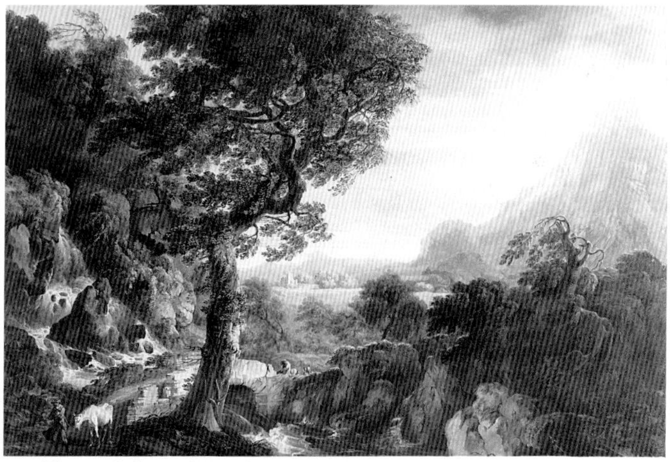

Thomas Roberts, A Land Storm. *Oil on canvas 96 x 133.5 cm. (sight). Private collection.*

Madden, (1686-1765), one of the founders of the Dublin Society grew up, and where he caused improvement to be made.[9] Thus the good doctor was practising what he preached! Only scant traces of anything constructed remain today, but of course the view is accurate.[10]

Moving further north along the east side of Upper Lough Erne, one arrives at a peninsula on which is situated the picturesque Belleisle, in 1770 the seat of Viscount Belleisle. A view from this property, and another towards Belleisle from the west side of the lake are in the collection of the Yale Centre for British Art, New Haven, Connecticut, USA. They had been acquired with a solid attribution to William Ashford, but they are unequivocally the work of Roberts.[11] The view towards Belleisle includes one of the loveliest depictions of a hunt in an Irish eighteenth-century painting. The hunt traverses the entire foreground of the picture, on the west bank of the lake, in the lee of that well known landmark, Knock Ninney.

Moving northwards, and to the west, the voyage with Thomas Roberts takes one through Enniskillen and on to the eastern shores of Lower Lough Erne. The view of the lake from Castle Archdale exhibited at the SAI in 1770, (no 46), and that exhibited in 1771, (no 44), remain untraced. They should be very attractive.

On the progress towards the Atlantic, the next recorded Roberts view is of Belleek, where Lower Lough Erne ends and becomes a river. In this view on an island opposite the manor house is an ornamental tempietto; there is no trace of it there today, and indeed in another late eighteenth-century view it does not appear. Perhaps, it was inserted by artistic licence.

Some miles downstream, at the estuary of the rapid flowing river, is the town of Ballyshannon, a gateway to County Donegal. In Roberts' painting one sees abundant fishing activity. For some decades now, that has all gone, because the falls of Ballyshannon were harnessed to provide a hydroelectric power installation, a joint venture of the Electricity Supply Boards of the Republic of Ireland and of the province of Northern Ireland.

How many of the paintings referred to above were actually commissioned? With lack of documentation, and with much more of Roberts' work to be rediscovered, this question can not be answered satisfactorily, especially when useful provenance is very scant indeed. It is reasonable to suggest that the four paintings of Dartrey and its surroundings which were together in the possession of descendants of the Dawson family, until recently, were a specific commission.

Owners of properties depicted by Roberts, or of persons living in the area, may well have bought pictures from the artist, when they saw the completed views.

There are extant some versions of views; one may mention in particular Views from and to Belleisle, and of the town of Ballyshannon.

It is reasonable to speculate that Roberts did more paintings 'On the Road to Donegal'. The documented views from Castle Archdale are, for example, currently untraced. On Lower Lough Erne, Castlecaldwell, sitting on top of a strong peninsula, would have been a very fine subject; the town of Enniskillen, situated where Upper and Lower Lough Erne are distinguished, with its castle and other fine buildings, would have been quite a challenge; on Upper Lough Erne, a fine sight would have been old Crom Castle.

In the series of paintings described above, there is no marked sign of artistic development. Consequently, they should be dated around 1770, when the first Lough Erne view was exhibited. Vernet, whose work is so well documented, must have done on average a painting every week, and some of them are quite large. Allowing Roberts two excursions on his north-west route, 1770-1772 should cover the paintings done on that way.

Around Dublin

Sailing into Dublin Bay is a truly beautiful experience; looking out to Dublin Bay from the city reveals lovely vistas. Dublin is truly blessed insofar as, within an arc of no more than twenty miles, one can experience a myriad of the wonders of nature.

About fifteen miles to the south, and a few miles inland, one is in the middle of the Powerscourt demesne, which itself is a microcosm of contrasts. Successive Viscounts Powerscourt added to the beauty of the property and welcomed visitors, especially artists. Related by marriage to the old owners, the present proprietors, the Slazengers, continue the tradition, making only a modest entrance charge to help defray the immense costs of maintaining the wilder parts of the property and one of the foremost formal gardens in the whole of Ireland.

While there are small landscapes which include as backdrops the Small Sugar Loaf and the Large Sugar Loaf mountains, at present no really major painting by

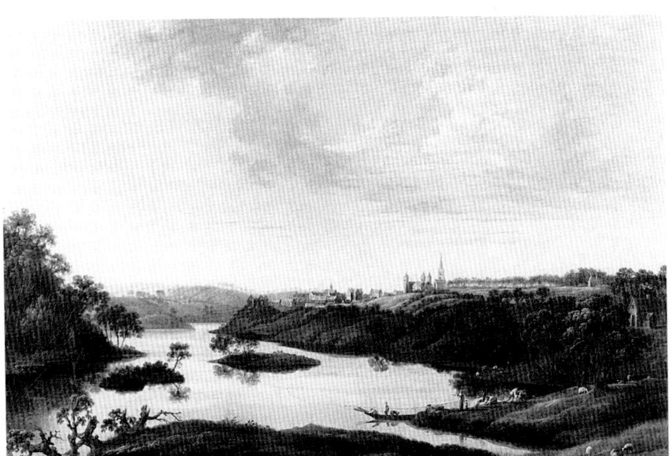

Thomas Roberts, A view of Belturbet, County Cavan,
Oil on canvas, 62 x 96 cm. Private collection.

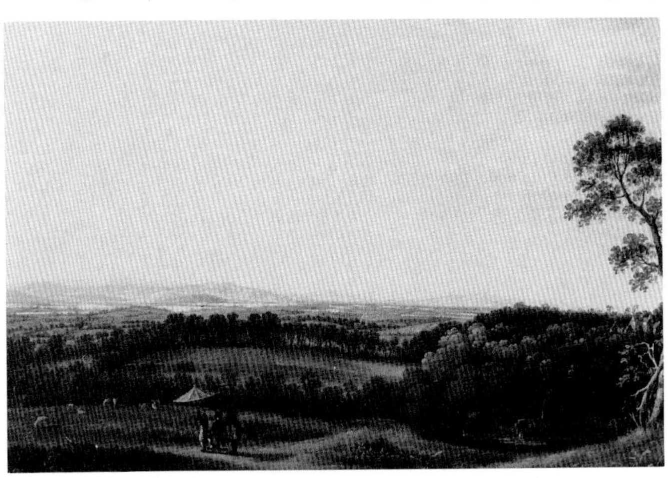

Thomas Roberts, Castle Watter, County Fermanagh.
Oil on canvas 39 x 61 cm. Private collection.

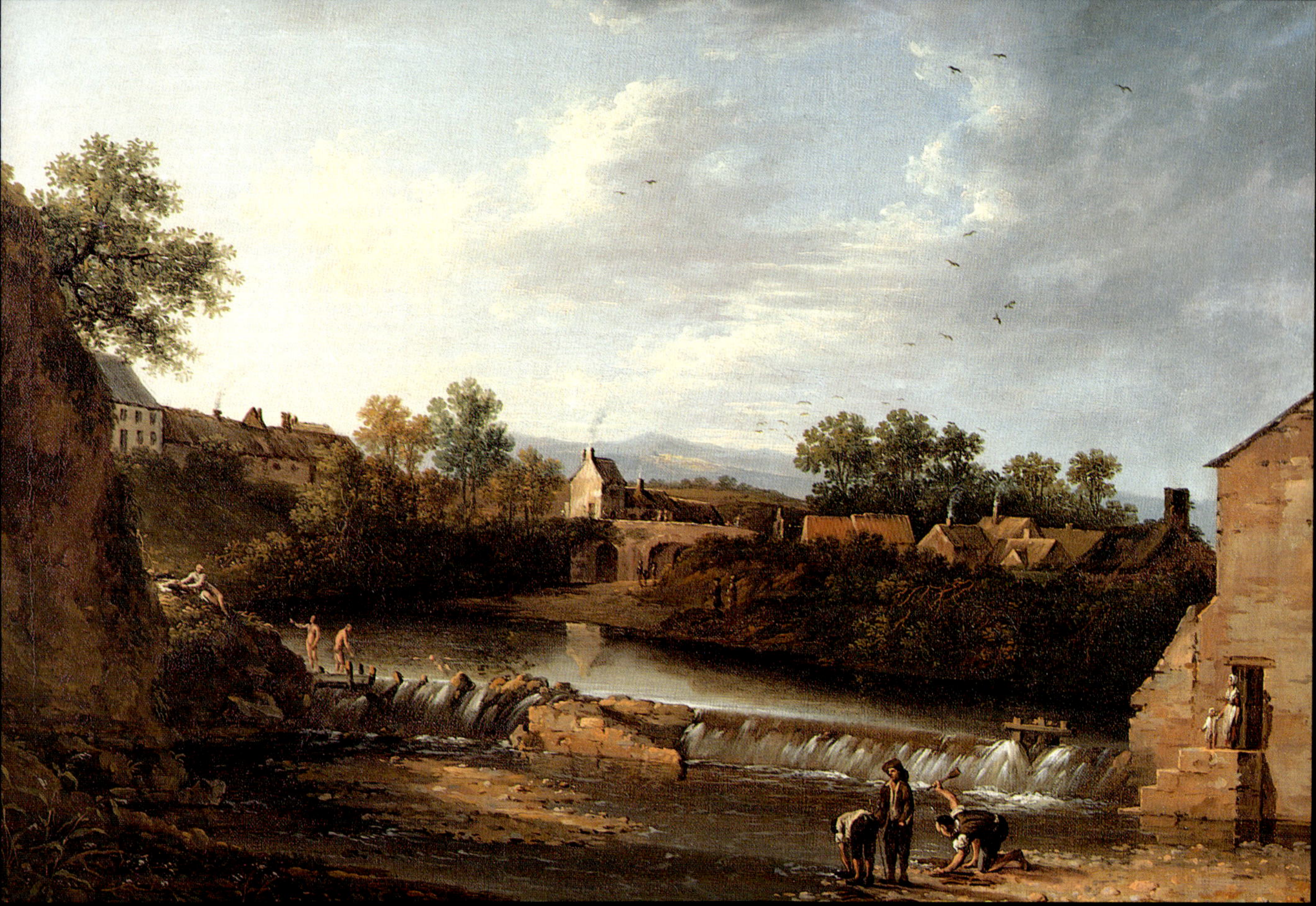

Thomas Roberts, Clonskeagh Bridge, County Dublin. *Oil on canvas, 43 x 63 cm. Private Collection.*

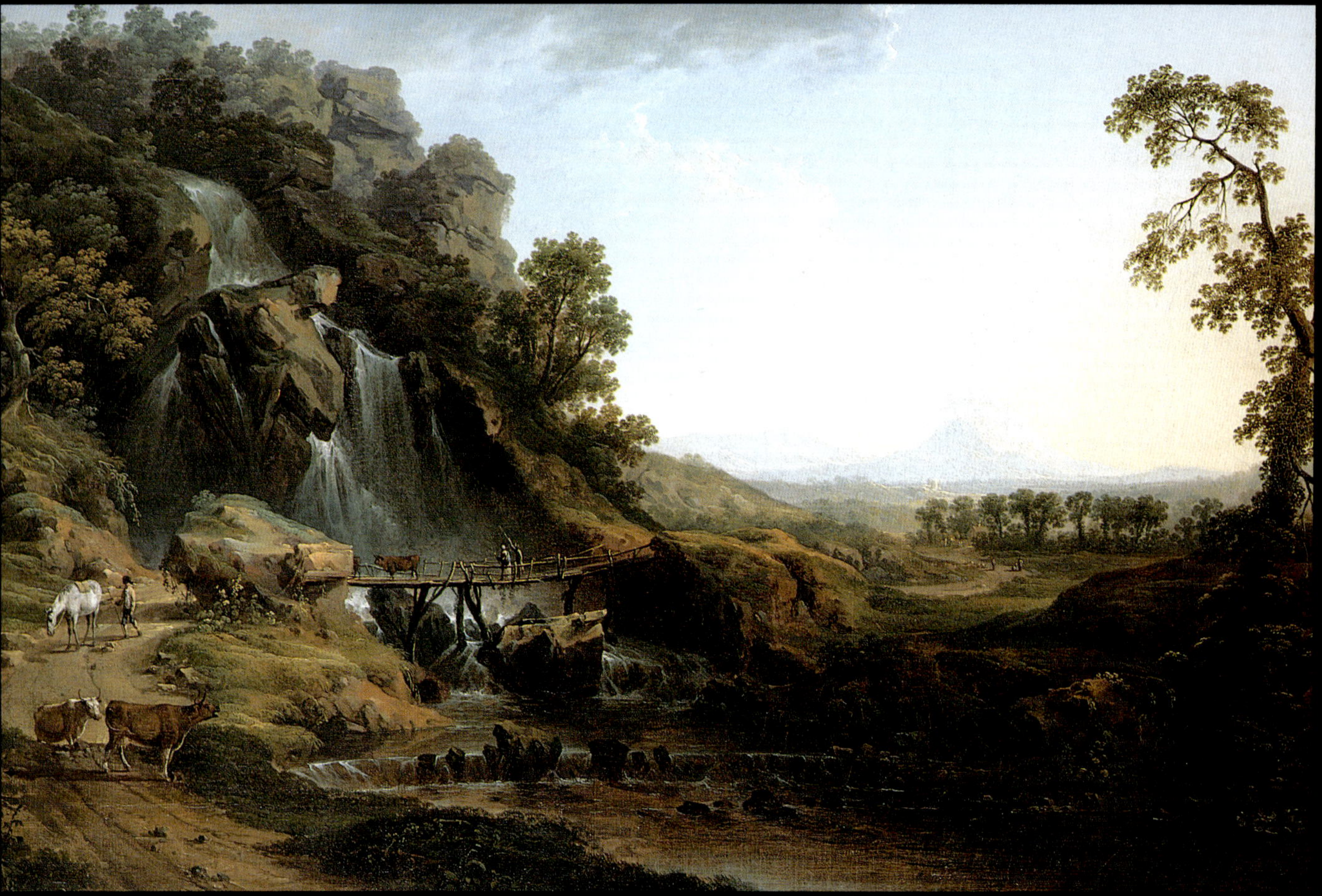

Thomas Roberts, Ideal Landscape. *Oil on canvas, 57 x 91 cm. Private collection.*

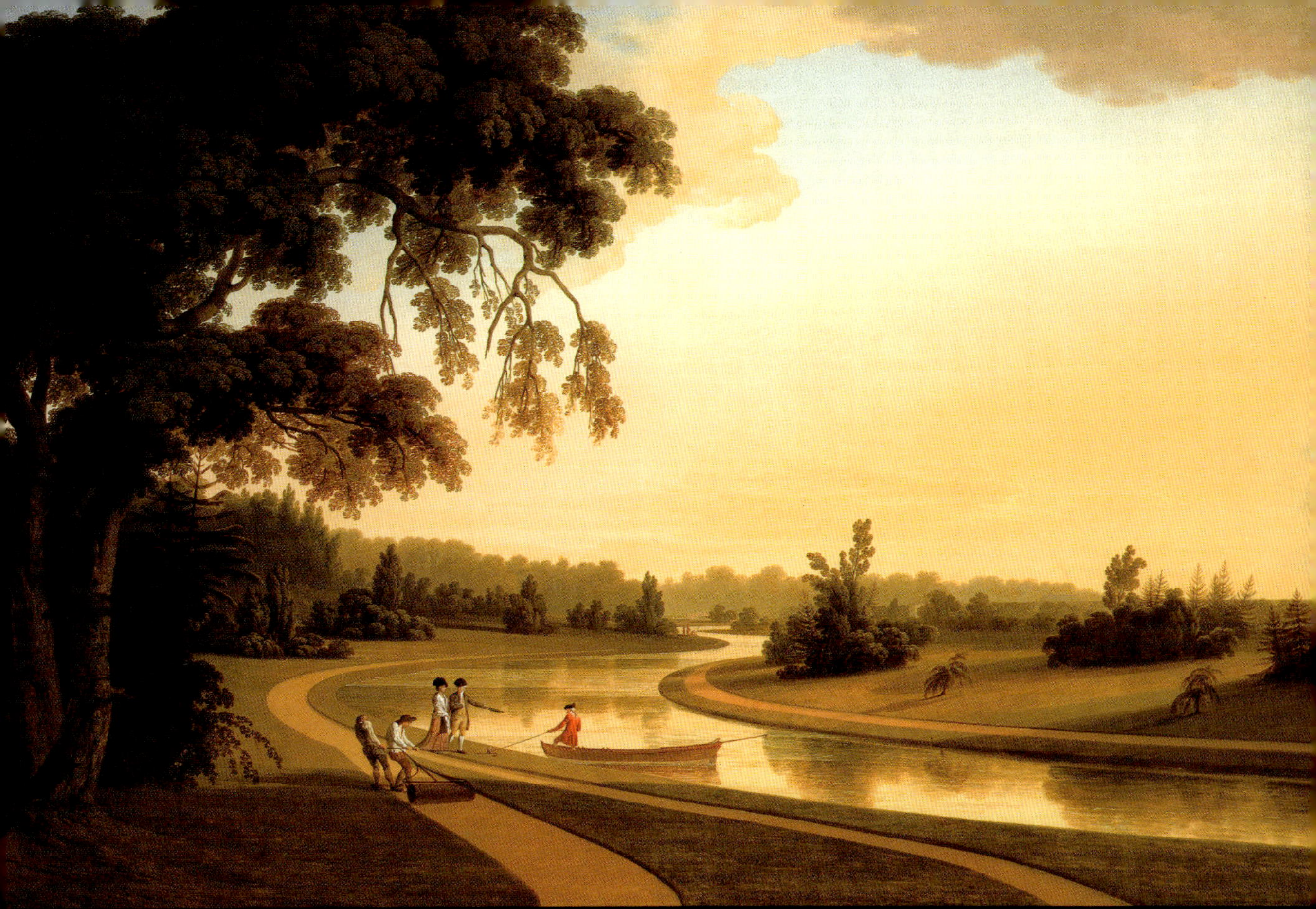

Thomas Roberts, Sheet of Water at Carton, County Kildare. *Oil on canvas, 112 x 153 cm. Private collection.*

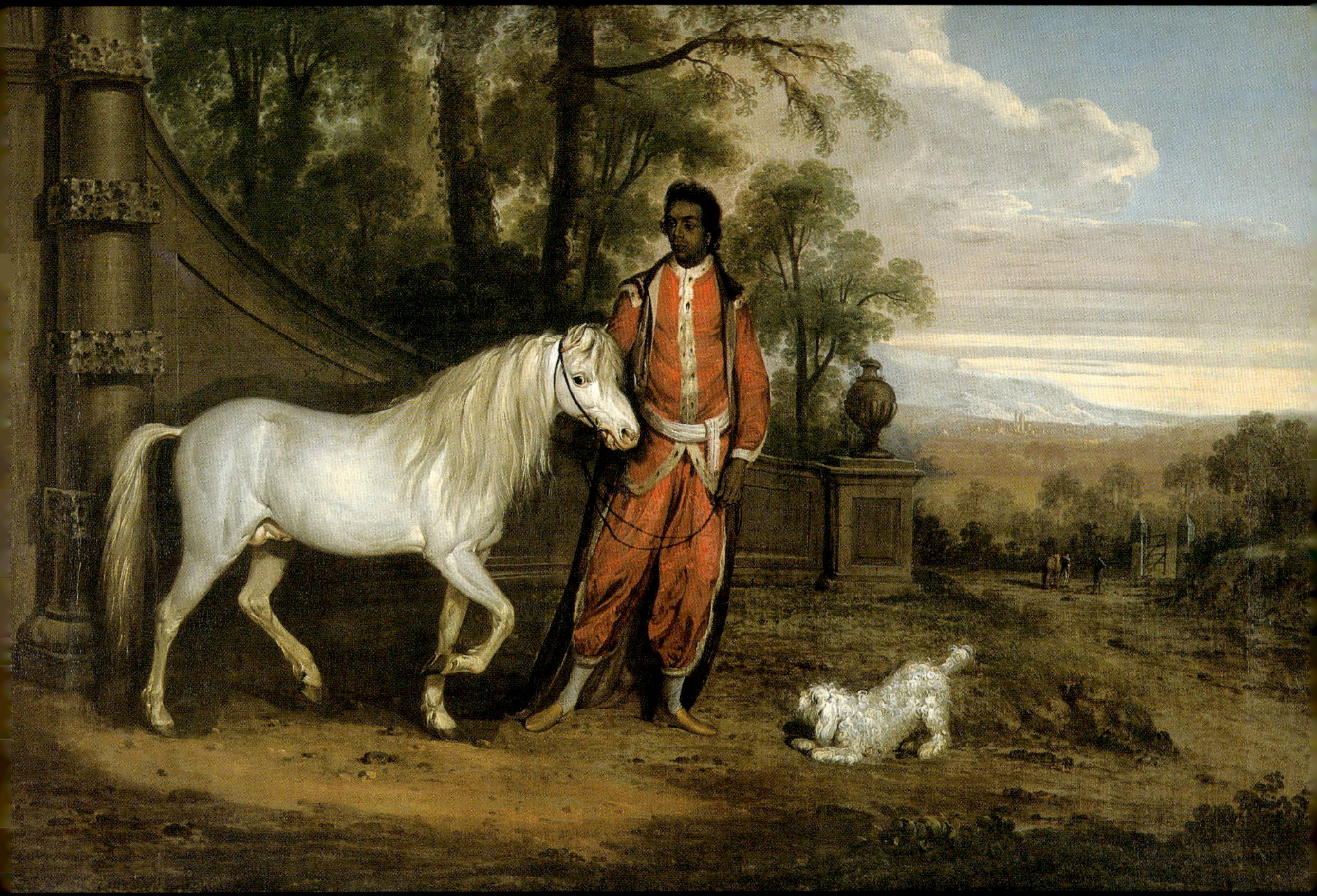

Thomas Roberts, Portrait of bold Sir William (a Barb), an East Indian black, and French dog, in the possession of Gerald Fitzgerald. *Oil on canvas, 62.2 x 92.6 cm. Private collection.*

THOMAS ROBERTS, 1748-1778

Roberts within the Powerscourt estate is known. Recorded are *A View in the Dargle* (SAI 1769, no 66) and *A View of Tinneyhinch Mountains* (SAI 1769, no 67); what is certain is that they would have been quality pictures and, perhaps, important works. Other County Wicklow views are also recorded.

Rathfarnham today is a residential suburb of Dublin, but in 1769 when Roberts exhibited *A View of Rathfarnham Castle, the Seat of the Earl of Ely* (SAI 1769, no 63) the castle, about six miles south west of the city, had a magnificent demesne, and was out in the country. Recently a private collector acquired a large painting, beautifully executed, which must surely be the exhibited work. It is a splendid panorama of the whole area, with the castle acting as a small-scale focal point.

While Rathfarnham is in the valley of the river Dodder, the lower reaches of the better known river Liffey are an artist's delight. So it is not surprising to find Roberts along that water with his painterly equipment. There are several single canvases of the area around Lucan, but the set of four, including one showing old Lucan house, was a very fortunate acquisition by the National Gallery of Ireland in 1983. The set remained in the new (present) house by family descent until the contents were sold in 1925 (a photograph in the sale catalogue shows them hanging in the Dining Room); at that sale they were bought by a member of the family who sold them by private treaty to the Gallery. The view showing old Lucan House is historically very important; it must be dated to the early 1770s, when the proprietor, Agmondisham Vesey, was designing his new house (with some advice from Sir William Chambers). The old house was certainly more romantic than the new Palladian villa, which is superbly maintained by the Italian Government as the official residence of its Ambassador. Mrs Vesey, a noted blue-stocking both in London and Dublin, missed the nooks and crannies of the older building.

Apart from lending scale in landscape painting, figures can take on a life of their own. In the bottom right hand corner of this picture a group of men appear to be quarrying stone close to the road. They are depicted with deft, quick brushstrokes, and lend an air of vivacity to the composition.

The three other views in this set show parts of the demesne attached to Lucan House; they are all of high quality.

While Agmondisham Vesey, an amateur architect, sought the opinion of Sir William Chambers, a more famous Irishman actually employed the great English architect on a number of projects. That of particular interest here is the Casino, a building of exquisite design, which Lord Charlemont (frequently referred to as 'The Volunteer Earl') caused to be constructed in his park, about four miles north east of the city centre. Roberts painted a splendid canvas in which the Casino seems perfectly at home in its setting, overlooking Dublin Bay. The picture, which belongs to the Whitworth Gallery, of the University of Manchester, was, until a few years ago, understandably attributed to William Ashford.

Roberts painted other pictures for Lord Charlemont, and one eagerly awaits their re-emergence from oblivion.

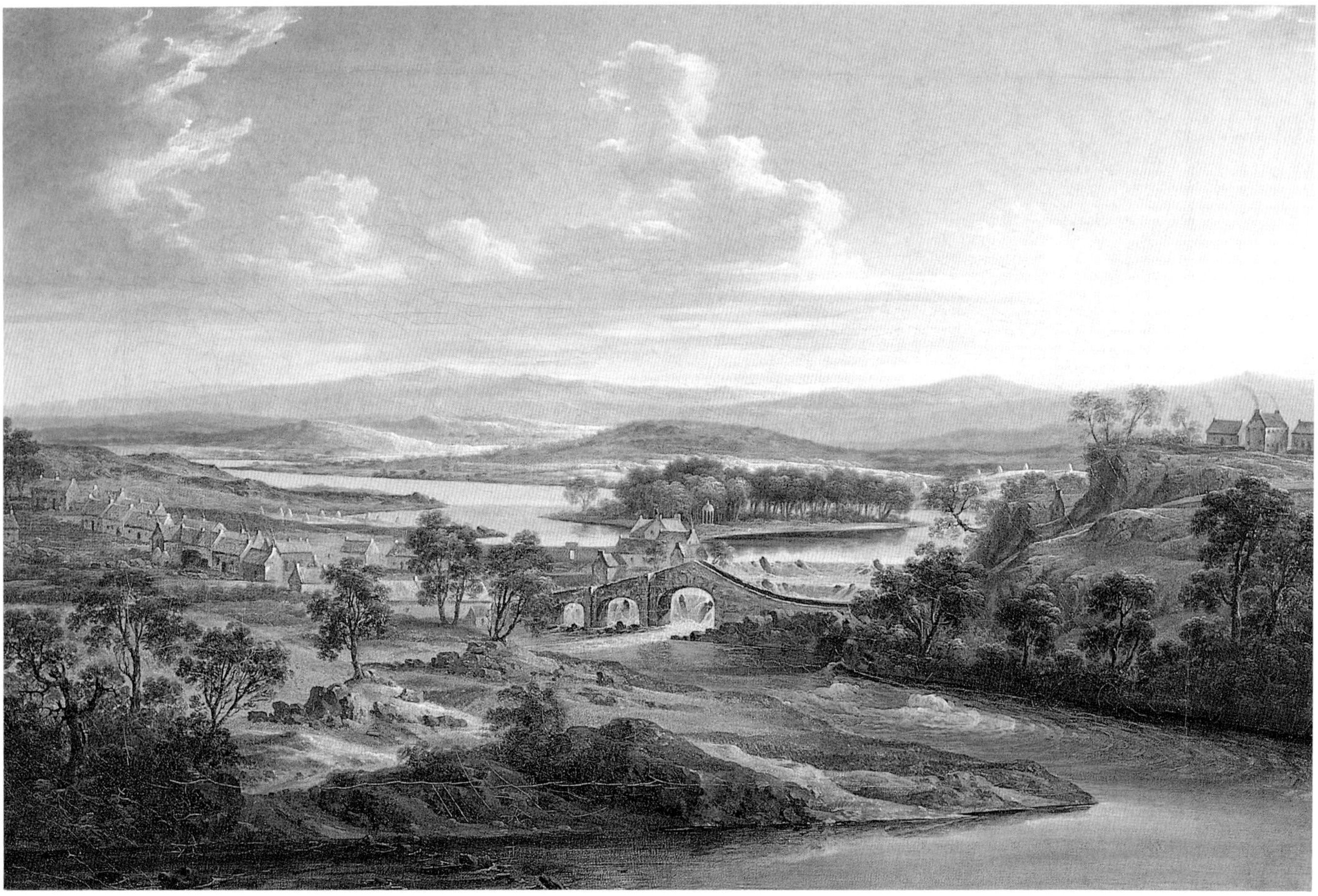

Thomas Roberts, A view of Belleek. *Oil on canvas, 45.5 x 64 cm. Private collection.*

THOMAS ROBERTS, 1748-1778

Ireland's premier peer, the first Duke of Leinster, remade the great park at Carton, County Kildare, in the then fashionable Capability Brown style. His expenditure must have been substantial, since, apart from earth-moving, the new, splendid features included a most gracious bridge built in stone to the designs of the distinguished Irish architect, Thomas Ivory. Carton Park was a triumph. It was the second Duke who commissioned from Thomas Roberts six large views of the demesne, within at least three years of receiving his inheritance in 1773. It has as its centrepiece the beautiful bridge designed by Ivory. The best-loved Roberts is undoubtedly that in which the second Duke and his Duchess are about to step into a punt from the finely manicured lawns, in order to glide along the tamed watercourses. Thomas Roberts managed to complete only four of the large canvases, one of which is dated 1776. By 1777 the artist was recorded as being in London on his way to Lisbon, in order to seek a cure for the tuberculosis which he had contracted. In 1778 Roberts died in Lisbon. To complete the series of six canvases the Duke commissioned the remainder from William Ashford, and his two paintings are in the collection of the present Duke of Leinster. Regrettably the four Roberts are in four different private collections. The second Duke, as Marquess of Kildare, spent a substantial part of his Grand Tour in Turin, at least from October 1767 until March 1768.[12] Kildare wanted to enrol in the highly respected Accademia Reale di Savoia, which survives to this day as the Academia Militare.[13] However, his father would not permit this, even for the minimum period of six months. The first Duke of Leinster wanted his eldest son and heir to proceed to Vienna, to participate in the activities around the imperial court. Nonetheless, Kildare became a noted and respected person at the court of the King of Sardinia, going out 'a hunting' with King Carlo Emanuele III, his heir, the Duke of Savoy, and a younger son of the king, the Duke of Chiablese.

During these hunting expeditions Kildare would have seen such royal palaces as Stupinigi, Mirafiori, Venaria Reale, Vigna di Madama Reale, Rivoli, Moncalieri, and others. Frequenting various indoor activities of the court, the young Irishman could not have but noticed the pride which the House of Savoy had in the great works of architecture and decoration which they had commissioned. It is sufficient to note the series of canvases depicting these accomplishments by the Maestro delle Residenze Sabaude, c.1670,[14] or the later paintings by Panini, *View of the castle of Rivoli from the east*[15] and *View of the castle of of Rivoli from the south,*[16] dating from the late 1720s.

It is clear from the copious correspondence from Kildare to his mother that he was really enjoying life at the court in Turin. And from other sources it is clear that he was extremely popular. Several Englishmen living in Turin thought of petitioning the King to appoint Kildare as the Minister Plenipotentiary to the court of Savoy. Kildare protested that he was too young, and too inexperienced for such as assignment. Moreover, he was anxious to return to Ireland in order to marry his

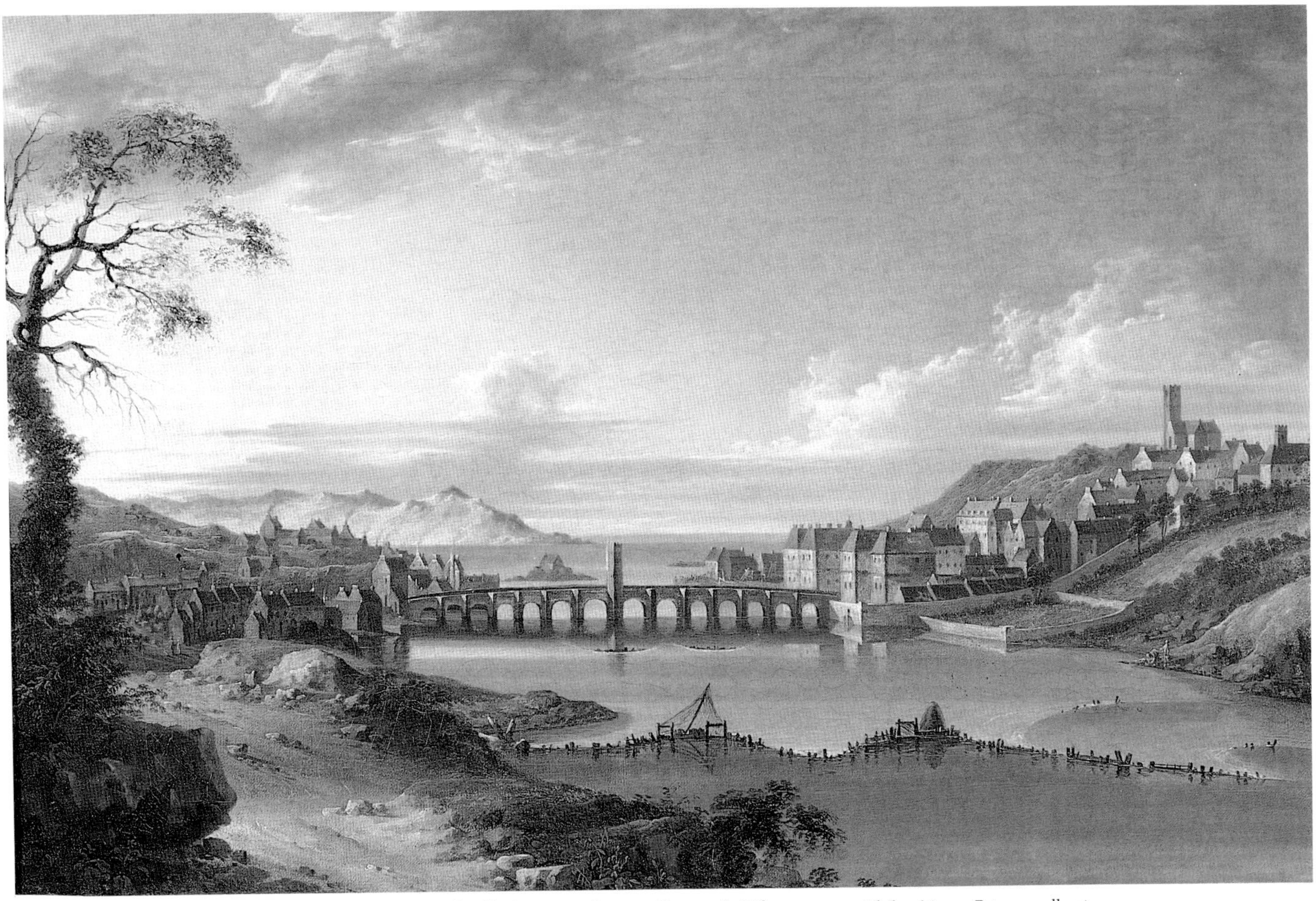

Thomas Roberts, A view of Ballyshannon, County Donegal. *Oil on canvas, 45.5 x 64 cm. Private collection.*

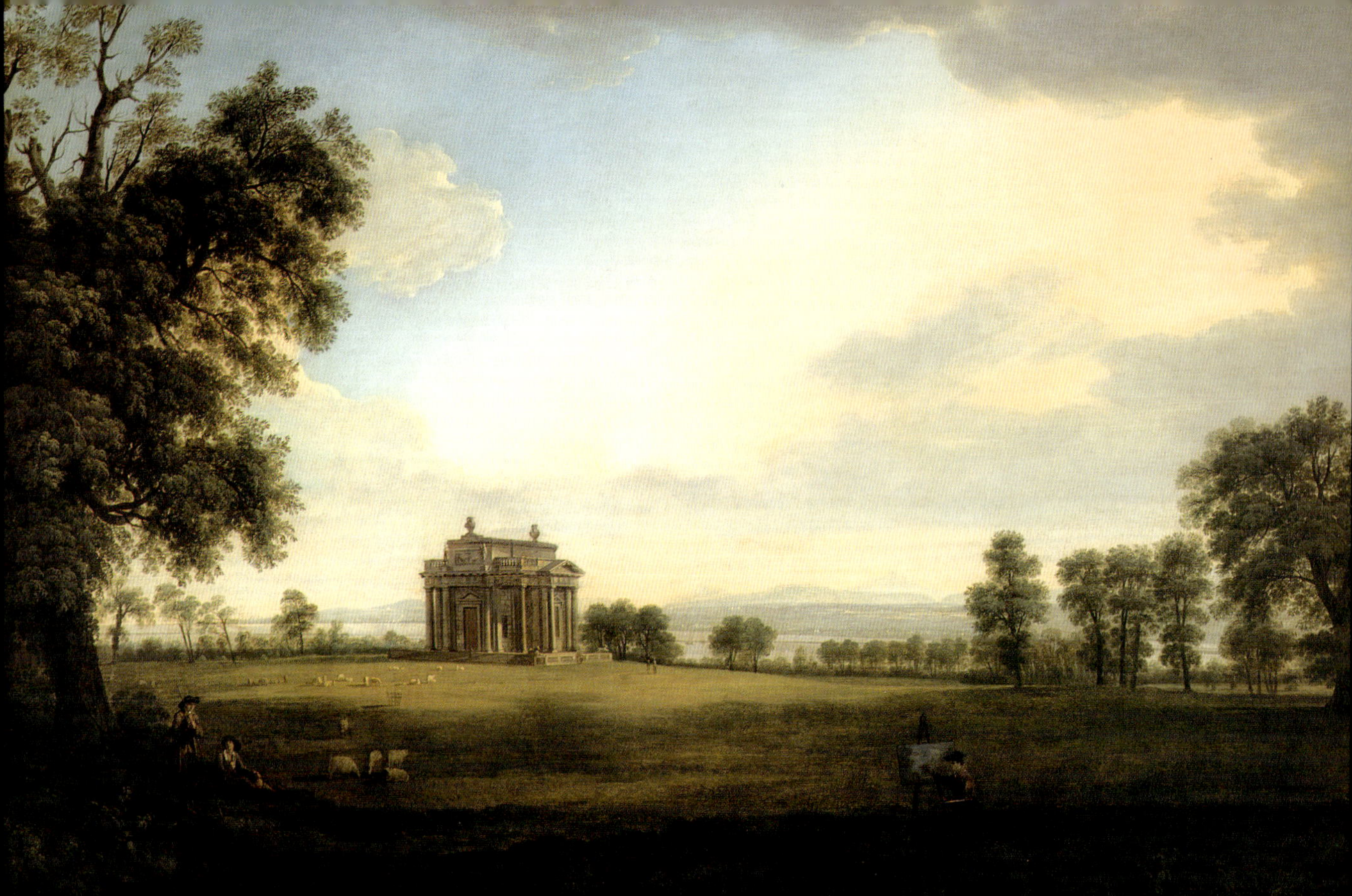

Thomas Roberts, The Casino at Marino, County Dublin. *öil on canvas, 62.3 x 96.3 cm.*
Whitworth Art Gallery, University of Manchester.

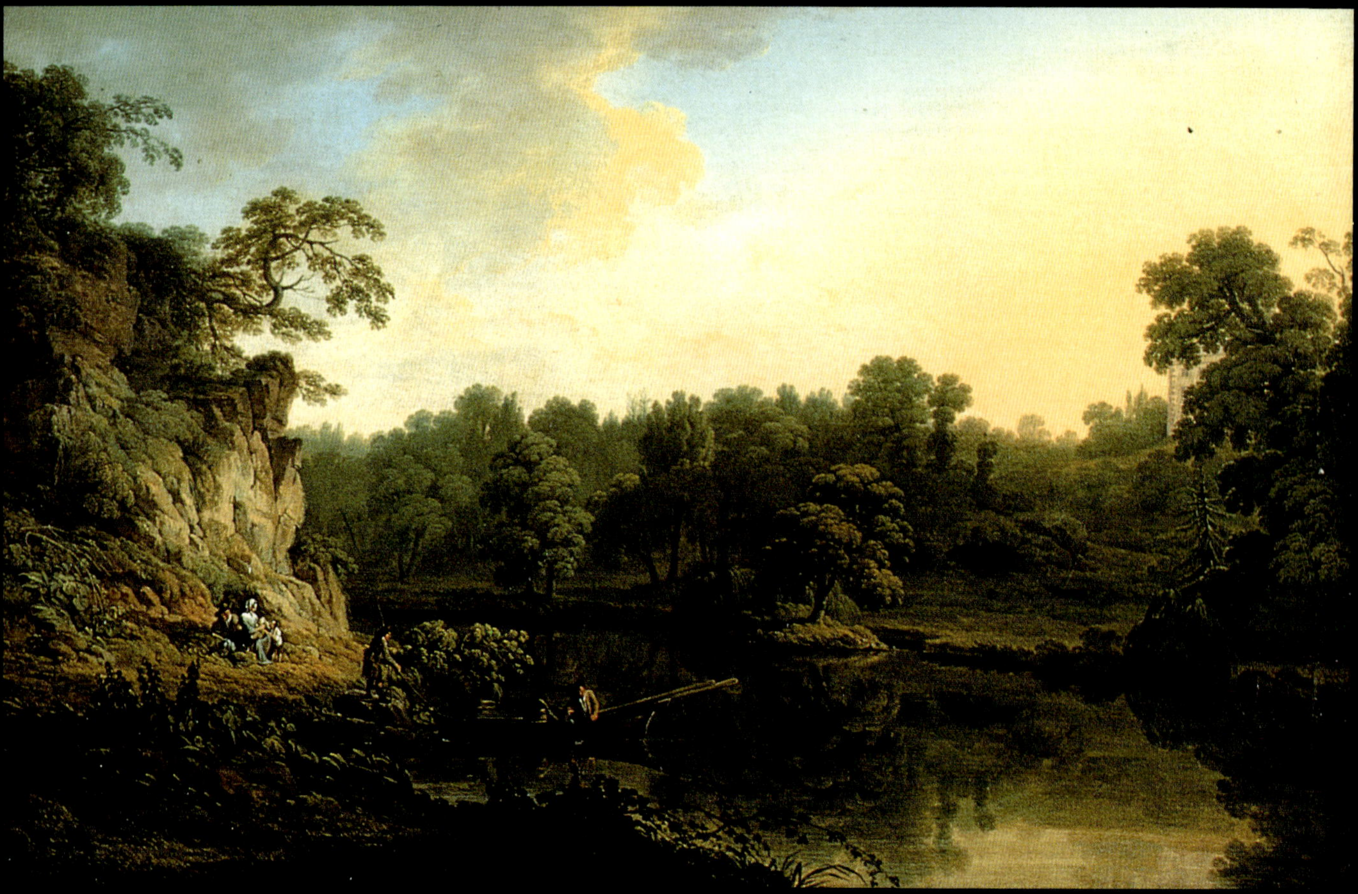

Thomas Roberts, Beau Parc, County Meath, seen from the river Boyne, *oil on canvas, 62 x 95 cm (sight). Private collection.*

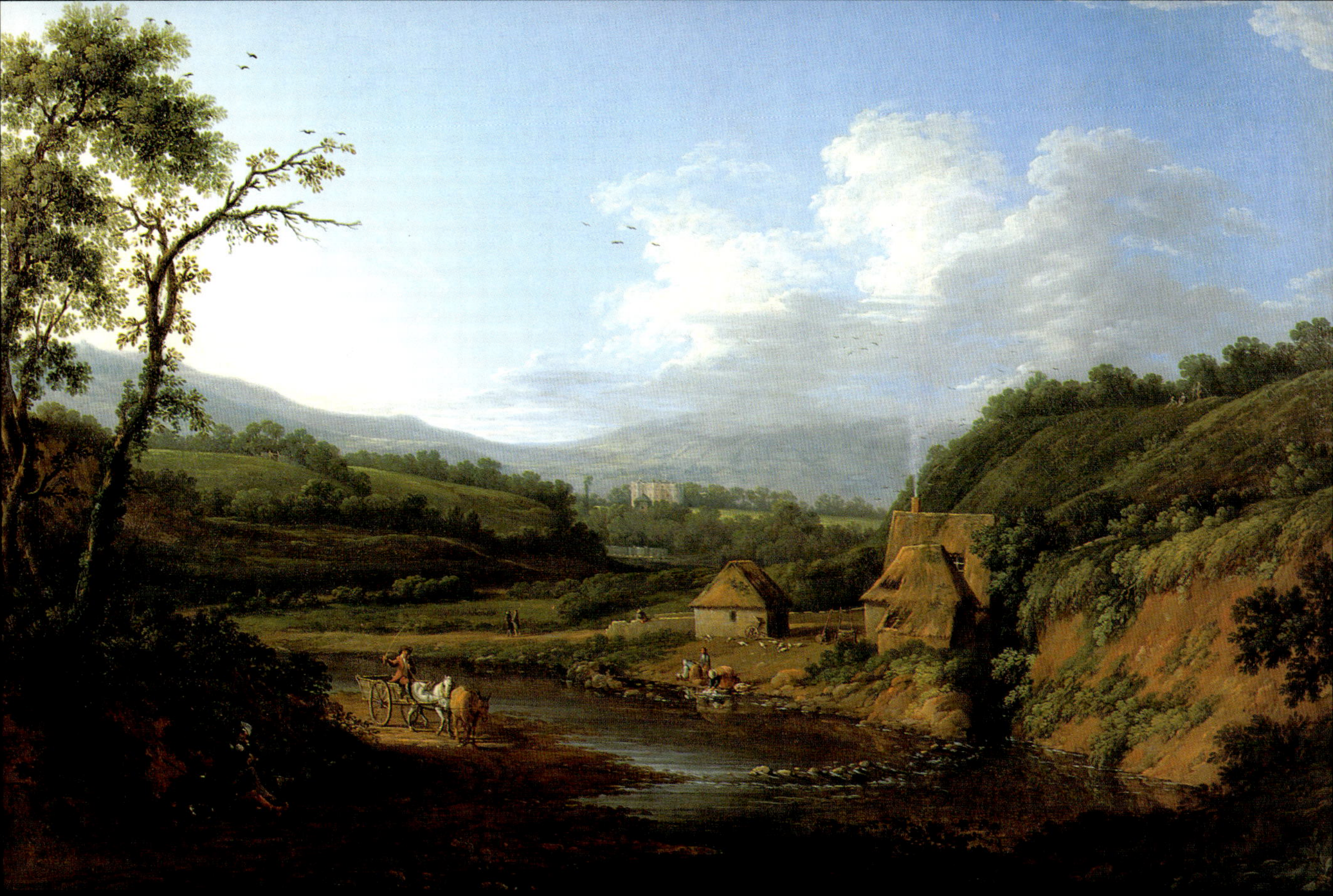

Thomas Roberts, An extensive view with Rathfarnham Castle, County Dublin. *Private collection.*

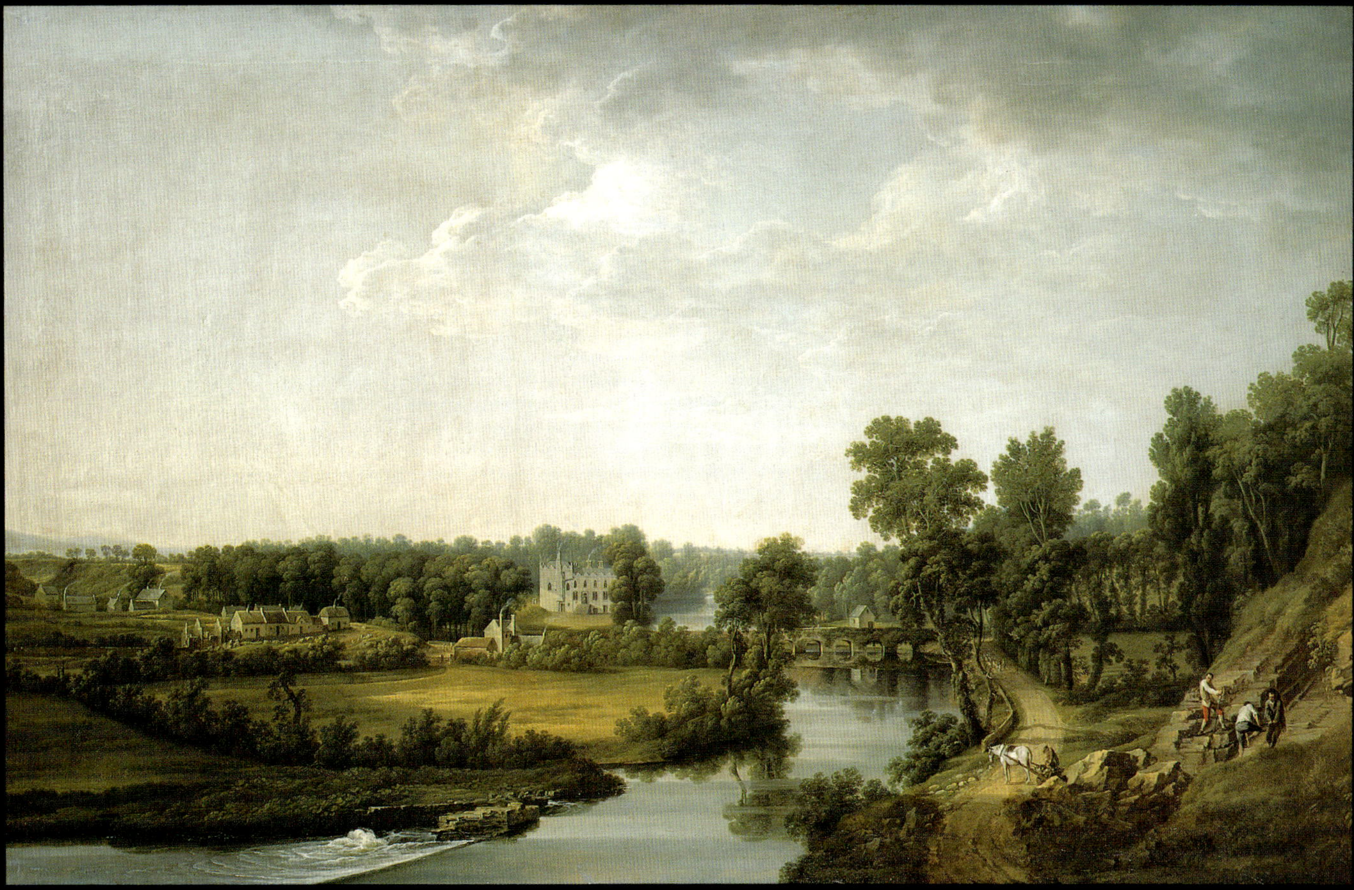

Thomas Roberts, A view of Lucan House, village and demesne, County Dublin. *Oil on canvas, 60.5 x 100 cm. National Gallery of Ireland, cat.no. 4463.*

THOMAS ROBERTS, 1748-1778

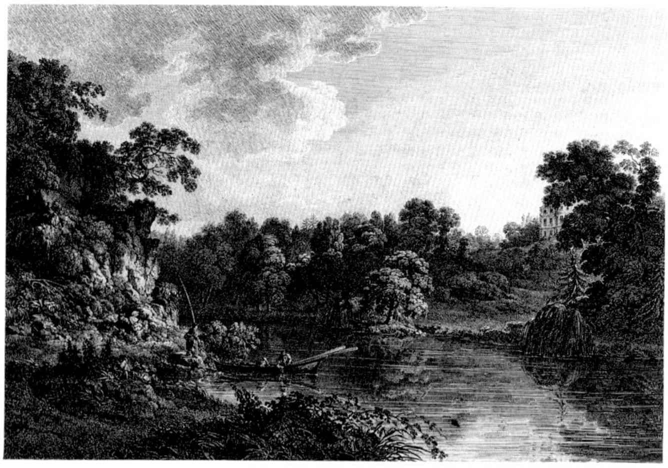

Thomas Milton, after Thomas Roberts, Beau Parc,County Meath. Aquatint, 13.2 x 19.1 cm. National Gallery of Ireland, cat.no. 20,277.

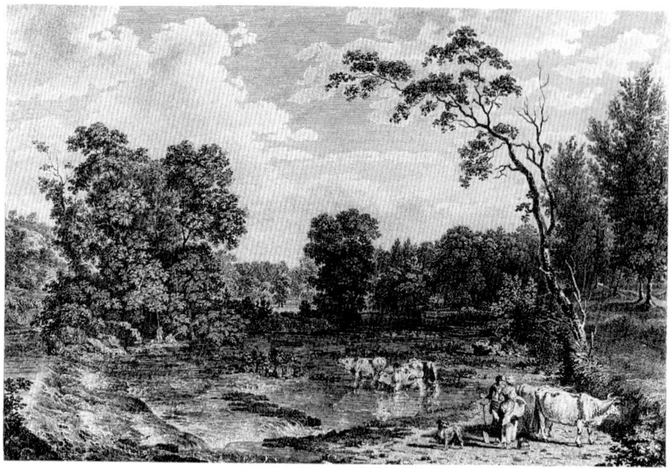

Thomas Milton, after Thomas Roberts, Lucan, County Dublin. Aquatint, 13.2 x 19.1 cm. National Gallery of Ireland cat.no. 20,295.

first love. Is it too far-fetched to suggest that the paintings of the buildings, gardens and parks which he saw in the countryside around the capital, gave him the idea to call upon Thomas Roberts to portray the magnificent demesne of Carton House which he inherited in 1773?

For a long time Roberts was known principally through the famous set of four views in the Carton House demesne.[17] On these views the public image of Roberts' work was founded. They were, however, untypical since Carton was *the* outstanding park created in the Capability Brown mode, in the entire island; moreover, it was well known, being less than twenty miles due west of Dublin, just within the confines of County Kildare. The great lime walk advancing westwards finished with a gate in the small town of Maynooth. At the western end of the town, on land provided by the FitzGeralds, was the royal foundation, St Patrick's College, initially a rather small national seminary, but later a major pontifical university. The students from the college were free to enjoy this great park; they could scarcely get up to much mischief, since they were obliged to wear clerical attire, down to the time when Carton was sold by the Leinster family.

It would appear that the very beautifully landscaped park at Carton drew out of Roberts the style of painting which is now seen to be unique within his *oeuvre*. So much has been learned in the past twenty years and Roberts is now known to have painted prolifically in a style quite different to his last commission.

Eyes trained on these four paintings found it difficult to give the name of Roberts to other works, whether larger or smaller. Many were assigned to William Ashford, an excellent artist, prolific and long-lived, who became first President of the Royal Hibernian Academy in 1823. Few of Roberts' works were engraved; two lovely aquatints by Milton show the weir in the Lucan House estate and a view of Beau Parc from the north side of the river Boyne.

About twenty years ago connoisseurs began to assess Roberts more critically, and, apart from signed works, there is a growing number of paintings which are securely attributed to Roberts. Despite the brevity of the artist's life, and presuming that he could have painted very little during his period of illness in 1777 and 1778, the number of pictures should increase steadily.

Michael Wynne

Dr Michael Wynne is the Keeper of the National Gallery of Ireland.

NOTES

1. Following the destruction of this house, the paintings had a somewhat chequered history until they were bought by the Irish government; they now embellish Arus an Uachtaráin (official residence of the President of Ireland).
2. Michael Wynne, 'Thomas Roberts, 1748-1778. Some reflections of the bicentenary of his death", *Studies*, Winter 1977, pp. 299-308.
3. Anne Crookshank and The Knight of Glin, *The Painters of Ireland, c 1660-1920,* London 1978, p. 127; ill., p. 128.
4. Michael Wynne, *Thomas Roberts, 1748-1778, Irish landscape artist.* Catalogue of exhibition held in The National Gallery of Ireland, Dublin 1978.
5. *Ibid.*, no. 20.
6. *Prospects of Town and Park. A Loan Exhibition of View Paintings to Mark the 85th Year of The National Art-Collections Fund,* Colnaghi, London 1988, no. 18.
7. Thomas Milton, *Seats and Demesnes of the Nobility and Gentry in Ireland,* London 1783-1794, pl. XI.
8. Photograph in Cynthia O'Connor Gallery archives.
9. Edward Malins and The Knight of Glin, *Lost Demesnes, Irish Landscape Gardening, 1660-1845,* London 1976, pp. 43-44.
10. Major John Madden, the present head of the family, told the writer that at a certain date the above property and that of Roslea Manor were sold and the proceeds used to buy a large property with better land, Hilton, in County Cavan.
11. Wynne 1977, p. 300.
12. Brian FitzGerald (ed.), *The Correspondence of Emily, Duchess of Leinster, 1731-1814,* Vol. 3, Dublin 1957, pp. 493-536.
13. Walter Barberis, *Le armi del Principe. La tradizione militare sabauda,* Torino 1988, pp. 177-185.
14. Michela de Macco and Giovanni Romano (ed.), *Diana trionfatrice. Arte di corte nel Piemonte del Scicento,* Exhibition catalogue, Parco del Valentino, Torino, 1989, nos. 345-46, 348, 351, 356-57, 359.
15. Gianfranco Gritella, *Rivoli. Genesi di una residenza sabauda,* Modena 1986, p. 102.
16. *Ibid.*, p. 95.
17. The paintings were kept at Carton until the dispersal of the contents of that house, when they were bought by the Hon Desmond Guinness, of nearby Leixlip Castle, who consigned all four for auction in London in 1983.

TEN YEARS OF EARLY IRISH METALWORK

Since 1984 many new developments in Early Irish Art scholarship have taken place. **Michael Ryan**, who wrote in our first issue, assesses the position ten years later.

Since the publication of the first issue of *Irish Arts Review* in 1984 something of a revolution has taken place in the field of early Irish art – new finds, new excavations and a significant increase in the amount of publication, especially in areas which had been neglected, have changed the way we must look at most important issues. In the same period a notable international conference on insular art has been founded, the proceedings of which are bringing new research to a wide audience.[1] We have seen renewed interest, after a considerable lull, in sculpture, led by Peter Harbison's work which has provoked a number of important responses, including that of Professor O Murchadha on the inscriptions on the Kinnitty Cross and the Cross of the Scriptures at Clonmacnoise, long thought to be illegible.[2] The publication of the facsimile of the Book of Kells is beginning to spark the scholarly response which many had hoped for and a steady stream of papers relating to the important field of metalwork has brought attention to a resource for evaluating aspects of the culture of the period which has often been overlooked by those who approach the subject solely from the point of view of the art historian or archaeologist. Welcome light has been shed on the visual arts by work in neighbouring disciplines, in particular Dáibhí O Cróinín's re-reading of the sources for the crucial period of development in the late seventh/early eighth century which enables us to put old controversies about the art of the Lindisfarne and Echternach Gospels into a more balanced perspective.[3] A new approach to the understanding of how early Irish society functioned has done much to place the artist-craftsman in his correct position in the scheme of things. While some myths are tenacious and some new implausibilities have been given currency, in general our interpretations of early Irish art have begun to carry more conviction. We now rely more on an understanding of structure, manufacture and analysis of motif. Above all, the function of a work of art is given its proper stress; we see how the artist related ornament to the purpose of the piece, but we also see how a given object might have had a variety of social purposes which transcended immediate practical considerations. A gospel book proclaimed the status of a church, a founding saint or patron, or signalled an aspiration to higher status. A personal ornament announced the prestige or the pretensions of the wearer, or the subordinate status of one who received it as a gift.

Our reception of early Irish art suffers from an inherent modern bias to look at the arts in categories such as 'fine' and 'decorative'. Thus painting and sculpture are 'fine' and goldsmithing, for example, is not. Such divisions would have been meaningless in Early Medieval Ireland where the artificer in metal, the forger and decorator of the weapons and accoutrements of the nobles, enjoyed a high, although not noble, status. His patterns were often borrowed by the illuminator and sculptor. Early Irish art, although best known from pieces made for the church, is firmly rooted in its inheritance from a barbaric, aristocratic society. Christ as hero or lord with a following of clients, much like a secular ruler, was never far from the thoughts of many early churchmen.

Early Irish art is intricate, allusive and richly symbolic. Much of its meaning has been lost because there was no artistic continuity between our own and early times. It is often only accessible to the modern viewer on a purely sensual level because its conventions are not fully understood. As a result, outside the arcane world of the specialist, its reception has frequently been one of admiration for its ornamental skill but little beyond that. Because the great rediscoveries of the nineteenth century inextricably linked early Irish art with emergent nationalism, national pride has come to play a significant part in how it is assessed. A consequence of this has been the inappropriate weighting of scholarly debate (especially about the relative importance of Anglo-Saxon influences) and also, paradoxically, an undue stress on fairly marginal aspects of the style and sometimes downright misunderstanding.

Amongst the commonest myths is the assumption that pieces – manuscripts, metal objects and the like – took an immensely long time to complete. So long in fact that it would have allowed no time in the average life to master an art, develop a style and achieve an output to attract patronage. There is no allowance in this view for teamwork, the use of shortcuts and sheer mastery of technique, and little for the formal training that early Irish law recognises. Françoise Henry suggested that the Cross of Cong took almost a decade to manufacture despite the fact that most of its components are cast and could have been prepared from pre-existing models – Raghnall Ó Floinn has pointed to the existence of a fragment of a cross of similar type in the National Museum which suggests strongly that the Cross of Cong was by no means unique.[4]

Another misconception is that all products are about on a par – that the quality of workmanship was uniformly high. Here too there is no allowance for great differences in the abilities of artists, for the fact that there was much production for daily use, for poorer patrons and even that there were ways of replicating components (by casting and die-stamping, for example) which could be used in fabricating objects of different types. Such replication of multiple copies of components was widely practised in the eighth and ninth centuries. This is brought into sharp focus by the Lough Kinale book shrine which bears an appliqué cross with round bosses on the front. Detached bosses of this type have been found both at Clonmacnoise and in Norway, where so much Irish metalwork ended up during the Viking Age. Pyramidal bronze bosses, almost certainly detached from processional crosses, have been found both in Ireland and in Norway. These, Peter Harbison has shown, were represented in sculpture on the arms of crosses carved on Pictish slabs of the eighth or ninth century. In metalwork they appear in miniature on the arms of the little wood and metal cross of about 800AD from Antrim (now in the Hunt Museum in Limerick). The supply of liturgical objects for the many churches of the time required the development of fairly standard products. This fact alone opens up the possibility of establishing a form of lineal relationship between objects, and of defining the products of distinctive workshop traditions.

Just as we know that some manuscripts were collaborative efforts, some metalwork objects may also have been made by teams. Some great pieces used such varied techniques, enamelling, casting, engraving filigree, that it is easy to conceive of the work being broken down and shared out among

TEN YEARS OF EARLY IRISH METALWORK

specialists and trainees. Proving it is a different matter, although we know that the Shrine of Saint Patrick's Bell was made about 1100 AD by a team of father and sons. There is clear evidence from code-markings on some objects, that literate individuals were involved in their creation. The Derrynaflan Paten for example, had a letter assembly code engraved on its components. Roman numerals have been noted on parts of the Ardagh Chalice. These must surely have been suggested by clerics.

Modern research has shed a great deal of light on how the illuminators and metalworkers of early Ireland worked. The manuscript painter ruled careful grids in drypoint, and laid out elaborate scrolled patterns by compass for freehand finishing. The metalworker often did exactly the same. The engraver of the discs in the hoard of door furniture from Donore, Co Meath, set up an elaborate compass-drawn grid for his complex scrolled patterns, incised through a film of tin-plating to reveal the underlying bronze. The ornament is uncannily like that of the Lindisfarne Gospels painted in the north of England at the turn of the seventh century. The relationship between kingly families and churches in Ireland and Northumbria raise anew intriguing questions about the flowering of the arts in the eighth century. Both the manuscript and the metalwork from Donore share their decorative idiom with the contemporary 'Tara' Brooch, a small, cast-silver personal ornament with filigree, glass and amber embellishments. Despite years of over-popularisation, it remains one of the most delicate, elegant and sophisticated pieces of jewellery of early medieval times. Its animal patterns seem to have a Christian symbolic significance which may have been intended to protect the wearer from harm. The symmetrical opposition of two beasts which is so much a feature of the decoration of the broad surfaces of brooches of Tara type, seems to be a version of the 'Tree of Life' motif which has obvious Christian overtones. The temptation to regard the ornament of manuscripts and metalwork as 'barbaric' style pressed into service by the church obscures the more likely explanation that much of it is borrowed Christian iconography brilliantly and elaborately reinterpreted by original craftsmen perfectly capable of assimilating and recreating the whole variety of their artistic experience.

A number of metalworking sites have been excavated. Some of these were high-status secular dwellings. Of these the royal crannog of Lagore, near Dunshaughlin, Co Meath excavated in the 1930s is perhaps the best known. Here, the fragments of unfinished processes and other debris are almost certainly the residue left by the execution of commissions on site by the craftsmen working for a potentate. As a royal residence, any quasi-industrial work there was likely to be secondary to the business of kingship. Current excavations by John Bradley at the crannog of Moynagh Lough, near Nobber, also in Co Meath, have revealed a site where fine metalworking was carried out over a long period – furnaces, mould fragments, slags and finished objects were found. We may well have here the residence of a metal-worker who had attained considerable wealth and status. Nevertheless, agriculture remained important to the occupants, and so it is possible that in the secular world, artistic activity was by no means full-time.

Investigations of monastic sites like Armagh and Clonmacnoise as well as lesser known places such as Movilla in Co Down have added to what we know from the poorly documented discoveries made at Nendrum, Co Down in the 1920s. These have established the significance of metalworking on ecclesiastical sites. The evidence of excavation and the sheer volume of discoveries from all other sources in recent years (the Derrynaflan Hoard, the Lough Kinale book-shrine, the Donore Hoard, the Blackwater Shrine, and many smaller objects and fragments) show that the original production of the workshops was considerable.[5] The art in metal, although predominantly in bronze, is nevertheless testimony to the wealth of the church in particular, and also of leading kings who, from the ninth century onwards, are recorded as endowing the enshrinement of relics. The aristocratic and wealthy society which supported these artists was, in its way, cosmopolitan, and this did not fail to have its effect on the arts of the time.

The Derrynaflan Paten, a work of the mid- to later eighth century, clearly owes its decorative layout to late Roman silver platters with animal and other scenes around the rim. Such plates are known to have been adapted for liturgical use in Early Medieval Europe in the period between the fourth and the seventh centuries, and so we cannot say if the paten is based on an imported model or one seen abroad by its patron or fabricator, or whether it is merely an Irish representative of a tradition which had long been fully assimilated in the western church as the appropriate style for patens. The paten with its elaborate polychrome ornament of gold filigree, gilt-bronze, cast studs of glass imitating gemstones and stamped foils is sumptuous. It is the acme of its tradition, matched only by the Ardagh Chalice in complexity and employment of skill.

One of the most striking things about the ninth century chalice from the Derrynaflan Hoard is how much of its filigree ornament of beasts and birds differs from the interlaced and contorted animals of works such as the Book of Kells and the Ardagh Chalice. On closer examination we can identify griffons and other quadrupeds which appear on Early Christian sarcophagi in Gaul and Italy. Drawn in a naturalistic way on a sacred vessel with all the skill of a good cartoonist, they must mean something profound, they are not mere doodles. The Derrynaflan Paten reinforces this view because its little filigree scenes also borrow from the repertoire of Mediterranean Christian symbolism. They are more ornamental than on the later chalice but still not subordinated to decoration. Symbolic references to baptism, the eucharist and redemption, the beasts of Genesis and the Psalms can be identified. We are looking at the works of a sophisticated and conscious tradition addressed to a knowledgeable and appreciative audience. It was not a popular art, its audience was very small and the number who handled sacred vessels, and could see and appreciate their detail, was very restricted. The paintings of the Book of Kells are nowadays seen as complex comments on the adjacent texts. Tracts were read at Mass and the Book could have been exposed so that the paintings – the Temptation, the Virgin and Child, the Evangelists for example – could, perhaps, have been used to reinforce a text, although there is little evidence of this practice in the liturgy of the period. Much of its ornament could only have been seen by a reader. The driving force in elaborate ornamentation was therefore devotion, the work being prayer made visible. The same impulse informed the metalworker, who lavished great detail on surfaces of sacred vessels which would not usually have been seen. An example of this is the

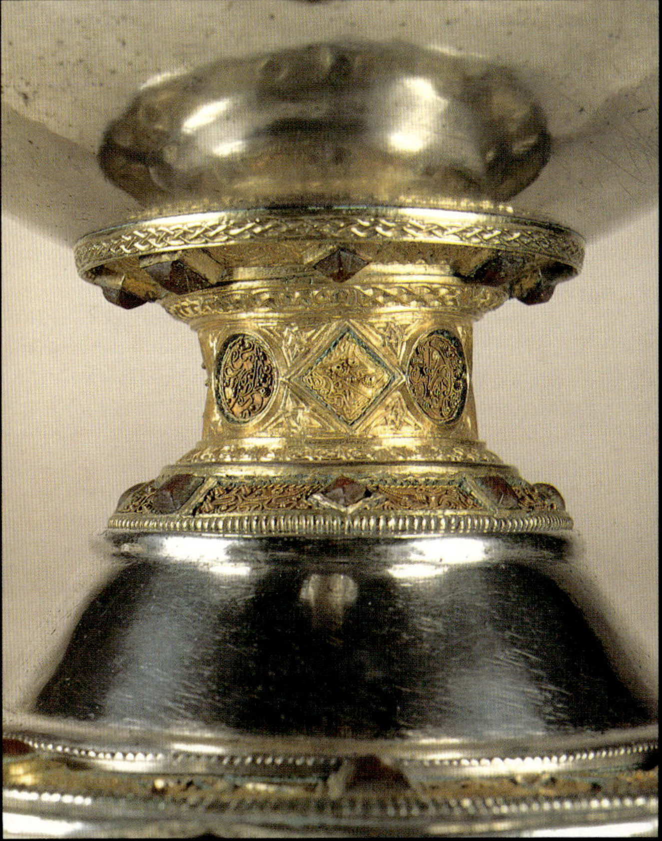

The Derrynaflan Chalice: detail of the stem.
National Museum of Ireland.

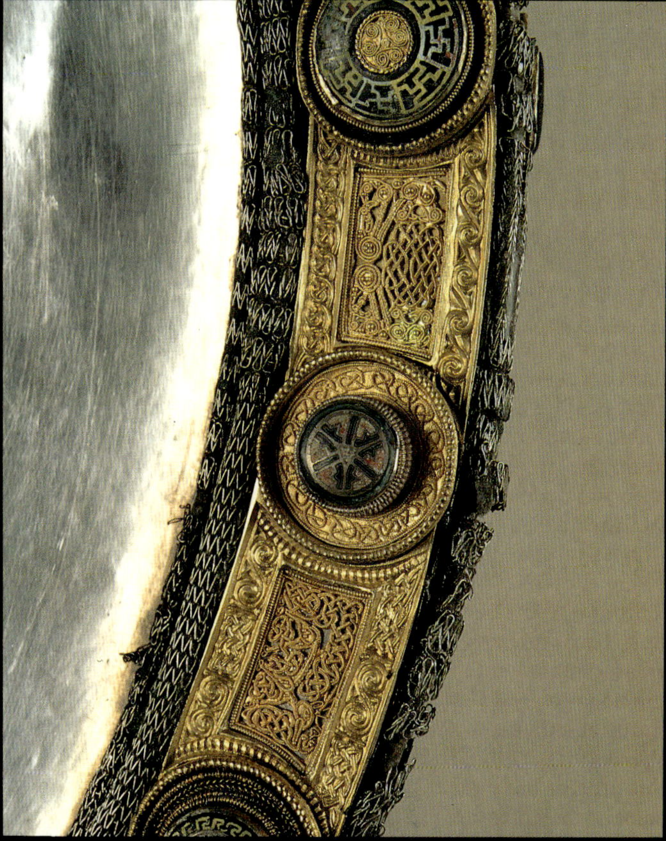

The Derrynaflan Paten: detail of stag and snake filigree panel.
National Museum of Ireland.

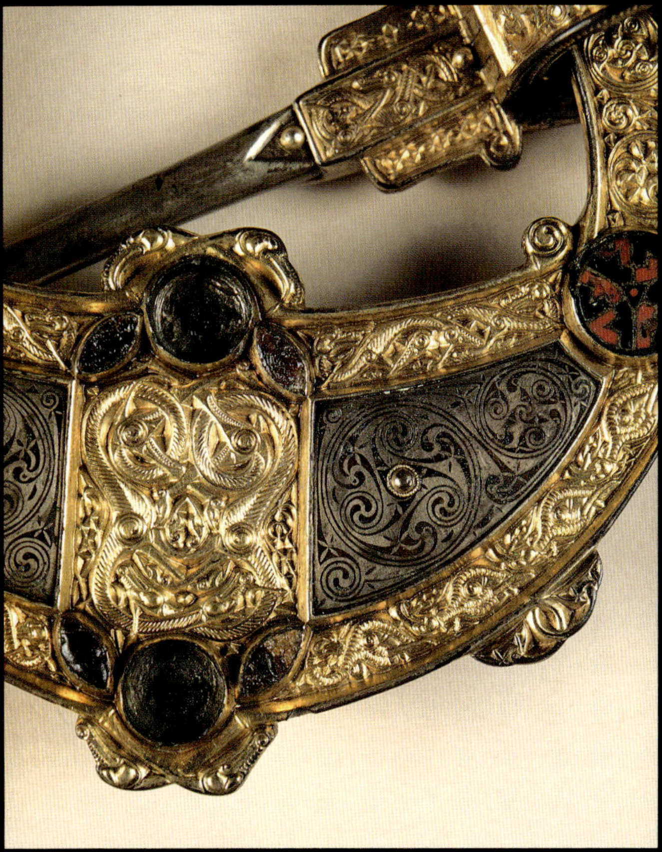

The Tara Brooch: view of bird frieze on reverse.
National Museum of Ireland.

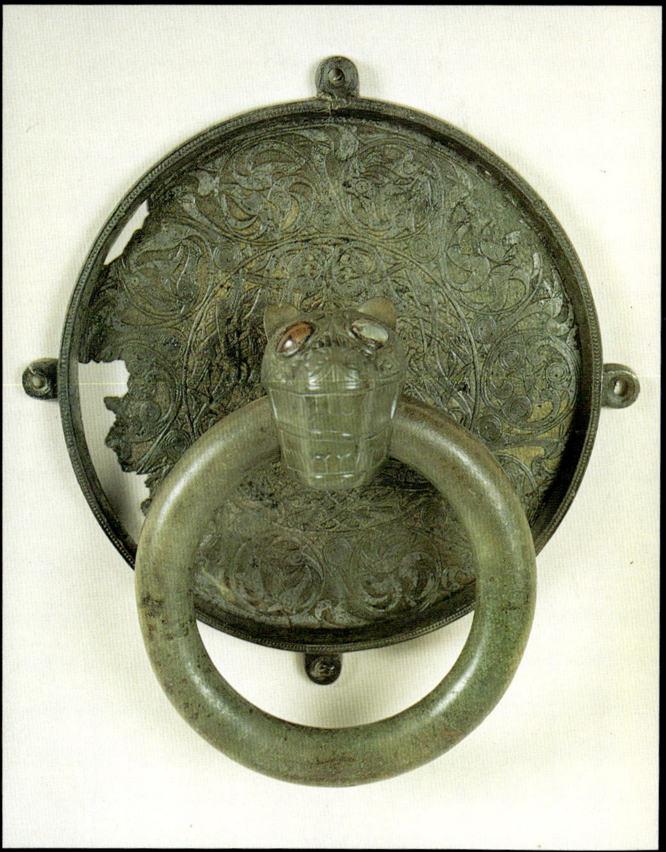

The Donore handle: general view of assembly of handle and disc,
National Museum of Ireland.

TEN YEARS OF EARLY IRISH METALWORK

decoration of the underside of the Ardagh Chalice which was made at a time when the cup was not elevated during the celebration of the eucharist. The ornament hides an ugly feature of the construction of the cup.

From the later ninth century onwards, high crosses bearing programmes of scriptural scenes which could have been used didactically were raised on monastic sites. These represented a significant departure from the modest scale and miniature effects of the metalworker and illuminator, and they began to appear at a time when stone churches first became widespread. There is no necessary link between stone sculpture and novel architecture except that both represent a turning towards greater monumentality, a greater sense of the need to proclaim to a wide public the status of monasteries which had achieved a powerful position in secular society. But this process did not require the abandonment of the miniature effects of the metalworker. The new expressions in stone seem to have become common during the ninth and tenth centuries. While this coincides with intense phases of Viking activity we cannot regard them as having supplanted earlier artistic traditions. Indeed the building of churches and the commissioning of crosses indicate that there was more patronage available for artists, and historical evidence, such as it is, supports this view. Shrines for the Books of Durrow and Armagh were endowed at this time by leading midlands kings one of whom, Flann Sinna, also patronised the sculptor who carved the Cross of the Scriptures at Clonmacnoise. One of the most persistent of popular myths has been the assumption that the Vikings all but extinguished artistic activity in Ireland and that it had to be revived in the centuries after Clontarf. This seems not to have been so; we can still identify peaks of achievement in the later seventh and eighth centuries, on the one hand, and in the later eleventh and twelfth centuries, on the other. The stylistic evidence for continuity between the two periods is substantial and while the artists of the Renaissance of the eleventh and twelfth centuries drew on late Viking Age influences, they married them to their native style, and to borrowings from Romanesque Europe, to forge the last great animal art style in the west.

Because they were deposited in hoards, the great works in metal survived, when many church treasures elsewhere were recycled or lost. They have, therefore, no very close contemporary analogues in Western Europe. While we can trace their relationships in a general way, we are forced to wonder if these great achievements of the metalworkers' art are not at the end of a development. In short, is Irish art a dead end? Is it interesting to the scholar in that it preserves in a fossilised and provincial form what has been destroyed elsewhere; yet it may not have contributed to mainstream later European art? The Irish script which had appeared by the seventh century was very significant in the development of lettering in Anglo-Saxon England and on the continent, and Irish manuscript decoration had an important role to play in the development of style both in England and in the Merovingian world. There is still much dispute about the relative strength of Irish and Anglo-Saxon influence in the emergence of style in these islands from the early seventh century (when missionaries from Iona first began to work amongst the Northumbrians), until the Viking Invasions and beyond. It is, however, difficult to trace Irish metalworking influence in Europe, although an Irish-style reliquary, recently recognised at Bobbio, may have been made abroad.

The catalogue of Irish objects identified in European treasuries has increased significantly in recent years – in Italy intact eighth century shrines at Bologna and Abbadia San Salvatore as well as the Bobbio fragments; an important shrine fragment in Brussels as well as a twelfth century horn-reliquary to add to the material already known.[6] There is, however, no clear evidence of Irish influence on European metalwork to match that which we know Anglo-Saxon style had on some Carolingian workshops, but we cannot infer that the surviving Irish exports to the continent represent either the original total or that the full corpus has yet been identified. In the past exaggerated claims have been made for the influence abroad of Irish early medieval sculpture. The richness of the iconographical tradition of Irish high crosses appears, however, to be a reflection of the cosmopolitanism of the ninth-century Irish church, and not the first working out of the themes and layout of Romanesque sculpture for re-export to Europe, as it were. It would be extremely rash to assume that medieval Europe owed a great deal to Irish endeavour in the visual arts as distinct from literary and intellectual pursuits, but there is likely to have been some influence. The conclusion is inescapable, however, that influences flowed mainly into Ireland from Europe and were there transformed. Christianity set much of the agenda for the native craftsmen and it by definition, was an import.

Michael Ryan

Dr Michael Ryan is an archaeologist who has published extensively on early Irish art and has edited, amongst other books, Ireland and Insular Art *and* Treasures of Ireland *and* The Illustrated Archaeology of Ireland. *He is currently seconded from the National Museum to the Directorship of the Chester Beatty Library. He was awarded the Frend Medal of the Society of Antiquaries of London in 1989 for his contribution to the archaeology of the Christian Church.*

NOTES

1. *Ireland and Insular Art* (ed. M. Ryan), Dublin 1987 and *The age of migrating ideas: proceedings of the second international conference on insular art* (eds. M Spearman and J. Higget), Edinburgh 1993.
2. In eg L. De Paor 'The High Crosses of Tech Theille (Hihilly) and Kinnitty, and related sculpture' in *Figures from the past: studies on figurative art in Christian Ireland* (ed E. Rynne) Dublin 1987, 131-58.
3. 'Rath Melsigi, Willibrord and the earliest Echternach manuscripts', *Peritia* 3 (1984), 17-49.
4. *Irish Art in the Romanesque Period 1020-1170 AD*, London, 1970, 77, 111 and R Ó Floinn in M Ryan (ed.) *op. cit.* at p.186.
5. M. Ryan, (ed) *The Derrynaflan Hoard I*, Dublin 1983: 1987 'The Donore hoard: early medieval metalwork from Moynalty, near Kells Co. Meath' *Antiquity* 61, March 1987, 57-63: E.P. Kelly 'The Lough Kinale Book shrine' in Higget and Spearman (eds): Cormac Bourke, 1991, 'The Blackwater shrine' *Dúiche Néill J. Of the O Neill Country Historical Society*, 6, 103-106.
6. M. Blindheim, 1984 'A house-shaped Irish-Scots reliquary in Bologna and its place among the other reliquaries', *Acta Archaeologica* 55, 1-53: F. Mancinelli, 1974 'Reliquie e reliquiari ad Abbadia San Salvatore' *Pontificia Accademia Romana di Archeologia rendiconti*, 46, 251-271: M. Ryan. 1990 'Decorated metalwork in the Museo dell'Abbazia, Bobbio, Italy', *J. R. Soc. Antiq. Ireland* 120, 102-111: M. Ryan, 'The Horn Reliquary of Tongres-Tongeren: A 12th century Irish object'. *Musea* (Bulletin of the Musées Royaux d'Art et d'Histoire, Brussels), 56 (1986), 43-55: Ryan 'A gilt-bronze object in the MRAH'. *Musea* 56 (1986), 57-60.

A VICTORIAN WATERCOLOURIST

Patricia Butler writes on Louisa Anne, Marchioness of Waterford (1818-91), philanthropist and painter.

The Victorian age produced a profusion of gifted amateur lady watercolourists of which Louisa Anne, Marchioness of Waterford is a richly talented example. Born into a distinguished family and a correspondent of the Pre-Raphaelites and John Ruskin, she was acknowledged within her own lifetime as a watercolourist of exceptional talent and ability.

Lady Waterford was born in Paris in the splendid Hotel Charost (in the Faubourg St Honoré) which had formerly belonged to Napoleon's favourite sister, Pauline. She was the second daughter of Sir Charles Stuart,[1] an able if somewhat eccentric man, who was, at the time of Louisa's birth, British ambassador to the recently restored court of Louis XVIII in Paris. His wife, Lady Elizabeth Yorke's[2] lack of good looks was more than compensated for by her zest and energy for life. The fact that such a physically undistinguished couple should produce two such outstandingly beautiful daughters[3] was to many people something of a mystery. A guest was heard to remark at a ball: 'How beautiful they are' and, looking more closely at their mother, commented 'Isn't it strange considering?'[4]

Lady Waterford was six years old when the family returned to England at the end of her father's ambassadorship. For four years, they lived at Bure near Christchurch on the south coast of Dorset.[5] In 1828 a new administration took over the government headed by the Duke of Wellington under whom Sir Charles had served in the Peninsular War.

After his re-appointment as Ambassador to France, Sir Charles and his family returned to Paris bringing with them the family governess, Miss Hyriott'[6] It was she who continually encouraged the girls to draw and paint. Louisa, now aged ten, was 'already devoted to her paint boxes'[7] and, according to friends, capable of copying a family portrait by Reynolds with a certain degree of skill and accuracy.

With the collapse of the Duke of Wellington's government, the Stuarts were recalled to London taking up residence at 4, Charlton House Terrace. In 1835, Charlotte was married to twenty-two year old Charles Canning,[8] later to become Governor General and first Viceroy of India. Like her sister, Charlotte was to become a keen artist and was later to record in watercolour, scenes in India that were both technically accomplished and attractive.

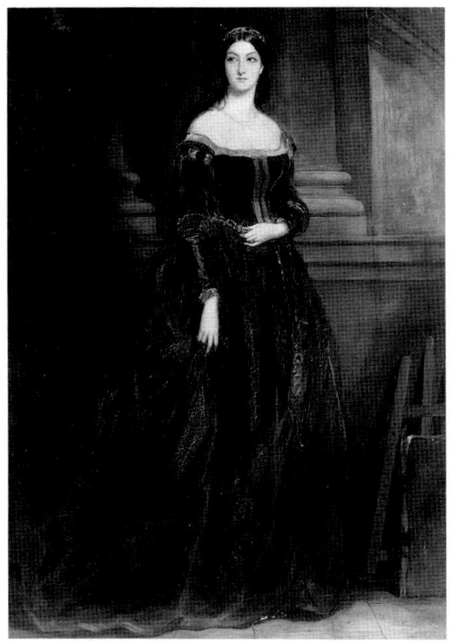

Sir Francis Grant, PRA (1803-1878), Portrait of Louisa Anne, Marchioness of Waterford (1818-1891). *National Portrait Gallery, London.*

In the year of her sister's marriage, Lady Waterford, an outstandingly beautiful girl,[9] was presented at Court. At the end of the season, she and her parents prepared to depart for a tour of southern Europe which was to include Italy. However, shortly before they were due to leave, her father departed for Iceland in the middle of the night with no explanation, and mother and daughter had to await his return. They finally left a year later. Spending the winter in Rome, Lady Waterford became immersed in studying the paintings which surrounded her, haunting the galleries and watching other artists at work. On her return to London, she had the distinction of being painted by many leading artists including Swinton, Watts, Sir Edwin Landseer and Sir Francis Grant.[10] A year later, in 1839, she and her mother travelled north to Scotland to attend the famous Victorian romantic folly, the Eglinton Tournament held at Eglinton Castle, Ayrshire.[11]

It was here that she first met the dashing 'wild Lord Waterford', third Marquis of Waterford whom she was later to marry.[12] Lady Waterford's father was somewhat dubious about the intended liaison. Lord Waterford's exploits,[13] fearlessness and somewhat rough manners had instilled a sense of unease in Sir Charles' cautious Victorian soul. However, Charlotte did her best to set his mind at rest: 'Lord Waterford has become much more gentle and amiable and he is so devoted to Louisa that he will do many things to please her and is certainly not exigeante . . .'[14]

The couple were married by special licence in the Royal Chapel of Whitehall on June 8, 1842, where no marriage had taken place for fifteen years. The ceremony was conducted by Lord Waterford's uncle, the Archbishop of Armagh. A few days later, the young couple left for Curraghmore in County Waterford, Lord Waterford's estate in the south of Ireland. On arrival at Kingstown[15] aboard the Osprey which was 'gaily decorated with flags',[16] the handsome couple were met by friendly, enthusiastic crowds.

At Curraghmore, Lady Waterford received a warm welcome and settled in easily and quickly. But within a week, tragedy struck. Whilst out driving with her husband in a phaeton pulled by two horses, she met with an accident, which left her unconscious for three days.

After a few weeks, and having made a full recovery, Lady Waterford set about trying to improve the living and working conditions of her tenants on the estate. Her husband lent his full support and, possessing a strong practical business head, implemented many of her schemes. Between them, they started a local industry for the manufacture of woollen goods and organised a 'Curraghmore Clothing Club'.[17] The local forge was converted for the manufacture of woollen goods which gave employment to thirty local women using spinning wheels and card-looms. The cottages of the tenants were improved. Lime was supplied to whiten their walls, seeds for the gardens with prizes being awarded for the best kept. Plans to build two churches were followed through, one being sited close to the entrance gates at Curraghmore and the other at Ghilcoe, near the place where Lady Waterford's riding accident had occurred. The terraced gardens, which still surround the house today,were planned and laid out by Lord and Lady Waterford with further plantings of trees taking place in the surrounding villages and on the vast estate itself.

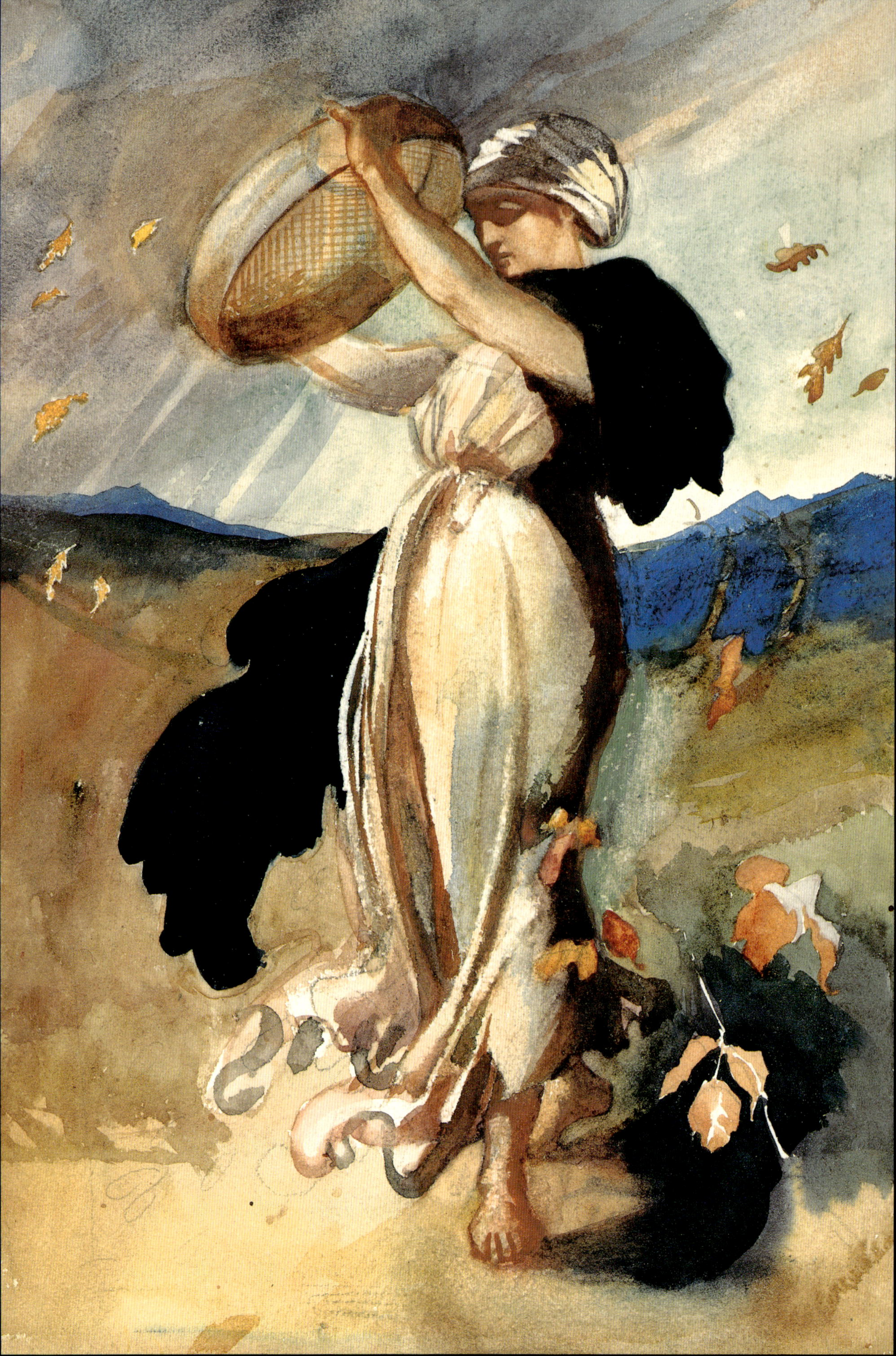

Louisa Anne, Marchioness of Waterford. Autumn with a sieve. *Watercolour on paper. 32.7 x 22 .9 cm. Victoria and Albert Museum, London.*

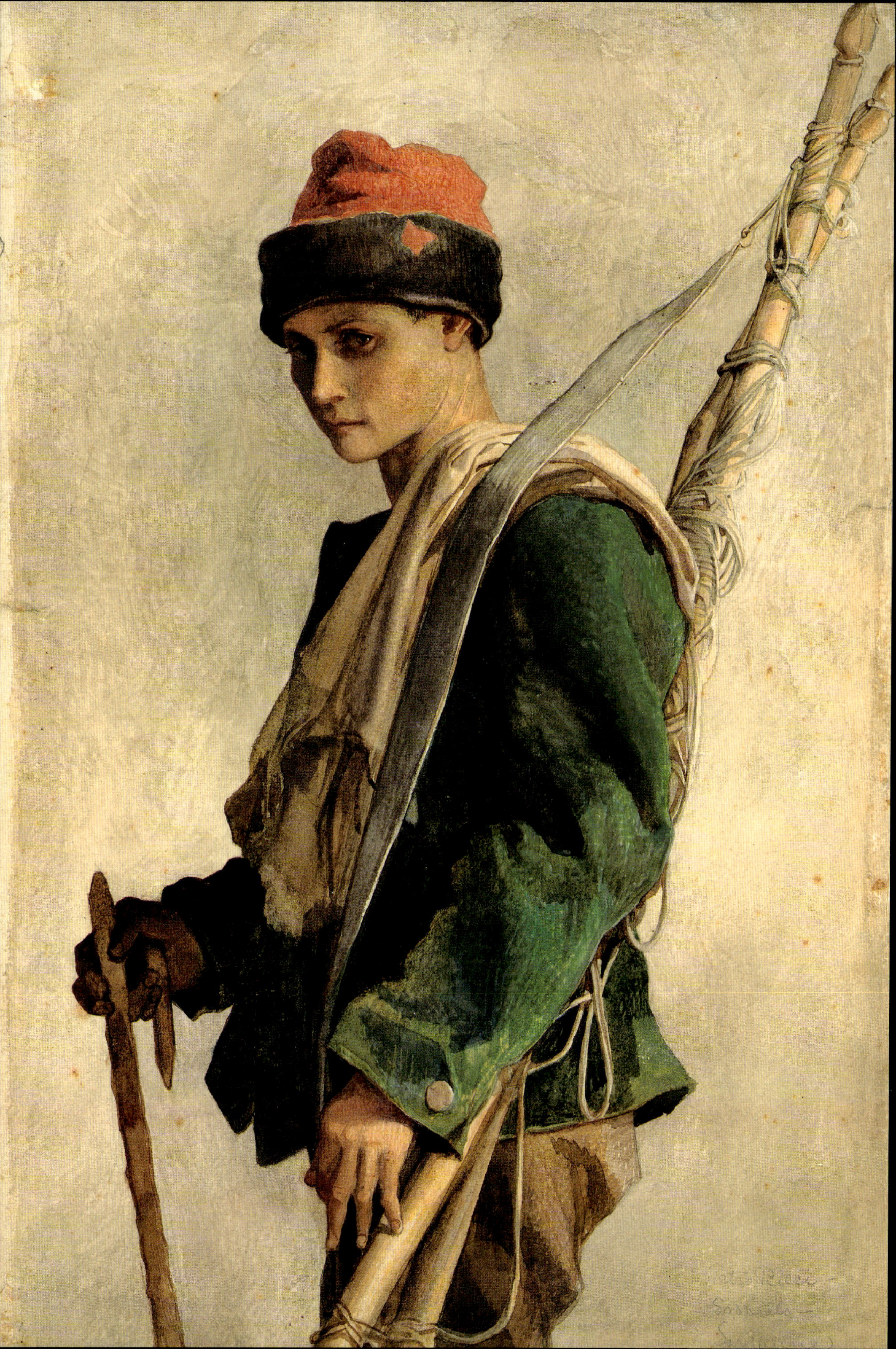

Louisa Anne, Marchioness of Waterford. Pietro Ricci, A Fisherman of Sospello near Menton.
Watercolour on paper. 47.3 x 32.4 cm. Victoria and Albert Museum, London.

A VICTORIAN WATERCOLOURIST

Despite all these activities, Lady Waterford still found time to indulge in her favourite recreation of painting and sketching, and developed the habit of carrying around with her a small sketch book. Often in the evening after 'a temperate meal of tea, chicken and roast potatoes (instead of dinner I like it so much better, but never expected to find a kindred spirit),'[18] she would sketch her husband quietly reading or writing by candlelight and complete her watercolour sketches of the villagers and tenants who worked in the house and on the estate. Her friend Grace Palliser, also an art lover,[19] frequently came to stay. She and Lady Waterford would spend whole days in a little painting room, working feverishly, only going out for walks at dusk. Many delightful sketches such as On the Terrace at Curraghmore, Supper after Hunting or The Stable School[20] demonstrate her ability to capture a scene, often intently observed. Designs for stained glass windows for the two new churches were also drawn up and completed. Writing to Lady Jane Bouverie in 1843, Lady Waterford mentioned that 'The first of my windows has been completed in the church, another is being burnt and leaded and I hope to complete the six before I go to London'.[21]

In the summer of 1844, she and Lord Waterford travelled to Europe ultimately to take the waters at Carlsbad. Lady Waterford's sketch books during this period reflect her enthusiasm for such cities as Berlin, Prague and Heidelberg. Many of the sketches are of architectural details which were later to be incorporated into improvements at Curraghmore. However, their trip was short lived. Lord Waterford's presence was urgently required at home.

In Ireland, famine was rife. The spring of 1848 brought a grim reminder of a general insurrection with the great house at Curraghmore having to be fortified by cannon. General Charles Stuart, a visitor to Curraghmore in the same year wrote: 'The police station at Curraghmore close to the park gate had been defended by a gallant old clergyman and his son against an armed rabble. A detachment of troops was quartered in the outhouses of Curraghmore for its defence, and a six pounder gun had, through the energy of Lord Waterford, been hoisted up to a commanding position in the house . . .'[22]

In June, Lord Waterford decided that it would be safer if his wife were to travel to England. Lady Waterford insisted on being kept in touch with the happenings at home. Her housekeeper, Mary Smith writing to her from Curraghmore on 2 August described the scene: 'We are still going on with barricading the windows. There is now a watchword for every night, so we have it all soldier like . . . I think my Lord only came home just in time to protect us'. Lady Waterford was unhappy in England. At the end of August, she returned to Curraghmore and in September wrote: 'We live in a state of siege, twenty-five soldiers quartered in the house, sixteen or eighteen specials also watching day and night on the housetop ... I have been busy colouring and correcting for publication my Babes in the Wood. As for coming over to England again, I cannot think of it till I hear of real peace'.[23]

A year later the 'troubles' had to some extent subsided and life at Curraghmore began to return to normal. In the years that followed, Lady Waterford made several journeys to England, visiting art exhibitions and generally keeping in touch with the artistic trends of the day. Attracted to the Pre-Raphaelite movement, in the summer of 1853 she paid a visit to Holman Hunt's studio at 5, Prospect Place, Cheyne Walk, London. Hunt sets the scene: '"Light of the world", stood upon the easel ... carriage wheels stopped at the side entrance to my studio and a loud knocking was followed by the names of the Marchioness of Waterford and Lady Canning. I received the ladies ... I had not made any effort to find chairs with perfect seats ... and when Lady Waterford taking a chair by the back placed her knee in the perforated seat ... she stood looking and talking, it might have been thought that the chair had been prepared for that special purpose'[24]. The following February, Lady Waterford's name was put forward for participation in a sketching club inaugurated by Millais. Sadly, this did not materialise, but Millais continued to praise her work, finding 'her drawings magnificent, so I could praise honestly'[25].

It is probable that around this period, she met John Ruskin for the first time. She may have been introduced by her cousin, Earl Somers who had been at Christ Church, Oxford, with him. Ruskin suggested that she should take lessons in drawing from Rossetti. However, Rossetti declined to offer instruction. This is confirmed in an entry in Ford Madox Brown's diary dated 13 July, 1855. 'After breakfast

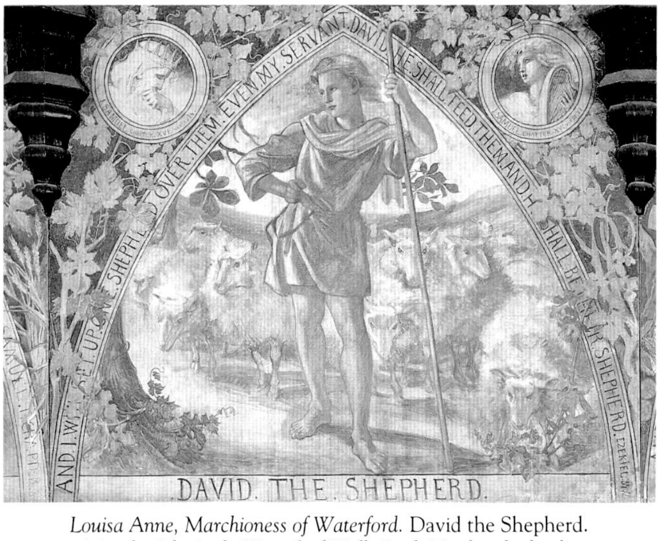

Louisa Anne, Marchioness of Waterford. David the Shepherd. *Mural – The Lady Waterford Hall, Ford, Northumberland.*

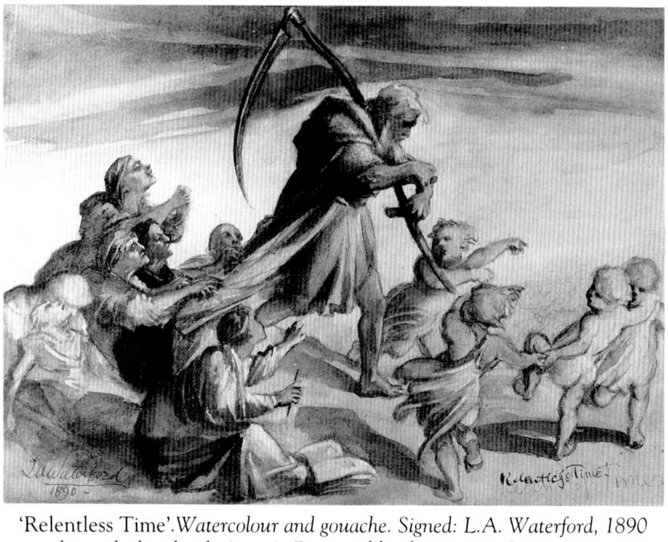

'Relentless Time'. *Watercolour and gouache. Signed: L.A. Waterford, 1890 and inscribed with title (twice). Presented by the artist to Queen Victoria, August 1890. Collection: Her Majesty the Queen. Royal Library, Windsor Castle*

concocted a letter with D.G.R. for the Marchioness of Waterford declining to give her lessons *à domicile* by my advice'[26]. Nevertheless Lady Waterford's work improved steadily. Ruskin remained scant with his praise insisting that it lay within her power to practise and persevere more. 'Everyone who has seen your drawings likes it exceedingly: I should praise it much more if I were not tacitly comparing it with what I am sure you can do'[27]. He advised her 'that the pen drawings may be softened with the knife to almost any extent as you would scratch out a mistake in a word; it is better of course not to have much to do after the operation, or one is liable to blots and holes and other catastrophes. But the knife, lightly used, helps in reforming the work exceedingly when it is done'[28]. Ruskin stressed the importance of accurate drawing, study of the human figure and above all, faithfulness to colour ('to colour well, requires your life').

Meanwhile, Lady Waterford's health had been deteriorating. In December 1857, at Curraghmore, she became ill with a chest condition. In February on her doctor's advice, she and her mother went abroad. Her sketch books vividly record their visits to Verona, Venice, Mantua and Menton and reveal a fluent, if somewhat elaborate brush style. Two boldly executed watercolours, now in the possession of the Victoria and Albert Museum, London reveal a number of influences. With its Pre-Raphaelite bright colouring and detailed handling, *Pietro Ricci. A Fisherman of Sospello near Menton* is tightly construed and differs in feeling from her striking study of Autumn with a Sieve where fluidity and movement is combined with the classical tradition. Ruskin approved of her enthusiasm for classicism, particularly towards the Venetian Renaissance. Lady Waterford was somewhat amused and pleased to find a critic enquiring at the opening of an exhibition 'Who is Mr Waterford[29], this new genius reviving the glories of the Venetian School'[30].

In the late winter of 1858/59 on the 29 March, Lord Waterford was tragically killed in a riding accident at Corbally, Carrick on Suir, just a few miles from Curraghmore[31]. In June of that year, childless and with her sister far away in India, Lady Waterford decided to leave Curraghmore to live at Ford Castle, Northumberland, which had belonged to her late husband.

There, full of determination and courage, she began carrying out improvements[32]. These included building a school, rebuilding many of the village houses and setting in motion major alterations to her somewhat forbidding northern fortress. In 1861, her sister[33] died and six years later, her mother. This left Lady Waterford bereft of any close relatives. Struck by tragedy, she once again showed extraordinary courage. From her mother, she had inherited the estate of Highcliffe Castle in Hampshire[34]. There, just as she had done at Ford, she began to take a strong interest in the local school and other enterprises. For the rest of her life, Lady Waterford was to follow the pattern of spending the summer months at Highcliffe Castle and the rest of the year at Ford.

At Ford, her main task was the completion of the murals for the local village school, a task which was to take her twenty one years to complete[35] and which amounts to her greatest achievement. Although they have been frequently described as frescoes they were not painted directly on to the walls of the school. Instead, working from her studio at Ford Castle, Lady Waterford executed the murals in both watercolour and gouache on 'large sheets of paper stretched on wooden frames, (these were made to fit the school walls) the paper was then washed over with distemper and the painting in watercolours done in a very large bold manner on the distemper, giving very much the effect of fresco'[36]. The murals, comprising scenes from the Bible,[37] and using local school children and their families as models, demonstrate Lady Waterford's mastery in handling figures, particularly children, who are conveyed with great tenderness and charm. A firm believer in accuracy and with a strong eye for detail, it was reputed that when creating the cartoon of *David the Shepherd*, she insisted on having live sheep brought upstairs into her drawing room from which to draw[38].

This cycle of remarkable 'frescoes' captured the attention of the art world, including Edward Burne-Jones, who urged her on in order that she might leave something outstanding for posterity and so the world might know 'there lived an artist as great as Venice ever knew'[39]. G F Watts offered help and advice, whilst Sir Edwin Landseer reported the cycle as being 'very encouraging'. Ruskin was less enthusiastic. 'He condemned my frescoes and has certainly spirited me on to do better'[40].

Towards the end of her life in July, 1890, Lady Waterford was invited by Queen Victoria to spend a night at Osborne House on the Isle of Wight. In a letter to a friend, she described the evening: 'I was asked to bring a portfolio which I did, and, to my horror, it was displayed in the drawing room in the evening while I sat on a sofa by the Queen. She liked *Relentless Time*[41] so I gave it to her, and she gracefully accepted it'[42].

In the autumn of that year, Lady Waterford's health began to decline. The winter was spent, in keeping with tradition, at Ford Castle. There she was cared for by two good friends. After several weeks of being confined to bed, she died peacefully on 12 May, 1891. Buried at Ford, a simple recumbent cross designed by Watts marks her grave[43].

Lady Waterford's relationship to her art was a complex one made up of many contradictory strands. On the one hand, she was obliged by birth to occupy a responsible role in upper class society whilst friends such as Ruskin encouraged her towards the rewards of socialism. Her strong Christian beliefs preached self denial and humility whilst she could obviously observe for herself the sharp inequalities of the time.

A follower of the classical tradition, interested in the Italian Renaissance style and the Pre-Raphaelites, Lady Waterford could not afford to ignore modern techniques and subject matter. Whilst always insisting on being viewed as an *amateur*, she was frustrated at not receiving the acknowledgment and praise her obvious talent deserved. Nevertheless her work is a fascinating contribution to the appreciation and understanding of Victorian art and the role a woman could occupy in it.

Patricia Butler

Patricia A Butler, art historian, is consultant to the Prints & Drawings Department, National Library of Ireland and is currently working on the NLI Brocas collection. Her publications include a Guide to Art Galleries in Ireland (1978) *and* Three Hundred Years of Irish Watercolours and Drawings, c.1660-c.1960. *(London 1990, Reprint, 1991).*

ACKNOWLEDGEMENTS

The staff of The National Gallery of Ireland; The Victoria & Albert Museum; The British Museum; The National Portrait Gallery; David Ker Fine Art; The Royal Collection, Windsor Castle, Berkshire; Bodleian Library, University of Oxford; Wesley College, Mass., USA; Wray Galloway; The Lord Joicey; Huon L. Mallalieu; Dr Charles Mould.

NOTES OVERLEAF

A VICTORIAN WATERCOLOURIST

NOTES

1. Sir Charles Stuart - Baron Stuart de Rothesay (1779-1845) was the eldest son of Sir Charles Stuart (1753-1801). A diplomat, he became joint Charge d'Affaires at Madrid in 1808, Envoy to Portugal (1810), Minister at the Hague (1815-16), Ambassador to Paris (1815-30), Ambassador to St. Petersburg (1841-45).
2. Lady Elizabeth, Margaret Yorke, third daughter of Philip Yorke, third Earl of Hardwicke (1757-1834). Her father has been lord lieutenant of Ireland under both Addington and Pitt.
3. The Hon. Charlotte Stuart (1817-61), Lady Waterford's elder sister by a year had also been born in Paris. She later became Viscountess Canning, wife of the first Viceroy of India. Her work in watercolour was greatly admired by John Ruskin. See Augustus J C Hare, *The Story of Two Noble Lives being Memorials of Charlotte, Countess Canning and Louisa, Marchioness of Waterford.* London 1893, (Vols. I-III). Vol. II. p.478.
4. See Hare, Vol. III. p.14.
5. Bure formed part of the family estate of Highcliffe, Hampshire. It had been owned and developed by Lord Stuart's grandfather, the third Earl of Bute, distinguished politician, botanist and eventual founder of the Royal Botanic Gardens, Kew. Highcliffe was enlarged and modernised by Lord Stuart and became known as Highcliffe Castle.
6. Sir Charles Stuart was created Baron Stuart de Rothesay of the Isle of Bute in 1828. He died on 6 November, 1845.
7. See Hare. Vol. I. Chapter II. p.153.
8. Charles John Canning, Earl Canning (1812-62) third son of George Canning (1770-1827) Prime Minister in the reign of George IV became Governor-General of India.
9. DG Rossetti in a letter to his mother dated 'Sunday night, 1st July 1855' described Lady Waterford as being 'an excellent artist and would have been really great... if not born such a swell and such a stunner'.
10. Sir Francis Grant, PRA (1803-1878) was born in Kilgraston, Perthshire, Scotland, the youngest son of the laird. During the 1830s, he began to practise as a professional portrait painter. Using a flattering portrait style coupled with good social connections, his work quickly became popular. By 1840, he was rated to be one of the most fashionable painters of the day numbering amongst his sitters, Queen Victoria, Palmerston and Sir Edwin Landseer. He exhibited at the RA (1834-79), elected ARA, 1842, RA, 1851 and PRA, 1866.
11. The Eglinton Tournament involved two years of preparation and was an attempt by some of the young men of the day to revive the sport of medieval jousting. In the autumn of 1839, the tournament attracted an estimated crowd of 100,000 people.
12. Henry de la Poer, third Marquis of Waterford (1811-59) succeeded his father at the age of fifteen. Wealthy, he enjoyed racing and hunting and owned at least three horses which ran in the Grand National. It was estimated that at the time of his marriage to Lady Waterford, his holdings in County Waterford alone comprised approximately 40,050 acres.
13. Sometimes known as the 'Mad Marquis', Lord Waterford was reputed to have ridden his horse up the steps of the Old Court House in Waterford, jumped over the Grand Jury balcony and returned safely to Curraghmore. See *The Clonmel Historical and Archaeological Society Journal.* Vol. I. No. 2. 1953-54. pp.61-63.
14. Letter from Charlotte, Viscountess Canning to Lord Stuart de Rothesay, 19 April, 1842.
15. Kingstown, now known as Dun Laoghaire, County Dublin.
16. See *Illustrated London News*, 25 June, 1842.
17. 'The Curraghmore Clothing Club' – In a letter to her sister dated 18 July, 1849, Lady Waterford writes: 'I have bought a quantity of factory cotton to be given out for work to Kilmacthomas seamstresses. It is very strong and will make very neat clothes, shirts and shifts. The workers are to have the work cut out and sent to them, cottons, buttons, needles, tape and thread furnished so that they may get the payment for the work intact'.
18. Letter from Lady Waterford to Lady Sarah Ingestre dated 4 January, 1843. Rockwell.
19. Grace Palliser, Derryluskin, County Tipperary.
20. The Stable School, Curraghmore, County Waterford possibly began in a building sited immediately inside the main entrance gates to Curraghmore. It was built in 1820 by Lady Waterford's mother-in-law as a school for children of dependants.
21. Lady Waterford completed six side windows for Clonegam Church on the estate of Curraghmore.
22. See General C. Stuart. *A Short Sketch of the Life of Lady Louisa*, Marchioness of Waterford. Published 1892, p. 10.
23. Letter from Lady Waterford to Lady Jane Ellice, 19 September, 1848. Curraghmore. The MS for *Babes in the Wood* is now in the collection of the Yale Centre for British Art, Conn., U.S.A. Published Joseph Cundall, London, 1849. Further editions, 1851, 1861. Lady Waterford always maintained that this work would receive a great deal of criticism when published. However, when it did appear she was proved wrong as it became an essential part of the Victorian child's nursery. Lady Waterford also illustrated at least one other book – *Life Songs* – Illustrated and illuminated by the Marchioness of Waterford and the Countess of Tankerville. Published James Nisbett & Co., London, 1884.
24. See W Holman Hunt, *Pre-Raphaelitism and the Pre-Raphaelite Brotherhood*, London, 1914, vol. i, p.256.
25. According to Millais, Lady Waterford was 'the noblest woman I ever saw'. See *The Life and letters of Sir John E. Millais*. ed. J.G. Millais, 1899, vol. i p.363.
26. See *Madox Brown's Diary. Ruskin, Rossetti: Pre-Raphaelitism*, ed. W.M. Rossetti. 1899, London, vol. i, p.38.
27. Letter to Lady Waterford from John Ruskin dated 19 November (1858) W.18.
28. Letter to Lady Waterford from John Ruskin dated 27 January (1858),W.13.
29. Lady Waterford's name was accidentally printed on the catalogue as 'Mr. L. Waterford' (Exhibiton Catalogue, Dudley Gallery, London, dated 1887).
30. Letter from Walter Severn, President of the Dudley Gallery, London to Canon Hastings M. Neville, 5 April, 1895.
31. Henry, third Marquis of Waterford died in 1859 and was buried at Clonegam Church. A recumbent figure in bronze of Lord Waterford was executed by the Italian sculptor, Baron Carlo Marochetti (1805-67). After Lord Waterford's death, he was succeeded by his brother who inherited the house and estates of Curraghmore. He died in November 1866, twenty five years before Lady Waterford's death in 1891.
32. Whilst alterations to Ford Castle were taking place under the guidance of Edinburgh architect, David Bryce, Lady Waterford lived at Ford Cottage below the Castle walls.
33. Charlotte, Viscountess Canning died in 1861 from malaria contracted on a journey from Darjeeling to Calcutta. She was buried at Barrackpur.
34. On Lady Stuart's death in June, 1867. Highcliffe Castle and estate Hampshire was left to Lady Waterford, her only surviving child.
35. The murals for the school at Ford, Northumberland were begun on 11 March, 1862 and finally completed on the same date in March, 1883.
36. Report from Miss Denison. See Hare.Vol. III. Chapter X. p.218.
37. The *Story* in nearly every case is taken verbatim from the Revised Standard Version of the Bible. The mural illustrated here is *David the Shepherd* and the text reads: 'And I will set up one shepherd over them...even my servant David, he shall feed them, and he shall be their shepherd' – (Ezekiel 34, v.23). The model for David the Shepherd was Peter Rule, who later became a butcher. His family were slaters and, according to Lord Joicey probably worked on the roof when the school was being built.
38. Report from Miss Denison. See Hare. Vol. III. Chapter X. p.218.
39. See Hare. Vol. III. Chapter X. p.218.
40. Letter from Lady Waterford to Mrs Bernal Osborne dated 22 February, 1865. Ford Cottage.
41. *Relentless Time.* Watercolour and gouache. Signed: L.A. Waterford, 1890, and inscribed with title (twice). Provenance: Presented by the artist to Queen Victoria, August, 1890. Collection: Her Majesty the Queen. Royal Library, Windsor Castle.
42. Letter from Lady Waterford to the Hon Mrs R. Boyle 16 August, 1890. Highcliffe.
43. A year after Lady Waterford's death, an exhibition of her work was held at 8 Carlton House Terrace, London where over 300 examples of her work were exhibited together with several of her sketchbooks.

THE IRISH AT ANTWERP

Irish artists at the Royal Irish Academy of Fine Arts in Antwerp, now Cultural Capital of Europe, included Osborne, Moynan and O'Conor. **Jeanne Sheehy** discusses this significant 'Antwerp School' of realist landscape painters.

The Royal Academy of Fine Arts at Antwerp inherited the French system of the *Prix de Rome,* instituted throughout Napoleon's Empire. The highest competition in the school was in history painting, and fine art training aimed to teach students figure painting and historical composition.[1] Though foreign students were not eligible for the *Prix de Rome,* they were taught in the same classes, and so were affected by it. A programme of re-organisation was carried out 1841-55, which strengthened teaching in landscape and animal painting and added extra studios, so that students who had completed their basic training could work in small groups under the direction of a master, after the manner of the German schools. The reputation of the Antwerp Academy was greatly enhanced by the reforms, and attendance nearly doubled within two years.[2]

The academy attracted foreigners as early as the 1840s, but it was only in the 1870s and 1880s that it achieved status as a major international school of art. Among the foreign students, between 1849 and 1891 there were twenty-six giving Irish addresses.[3] The first Irishman to register was Hugh Newell, from Belfast. He spent the year 1849-50 at Antwerp and then went on to the studio of Couture in Paris, before emigrating to America.[4] Another Irish Antwerp student who made his career outside Ireland was William Spread, from Queenstown, Co Cork. Spread spent two years at Antwerp, and then settled in London as a painter of architectural views and as an aquafortist.[5] A number of names in the Academy registers have not been possible to trace, or did not pursue careers as artists.[6] One Irishman, Michael Healy from Cork, trained there as a sculptor.[7]

It was not until the 1870s that a sufficient number of Irish artists went to Antwerp for it to have much impact on Irish painting. Thirteen of the Irish registered at the Academy between 1877 and 1891 could be said to belong to a fairly coherent group, the 'Antwerp School'. The same was true for England and Scotland – it was the naturalist generation of the 1870s and 1880s who went there in large numbers, and whose work shows common characteristics attributable to their Antwerp background. The Irish who were there in the same period were part of the same tendency.[8] They were Joseph Malachy Kavanagh, Henry Allan, Walter Osborne, Nathaniel Hill, Norman Garstin, Hugh Charde, Richard Thomas Moynan and Dermod O'Brien. Roderic O'Conor can also be added to the list – though his work became more modernist and adventurous than the others', it developed, as did that of Gauguin and Van Gogh who influenced him, out of the naturalist school prevalent in Europe at the time. The Antwerp painters are not an exclusively Irish school, but a European one. In Britain many of them settled at Newlyn, in

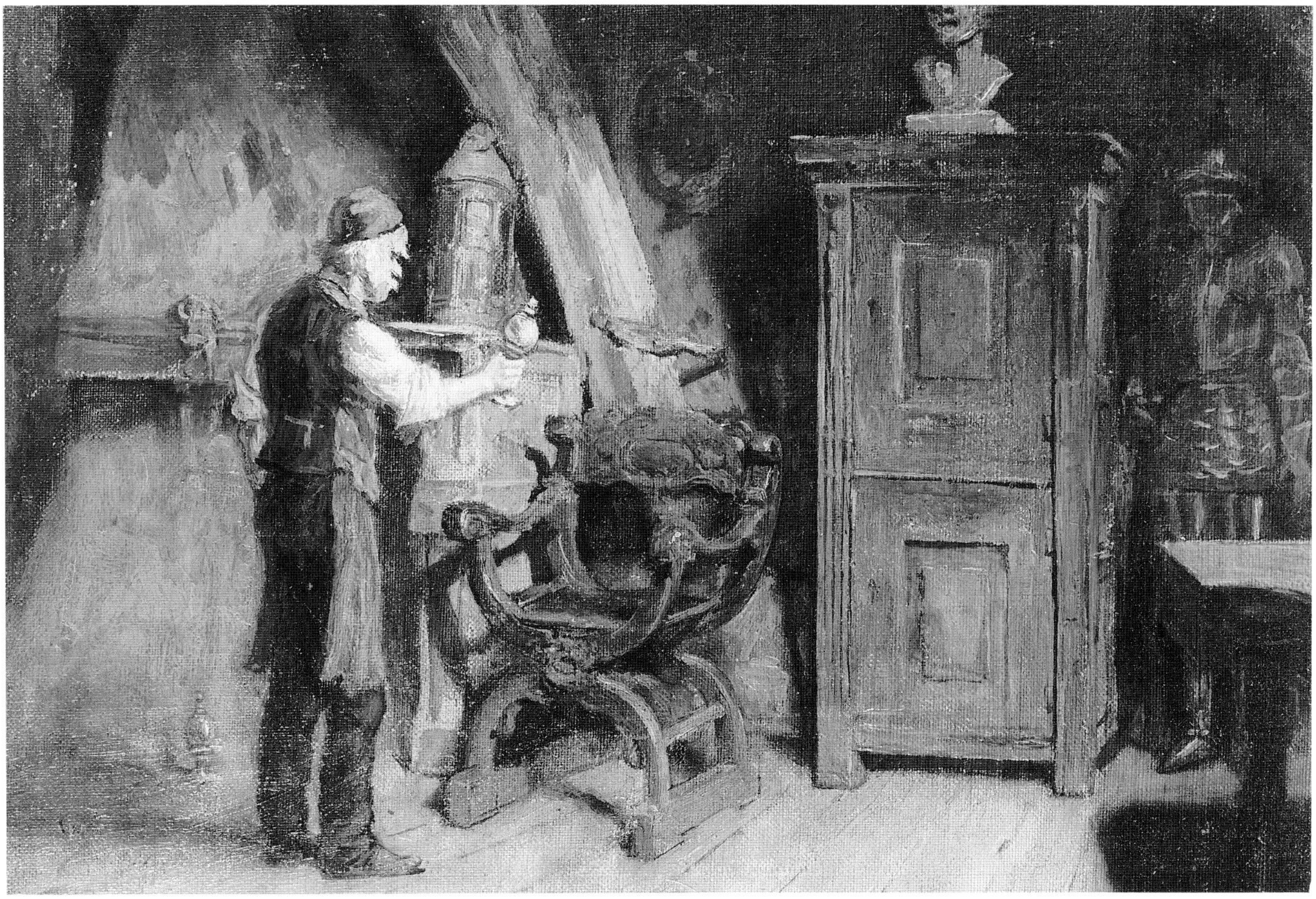

Henry Allan, A Dutch (Flemish?) Interior. *National Gallery of Ireland.*

THE IRISH AT ANTWERP

Cornwall, and they and others were involved with the New English Art Club. They have in common the realism of their subject matter, freer brushwork, more adventurous colour, and a liking for *plein-air* work.

The first Irishman of this generation was Vincent Gernon. In June 1887 he registered in the intermediate class.[9] This was the class in drawing from the antique (known as *antiek*), taught by Polydore Beaufaux. Plaster casts of classical antiquities such as the *Dying Gladiator* were placed under strong light which threw them into high relief. Students in this class also did compositional sketches at home, learning to draw freely by working on a very large scale.[10] Each year, at the end of the winter course, there were *concours* in which students were awarded marks, and placed in order of merit. Gernon competed in the *concours* for *antiek*, but not in any others. Like most of his contemporaries he spent a lot of his time working the the country round Antwerp, especially along the river Scheldt.[11] Among Gernon's fellow students in the *antiek* class was Thomas Gotch, the first of the Newlyn artists to go to Antwerp. Another, Frank Bramley, was in the life class from 1878, and took the top prize one year.

By the summer of 1880-81 there was a whole British colony at Antwerp, including five men who were to be associated with the Newlyn colony – Leghe Suthers, Ralph Todd, Fred Millard, Blandford Fletcher, and an Irishman, Norman Garstin. Garstin spent three sessions in *antiek*, which suggests that he was in need of fairly basic training.[12]

There was a fresh wave of 'Anglais' (this term covered anyone from the British Isles) in 1881. On 29 September 1881, Walter Osborne, Nathaniel Hill and J M Kavanagh registered at the Academy, and were immediately absorbed into a vigorous international art colony. Among the English were groups of students who had come from the Government Schools of Design in London and Birmingham 'fleeing south Kensington and her system', who wrote home enthusiastically about the teaching at Antwerp:

> *you may imagine that we have got on pretty well for one week having done four drawings, whereas at Kensington if we worked very hard, we might have succeeded in half finishing one!*[13]

Discipline at the school was very strict, and the timetable rigid. Work began at 8.00 am, a 6.00 am start having been abandoned the previous year 'because the English students did not find that hour convenient'. There was an afternoon session, and lectures in the evening. There does not seem to have been a language problem – most Flemish people spoke French if required, and the educated classes spoke nothing else.

Hill and Kavanagh registered in the drawing class, where they spent two weeks demonstrating their proficiency before they were allowed into the senior class, painting and drawing from the live model. Osborne went straight into the life class. Students were required to work quickly, with the emphasis on vigour of execution. It was very different from the art schools and academies of the British Isles:

> *There is no 'stippling' here, you have to pile on the chalk and lump on the paint and if a student shews anything individual M. Verlat recommends him to stick to it, this is again the opposite of Poynter's system who has an idea that his style and method is infallible.*[14]

The Antwerp school was famous for encouraging vigorous handling of paint, and adventurous colour. Many commentators on the school remarked on the teaching of Josef Van Lerius, who, as *Professor of the Principles of Painting and Genre*, presided over the life class 1854-76. Van Lerius's teaching methods were legendary. The first thing he did when he encountered a new pupil was to tell him to throw away his palette and get one twice the size. 'Do you call this a palette?', he would say. He encouraged pupils to lay the colour on very thick, especially in the highlights, to such an extent that to use up a tube of paint at one sitting was considered evidence of high skill.[15]

Van Lerius was succeeded by Charles Verlat, *Professor of Painting* from 1876 until 1885, and Director after that, though he continued to teach. So influential was he that the Newlyn artists referred to 'Verlat's Academy in Antwerp'.[16] He carried on the Antwerp tradition of *attack* in painting. He was very proud of the speed and facility with which he worked, and boasted that he never spent more than a couple of hours a day at his easel.

In the life class there were three categories of work from living models: *Torse*, a nude model in an academic pose, like the *académie* of the French system; the *Clothed Model*, often dressed in working clothes, a milkmaid, or a sailor, for example; finally there was the *Group*, a pair of wrestlers, perhaps, or a mother and child. At the end of the session, early in 1882, Hill, Kavanagh, Osborne, and another Dubliner, John Greene were all in the *concours*. Marks were out of 60, and Osborne did best, with 57.3 for painting, and 52.5 for drawing. Hill only got 48 for painting, but did better with 56.1 for drawing. Kavanagh got 42.3 for painting, and 54.6 for drawing. Greene was lowest, with 46.5 for painting, and 48 for drawing.

At the end of May all four registered once again in the life class. While Hill and Kavanagh stayed on at 49 Kloosterstraat, where Osborne also had lodged the previous winter, Osborne and Greene moved to 12 Keizerstraat. It was just round the corner from the school, a large rambling house with a courtyard which had been the seventeenth century town house of Nicolas Rockox, patron and friend of Rubens. Some students from the Birmingham school of art, William Spittle and Fred Davis, also had lodgings there, and Fred Hall. In this way students formed themselves into groups which were to last beyond the student days – for Osborne, Fred Hall was another link with the Newlyn group, with whom he had so much in common, and he was to exhibit regularly with the Birmingham Society of Artists. Osborne and Hill also became friendly with Blandford Fletcher, who probably introduced them to Pont Aven, and with whom they later went on painting expeditions in rural England. It was through Fletcher, and his friend Francis Bate, who was its first secretary, that the Irish artists became involved with the *New English Art Club*.

What little free time students had was spent sketching picturesque subject in the old city, and out in the country, especially along the Scheldt. Walter Osborne's *Antwerp from a Bend of the Scheldt*, for example, shows the towers and spires of Antwerp seen from across the river. They went out to the villages round Antwerp in search of farmyard scenes such as Nathaniel Hill's *Feeding Time in a Flemish Farmyard*; Kavanagh's *A Corn-field near Antwerp*; Osborne's *Interior of a Cowshed, Merxem, near Antwerp*; or Allan's *Berchem near Antwerp*.[17] They wandered round Antwerp looking for picturesque corners – both Osborne and Kavanagh painted in a courtyard beside the church of St Jacques, Osborne's *Beneath St Jacques, Antwerp* and Kavanagh's *Under the Shadow of St Jacques, Antwerp*. In the longer breaks between the

THE IRISH AT ANTWERP

summer and winter courses, in the spring and autumn, students went further afield – to the Belgian *Kempenland,* a favourite haunt of the Belgian realists, to Bruges and Dinant or as far south as Pont-Aven in Brittany.

These sketching trips served several purposes. Artists collected interesting settings, landscapes and interiors, to use as backgrounds for genre painting, or they sketched figures which would later be worked into larger compositions, like Walter Osborne's *Moderke Verhoft,* painted at Calmphtout. For Norman Garstin it seems to have been these painting excursions that were the important part of his Antwerp education. He never managed to get into Verlat's life class, and spent the last six months of his stay painting in the country with Theodore Verstraete.

Hill, Kavanagh and Osborne[18] had all moved on to Pont Aven by the time Roderic O'Conor and Richard Thomas Moynan arrived at Osborne's former lodgings, 12 Keizerstraat, in time for the winter course of 1883-84. O'Conor went straight into the life class, so he must have been able to prove a certain level of proficiency. Moynan started out in *antiek,* though he soon moved to *natuur.* Among their fellow students was the Scottish painter Edward Hornel.[19] Next to arrive from Ireland was Henry Allan from Dundalk, who was in the *antiek* class for two sessions 1884-85, before he moved to *natuur.* This was a time of great chaos in the school, and standards were considered to be so low that it was decided not to hold any *concours* in 1886 – students were either deemed competent to proceed, or were sent back to the elementary classes. Allan was allowed to pass, but Vincent Van Gogh, in *antiek,* was among those sent back to the elementary class.[20]

By the time Dermod O'Brien arrived in Antwerp in May 1887 the reforms were in place. The summer course which he took was the last one, from then on they were yearly. In spite of a poor showing in the *antiek concours,* at the beginning of the new academic year he was in the *Class for Drawing and Painting from the Life,* taught by Verlat. O'Brien spent four years at Antwerp, improving steadily until he was among the top competitors in the *concours.* He was the last of the Irish 'Antwerp School'. In the life school, in 1890, he painted *The Fine Art Academy, Antwerp* – it was probably his entry for the *Group* part of the *concours.* It is initialled by his fellow students, and shows a typically 'realist' model, a woman in working clothes with a little girl. On the wall are prizewinning life studies by previous students.[21]

How did the Antwerp Academy come to turn out a whole generation of 'realists', painters of landscape and peasant genre? It was, one the face of it, the most conservative of institutions, with a syllabus centred round the high tradition of history painting. However it offered a range of teaching that was not available in Great Britain or Ireland, and compared with the *Ecole des Beaux Arts* in Paris it gave budding realists

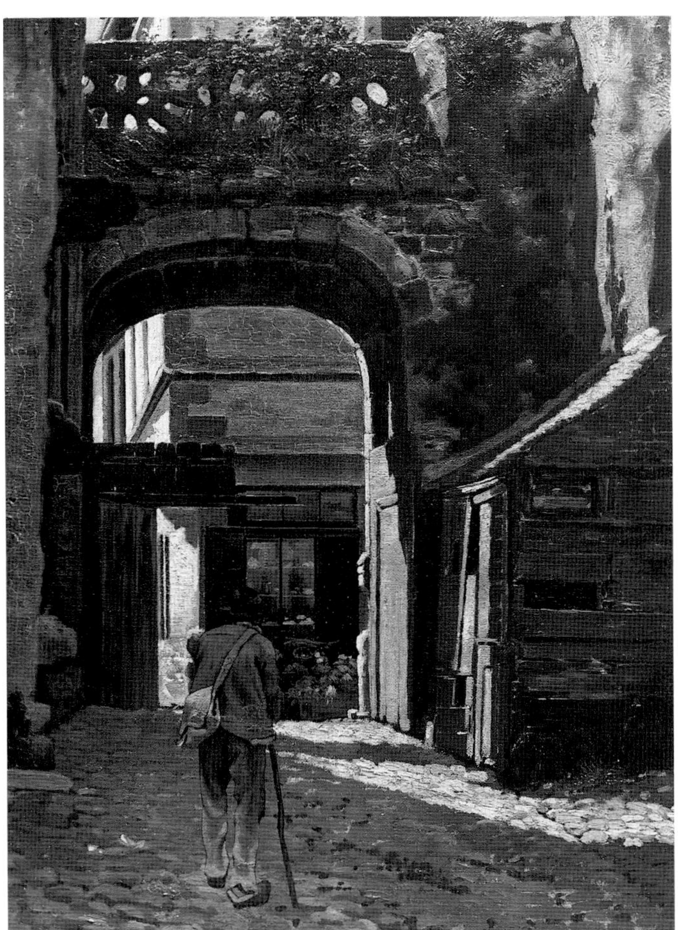

J.M. Kavanagh, The Old Convent Gate, Dinant, *1883. National Gallery of Ireland.*

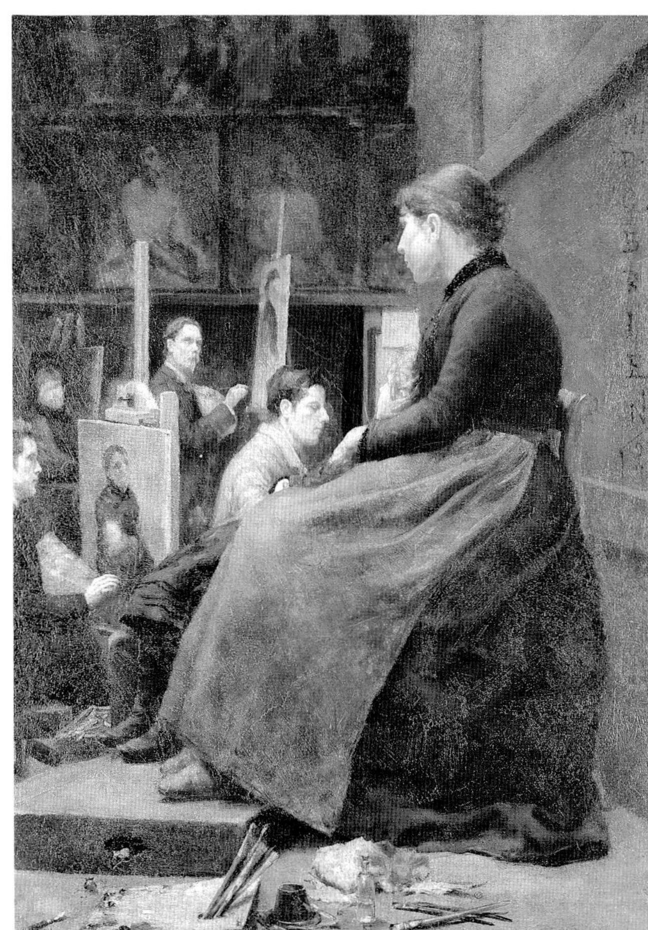

Dermod O'Brien, The Fine Art Class, Antwerp. *1890, Ulster Museum, Belfast.*

THE IRISH AT ANTWERP

a remarkable amount of scope. In the life classes, models and groups dressed in contemporary working costume are to be found as early as 1856, and the genre is still going strong in Dermod O'Brien's painting of the life class at Antwerp in 1890. There were also classes in landscape and animal painting from the 1840s onwards.

Charles Verlat was a powerful teacher, with realist tendencies inherited from his northern background and his French training. He was a great admirer of Courbet, and an advocate of *plein-air* painting. Courbet himself is an important factor. He attended the *International Congress of Artists* held in Antwerp in 1861, specifically, it seems, to represent the realist point of view.

There was a strong Belgian realist school, painters of genre, of peasants and fisher folk like the Hague School across the border in Holland. Antwerp was on the edge of the Kempenland which was the Belgian equivalent of the Parisians' Brittany, frequented by Belgian realists. Many Antwerp students came under the influence of landscape and genre painters who had themselves been pupils at the school – especially Henri de Braekeleer, Jan Stobbaerts, Theodore Verstraete and Piet Verhaert. Finally there was the realist tradition associated with Netherlandish painting through the ages, and the Dutch tradition of landscape, seascape and genre.

A large proportion of Antwerp students of this period went on to France – some to the studios of Paris, and many to Brittany, especially to Pont Aven, where they joined forces with Anglo-French naturalists like Edward Stott or Stanhope Forbes. They became acquainted with developments in French naturalism, especially the work of the much admired Jules Bastien Lepage. English naturalism of the end of the century has been attributed solely to French influence, and Antwerp forgotten. In fact, it was their Antwerp experience that turned the artists in question into painters of landscape and peasant genre. France merely reinforced the lesson.

Jeanne Sheehy

Jeanne Sheehy is an art historian and lecturer. Among her recent publications is Walter Osborne, *(Dublin 1992).*

NOTES

1. See *Historiek Nationaal Hoger Instituut voor Schone Kunsten 1663-1884/1945.* (Antwerp 1985), pp. 24-28; Louis Alvin, *Les Academies et les Autres Ecoles de Dessin de la Belgique.* (Brussels 1865).
2. *Académie Royale des Beaux-Arts, Anvers, Annual Prizegiving.* (Antwerp, yearly), 1843, pp. 4-13; 1846, pp. 17-19; 1847 p. 4, 1853, p. 13 and 1865.
3. Erin Corr (1803-1862), born in Brussels of Irish parents, taught metal engraving at Antwerp around 1860. He may have been a factor in the Antwerp Irish connection.
4. Information about inscriptions comes form the Ms Registers of *Académie Royale des Beaux Arts,* 1837-96, *Nationaal Hoger Instituut voor Schone Kunsten,* Antwerpen.
5. William Spread (c. 1850-1909), aged 24, Queenstown, Co. Cork, *antiek,* summer 1875, winter 1875-6. *Concours* 1876: drawing from the antique 45/60, expression 34.6/40, perspective 18.5/20 and history 12.8/20. Painting from life 27/60. *Concours* 78, 58.5/60 for painting from life and 45/60 for life drawing. *Natuur,* summer 1878.
6. Robert Apliton, aged 56, Cork, *natuur,* winter 1868-69. Henry English, aged 20, Waterford, *antiek* summer 1874, Winter 1874-75. *Concours* 1875, 10th in drawing. William Desart, aged 25, Ireland, *antiek,* summer 1865. Peter Keelan, aged 22, Dublin, *antiek,* winter 1878-79. *Concours,* 1879, 12/60. *Antiek,* summer 1879, winter 1879-80. *Concours,* 1880, 37.5/60. Thomas Burrowes, 25, Dublin, *antiek,* winter 1881-82, summer 1882, winter 1882-83, summer 1883. Edwin Hill, aged 21, place of origin given variously as London and Dublin, *landscape and animal class,* summer 1882, winter 1882-3; *antiek* summer 1883, winter 1883-4, winter 1884-5, summer 1885, winter 1885-6. Frederic Bentz, *antiek* winter 1882-83. George W Yeates, aged 22, *antiek,* summer 1883. Martin Russell, 46, Cork, *antiek* 1887-8, 1888-89, 1889-90. *Concours* 1890, 1/18th for standing model, 17.2/14th for lying model, 1/19th for group. *Antiek* 1990-91.
7. Healy was in the sculpture class 1867-74. It would be interesting to know more about him. He spent seven years at Antwerp, assiduously attending class, then seems to disappear completely from view.
8. See Ethna Waldron, 'Joseph Malachy Kavanagh', *The Capuchin Annual,* (Dublin 1968), pp. 314-27. See also Julian Campbell *The Irish Impressionists,* (National Gallery of Ireland, Ulster Museum, Belfast, 1984-85).
9. Vincent Gernon, aged 21, Dublin, *antiek* summer 1877, winter 1877-8, summer 1879, winter 1879-80. *Concours,* 1879, 58.2/60 historical composition, 45/60 drawing from the antique.
10. Thomas John Lucas, 'Art Life in Belgium', *The Portfolio,* vol. X, (1879), p. 179.
11. See Ann M Stewart, *Royal Hibernian Academy of Arts. Index of Exhibitors 1826-1879.* (Dublin 1985-87).
12. Norman Garstin, aged 32, Limerick, *antiek, summer 1880,* winter 1880-81, summer 1881. John Greene, Dublin, aged 20, antiek, winter 1880-81, summer 1881.
13. William Blandford Fletcher, letters home, 1880. Private Collection.
14. Blandford Fletcher letter, 16 May 1880, loc. cit.
15. Lucas, op. cit. p. 180.
16. For Newlyn artists see Caroline Fox and Francis Greenacre, *Painting in Newlyn 1880-1930,* Barbican Art Gallery, London, 1985.
17. See Stewart, op. cit. above.
18. Walter Osborne, *natuur,* winter 1882-3, but did not join *concours.* Hill and Kavanagh, joined *concours* 1883. Hill got 59.1 for painting (he came second in the section for painting a torso from life, 19.7/20, out of 39 competitors) and 52.5 from drawing, Kavanagh 49.5 for painting, 50.4 for drawing. Another Dublin student, Henry Tisdall, who had joined the life class the previous autumn, got 50.1 for painting and 53.4 for drawing.
19. Roderic O'Conor, from Roscommon, *natuur* winter 1883-84. *Concours* 36.3 for painting, 38.4 for drawing. *Natuur* summer 1884. Moynan, *antiek,* then moved to *natuur,* winter 1883-84. *Concours* first place in the life painting, with 60/60, 42.6 for drawing. *Natuur* summer 1884, winter 1884-5.
20. Henry Allan, pass in life painting torso, group, and *matelot,* 1886. Allan, *natuur,* 1886, winter 1886-87. *Concours,* 1887, 19.2/20 painting from the living model, *Laitière,* 8th in a class of 31; Overall 56.4 for torso, 55.2 for group, 57.6 for *laitière* and 53.1 for life drawing – 4th in a class of 37.
21. William O'Brien, aged 21, Limerick, *Painting and Drawing the Figure from the Antique.* Two *concours,* in the first he came 10th, with 13.3/20, in the second 13th, with 10/20. Academic year 1887-1888 *Class for Drawing and Painting from the Life Concours,* under the three headings: torso 17/11th, clothed model 17.1/9th, and 17.7/14th, overall 10th in the class. *Concours,* 1888-89, 55.2/60 (group), and 55.8/60 (torso) for painting, 8th in class, and 53.7 and 59.7 – 4th in Siberdts, drawing class. 1889-90, 5th in the class – 17/5th standing model, 19.4/3rd lying model, for some reason *hors-concours* in the group section, 20/1st drawing from life 1, 17/10th drawing from life 2. Finally registered 1890-91 – but does not appear to have joined *concours.*

EDWARD MARTYN AND GUESTS AT TULIRA

J C M Nolan discusses Edward Martyn, patron of the arts of the Celtic Revival and host to artists and writers in Tulira Castle, County Galway.

W B Yeats is the person who threatens to pervert a balanced understanding of Edward Martyn (1859-1923). It suited Yeats' Irish cultural theories to link closely together Martyn and George Moore as two ludicrous landlords from the West of Ireland. In one of the most malicious speeches in his play *The Cat and the Moon* (1917), Yeats caricatured the pair as peasant saint and peasant sinner:

> *Did you ever know a holy man but had a wicked man for his comrade and his heart's darling? There is not a more holy man in the barony than the man who has the big house at Laban, and he goes knocking about the roads day and night with that old lecher from the county of Mayo, and he a woman-hater since the day of his birth ... The old lecher does be telling over all the sins he committed, or maybe never committed at all, and the man of Laban does be trying to head him off and quiet him down that he may quit telling them.*[1]

Yeats came to associate Martyn with the system of Irish Catholicism for which he had no intellectual sympathy; further to his reflections on the mixture of gentry and peasant strains in both Martyn and Moore, he wrote:

> *The whole system of Irish Catholicism pulls down the able and well-born if it pulls up the peasant, as I think it does. A long continuity of culture like that of Coole could not have arisen in a single Catholic family in Ireland since the Middle Ages.*[2]

With the Nobel Prize for Literature in his back-pocket, Yeats delivered his most crushing blow to Martyn and to the Catholic tradition which Martyn had come to represent; 'An unhappy, childless, unfinished man, typical of an Ireland that is passing away'.[3]

The beginning of Yeats' fierce animosity towards Edward Martyn can be traced back to 1896. In that year, Yeats and the critic Arthur Symons visited Martyn in Tulira Castle, Co Galway, as part of a tour of the West of Ireland about which Symons was to write in his London magazine *The Savoy* later in the same year. At this stage, Yeats had not yet met Martyn's closest neighbour and friend, Lady Augusta Gregory of Coole Park. In *The Savoy*, Symons described Tulira Castle as 'a castle of dreams', where 'in the morning, I climb the winding staircase in the tower, creep through the secret passage, and find myself in a vast deserted room above the chapel which is my retiring room for meditation; or following the winding staircase, come out of the battlements, where I can look widely across Galway, to the hills.' Symons went on to say that Edward Martyn played Vittoria and Palestrina on the organ in the half-dark Great Gothic Hall of the nineteenth-century part of Tulira: 'I wander between the pillars of black marble, hearing the many voices rising into the dome.'[4]

Yeats, too, admitted to having been touched by a sense of romance in Tulira, as he remembered 'the many rookeries, the square old tower, and the great yard where medieval soldiers had exercised' but also remembered vividly his sense of irreverence on the occasion: 'Symons lectured me on my bad manners because, when Martyn showed us two rooms and said we had to choose, I proposed tossing a halfpenny.'[5] Yeats, however, seems to have felt the lure of the tower – in the vast deserted room above the chapel in the Tulira Tower, he 'decided to invoke the lunar tower, which was, I believe, the chief source of my inspiration.' Yeats recorded that he made his invocation of the moon

> *night after night after night just before I went to bed, and after many nights – eight or nine, perhaps – I saw between sleeping and waking, as in a kinematograph, a galloping centaur, and a moment later a naked woman of incredible beauty, standing upon a pedestal and shooting an arrow at a star. I still remember the tint of that marvellous flesh which makes all human flesh seem unhealthy.*[6]

Yeats did not keep these dreams to himself during his stay at Tulira and talked freely about them to his companions. Symons admitted to having had a similar dream the night before of 'a clothed woman of great beauty'.

But Edward Martyn was not prepared to join the dreaming set, and a very early clash of personality was, in due course, recorded by Yeats: 'Martyn was really angry. I had known that a room over a chapel must be left empty, and that an action such as mine might be considered

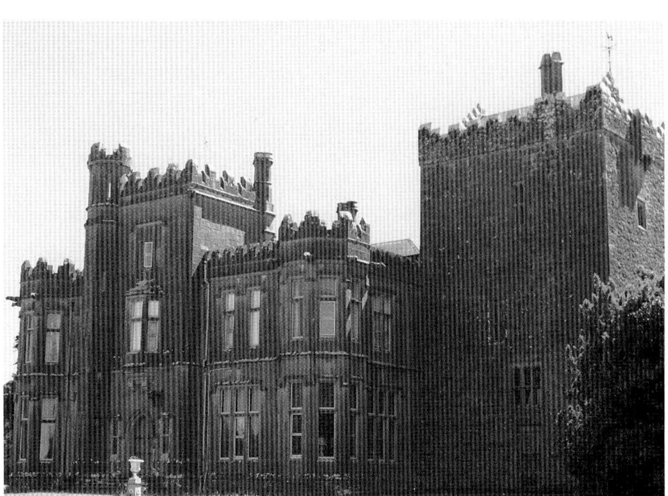

Photograph taken in 1989 of Tulira, showing the contrast between the old tower and Ashlin's Neo-Gothic extension.

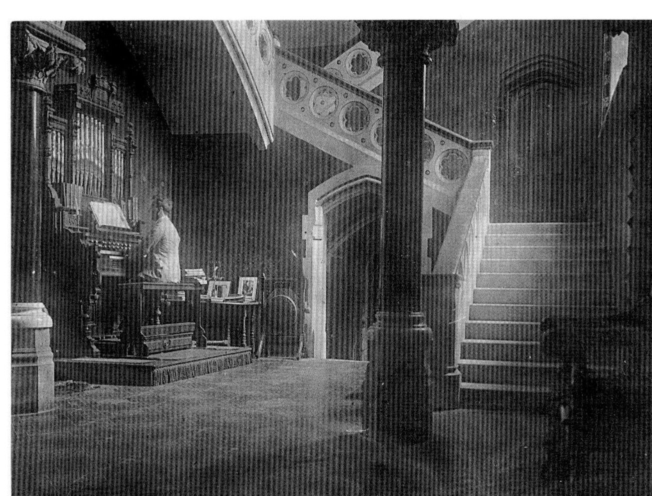

The Great Hall in Ashlin's extension, c.1914. The identity of the organist is unknown. Photograph by Arthur Brandreth.

EDWARD MARTYN AND GUESTS AT TULIRA

to obstruct the passage of prayer. I was forbidden even to speak of invocation.' As he remembered this early confrontation, Yeats made one of the very few admissions that Martyn and he might well have shared a common ground: 'I was sorry, for I know I must have much in common with Martyn who spent hours after we had all gone to bed, reading St Chrysostom.'[7]

What the two had in common was a strong interest in religion; but working in very different traditions was to keep them apart.

Then there was the vexed question of Martyn's country house. George Moore recalled: 'walking on the lawn, I remember trying to persuade him that the eighteenth-century house which one of his ancestors had built alongside of the old castle, on the decline of brigandage, would be sufficient for his want.' Moore did not record Martyn's reply to this suggestion but made much of Mrs Martyn's great ambition to replace the eighteenth-century house with a modern mansion. 'Edward must build a large and substantial house of family importance, and when this house was finished he could not do otherwise than marry.' Martyn's dedication, from youth, to a celibate life could not accommodate his mother's dream of a vast family house, and so Moore reported that 'even before the modern house was quite finished ... Martyn decided to live in the old Tower ... with the bed as narrow as a monk's and the walls whitewashed like a cell and nothing upon them but a crucifix.'[8]

Now Yeats intensely disliked the nineteenth century neo-Gothic extension from his very first sighting of it. It had been designed by the church architect George Ashlin and had cost Martyn about £20,000 during the early 1880s: 'among the worst inventions of the Gothic Revival.' In this Yeats claimed to be sharing Martyn's own opinion: 'He hated that house in all its detail ... all except an ancient tower where he had a study.'[9] In 1925, after Martyn's death, Yeats utterly condemned George Ashlin's extension (without mentioning the architect by name) 'a pretentious modern Gothic once dear to Irish Catholic families,' and went on to dismiss the decoration of the Great Gothic Hall which had been carried out in the early 1890s by 'that dreary decorator Crace.'[10]

So what *was* Edward Martyn's view of Tulira? Yeats and Moore seemed incapable

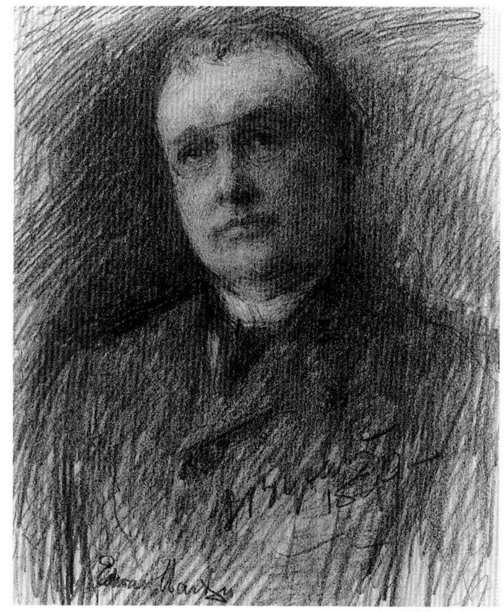

John B Yeats, Edward Martyn: Philanthropist and Playwright. *Pencil and wash. Signed: 1899. Acquired at Coole Park sale in 1932. NGI cat.no. 2941*

of making the distinction between Martyn's rejection of his mother's view of Tulira as the family home for her grandchildren, and his eventual bending of Tulira to his own purposes as a home for guests who were willing to share his supreme passion for the Celtic Arts. Part of Martyn's confident strength as patron of the arts must have derived from his intense pride in family traditions at Tulira, and it is not surprising that he should have felt the urge to celebrate such a pride by commissioning Crace to decorate the Great Hall of Ashlin's mansion.

The Martyn tradition had originated when the Martyns (one of the successful and prominent merchant families of Galway City who were designated 'tribes') became the owners of the De Burgo Castle in Tulira around 1598. The armorial bearings of the family were believed to have been given by Richard I to Oliver Martyn who was believed to have accompanied the King on his expedition to the Holy Land. In Crace's decoration in the Great Hall, there are many variations of the Martyn coat-of-arms, this commission coming from Edward Martyn himself and not from his mother.[11]

There was another sign of family pride in Tulira; a facsimile of Queen Anne's Act which singled out the Martyns of Tulira for very special treatment. The Queen Anne Act was passed for 'explaining and amending the Act to prevent the growth of Popery', and, in it, there was a reference to an Oliver Martyn, 'a person who, during the rebellion, behaved himself with great moderation, and was remarkably kind to Protestants in distress, many of whom he supported in his family and by his charity and goodness, saved their lives.' As a result of such Christian behaviour, the Martyns of Tulira were confirmed by Queen Anne in 'their very extensive estates and in all their rights as citizens, proprietors, and Catholics.'[12] The facsimile of the Queen Anne Act used to hang in Tulira's drawing room and must have served as a reminder to his guests not only of the unbroken Catholic tradition of the family but of the ancient reputation for generosity and hospitality in Tulira; a tradition which Edward Martyn was very happy to continue by opening the door of his mansion to all who were interested in the arts.

While Mrs Martyn still lived, Martyn had to restrict the range of his guests – indeed, George Moore was banned from setting foot in Tulira after the publication of his novel *Drama in Muslin*, which contained some criticism of the priests of the local parish church at Ardrahan. Consequently he was able to join Edward in the house only after Mrs Martyn's death.[13] Obviously, Symons and Yeats visited in Mrs Martyn's lifetime, and they were very aware of Martyn in his ancient tower, withdrawn from his mother's world.

In reality, there could be no total escape into the tower because, to preserve his position as one of the leading Catholic landlords in the West, Martyn had to assert himself when the Land War was being savagely waged, especially in the West where no distinction was made between Protestant and Catholic landlord. Martyn served on the Grand Jury in Galway and it was said that 'in his early years he was the most extreme in his landlord views ... in measuring out compensation for malicious injuries.' An early form of his will revealed that Martyn had a fear of being murdered by his tenants since he directed that, in that event, the provisions in the will about remission of rent and relief of the poor should not be effected.[14]

It was during this period of agrarian unrest that Martyn began his two great collections in the Ashlin extension – his library and his pictures. The library itself was finally given to his great friend, Father Cyril Ryan, Provincial of the Carmelites, in St Teresa's, Clarendon Street, Dublin, and much of it still remains to reveal the great breadth of Martyn's intellectual

EDWARD MARTYN AND GUESTS AT TULIRA

interests.[15] One catches something of Martyn's own early excitement at the building-up of his library in a draft of an unpublished short story, found among his papers, where Tulira is thinly disguised as 'Crofton Court':

> *'Among the classical authors ... Pollux and Apuleius ... the works of St Augustine, the sermons of St John Chrysostom, St Basil's Homilies, and the liturgy of the Greek Church ... all the great English writers ... many of the French ... The Germans Winckelmann and Goethe ... Plato, Schopenhauer ... Classical Archaeology ... portfolios with photographs of the great pictures and statuary in every gallery in Europe ... coloured plates illustrating Byzantine Architecture.*[16]

There is little doubt that Martyn read and studied his books – he shows much learning in his great prose fantasy novel *Morgante the Lesser* which he published in 1890 under the pen-name *Sirius*. (Certainly without his library it could not have been written). One tiny detail in its history shows how Martyn sought to preserve his collection – when he heard that some of the books were on the Catholic Index, he wrote to Rome for permission to retain them on his shelves![17]

We can look to Yeats for a report of Martyn's picture collection in its early stages. During that first visit with Symons, Yeats noted the pictures and disapproved of Martyn's first purchase, a large coffee-coloured sea picture by Edwin Ellis, but very much approved of the other pictures on the walls: Degas, Monet, Corot and Utamaro. Yeats wrote, 'Of these pictures he talked with more intelligence, more feeling than when he talked about literature.'[18] These latter were pictures bought under the influence of George Moore. Predictably Mrs Martyn was not very keen about the Degas Ballet Girls. As the Countess of Fingal reported: 'These last shocked Mrs Martyn greatly.'[19]

Martyn developed early a strong interest in buying pictures from living artists, an experience which he first relished when he bought his two Degas pictures from the artist himself in Paris in 1886, under the watchful eye of Moore. Yeats noted a strong interest in the work of Beardsley: 'Edward, who admired Beardsley for his saturnine genius, had commissioned from him a great stained-glass window for the hall.'[20] Unfortunately Beardsley died before he could execute such a commission and, somewhat surprisingly, no

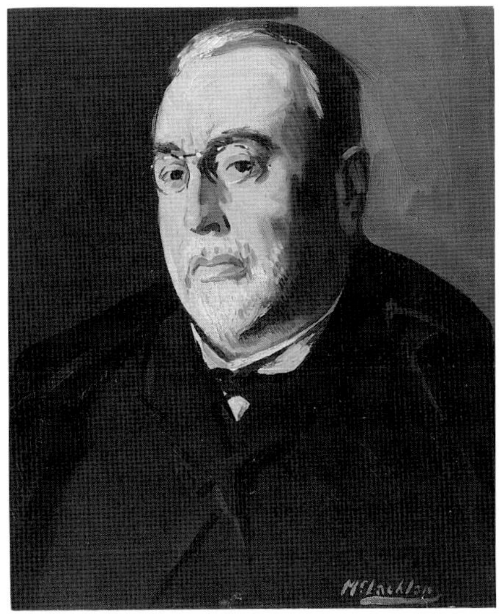

Norman McLachlan, Edward Martyn: Dramatic Author, Nationalist, Philanthropist. *Oil on canvas. Presented by Joseph Holloway in 1934. NGI cat.no. 975*

Beardsley survived in the Martyn Picture Collection.

Edward Martyn as Collector can be studied only in the context of the list of the forty-five items which were received by the National Gallery of Ireland shortly before Martyn's death. The work of Irish artists, mostly bought by Martyn from the artists themselves dominates the list; with artists such as Hone, Duffy, Leech, Henry, May Guinness, Dermod O'Brien, AE, and Jack Yeats featured among others. The only trace of Martyn's supposed interest in English symbolist art was *Before the Dawn: Female Head* by Simeon Solomon. The Martyn Bequest (probably because it was largely based on the work of living artists) seems not to have much impressed the National Gallery who accepted only about six of the pictures (mainly the Parisian purchases); most of the rest were stored by the Municipal Art Gallery with a few items (including AE's *An Enchanted Sea*), being assigned to the Carmelites of St Teresa's, Clarendon Street, Dublin.[21] Martyn meant his collection of pictures to belong to the Irish nation and saw to it that they were removed from Tulira before his death. Lady Gregory recorded in her *Journal* that she saw them, by courtesy of James Stephens, in the locked-up National Gallery on 12 June 1923.[22] It is sad that only a few of the pictures have been on display to the public over the years.

There were two major areas of patronage which began from invitations to visit Edward Martyn at Tulira round about the turn of the century. One invitation was to Christopher Whall (1849-1924), the acknowledged father of the English Arts and Crafts Stained Glass Revival. He came to discuss stained glass commissions for Martyn's local parish church at Laban, near Ardrahan, a church of Gothic design, built about 1856, where the Martyns of Tulira had already been prominent patrons of religious arts. Indeed, the high altar of Sicilian marble had been the gift of Mrs Martyn.[23] Edward Martyn's quest with Whall was not just to produce stained glass for Ardrahan, but to found (with Whall's advice and help) a flourishing native school of stained glass. This he saw as an alternative to the poorly-made foreign stained glass which was much in demand for many of the hastily-erected Catholic churches of this period of the Irish Catholic Revival. Martyn achieved both his aims. He successfully commissioned for Ardrahan church two lights from Selwyn Image, an old friend of Whall, and a St Elizabeth window from Whall and he persuaded Whall to send over to Dublin, the artist Alfred Ernest Child. In 1901 Child became Instructor in Stained Glass at the Dublin Metropolitan School of Art on the course which had been set up with the support of Martyn's friend, T P Gill. About the same time, Martyn (with the help of Father Jeremiah O'Donovan, Administrator) was busy persuading Bishop Healy of Clonfert to commit himself to the principle that the new neo-Gothic cathedral of Loughrea (only a few miles from Tulira) should have stained glass windows exclusively executed in Ireland by well-trained Irish craftsmen. As a direct result of Martyn's vision and influence, there was set up the all-important Tower Glass Company (An Túr Gloine) under Child's management and day-to-day running by Sarah Purser, the Dublin portrait painter.[24]

Patrick Egan sums up the Martyn situation as follows: 'The inducement he offered was the prospect of an ongoing stream of orders from Loughrea Cathedral, funded by himself and the Smith family.'[25] That stream of stained glass artists at Loughrea included the great Michael Healy.

It is not clear if Healy ever visited Tulira but it seems likely that he must have been invited on the strength of his early contributions to stained glass in St Brendan's, Loughrea. These comprise *The St Simeon* Baptistry Window (1904), the side altar

EDWARD MARTYN AND GUESTS AT TULIRA

Windows of *The Virgin and Child* (1907) and of *The Holy Family* (1907), and the *St Anthony* east aisle Window (1907) which Patrick Egan identifies as 'a gift from Edward Martyn'. After Bishop Healy had departed from Clonfert to Tuam in 1903, and Father Jeremiah O'Donovan had departed his job as Loughrea Cathedral's Administrator, Bishop O'Dea succeeded to Clonfert, and the new Bishop seems to have much relied on the advice of Edward Martyn, especially in his commissioning of William A Scott (the architect of Spiddal Church) to design the furnishing and the massive gate entrances to the cathedral. There seems to be little doubt that Edward Martyn of Tulira was the prime cause of much Celtic art in Loughrea Cathedral, the evidence of which still testifies eloquently to a great patron of religious art.

The second area of Martyn's patronage lies in church music. During his travels in Europe in the 1890s, Martyn had been very much impressed by the singing of the liturgical music of Palestrina and Vittoria in such places as Cologne Cathedral and the Church of St Gervais in Paris.[26] Consequently he longed to find a way of founding an Irish *schola* of male voices to sing this music in Irish churches. The opportunity presented itself to Martyn when he attended St Teresa's, Clarendon Street, Dublin, on 16 October 1898, for the reopening of the Carmelite Church where he heard the choir sing Palestrina's *Missa Papae Marcelli* under the direction of Dr Vincent O'Brien. Colum O'Brien, the eldest son of Vincent O'Brien, has spoken about this event which marked the beginning of the very close friendship between Martyn and O'Brien.

> *The young conductor was introduced to him and together they walked to Martyn's flat ... The reserved, scholarly Martyn ... outlined his long and carefully considered plan for the reformation of Liturgical Music in Ireland. Thus was born 'the unique Palestrina Choir.*

Colum O'Brien goes on to say that his father often spent Summer vacations at Tulira, whereby began

> *a strong, intimate friendship ... between the wealthy man of letters, Martyn, and the gifted young choirmaster in whose character he had taken a guiding interest.*[27]

There seems little doubt that Edward Martyn and Vincent O'Brien must have played Palestrina on the organ in the Great Hall at Tulira; not now as on some Parsifal-set (as Yeats and Symons discerned during their famous visit) but as practice for the performance of the Palestrina Choir in the Pro-Cathedral, Dublin, under the patronage of Archbishop Walsh. Martyn seems to have found in severe polyphonic music the great antidote to his impatience with so much flux and change in the world (not just in Ireland). He must have been overjoyed when he discovered that his spiritual passion was in total harmony with the reform of church music in the liturgy, as decreed by Pope Pius X for the Universal Church, just a few years after the foundation of the Palestrina Choir.

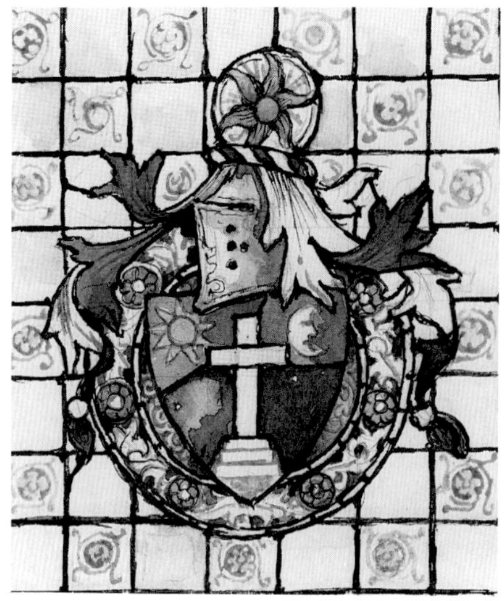

J D Crace's Designs for the Stained Glass Windows in the Great Hall, Tillyra *which featured the Martyn armorial sign. Original colour drawing in RIBA Library, London*

While Vincent O'Brien seems to have turned out to be Martyn's most successful protegé, there were other young men whose talent he was pleased to nurture as guests at Tulira. Robert Elliott, the very well-informed and eloquent art critic, wrote much about the patronage of church art in *The Irish Rosary* and in *The Leader*. His selected essays *Art and Ireland* were prefaced by Martyn in 1906. O'Brien Butler from County Kerry was the composer of the Celtic opera *Muirgheis* (1903) which Martyn much admired in its performance in the Theatre Royal, Dublin, 1913; this composer's death on board the *Lusitania* was described by the grieving Martyn as being 'to the irreparable detriment of Irish Music'.[28] After much searching for the Irish Ibsen, Martyn was to proclaim Henry B O'Hanlon's play *The All-Alone* (which was performed at the Irish Theatre in Hardwicke Street in June 1918) as truly Ibsenite.[29] These three guests were not to achieve the greatness predicted by Martyn; but they are reminders of Martyn's generous patronage of a range of the arts in Ireland, among the young and promising.

Back in the 1890s, Martyn had become involved in the work of the Gaelic League, especially in the area of the preservation of Irish folk music, and became most enthusiastically involved in and reported on the Feis Ceoil whose first competition was held in May 1897. Martyn's love of Irish folk music grew enormously, so much so that he often tried to set Irish folk music in the context of world culture. This wider term of reference was most clearly revealed in the statement made in connection with the traditional singing of Bartly Walsh whom Martyn first heard at the Tuam Feis; 'It reminds me of beautiful Gregorian singing, or of Orientals chanting in old mysterious tonality.'[30]

By the time of Mrs Martyn's death in 1898 and the passing away of the stern disciplinarian of Tulira, Martyn was ready to express his growing love of things Irish in political terms. There was an event in Tulira which marked the new phase in his life. During a period of absence from Tulira caused by his taking part in Nationalist demonstrations to mark the rebellion of 1798, a concert was held there by the local Glee Club, organised by the local Protestant rector of Ardrahan. Some of the gentry who attended the concert took exception to the absence of the National Anthem from the programme, held, as it was, in the country house of a local magistrate and Deputy Lieutenant for the county. When, as Her Majesty's Lieutenant for the County of Galway, Lord Clonbrock challenged Martyn on the issue, Martyn took the opportunity to resign his commissions (in spite of a protest from the local Protestant rector) and to espouse the Nationalist cause in a public way.[31] From 1898 onwards, Martyn continued to feel the need to assert himself as a Nationalist landlord in the midst of an Unionist gentry. His most famous self-assertion took place, not in Tulira, but in the Kildare Street Club where attempts to expel him for his excessive disrespect for the British Army failed in a sensational court case in 1906.[32] That Martyn 'the Nationalist' continued to function within his class in all sorts of ways, reveals him as

EDWARD MARTYN AND GUESTS AT TULIRA

a robustly stubborn individual who was confident in his role, not so much as a landlord (he reduced his estate greatly by selling off to tenants under the terms of the Wyndham Acts), but as the Celtic Revivalist of Tulira opposed, most of all, to the abundance of English bad taste in the arts of Ireland!

Martyn's first play *The Heather Field* was produced in 1899[33] as part of the first season of the Irish Literary Theatre. It dealt, in a symbolist style, with the problem of an Irish Catholic landlord's ineffectuality set in the context of the extraordinarily beautiful landscape of the West of Ireland. Martyn, the Celtic Revivalist, could never be described as 'ineffectual' in those projects such as the Stained Glass Company and the Palestrina Choir, both of which succeeded and survive to the present day. Martyn's reputation for ineffectuality was associated with his ventures as a dramatist and as an Irish Theatre Director. The great battle which developed between Martyn and Yeats over the nature of an Irish Literary Theatre was totally lost by Martyn; and so the direction of the Irish Theatre passed totally away from Tulira and settled in Coole Park where Yeats and Lady Gregory set up their headquarters after 1902. Martyn's ambition for an European Revival in the Irish Theatre was not extinguished until 1921, when he admitted defeat in an article on the future of the Irish Theatre. Writing in the first issue of the monthly journal *Banba*, he (somewhat unjustly) blamed the actors 'a class of people for the most part whose very last thought is reform'.

In the years of the Irish Theatre (1914-1920) at Hardwicke Street, Martyn ran the Theatre with his fellow directors, Thomas McDonagh and Joseph Plunkett, not from Tulira but from the flat above the tobacconist shop in Leinster Street, round the corner from the Kildare Street Club.[34] George Moore described this flat as the equivalent of his Ancient Tower in Tulira:

> *Two short flights of stairs, and we are in his room. It never changes – the same litter, from day to day, from year to year, the same old and broken mahogany furniture, the same musty wall-paper, dusty manuscripts lying about in heaps, and many dusty books ... old prints that he tacks on the wall ... a torn, dusty, ragged screen ... between the folds of the screen ... a small harmonium of about three octaves, and on it a score of Palestrina ... on the table is a candlestick made out of white tin, designed probably by Edward himself, for it holds four candles. He prefers candles for reading,but he snuffs them when I enter and lights the gas, offers me a cigar, refills his churchwarden, and closes his book.*

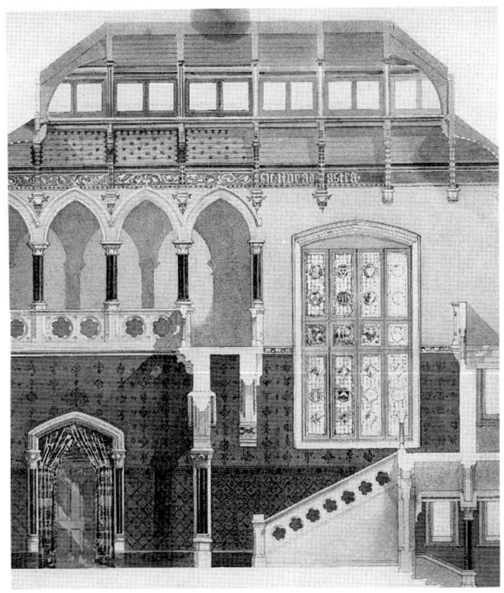

J D Crace's Design for the Stair Hall, 'Tillyra Castle' (sic) Co Galway, *reproduced from* The Craces: 1768-1899, *ed. Megan Aldrich (Murray, London, 1990), p.133. Original colour drawing in RIBA Library, London.*

The self-possession of Martyn fascinated George Moore and he marvelled at the 'originality' of Martyn's behaviour in Leinster Street: 'Is there another man in this world whose income is two thousand a year, and who sleeps in a bare bedroom, without dressing room, or bathroom, or servant in the house to brush his clothes and who has to go to the baker's for his breakfast?'[35] While Moore was capable of this kind of grudging admiration of Martyn's so-called eccentricity, Yeats' approach was to speculate much on the ambiguities of the Martyn/Moore relationship. After both men had died he concluded that Martyn and Moore had much in common and felt extremely comfortable in his self-appointed judgement-seat:

> *I have been told that the crudity common to all Moores came from the mother's family, Mayo squireens, probably half-peasants in education and occupation, for his father was a man of education and power and old descent. His mother's strain seems to have affected him and his brother as the peasant strain has affected Edward Martyn. There has been an union of incompatibles and consequent sterility.'*[36]

In his attempts to fathom Martyn's complex personality, Yeats' damning conclusions show little understanding and sympathy: 'I used to think that the two traditions met and destroyed each other in his blood, creating the sterility of the mule ... His father's family was old and honoured; his mother but one generation from the peasant.' At this point Yeats yields to the irresistible temptation to generalise about Ireland's cultural history on the basis of what he has decided was the trouble with poor old Martyn and Moore: 'Both men are examples of the way Irish civilisation is held back by the lack of education of Irish women.'[37] This assertion has influenced numerous scholars in their view of Martyn, though less so in the case of Moore. Yeats' judgement enormously influenced the way in which some critics have compared Tulira and Coole Park as Irish country houses. Joseph Ronsley is the critic who has spelt out this utterly unresearched view of Tulira: 'Martyn's Tulira betrayed an insincerity and a pretentiousness ... No sense of history or tradition enlivened the house. Nearly everything in it was hated by its owner, but hated with a kind of relish because it fed on hatred of life itself ... Lady Gregory, unlike Martyn, loved her house, and loved it more as it grew more rich in associations.'[38] A comparison between the two houses as images of Irish cultural life at the time of the Revival can be made: Coole, largely the creation of a most gifted poet in such poems as *Coole Park and Ballylee, 1931* with the house imagined as a kind of Irish Urbino, a peak of Anglo-Irish high culture in one of its loveliest forms; in contrast to Tulira, the home of a rich Catholic landlord determined to use his house as main base and meeting point for his many cultural and philanthropic enterprises which were designed to reform an insular Irish Catholicism. This was often made to seem extremely inferior to the splendour of the Yeatsian myth of the eighteenth century Anglo-Irish gentry on whom the middle-aged Yeats yearned to forge his ideals for Ireland.[39]

Denis Gwynn has written about the many happy years when Martyn opened up Tulira to all interested in Celtic Revival; thus Martyn made Tulira into a place of hospitality for Irishmen of all classes passionately interested in the creation of the arts. Gwynn wrote: 'They had been welcome at all items of the year, and frequently when he was not there himself, he would urge his friends who needed a holi-

EDWARD MARTYN AND GUESTS AT TULIRA

day to treat it as their own ...'[40] Dermot Coffey speaking in Philip Rooney's excellent feature programme, *The Turret Room* provided interesting insights into the domestic routine of Tulira at the turn of the century. 'I first knew Edward Martyn in 1900 or 1901 when I was still a child. My people were much interested in the Irish Literary Revival and through that we got to know him, and we used to stay with him in Tulira ... As servants he had an old butler called Gantly and a cook and a housemaid. A very small staff for so large a house ... He used, I believe, to get up very early in the morning and write till breakfast, which he had at ten or later. He did not expect his guests to keep these hours. He ate an enormous breakfast and took a great deal of exercise, mainly walking. He never had afternoon tea but ate a very large dinner at about seven ... his voice had a rich western tone which was pleasing, and seemed to fit his personality. He had a broad sense of humour.' Once on a walk with young Coffey, Martyn said: 'We'd better be getting back as your mother is here, so we must get into evening clothes. Women like that sort of thing – that's what makes them such a nuisance.' When Coffey assured Martyn that his mother was not like that, Martyn said: 'Really Dermot? Really! I didn't know such sensible women existed.'[41]

Another testament to the genial side of Martyn at Tulira was provided by J J Horgan: 'Martyn was at his best in his country house, Tulira, County Galway, where his genius for hospitality and kindness had full scope.'

> *Martyn objected to oil lamps and Yeats, in the rather dim mellow candlelight, after dinner, sat wrapped in clouds of tobacco smoke from Martyn's churchwarden pipe, descanting like a prophet, in that delicate and fastidious language of which he was the master, on the eternal verities in art and beauty. From time to time Martyn would burst in with some matter of fact, and sometimes slightly malicious, comment, which brought the proceedings down to earth.*[42]

Martyn's final years in Tulira were bleak and desolate. Lady Gregory noted in her *Journal:*[43] 'He is anxious about money, has fears of his investment in the English railways, and is very crippled by rheumatism' (25 September 1921). Later Lady Gregory noted that Martyn wanted to sell Tulira to the Hemphills (his first cousins). In 1921, as part of the guerrilla war between the Free State Army and the Republican irregulars, country houses were put on a 'hit list' by the Republicans; three examples of wanton destruction by burning, quite close to Tulira, were Palmerston (Lord Mayo), Kilteragh (Sir Horace Plunkett) and Moore Hall (birthplace of George).[44] As the threat to Tulira grew, Martyn himself became ever more seriously ill. Lady Gregory visited Tulira to see Edward Martyn on the 8 September 1923 – it was to be her last visit to Tulira in Martyn's lifetime. She wrote in her *Journal:*

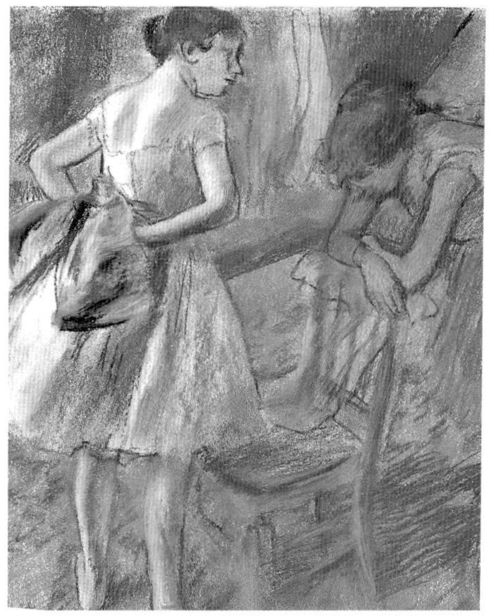

Edgar Degas (1834-1917),
Two Ballet Dancers, *Pastel on paper, 48.5 x 64cm. Bequeathed to the NGI (No 2740) by Edward Martyn in 1924.*

> *In the bow window of the library I saw Edward sitting ... he stayed quite quite immovable, like a stuffed figure, it was quite uncanny ... I touched his hands (one could not shake them, all crippled, Dolan says he has to be fed) and spoke to him. He slowly turned his eyes but without recognition. I went on talking without response till I asked him if he had any pain and he whispered: "No, thank God". I didn't know if he knew me, but talked a little, and presently, he whispered: "How is Robert?" I said: "He is well, as all are in God's hands, he has gone before me and before you." Then I said: "My little grandson, Richard, is well", and he said with difficulty and in a whisper: 'I am very glad of that.' Then I came away, there was no use staying ... Dolan had tea ready but I could not have touched anything, it seems such a house of death. Poor Edward every moment was picking at the rug over his knees.*

On the 7 December 1923, Lady Gregory noted in her *Journal* the fact of Edward Martyn's death. 'I heard of Edward Martyn's death, it had taken place that morning, the doctor told Mr Bagot a tumour had been taken from his head on Saturday. Dr McGuinness had come from Dublin for the operation and he lost a good deal of blood. Father Kelly said that he had recognised Father Carr, which he had not done for some time.' On the 11 December 1923 Lady Gregory noted in her *Journal:* 'Poor Edward. His body has been taken to Dublin to be dissected, by director of his will. He directed the Dr should visit it each day till removal to make sure he was really dead. But if he meant by giving it to the School of Medicine to perhaps save some sufferer for what he has gone through (no doctor seeming to know what was wrong or be able to help him) it was a fine thing to do.' But the significance of Martyn's donation of his body to St Cecilia's Hospital for dissection and his subsequent burial in a pauper's grave (all strictly prescribed in his will) cannot be reduced to an overwhelming desire to be useful to science.

Martyn's dream of an unknown grave among paupers was described by Denis Gwynn as 'his supreme gesture of indifference to the vanities of human life, the last act of relentless discipline over his body which he had regularly controlled.'[45] There seems little doubt about the fact that Martyn, by this act, seems to have wanted to free himself from Tulira itself and its associations with the landlord class whose decay was both inevitable and welcome to him. As a member of the Irish gentry, Martyn never felt Yeats' need to proclaim the graciousness of the Irish Country House surrounded mainly by clerically-dominated philistines. Certainly the Tulira Tower was never in need of poems in order to establish it as a significant poetic image, as Yeats chose to mythologise his newly-acquired and restored Ballylee Tower on the Coole estate. The Tulira Tower was a cockpit for Martyn the reformer. The freedom from Tulira, which his burial in an unknown grave gave Martyn, should be considered alongside his gift of his library and papers to the Carmelites and of his pictures to the National Gallery. Here is the last demonstration of Martyn's altruism as public moralist – a public role very far removed from the brief reign of W B Yeats as Senator of the Irish Free State. Is it surprising that virtually nobody in the Ireland of the 1920s was ready to respond to

EDWARD MARTYN AND GUESTS AT TULIRA

Martyn's message?

Edward Martyn had many dreams of reviving the arts in Catholic Ireland and often generously invited his guests to share his dream; not in the Tower where he resided alone but in the splendid George Ashlin extension with its library, pictures and organ in the Great Hall. Many of the reforms initiated by Martyn had fallen short of his dreams at the time of his death – the cultural reasons for the few successes and many failures have never really been fully researched by scholars of Anglo-Irish Literature who have tended to accept lazily Yeats' verdict on Martyn 'the sterility of the mule'[46] which is, of course, the winner's version! Meanwhile Martyn's many writings especially for fugitive nationalist reviews and newspapers remain virtually ignored by the scholars. Martyn's Tulira no longer exists, even though the buildings survive.

The invitation from the ghost of Martyn, some seventy years after his death, is certainly not to sink with an Ireland that is passing away; a proper response to the invitation should become the urgently-felt need to look objectively at the evidence of his successes and failures, to sift through the many misrepresentations of his reforms for the arts in Ireland, to recapture something of the dreams of an Irish Maecenas before the role of patronage was taken over by bodies such as the Arts Council.

In 1963 F S L Lyons suggested, in his O'Donnell Lecture, in Trinity College, Dublin that Martyn's cultural failure was not his fault, but the result of his living into a nationalist period of Irish history when integration with European civilisation (according to Martyn, the key to Irish cultural development) came to seem impracticable and undesirable in the political struggle against England.[47]

Is the Ireland of the 1990s ready for the tasks of transforming Martyn's dreams into reforms? That is still the most pressing question in need of thorough discussion among guests at Tulira!

J C M Nolan

J C M Nolan is preparing a biography of Edward Martyn (1859-1923).

NOTES

1. W B Yeats, *Autobiographies*, London 1955. Yeats quotes from and comments on this extract from the play on p.402.
2. W B Yeats, *Memoirs*, ed. Denis Donoghue, London 1972, pp.270-71.
3. W B Yeats, *The Bounty of Sweden*, Cuala Press, Dublin 1925, pp.51-52. This indictment of Martyn was not actually part of the Yeats address to the Swedish Academy on his acceptance of the Nobel Prize for Literature in early 1924; but the great poet could not resist adding it as a footnote to the published address.
4. Symons' articles appeared in *The Savoy* (October, November and December, 1896). They were reprinted in his *Cities and Sea-Coasts and Islands*, Collins, London, 1918, pp.302-44.
5. Yeats, *Memoirs*, p.100.
6. Yeats, *Autobiographies*, pp.372-73.
7. Yeats, *Memoirs*, p.101.
8. George Moore, *Hail and Farewell*, ed. Richard Cave, Gerrards Cross, 1976, pp.184-95.
9. Yeats, *Autobiographies*, p.386.
10. Yeats, *The Bounty of Sweden*, pp.51-52.
11. She was a Smith of Masonbrook, whose father had made a speedy ascent from peasant to land-property speculator and had used his financial success to bid successfully for the marriage of his daughter into the Martyn gentry.
12. Rev. J Fahey, *The History and Antiquities of the Diocese of Kilmacduagh*, Gill, Dublin, 1893, pp.248-49 for much back ground on the Martyn family and the Queen Anne Act.
13. J Hone, *The Life of George Moore*, London, 1936, p.124.
14. Denis Gwynn, *Edward Martyn and the Irish Revival*, London, 1930, p.105. Due to the loss of the Martyn Papers while in the custody of the Carmelites of Clarendon Street, Gwynn's totally unscholarly memoir has become indispensable for the Edward Martyn researcher, in view of the lengthy quotations which Gwynn copied out from the last papers.
15. Gwynn, pp.345-46.
16. Gwynn, pp.59-73.
17. Gwynn, p.80.
18. Yeats, *Autobiographies*, p.387.
19. The Countess of Fingal, *Seventy Years Young*, London, 1937 and Dublin, 1991, p.52.
20. Yeats, *Autobiographies*, p.387.
21. National Gallery of Ireland Archive: Papers about the Martyn Bequest. I am most grateful to Adrian Le Harivel for giving me access to these papers. I am also grateful to Barbara Dawson and Patricia Flavin of the Hugh Lane Municipal Gallery of Modern Art for information about the Martyn Bequest pictures in their care.
22. *Lady Gregory's Journal*, ed. D J Murphy, Gerrards Cross, 1978, Vol 1.
23. Rev J Fahey, *History*: p.430.
24. *Gazetteer of Irish Stained Glass*, ed. Nicola Gordon Bowe, David Caron and Michael Wynne, Dublin, 1988, pp.12-20.
25. Patrick Egan, *St Brendan's Cathedral, Loughrea* (Irish Heritage Series: 56), Dublin 1986.
26. Martyn's articles appeared in *The Speaker* (London): Feb, 1895 & Aug 1896.
27. Radio Script: Vincent O'Brien (part 1). I am deeply endebted to Mr Colum O'Brien for a copy of the typescript and for his invaluable comments on it. Mr and Mrs Oliver O'Brien have also been most generous in providing me with copies of Martyn's letters to Vincent O'Brien still in their possession.
28. Gwynn, p.265.
29. WJ Feeney, *Drama in Hardwicke Street*, AUP, 1986 contains information about O'Hanlon the playwright, pp.202-23.
30. Gwynn, pp.269-74.
31. Gwynn, p.108.
32. Mark Bence-Jones, *Twilight of the Ascendancy*, London, 1987, pp.110-13.
33. *The Heather Field* and *Maeve*, London, 1899 has an over enthusiastic Introduction by George Moore. Jan Setterquist, *Ibsen and the Beginnings of Anglo-Irish Drama 2: Edward Martyn*, Dublin 1960 is a comprehensive study of Martyn's debt to Ibsen in these and later plays.
34. Dr Feeney, in his *Drama in Hardwicke Street*, explores painstakingly Martyn's role in his amazing Fringe Theatre in revolutionary Dublin.
35. Moore, *Hail and Farewell*, pp.594-95.
36. Yeats, *Memoirs*, pp.270-71.
37. Yeats, *Memoirs*, p.271.
38. Joseph Ronsley, *Yeats' Autobiography: Life as Symbolic Pattern*, Harvard, 1968, pp.111-12.
39. In Seamus Deane's *Celtic Revivals* (London, 1985), pp.30-37 and in Antony Coleman's essay 'The Big House, Yeats and the Irish Context' in *Ancestral Voices*, Dublin 1992, pp.123-45, Yeats' excursions into the creation of his own Anglo-Irish cultural history have at last been subjected to some trenchant intellectual analysis.
40. Gwynn, pp.35-36.
41. *Capuchin Annual, 1962*, pages 71-80. I am indebted to Brian Lynch of RTE Archive who made available a tape of Philip Rooney's radio programme, relayed on 22 April 1956, *The Turret Room*. Dermot Coffey's daughter, Miss Saive Coffey, has been kind enough to write to me about her grandmother's involvement as Secretary of the Irish Literary Theatre in 1899.
42. JJ Horgan, *Parnell to Pearse*, Dublin, 1948, p.117.
43. All these quotations from *Lady Gregory's Journals* are taken from D J Murphy's edition, as above.
44. Mark Bence-Jones, *Twilight of the Ascendancy*, pp.230-35.
45. Gwynn, p.343.
46. Yeats, *Autobiographies*, p.388.
47. Professor Lyons' paper, 'George Moore and Edward Martyn, was published in *Hermathena*, 1964, pp.9-32.

AN TUR GLOINE STAINED GLASS IN ARIZONA

The stained glass windows in Brophy College Chapel, Phoenix, Arizona, were commissioned by Irish-American Mrs Amelia Brophy in the 1920s and 1930s. **David Caron** examines these windows by Michael Healy, AE Child, Hubert McGoldrick, Ethel Rhind and Kitty O'Brien, members of *An Túr Gloine.*

During the late 1920s and 1930s five stained glass artists (Michael Healy, AE Child, Kitty O'Brien, Ethel Rhind and Hubert McGoldrick) designed and executed a series of ten windows for a school chapel in Phoenix, Arizona. This series of windows is one of the most interesting in the history of twentieth-century Irish stained glass for several reasons. First, it was the largest single overseas order to be undertaken at *An Túr Gloine* (Tower of Glass) Studio in Dublin. Second, the subject of the series, the Apostles' Creed, is highly unusual, and this was the only instance when it was attempted at *An Túr Gloine*. Third, the series is exceptionally well-documented with over one hundred items of correspondence extant in Phoenix, and eight sketch designs (some rejected) for individual windows in the collection of the National Gallery of Ireland.

Since the Phoenix commission is so well documented, compared to the relative lack of information about most *An Túr Gloine* windows, it provides a valuable insight into the commissioning process. Normally much of this would have been conducted in person at the studio, with Sarah Purser (the well-known painter and unofficial manager of *An Túr Gloine*) liaising with donor and artist, but because this was an overseas commission, all details had to be ironed out through the post.

Previous to the Phoenix series, the artists of *An Túr Gloine* had designed windows for several countries, including Britain (many orders), Canada, India, New Zealand, Singapore, Turkey and the United States. In each case the artists had to contend with the difficulty of designing a window for an unseen destination having to rely on the donor to describe the architectural style and features of the church or building, the location and aspect of the proposed windows, any climatic considerations (such as Arizona's intense sunlight eleven months of the year), and all other salient factors. It appears that in all cases, with the possible exception of some of the British windows, that the artists never saw their works *in situ*.

An Túr Gloine's largest foreign commission prior to Phoenix, was for a convent chapel in Newton, a suburb of Boston. This commission (for which there is virtually no surviving documentation), comprises eight windows which had been designed by six artists, most of whom were to contribute windows to the Phoenix series. In general the Newton windows form a much more homogenous group, perhaps reflecting the fact that they were all executed in the studio during a single year, 1927, whereas the Phoenix windows span almost a decade. The Newton commission was also more standard, in that seven of the windows (the eighth is a rose) depict saints, as indeed do the vast majority of all *An Túr Gloine* windows, whereas the Phoenix series required the artists to combine often obscure symbols and pictoral vignettes in order to illustrate the text of a prayer.

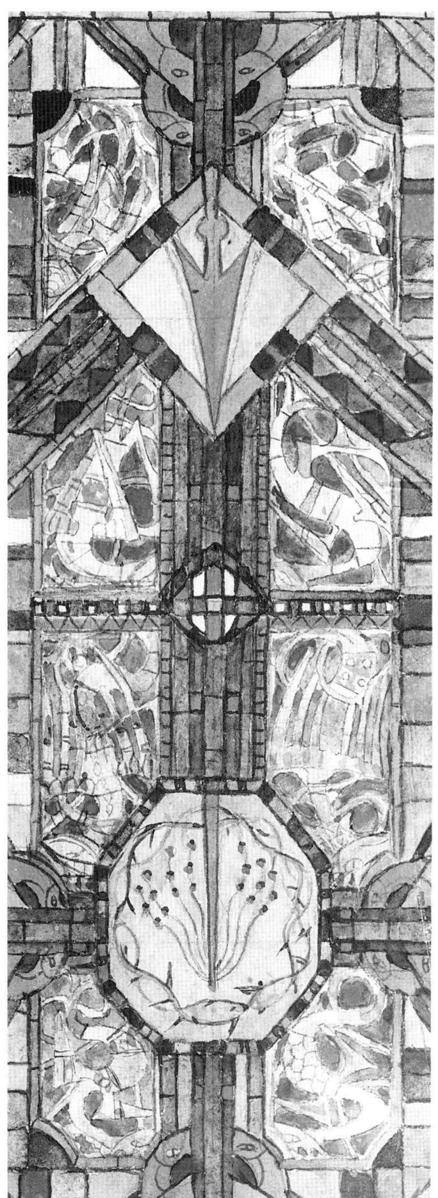

Michael Healy, Instruments of the Passion, *25 x 13.8 cm. Watercolour on paper, NGI cat no. 18,369.*

It should be noted at the outset that the quality of the individual Phoenix windows varies considerably; there are some disappointing works (particularly those of AE Child), but there are also a pair of very fine windows by Hubert McGoldrick, and a stunning work by Michael Healy.

Four individuals were involved in the protracted negotiations relating to the Phoenix commission. These were Ellen Brophy, the American donor; John Kibbey, her architect; Sarah Purser; and AE Child, the English-born stained-glass artist and official manager/secretary of *An Túr Gloine*.

Ellen Amelia Goodbody Brophy (1871-1934) was the widow of a prominent Arizona banker, William Henry Brophy (1863-1922).[1] William Brophy, a native of Baltinglass, County Wicklow, had been orphaned as a child and raised by his grandmother (an elder sister of Cardinal Cullen), and at the age of nineteen he borrowed money and emigrated to the USA. William Brophy initially made his fortune in mining which he then invested in banking and land purchase around Phoenix. In 1891 he married Ellen Goodbody of Illinois, the daughter of Francis Alexander Goodbody who was a railroad contractor. As a child, she travelled with her father while he worked on the opening of the railroads in Texas, Arizona and Southern California. William and Ellen Brophy were to have three children, two of whom died young. Mrs Brophy devoted much time to charitable and philanthropic activities which were recognised by Pope Pius XI who bestowed on her the *Pro Ecclesia et Pontifice*.

In 1922 William Brophy drowned in a boating accident off the coast of Mexico. Partly because of a desire to commemorate her late husband, and partly because of a need to establish a good Catholic school in Arizona, Ellen Brophy set about founding

AN TUR GLOINE STAINED GLASS IN ARIZONA

a Jesuit school in the state capital, Phoenix. An architect friend of the Brophys, John Rinker Kibbey, was employed, and after much deliberation, a school (incorporating a chapel) was built some four miles from the centre of Phoenix. John Kibbey had travelled extensively in Spain and Mexico[2] and the influence of his peregrinations is evident in the architectural style of the building on the forty-acre campus.

When I visited the school I was struck by the stylish, though somewhat restrained, interpretation of Mexican Mission architecture, and the dramatic contrast between the exterior and interior of the chapel. Outside, the overall impression is of crisp, white stuccoed walls, arched verandas and terra-cotta tiled roofs, all set among soaring palm trees and manicured lawns. Entering the chapel though the large wooden doors, one leaves behind the glaring sunshine and it takes several minutes to adjust to the interior darkness, pierced only by the sonorous, jewelled windows.

It was Ellen Brophy who decided that all the stained glass would be Irish;[3] this was a rather curious decision as it had already been determined by her, in conjunction with her architect John Kibbey, that the chapel and all its interior decorative elements (altar, panelled ceiling, etc) would be treated as a pastiche of a Mexican Mission church. Ellen Brophy, accompanied by her nieces, visited Ireland on at least two occasions and became firm friends with Sarah Purser, who undoubtedly encouraged her to commission the windows from *An Túr Gloine*.[4] Sarah Purser also succeeded in getting Ellen Brophy to become a member of The Friends of the National Collections which Miss Purser had founded to purchase works of art, and to campaign for the return of Hugh Lane's collection to Dublin.[5]

In the archive of Brophy College, the first document relating to the stained-glass commission is a letter from Ellen Brophy to Sarah Purser dated 15 August 1927. In this letter Mrs Brophy requested an estimate for the cost of stained-glass windows for her prospective memorial chapel. 'I am anxious to introduce your glass to this part of America. There are some good churches going up in Los Angeles (where Mrs Brophy normally resided) with the usual hideous windows. If I can show the padres in this part of the country the beauty of your glass I feel I shall be a public benefactor.' She enclosed a drawing and dimensions of a window for the purpose of the estimate and stated that the chapel would have a total of fourteen windows. (The order was subsequently reduced to eleven, though, finally, only ten windows were made,[6] each costing £100). In terms of subjects, Ellen Brophy's initial idea was to have 'original designs portraying the lives of our early Spanish Jesuits who lived in Arizona during the seventeenth century'.[7] It is almost certain that Ellen Brophy had already seen examples of *An Túr Gloine* glass in Ireland, and from the chatty final sentence of her letter it is clear that she was on friendly terms with Miss Purser: 'Hoping you are well and that the entrance of the Republicans into the Dial [sic] is not causing an unsettling of affairs'.[8]

In the following August, 1928, Ellen Brophy is known to have visited the studio in Dublin,[9] and at an *An Túr Gloine* Committee Meeting held on 13 August it was decided that 'Mr Healy and Mr McGoldrick or one of them should prepare a finished sketch of St Ignatius to be sent to Mrs Brophy'.[10] Healy did produce a crayon-and-watercolour sketch design (now in the National Gallery of Ireland),[11] though, by November, Mrs Brophy had decided against depicting Jesuit saints.[12]

During 1929 and early 1930 Ellen Brophy changed her mind several times, and letters attempting to clarify the subjects to be commissioned were dispatched by Mrs Brophy, John Kibbey, Miss Purser and AE Child. Windows depicting the

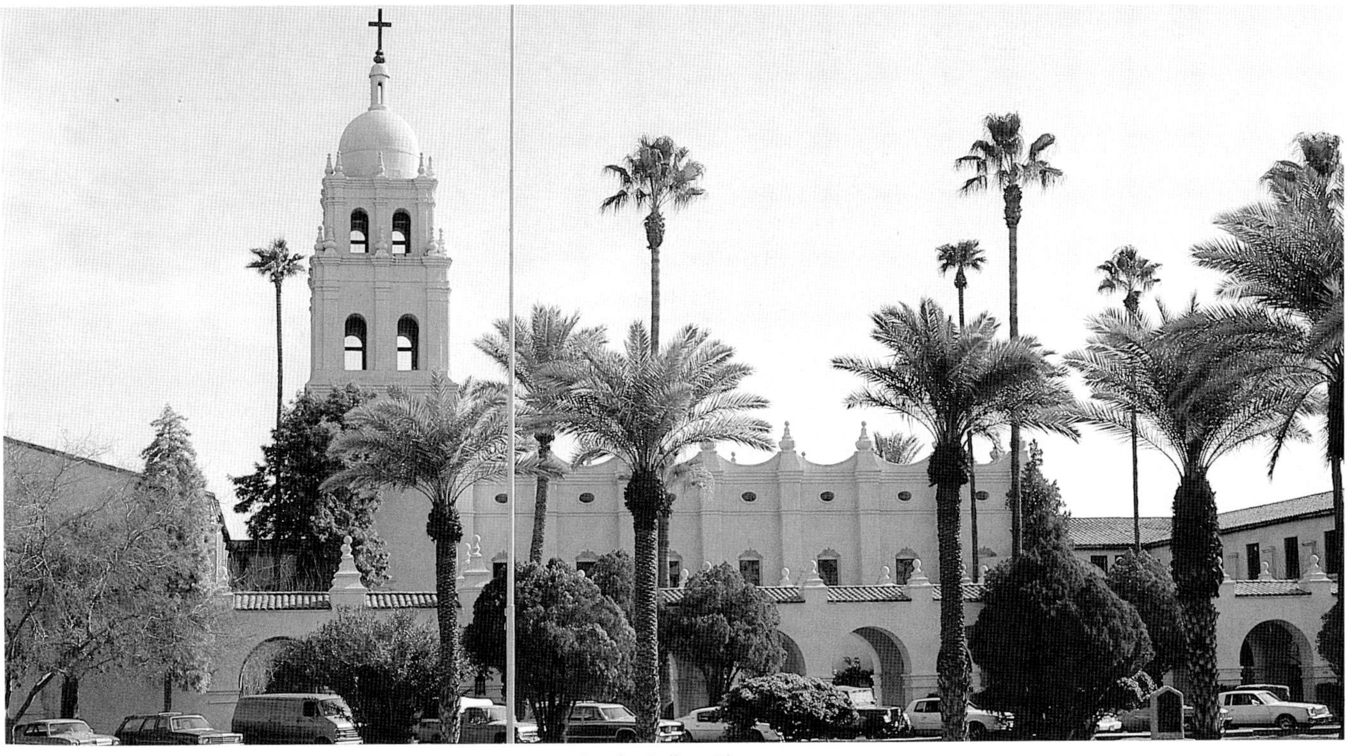

Brophy College, Phoenix.

AN TUR GLOINE STAINED GLASS IN ARIZONA

Blessed Virgin and St Joseph were considered,[13] then the Blessed Virgin and St William,[14] then St Helen and St William in conjunction with the symbols of the Evangelists;[15] and yet another scheme was to incorporate 'angel heads in all of them ...'[16] The confusion was exacerbated by the fact that it took five weeks for letters to travel from Los Angeles to Dublin and, inevitably, letters crossed in the post.

In 1929 Kibbey wrote to Child describing the chapel. (This was after Kibbey had received the first sketch designs, including presumably Healy's *St Ignatius*, which he deemed to be 'quite in opposition of everything else in the building').[17] Kibbey informed Child: 'the character of the building is Mexican Mission. This is similar to Spanish Renaissance but is much cruder in execution of form and detail that would be found in Spain. There are no examples of either stained glass or of illuminated ceilings in any of the Mexican Missions that can serve as a precedent for us, so that we can only do what the Mission priests of former years did, i.e. go back to Spain for our inspiration, and try and modify our designs to fit in with and conform to the conditions that would have existed'.[18]

Kibbey sent to Child samples of the original colours used in the chapel ceiling as possible aids in selecting the window colours.[19] He also directed the artists of *An Túr Gloine* to study the windows at the Cathedral of León in Spain: 'Try and absorb their spirit, not in actual design but character and colour ...'[20] Not surprisingly none of the artists had been to León, though Sarah Purser had examined the windows at Seville and Avila.[21] After considerable difficulty the studio obtained from Spain a copy of *Arte y Decoracion in Espana*, Vol III, which contained colour plates of the León windows. Kibbey had suggested the volume as an inspiration source.[22] However Sarah Purser and the artists did not find it particularly helpful: 'We were afraid to go on till we had seen it – but we do not see very well in what it differs from ordinary 13th century work all over the continent – and it is figure work not ornament, which then, as afterwards, was always done in *grisaille* with very little colour introduced, which was what we were aiming at. The tomato-red effect in the plates is due to the printing I think – however we have kept as near as we could to that tone and the colour patterns your architect sent us ...'[23]

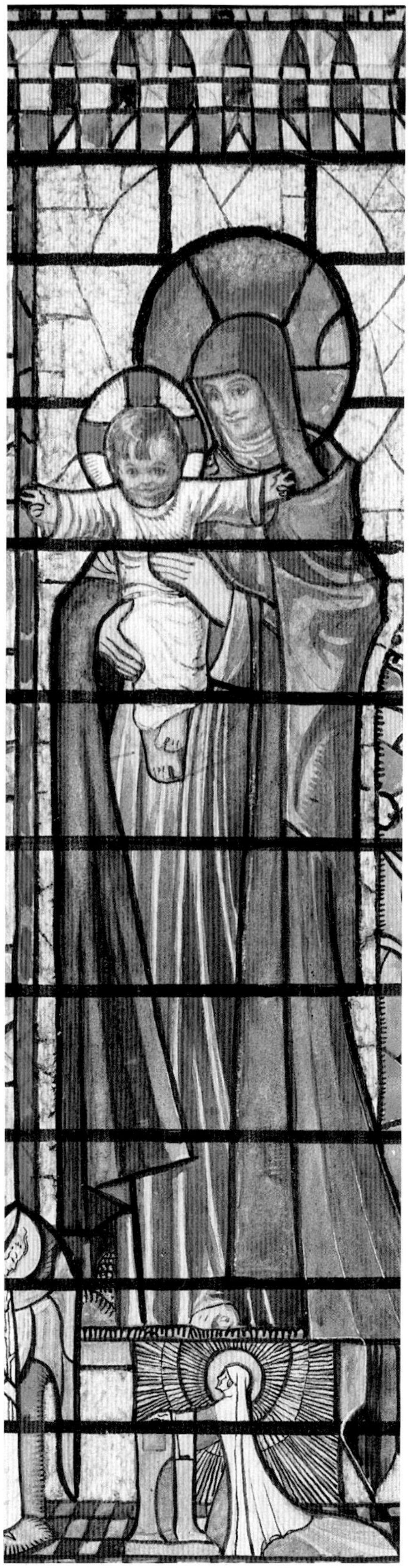

Hubert McGoldrick, Virgin and Child *(above);* the Annunciation, *20.7 x 7.8 cm. Ink and watercolour on board, NGI cat. no. 18,416.*

While Kibbey concerned himself primarily with the aesthetic aspects of the stained-glass scheme, Ellen Brophy directed her energy into the selection of subjects to be treated in the ten windows. By late Spring 1931 the overall scheme, if not all the individual subjects, had been determined. Mrs Brophy's idea was to illustrate, through the depiction of symbols, the Apostles' Creed, and to this end she solicited the assistance of 'a bright young Rector of the University here, who is rather keen on such things and from whom I shall get splendid assistance'.[24] Sarah Purser also enrolled two erudite priests to advise in the matter, Fr Aubrey Gwynn, SJ[25] and Fr Bertie O'Connell, a Dublin Diocesan priest.[26]

The subjects of the ten windows are listed below (starting at the front of the church near the pulpit and proceeding counterclockwise). All of the windows are positioned at clerestory level and each of the rectangular windows (measuring 7'9" by 3'2"), is divided horizontally in half. The majority of windows feature two main symbols or images, one in each half. They are:-

1. AE Child, *Alpha and Omega*, c. 1930.
2. AE Child, *Symbol of the Holy Trinity (triangle) with omniscient Eye of God; Sceptre and Crown*, 1934.
3. Michael Healy, *IHS Sacred Heart*, 1937.
4. Hubert McGoldrick, *Symbols of the Blessed Virgin*, c. 1934.
5. Kitty O'Brien, *Host and Chalice; Wheat and Grapes*, 1937.
6. Kitty O'Brien, *Pelican and Lamb*, 1937.
7. Hubert McGoldrick, *Dove; Fire and Torch*, c. 1934.
8. Ethel Rhind, *St Peter's Archbasilica, Rome; Fountain of Grace*, c. 1934.
9. AE Child, *Smoking Thurible; Crossed Keys*, c. 1934.
10. AE Child, *Butterfly; Crossed Palm and Crown*, 1932.

The first window of the series to be completed, *Alpha and Omega* by AE Child, left the studio in April 1931.[27] The imagery was selected to represent the first article of the Creed: 'I believe in one God the Father almighty, maker of heaven and earth, and of all things visible and invisible.' The overwhelming colour of the window is ruby. Above and below, the two Greek letters sit in dark blue hexagons surrounded (surprisingly) by much gold Celtic-style interlacing. The design and treatment of *Alpha and Omega* is unchar-

AN TUR GLOINE STAINED GLASS IN ARIZONA

acteristically crude and heavyhanded. Child was at his best when working in the manner of his teacher, Christopher Whall, who employed subtle colours, made frequent use of white glass quarries, and often included decorative motifs inspired by nature. The treatment of *Alpha and Omega* is without precedent in Child's *oeuvre* and it would seem that his unusual work was the result of his attempt to take all of the architect's advice and criticism on board.

After the installation of *Alpha and Omega* in Brophy College chapel, much discussion ensued as to whether the window was too dark in tone.[28] Sarah Purser became quite impatient: 'Dear Mrs Brophy, I do think you are somewhat like Aesop's old man and his ass!! In this world, especially in matters of taste, there is no use trying to please everyone. If you are pleased as we (the artists) are pleased, it will be well above the average of satisfaction'.[29] In reply, Ellen Brophy conceded that: 'As far as design and other details are concerned, you are to have *carte blanche*, and when the question of density of light is decided on, you will have no more interference from me'.[30]

It appears that around July 1931 Michael Healy submitted a second sketch design to Ellen Brophy, this time for a window depicting the *Suffering of Christ*. Mrs Brophy wrote back to Sarah Purser: 'I found your last two sketches [the other sketch was by McGoldrick] extremely interesting, but cannot imagine the one of the *Sufferings of Christ* [Healy's sketch] fitting in with the designs I have already received. It seems a bit impressionistic and brilliant. However, it is, as you say, most interesting and might not be as great an innovation as I think'.[31] *The Sufferings of Christ*, or more accurately *The Instruments of the Passion*[32] was never executed[33] though the basis of the design has been adapted for the *IHS Sacred Heart*, the window which Healy executed for the chapel in 1937. Another, less symmetrical, sketch design by Healy for Brophy College, depicting *Symbols of the Blessed Virgin; the Burning Bush and Lily among the thorns* may also date from around this time.[34]

By March 1932 Sarah Purser was able to report to Ellen Brophy that the second window, also by Child, 'is well on its way to completion – something the same as the first in design and colour but slightly less dense and more translucent ...'[35] *Butterfly; Crossed Palms and Crown* was despatched in April and scheduled to arrive in Los Angeles a month later.[36] Again ruby is the dominant colour and the images sit in blue hexagons, however the Celtic-style interlacings have been replaced by symmetrical foliate designs.

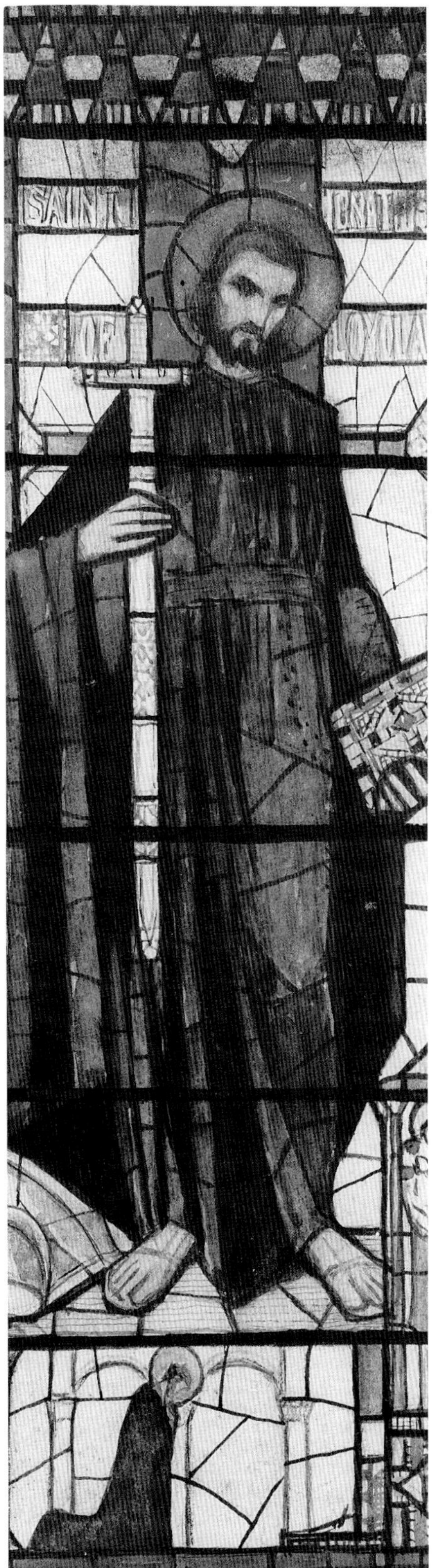

Michael Healy, St Ignatius of Loyola with sword and book *(top) and* Kneeling before the Virgin *(bottom), signed: Michael Healy, 30.7 x 14.1 cm. Crayon and watercolour on paper, NGI cat. no. 18,482.*

In June 1933 Ellen Brophy sent a cheque for a further three windows to be undertaken. These were to be *Smoking Thurible; Crossed Keys* and *Symbol of the Holy Trinity (triangle) with omniscient Eye of God; Sceptre and Crown*,[37] both by AE Child, and *St Peter's Archbasilica, Rome; Fountain of Grace*, by Ethel Rhind. In the first of his pair of windows, Child shifted the colour emphasis from ruby to emerald and reintroduced some Celtic-style ornamentation to produce his most satisfactory window. Child's other window, again overwhelmingly red, disappoints largely because the glazing bars crudely cut across the images.

Ethel Rhind's window is among the most illustrative of the ten Phoenix windows, and, unlike Child, she was entirely comfortable utilising a vivid palette. In the upper half of the window she includes a detailed vignette of Maderna's facade of St Peter's; below is an ornamental fountain at which two hovering doves drink. The background design, which is filled with vigorously sprouting vegetation, is clearly derived from Child's three windows.

The next two windows to be designed, one celebrating the Blessed Virgin and the other celebrating the Holy Spirit, were both the work of Hubert McGoldrick. Unfortunately there is no correspondence relating to these or the subsequent windows and it is assumed that this is due to Ellen Brophy's increasingly poor state of health.

The composition of McGoldrick's two windows is very similar; both are predominantly blue and, of all the windows in this church, are the most reminiscent of medieval glass, yet at the same time are distinctly in the style of McGoldrick. They both feature several symbols, a pair of figures in profile (the only figures to appear in any of the Phoenix windows), and a broad abstract border composed of cullets, some painted with irregular checkerboard patterns. McGoldrick's characteristic matting technique, including liquid mats that were allowed to 'run', is also in evidence. Of the pair, the more resonant is *Symbols of the Blessed Virgin*. Here McGoldrick features the burning bush, Immaculate Heart of Mary, the Angel Gabriel appearing to

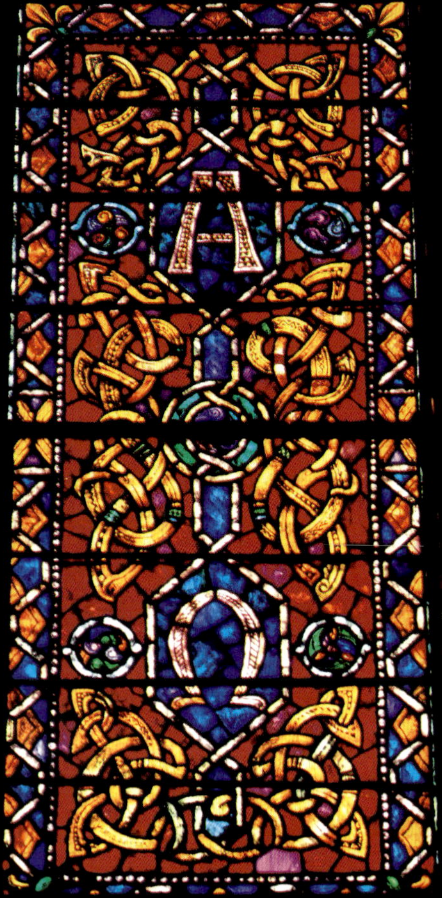

A E Child, Alpha and Omega *c. 1930-1, Brophy College, Phoenix.*

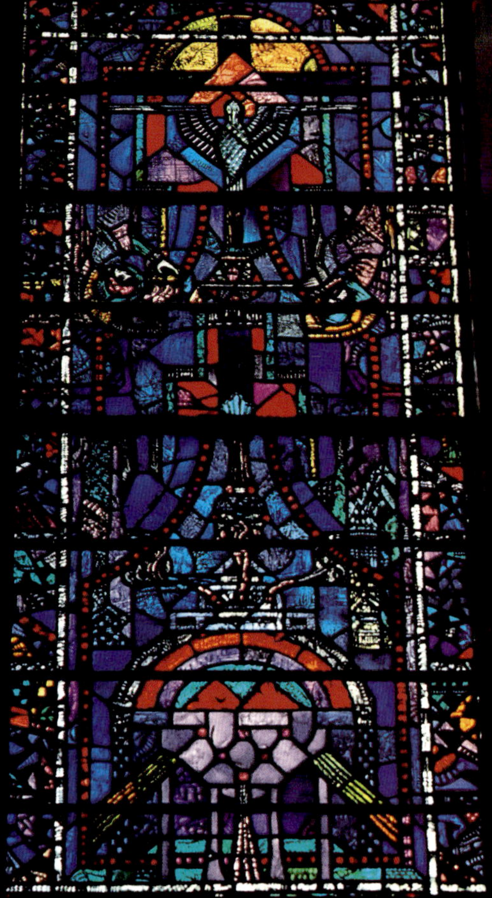

Hubert McGoldrick, Dove; fire and torch *c. 1934, Brophy College, Phoenix.*

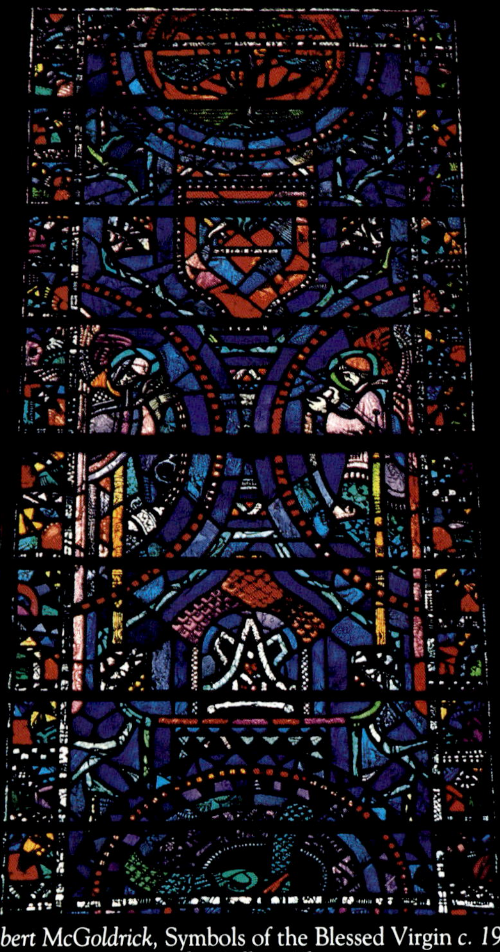

Hubert McGoldrick, Symbols of the Blessed Virgin *c. 1934, Brophy College, Phoenix*

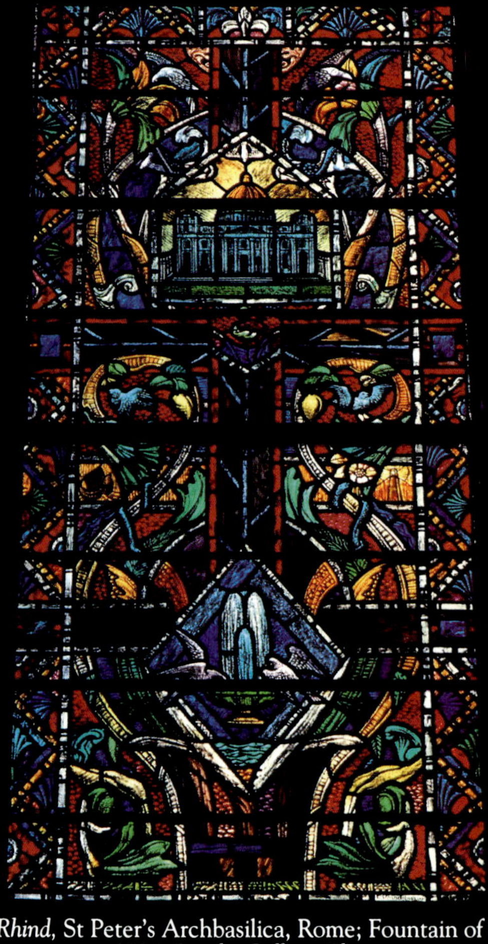

Ethel Rhind, St Peter's Archbasilica, Rome; Fountain of Grace, *c. 1934, Brophy College, Phoenix.*

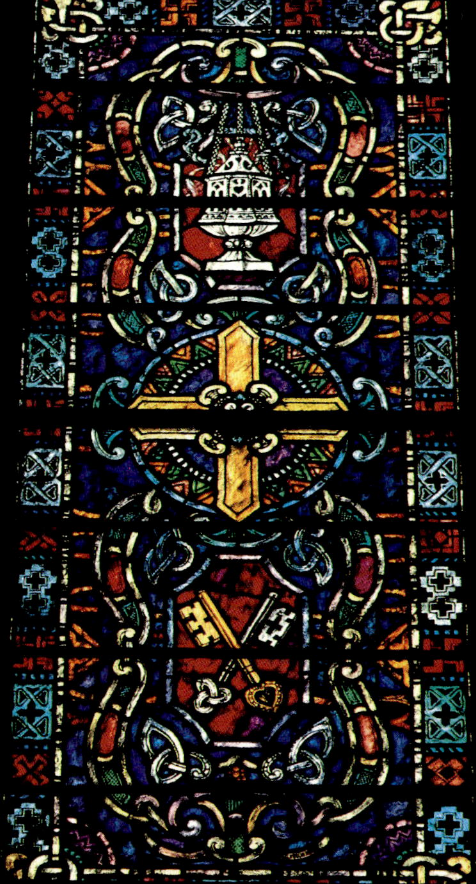

A E Child, Smoking Thurible; Crossed Keys,
Brophy College, Phoenix.

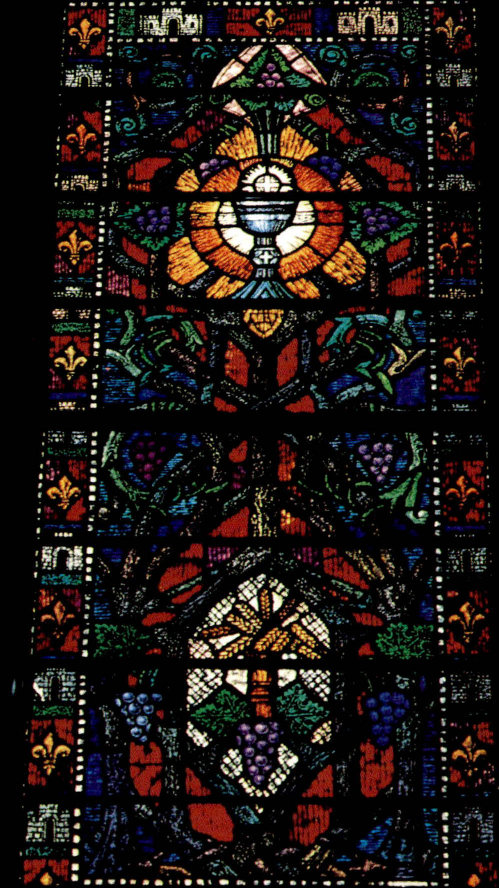

Kitty O'Brien, Host and Chalice; Wheat and Grapes, *1937,*
Brophy College, Phoenix.

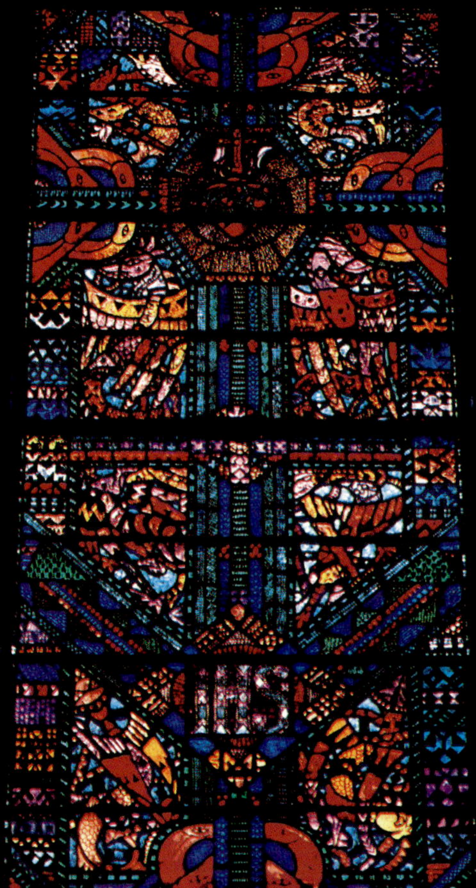

Michael Healy, I H S; Sacred Heart, *1937,*
Brophy College, Phoenix.

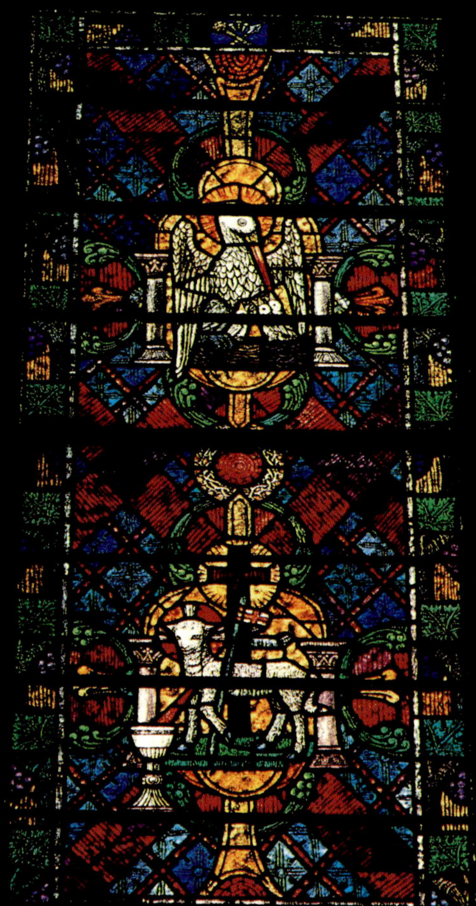

Kitty O'Brien, Pelican and Lamb, *1937.*
Brophy College, Phoenix.

AN TUR GLOINE STAINED GLASS IN ARIZONA

Mary, letters M and A interwoven, and the serpent crushed by Mary.

In July 1934 McGoldrick's two windows, along with Child's second pair and Rhind's sole window, were dispatched from the studio to Los Angeles via Liverpool.[38] Unknown to the artists of *An Túr Gloine*, Ellen Brophy had died some three weeks earlier on 23 June. Mrs Brophy's death may have placed the completion of the series in doubt. However the following year *An Túr Gloine* received a further cheque to proceed with the remaining windows,[39] presumably from Ellen Brophy's only surviving child, Frank Cullen Brophy.

The final three windows comprise a pair by Kitty O'Brien and a single window by Michael Healy. O'Brien's windows are designed in a similar vein to those of Child and Rhind. Their vivid, mostly unadulterated primary colours and the naturalistic though somewhat naive illustrative style convey a certain robust charm.[40]

Michael Healy's window, *IHS Sacred Heart*, is indisputably the highlight of the Phoenix series. The dominant colours in this refulgent window are ruby and emerald, with virtually none of Healy's characteristic aciding incorporated, no doubt on account of the intense sunlight. The highly symmetrical composition features, aside from the Sacred Heart (centre top) and IHS monogram (centre bottom), eight fantastic creatures, each part-serpent, animal and bird. These creatures, all different and some quite fearsome, are clearly derived from native American-Indian art which Healy absorbed and then reinterpreted to dramatic effect. The window is a *tour-de-force*, and though distinctly the work of Healy, is at the same time, without parallel among his life's *oeuvre*. It was dispatched from the studio, along with O'Brien's two windows, in June 1937.[41]

The Phoenix series was to be the last significant collaborative commission undertaken at *An Túr Gloine*. Within a few years AE Child and Michael Healy had died, and Sarah Purser, Ethel Rhind and Hubert McGoldrick had retired, and so this remarkable group of windows can be seen as a memorial not only to William Brophy and his philanthropic wife Ellen, but also to the unique artistry of those who worked at *An Túr Gloine*.

David Caron

David Caron was educated at the National College of Art and Design, Dublin (BSc in Visual Communications), Pratt Institute, New York (MS in Communications Design), and Trinity College, Dublin (PhD). The subject of his PhD was 'An Túr Gloine and Michael Healy (1873-1941)'. He is the author, along with Dr Nicola Gordon Bowe and Dr Michael Wynne, of Gazetteer of Irish Stained Glass. *He currently lectures in Graphic Design at Limerick School of Art and Design.*

NOTES

1. All biographical details of William and Ellen Brophy are from: *The Brophy Family and the Founding of Brophy College* by William Henry Brophy III. This booklet was privately printed in 1972 and a copy is in the author's possession.
2. W H Brophy III, *The Brophy Family and the Founding of Brophy College*, 1972, p.12.
3. Ellen Brophy (EB) to Sarah Purser (SP), 15 August 1927. Carbon copy of letter in Brophy College, Phoenix (BCP).
4. A visit by Ellen Brophy in August 1928 is referred to in a letter from SP to EB, dated 6 February 1929. Visits to Ireland with her nieces are referred to in EB to SP, 12 August 1931. Letters in BCP.
5. SP to EB, 6 January 1932, BCP.
6. The eleventh window, which is located in the choir loft, was never executed. In 1985 an Arizona stained glass artist, William Lupkin, was commissioned to design and execute the final window. Mr Lupkin was also responsible for restoring the *An Túr Gloine* windows in the same year. An article by him on the Brophy College windows titled 'Irish Jewels in the Valley of the Sun' can be found in the American journal *Stained Glass*, Summer 1986, pp. 106-10.
7. EB to SP, 15 August 1927, BCP.
8. Ibid.
9. Ellen Brophy's visit is referred to by Sarah Purser in: SP to EB, 6 February 1927, BCP.
10. Minutes of meeting held on 13 August 1928. *An Túr Gloine* Share Register and Minute Book (SRMB) which is in NGI.
11. *St Ignatius of Loyola with sword and book (top) and kneeling before the Virgin (bottom)* signed: *Michael Healy*, 30.7 x 14.1 ($12^{1}/_{8}$" x $5^{1}/_{2}$"), crayon and watercolour on paper, NGI cat no 18,482.
12. Minutes of Meeting held on 16 November 1928: 'An Túr Gloine agreed to accept Mrs Brophy's offer to supply the windows in good quality ornamental design with religious emblems introduced ... and if the Blessed Mother design is accepted that Mr McGoldrick will do this window ...' SRMB, NGI. In the NGI there is a sketch design by McGoldrick which appears to have been designed for Brophy College: 'Virgin and Child above the Annunciation', 20.7 x 7.8 ($8^{1}/_{4}$" x $3^{1}/_{8}$"), ink and watercolour on board, NGI cat no 18, 416.
13. SP to EB, 6 February 1929, BCP. In the NGI there is a sketch design by Kitty O'Brien which appears to have been designed for Brophy College *St William of York*. 27 x 15 ($10^{5}/_{8}$" x 6"), pencil and watercolour on paper, NGI cat no 19,079.
14. AE Child (AEC) to John Kibbey (JK), 8 June 1929, BCP.
15. JK to AEC, 15 October 1929. Carbon copy of letter in BCP.
16. SP to EB, 3 February 1930, BCP.
17. JK to AEC, 24 May 1929. Carbon copy of letter in BCP.
18. Ibid.
19. Ibid.
20. Ibid.
21. SP to EB, undated page from a letter, probably c. August 1929, BCP.
22. AEC to JK, 19 August 1929, BCP.
23. SP to EB, 19 August 1929, BCP.
24. SP to EB, 16 May 1931. BCP.
25. SP to EB, 3 February 1920, BCP. Fr Aubrey Osborn Gwynn (1892-1982) was the son of Stephen Gwynn MP, the well-known writer. When Sarah Purser sought his advice in 1930 he then held the position of Lecturer in Medieval History at UCD.
26. SP to EB, 16 May 1931, BCP. Sarah Purser wrote of Fr O'Connell as 'a very great authority on all liturgical matters.'
27. AEC to EB, 27 April 1931, BCP.
28. EB to SP, 24 November 1931. Carbon copy of letter in BCP.
29. SP to EB, 6 June 1932, BCP.
30. EB to SP, 12 February 1932. Carbon copy of letter in BCP.
31. EB to SP, 12 August 1931. Carbon copy of letter in BCP.
32. The sketch design for this window is in the NGI *Instruments of the Passion*, 25 x 13.8 ($9^{7}/_{8}$" x $5^{1}/_{2}$"), watercolour on paper, NGI cat no 18,369.
33. The window was executed by William Lupkin in 1985. See note 6.
34. The sketch design for this window is in the NGI: *Symbols of the Blessed Virgin; the burning bush and lily among the thorns*, 25.4 x 10.6 (10" x $4^{1}/_{4}$"), crayon and watercolour on board, NGI cat no 18,410. It was McGoldrick who actually designed and executed the window of this subject for the subject for the chapel.
35. SP to EB, 22(?) March 1932, BCP.
36. AEC to EB, 16 April 1932, BCP.
37. AEC to EB, 29 June 1932, BCP.
38. *An Túr Gloine* Work Journal (ATG WJ) no 2, p. 68, order no 661. The studio's three work journals are in the NGI.
39. Ibid.
40. There are sketch designs for both these windows in NGI: *Host and chalice; wheat and grapes*, 25.5 x 12 (10" x $4^{3}/_{4}$"), watercolour on board, NGI cat no 18,477; *Pelican and Lamb*, 27.4 x 15.5 ($10^{3}/_{4}$" x $6^{1}/_{8}$"), watercolour on board, NGI cat no 18,481. There are two other sketch designs by O'Brien for proposed windows in Brophy College Chapel which were never executed: *The Crucifixion, a Font and the interior of a Spanish Mission church*, signed: K O'Brien, 24.6 x 12.4 ($9^{3}/_{4}$" x $4^{7}/_{8}$"), ink, pencil and watercolour on paper, NGI cat no 19,105; *Holy Dove and Fire, with the exterior of a Spanish Mission church*, signed: K O'Brien, 22.1 x 12 ($18^{3}/_{4}$" x $4^{3}/_{4}$"), ink, pencil and watercolour on paper, NGI cat no 19,106.
41. ATG WJ no 2, p 68, order no 661, NGI.

WILHELMINA GEDDES' OTTAWA WINDOW

Shirley Anne Brown
discusses Wilhelmina Geddes' sole North American commission, a First World War memorial window in Canada, commissioned by the Duke of Connaught and produced at *An Túr Gloine*.

In the past several years, there has been renewed interest in the life and works of Wilhelmina Geddes, the admittedly eccentric, but remarkably talented Irishwoman who, for fifteen years before she moved to London in 1925, was an active member of *An Túr Gloine*.[1] The majority of Geddes' surviving stained glass windows are in Great Britain and Ireland, with one window in Ypres, Belgium, and two in Wellington, New Zealand. Her sole North American work is the First World War Memorial Window commissioned by the Duke of Connaught for St Bartholomew's Church in Ottawa, Ontario, Canada.[2]

St Bartholomew's sits unobtrusively on the corner of Victoria and McKay Streets in Ottawa.[3] This small Anglican church was begun in 1867, the year of Canadian Confederation, as the parish church for Rideau Hall, the official residence of the Governor-General. It was built on the model of a Victorian country parish church. Today, passers-by are few, and almost no one realizes that this neo-Gothic structure possesses a most remarkable stained glass window.[4]

On Sunday morning, 9 November, 1919, St Bartholomew's was filled to overflowing. At the appointed time, the Governor-General of Canada, the Duke of Devonshire, escorted the Prince of Wales into the church, accompanied by representatives of Princess Patricia's Canadian Light Infantry. The future Edward VIII had come from England specifically to unveil the new East Window, a memorial to lives lost during the war which had ended only a year before.

The next day's report in the *Ottawa Citizen* described how an audible gasp swept through the congregation when the Prince pulled the cord and the drapery covering the window fell away. It does not opine whether it was a gasp of appreciation or astonishment at what they saw before them. Instead of the usual Late Victorian sentimentality common in Canadian stained glass of the day, this unassuming little church now housed the most expressive tribute to human heroism and sacrifice that Ottawa, perhaps even Canada, had seen.

The subject of the three-light window is the welcoming of a slain warrior into the eternal company of soldier-saints, champions, and angels. The warrior, who personifies all the memorialized men, strides in from the left, wrapped in a crimson cloak, carrying a broken spear. He is conducted by Raphael, the Angel of Healing, and by Gabriel, the Angel of the Annunciation. Behind them, the Angel of Death, in dark clothing, bears a cup in his hand; the Angel of Peace hovers above. In the middle window, they are met by three Roman soldier-saints – Longinus, Sebastian, and Martin – while above them looms Michael, the militant Archangel, carrying a sceptre and a sword. To the right are English and French national saints – Edmund, Joan of Arc, and Louis, with Saint George above on horseback. A close look at the background reveals the knights of the legendary King Arthur. The acts and martyrdoms of the saints are shown on their banners while the knights carry pennons painted with their exploits or emblems. Almost all the figures are accompanied by identifying inscriptions. In the tracery Angels of War and Peace descend from the crenellated towers of the heavenly citadel.

The base panels contain the memorial inscription, an effigy of the recumbent soldier, and mourners. The inscription reads:

> *This window was erected by Arthur, Duke of Connaught, Governor-General of Canada, to the Glory of God and in affectionate memory of the members of his staff who fell in the Great War 1914-1918. May their names live forever more.*

But the Duke of Connaught was not in Ottawa on that chill November day. At the age of 69, his health required that he spend the winter months in the relative warmth of the south of France. Born in 1850, the third son of Queen Victoria, Prince Arthur had accepted the post of Governor-General of Canada in 1911, returning to England in 1916. It was he who presented the window to St Bartholomew's Church where he and his family had worshipped regularly during their five-year stay in Ottawa.[5]

The Great War had broken out during the Duke's term in Canada and soon took sad toll of his household. Since most of his personal staff were experienced professional military men, they went off to assume various active commands, including that of the Princess Patricia's Canadian Light Infantry. A bronze plaque on the wall indicates that the memorial commemorates ten men from the Duke's personal staff who were killed during the war, three of whom had been with the 'Princess Pats', as the regiment had quickly become known.[6]

When she received the commission, Wilhelmina Geddes was a relatively unknown thirty-two year-old Irish woman from Belfast. The Ottawa window was her first large stained glass commission and was produced in the Dublin studios of *An Túr Gloine*, the Tower of Glass. It is not known exactly why the Duke of Connaught gave the commission for the Canadian memorial window to this progressive artists' cooperative which was very much involved in the Irish Celtic Revival and the Arts and Crafts Movement.[7]

As Prince Arthur, the Duke had visited Ireland many times and had served as Commander-in-Chief of the British Forces there from 1901 to 1904. During his period of residence in Dublin, his family had naturally become involved in Anglo-Irish society, making friends and contacts with the literati and the aristocratic women who were the main patrons of the revival of the arts in Ireland. It is probable that the commission was directed through one of them. Geddes' letters indicate that the most likely contact was Lady Leslie, an American woman living in Ireland who was a confidante of the Duke and his wife, and also very close to Sarah Purser, who headed the Tower of Glass.[8]

Purser gave the commission to Wilhelmina Geddes who had been invited to join the group in 1910. Prior to her coming to Dublin from Belfast, Geddes had not been trained as a stained glass artist, but she learned the techniques from the other artists in the cooperative. Her remarkable talent developed rapidly and the series of windows which she created during the late 'teens heralds the arrival of her fully-developed style. The memorial window in St Anne's Church on Dawson Street in Dublin, installed in 1918, shows St Michael flanked by smaller figures of warrior saints and angels, and nine exquisitely-painted, dramatic interludes from their lives. Three windows were completed in 1920 for All Saints Church in Blackrock, County Dublin, although only two now

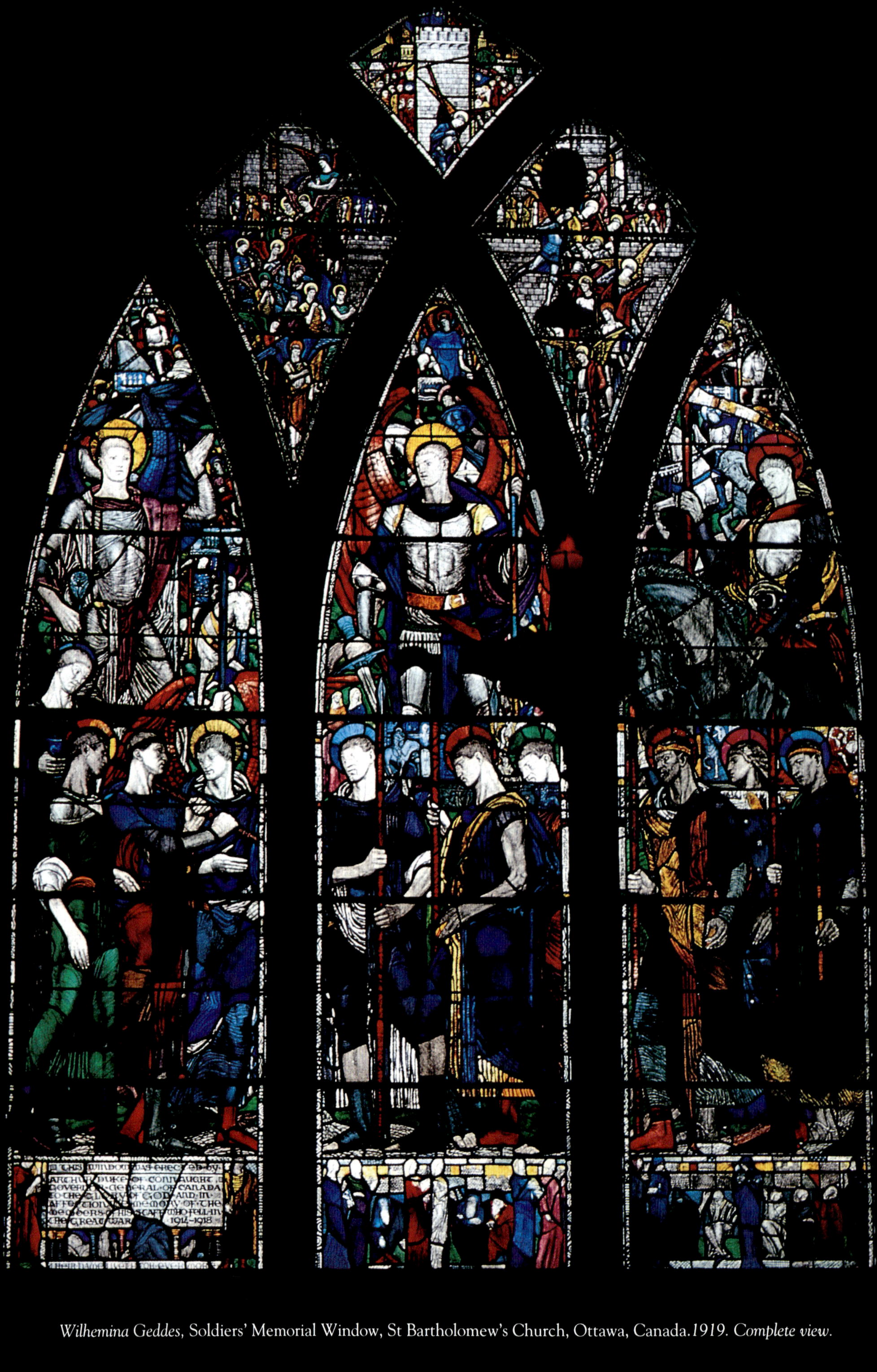

Wilhemina Geddes, Soldiers' Memorial Window, St Bartholomew's Church, Ottawa, Canada.*1919. Complete view.*

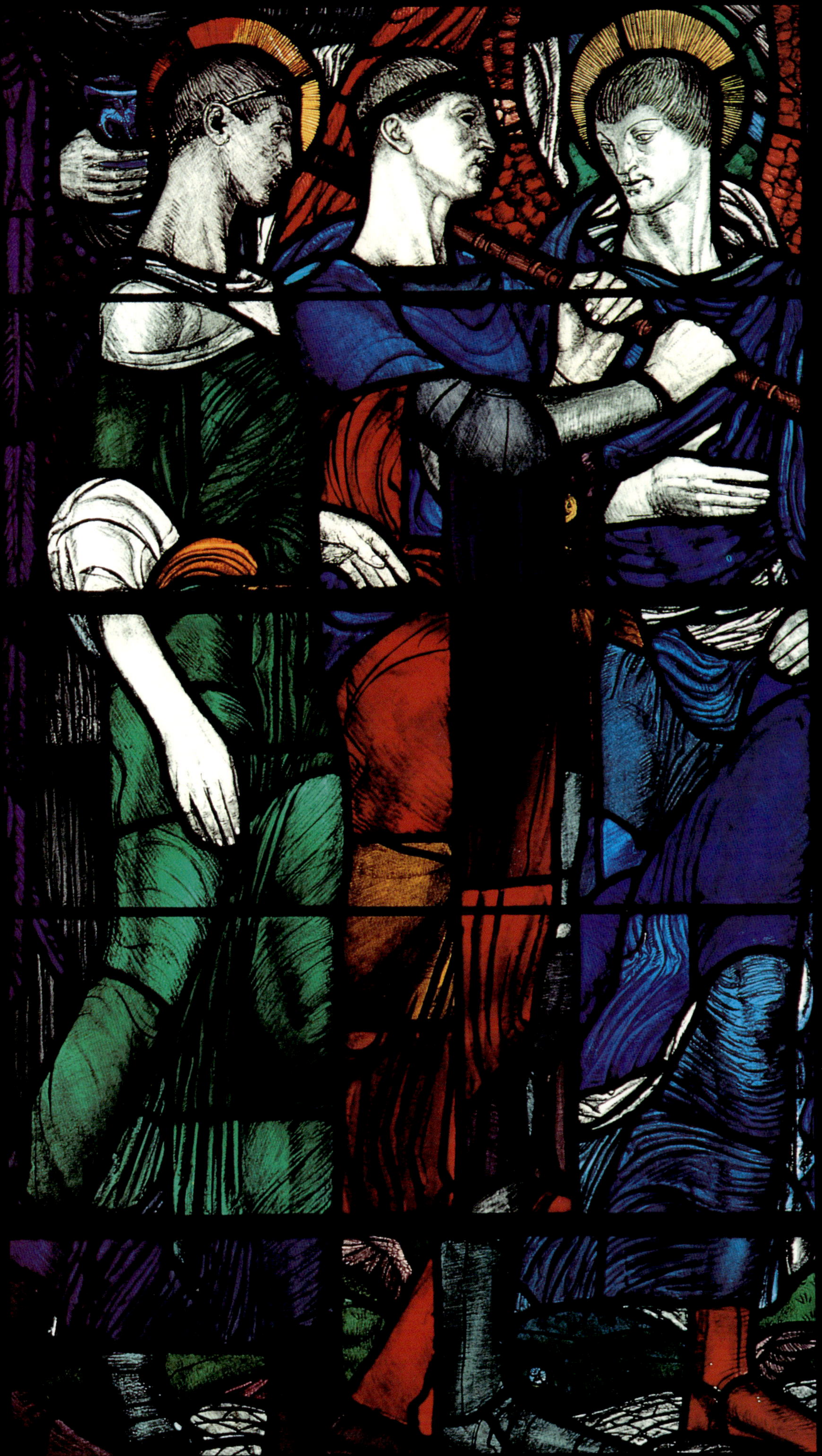

Detail: Raphael; Slain warrior; Gabriel

WILHELMINA GEDDES' OTTAWA WINDOW

exist: St Michael and St Raphael. There also, the central figures are surrounded by smaller figures, evoking a complexity of both iconography and surface design. The Ottawa window shares a close kinship with these examples, in particular with the Dawson Street work.

According to the order books of the Tower of Glass, the Ottawa window was confirmed in May 1917, and it has always been assumed that it took two years to complete. But a recent look through Geddes' remaining correspondence, now in the National Library in Dublin, indicates that she had started work on the design before the end of 1915.[9]

The records of the Princess Patricia Infantry yield the information that the first of the Duke's household staff to fall during the war had been Captain DOC Newton. Deployed near St-Omer, on the second night of trench warfare for the regiment, 9 January, 1915, Newton got lost between the lines, was mistaken for the enemy and was shot by one of his own nervous sentries.[10]

But it was the death of Lieutenant-Colonel Farquhar, the Duke's Aide-de-Camp and a personal friend, which brought the realities of the war home to Ottawa. Farquhar had been chosen as commander of the Canadian regiment and he died in action on 20 March, 1915, at Voormezeele, behind the trench lines at St-Eloi.[11] Notification of his death caused a shockwave to pass through the Governor-General's household in Ottawa and a memorial service was held for him at St Bartholomew's. It was his death which must have provided the impetus for the commissioning of the memorial window, even though it was not confirmed for another year and a half. The third household staff member assigned to the Princess Pats to lose his life was Captain Herbert Buller who replaced Farquhar as commanding officer and died on 2 June, 1916, in Sanctuary Wood during the Battle of Mount Sorrel.[12]

Geddes knew that her designs adopted a different aesthetic from the stained glass produced by the large commercial houses. The human figure always dominates Geddes' compositions, and she created a new male prototype for stained glass – modern-looking figures, close-shaven, classically-derived young men, serious and thoughtful – very different from the vacuous Late Victorian model. Their sinewy bodies are covered with wet-fold drapery, reflecting her consummate skill in life-drawing. Her incorporation of handwritten names and small poignant figurative details was to remain a hallmark of her style.

Geddes' stained glass designs have a strongly graphic quality, reflecting her lifelong commitment to printmaking, watercolour, and drawing. She painted her glass heavily with the traditional brown-black paint and wash, creating strong outlines, linear drapery patterns, and sensitive facial nuances.

With its intense colouration, the Ottawa window conveys a deeply spiritual, solemn intensity. Geddes saw herself as part of the centuries-old tradition of artists who worked with coloured glass. After her first visit to France in 1914, she said: 'I believe that strength of design and intensity of colour are the qualities to be aimed at in stained glass. I go back to the thirteenth century, where the figures are not only more impressive but more modern than anything that has been done since in the medium.'[13]

In order to achieve the results that she wanted, Geddes adhered to the Arts and Crafts philosophy that each window is the work of one artist who makes the sketch and prepares the cartoon, then selects and paints every piece of glass him or herself. Only the cutting and leading could be handled by someone else. Because of her intense involvement in both the design and production of her windows, Geddes required a lengthy period of time for her commissions.

In a letter, written at Christmastime 1915 from Belfast to Sarah Purser in Dublin, Geddes admitted she knew nothing about the taste of the Canadian public and expressed her anxiety and uncertainty:

> *Do you think Canadians are too stupid to like my little picture? I sometimes think it is stupidity complicated with conceit, not pure stupidity, that makes people like the worst best (as most resembling what they'd do themselves I suppose). Would Canadians be worse than Belfast people? I don't know much about them, except that they have a passion for telling the history of their lives at infinite length to strangers in boarding houses where they come to stay. Australians do it too.*[14]

In spite of her reservations, she continued with the work on the Ottawa sketches. They caused her no end of frustration and it was almost two years before she produced a sketch which she considered satisfactory. From her letters and the five preliminary sketches which still exist, we get a reflection of Geddes' artistic struggles with this window. Always in fairly fragile health, she would work in spurts, spending consecutive days and nights dithering over her designs, and then doing nothing for weeks. This may very well have caused the delay in the confirmation of the order.

One of the two sketches in the National Gallery in Dublin is either an early or an alternative version.[15] Here the composition is conservative and straight-forward. The core of the final iconography is in place already with the inclusion of St George, St Michael, and the Angel of Peace as dominant figures, the battalion of tiny angels in the upper background, and the effigy and mourners at the base.

The rudimentary pencil sketch[16] shows Geddes moving in the direction of the final design with an increased number of main protagonists placed in two rows, and with the introduction of the mounted figures. Geddes complained endlessly about the design of the horses and her feeling that their white colour would dominate the colour scheme.

The new disposition of figures was retained through subsequent alterations, as can be seen in the second sketch in Dublin.[17] The main procession of warrior saints, companion angels, and the 'deader' (as Geddes called him) are set into their final locations, as are St George and the Angel of Peace; St Michael impinges rather awkwardly into the lower range; the small angels are more evenly distributed through the traceries. It is a surprise to see the lion in the lower left light. It seems to have been suggested by someone other than Geddes, for she complained about it to Sarah Purser, saying it made no sense, and several times requested permission to remove it.

The crayon sketch[18] indicates the next stage where she in fact has eliminated the bothersome lion and moved St Michael into the upper tier of figures, creating a definite division in the composition. This was to be the final version which was then refined into the cartoon.[19] This latest surviving design is very close, but not identical, to the actual window. The predella panels are blank in all the sketches, possibly because of the uncertainty over the length of the inscription. No sketches exist for the predella figures which were to appear in the actual window.

WILHELMINA GEDDES' OTTAWA WINDOW

There is considerable, but fragmented, discussion of the iconography of the Ottawa window in the Geddes correspondence with Sarah Purser, but no clear indication emerges as to who might have dictated the subject-matter. It does seem that the general idea was set by the patron or his agent but that considerable leeway was given to the studio. Geddes was worried very early on that, with St Michael so prominently displayed, the window would take on the character of a *Last Judgement,* an idea she did not like particularly. At one point after the rejection of her suggestion that the deceased be shown ascending to heaven on winged horses, she sarcastically commented that, if a welcoming committee of saints was to comprise the main design, the deceased warrior might as well be shown shaking hands with them.

The Arthurian material in the background does not appear in any of the existing sketches before the cartoon stage, although it was first discussed in 1917. Geddes herself suggested the division of the Grail knights from the warrior knights and from King Arthur.[20] She mentioned the figure she would rather not include, such as the lion, the large horse, and Joan of Arc, who she felt was 'unwarlike' because of her gender. The details of the iconography, like the design itself, seem to have evolved through trial and error, over a lengthy period of time and through the daily mail between Belfast and Dublin.

Geddes' work is deeply religious, with a strong expression of emotion and sentiment, but not usually theological or liturgical. Perhaps this was an expression arising out of her strict Methodist upbringing. The prominent warrior saints were chosen to represent heroic kings of England and France and warriors of both sexes, although Geddes personally felt that a female warrior was out of place. Each hero is identified by name and the exploits of each one are depicted in the background. Near Longinus' head, he can be seen as the mounted Roman soldier present at Christ's crucifixion. On either side of Sebastian's massive neck the banner carries a row of kneeling archers, a reference to his martyrdom. To the left of Martin's head, the mounted soldier is dividing his cloak to share with the beggar. The funeral of St Edmund is seen near the English king's shoulder, while above that, a tiny Joan of Arc appears in full armour. At the right edge of the right light, the crusading

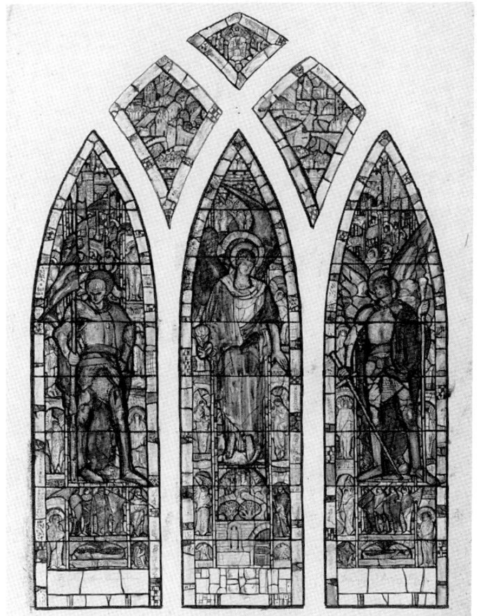

Sketch A for Memorial Window. Saint George, Gideon's Angel and Saint Michael. *NGI cat.no. 18,433*

St Louis of France is shown in the thick of battle. Astride a magnificent white steed, St George in purple armour dominates the upper part of the right window; his banner shows him as a knight at full tilt, undoubtedly a reference to the legend of his rescuing a maiden from a dragon. As the patron saint of England, he was a natural choice for the window, and was placed on the second tier of main figures, along with the Angel of Peace and Michael the Archangel.

Wilhelmina Geddes was a well-educated woman, and often made literary references in her work, often in the choice of the subsidiary figures. In the Ottawa window, the inclusion of several characters from the legend of King Arthur and the Knights of the Round Table should not be seen merely as a rather obvious play on the patron's name, Arthur. Popularized during the nineteenth century through the revitalization of Malory's *Morte d'Arthur* and Tennyson's *Idylls of the King,*[21] the legendary heroes were widely interpreted as reflections of heroism and warrior ideals, models for all that was worthy in British culture and history.[22]

Geddes seems to have relied on Malory's version rather than Tennyson's epic-length poem for her source. Above St George, the model of English military prowess, Geddes included the knights Tristram, Lancelot, and Palomides, embodiments of the tireless fighting man. In the upper part of the left window section, around the figure of the Angel of Peace, the Quest for the Holy Grail is featured, with the three successful knights: Percival, Galahad, and Bors. The ship with the angel-guide carrying the three knights towards the vision of the Holy Grail appears three times, on a small scale. With the attainment of their Quest, these men reached their own inner peace, a peace also reached by the memorialized soldiers.

In the centre window, the background concentrates on the death of King Arthur. Between the sweep of St Michael's great crimson wings, Arthur rides in full armour. His banner carries the scene of the women mourning around his body as it is borne away in a boat to Avalon, with Sir Bedevere and an angel as solemn witnesses. There is a row of female half-figures just above the haloes of the lower tier of saints with the inscription: 'These are they that I fought for in righteous combat'. They are accompanied by Sir Gawain on a white horse. This refers to the vision and words of Sir Gawain which came to King Arthur the night before he was mortally wounded in combat against his son Mordred.

Along the base of the windows, a procession of singers and mourners accompanies the recumbent figure of a dead soldier – men too old to fight join the poignant procession of grief. The list of the commemorated deceased was not inserted into the window, but was placed instead on a separate plaque. When the commission for the window was finalised in 1917, and actual work could begin, the war was still raging and there was no way of knowing how long the list was going to be. Geddes was relieved by the decision to separate the dedicatory and memorial inscriptions, since there was a danger that it would take up too much space and destroy the design of her predella panels.[23]

Geddes' familiarity with historical art is revealed by her occasional quotes from famous paintings or sculpture. In the Ottawa window, the row of archers near St Sebastian are variations on the kneeling archers from the pediment of the archaic Greek Temple of Aphaia at Aegina. The figures of the old men sitting so dejectedly in the base panels are not unlike some of the seated figures in the spandrels of Michelangelo's Sistine Chapel ceiling. As far as we know, Geddes visited neither Munich, where the statues are, nor Rome, but reproductions of famous works of art were plentifully available.

The St Bartholomew's parishioners seem

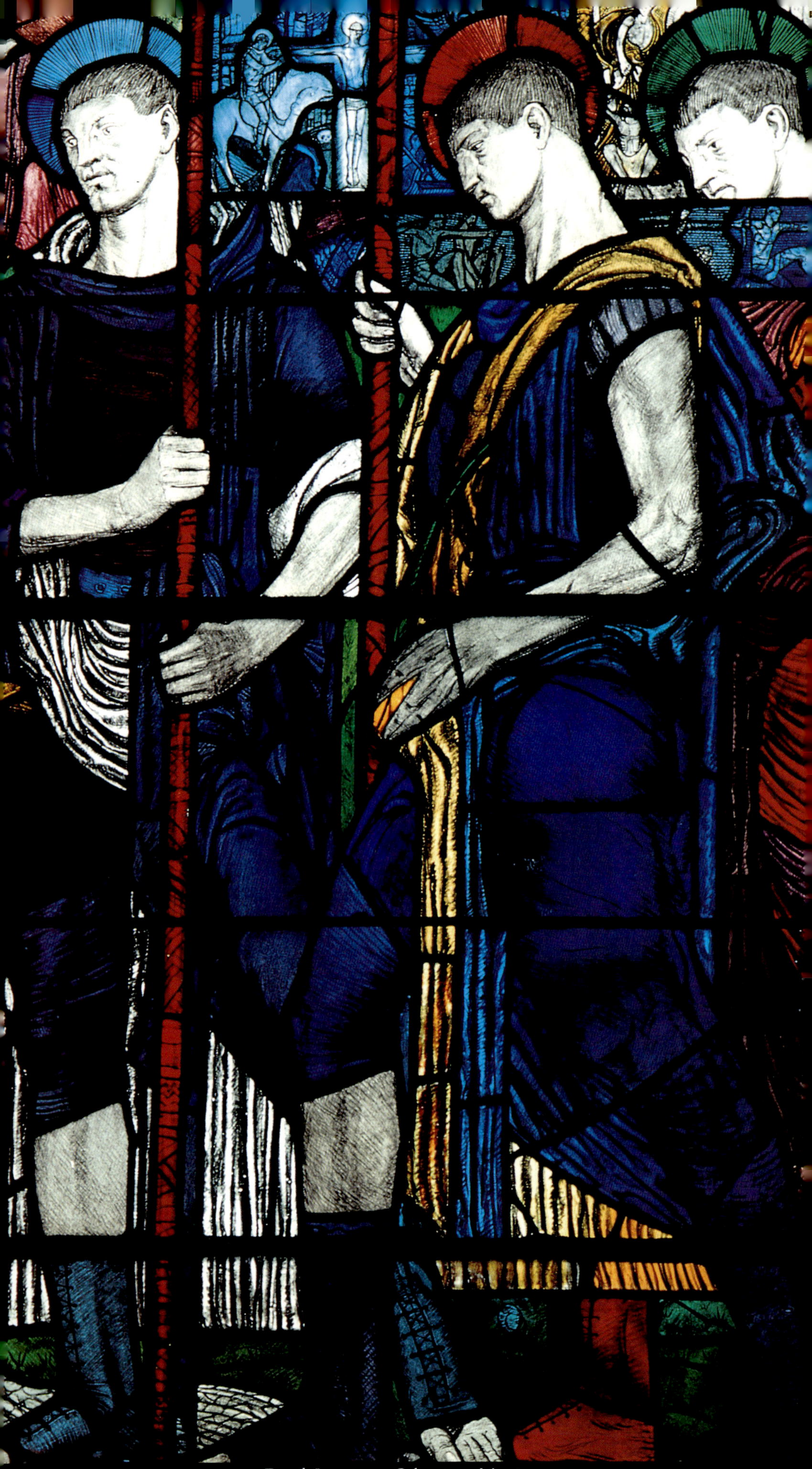

Detail: Longinus · Sebastian · Martin

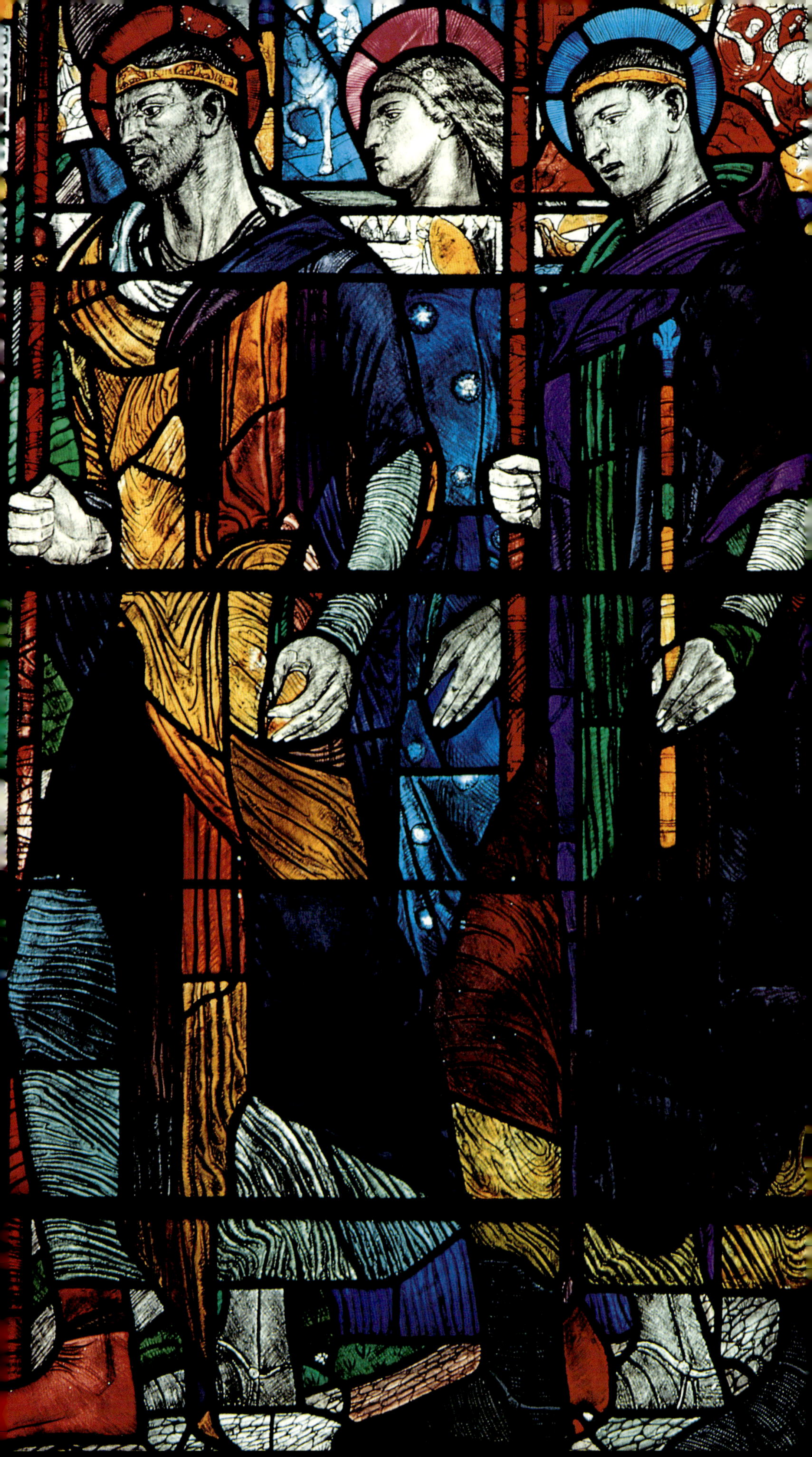

Detail · Edmund · Joan of Arc · Louis

WILHELMINA GEDDES' OTTAWA WINDOW

not to have been consulted about the details of the memorial window ordered by the Governor-General and the gasp uttered when they first saw it must remain enigmatic. It may be telling that there were no more Canadian commissions for Wilhelmina Geddes. Years later, there is a hint that Geddes felt a certain ambivalence about the tendering of the Ottawa commission and the publicity that had surrounded it. When she was working on the War Memorial window for Ypres Cathedral, she wrote that she had been recommended by 'people who liked my work – no Duke and no Duke's windows had anything to do with it. At present there won't be any newspaper Splosh about me ...'[24]

Nevertheless, Geddes' window did have a lasting and dramatic effect upon what could be accepted in stained glass windows in Canada. The Ottawa window was hailed as a 'courageous adventure in the medium' by Charles Connick, an influential stained glass artist from Boston. Aesthetic doors were opened enabling other artists trained in the Arts and Crafts tradition to gain commissions. Examples include the memorial windows by Frank Hollister and Gladys Allen installed in 1928 in the Peace Tower Chapel in the Canadian Houses of Parliament. The English Bromsgrove Guild headed by A J Davies received commissions in the 1920s and 30s in Toronto and Montreal. In the 1930s, the Canadian Yvonne Williams could succeed with her strong new ideas. But none of these have the revolutionary strength and directness of the Geddes vision. It is time that the window placed in the little-known St Bartholomew's Church on a quiet Ottawa Street was given its due not only as a war memorial, but as a turning point in the history of stained glass in Canada. It is also time that the influence of Wilhelmina Geddes on other stained glass artists was reassessed.

Shirley Ann Brown

Shirley Ann Brown is Associate Professor and Director of the Graduate Programme in Art History at York University in North York (Toronto), Ontario. She is Founder-Director of the Registry of Stained Glass Windows in Canada, established in 1987. Having received her PhD in the history of medieval art and architecture from Cornell University, she has lectured widely and published books and articles on the Bayeux Tapestry and early medieval insular art. Simultaneously, Dr Brown has produced studies of the Canadian stained glass commissions of European firms and artists, including Henry Holiday, C E Kempe, and Franz Mayer. Publishing regularly in Rotunda, *the quarterly of the Royal Ontario Museum, she is currently working on a book on the history of stained glass in Toronto.*

ACKNOWLEDGEMENTS

The research for this study was made possible by the generous support of the Social Sciences and Humanities Research Council of Canada and by Atkinson College and the Faculty of Fine Arts, York University, Toronto. I would like to thank Dr Nicola Gordon Bowe and Mrs Elizabeth Kerr for their assistance with locating and dating sources and sketches for the Ottawa window. Rev Desmond Kimmitt, Rector of the church, kindly allowed me photograph the window on several occasions

NOTES

1. Recent works on Geddes include: Nicola Gordon Bowe, 'Wilhelmina Geddes: Ireland's Extraordinary Artist', *Stained Glass*, vol 76 no 1, (1981) pp 41-43; *Centenary Exhibition of Wilhelmina Geddes (1887-1955)*, Belfast, 1987. (Exhibition catalogue); 'Wilhelmina Geddes', *Irish Arts Review*, vol.4 no.3, (1987) pp.53-59; 'Wilhelmina Geddes 1887-1955. Her Life and Work — A Reappraisal', *The Journal of Stained Glass*, vol.XVIII, no.3, (1988) pp.275-301.
2. See the window locations list in Nicola Gordon Bowe, David Caron and Michael Wynne, *Gazetteer of Irish Stained Glass*, Dublin, 1988, pp.31-87.
3. This church is often mislocated in references. It is not to be confused with the Peace Tower Chapel in the Parliament Buildings, which is the official war memorial for the country.
4. After a flurry of publicity when it was installed, the window seems to have been generally ignored by the North American press. It is referred to fairly often in Irish and English references to Geddes' work but has not before received a detailed study.
5. For a biography of the Duke of Connaught see George Aston, *HRH the Duke of Connaught and Strathearn*. London, 1929.
6. The complete list is as follows:
   Lt-Colonel FD Farquhar, DSO, Coldstream Guards. Commanding Princess Patricia's Canadian Light Infantry.
   Captain T Rivers Bulkeley, CMG, MVO, Scots Guards.
   Captain Herbert Buller, DSO, Rifle Brigade. Lt-Colonel Commanding Princess Patricia's Canadian Light Infantry.
   Captain Lord John Hamilton, Irish Guards.
   Captain Lord Spencer Compton, Royal Horse Guards.
   Captain Newton, Middlesex Regiment. Princess Patricia's Canadian Light Infantry.
   Major the Hon J Campbell, Coldstream Guards.
   Major and Brevet Colonel Walter Long, CMG DSO, Scots Greys. Temporary Brig.-General Commanding 56th Brigade.
   Major the Hon G Boscawen, DSO, Royal Field Artillery.
   Captain Angus Mackintosh, Royal Horse Guards.
7. See Nicola Gordon Bowe, 'The Irish Arts and Crafts Movement (1886-1925)', *Irish Arts Review*, (1990-91) pp.172-85.
8. Lady Leslie was born Leonie Jerome. She was the sister of Jenny Jerome, who married Lord Randolph Churchill and became the mother of Winston Churchill. The close relationship between Lady Leslie and the Duke and Duchess of Connaught has been attested to by the Leslie family. Her name appears in a letter written by Geddes on 19 September, 1917 from Belfast in which she wonders whether Lady Leslie will be in Dublin to vet the cartoons for the window before the glass is cut. Another reference occurs in a note of 8 October, 1917 which discusses 'Lady L's' letter which relays the decision that the names of the deceased will be placed on a plaque rather than painted on the window.
9. The first reference to the Ottawa commission is in a letter from Geddes to Sarah Purser, written at Portrush on 4 August, 1915, in which it is compared to the St Peter window in Christchurch Presbyterian in Rathgar. This was drawn to my attention by Nicola Gordon Bowe.
10. Ralph Hodder-Williams, *Princess Patricia's Canadian Light Infantry 1914-1919*. London & Toronto, 1912, p.24.
11. Hodder-Williams, pp.43-44.
12. Hodder-Williams, pp.124, 136.
13. From Bowe, 'A Reappraisal ...', 1988, p.280 and notes.25,26.
14. My thanks go to Mrs Elizabeth Kerr, Geddes' niece, for help in dating the Geddes' letters.
15. Catalogue no. 18.433. 44 x 29.8cms. Ink , pencil and watercolour on board.
16. In the collection of Mrs Elizabeth Kerr in London.
17. Catalogue no.18.434. 38 x 30.5cms. Ink, pencil and watercolour on board.
18. From Mrs Kerr's collection.
19. The cartoon itself has disappeared, but the photograph is in Mrs Kerr's collection.
20. Letter of 12 June, 1917 in a discussion of a sketch.
21. An example of the longevity of the interest in Arthurian legends is the beautiful edition of Malory's *Morte d'Arthur*, with initials by Graily Hewitt, printed at the Ashendene Press in 1910-13.
22. See Debra Mancoff, *The Arthurian Revival in Victorian Art*. New York & London, 1990.
23. Letter of October 8, 1917 to Sarah Purser.
24. Letter to Sarah Purser, 1 November, 1934, as quoted in Bowe, 'A Reappraisal ...', 1988, p.287.

'LOVING PERSPECTIVES'

David Scott discusses eroticism and the vanishing point in the work of the Belgian artist Paul Delvaux.

Paul Delvaux seems to have been interested in perspective-related phenomena even before he became involved in art and drawing. He grew up in Edwardian Belgium at a time when railways, tramlines and telegraph poles were transforming the urban and, to a lesser extent, the country scene. Such motifs were to appear and reappear obsessively in his mature paintings. Delvaux's initial training as an architect was also significant; he entered the Académie des Beaux-Arts in Brussels to study architecture under Joseph van Neck in 1916. Part of his training involved the copying of numerous architectural works and from this he seems to have learnt much about perspective and three-dimensional form – and the relationship between the two. When, soon after, Delvaux switched to the study of art, he was taught by artists who continued to stress the importance of academic drawing. The teaching he received was also academic in its stress on the human figure, the creation of the illusion of three-dimensional form, the observance of the laws of perspective, and the use of architectural forms (very often classical). The originality of Delvaux lies in his adaptation of these conventions to quite unexpected ends – in a word, to the creation of poetic and surrealist effects.

The painting which first fully manifested the style which was, henceforth, to be recognized as Delvaux's own, was *Le Cortège en dentelle* of 1936. The preoccupations of this painting – the placing of nude and clothed women in a strongly perspectival environment – were still to be clearly evident in his works thirty and forty years later – and were fundamental to Delvaux's art. An analysis of the relationship between these two elements – the nude and exaggerated perspective – leads to a clearer understanding of Delvaux's style as a painter and, in particular, of how it seems to have been created through an amalgamation of academic and surrealist elements. In this way it is an excellent introduction to Delvaux's art.

Delvaux's first paintings, executed in the early 1920s, are mostly landscapes or cityscapes, post-impressionist in style but muddy in their tones. These works give way, in the later 1920s and the early 1930s, to a more expressionist style and to an already obsessive focus on the female nude. Whereas the early landscapes were small in scale, the expressionist nudes were often huge: one, *Maternité*, 1930 (later destroyed) was two metres square. Whereas the landscapes and views of Brussels stations – most notably, the *Vue de la Gare du Quartier Léopold* of 1922 – are conventional in their creation of the illusion of visual depth, the pictures of nudes become notably flat. Their large surface area is almost completely filled by the women themselves; background figures, squeezed in round the edge, appear as if on wallpaper rather than as if they were conceived as being situated in three-dimensional space. All this changed quite suddenly in Delvaux's painting around 1933-34.

There were a number of reasons for this sudden change. The first was Delvaux's discovery, in 1932, of the Musée Spitzner at the Brussels fair which included, among its exhibits, wax models of human deformities, a child's head preserved in a glass jar, a tanned human skin and a didactic portrayal of all the symptoms of venereal disease. It also included paintings of Charcot, the famous doctor, examining an hysterical woman in front of medical students, and of Louis Pasteur at the bedside of a sick child. What struck Delvaux about these paintings was their realism. Although Delvaux's first painting of the Musée Spitzner, completed that year (later destroyed) portrayed its figures in a flattened, virtually depthless space, his work of the next two years began to create a sense of pictorial depth and, with it, some of the impact of the 'realist' paintings exhibited in the Musée Spitzner.

An important event for Delvaux at this time was the death of his mother in the night of 31 December 1932 and 1 January 1933. Delvaux seems to have experienced a classic oedipal relationship with this woman who, while adoring him, her eldest son, seems to have profoundly traumatized him through her condemnation of the temptations of the flesh. She never really approved of his vocation as an artist, especially disliking the nudes which he featured in his paintings from the late 1920s. The repressive effect she had on her son's sexual and emotional life was to have a deep impact on his artistic development. Her death, though also traumatic for Delvaux, must have come as a release for the thirty-six-year old artist, still a bachelor, and this seems to have been reflected in the radical change in his painterly style over the next couple of years.

Also important in this period was Delvaux's rediscovery of the work of Giorgio de Chirico. Although Delvaux may have seen the Italian artist's work on a visit to Paris around 1927, it was only when he saw it again in 1934 at the Surrealist exhibition in Brussels that he recognized its importance for his own artistic development. De Chirico's works of his 'metaphysical' period, with their views of arcades and railway stations, their extreme contrast of light and shadow, their isolated human presences and their fleeing perspectives expressed a sense of anxiety and eroticism, even of poetry, which was a function of an exaggerated use of the conventions of pictorial representation.

At the moment when Delvaux was, in the mid-1930s, establishing the essential characteristics of his style as a painter, he was also embarking on an investigation of painterly conventions. The symptoms of this are the mirrors and paintings within paintings, and the appearance of the artist himself, clothed or unclothed, within the pictorial frame. Delvaux seems to have learnt at this time from the art of Magritte – they exhibited together in 1936, but Delvaux had been familiar with Magritte's work for years before this. Like that of Delvaux, Magritte's painting combines naturalism of representation with the juxtaposition of logically incompatible elements. In addition, Magritte's pictures exploit these features as a means of exploring, and often disconcerting, the viewer's expectations. In Magritte, as in Delvaux, it is this interference with the conventions of academic painting that creates the surrealist effect.

Delvaux's renewed interest, around the mid-1930s, in pictorial depth led to a fresh awareness of the importance of the relationship between figure and background, particularly for creating surrealist effects. He wanted to explore irrational or unconscious aspects of experience while still maintaining a high level of realism in his pictures. The result was the setting up of tensions – between foreground and background, between figure and decor, between person and object – that are often disturbing or surrealist in their effect. These tensions were to find both their origin and their expression in the lines which are so often the means by which the

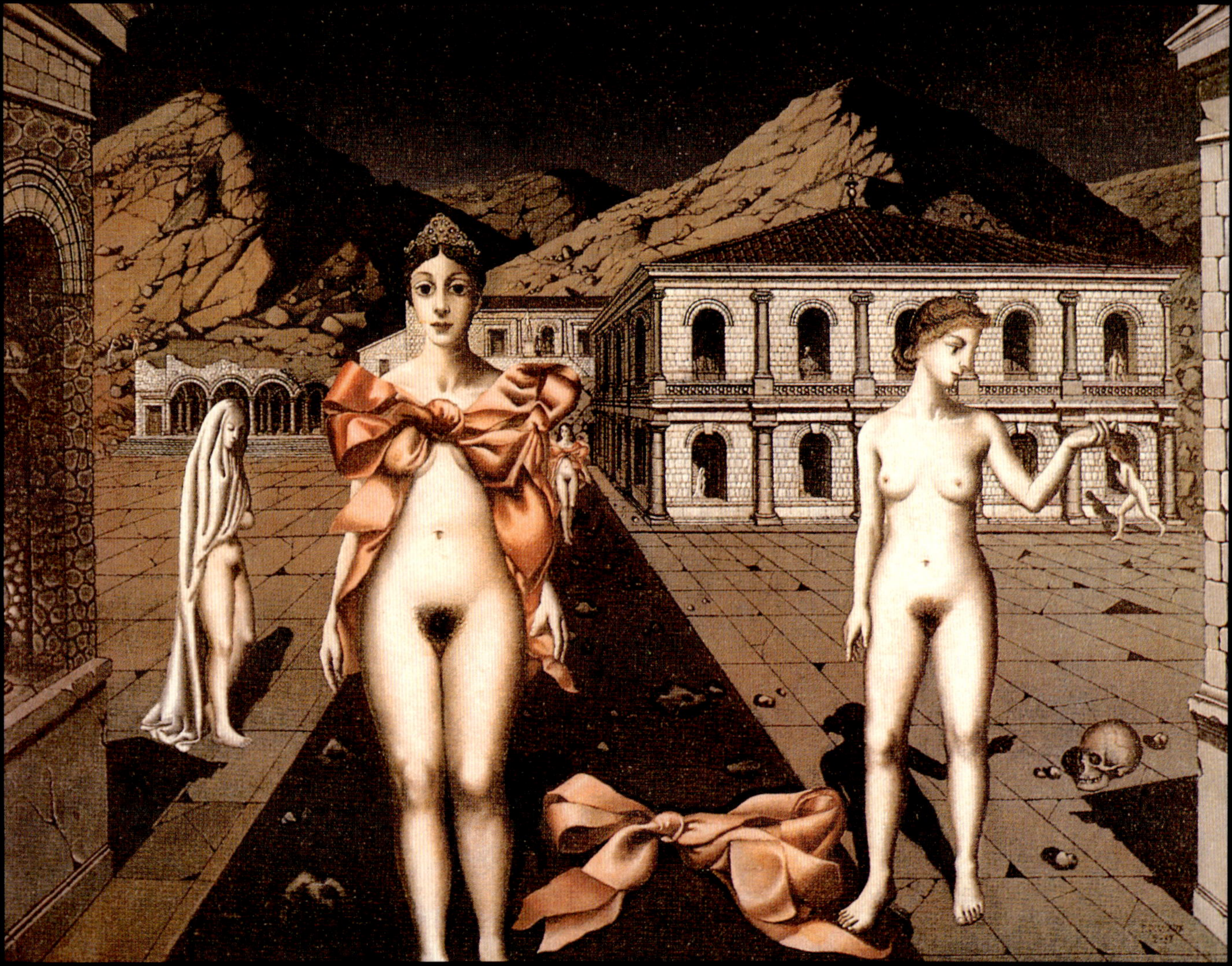

Paul Delvaux, Les Noeuds Roses (Pink Bows) *1937.Oil on canvas, 121.5 x 160 cm.*
Koninklijk Museum voor Schone Kunsten, Antwerp.

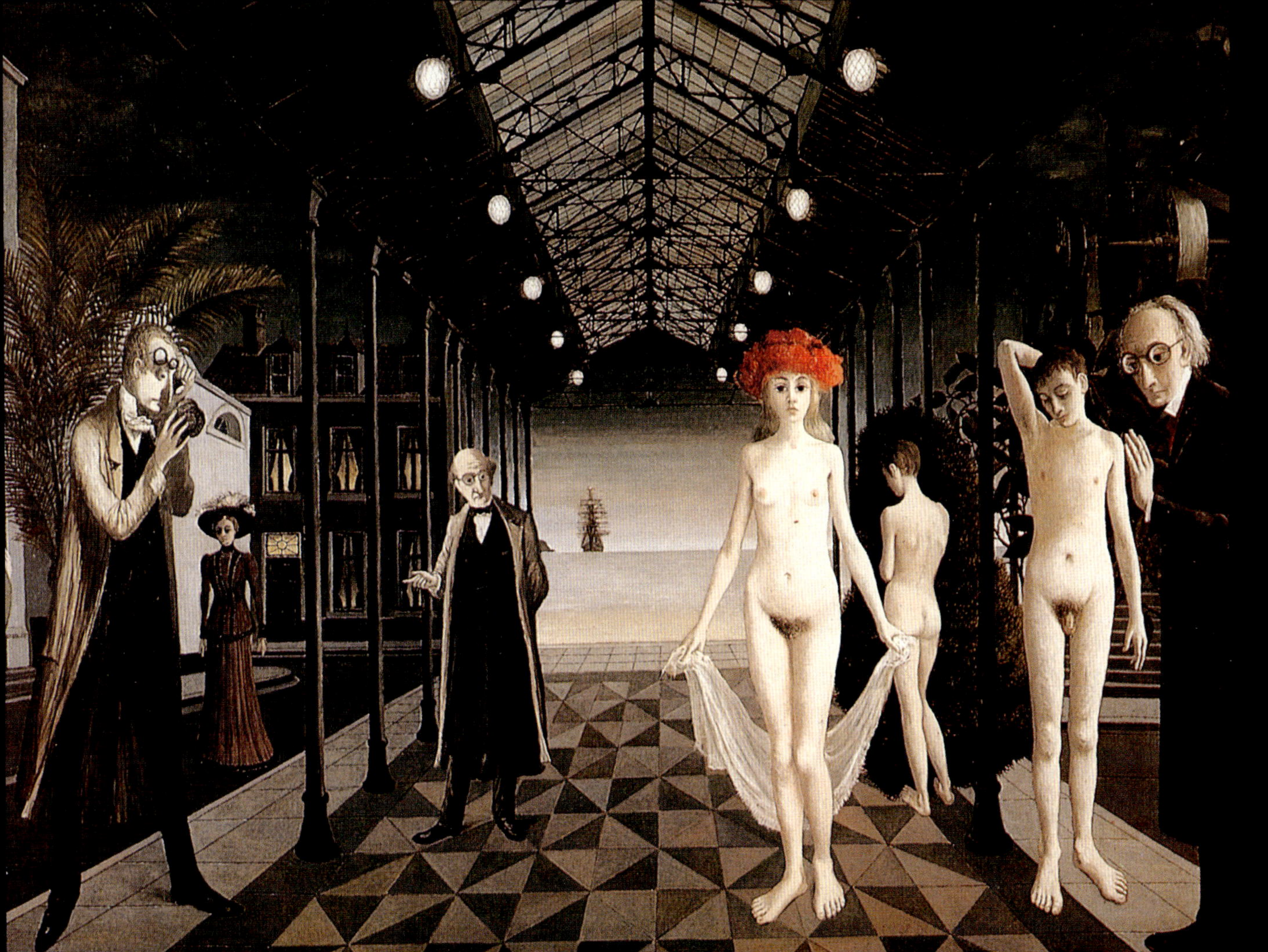

Paul Delvaux, Hommage à Jules Verne (Homage to Jules Verne) *1971. Oil on canvas, 150 x 210 cm.*
Fondation Paul Delvaux, Saint-Idesbald.

'LOVING PERSPECTIVES'

opposing or complementary spaces of Delvaux's pictures are connected.

Delvaux's early interest in lines found a natural expression in drawing for which he showed a precocious aptitude. His early training as an architect and his subsequent studies at art school led him to appreciate the analytical purpose of drawing – the recognition of linear structures beneath masses, whether of the skeletal and muscular framework of the human body or the mathematical forms that governed architecture. But Delvaux was also fully aware of drawing's immense erotic potential as can be witnessed, for example, in his obsessive interest in curvilinear forms, especially of the human body. Hair, for example, especially pubic hair,is often a central motif in his pictures. As many hundreds of sketches attest, drawing was, for Delvaux, erotic both as a practice and in so far as it produced sexually-stimulating images, ones that were a function of the curved line, as embodied in the female anatomy, or in the straight line, as in architecture and perspective.

Delvaux made it a principle of his art from the 1930s onwards to set up tensions between body and background, nude and perspective – elements which he contrives to render equally fascinating to the viewer of his pictures. The basis of the fascination seems to be erotic in that the nude body eroticizes its environment. The viewer, while absorbed by the objects in the foreground of the picture, is nevertheless enticed by the perspectival lines to look through or beyond them. The perspective's magnetic effect is also, of course, the function of a lack in the foreground image, a male or other principle to complement the female one so often reiterated in Delvaux's foregrounds. For whom is the nude waiting, why is she alone, what clues in the background clarify her situation and satisfy the viewer's curiosity? Do the perspectives back into the picture reveal a past – historical (or archeological), intertextual (to other paintings – by Delvaux or other artists), or psychological (the unconscious of the foreground's consciousness)? Do they lure the viewer's gaze into the realm of desire, where satisfaction may be imagined, like the vanishing point, as the unity of complementary or incompatible elements?

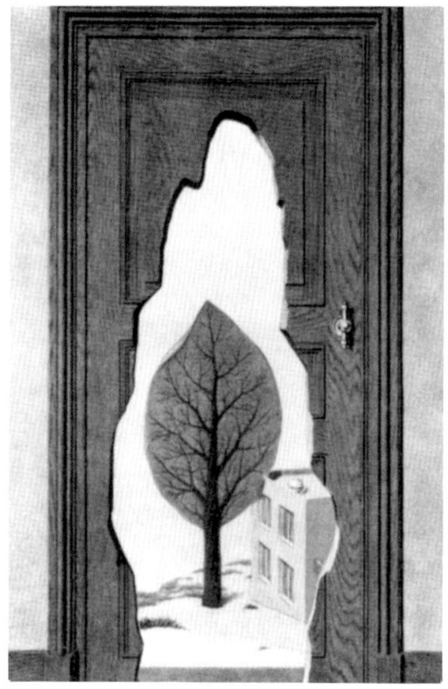

Rene Magritte, La Perspective Amoureuse (Loving Perspective) *1935. Oil on canvas. Robert Giron Collection , Brussels.*

An answer to these questions may be offered by comparing of one of Delvaux's first truly surrealist paintings, *Femme dans une grotte,* 1936, with a work by Magritte of the previous year with the revelatory title of *La Perspective Amoureuse.* In offering release for both his protagonist's and his viewer's desires, Magritte establishes the principle of the loving perspective, taken up by Delvaux throughout the rest of his career. In Magritte's picture, the desiring consciousness of the hero/ protagonist has smashed through the resistance placed in its/his path in the form of the doorway to the open perspectives beyond. In Delvaux's picture *Femme dans une Grotte,* the phallus-shaped aperture of *La Perspective amoureuse* becomes the entrance to a cavern in which a naked woman admires herself in a looking glass. While the viewer's gaze is divided between the woman and her reflection in the mirror, it is also drawn to the band of lace which hangs loosely round the glass and slithers like a serpent towards the woman's right breast. But the gaze is also drawn towards the cave mouth (which is also the principal source of light in the picture) in the expectation, perhaps, of the appearance of some masculine principle, for the arrival of some Adam to satisfy the desire of the Eve who is in danger of being seduced by the serpent of her own vanity. The cavern opening, as well as being phallic in outline, is also a vagina-like entrance to the cave, an image synonymous with the womb. But this entrance opens only onto a stony desert. The system of tensions Delvaux sets up here – woman/reflection, serpent/woman, entrance/cave, female pres-

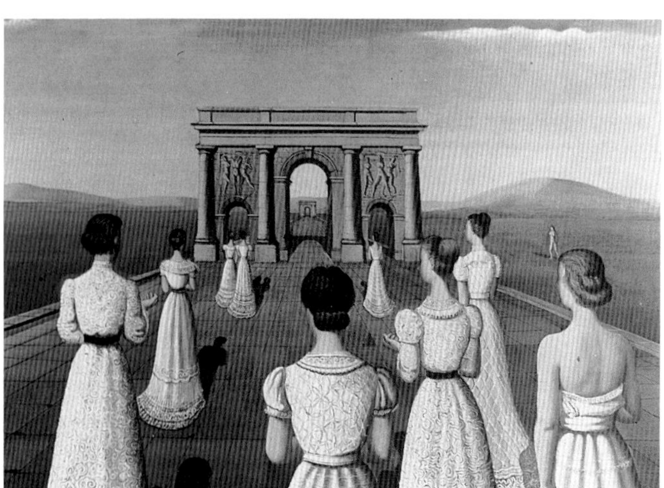

Paul Delvaux, Le Cortège en Dentelle (Procession in Lace),*1936. Oil on canvas, 115 x 158 cm. Städtische Galerie, Hanover.*

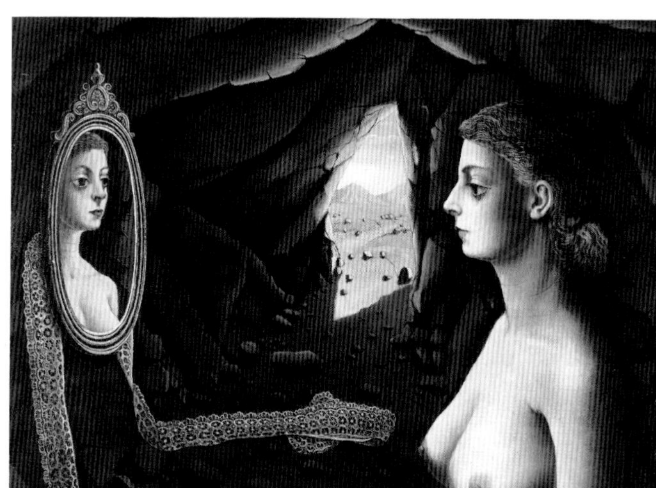

Paul Delvaux, La Femme dans une Grotte (Woman in a Mirror) *1936. Oil on canvas, 71 x 91.5 cm. Thyssen-Bornemisza Collection, Lugano.*

'LOVING PERSPECTIVES'

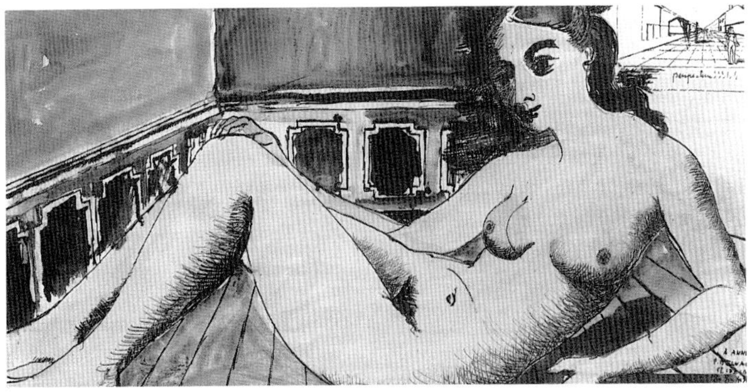

Paul Delvaux, Nu Allongé *(Reclining Nude) 1946.*
Ink and watercolour, 31 x 60 cm. Private collection.

ence/male absence – is shaped by the conventional resources of pictorial composition – reflection, perspective, foreground/background distinction – but, by playing on the viewer's conscious or unconscious desires to resolve them, he creates effects of surrealist intensity.

The role of perspective in creating this intensity seems to be clarified by a watercolour of 1946 *Nu Allongé*. In this work, a nude reclines on the bare floorboards (perspectively aligned) of a room decorated in crimson. An effect of claustrophobia is created by the disparity in scale of certain features of the room – a skirting board that is oversized, the nude seeming too large for her environment. The only opening is provided by the drawing pinned to the wall in the top left-hand corner of the room, which depicts a nude standing in a strongly perspectival setting. Beneath the sketch Delvaux has written 'Perspective!!!!!', thus stressing the importance of the latter in enhancing the erotic and surrealist intensity of his work.

In *Le Cortège en dentelle*, the first of Delvaux's pictures to establish an exaggerated perspectival environment for his female figures, the latter are fully and beautifully dressed. Yet we sense that the triumphal arch towards which they seem to be drawn implies a passage of initiation which will involve the removal of their clothing. This likelihood would seem to be supported by the images of naked women in erotic poses carved as a relief on the archway, by the distant woman to the right who, because naked, seems already to have made the transition, and the woman in the lower right hand corner of the picture who has, in anticipation of her passage through the arch, bared the upper part of her body. The fact that there is a second archway in the distance, which we presume will also be traversed by the women of the foreground, leads the viewer to ponder what form of rite of passage it will elicit. The mystery of this far gateway is further heightened by its position in the picture – on the threshold of the vanishing point.

The erotic function of the central perspectival axis is more explicit in a major picture by Delvaux of the following year. *Les Noeuds Roses* (1937), which establishes an iconography of red carpets and pink or purple bows that was to contribute to the eroticisation of Delvaux's paintings over the next forty years. *Les Noeuds Roses* also consecrates a tendency, that of making the triangle of female pubic hair the central image of the picture, establishing a tension between it and the perspectival triangle along whose axis it is placed. In *Les Noeuds Roses*, the procession of *Cortège en Dentelle* seems to be read in reverse, the now naked beauties progressing, one by one, from the background to the foreground, divesting themselves of the last attribute of their virginity (the pink bows) as they walk along the red carpet which flows like a stream of menstrual blood

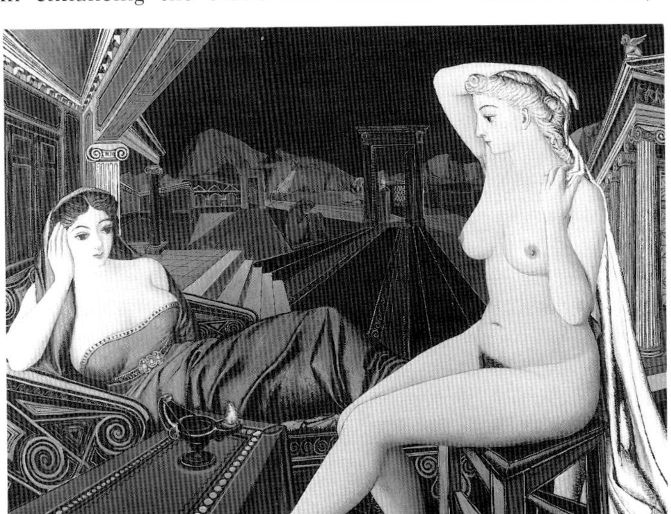

Paul Delvaux, La Ville Noire (The Dark City). *1946.*
Oil on canvas, 122 x 183 cm. Private collection.

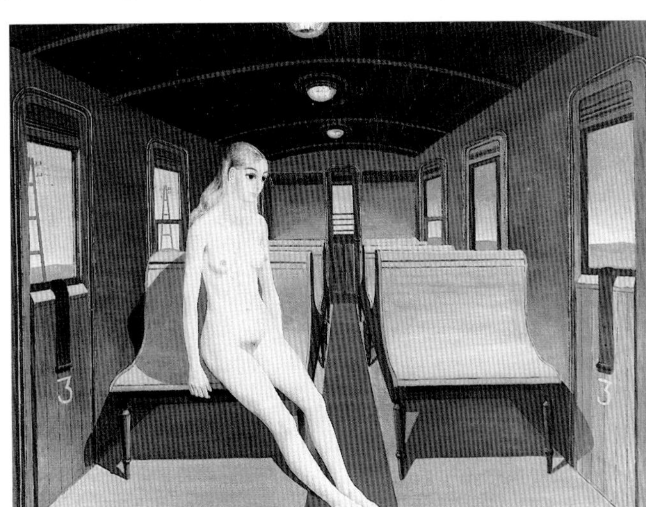

Paul Delvaux, Le Dernier Wagon (The Last Carriage), *1975.*
Oil on canvas, 150 x 190 cm. Fondation Paul Delvaux, Saint-Idesbald.

'LOVING PERSPECTIVES'

beneath their feet and legs. The palaces in *Les Noeuds Roses* propose a similar set of contrasts to those of the triumphal arches in *Le Cortège en Dentelle* – pilasters alternate with arches, that in the left foreground being illuminated by a phallus-like gaslight. The lamp of desire thus continues to burn as the women cast off their bows, having experienced the 'little death' of orgasm perhaps symbolized by the skull placed next to the naked woman in the right foreground.

In some of Delvaux's paintings of the mid-1940s, perspectival views are complicated by the use of a kind of bifocal or multifocal perspective – as in *La Ville noire* of 1946. Here Delvaux uses a multiplicity of perspectival views which lead off not only into the central distance but also sidewards and in various directions – even forwards out of the picture towards the viewer. This development is particularly evident in *La Ville Noire* in which at least three different vanishing points are proposed and in which several other series of converging lines lead the eye of the viewer in different directions. The jagged, zig-zag framework of landscape and architectural features contrasts strikingly with the rounded, fully three-dimensional forms of the female figures. This is especially true of that of the stately nude in the foreground whose body constitutes, in effect, the starting point of many of the perspectives developed in the background of the picture. Once again, these draw attention away from the sumptuous nude, with the triangle of her pubic hair clearly visible, to narrow gates or other orifices in the landscape, eagerly penetrated by the viewer's gaze. Once again the dynamics of voyeurism are picked up and accelerated by Delvaux's use of perspective, in this case, multifocal.

In his paintings of the 1960s and 1970s, Delvaux manages to combine and reinterpret elements that were fundamental to the structure and iconography of pictures painted thirty to forty years before. In *Le Dernier Wagon* of 1975, for example, Delvaux has managed to reduce to its bare essentials the formula of the nude in the tram or train, or by the tram or railway line, which achieved classic status in his work of the 1940s and 1950s. The exaggerated perspectival tendencies reappear, enhanced by the economy of the composition and the sobriety of the colour scheme (only the narrow red carpet enlivens the neutral greys, blue and olive of the scene). The tension between the nudity of the woman and the blood-red carpet on which her feet lightly rest is increased by the way the latter leads the eye back to the narrow, vagina-like exit at the back of the carriage in a perspective which, as in *Les Noeuds Roses*, is the inverse of that proposed by the triangle of pubic hair between the nude's white thighs. Meanwhile, outside the carriage, the phallic telegraph poles recede into the distance, their taut wires disappearing to a vanishing point which presumably coincides with that perceived through the window of the doorway at the back of the carriage. In this way Delvaux succeeds in expressing sexual expectation on the part of the young woman without the appearance of any male figure.

To conclude this rapid survey of the loving perspective in Delvaux's painting, let us turn to one of his last masterpieces, *Hommage à Jules Verne* of 1971. Here, Delvaux uses five clearly-demarcated perspectival bands to clarify the layers of meaning implicit in the painting. Reading from left to right, these five parallel perspectives include the street scene of Delvaux's Edwardian childhood – perhaps the primal scene of the artist's oedipal desire – in which mother-figures in early 1900s dress, walk up and down in a respectable bourgeois quarter. Then appears the first of two bands of pavement running down either side of the central scenario on which stand characters from Jules Verne's novels; these include Otto Lidenbrock and Palmyrin Rosette. For Delvaux, the Jules Verne characters represented the principle of rational observation and enquiry, an obsession with weighing and measuring almost completely oblivious to the life of the body. In the central band, beneath a glass canopy, stands the current object of desire, a Venus of 1971, her Twiggy-like figure and pert, Jean Shrimpton-like face crowned by an absurd but gorgeous coral- coloured hat. As her white bathing towel suggests, she has just stepped, like Aphrodite, from the waves, or has swum ashore from the galleon in the distance. To her left, a couple of adolescent boys stand just at the margin of the central bay, between desire and reason, the foot of the boy in the foreground straddling the rationalist world of the Jules Verne character. Meanwhile, on the extreme right, a steam engine pumps away, its belts and axles expressing some of the tensions of the scene. These latter are created by the surrealist juxtaposition of bands of incompatible elements which express, for example, love for the young woman and guilt in relation to the mother; instinctual knowledge versus scientific; the apparent indifference of old men to beauty, the latter's often castratory effect on the young male. This surreality is made legible to the viewer by the fan-like perspectival composition of the foreground which directs the gaze from left to right, urging it to rest momentarily on the central nude figure from which it is irresistibly drawn to the distant galleon and to the vanishing point of the horizon. In this way, combining all the techniques of visual representation known to academic art, and in particular its use of the convention of perspective, Delvaux is able to give coherence to a surrealist juxtaposition of objects, creating a paradoxical harmony of order and eroticism to which, over forty years, his painting has become the monument.

David Scott

Professor David Scott is Head of the Department of French, Trinity College, Dublin. A specialist in literature, modern art and textual and visual studies, his book Paul Delvaux: Surrealizing the Nude *was published by Reaktion Books, London, in 1992. An editor of the journal* Word & Image, *he is currently researching books on the semiotics of the postage stamp and on early modern European poster design.*

JOHN HUGHES: THE ITALIAN CONNECTION

Sighle Bhreathnach Lynch explores the influence of Italian Renaissance sculpture on the Dublin sculptor John Hughes.

John Hughes (1865-1941) is perhaps best remembered as the sculptor responsible for the highly unpopular monument to Queen Victoria which once graced the lawn of Leinster House. Described as 'an obese statue ... looking like a Wagnerian Rhinemaiden and certainly the ugliest monument in the city' it was a large seated figure of the Queen, remarkable above all for its heavy, ponderous appearance.[1] Also included were figures of *Erin* leaning on a harp and holding a laurel wreath for a dead Irish soldier, and allegorical figures representing *Fame* and *Peace*. These figures show a singularly impressive naturalism which demonstrates more convincingly the sculptor's undoubted talents.

During his career Hughes did indeed produce some fine pieces of sculpture. An impressive work from his early period is the bronze and limestone monument to Charles Kickham, the Irish patriot, poet and novelist. Kickham is represented as a seated figure, a scroll of paper resting on his knee, a pen in the right hand. His pose and expression show a passive dignity in keeping with the writer's gentle character. When unveiled in 1898 the work was enthusiastically described as 'a handsome work'.[2] Two later monuments further demonstrate the artist's prowess in this category of sculpture, a marble monument to Dr George Salmon (1905/10) in which the seated figure is treated in a convincingly lively manner, and a full-length imposing bronze and Portland stone memorial to William Gladstone (1910/19). There is also an outstanding body of work done for Loughrea Cathedral, Co Galway, a highly impressive bronze fountain group for the gardens of Heywood House (designed by Edwin Lutyens in Co Laois)[3], as well as some small, finely-wrought, idealistic works and a number of successful portraits.

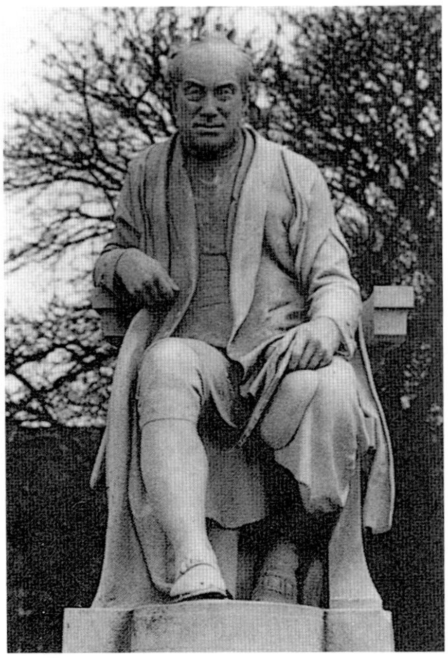

John Hughes, Monument to George Salmon, *c. 1911. Marble. Height 3.7 metres (overall). Reproduced from Anne Crookshank and David Webb,* Paintings and Sculptures in Trinity College Dublin, *Dublin 1990.*

What is remarkable about Hughes' *oeuvre* is the calibre of his naturalism which was based, in the main, on Italian fifteenth- and sixteenth-century artistic sources. The manner in which he used these sources not only enriched the quality of his work, in some cases to an outstanding degree, but also demonstrated a first-hand knowledge of the originals. I propose to examine the extent to which his work is dependent on Italian prototypes and to investigate how he came to be so familiar with these art forms.

John Hughes' connection with Italian art is, however, decidedly problematic for the art historian. If one is to believe that Hughes' visits to Italy were a crucial factor in the development of his artistic style, there is scant documentation of his first

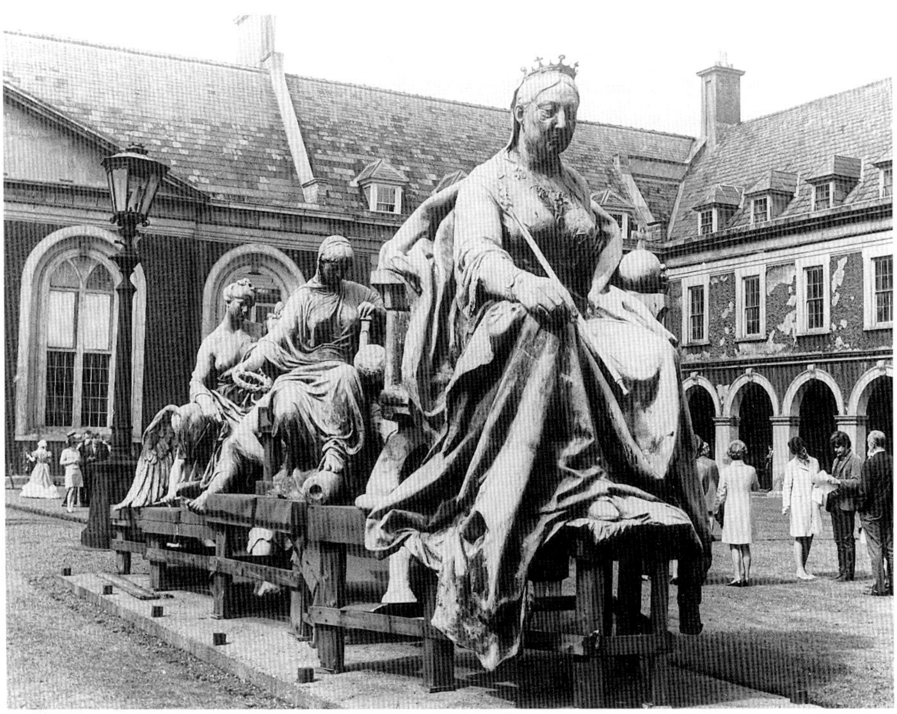

John Hughes, Monument to Queen Victoria. *At the Royal Hospital Kilmainham before being presented to the people of Australia by C J Haughey.*

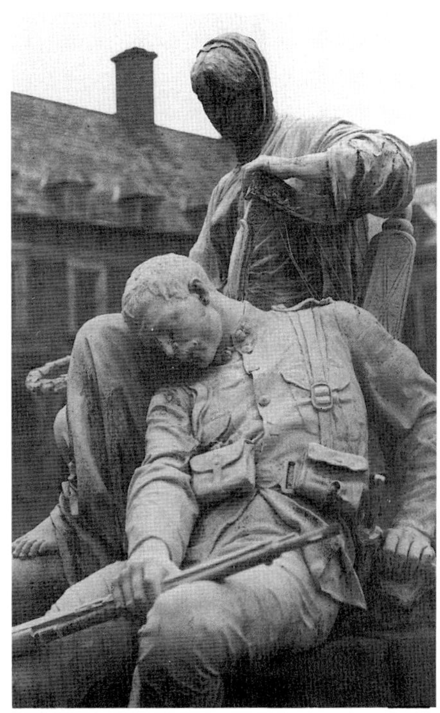

John Hughes, Monument to Queen Victoria (detail). *Reproduced from Jeanne Sheehy,* The Rediscovery of Ireland's Past :The Celtic Revival 1830-1930, *London 1980*

JOHN HUGHES: THE ITALIAN CONNECTION

five visits to that country.[4] It is tempting, therefore, to concentrate solely on his later visits made during the 1920s and 1930s, a time when his artistic output had dropped considerably, since there exist some letters written by him during this period which shed some light on his travels, his feelings about Italy, its people, and, in particular, its art. Yet it is the undocumented early visits which coincide with the decades in which the artist was producing the bulk of his sculpture, that is, from the 1890s up until the end of the First World War. While it is useful to piece together what flimsy evidence does exist about his journeys to Italy, there is another means by which his close contact with Italian art can be revealed. A thorough stylistic analysis of some key-works can serve to identify several precise Italian sources and help to explain how, aside from the visits, he was so well-versed in Italian Renaissance sculpture.

John Hughes was born in Dublin in 1865, son of a carpenter. He attended O'Connell Schools in North Richmond Street and the Dublin Metropolitan School of Art records show that he first registered there as a part-time student in 1878.[5] The school at that time was affiliated to the National Art Training School at South Kensington and in the 1890-91 session Hughes won a scholarship to the London school. The Annual Report for the Dublin Art School for that same session comments on Hughes' student work at the time. Having noted his winning of the scholarship, the report continued with a comment on the work which had earned him the gold medal — a plaster centre-panel for a mantelpiece:

> *It is in its way very remarkable. The figures are full of style, are excellent in relief and indeed might have been done by a clever Italian sculptor at the beginning of the sixteenth century with much mannerism and great skill.*[6]

Thus already, even as a young student, Hughes would seem to be displaying a natural affinity with the art of Renaissance Italy without ever having set foot outside Ireland. One explanation for this early familiarity may be found in the sculpture casts in the School of Art which were keenly studied and copied by the students. The bulk of this collection consisted of reproductions of well-known ancient classical works. Included among them were the *Laocoön* and the *Farnese Hercules*, works which in their time had inspired

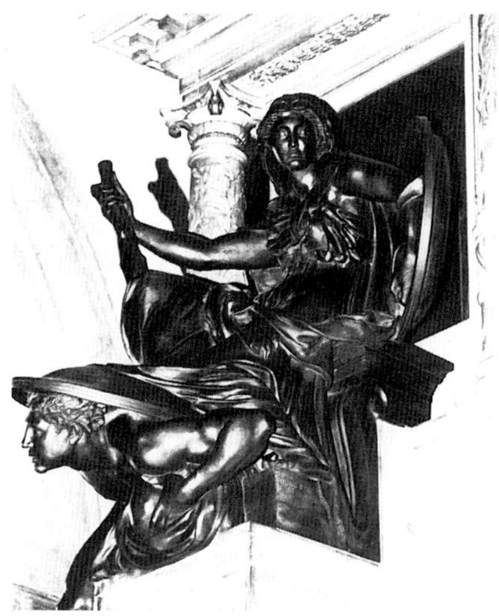

Alfred Stevens, Valour and Cowardice, *1857. Wellington Monument, St Paul's Cathedral, London. Reproduced from Susan Beattie,* The New Sculpture, *New Haven and London, 1983.*

Renaissance sculptors. A small but selective collection of Renaissance sculpture was also available for study. Among these works was a copy of Donatello's *Saint George* statue in Florence and some works by Michelangelo – a bust of Brutus, a *Virgin and Child* relief and individual section of the *David* figure. Significantly too, examples of decorative Renaissance work including portions of the so-called *'Paradise Doors'* by Lorenzo Ghiberti, also formed part of the cast collection.[7] There can be little doubt that the young Hughes drew on these works for stylistic ideas.

However, I believe that it was the two years spent in the South Kensington school which were crucial to the development of his style; one steeped in the classical Italian tradition. Two factors contributed to this, the most important being his close contact with the cast collection of Italian Renaissance works as well as original sculptures which were on display in the Victorian and Albert Museum.[8] The casts included such works as the baptismal font at San Giovanni in Siena; the second pair of baptistry doors by Ghiberti; Jacopo della Quercia's doors in Bologna; Donatello's bronze *David*; Verrocchio's *Boy with a Dolphin*; Michelangelo's *David*; and Giambologna's figure of *Mercury*. It was a magnificent collection with which to familiarise oneself with the art of the Italian past. Students were actively encouraged to study the casts.

A second influence on Hughes' style was his contact with the work of the English Victorian sculptor, Alfred Stevens. Stevens had been to Rome in the 1830s, and had worked for a short period in the studio of the Danish neo-classical sculptor, Bertel Thorvaldsen. However, rather than being influenced by neo-classical art, with its conscious imitation of the purity of ancient Greek forms, Stevens steeped himself in a study of the more dynamic forms of Italian High Renaissance art.[9] His most public work in England was his contribution to the Wellington Monument in Saint Paul's Cathedral – two great figure groups of *Valour and Cowardice* and *Truth and Falsehood* (1857-75). These display an undoubted debt to Michelangelo in the grandeur of pose and gesture as well as in the mood of heroic contemplation which they evoke. Writing to Sarah Purser in 1927, Hughes was to single out this monument and call Stevens 'the greatest designer since the Renaissance'.[10]

Hughes' first trip abroad occurred between 1892 and 1893. He had won a travelling scholarship worth £50 while at South Kensington. This enabled him to visit France and perhaps Italy, although there is no clear evidence to confirm this.[11] What is not doubted is how he spent his time in France. He studied for a short time at the Académie Julian and at the studio of Colarossi in Paris.[12] Here he had the opportunity to study at first hand contemporary French art practice and the work of the major French sculptors of the age. Among the best-known pieces of sculpture on public display was Jean-Baptiste Carpeaux's group, *Ugolino and his Sons* (1862). The great brooding figure of Ugolino is an example of Michelangelo freely interpreted; and Carpeaux's figures of *Science* and *Agriculture* on the pediment of the Pavillion de Flore of the Louvre (begun 1863) are variants of Michelangelo's Medici tomb designs. At the Paris Salon of 1872, Antonin Mercie had achieved public success with a representation of David with the head of Goliath, a work which combined the style of Donatello's earlier figure with a fresh elegance and grace. Aimée-Jules Dalou's figures also showed a closely-observed naturalism coupled with neo-baroque fullness and dynamism. However the most famous contemporary name in French sculpture was that of Auguste Rodin, who had achieved notoriety with his *Age of Bronze* (1877), a work which went even further in its obser-

JOHN HUGHES: THE ITALIAN CONNECTION

vation of nature than Dalou, and which also relied on Michelangelo in a pose which recalled the so-called *'Dying Slave'*.

Two early statuettes by Hughes point to his absorption of Italian Renaissance forms. These were executed by him during his successful years in Dublin (1894-1901) when he was teaching in the Dublin School of Art, exhibiting with the Royal Hibernian Academy (he was elected to full membership of the Academy in 1900), and busy carrying out prestigious commissions including the monument to Charles J Kickham. Both were uncommissioned works and they reflect the general interest in the 1890s for small portable bronzes which made sculpture (at least in theory) accessible to all. Sculptors saw the modelling of such pieces as a means of free expression for their ideas, normally not possible in commissioned work. In Hughes' case they also point to a personal interest in the depiction of the male nude.

The first of these statuettes, called *L'Ame du Vin (The Spirit of Wine)* was exhibited in London in 1898 and at the Royal Hibernian Academy a year later. The work is based on some lines from Baudelaire's *Les Fleurs du Mal*, and inscribed on the decorative base is the poet's description of man's manufacture of

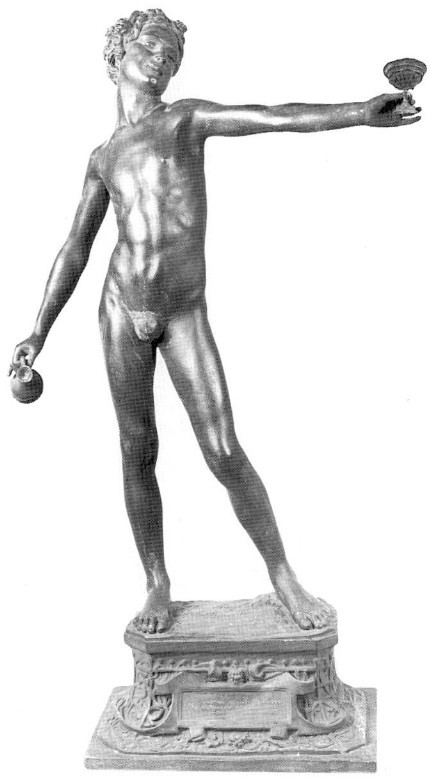

John Hughes, L'Ame du Vin, *1898. Bronze. Height 73.7 cm. Courtesy of National Museum of Ireland.*

wine as a blest offspring of the sun.[13] A young naked Bacchus is depicted as a full-length standing figure, holding out a drinking vessel, as if offering wine.[14] A small jug is held in the other hand. The boy appears to be in a state of dreamy intoxication. It is a work which celebrates the beauty of the male nude, and the gentle incline of the head, shoulders, hip and leg all combine to suggest the natural unconscious grace of youth. While the figure recalls Michelangelo's *Bacchus* (then on public display in Florence and widely-known through reproductions), an examination of the two works shows some significant differences. Michelangelo's figure is a fully-grown young man and is so intoxicated that he is almost reeling over. Hughes' pubescent boy is far less fleshy and the pose is more stable. A closer study of the work in fact reveals a greater reliance on two other well-known *Davids*, the bronze by Donatello and the marble by Michelangelo, both on display in the V&A in cast form during Hughes' student days in London.[15] The positioning of the lower torso is almost identical in all three sculptures, with the Michelangelo and Hughes figures being particularly close. The sensuous treatment of the body of the young Bacchus, however, recalls of *David* of

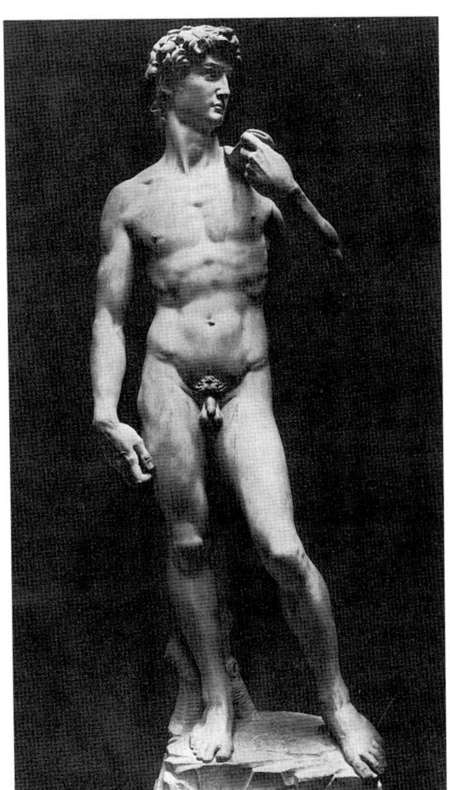

Michelangelo, David. *518cm. Accademia, Florence.*

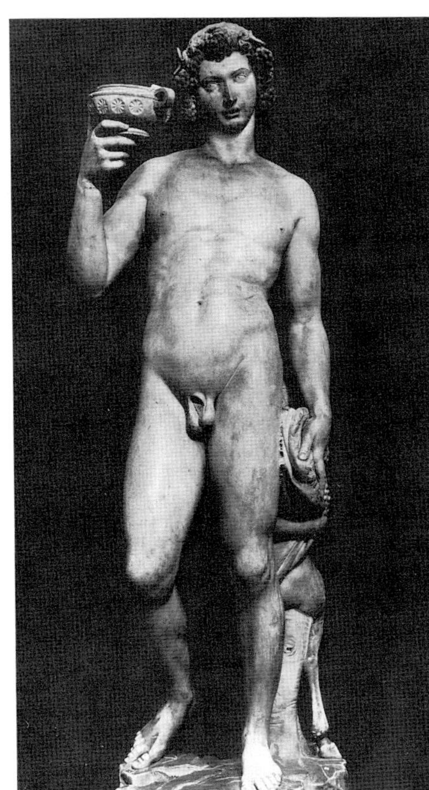

Michelangelo, Bacchus *204cm. Bargello, Florence*

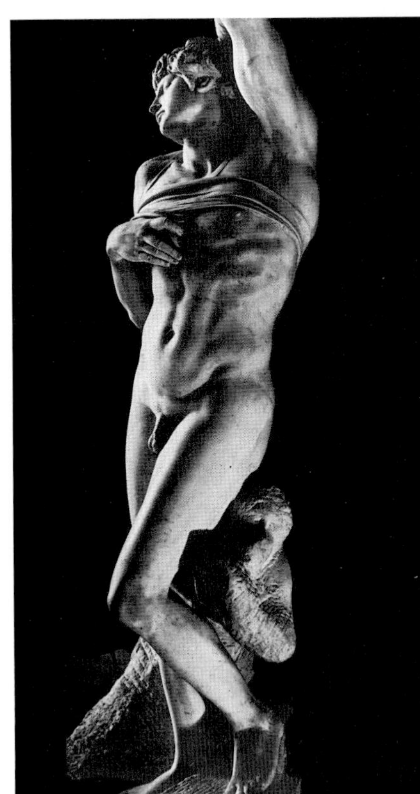

Michelangelo, Dying Slave. *231cm. Louvre, Paris.*

Donatello. In both cases the softness of living flesh has been perfectly rendered. Like Donatello, Hughes, too, contrasts the smoothness of the flesh with the sharply chiselled details of the hair.

The second of Hughes small sculptures, *The Mandolin Player*, is thought to be a work exhibited at the RHA in 1900 under the title of *Napoli*. It depicts what Hughes described as 'a sort of Neapolitan gutter-snipe'.[16] This takes the form of a young male nude, whose nudity is emphasised in a novel way by the inclusion of a jaunty hat on the upraised head. One hand rests on his chin, the other is outstretched holding a small mandolin.[17] The mouth is open as if in song, the eyes half-closed in intense concentration. On this occasion, while Hughes used the same young model as for his *L'Ame du Vin*, the figure is developed to adopt a more active pose, to one in action. Rodin's well-known portrayal of *Saint John the Baptist* as a nude in motion may have provided the starting point. But Hughes goes further in that his figure seems to be already stepping off the base into our space. It is a most vital representation both in its expression and pose, and the echoes of Italian prototypes enhance the work. The forward thrust of the chest showing a resulting anatomical stress recalls Michelangelo's *'Dying Slave'*, on display in cast form in the V&A since 1863, and the counterbalance between the forward projecting limbs on one side of the body and the reversing rearward twist shows a knowledge of Cellini's *Perseus*, also available in cast form.[18] The fact that these early bronzes recall Donatello and Michelangelo's *David* figures may also suggest that Hughes had the opportunity to study them in the original in Florence. Lady Beatrice Glenavy, a former pupil and friend of Hughes in Dublin, remembered his making a trip to Italy in 1897.[19] Another friend, George Russell, writing in *The Arts and Crafts Journal* in 1901 stated that Hughes' talent was due to his 'long study in London, Paris and Italy'.[20] The use of the word 'long' suggests more than a passing acquaintance with Italy before 1901. It is also clear from a later letter written by the artist to Sarah Purser that he deeply admired both these artists.[21]

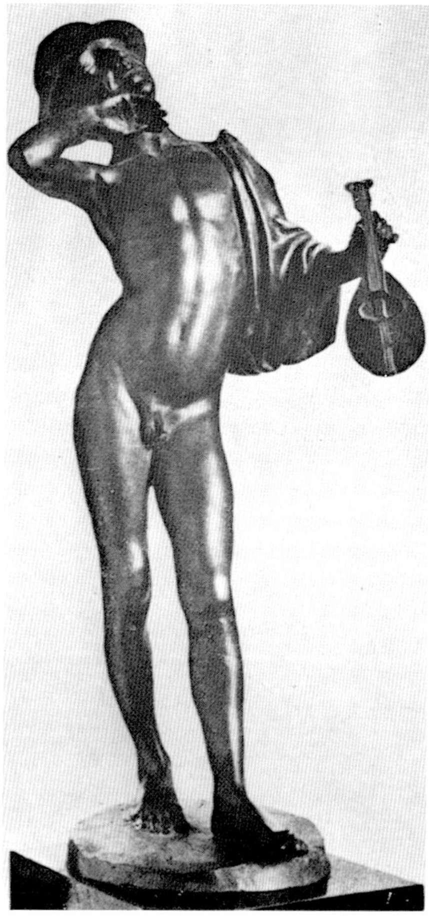

John Hughes, The Mandolin Player (Napoli), 1900. Bronze. Height 49.5 cm. Reproduced from Alan Denson, John Hughes: A Documentary Biography, *London 1969.*

In October 1901 Hughes resigned his post as instructor in modelling in the Dublin Art School in order to devote his attention to the monument to Queen Victoria. He had decided to move to Paris to carry out the work and had settled there by 1903. From there he was to travel to Italy on several occasions before 1920. During this period, while busy on the monument, itself a splendidly baroque concept, he was also engaged on an important commission in Loughrea Cathedral. Thanks to the enlightened patronage of Edward Martyn, one of the guiding forces behind the Celtic Revival, and to an equally enlightened clergy, this church

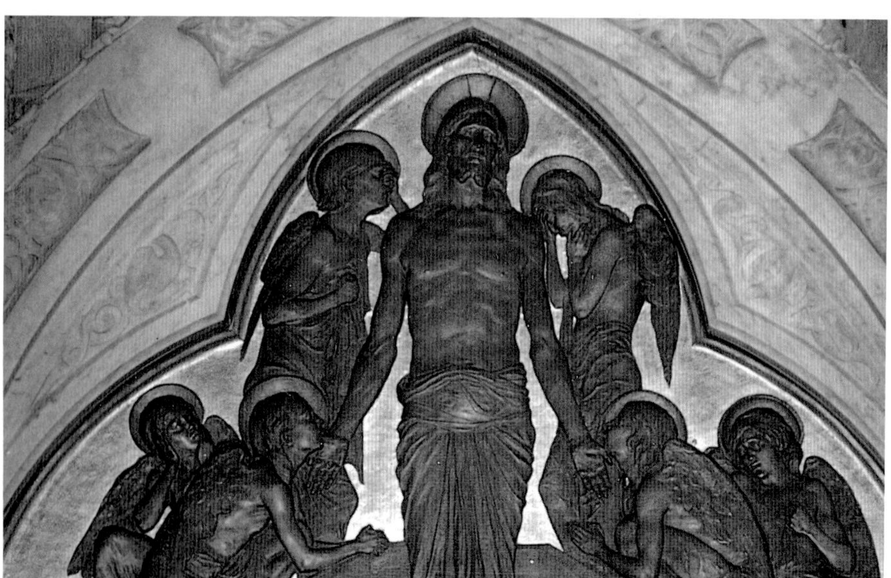

John Hughes, Man of Sorrows, *1901-05. Bronze. Height 137 cm. width 205cm.*

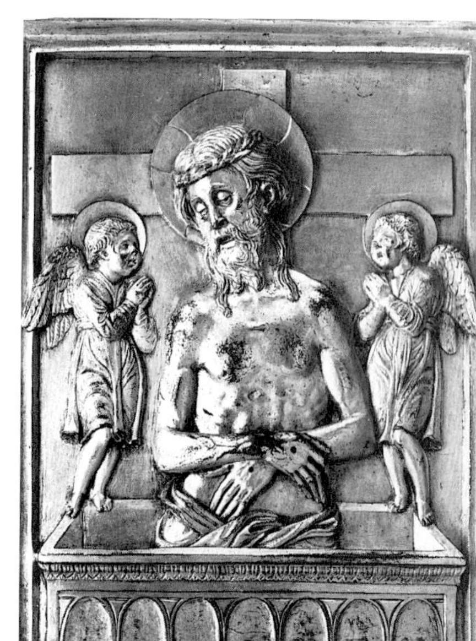

Bartolomeo Bellano, Cristo Passo. *Reproduced from* Italian Renaissance Sculpture in the Time of Donatello, *Exhibition Catalogue, Detroit, 1985.*

JOHN HUGHES: THE ITALIAN CONNECTION

was to become a veritable treasure house of sculpture, stained glass, wood-carving, metalwork and textiles. Early in 1901, Bishop Healy commissioned Hughes to do the modelling and carving work for the church – the artist being considered, at this point in his career, to be the country's foremost sculptor. His contribution to the Cathedral consists of a magnificent bronze high altar relief and tabernacle door, a freestanding marble *Virgin and Child* for a side altar and, possibly, the designs for the bronze altar rail panels which were executed by his assistant, Michael Shorthall.[22]

In 1902, while in Paris, he made a small clay sketch for his *Man of Sorrows* relief and the finished bronze was placed on the high altar some three years later. It is a large work, measuring over 140cm high by 203cm wide, depicting Christ, standing in an open tomb, surrounded by weeping and grieving angels. The subject, common in medieval times, was an unusual choice for a high altar in the early twentieth century but it served as a vivid reminder to all facing the altar of Christ's suffering for mankind. Hughes appears to derive his image from a rather interesting prototype. In fifteenth-century Italian art, the Dead Christ, shown half-length in the sarcophagus, surrounded by mourning angels, was a popular depiction, especially in Padua where it became known as the *Cristo Passo*. Donatello had developed the type and it was subsequently disseminated throughout the Veneto by painters including Giovanni Bellini and the sculptor Bartolomeo Bellano, a pupil of Donatello. Like Donatello, Hughes makes use of the traditional gestures of grief – the bowed head, the hands covering the face – but his angels are more restrained and tender in their grief and their modelling is more naturalistic. His treatment of the haloes is similar to that of Donatello, as is the deeply modelled 'rosy' treatment of drapery. Another Donatellesque feature is the representation of Christ as an older man, complete with lined face and matted beard. This is how Donatello had depicted the figure in the *Lamentation* and *Resurrection* panels of the pulpits in the church of San Lorenzo in Florence.

The stylistic link with Padua is maintained in the bronze reliefs on the altar rails of the high-altar. In each panel is depicted a small cherub singing or playing a musical instrument. The design is copied from Donatello's cherubs of the high altar in the Santo. I believe that this close

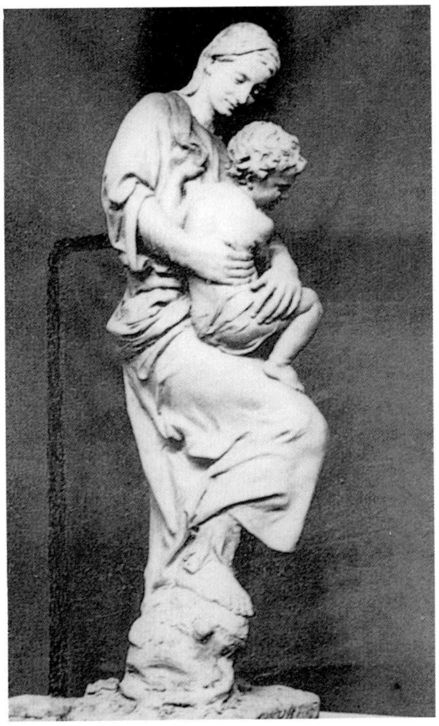

John Hughes, Virgin and Child. *Clay. Height 143.5 cm. Reproduced from Alan Denson*, John Hughes: A Documentary Biography, *London 1969.*

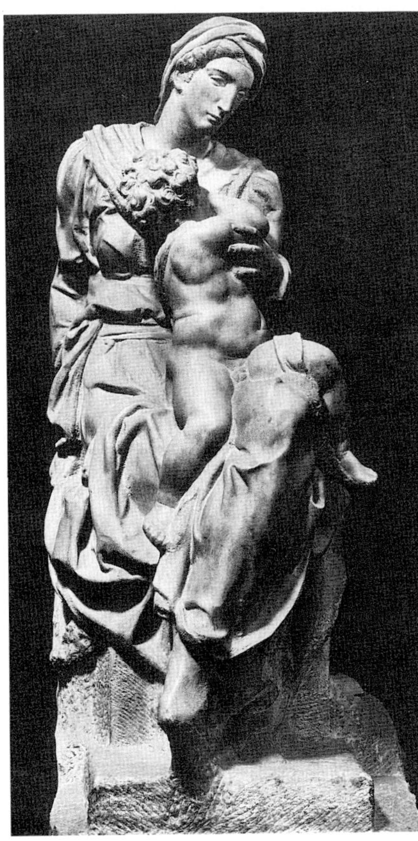

Michelangelo, Virgin and Child. *227.5cm. San Lorenzo, Florence.*

knowledge of Donatello's work at Padua derives originally from Hughes' study in the cast room in the V&A. Casts of the Paduan bronzes were in place there from 1870.[23] However, remarks by Beatrice Glenavy in her autobiography indicate that Hughes may also have visited the area on one of his early trips. She writes:

> *I found it all marvellous – the feeling of coming down from the sun-on-snow air of the Alps to the perfumed warmth of Italy and then the lovely Italian towns and places that John Hughes had talked so much about in the modelling room.*[24]

Another superb contribution to the decoration of Loughrea Cathedral is his freestanding marble of *The Virgin and Child* placed on a side altar. When precisely Hughes was given the commission is unknown but the work was *in situ* before 1909.[25] This group is a superb re-interpretation of the old theme of Virgin and Child but one rarely attempted by Irish sculptors and never in this way. From a photograph of the clay model, sent by Hughes to Hugh Lane, it is clear that from the beginning the statue was conceived to be viewed from several different viewpoints. This is indicated by the treatment of the Virgin, who is given a dynamic twisting pose, which is in turn echoed by that of the Christ child. Such a presentation demands that the spectator must move around the sculpture in order to appreciate it fully. Yet Hughes must have been aware of the final location of his statue – in front of a shallow niche on the altar wall, with no chance to show off the complexity of the composition.

The successful integration of the two figures demonstrates the artist's masterly adaptation of Renaissance Italian types in both painting and sculpture. He may have been aware of the *Foligno Madonna*, a painting by Raphael, on public display in the the Vatican Museum.[26] The pose of this Renaissance group is similar to the Hughes group, even allowing for dissimilarities in the upper torso of the child and the fact that Raphael's Madonna is a seated rather than standing figure, as in Loughrea. The smiling chubby-cheeked child certainly recalls Raphael's treatment of children. A close examination of the Hughes group also reveals a thorough knowledge of Michelangelo's *Virgin and Child* group in the Medici chapel in Florence, perhaps in this case studied *in situ*. The profile, the inclination of the head, and the headdress are treated in a

JOHN HUGHES: THE ITALIAN CONNECTION

similar manner. The twisting shoulders of Hughes' Madonna also recall Michelangelo, although in Hughes's case the pose is reversed.

In 1913, some years after the work in Loughrea was completed, Hughes executed a bronze fountain piece, comprising a crouching young woman with a small child perched on her shoulders, holding aloft a fish. It is a superb example of the artist's virtuosity, both technically and stylistically. It is thought to be one of his last commissions. Fountain statuary was a speciality of Renaissance sculpture and Hughes' work looks to such prototypes for inspiration. In its variety of viewpoints the work recalls the fifteenth-century fountain piece, *Putto with a Dolphin*, by Andrea del Verrocchio. This was designed as the central decoration of a fountain in Lorenzo de Medici's country villa at Careggi and consisted of a small chubby-limbed winged putto clutching a wriggling fish. What is remarkable about Verrocchio's figure is the fact that it was designed in the round, one of the first statues of the Renaissance to have multiple and merging viewpoints. Hughes' fountain-piece is treated in a similar manner and his plump child, also grasping a fish, is a free variant of the Renaissance model. Hughes' undoubted debt to this striking composition may be traced once more to the cast court in the V&A. A cast of Verrocchio's sculpture had been on display since 1888 and Hughes would have had the opportunity to study it at leisure. In my opinion, the source of the crouching female figure beneath is also reliant on the V&A cast collection. While Hughes' figures bears a striking resemblance to a sixteenth-century work, *Kneeling Venus*, by Giambologna, closer to it is a later freely worked copy of the Giambologna original in the V&A. This figure, unlike Giambologna's, rests the full weight of her body on one leg. Hughes uses this format in his representation too. However, there the resemblance ends. The smooth rounded surfaces, the fluent contours, and the impersonal face of the Giambologna copy are not part of Hughes' interpretation. In his figures the contours and surfaces are in keeping with his keen sense of naturalism. This is especially apparent in the treatment of the heads and hands. The Giambolognesque dimpled hands, with their interminable serpentine fingers, firmly belong to Florentine sculpture of the age of mannerism.

Although this work is considered to be one of his last, Hughes lived on for another twenty years, travelling to Italy on several occasions. These visits are better chronicled and offer an interesting insight into his views on Italian art. In a Christmas letter to Sarah Purser in 1933, he expressed his views on the early Renaissance sculptor, Jacopo della Quercia:

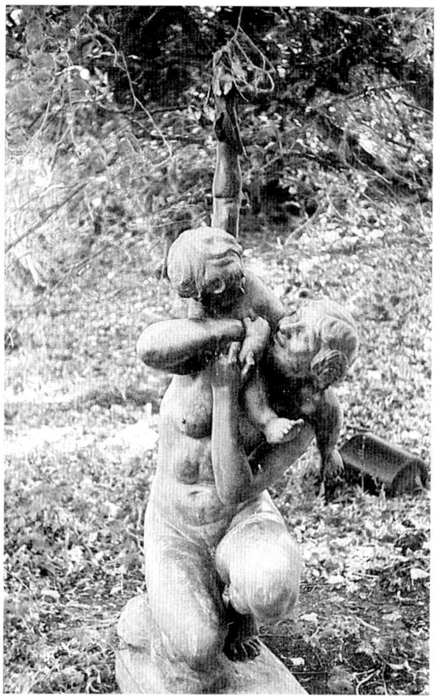

John Hughes, Fountain Sculpture, *1913. Bronze. Height 178 cm. (overall).*

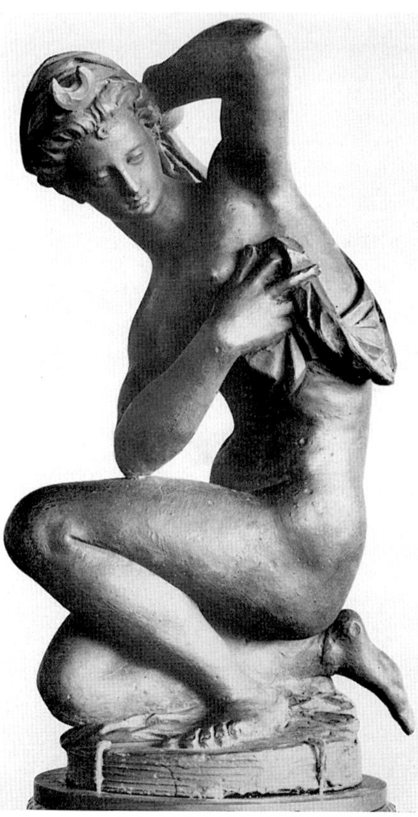

Diana, *a 'freely worked copy of Giambologna's Kneeling Venus in the Victoria and Albert'. Reproduced from* Victoria and Albert Yearbook, *No. 2, London, 1970.*

> *He was born in Siena one hundred years before Michelangelo. There are four small figures in relief of prophets on the font in the baptistry at Siena by Jacopo and they are grand in style as any thing Michelangelo ever did and don't you think that wonderful? Donatello never did anything half as grandiose and majestic. Jacopo was a greater sculptor.*[27]

There is also a reference to an exhibition of Caravaggio's work which he had seen in Florence some years previously. Hughes, who considered Caravaggio to be the precursor of Rembrandt, was deeply impressed by his work and wrote 'What a passionate painter he was'.

In spite of only tantalising glimpses of his response to what he saw on his Italian trips, there is evidence of his strong feelings for that country and its people. Between 1920 and 1926 he took up residence in Florence with his two sisters, Mary and Jane. A letter written by him to Oliver Sheppard in the summer of 1922 is revealing. He writes 'I have a modest furnished flat here on the side of a hill. I live amongst the people. They are very like the Irish, good humoured and kindly. I like them well'.[28] He then goes on to describe a visit to southern Italy which obviously delighted him; so much so that the writing at this point achieves an almost poetic lyricism:

> *I saw the island of Sicily rising out of the sea at dawn of a June morning, the sun touching with gold the surface of its wild mountains. I spent a month there. The Greek temples at Sergenti, the classic remains at Syracuse and Taormina. The beautiful things in Palermo in Monreale are something to dream of for the rest of one's life.*

The letter incidentally makes clear that he had not lost touch with what was happening in Ireland. He writes:

> *Mike Collins has a man's head on him judging by his picture which I saw the other day in the Piazza here. He will want to be as good a man as he looks to run the show in Ireland now. The northern frontier is an absolute impossibility, I hope it may soon cease to exist ... When I read the leading*

JOHN HUGHES: THE ITALIAN CONNECTION

articles in the Giornale d'Italia and the Corriere della Sera all about the magnificent Irish race I take off my hat to myself and invite myself to have a glass of Chianti and a cigar.

It is thought that Hughes made other visits to Italy in the 1930s, perhaps to the south of the country in 1932 with his two sisters, and a later visit in 1935 or 1936. Unfortunately these last visits are as poorly documented as the early ones and leave no clue as to what he saw on his travels.

Although now neglected, the work of John Hughes serves as a reminder of a vigorous academic talent. The variety of his sculpture, from the delightful statuettes to the splendour of the work at Loughrea Cathedral, is impressive for its display of artistic ideas as well as for its mastery of technical skills. Hughes was an artist who usefully absorbed the lessons of other great artists before him. Visually stimulated by all that he came in contact with, his own sculptural ideas were formed and nourished by these encounters. But like all good artists he freely interpreted what he had seen. In the foundation group, for instance, he maintains his closeness to natural forms while investing the work with the dynamism inherent in the multi-faceted compositions of the Renaissance. The *Man of Sorrows* relief demonstrates the extent to which the ideas of Donatello stirred Hughes's creative imagination and served to enrich the work. I believe, that while the visits to Italy must have been of great importance to his stylistic development, the opportunity to study the superb collection of Renaissance casts at close quarters in London had an equally far-reaching effect.

Sighle Bhreathnach-Lynch

Dr Sighle Bhreathnach-Lynch is a Lecturer in the History of Art Department in University College Dublin.

ACKNOWLEDGEMENTS

I would like to thank Alan Denson for his encouraging and helpful comments during the original writing-up of this topic. A word of thanks is also due to Padraig Ó Snodaigh, formerly of the National Museum of Ireland for arranging a special viewing of the statuettes, *L'Ame du Vin* and *The Mandolin Player*.

NOTES

1. See Brian Lalor, *Ultimate Dublin Guide*, Dublin, 1991, p.273. When unveiled in 1908 this monument was initially well-received. However by the late 1920s it was seen as a work misrepresenting the national outlook towards British rule in Ireland. It was removed to the Royal Hospital Kilmainham in 1948 and was later presented to the citizens of Australia as a gift from the Irish nation.
2. See *The Nationalist* (Clonmel), 30 November 1898, p.3.
3. This group was originally placed in the centre of the pool. It has since been replaced with one of children bearing an ornamental bowl. The Hughes statue is now in a private collection elsewhere in Ireland. Its present location is under a large tree. For a history of the garden see also John A Ryan, 'The Garden at Heywood', *Irish Arts Review 1991-92*, pp. 95-98.
4. The definitive research on John Hughes which has been carried out by Alan Denson has yielded little about this area of his life. See Alan Denson, *John Hughes A Documentary Biography*, London, 1969
5. This is recorded in the *Index Register* for that year, now located in the archives of the National College of Art and Design, Thomas Street, Dublin.
6. See *Annual Report and List of Prizes Metropolitan School of Art Session 1890/1*, Dublin, 1891, p.3.
7. These works are listed in the following publication: *A Catalogue of Casts, Drawings, Photographs and other Examples in the Metropolitan School of Art, Dublin*, 1886.
8. When the Museum of Manufactures (as the Victoria & Albert Museum was first known) was established in 1852, casts were regarded as a crucial part of the collection. The 'application of fine art to objects of utility' was among the Museum's essential aims, and casts of architectural and ornamental work existed as educational tools. In the early 1860s, the collecting policy broadened to include figure sculpture and part of that policy was a sustained programme of reproducing Italian Renaissance works. This resulted in an outstanding collection of Italian sculpture, the most comprehensive outside Italy. For further information see Malcolm Baker's pamphlet, *The Cast Courts*, V&A publication.
9. For an account of Alfred Stevens' contribution to nineteenth-century British sculpture see Susan Beattie, *The New Sculpture*, New Haven and London, 1983.
10. National Library of Ireland, Ms.10201 (12), Sarah Purser correspondence, letter, December 1927.
11. Alan Denson suggests that he travelled to France and to Italy. See Denson, 'John Hughes, RHA 1865-1941. A Neglected Irish Sculptor', *Capuchin Annual*, 1975, pp.126-37.
12. Ibid.
13. It is not known precisely why this poem by Baudelaire was chosen. However Hughes was remembered by his student, the artist Beatrice Glenavy, as a deeply cultured and well-read man. Perhaps this was a favourite poem. See Beatrice Glenavy, *Today We Will Only Gossip*, London 1964.
14. The genital area was covered later in a fit of prudery by the National Museum.
15. A cast of Donatello's *David* was in place in the Museum in 1885 and the Michelangelo figure had been in the collection as early as 1857 (this information is documented on plaques placed beside each work).
16. This comment is in a letter to Sarah Purser, written in 1933, which forms part of a private collection of Hughes' correspondence, quoted by Denson, *John Hughes, A Documentary Biography*, op.cit., p.166.
17. During its long years of storage in the basement of the National Museum of Ireland, the mandolin at some stage became detached from the figure.
18. This cast was on display from 1882.
19. Although Denson believes that he had already been to Italy, Beatrice Glenavy thought the 1897 trip was his first visit to that country. See Denson, *John Hughes A Documentary Biography*, op. cit., letter from Glenavy to Denson, 5 September 1956, p.382.
20. This remark is to be found an 'Irish Sculptor – John Hughes, RHA', published in *Journal and Proceedings of the Arts and Crafts Society of Ireland*, Vol.1, No.3, 1901, pp.243-48.
21. Titian, Leonardo and Mantegna are also mentioned. This list is quoted in a letter to Sarah Purser (1933) which is in a private collection of Hughes' correspondence. See Denson, op.cit., p.167.
22. Both Alan Denson and Thomas McGreevy are of the opinion that the designs are by Hughes. See Hughes, op.cit. and Thomas McGreevy, 'St. Brendan's Cathedral, Loughrea 1897-1947', *Capuchin Annual*, 1947, pp.353-73. Monsignor Patrick Egan and Dr Paul Larmour, on the other hand, believe that the architect supervising the interior of the church, William Scott, may have been responsible for the designs. See Patrick K Egan, *St. Brendan's Cathedral, Loughrea, Co Galway*, Dublin, 1986 (not paginated) and Paul Larmour, *The Arts and Crafts Movement in Ireland*, Belfast, 1992, pp.130-33.
23. A marble version of the *Man of Sorrows* theme (c.1438), designed for an altar front by Donatello and executed by his workshop, was also in the V&A sculpture collection from 1861.
24. Beatrice Glenavy, op.cit.
25. See Patrick K Egan, op.cit.
26. A copy of the *Handbook for Travellers*, Vol.2 (Central Italy and Rome), by K Baedeker, for 1893, lists the Vatican collections as being open to the public.
27. These comments are quoted in a letter from a private collection of letters, Denson, op.cit., p.169.
28. Ibid., p.153.

THE POLITICS OF THE STREET MONUMENT

Paula Murphy examines the political significance of Dublin nineteenth-century street monuments.

According to Pliny 'the Greeks were the first who conferred statues as a mark of honour'[1], a status that inevitably incorporates the possibility of subsequent rejection. The politics of public statuary have been particularly evident in recent years with the collapse of communism. Russia, which had witnessed the tearing down of images of members of the Tsarist regime after the Revolution in 1917, now saw the removal of statues of communist leaders. Such monuments, in their choice of style, scale and position, have considerable propagandist strength and a silent, statuesque likeness of a particular individual enables the continued exertion of power.

In Dublin public statuary has wielded similar power and has witnessed similar opposition. Throughout the nineteenth and twentieth centuries attempts to destroy monuments representative of British dominance in Ireland have been numerous. Successful attempts include the destruction of the statue of Lord Gough in the Phoenix Park, which, targetted many times since its installation in 1880, was finally blown up in 1957, while Nelson's Pillar in O'Connell Street was destroyed just nine years later in 1966. Some monuments were removed from their prominent positions before activists could manifest their grievance. Such works were placed either in a less obvious and more secure site, as was the case with the Albert Memorial on Leinster Lawn, which was removed from its central position, and relocated alongside the Museum Building in 1924. Alternatively, monuments were dismantled and placed in storage, as happened to John Hughes's monument to Queen Victoria.

A guide book for visitors to the Great Industrial Exhibition of 1853 in Dublin listed the public monuments which could be seen.[2] As might be expected, they were few in number and regal in character. In addition, a contributor to *Dublin University Magazine* in 1856 drew attention to the fact that 'No public statue of an illustrious Irishman has ever graced the Irish capital. No monument exists to which the gaze of the young Irish children can be directed, while their fathers tell them, "this was to the glory of your countrymen".[3] However, the second half of the nineteenth century saw a significant change in the images that peopled the streets of Dublin.

The nature of the public monument was called into question in relation to its two-fold objective – as a commemoration and as an adornment of public thoroughfares. The type of figure considered acceptable for public commemoration was addressed in the early 1860s when a memorial fountain to Sir Philip Crampton was unveiled in College Street. The appropriateness of such a public testimonial to an eminent surgeon, whose merits were confined to a limited circle, was questioned.[4] Generally memorials of a professional character were deemed more fittingly displayed in the environs of a relevant building, whereas, it was mooted that the streets should function as repositories for commemorations of a public nature, capable of swaying the thoughts and moulding the conduct of the general public.

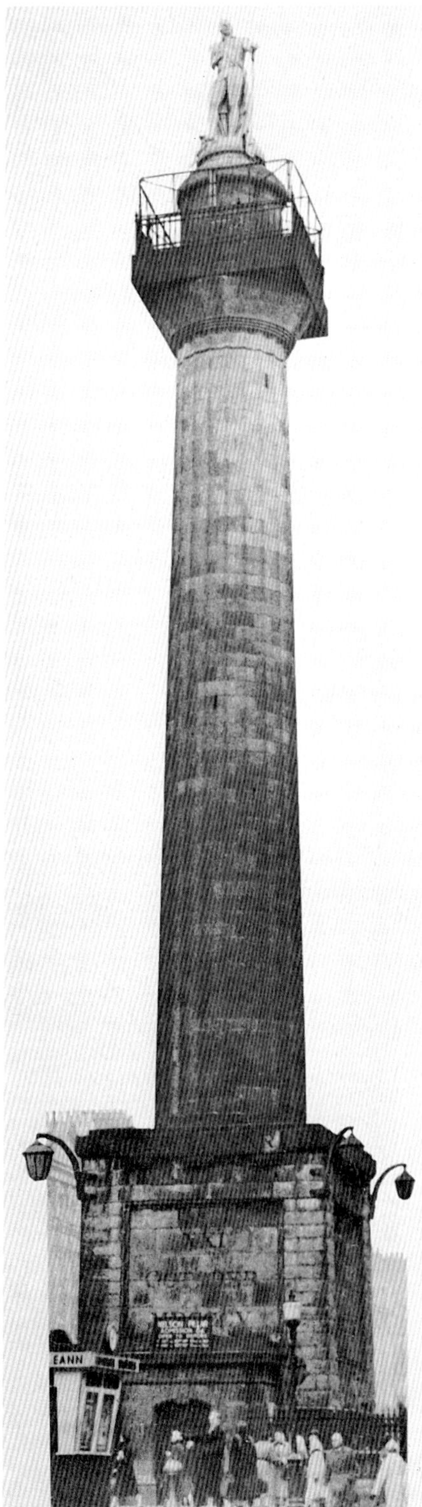

Thomas Kirk, The Nelson Column, *1808. O'Connell Street, Dublin. (now destroyed).*

The royal monuments to be seen in central Dublin in the first half of the nineteenth century dated from the 1700s and functioned not just as works of art, but as constant reminders of Ireland's continuing domination by a foreign power. Grinling Gibbons's statue of King William III, erected in 1701 in College Green at the expense of Dublin Corporation, was the most controversial monument in the city, serving, as it did, as the focal point of an annual commemorative procession culminating in its decoration, with orange lilies and a flaming sash, and the firing of volleys. In 1806, the Lord Lieutenant attempted to discourage such political taunts, by refusing to be present at the procession and by banning the firing of volleys. In 1822 his successor tried to dissuade the Orange Order from decorating the statue and, in 1836, Irish radicals made three attempts to blow it up. Other royal monuments were less unashamedly public. The equestrian statue of George I, moved from Essex Bridge to the gardens of the Mansion House in 1753, was positioned on a pedestal overlooking Dawson Street, but separated from the people by a railing. Here again both the Corporation and contemporary politics had a significant role, identified on the inscription: 'Be it remembered that, at the time when rebellion and disloyalty were the characteristics of the day, the loyal Corporation of the City of Dublin re-elevated this statue of the illustrious House of Hanover'.

These statues were joined early in the nineteenth century by commemorative monuments of military heroes. Victorious campaigners achieved virtual deification when Viscount Nelson was placed on a triumphal column in the centre of Sackville

THE POLITICS OF THE STREET MONUMENT

Street in the heart of the city and when in 1808, the Duke of Wellington was commemorated by a gigantic obelisk in the Phoenix Park. Both monuments, rising to a soaring height and visible from some considerable distance, employed scale in an aggressive manner. The Nelson monument was controversial from the start. Political, artistic and situational objections were raised, and several Corporation Bills were introduced requesting its removal.[5]

The public concern that the Irish people honour Irish men was initially manifest in statues of such uncontroversial figures as Thomas Moore, Oliver Goldsmith and Edmund Burke. Creative writers and thinkers struck a less pompous note on the streets of Dublin and indicated a link with the new French practice of commemorating men of letters. The Moore statue was erected in College Street in 1857. A Dublin-born, nationalist balladeer, he had shown real concern for the plight of Irish Catholics. While the subject was acceptable, the choice of sculptor was controversial, with the commission being awarded to

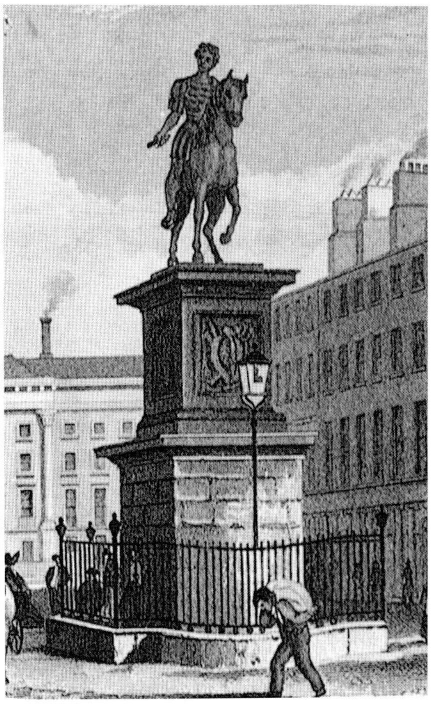

Grinling Gibbons, Statue of William III, *College Green, Dublin. Erected 1701.*

Christopher Moore in 1853 after a competition, in which it had been generally considered that John Hogan's model was the most successful.[6] In this instance 'politicking' activated itself at committee level,[7] resulting in a statue that was described as 'A stigma on our national taste'.[8] There were calls for its removal and as a result of this 'failure' the method of selection of monument committees was much questioned.[9]

By comparison with Moore, the Goldsmith (1864) and Burke (1868) statues, the work of John Henry Foley, moved from inception to erection without incident. Commissioned for the strip of lawn before the entrance front of Trinity College, where both men were educated, these could be considered as private works. However this area was leased by the Corporation and both statues were paid for by public subscription. The commission of a commemorative statue of Oliver Goldsmith in 1861 can only be described as playing safe. Edmund Burke, on the other hand, was a more interesting

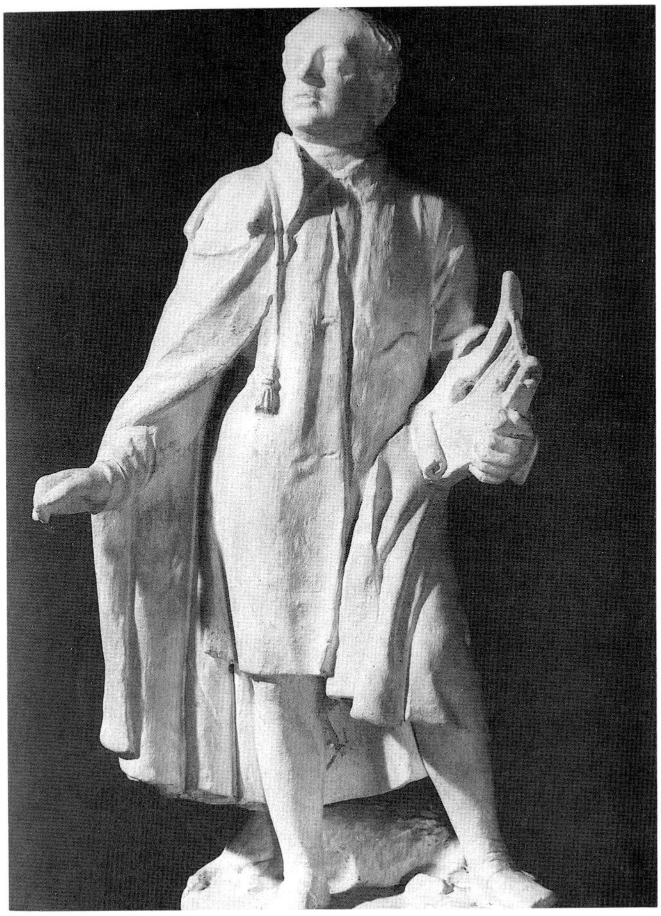

John Hogan, Sketch model in plaster for monument to Thomas Moore. National Gallery of Ireland.

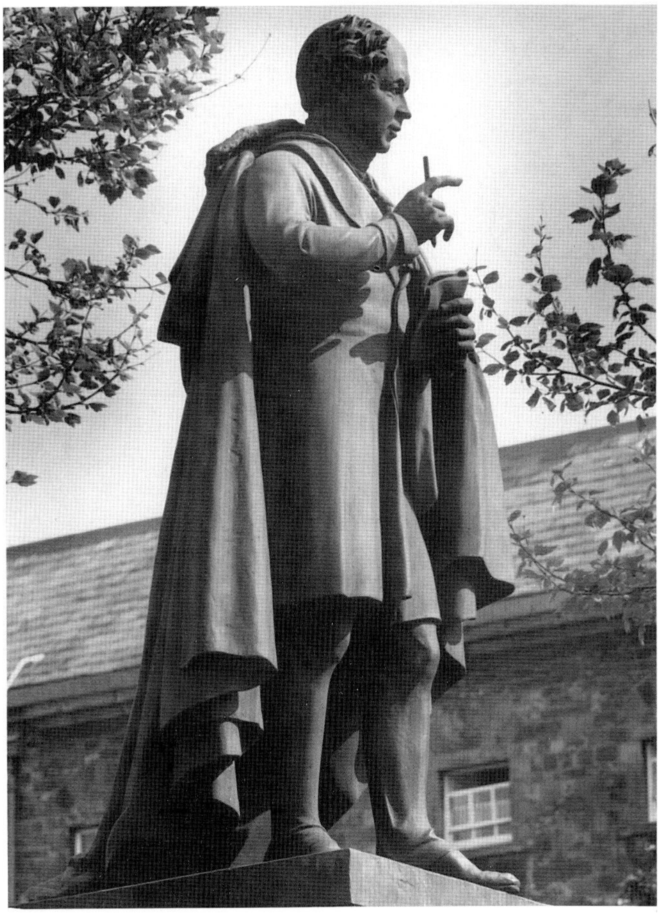

Christopher Moore, Thomas Moore. *Bronze, 1857. College Street, Dublin.*

THE POLITICS OF THE STREET MONUMENT

choice. Born in Dublin to a Catholic mother and a Protestant father, he had, throughout his career, revealed constant concern for Ireland and particularly for the difficulties suffered by Irish Catholics.

It is of interest to consider who was not chosen for this particular site. Theobald Wolfe Tone, who died just one year after Burke in 1798, was also born in Dublin, educated at Trinity College and played a significant role in Irish national politics. However his revolutionary republican beliefs, coupled with his activist involvement, made him, at this stage, too controversial a figure for a lofty public pedestal. The foundation stone for a Tone memorial was not to be laid until his centenary year.[10] The more recently deceased Thomas Davis was also a graduate of Trinity College and seems likewise not to have been a contender for one of these pedestals. Davis, who died in 1845 at the age of 31, was influential in his day as a literary and political nationalist. He was, however, active on a narrow stage, living and working, as he did, in Dublin rather than in London, and it was as yet too early to recognise someone who came to be described as 'the purest Irish patriot'.[11] While Goldsmith and Burke had prominent public locations, contemporaneously a statue of the Earl of Eglinton and Winton was erected in the then private St. Stephen's Green. This bronze work, modelled by Patrick McDowell in 1866, was visible from the street, but nonetheless behind railings and in a space that was closed to the public.

Nationalist commemorations of a more political nature were instigated with the commission of the O'Connell monument for Dublin in 1864. This was not the first statue of O'Connell since one was already in place in Limerick and another in execution for Ennis. However these two commemorations had a domestic flavour smacking almost of parochialism. A further dedication in the form of a tomb monument was in construction in the cemetery at Glasnevin on the outskirts of Dublin. Designed by the antiquarian George Petrie, this was to have been a celtic revival architectural complex, but ultimately only the round tower was erected. Completed in 1860, and markedly out of proportion in the grave-yard, it stands as a giant symbol of celtic triumphalism, and might be viewed as a response, of an oppositional nature, to Wellington's obelisk in the Phoenix Park.

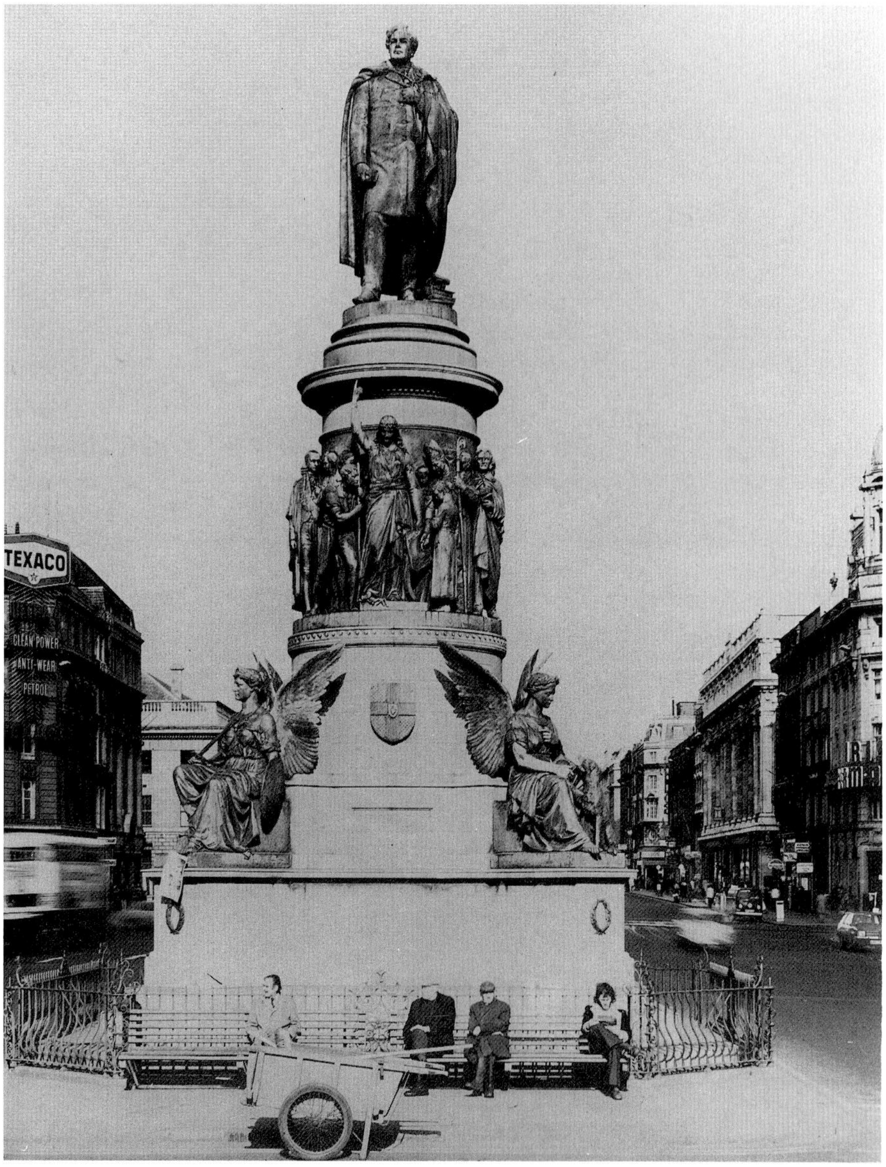

John Henry Foley, The O'Connell Monument, *1864-82.*
O'Connell Street, Dublin

The monument for the central thoroughfare in the capital city carried much wider national significance, in this instance of a Catholic nature. This was the first Catholic figure to be given such a public commemoration, and the only statue of a Catholic erected on the streets of Dublin in the nineteenth century. Such was the importance of this commission that it was accompanied by a very public debate which highlights issues of Irishness and insecurity.[12] The competitions to find a sculptor were unsuccessful and with a sweeping rejection of the work of resident artists, the commission was offered to Foley. While nationalism as a fundamental concern in the selection of an artist was considered to be both isolationist and restricting,[13] nonetheless those who felt 'that nothing great can be done upon our own soil and that everything great is to be sought in foreign lands' were instrumental in reinforcing a troubling sense of inferiority amongst the Irish.[14]

Foley exhibited his model for the work in Dublin in 1867. He was, however, slow to complete the commission and the monument was not erected until 1882, eight years after his death. By this time the memory of Daniel O'Connell was no longer simply that of a glorified nationalist hero, and the unveiling, though treated as

THE POLITICS OF THE STREET MONUMENT

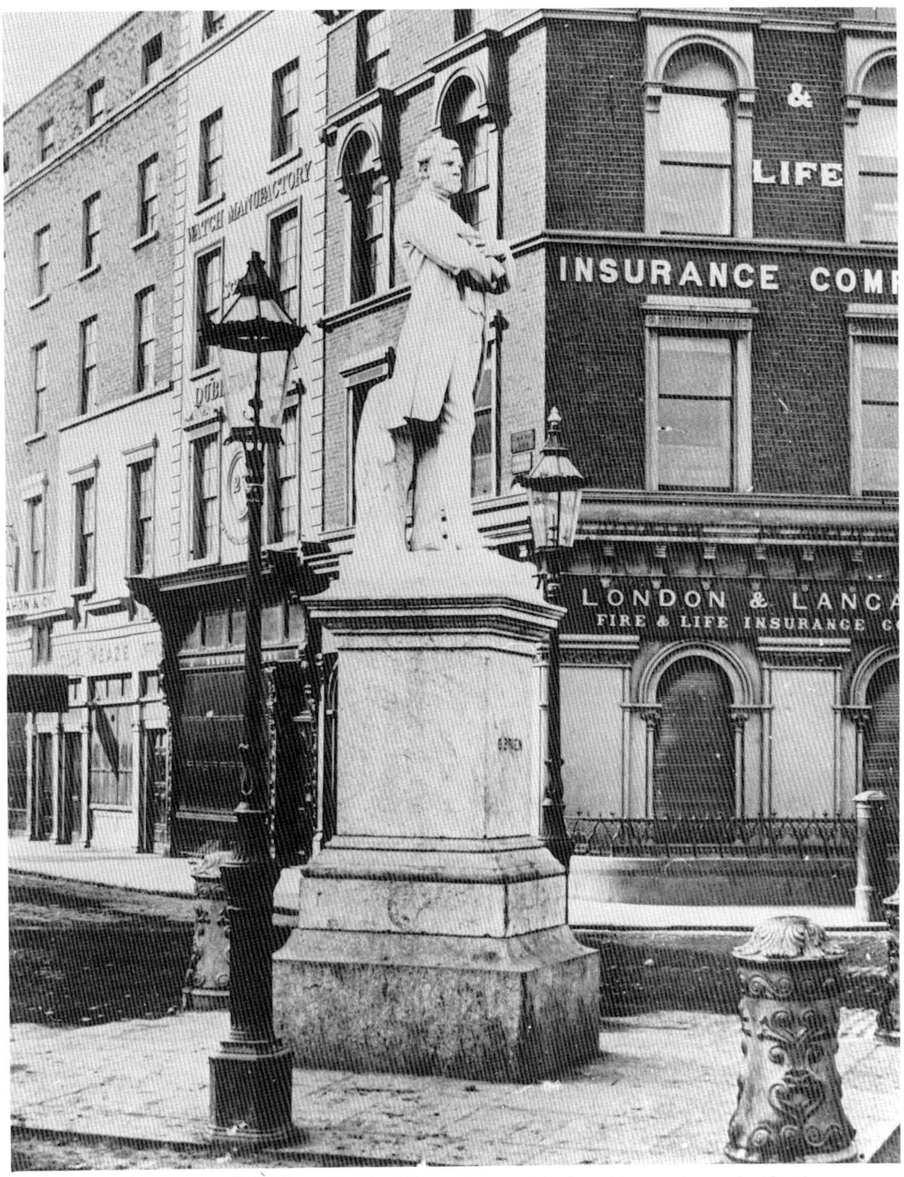

Thomas Farrell, William Smith O'Brien, *in its original position on the south side of O'Connell Bridge (unveiled 1870). Moved in 1929 to O'Connell Street, Dublin.*

an occasion of public celebration, produced mixed feelings. The newspapers felt it necessary to warn the anti-O'Connellites of the need to behave with propriety.[15]. The confrontational nature of the statues on the streets of the capital became more evident as the century was drawing to a close. Just days after the O'Connell unveiling a crowd of several hundred people surrounded the statue of William III in College Green yelling and throwing stones. The rioting and damage to the monument resulted in arrests.[16]

The considerable delay in the completion of the O'Connell monument resulted in other statues being finished before it. The most significant of these was the statue of William Smith O'Brien by Thomas Farrell erected in 1870. The siting of this work on the opposite side of O'Connell Bridge was not without irony. O'Connell and O'Brien had worked closely together towards similar nationalist ends, but later found themselves in dispute over the use of physical force, which led to a break between O'Connell's Repeal Association and the Young Irelanders, and an ensuing rivalry between the two men.[17]

O'Brien was a controversial figure whose revolutionary principles followed those of Wolfe Tone. While Tone himself was not yet commemorated on the streets of Dublin, O'Brien, dying in 1864, was a more immediate hero and suitable for recognition. After his death a group of his followers formed a committee to organise the erection of a statue to his memory. Such were the conflicting opinions held about William Smith O'Brien that the expectation of problems at the unveiling ceremony were not unfounded. In anticipation of this, processions were prohibited and bands were prevented from playing while marching. However, while the crowd of some 20,000 people was considered unsettled, disorganised and uncontrollable,[18] it gained this reputation more on account of its rowdy support for the more revolutionary amongst the speakers at the ceremony, than for any incidents of actual violence. In the course of the speeches attention was drawn to the statues on the streets of Dublin that represented men who served and loved England, rather than Ireland, and monuments that highlighted 'the haughty mastery of the English people and our servility and helplessness'.[19]

Those who favoured the O'Brien commemoration later delighted in the decision to erect a public statue of Henry Grattan,[20] although not in the choice of sculptor, when once more a resident Irish sculptor was passed over in favour of Foley. The Grattan statue has interesting origins, as the money used for the commission was raised for a different dedication.[21] A M Sullivan, editor and proprietor of *The Nation,* had been arrested in 1868 for an article he had written about the Manchester Martyrs, who were hanged in November 1867. While he was in prison his friends raised money for a testimonial to him. On his release Sullivan decided to dedicate the funds towards a statue of Grattan, and Dublin Corporation offered a site in front of the Old Parliament House. This was an appropriate site, not only with regard to Grattan's student days in Trinity College and his triumphs in the Parliament building, but also because the Corporation had previously granted this same location for the proposed Albert Memorial in 1864.[22] It was hoped that the Grattan statue, portraying a staunch Protestant and a Home Ruler, would be a uniting force in the city. Certainly members of different political parties, different religions and different classes were all present at the unveiling ceremony on 6 January 1876, which was carried out without political harangue.[23] In his speech from the platform, Sullivan indicated his wish that the youth of Ireland 'might learn lessons of concord, of good-will of public virtue, of toleration and of patriotism' from the presence of Grattan in their midst.[24]

In contrast, at the beginning of the decade, a statue of the Earl of Carlisle by Foley was unveiled without ceremony in the Phoenix Park by the Lord Lieutenant, Earl Spencer. The Earl of Carlisle had been a popular Lord Lieutenant in Ireland and while it was suggested at the time that no ceremony would do him justice,[25] the absence of public ceremony may have been politically motivated, perhaps inspired by the fear of political demonstration. After all, just seven months later some 20,000 people would throng the streets of Dublin for the unveiling of the O'Brien monument. Given that these two figures, the one revolutionary, the other representative of the crown, could not co-exist on the public thoroughfares, O'Brien, pointing to the future, was positioned in the heart of the city, while Carlisle was assigned to a park on the city outskirts. Carlisle would be joined later in the Phoenix Park by an equestrian statue of Lord Gough, after vain attempts to place this work more centrally, firstly in Foster Place and secondly on Carlisle Bridge.

Different emotions were aroused by the Gough memorial. Gough was Irish born, like Wellington, and served as Field Marshal in the British army; according to the inscription on the plinth of the monument, he 'added lustre to the military glory of this country which he faithfully served for seventy-five years'.[26] Such laudatory commendation might seem more fitting to a monument raised in England, and it was suggested that the statue might be more suitably sited in London.[27] The equestrian portrait was a private commission financed by friends of Gough. The unveiling on 21 February 1880, by the Duke of Marlborough, was a 'distinguished' and 'military' affair, with the Lord Lieutenant describing the Phoenix Park as the 'Champ de Mars of Dublin'.[28]

If Gough himself was an unacceptable figure to many of the Irish, the very nature of the commemoration must have emphasised his unacceptability. The antique equestrian monuments which inspired it, were symbolic of imperialism and were used for royal and military persons. Foley was keen to execute an equestrian statue for his native city. He declared his position

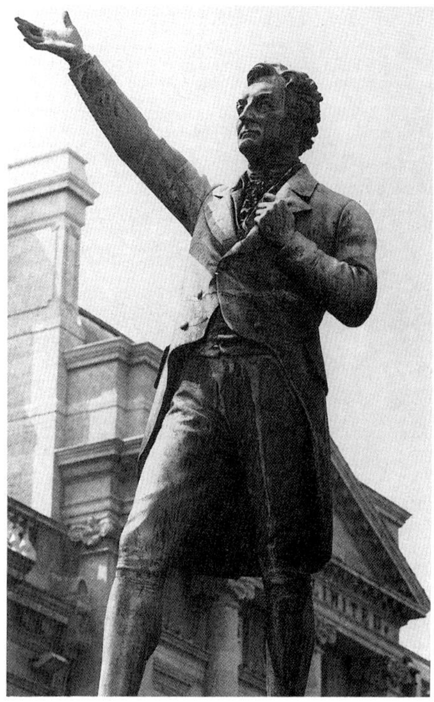

John Henry Foley, Henry Grattan, *1874. College Green, Dublin.*

in a letter accepting the commission: 'I need scarcely repeat how gratifying the task would be to me, and how willing I am to forego all consideration of profit in my desire to engage myself upon it ... I feel that the time has arrived for our native country to add to the memorials of her illustrious dead an Equestrian Statue, and that Lord Gough at once presents a worthy subject for such a memorial'.[29] Foley reveals here the extent to which he was out of touch with the changing attitudes in Ireland.

The controversy surrounding the site for Dublin's Albert Memorial was already being aired in the press in January 1862. The commission was given directly to Foley, who made use of a simple variant of the imposing monument in Hyde Park, London. A site for the monument was secured on Leinster Lawn and the unveiling ceremony, which was never in fact to take place, was scheduled for 6 June, 1872. Foley's tardiness in completing the work was yet again in evidence, and on the day in question the Duke of Edinburgh viewed, rather than unveiled, an incomplete monument.[30]

While statues of nationalist figures mark the central thoroughfares in Dublin, the monuments commemorating those who represented the Crown and British imperialism were assigned to more remote locations,sites that were less public and therefore less likely to occasion opposition or encourage demonstrations. However, even in their discreet locations, Foley's statues of Carlisle and of Gough were blown up, in 1958, and 1957 respectively, while the monument to Prince Albert was relocated in a more secure and less accessible position.

Joining the nationalist heroes on the streets of Dublin in the last quarter of the nineteenth century was a commemoration of Sir John Gray, who had actively involved himself in improving the quality of life for those who lived in the city. The public nature of the Gray commemoration was unique, as, 'do-gooder' portraits are more usually site-specific. Instances of this can be seen in the statue of William Dargan (1864) in the forecourt of the National Gallery, Sir Benjamin Guinness (1875) in the grounds of St Patrick's Cathedral, and Lord Ardilaun (1892) in St Stephen's Green, all of which combine public with private characteristics. Sir John Gray was the instigator of the O'Connell Monument and, more importantly, of the Vartry drinking water scheme. While it was for his 'public duty spiritedly undertaken' that a testimonial was first suggested in 1861,[31] there was also political motivation, as the improvement of water facilities in the city was a strongly nationalist issue which met with fierce opposition. It is likely, therefore, that his nationalist ideology secured for him the significant location, for this remained the only testimonial to civic spiritedness to be located on a public thoroughfare. The next O'Connell Street commission would commemorate another political figure, Charles Stewart Parnell.

Shortly before the decision was arrived at to commemorate Parnell, another controversy developed in connection with a proposal to erect a statue of Gladstone in Dublin. The Trustees of the Gladstone National Memorial Fund, set up in 1898, proposed three monuments, one each for London, Edinburgh and Dublin. The suggestion met with outrage by many in Dublin and newspaper articles drew attention to the inappropriate nature of such a commemoration, particularly when, as yet, there was no statue of Parnell.[32] Dublin Corporation passed a motion in 1898 stating 'that no statue should be erected in Dublin in honour of any Englishman until as least the Irish people have raised a fitting monument to the memory of Charles Stewart Parnell ...'[33] While the decision of

THE POLITICS OF THE STREET MONUMENT

the Corporation did not rule out the possibility of a Gladstone commemoration being erected at a later date and Gladstone's son, Herbert, was of the opinion that the Irish would want to remember his father,[34] this was not to be the case.[35]

The foundation stone for the Parnell commemoration was laid on 8 October, 1899 at the north end of O'Connell Street, and the ceremony and its attendant friction between Parnellites and anti-Parnellites were described in the newspapers the following day. As had been the case with the erection of the Grattan statue in 1876 it was hoped that 'the Parnell monument might be the means of bringing Irishmen together again'.[36] In the last days of the century, in November 1899, the Lord Mayor of Dublin, in the company of John E Redmond, MP travelled across America on a fund-raising expedition for the Parnell monument. A substantial amount of money was raised and 'as no Irish sculptor of sufficient ability (was) living' according to John Redmond,[37] the commission was given to the Irish American, Augustus St Gaudens. The statue was unveiled on 1 October, 1911. The portrait of Parnell and the accompanying Nelson and O'Connell, the 'three old rascals'[38] on O'Connell Street, were drawn on by W B Yeats to illustrate his contribution to the Senate debate on divorce in 1925. He suggested that their public presence was 'encouraging', given their adulterous behaviour, and that these 'three very salutary objects of meditation (might) make us a little more tolerant'.[39]

The Parnell statue was unveiled just three years after the neo-Baroque extravaganza commemorating Queen Victoria had been placed on Leinster Lawn. This was the work of John Hughes (see Sighle Bhreathnach-Lynch, *John Hughes: The Italian Connection* in this issue) and showed the queen seated on a high pedestal on the base of which were positioned allegorical figures of *Peace* and *Fame* and *Erin*, presenting a wounded Irish soldier with a laurel wreath. While Parnell still stands in his original location in O'Connell Street, closing off the north end of the central area of the city, the Victoria monument was dismantled in 1948.[40] Initially stripped of majestic decorum, the bronze statue of the queen languished in storage at the Royal Hospital Kilmainham, and was subsequently donated to the Australians, and unveiled in Sydney in 1987. Queen Victoria sits once more on a pedestal, if a lesser one than her original perch, while, ironically, the figures of Erin and the Irish soldier lie discarded in the tall grass on the premises of the National Museum overflow building at Daingean.

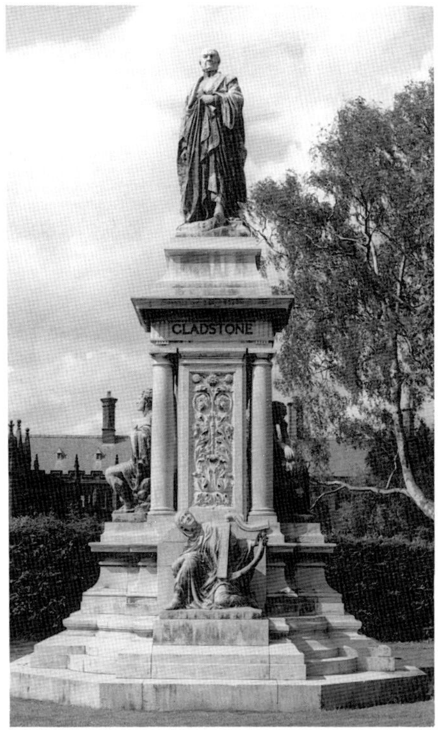

John Hughes, Gladstone Monument. *Erected 1925, Hawarden. Originally intended for Dublin.*

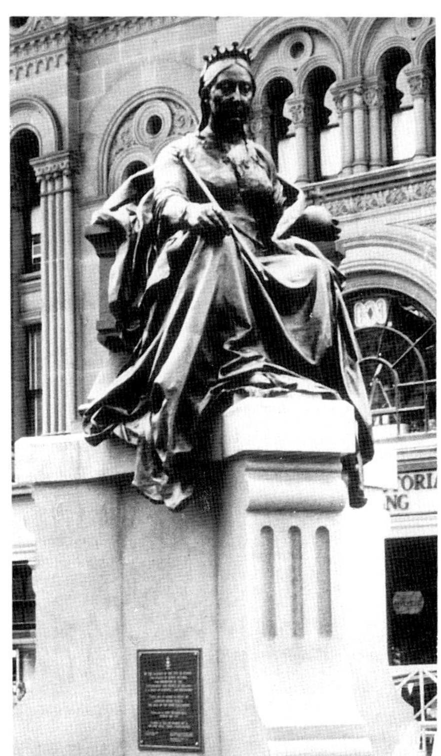

John Hughes, Queen Victoria. *From the Victoria Monument originally positioned in 1908 on the forecourt of Leinster House. Dismantled in 1948. The central figure from the monument was donated to Australia and unveiled there in 1987.*

The words of Lord Palmerston on the founding of the National Portrait Gallery in London in 1856 are of interest in relation to the range of portraits that were positioned on Dublin streets by the close of the nineteenth century. 'There cannot ... be a greater incentive to mental exertion, to noble actions, to good conduct on the part of the living, than for them to see before them the features of those who have done things which are worthy of our admiration, and whose example we are more induced to imitate when they are brought before us in the visible and tangible shape of portraits'.[41] The portrait statues positioned in Dublin reveal that the type of person considered worthy of admiration changed radically in the course of the century. These statues were of great import in their day and had particular significance in a country striving towards independence. Such public commemorations provide continuing evidence of changing attitudes in society.

Lord Palmerston's lofty ideals hardly withstand the passage of time. In the later twentieth century, while artistic or historic interest may occasionally attract a passerby to examine a nineteenth century street monument, it is more often the case that these works are passed unnoticed. The streets are certainly busier and the pace of life is faster. But it is also the case that the need to purge the streets of politically unacceptable monuments has destroyed something of their character. It is certain that some fine works have disappeared and along with them part of the heritage. The civic conflict – so much part of nineteenth century Dublin – could at one time be witnessed in the city's public monuments: sadly the terrorist's desire to obliterate the evidence of the past, ignores the place of history in the development of our culture. 'Statue and column, mausoleum and shrine, are trophies of a nation's triumphs or its tragedies'.[42]

Paula Murphy

Paula Murphy is a Lecturer in the History of Art Department in University College Dublin.

NOTES OVERLEAF

THE POLITICS OF THE STREET MONUMENT

NOTES

1. *The Elder Pliny's Chapters on the History of Art*, translated by K. Jex-Blake, 1968, p.23.
2. G K Whammond, *The Exhibition Guide through Dublin:* containing a description of the Public Buildings, Cathedral, Churches and Chapels, Dublin, 1853.
3. *Dublin University Magazine*, Vol.47, 1856, p.321. Review of J T Gilbert's *History of the City of Dublin*.
4. *The Dublin Builder*, August 15, 1862.
5. For further information on the Nelson monument, see Patrick Henchy, 'Nelson's Pillar', *Dublin Historical Record*, Vol X, No 1, March-May, 1948, p.53-63.
6. *The Dublin Builder*, April 1 1859.
7. The monument committee was divided between Lord Charlemont who favoured Christopher Moore for the commission and Lord Cloncurry who backed John Hogan. However it was Lord Charlemont who chaired the committee. See John Turpin, *John Hogan*, Irish Academic Press, 1982.
8. *The Dublin Builder*, March 1 1859. The attack on this statue has continued into the twentieth century. A biographer of Thomas Moore, Terence de Vere White, wrote in 1977 that this statue is 'a libel in metal, holding (Moore) up to posterity's ridicule and contempt'. Art historians have similarly dismissed the work: Jeanne Sheehy suggested in 1980 that it has 'deservedly been an object of derision ever since it was put up in 1857' and Homan Potterton in 1978 described it as 'the most dismal failure of all'. Both writers consider the Hogan model far superior. Comparison of these two images reveals however that the Hogan model is a studied essay in lyricism, an attempt to imbue the portrait with a sense of poetry, and these elements only operate in a superficial manner. The Christopher Moore work is a solid and worthy portrait, friendly and honest, rather than artificial and dainty, and much more in keeping with painted likenesses of the man.
9. Apathy, carelessness, incompetence and unscrupulousness were just some of the words used to describe committee members in an article examining the issue of competitions in *The Dublin Builder*, January 15 1865.
10. The foundation stone for a public monument to Wolfe Tone was laid in Dublin on August 15 1898 amidst a huge public celebration. The stone was presented by a nationalist association in Belfast and was laid at the junction of St. Stephen's Green and Grafton Street. The whole event was reported in *The Times*, August 16 1898. However sufficient money was not forthcoming, as communities around the country were committed to local memorials. The commemoration was reactivated in 1964 when a competition to choose an appropriate sculptor was held and was won by Edward Delaney. A Tone monument was finally unveiled at a different corner of the Green on November 18 1967.
11. R F Foster, *Modern Ireland 1600-1972*, The Penguin Press, 1988, p.311. Davis was eventually commemorated by a public monument in Dublin in 1966. Erected in College Green, this statue group is also the work of Edward Delaney. Davis had earlier been commemorated in a statue by John Hogan, completed in 1852. However with no site prepared for the work, it was positioned on Davis's grave in Mount Jerome, before being moved to the City Hall. For further information on this monument *see* Turpin, op.cit.
12. An extensive collection of documents preserved in the Archives of the City Hall in Dublin records the progress of the O'Connell Monument from its inception to its completion, amongst which Ms Ch 6/1 and Ms Ch 6/2 have been particularly relevant in the context of this study.
13. 'Genius knows no geography; it despises the conventional boundaries of states and empire ... if each nation were to isolate itself from the rest, and, surrounded by an impenetrable barrier of prejudice, were to reject the refining influence of the arts, sciences and literature of other countries, civilization would halt, and the world would soon relapse into primeval barbarism'. Letter from John F Fraser to the O'Connell Committee, June 4 1864, supporting the selection of Foley. Ms Ch 6/2, City Hall, Dublin.
14. Quoted in the report of committee member, Mr O'Sullivan, who, as a friend of John Hogan, was well versed in the problems faced by Irish sculptors, and was opposed to the idea that there was no talent in Ireland. Ibid.
15. *The Freeman's Journal*, August 14 1882.
16. *The Freeman's Journal*, September 5 1882.
17. The irony was reversed in 1929 when the O'Brien statue was moved to O'Connell Street. In its new location it is not only positioned behind the O'Connell Monument but is considerably dwarfed by it.
18. *The Irish Times*, December 27 1870.
19. Ibid.
20. A statue of Grattan, dated 1827, the work of Sir Francis Chantrey, had already been erected in the Royal Exchange, (which became the City Hall in 1852). However this was a private commission, paid for by friends of Grattan.
21. The Origins, Progress and Completion of the Grattan Statue, compiled by the Hon. John P Vereker, 1881. Ms 1703, Trinity College Dublin.
22. *The Dublin Builder*, February 15 1864.
23. *The Irish Times*, January 7 1876.
24. Op. cit. Ms 1703, Trinity College Dublin.
25. *The Irish Times*, May 3 1870.
26. *The Irish Times*, August 15 1986..
27. *The Irish Times*, February 23 1880.
28. *Ibid.*
29. A letter from J H Foley to David McBirney, Esq, dated August 25 1869, and published in the *Statement of Proceedings taken to erect the Gough Equestrian Statue*.
30. *The Irish Times*, June 5, 1872.
31. *The Dublin Builder*, August 15 1861.
32. *The Irish Independent*, August 8 1898, posed the question: 'Is it to be tolerated that such a man should have one of the prominent public places in the capital of Ireland for a statue ...', and further, described the proposal as 'a daring insult to the memory of Parnell'.
33. *Minutes of Dublin City Council.* Meeting held August 8 1898, Motion No. 287.
34. 'Sooner or later Ireland will put up a statue. When that time comes they will probably prefer to put up a statue of their own and make it a real Irish tribute'. Extract from a letter, Herbert Gladstone to his brother, Henry, dated July 3 1924, and quoted in Alan Denson, *John Hughes, Sculptor, 1865-1941*, A Documentary Biography, Kendal, 1969.
35. The Gladstone Monument was executed by John Hughes. The portrait figure is accompanied by allegorical statues: Erin, Classical Learning, Finance and Eloquence. A further attempt was made, in 1924, to have the monument erected in Dublin, in the Phoenix Park. However the Government declined to accept the offer and the Memorial Committee offered the monument instead to the Trustees of St Deiniol's Library at Hawarden, where it was erected in April 1925. One Trustee suggested that 'if at some future date, the political situation in Ireland makes it possible to erect the statue in Dublin, it should be released and presented to Ireland as originally intended'. See Denson, op. cit.
36. *The Irish Independent*, October 9 1899.
37. This quotation from Redmond's speech at the memorial meeting in Albany, reported in the *Albany, New York Times Union*, November 13 1899. The press reports of the Tallon/Redmond American journey can be consulted in *The Parnell Monument Fund* in the National Library of Ireland.
38. 'The Three Monuments', *W B Yeats, Collected Poems,* Dublin/London, 1933.
39. *The Senate Speeches of W B Yeats*, edited by Donald R Pearce, Indiana University Press, 1960, p.98.
40. Several contemporary newspaper reports, amongst which *The Irish Press*, July 7, and *The Irish Times*, July 23, detail the removal of the statue in 1948. Criticism of the statue and its location began earlier in the twentieth century. A particularly hard-hitting attack can be found in *The Star*, August 17 1929, where the monument is described as 'repugnant to national feelings'. The writer states that 'those who were responsible for the erection of the statue of Queen Victoria and similar monuments here were not representative of the Irish people'. (The idea for a Victoria commemoration originated with members of the Royal Dublin Society). The article continues: 'Monuments like (those to) Victoria and Nelson in the streets of the Capital evoke memories which it would be in the best interests of all to forget. There is no room in the new Ireland for the outlook and the attitude to things Irish which prompted their erection...'. This article is quoted in Denson, op.cit.
41. Lord Palmerston's words are now placed at the entrance to the National Portrait Gallery in London.
42. *Dublin University Magazine*, Vol.47, 1856, p.320. Op.cit.

IRISH ART AND DESIGN EDUCATION

This article aims to provide a survey of the development of professional art and design education in Ireland.

The Eighteenth Century

In the early eighteenth century the Dublin Guild of Cutlers, Painter-Steyners and Stationers had an indirect educational function through its master-apprentice system, but this did not extend to formal instruction in drawing. The Renaissance practice of teaching fine art in academies by means of life and antique drawing did not take root in Ireland until the early nineteenth century. In fact, the European academic tradition was not the most influential source for Irish art educational institutions. Far more important in both Britain and Ireland was the commercial imperative which recognised the study of drawing as being useful to economic development. Most of the art and design colleges and departments of today owe their foundation more to the traditions of artisan training and to state-supported technical education, than to continental Neoclassical ideas of art education.

Throughout Europe, training in the crafts, such as weaving, metalwork and ceramics, remained in the province of the guilds and small workshops until the industrial revolution. However, in the mid-seventeenth century, at the French Royal Manufactories of carpets, ceramics and furniture, it was realised that a training in drawing was essential to the creation of new patterns in two and three dimensions. In short, the role of creative visual ideas, grounded in the historical repertoire of classical ornament, was seen as essential to modern applications.

France led the European production of luxury craft products in the late seventeenth and eighteenth centuries.[1] French tapestries, carpets, silverwork, furniture and ceramic services were exported and copied all over Europe. The French established the Écoles Gratuites de Dessin – free drawing schools – which were a vital new ingredient of art education. The teaching methodology in these schools included the copying of casts and prints of ornament.[2] The inclusion of life drawing was important too because the ornamental artist had to be able to master the figure in designs for fabric, for carved and plastered panels and ceramic decoration. The theory was that craftwork was the manual realisation of drawing, and a crucial division between invention and realisation was thus underlined. This had long been the case in architecture but was now applied systematically to the applied arts. The education of the designer (one who made drawings for the decorative arts) was therefore of the greatest importance in defining style for the artisan, while training in manual skill remained in the domain of the commercial workshop.

John Turpin traces the history of professional art and design education in Ireland from the 18th century to the present day.

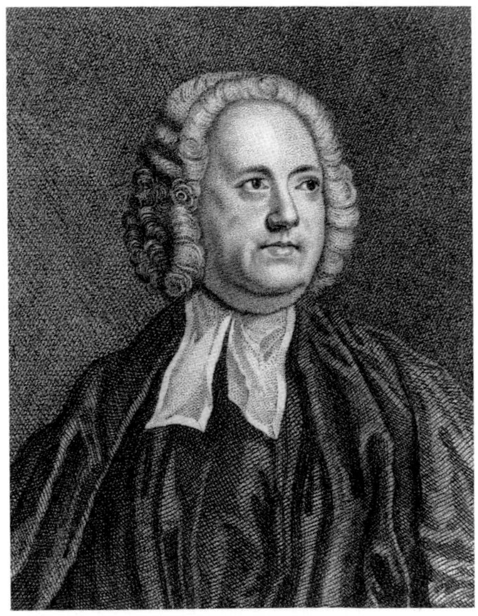

S Harding, Rev Dr Samuel Madden, *engraving. National Library of Ireland. By offering premiums for drawing to students, Madden can be considered the father of Irish Art Studies.*

Where does Ireland fit into European art education developments of the eighteenth century? The state-sponsored academies and free schools of drawing of France and other continental countries – had they any Irish equivalent? The absence of a resident monarch and court was a major disadvantage in the stimulation of the fine and applied arts; the very limited artistic culture was another. Aspiring young painters in the early eighteenth century went to London or to the continent to develop their style and find a wider market. The lack of developed taste for pictures and sculptures, the absence of princely pride, and the lack of artists all militated against the founding of a state academy of arts. Although there were some half-hearted attempts, the political will was not there.

However, the situation with regard to the training of artisans was very different. The central cause was economic. After centuries of strife the Irish agricultural and industrial economy was, in the early eighteenth century, very depleted. However, by the 1730s the landed gentry were firmly established on their estates, and increasing agricultural prosperity allowed them to apply themselves to the acquisition of luxury goods to fill their new houses. The demand stimulated production, with the Anglo-Irish nobility, gentry and professionals in town and country – notably in Dublin, Cork and Limerick – providing the market.

Anglo-Irish intellectuals, such as Swift and Berkeley, saw the value of developing the Irish economy which was, at the time, very backward compared to that of Britain. There was also a genuine desire to stimulate the fine arts as an aspect of civilised living. However, it is important to stress that this urge to improve the condition of the arts in Ireland came, not from an intellectual Renaissance ideal, but from economic good sense which aimed to enrich the country and its inhabitants by stimulating trade and manufacture, bringing peace, civilisation and prosperity to all. The principal agent of this practical-minded approach was the Dublin Society which was founded in 1731. This can bear comparison to other European economic societies (like the Society of Arts, London). The Dublin Society's educational aims reflected the practicalities of the French Enlightenment. The Society, led by men like Thomas Prior and Samuel Madden, avoided pure speculation, preferring to advocate ways and means of increasing national wealth and prosperity through stimulating improved methods of agricultural and industrial production.

Part of this economic approach took the form of the promotion of prizes for agricultural and industrial improvement, and for the best work in the fine and applied arts. Samuel Madden, a connoisseur of the fine arts, in his open published letters to the gentry, sought to cut down foreign imports and to stimulate native industry, mainly by providing patterns for woven and printed textiles, such as silk-poplin. (A very large industry was established by the Huguenots in Dublin.[3]) At first the Society paid the fees of boys sent to Robert West's private drawing school from 1746 and the Society took over the school in 1750. There were other practitioners who taught drawing, but their schools were short-lived.

In view of the Society's orientation to design for manufacture, it is not surprising that it was its School of Landscape and Ornament, founded in 1756, that was best attended.[4] The School of Architecture followed in 1764, and the School of Modelling much later in 1811 – a result of the greater emphasis on sculpture in Neoclassical theory and in Dublin's public buildings. Teaching in these schools (or classes) was carried out through the copying of plaster casts, original drawings and engravings of the best continental examples. There were annual competitions for prizes. This provided the young Dublin artisans who attended the free drawing schools with a knowledge of the Rococo and later Neoclassical styles including the classical architectural orders. It was also a training in technical drawing useful in draughting patterns for the textile industry and for all types of architectural applications in the building trades. This familiarisation with the international language of classical ornament and proportion was of enormous benefit to artisans of all descriptions.

A central factor in the unfaltering emergence and continuation of the Dublin Society Schools was the support of the Irish Parliament. The Parliament was anxious to increase the wealth of the kingdom and saw the Dublin Society as a means of awarding subsidies to stimulate economic growth. The drawing schools were involved in this useful economic process.

Accordingly, part of the Society's annual grant from parliament went towards the payment of salaries for the masters of the schools and to other running costs. Through its fine arts committee, the Society managed the schools well, using the money available to the best advantage. Original Old Master drawings were acquired for copying purposes, and the collection of antique casts was expanded. Tuition was offered free by the Society because its primary aim was to provide an education in drawing to sons of artisans who could not afford private drawing masters. Since the schools were free, state-supported, and aimed mainly to assist the craftsman, they can be compared readily to the French Écoles Gratuites de Dessin; the Dublin Society Schools mark the arrival of state-supported art education well before the School of Design in London in 1836.

In addition to the artisans from the applied arts and building trades, aspiring

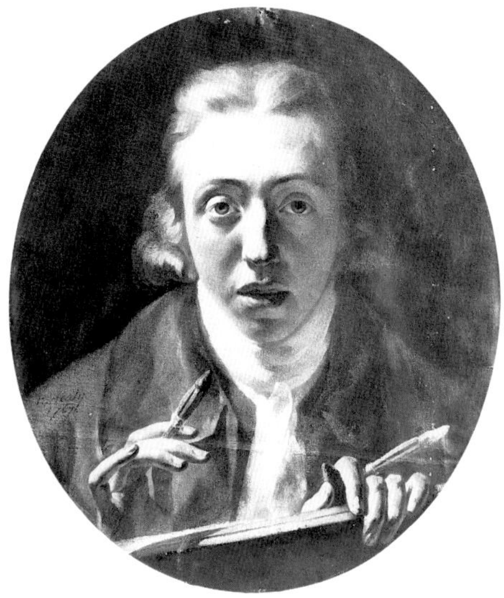

Robert Healy, William Healy, *black and white chalk on paper, date 1767. National Gallery of Ireland. Monochrome chalk drawing was the chief technique taught in the Figure drawing school of the Dublin Society.*

painters also benefited greatly. The emergence of the Irish school of landscape can, indeed, be traced to the Dublin Society where the pictorial conventions of Dutch and Italian landscape painting were taught by means of copying engravings. These artists then proceeded to Rome where they absorbed the tradition of ideal landscape. A key point is that since the schools did not form part of a classical academy, they were free from the dogma of the hierarchy of genres through which figure painting was exalted at the expense of landscape painting. In the Dublin Society Schools there existed a free tolerant approach which provided comprehensive art and design education at a basic level. The Irish landscape painting tradition had its roots in the teaching of the Society's schools which provided young Irish artists with artistic models with which to approach Irish subjects.[5]

The main problem about the curriculum in the eighteenth and early nineteenth centuries was that it did not include the teaching of painting. The schools were drawing schools only – largely because their aim was practical, to aid the making of plans, elevations and fabric patterns, and to assist the artisan including the commercial engraver. The teaching of High Art was never an aim, nor would it have been a priority for the pragmatic, practically-minded gentry who ran the Dublin Society. The result was, however, a void in Irish art education, whereby painters had to go abroad to complete their training.

From the late eighteenth century onwards the professional artists of Dublin felt the lack of an Irish academy for painters and of a school of painting. The Dublin Society obliged them by giving them access to its life class and by providing exhibition space to show their work. However, it was only with the founding of the Royal Hibernian Academy in 1823, and the establishment of its schools of the antique and of life drawing and painting, that it was possible for Irish painters to receive an education at home. The founding of the RHA introduced a duality into Irish art education which prevailed for the rest of the century. There emerged a pattern whereby students spent their initial period in the Royal Dublin Society Schools learning to draw, and then transferred to learn painting at the Academy. Modelling was, however, always taught at the Royal Dublin Society Schools and not at the Academy.

The maintenance of the life class was central to the Academy's teaching; the Royal Dublin Society also maintained a life class, (although at times it fell into abeyance as the Royal Dublin Society felt that the main responsibility for fine art education lay with the Academy). The British government criticised the fact that it was subsidising two life classes and argued for their amalgamation, but there was no agreement, following two state enquiries in 1857 and 1906, on which school should be eliminated.

Nevertheless, it is clear that, from the 1850s, the state saw the Royal Dublin Society School of Design and its successors as the focus of investment in Irish art education. Unlike other continental academies, the RHA was never to evolve into a state-sponsored art education establishment. It remained, like its British counterpart, primarily an exhibiting body.[6]

The Nineteenth Century

After the Act of Union of 1801, the British government no longer had faith in the Royal Dublin Society as an agent of public support for the economy, and its grant was consequently reduced. This put pressure on the Society which became increasingly isolated from those in power, and its political unionism did not recommend it to the Irish nationalist members of parliament. Lack of funds negated the Society's desire to expand design education to the more advanced level, which would have brought the schools into line with the new schools of design which were spreading all over England in the 1830s and 1840s. British parliamentarians and administrators realised that, despite the industrial revolution, the United Kingdom was far behind its rival France in terms of the education of artisans for mass-manufacture. The Royal Dublin Society wished to develop its design curriculum too, but lacked the necessary resources.[7]

The United Kingdom was no exception to the general nineteenth-century rule whereby the state extended its bureaucratic control over many aspects of national life – particularly education. The Royal Dublin Society's petition for extra support to develop its schools into a School of Design was rejected. Instead, the Board of Trade agreed to subsidise the schools, on its own terms, as a School of Design. The Board's successor from 1854, the Department of Science and Art, tightened its control by making the Royal Dublin Society Schools conform to a London curriculum which was geared exclusively to the education of artisans for industry. This was somewhat inappropriate for Dublin, where the main manufactures were brewing, distilling and biscuit manufacture. In 1877 the Dublin Science and Art Museum Act completed the process of creeping nationalisation and the school became a wholly state-controlled institution renamed the Dublin Metropolitan School of Art. From the 1850s, women were admitted and evening classes instituted for artisans. The social composition prevalent in the eighteenth and nineteenth centuries, which had been mostly Protestant artisan boys, now included many middle-class Protestant women.

In the second half of the nineteenth century, as a result of the policies of the Department of Science and Art, similar schools were established at Cork, Belfast, Waterford, Limerick, Clonmel and Derry under local committees receiving grants from the Department.[8] The movement for art education in Cork had begun earlier with the establishment of the Cork Society for the Promotion of the Fine Arts in 1816, supported by the gentry. A collection of plaster casts of the Vatican marbles, made under Canova's direction, was presented to the Prince Regent by Pope Pius VII in gratitude for the defeat of the French. This collection came to Cork on the petition of Lord Ennismore, a prominent County Cork art collector. The casts were displayed in the former Apollo theatre from 1818 which, thus, became the first drawing school in Cork. This was where the artists Daniel Maclise and John Hogan began their careers. This drawing school appears to have lost momentum, and the collection passed to the Royal Cork Institution, a literary society (founded in 1808) based at the old Custom House from 1832. In 1825 the Cork Mechanics' Institute was founded; it provided classes in drawing to apprentice craftsmen, but it did not last long.

The school of design movement in Ireland of the 1840s must be seen in the general context of the movement for higher education in Ireland. In 1845 Queen's College Cork was founded and became a constituent college, along with Galway and Belfast, of the new Queen's University

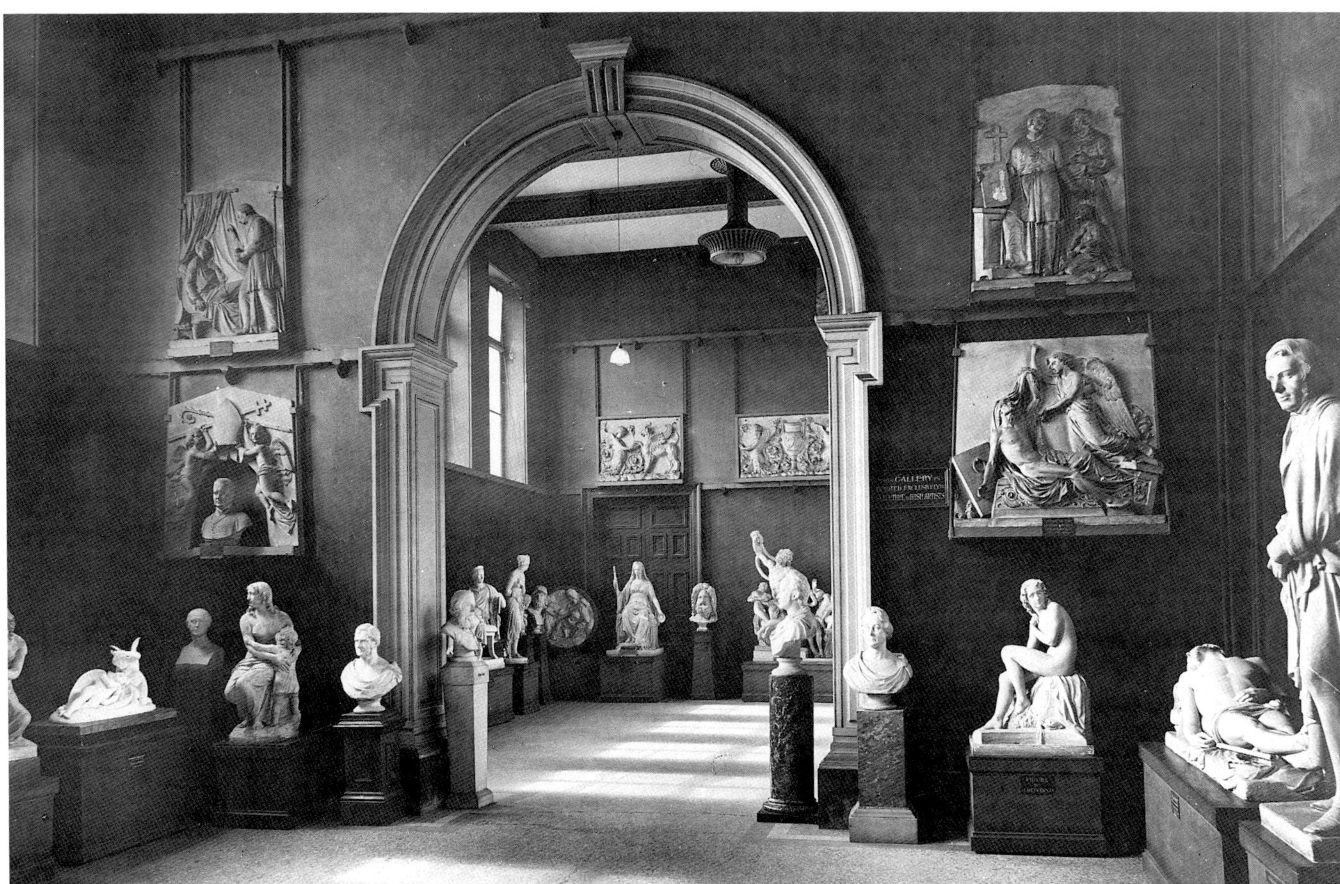

Crawford School of Art, Cork, the Sculpture Gallery 1884. *Crawford Municipal Art Gallery, Cork.*
The collection of Vatican casts laid the foundation of art education in Cork. Cast collections like these were essential for all art schools.

of Ireland. In 1849 leading Cork citizens appealed to the Board of Trade for support for the setting up of a school of design. The Board sent Charles Heath Wilson, of the London school of design, to Cork to report back. Finally, a Cork school of design was opened in 1850 using the Papal casts in the old Custom House; it was to remain the location of the Cork School of Art until 1979. A fine series of purpose built art galleries was added in 1884, paid for by W H Crawford, a local brewer, and opened by the Prince of Wales in 1885.[9]

Following the Famine of 1845-47, which was very bad in the south-west of the country, there was, in Ireland, the beginning of an awareness of the importance of industrial development and of technical training. Faith in Ireland's traditional agricultural economy had been undermined, and a national industrial exhibition was held in Cork in 1852 to promote the concept of industrialisation. There were further international exhibitions in Dublin in 1853 and 1865, and many other exhibitions of art and industry around Ireland which took on a major art educational function by introducing people to a wide range of art and ornament.

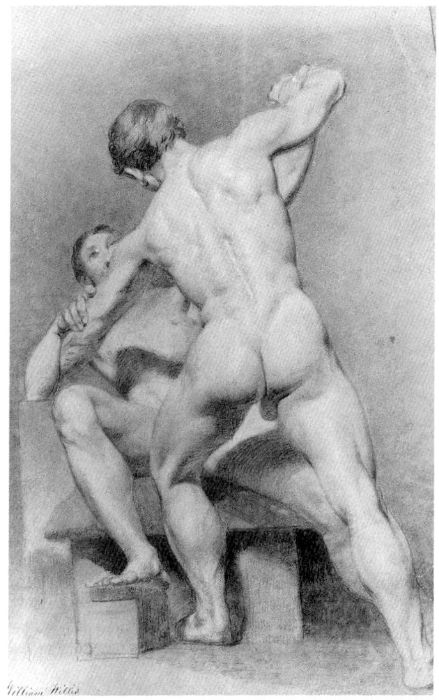

William Willes, Two Male Models, *Crawford Municipal Art Gallery, Cork. Willes was the first headmaster of the Cork School of Design in 1850. This is a good example of Victorian academic life drawing with poses evocative of high art.*

Cork

The initial curriculum of the Cork School of Design included drawing of ornament; geometric and perspective drawing; watercolour, tempera and oil painting; drawing of natural forms; drawing, painting and modelling from the cast. Life drawing, however, was absent, thus reflecting the utilitarian London curriculum. The first headmaster in Cork was William Willes, a Cork-born artist who had studied at the Royal Academy London; his tenure was short as he died in Spring 1851, although he had successfully established the School. During 1854 the School collided with the centralising and standardising regulations of Henry Cole of the Department of Science and Art, (as happened also at the Dublin School of Design in 1862 when Henry McManus the headmaster was forced to retire by the Department). The Department's grant to Cork was withdrawn, thus having the effect of also ending the local Corporation grant, which closed the School for a year.

Under a new Act of Parliament for establishing libraries and museums, local corporations had powers allowing them to fund schools of design. The rate-payers of Cork voted to support and revive the School, which was reopened in January 1856 with the appointment, as headmaster, of David W Reimbach from the Limerick School of Design. Between 1860 and 1889 the headmaster was James Brenan, Ireland's most important nineteenth-century art educator. He studied at the Royal Hibernian Academy Schools and went to London where he studied decorative art under the celebrated design theorist Owen Jones and Sir Matthew Digby Wyatt, assisting them in the decoration of the Crystal Palace. In 1855, he joined the Department's training school at Marlborough House, then took a teaching post at Birmingham School of Design, returning to South Kensington until 1860. He brought to Cork a full understanding of the South Kensington system of art education together with an appreciation of circumstances peculiar to Ireland. He was a very able art educationalist with a special interest in the application of art to industry.

Along with Alan Cole (son of Henry Cole) of South Kensington, Brenan devised a scheme for promoting design for lacemaking, particularly in relation to convent schools throughout the province of Munster from 1884. Antique lace specimens and designs were circulated and the small-scale industry grew extensively. This was developed largely to give employment to women in rural areas. On the 1 June 1889, Brenan became headmaster of the Dublin Metropolitan School of Art, where he continued his promotion of design for the lace industry which now included many centres in the north of Ireland. Lace was the first craft to be introduced into the Irish schools of art which were otherwise totally preoccupied with paper design. It was under Brenan's aegis that the new crafts were introduced in Dublin in the early years of the twentieth century.

Limerick, Waterford and Clonmel

In Limerick a School of Ornamental Art had existed from 1852 supported by the Board of Trade with David W Reimbach, from the staff of the Belfast School, as headmaster. He transferred to Cork as headmaster in 1856, and was succeeded by W L Casey; in 1896 the Corporation of Limerick took over management of the School. In Waterford, a School of Practical Art and Design was opened in 1852 through the Mechanics' Institute, and was supported by the Board of Trade; it ceased after some years but was re-established in 1881. Finally in Clonmel (which although small, was a major centre of coach building), a School of Art was established in 1854 in the Mechanics' Institute. James A Healy, formerly assistant to MacManus in Dublin, was headmaster. It did not last, probably because Clonmel was, as a town, too small to support a school, and because Cork and Waterford were able to provide for the region. This was the only example of an Irish state-supported art school disappearing permanently.

Belfast

The position of Belfast School of Design was different to other Irish schools because of the economic basis of the city.[10] Belfast, alone of all Irish centres was highly industrialised. The linen-damask industry, comparable only to the textile industries of the north of England, needed ornamental pattern for weaving, and for paper packaging in order to market goods. Already in 1847, one Belfast stationer had set up premises to print the decorated packages for exporting linen. It was to supply these commercial and industrial needs that the Belfast School of Design was founded in 1850 in rooms belonging to the Academical

Institution. Claude Nursey, former master at Leeds and Bradford Schools of Design, was headmaster, and he brought with him a knowledge of design for textiles. David Reimbach was his assistant.

An analysis of the first Belfast pupils in 1850 revealed that several established designers of 'sewed muslin' and damask were attending as students. Others were engravers, several of whom were 'designers of the paper bands and envelopes used in tying up rolls of linen'. The continuing demand from the linen industry and the ornamental printing trade led to a stipulation by many local manufacturers that all design apprentices should receive training in the school of art. Apprentices were released, and their fees supported the school. In 1855, Henry Cole of the Department of Science and Art cut the government grant from £300 down to £50 thus reducing the teaching budget of the school, which survived mostly on local subscriptions. Public opinion, as in the case of Cork in 1854, forced the government to review its position, and the annual grant was restored in 1860.

In 1863 a new 'constitution and rules were adopted', and the School was re-established as a Government School of Art, managed by a local committee which included the eminent Belfast architect Sir Charles Lanyon. Queen's College, (the University), also provided financial assistance and some accommodation for lectures, and many wealthy Belfast citizens established scholarships and prizes. The School was taken over by the Corporation of Belfast in 1901 and moved to new premises at North Street. In 1906 it became part of the Municipal Technical Institute buildings and additional craft classes were accommodated. In the nineteenth century, while general art provision did exist at the School for 'ladies and gentlemen,' it was its teaching of design for industrial mass production which distinguished it from all other Irish art educational institutions.

Derry

The last Victorian school of art to be founded was that at Derry, set up in 1874 with support from the Science and Art Department. The first headmaster in 1875 was the painter J Poole Abbey, originally educated at the Cork School of Design, who resigned in 1887 and later taught part-time in the Dublin School. He was succeeded by Robert J Douglas, of the Dundee School, and in 1889 by W E Crow of Manchester. In 1890 the Corporation of Derry agreed to support the school and it became part of the Municipal Technical School.

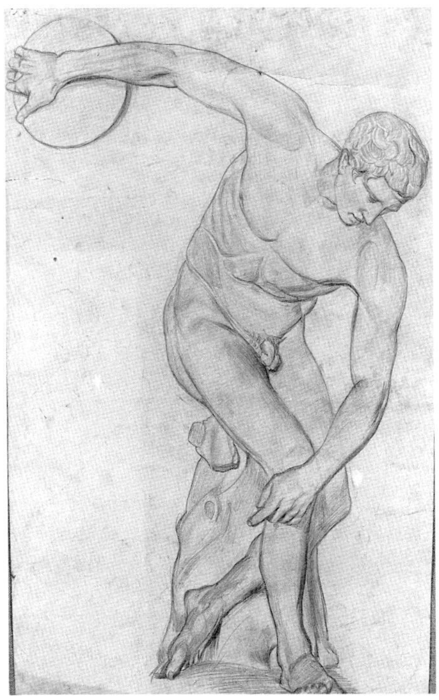

Harry Kernoff, The Diskobolos, *pencil drawing, National Gallery of Ireland. Every student had to master figure drawing in this way before being admitted to the Life Room. The emphasis on contour was a Neoclassical characteristic.*

It is clear from the staff appointments in these art schools that there was considerable movement of staff from British schools to Irish ones and also within Ireland itself. Whatever the faults of the South Kensington system, and of the closures demanded by Henry Cole's ruthlessness and by the inappropriateness of his utilitarian curriculum to Ireland in general, nevertheless, the policies of the Department laid the foundation of a network of regional art schools, and sustained the funding of the long established Royal Dublin Society Schools.

The last thirty years of the nineteenth century, notably the 1870s and 1880s, were the high-point of the RHA. Most of Ireland's important painters studied at its school. Having mastered the language of painting there, they proceeded to the Royal Academy of Fine Art at Antwerp or to the Académie Julian in Paris. They then commenced their independent professional careers by painting in Brittany, before returning to Ireland. The Academy schools were central to this peregrination and played a major role in forming the substantial group of Irish artists who brought French 'plein-air' painting to Ireland. The Academy provided an essential preparation or bridge to France and thus played a key role in facilitating the first phase of modern French-influenced painting in Ireland.[11]

The Turn of the Century

The early years of the twentieth century were very important for Irish art education. The teachings of William Morris and his associates had led to the English arts and crafts movement which was to have extensive influence on the continent and in North America. The Irish Arts and Crafts Society founded in 1894 set in train a chain of events which led to major innovations in Irish art education. Hitherto all Irish art schools, apart from the RHA, had followed the curriculum of the Science and Art Department. This was composed of a vast proliferation of individual subjects, such as the drawing of ornament and of still life, mechanical drawing and plaster-cast drawing. There was no craft experience although, as we saw, lace-making was taught locally in Ireland.

The revolt against this South Kensington system throughout Britain was led by arts and crafts educators, like Walter Crane and W R Lethaby. The result was the termination of the Science and Art Department and the transformation of the National Art Training School at South Kensington into the Royal College of Art in 1899. Other schools such as the Birmingham School of Art became major centres for arts and crafts thinking. Craft classes were now introduced into the curriculum of the art schools all over Britain. In this way the arts and crafts ideology came to dominate British art education until well into the twentieth century.

Conservative government policy during the 1890s tried to defuse the Home Rule movement in Ireland by means of capital investment and by administrative and educational reform. As a result of this, and of pressure from Irish members of parliament, the Department of Agriculture and Technical Instruction was set up in Dublin in 1900. The Technical Instruction branch controlled all Irish art schools (and even inspected the RHA schools). This marked the beginning of a specifically Irish state-controlled art education system. By

IRISH ART AND DESIGN EDUCATION

1913 the Department had re-styled the old Victorian curriculum as the Technical Schools Examinations in Art, which were to dominate all Irish art schools until 1980. In character they resembled their Victorian predecessor although they were significantly re-modelled in a fine art direction in 1936.

In the early twentieth century, the Department of Agriculture and Technical Instruction was anxious to develop the Irish economy in a manner similar to that envisaged by the old Irish parliament and the Dublin Society in the eighteenth century. In this way the development of a new crafts curriculum could be seen as expanding national industry. The Irish cultural revival, which was under way during these years, stimulated a major renaissance of the crafts: stained glass, fine metalwork and enamelling, embroidery and fine printing.[12] The Dublin Metropolitan School of Art played a key role in this – particularly through its newly-established departments of stained glass and metalwork. Students won many prizes in the National Competitions which were held annually at South Kensington. Belfast too, with its stronger industrial background, developed its crafts – notably silverwork, design for printing and design for textiles. There existed a comparable level of achievement between Dublin and Belfast which was to be removed by the Government of Ireland Act of 1920, when Belfast came under separate jurisdiction. The impetus given to the crafts in Ireland in the early twentieth century was to have a long-lasting effect, although the educational momentum declined in the 1920s and 1930s.

In the early years of the century the education of painters was to shift irrevocably from the Royal Hibernian Academy schools to the Dublin Metropolitan School of Art. This was largely the result of the Department's policy of developing the main state art school in Dublin into a comprehensive art educational establishment to include fine art as well as design. After the 1906 parliamentary enquiry, the government had little faith in the RHA schools which had been severely criticised for incompetence. It resolved to centre all its investment and student scholarships at the DMSA. The one great argument for the Academy schools – the education of artists by artists – had been undermined by the Department's employment of William Orpen to teach in the life class at the DMSA at a salary which the RHA could not afford. There was no able figure-painter and teacher at the Academy after the death of Osborne in 1903. Orpen's brilliant technique, derived from his experience at the Slade School, and his dynamic personality, made the DMSA a magnet which drew in able students. His pupils, and their pupils in turn, were to dominate the teaching of painting up to 1969.[13] The beginning of Orpen's regular teaching at the DMSA in 1906 marked the effective end of the Academy as the main centre for fine art education. The burning of the RHA school in the 1916 Rising further damaged its position, although the school continued in rented premises and was terminated only in 1941. With the opening of the RHA Gallagher Gallery in recent years, there are plans afoot today to revive the Academy's schools on a postgraduate basis.

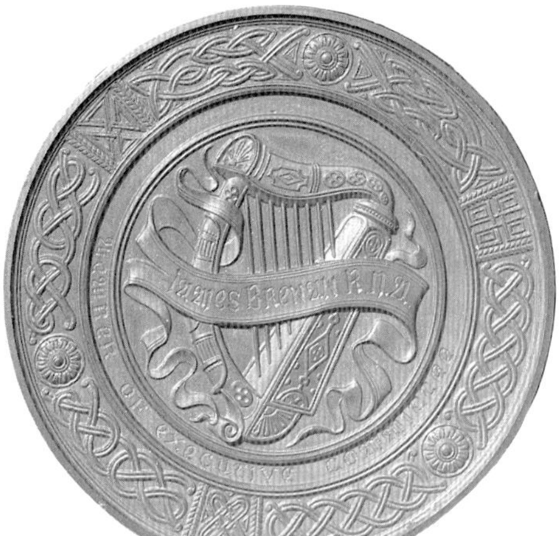

Cork Industrial Exhibition of 1883, medal award to James Brenan RHA as member of the Executive Committee, National College of Art and Design. The medal is an early example of the Celtic Revival in the applied arts. This movement began to gather momentum during the 1880s.

The government of the Irish Free State had little time or resources to allocate to the DMSA, which from 1924 was directly controlled by the Department of Education. This seemingly eccentric arrangement was similar to that of the Royal College of Art in London. Centralised government control of the DMSA and the RCA by the respective departments of state was a legacy of the Victorian period. This was in marked contrast to all other state art schools in Ireland – north or south. They were taken over by municipalities and run by Technical Instruction Committees. In the Free State, the Vocational Education Act of 1930 set up a country-wide system of Vocational Education Committees which were controlled by elected representatives while the Department of Education ruled on funding and appointments. Municipal control meant that local pride and local professional influence served to support art schools, such as those at Cork and Limerick, which fared far better in the new state than the DMSA which suffered from lack of adequate planning and funding by the Department.

Nevertheless, the Department of Education realised the necessity of reforming the system of art education and, in 1927, summoned a panel of French art educational inspectors to advise. Their report advocated an ideal French-style institution (which did not exist even in France), combining the fine and decorative arts, subject to a powerful art inspectorate, which did not exist in Ireland. Their impractical, if well-intentioned, report was ignored by the Department. It was not until 1936 that a reformed college structure with departments of painting, sculpture and design was set up with a professor to head each. The course was to cover three years leading to a diploma. The painting curriculum since 1920 had been dominated by Séan Keating, that of sculpture by Oliver Sheppard. The headmaster since 1918, George Atkinson, who had been formed by the RCA and the arts and crafts movement, advocated a major emphasis on design. The new professor of design, Bernardus Romin, was a Dutchman highly-skilled in the graphic techniques of the 1930s, but too dogmatic to be a good teacher. Many of the senior personnel of the National College of Art and of the Royal Hibernian Academy were the same people, which brought both institutions very close. Effectively, the NCA absorbed the Irish figurative academic tradition to itself. This fusion was in the long run to contribute to the build up of modernist pressure against the NCA leading to the student revolution of 1968-71.

Post-War Developments

Irish art education stagnated in the war years and afterwards. Thomas Bodkin's *Report on the Arts in Ireland* of 1949[14] pointed to what needed to be done – particularly the need for a revival of the crafts and design for industry. During the 1950s at the NCA a craft revival did take place, but on a piecemeal, subject-centred basis with little comprehensive curricular think-

IRISH ART AND DESIGN EDUCATION

ing. Most of the college's students still sat for the Department's Technical Schools Examination in Art. The managerial structure of the NCA run by the Technical Instruction Branch of the Department was not helpful.

Just as in the eighteenth century the main impulse for the development of education in design came from economic necessity, so also in the 1960s. Protectionism was to be abandoned in favour of membership of the European Economic Community – where Irish goods would have to compete in a free trade environment. In this new context, Córas Tráchtála (the Irish Export Board) saw the necessity of improving the design of Irish manufactures. A group of Scandinavian designers were called in to advise. Their report *Design in Ireland* (February 1962), was a devastating critique of Irish design and of Irish art and design eduction. This initiated a decade of debate on the need to overhaul Irish art education institutions which were agreed to be out-of-date. A series of government reports pointed out the necessary reforms – mainly that the National College of Art be established as an independent academic entity with adequate buildings and funding. Ministerial inaction provoked a crisis. A series of student occupations and closures of the college between 1968 and 1971 were the focus of national media and parliamentary attention. The crisis was essentially an academic one: the claims of modernism instead of traditional academic life drawing, together with the need for design to respond to modern industrial requirements.

It was also a crisis about control – should it be the Minister and his civil servants, or the academic body of staff and students who should determine the curriculum? Staff were divided among themselves as were the students, and all were suspicious of the Department which had done so little to act on the advice of successive government reports. The entire crisis was highly embarrassing for the Department. The outcome was the National College of Art and Design Act of 1971, which set up the college upon a new statutory foundation. In 1975 the college was restructured into the following faculties: Fine Art; Design; History of Art and Design and Complementary Studies; Art Education; and a Department of Foundation Studies. The upgrading of all diplomas to degree status followed between 1980 and 1990. Fine Art came to be dominated by the modernist idea-centred approach while the design departments related increasingly to industrial and commercial realities. History of Art and Design provided a theoretical and historical component of the degrees.

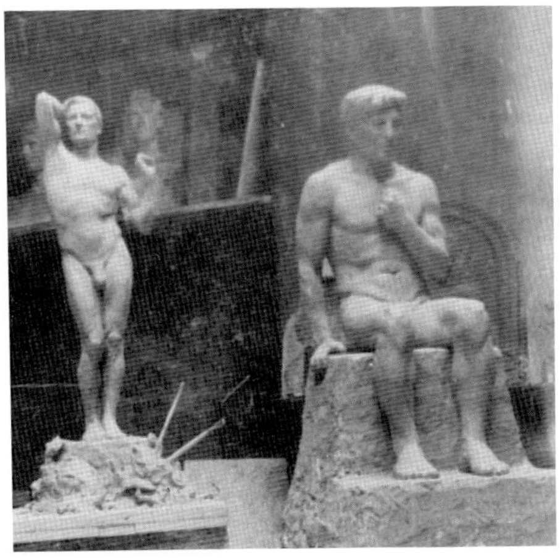

The Modelling Studio in the 1920s, Dublin Metropolitan School of Art. (D. White). *Modelling the male or female nude was the aim of sculpture teaching. On the left is 'Adam' by Kathleen Verschoyle and on the right 'Adam' by Hilda Roberts.*

The advent of Ireland's membership of the European Community led to funding for technical education throughout the Republic. This, in turn, led to the establishment of Regional Technical Colleges around the country. There were art and design departments in the RTCs at Waterford, Galway, Sligo, Carlow, Athlone and Letterkenny. The older traditional art schools at Cork and Limerick continued to grow and a new art school in Dun Laoghaire, Co. Dublin, emerged out of a vocational school. The College of Marketing and Design at Parnell Square (later at Mountjoy Square), can trace its origins to the schools of science and art set up in Kevin Street in 1888 under Dublin Corporation. The first design courses set up in 1962 were in retail display which led to significant growth in the next two decades, in parallel with the growth of the Regional Technical Schools throughout Ireland. These Irish departments of art, or schools of art and design, benefited by being part of the technical institutions since they thereby gained access to finance, such as the European Community Social Fund Scheme intended for skills training in technical education. The various British and Irish art departments which had originated as Schools of Design in the Victorian era, had gradually introduced fine art elements so that what were initially schools of design for manufacture became general all-purpose art schools. This enriched the cultural environment of the regions, although vocationalist opinion favoured design rather than fine art developments.

In order to validate the courses at the RTCs, which were mainly of a technical or business nature, the government set up the National Council for Educational Awards, informally in 1972, and statutorily in 1979. All the schools of art, departments of art, as well as the NCAD, were required to seek validation of their courses through this body. Diplomas, certificates and degrees in art and design subjects were awarded. This pattern was very similar to that of the Council for National Academic Awards in the United Kingdom which awarded degrees and diplomas outside the universities. The NCAD became an all-degree college, with degrees also at Cork and Limerick Colleges of Art and Design.

In terms of curriculum, all the normal specialisations of modern art and design are found around the country. At NCAD there is the greatest concentrated range including industrial design (engineering) which had been called for so often during the 1960s. This was taught from 1975 in conjunction with the National Institute of Higher Education (now University of Limerick). From the late 1980s, MA degrees were also awarded at the NCAD.

The story of the Belfast School of Art is completely unique in Ireland. Originating as a school of art on the top floor of the Municipal Institute, it got its own modern building in the 1960s and, in 1971 became a faculty of art and design of the Ulster Polytechnic. In turn this was amalgamated with the New University of Ulster at Coleraine in 1984. Thus the Belfast School of Art is now part of the University of Ulster and therefore gives its own degrees. It provided an important precedent for what was to happen all over the United Kingdom. The British pattern has been to absorb the art schools into polytechnics, which in the early 1990s have become independent universities with authority to award their own degrees. The Royal College of Art, as an exclusively postgraduate institution, is awarded this right under its independent Royal Charter.

Since the mid-nineteenth century the Irish experience has been very similar to that of Britain. In Ireland art and design

IRISH ART AND DESIGN EDUCATION

were taught together in institutions – often of a technical nature, with a centralised free-standing art college – the NCAD. This is very different to the continental experience where in general fine art and design are not taught together. There the historic fine art academies and the *atelier* system have modernised but nevertheless remain distinct. In Ireland and Britain, the state never took over the academies of art, which remain private, with a strong commercial dimension. On the continent, design means industrial and interior design as well as visual communications; fashion and craft schools are often specialised and separate from larger institutions; many of them are private. Degrees are not common and studio art at post-graduate level is little known. However, the basic primary qualification there entails a longer period of study than in Britain or Ireland.

As a massive state network of art education institutions, with undergraduate and postgraduate degrees, the British experience founded on the Schools of Design of the 1830s is the most extensive in Europe.

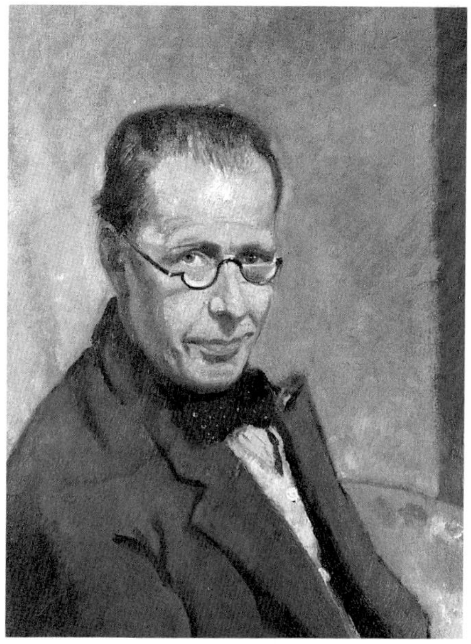

James Sleator, Sir William Orpen, *Hugh Lane Municipal Gallery of Modern Art. Orpen was immensely successful as a teacher of painting at the Dublin Metropolitan School of Art up to 1914 and his influence dominated the teaching of painting in Ireland from the 1900s to the 1960s.*

The Republic of Ireland has largely followed that pattern. In the near future, most art and design faculties in Britain will be part of the newly constituted polytechnic-universities; this will bring the British pattern, with its modular degrees, closer to the American, where art and design departments are often faculties of universities. In Ireland the recent arrival of greater autonomy to the Regional Technical Colleges under new legislation should improve the status of the art departments and of their qualifications. The country now has an extensive network of art education establishments, including the NCAD, one of the oldest art educational institutes in Europe, offering the widest range of art and design degrees in the country at undergraduate and post graduate level.

John Turpin

John Turpin took his degrees in art history at UCD and the Courtauld Institute of Art. He was appointed Professor of the History of Art at the NCAD in 1975 and Director in 1989.

NOTES

1. For a European background see, Nikolaus Pevsner, *Academies of Art,* Cambridge, 1940.
2. See *Academies of Art between Renaissance and Romanticism, Leids Kunsthistorisch, Jaarboek, V-VI,* 1986-87, SDU Uitgeverij, 'S-Gravenhage, 1989. This is a compendium of articles on continental art education, mainly on the eighteenth century.
3. Samuel Madden, *Reflections and Resolutions Proper to the Gentlemen of Ireland,* Dublin: A. Reilly, 1738, pp.186, 231.
4. On the Dublin Society and its work see, Henry F. Berry, *A History of the Royal Dublin Society,* London 1915; James Meenan and Desmond Clarke (eds.), *The Royal Dublin Society 1731-1981,* Dublin 1981; Anne Crookshank and the Knight of Glin, *The Painters of Ireland c.1660-1920,* London, 1978, ch.4.
5. On the individual schools see, John Turpin, 'The Dublin Society's School of Architectural Drawing', *Bulletin of the Irish Georgian Society,* XXVIII, 1985; – 'The Dublin Society's Figure Drawing School and the Fine Arts in Dublin, 1800-1849', *Dublin Historical Record,* XXXIX, 2 March 1986; – 'French influence on Eighteenth Century Art Education in Dublin', *Eighteenth Century Ireland,* Vol.5, 1990; – 'The Dublin Society School of Ornament in the Eighteenth Century', *Journal of the Royal Society of Antiquaries of Ireland,* Vol.116 (1986); – 'The School of Figure Drawing of the Dublin Society in the Eighteenth Century', *Dublin Historical Record,* XL, 1, December 1986, and XL, 2 March 1987.
6. See compendium of articles: 'The Royal Hibernian Academy of Arts', *Martello,* special issue, 1991; John Turpin, 'The Royal Hibernian Academy Schools, The First Eighty Years 1826-1906', *Irish Arts Review, Yearbook, 1991-92.*
7. See Clive Bell, *The Schools of Design,* London, 1963.
8. Walter Strickland, *A Dictionary of Irish Artists,* Dublin, 1913, II, pp.579-91 and 652-58. See also William P. Coyne, *Ireland, Industrial and Agricultural, Handbook for the Irish Pavilion,* Glasgow International Exhibition, 1901.
9. On the Cork School, see the *Illustrated Summary Catalogue of the Crawford Municipal Art Gallery,* compiled by Peter Murray, Cork: VEC, 1991.
10. *The Ulster College of Art and Design,* commemorative booklet, Belfast: The Education Committee, 1970.
11. *The Irish Impressionists,* exhibition catalogue, compiled by Julian Campbell, The National Gallery of Ireland, October 1984.
12. See Jeanne Sheehy, *The Rediscovery of Ireland's Past, the Celtic Revival, 1830-1930,* London: Thames and Hudson, 1980.
13. See Bruce Arnold, *Orpen, Mirror to an Age,* London,1981; and John Turpin, 'William Orpen as Student and Teacher', *Studies,* LXVIII, Nos. 271 and 272 (1979).
14. Thomas Bodkin, *Report on the Arts in Ireland,* Dublin: Stationery Office, 1949.

HENRY TRENCH (c.1685-1726) PAINTER AND ILLUSTRATOR

Nicola Figgis
discusses the importance of prizewinning drawings recently discovered in Rome, by the early 18th century Irish artist, Henry Trench.

The work of Henry Trench (c. 1685-1726), an Irish artist practising in the first quarter of the eighteenth century, has remained relatively unknown until recently. In 1978 Crookshank and Glin named a single decorative work by him which no longer survives.[1] Information from manuscript transcripts at the Brinsley Ford Archive, London, has helped to increase our knowledge of this artist.[2] In addition, a recent article on Lord Shaftesbury by Sheila O'Connell in the *The Walpole Society Journal*[3] not only provides information through account books and letters into Trench's connection with this patron and the period the artist spent in Naples, but also illustrates fifteen preliminary drawings for the second edition of Lord Shaftesbury's *Characteristicks*. These drawings are now in the possession of the British Museum. However, by far the best insight currently available into the ability of this artist may be derived from a study of five prizewinning drawings, which have recently come to light at the Archivio Storico, Accademia Nazionale di S. Luca in Rome. These attest to considerable skill in draughtmanship and prove that Trench's work was highly-rated by established artists.

Nothing is known of Trench's early years in Ireland. He was possibly descended from the Irish family from which stemmed the peerages of Ashdown and Clancarty.[4] Since he was referred to as a 'young artist' in 1712, and since he had already lived in Rome since around 1704, it may be assumed that he was born in the mid-1680s. Although Strickland states that he had arrived in Italy by 1700 the author has found no corroborative evidence to support this early date.[5]

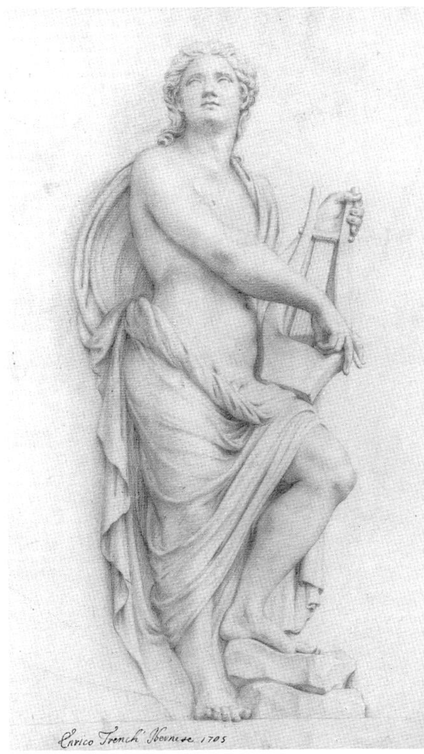

Henry Trench, Apollo, 1705, *red pencil on paper, 49 x 36cm, Archivio Storico, Accademia Nazionale de S Luca, Rome.*

It is known, however, that in Rome, Trench studied under Giuseppe Chiari (1654-1727), and also possibly under his master Carlo Maratta (1625-1713), who was influenced by the style of Raphael and the Caracci rather than the Baroque masters. Maratta was then Honorary Principal of the Accademia di S. Luca,[6] and it was there that Trench's work was first given recognition. In 1705, 'Enrico Trench Ibernese' was awarded First Prize in the Third Class of the *Concorso Clementino* for three drawings of the antique statues of *Cleopatra, Apollo* and *Bacchus*. In the following year, Trench received First Prize in the Second Class of the competition for his subject drawing on *The Slaying of Tarpeia*. His next prizewinning drawing was produced in 1711 and on that occasion he was awarded Second Prize in the First Class for his depiction of *Furious Camillus and the Teacher*.[7]

These drawings executed in red pencil are large in format, measuring as much as seventy-seven centimetres across. The earliest of them, the *Cleopatra* (37 x 53.5cm), *Apollo* (49 x 36cm) and *Bacchus* (49 x 38cm) convey a strong sculptural quality and a feeling for the antique marble. *Cleopatra* and *Bacchus* are highly finished

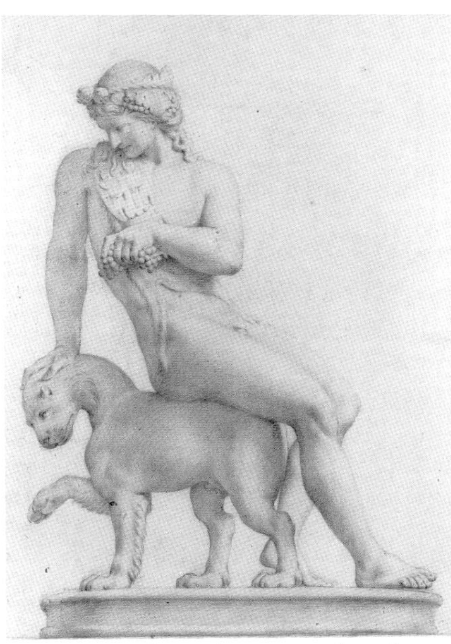

Henry Trench, Bacchus, 1705, *red pencil on paper, 49 x 38cm, Archivio Storico, Accademia Nazionale de S Luca, Rome.*

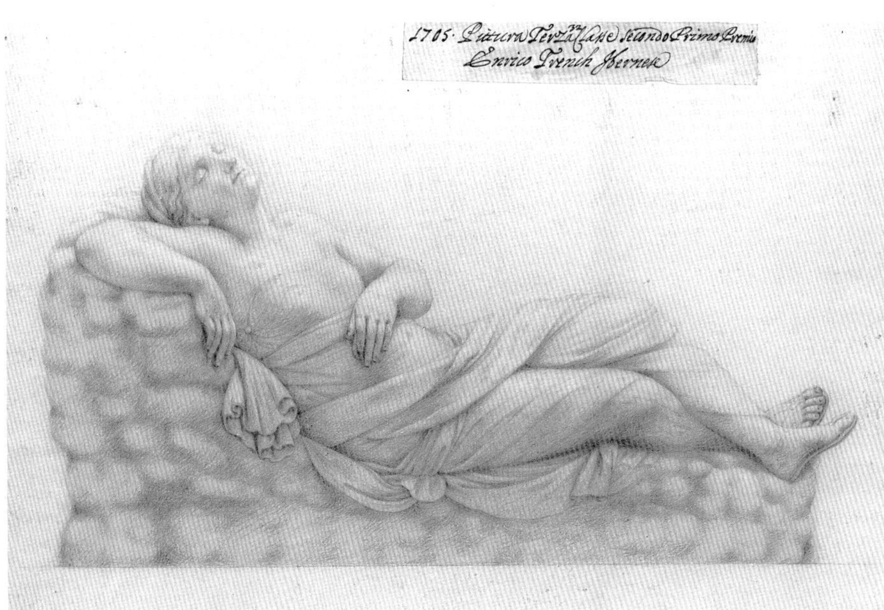

Henry Trench, Cleopatra, 1705, *red pencil on paper, 37 x 53.5cm, Archivio Storico, Accademia Nazionale de S Luca, Rome.*

HENRY TRENCH (c.1685-1726) PAINTER AND ILLUSTRATOR

and the strong diagonal hatching strokes give depth and shade. The head of the *Apollo* is the least finished although Trench clearly paid great attention to the copying of the antique draperies. *The Slaying of Tarpeia* (51 x 71cm) is a more complicated composition with the elements in the foreground seen in terms of visual cacophony, serving to convey the pain and drama of the punished treachery. A skilfully drawn horse and its rider on the right side bring the eye back to the walls of Rome and its distant buildings. *Furious Camillus and the Teacher* (53 x 77.5cm) is easier to read compositionally and the eye focuses on the plight of the unfortunate teacher. Both this work and the previous drawing show strong baroque tendencies in the use of the diagonals and spiralling movements. This is particularly apparent in Trench's sketch of *Hercules and the Centaur* which he submitted as an exercise with the *Slaying of Tarpeia*.

In the first half of 1707 in Rome, Trench was introduced to Sir John Perceval, later 1st Earl of Egmont, who was then on his Grand Tour. On 17 October 1707, having returned to England, Perceval wrote to the English portraitist, Edward Gouge, 'I hope the English gentlemen I left at Rome are well, and that Mr Gibbs finds scholars to his mind. Mr Trench too, I hope, minds his business and improves.' (Perceval subsequently wrote in a marginal note, 'Trench returned some years after and proved a very good history painter.') In a further letter, dated 3 December 1707, the British architect James Gibbs wrote, 'Mr Trench goes on in his study very well'.[8]

In early February 1712, Trench was recommended by the Rev Dr James Fagan, an Irish Catholic priest, to carry out drawings for Anthony Ashley Cooper, 3rd Earl of Shaftesbury (1671-1713), who was then living in Naples. Shaftesbury subsequently wrote to Fagan on 13 February and on 19 March enclosing the following memorandum for the artist:

> *Being satisfy'd, by good Testimony, of Mr Thrense's (sic) Sobriety, and Industry, and, by what I have seen in his hand, of his ability and improving Genius in Design I am ready to accept his Visit to me hither, having to that end order'd his travelling Expense to be advanc'd to him. And for the Month or two (or whatever longer time) he stays with me I shall take care he shall not have reason to esteem himself a Looser in his time or the profit of his Labour.*[9]

Shaftesbury also urged Trench to occupy his time before leaving Rome in copying from the antique:

> *But whatever time he has to spare (tho' it be but a few Days) he is desir'd to work as assiduously as possible in the same way, after the antient Statues, and in taking what he possibly can from the antient* Bassi Relievi, *both for the sake of the Figures as well as the Draperys, Dresses, Arms, Instruments, and Ornaments civil, military, and religious, which accompany the antient historical Pieces.*

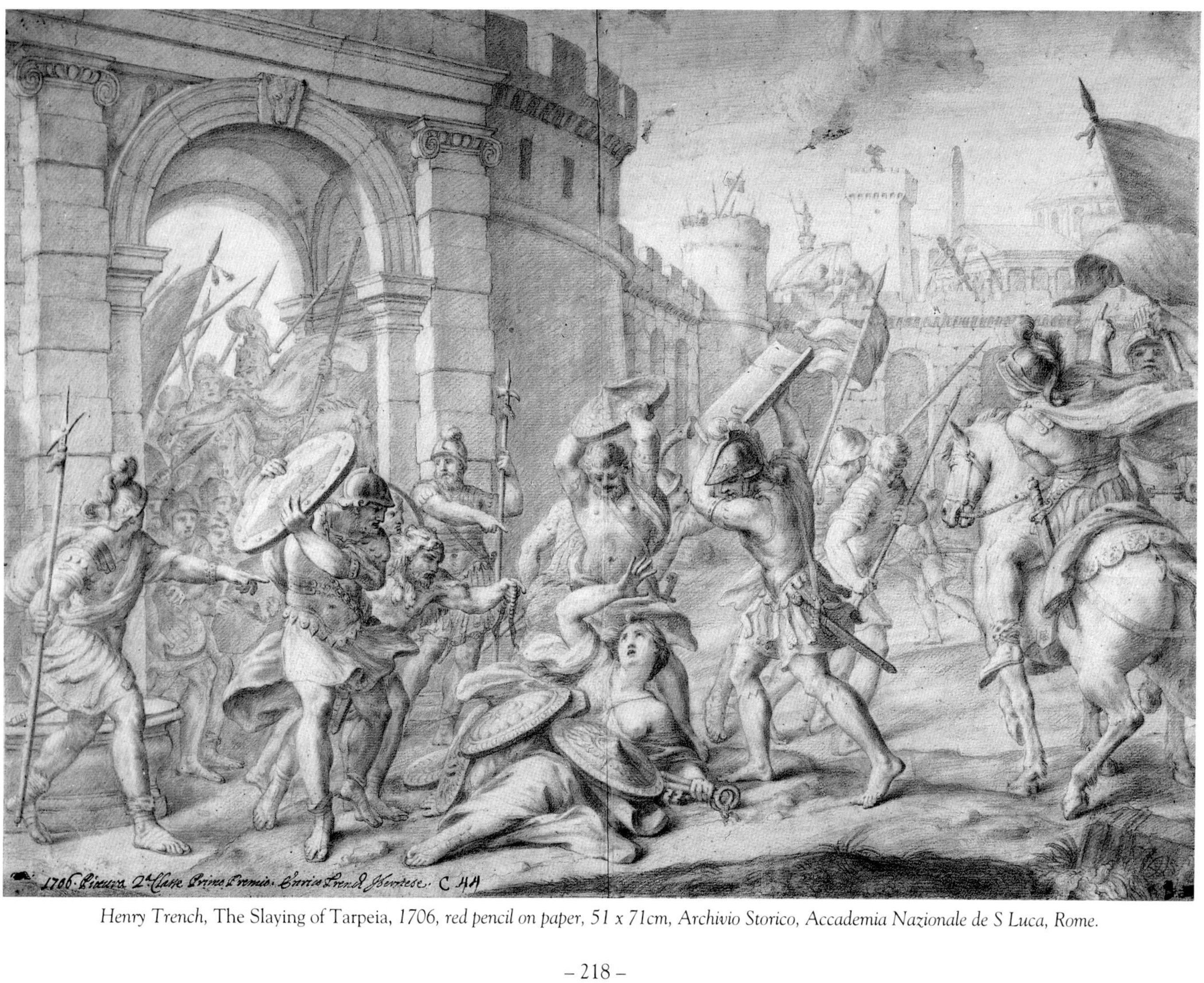

Henry Trench, The Slaying of Tarpeia, *1706, red pencil on paper, 51 x 71cm, Archivio Storico, Accademia Nazionale de S Luca, Rome.*

What Prints or Books soever Mr Thrense has of his own relating to these Subjects, he is desir'd to bring with him, and whatever may be farther usefull in his Study, he may purchase at my expense and bring also with him.[10]

Trench stayed in Rome for a further month presumably to carry out these instructions. He was also recorded on 28 March as visiting the Church of S Ignazio with John Talman (1677-1726), an English amateur artist, known for his sketches of baroque interiors. In the meantime in Naples, according to Shaftesbury's account books kept by his steward, Bryan Wheelock (d 1735), practical considerations were being given to Trench's arrival. On Saturday, 26 March 1712, four carlins were paid for 'Supporters of ye Boards for a Bed for Mr Trench' and on 1 April, a mat was purchased for the door 'into ye Room intended for Mr Trench'. The artist's arrival in Naples on Wednesday, 6 April was recorded by Wheelock who wrote, 'Paid a man that conducted Mr Trench from the inn to my Lords'.[11]

Trench remained in Naples until 16 September, working on the preliminary drawings for the second edition of Shaftesbury's *Characteristicks* which were later published in London, in 1714.[12] This was a collection of writings in which the philosopher argued that ridicule was the test of truth, that man possesses a moral sense and that everything in the world is for the best. Trench was commissioned to produce draft frontispieces and headpieces which were to be engraved by Simon Gribelin (1661-1733) in London. The small and fairly loosely-handled illustrations by Trench relate closely to the text. The drawings were carried out to strict instructions by Shaftesbury who later referred to them as those 'which I in a manner myself designed and drew'. His instructions for the engraver included such detailed specifications accompanying the draft for the frontispiece to Volume II as:

The Spiders Webb is not so exactly round and regular as it ought to be, in this emblematical kind. The Spider too in the Center must lye more round or orbicular (suitable to the orb hard by to which the Emblem relates) and the Flys caught in the Webb, must be much smaller in proportion and almost indiscernable.[13]

Throughout Trench's stay Wheelock kept record of such sundry items purchased for him as: chalk, 'Linnen', 'Soap for cleaning Mr Trench's Pensils' and, on 5 July 1712 no less a necessity than a 'Urinal with Cover for Mr Trench'. His academic and artistic needs were satisfied with 'Apuleius & Vitruvius in Italian', both Giovanni Bellori's *L'Historia Augusta* (1685) and *Le Vite di Pittori* (1672) as well as *Deorum dearumque Capita Ex vetustis numismatibus* by Abraham Ortelius (1573). Prints that he was given included those of the *Heliodorus* and a grotesque work after Raphael as well as a print of *St Jerome* by Dominichino.[14]

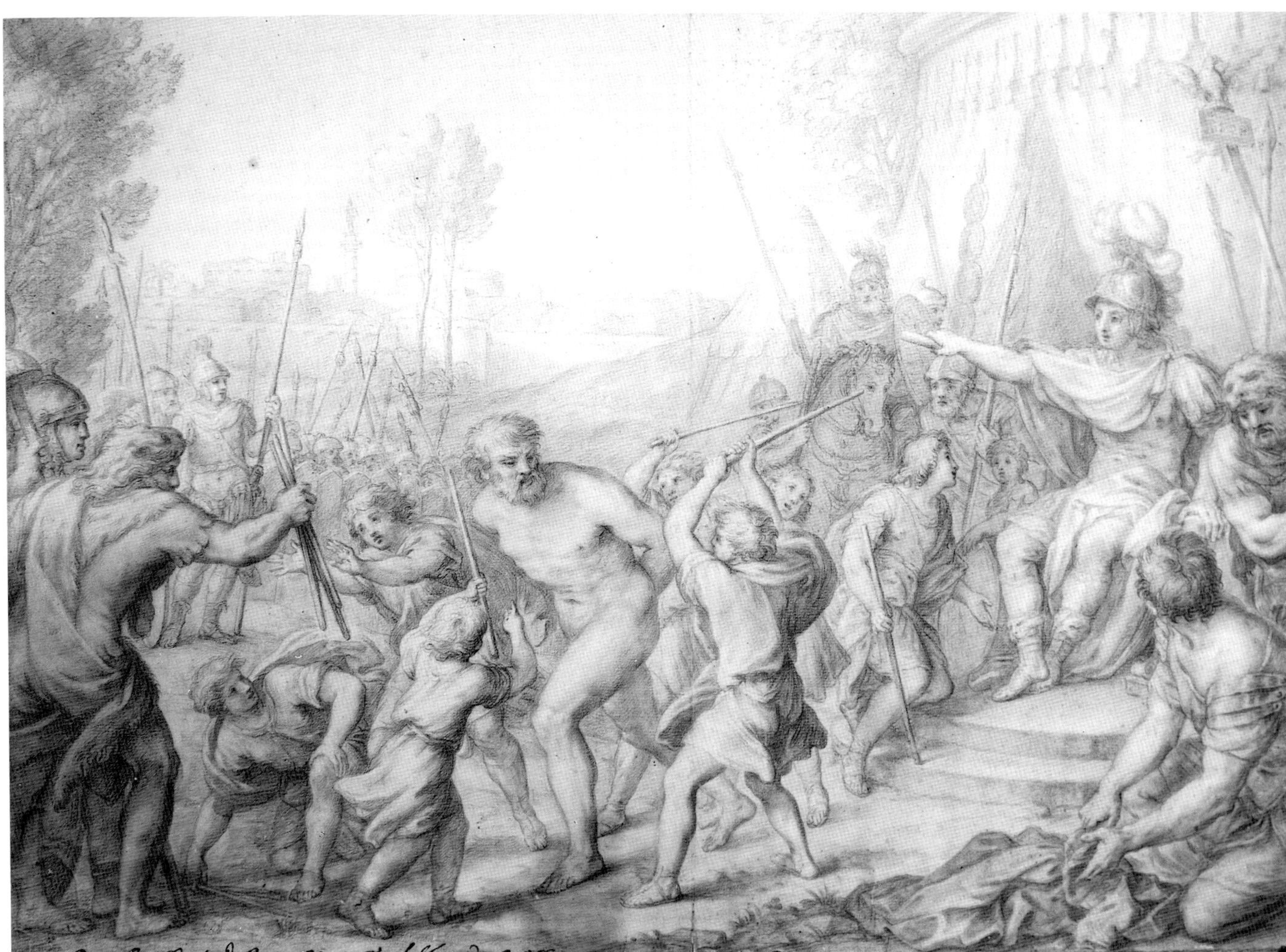

Henry Trench, Furious Camillus and the Teacher, 1711, *red pencil on paper, 53 x 77.5cm, Archivio Storico, Accademia Nazionale de S Luca, Rome.*

Whilst in Naples, Trench also acted as intermediary for Shaftesbury in the purchase of works of art for the Earl's friend Sir John Cropley, Bt.[15] On 20 June, Trench was paid five pistoles 'being a Present to him for his Trouble in Agency about the five pieces of Painting bought by my Lord of Signr Porcinari'.[16] These pictures included a landscape by Claude with figures by Luca Giordano, and two by Salvator Rosa. They were purchased from the Neapolitan art dealer Niccolò Porcinaro, originating from the great art collection of the Marques del Carpio, Viceroy of Naples.[17]

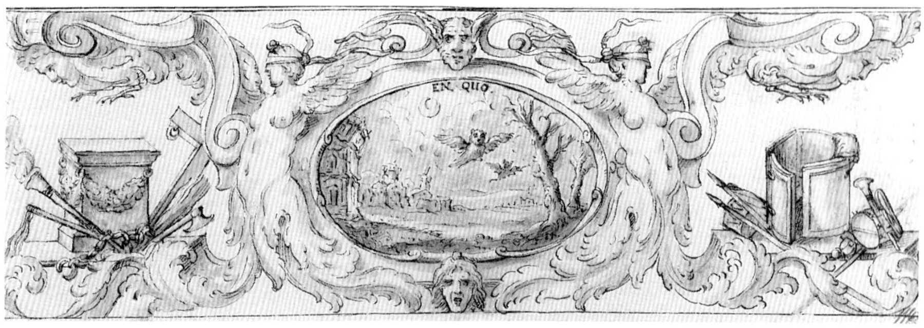

Henry Trench, Draft for the upper border of the Frontispiece of Vol I, *1712, pen and brown ink with grey wash touched with white, 7.7 x 19cm, Department of Prints and Drawings, British Museum, London.*

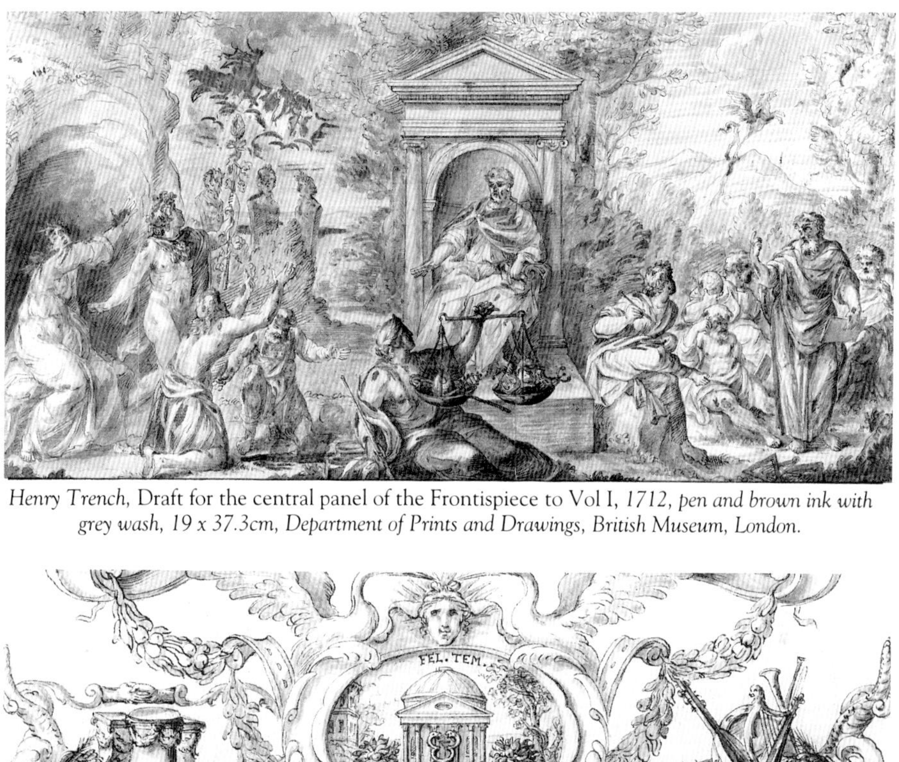

Henry Trench, Draft for the central panel of the Frontispiece to Vol I, *1712, pen and brown ink with grey wash, 19 x 37.3cm, Department of Prints and Drawings, British Museum, London.*

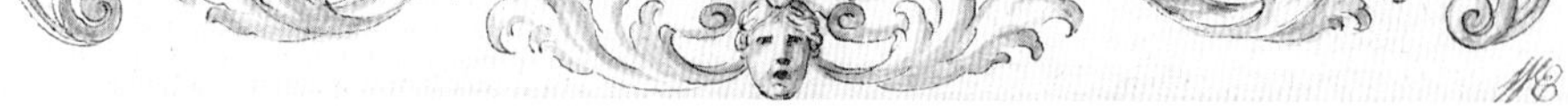

Henry Trench, Draft for the lower border of the Frontispiece to Vol I, *1712, pen and brown ink with grey wash, 7.1 x 19.6cm, Department of Prints and Drawings, British Museum, London.*

Trench returned to Rome on 16 September 1712, having been paid for prints and for the cost of his journey. He was also presented with five pistoles and asked to deliver a 'pair of Silk Stockins' to the English artist William Kent (1684-1748) in recompense for his drawing of *King Attila.*[18] The artist also brought with him a memorandum from Shaftesbury listing questions concerning new works of art and archaeological discoveries about which the artist was to send back information to Naples.[19] By Easter 1713 Trench had moved into lodgings in S Lorenzo in Lucina on the Seguita Piazza di Spagna verso i Greci.[20]

According to Vertue, in the following year Trench entered a further competition at the Accademia di S Luca, winning Second prize in the Third Class for a drawing of the statue of S Martina, at the Academy's church.[21] However, since there is no record of this at the Academy, it looks as if Trench was unsuccessful. In this year, William Kent was a prizewinner but according to Vertue 'it is generally allowed that Trench is ye better designer'.[22] Later that year, Trench's name was recorded in the visitors' list of Padua University on 16 September 1714. He may have accompanied Kent and his patron Thomas Coke, later 1st Earl of Leicester, who were touring northern Italy at the same time.[23]

Trench returned to London at the end of 1718, where he set up practice as a painter of historical subjects but according to Strickland he did not succeed. Vertue relates how he sought work from the 3rd Earl of Burlington, whom he would have met during his stay in Rome from September 1714 to February 1715, but Kent was preferred to him. Trench, as a result, 'took an occasion to write an expostulatory letter to this Nobleman setting forth the difference of merit on his side, more than Kents'. However, it had no effect except that 'Lord Burlington would read it to Kent, by way of mortification and mirth'.[24]

Trench returned to Italy in 1723 for a further period of study arriving in Rome on 23 October. There he stayed for a week before leaving for Naples, where he studied under Francesco Solimena (1657-1747) for two and a half years. Whilst there he acted as agent in the shipment of works of art for the Irish portrait-painter Hugh Howard (1675-1738), who had himself studied drawing and painting in Rome from 1697 to 1700. A letter from Trench written in Naples dated 26 May 1724, reveals much about his activities:

> *Sir,*
> *I received your letter dated ye 15 of March Old Stile in which was ye receipt for ye Prussian Blew; letters has been stopt at ye French Posthouse in Rome & layne long, the*

HENRY TRENCH (c.1685-1726) PAINTER AND ILLUSTRATOR

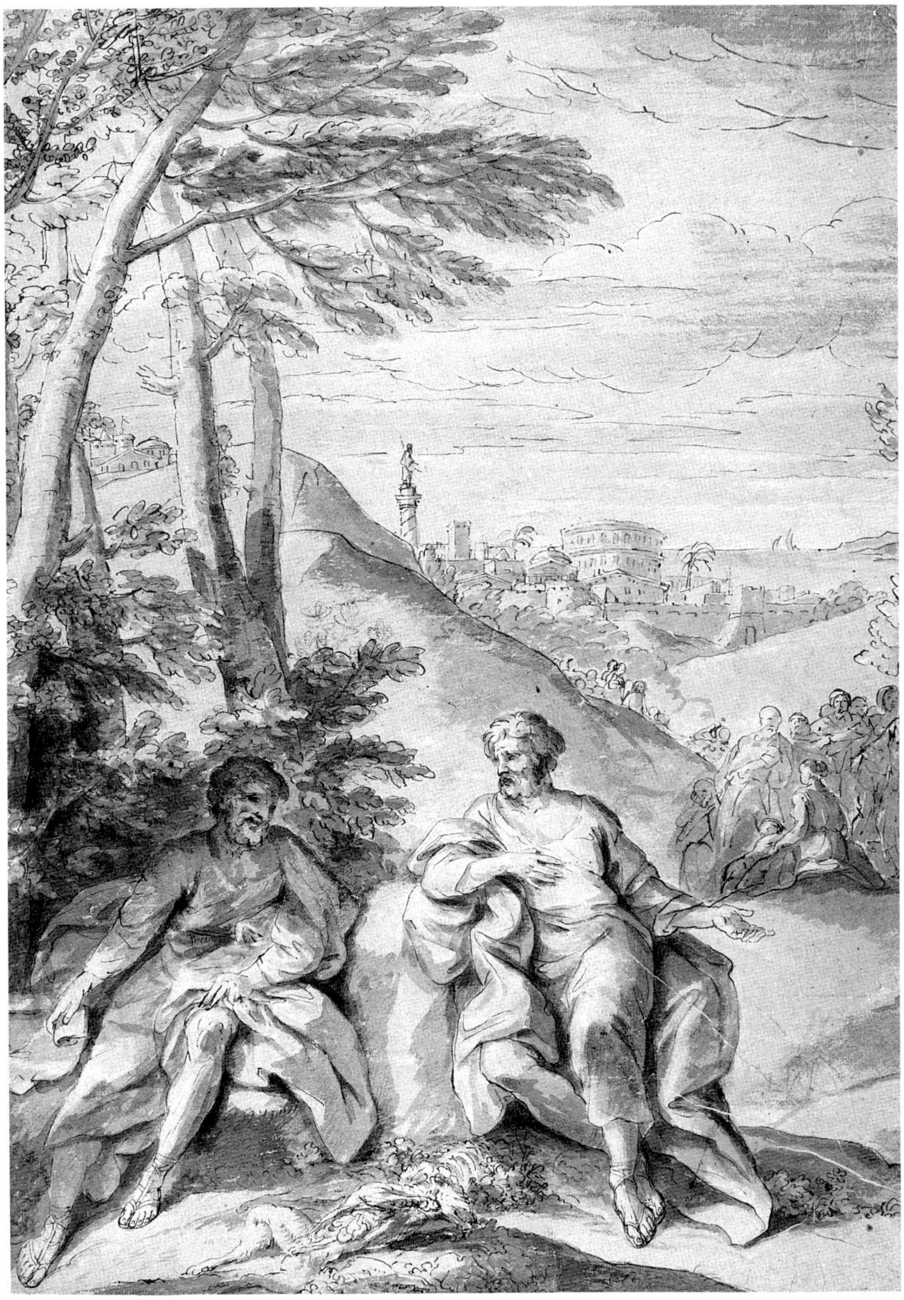

Henry Trench, Reading an Omen, *c. 1724, pen and wash and pen on grey paper, 57.5 x 46cm, Department of Prints and Drawings, British Museum, London.*

Misfortune was ye Postmaster being Bankrupt ... your Prints as well as other things was at Leghorne Six Months agoe ... ye picture of Caracci was for my Lord James Cavendish & only three sent to you as yett & I beleeve may by this time be arrived in London ... Ye Tables I bespoke and will be verry cheap, as I am informed, wch is 36 Ducatts of Naples; they are to be of Calabrian Marble little inferior to Verd Antick. I expect ye picture of Carolo Marratti is at Leghorne ... Sigr Solimeni is out of town some time; he has wrote to his brother & for ye pictures about foure Palmes he will have 500 Ducatts ye Peice ...[25]

Trench also saw to the export of his own paintings, including his copy of *Fernando Cortes* after Titian, which appears on a list of works in the collection of Hugh Howard, which was later bequeathed to his only brother, Robert, Bishop of Elphin, the father of Ralph, 1st Viscount Wicklow.[26] A further drawing by Trench originating from the Wicklow collection, entitled *Reading an Omen* probably datable to this second period in Naples, is in the collection of the British Museum.[27]

Trench returned to London in October 1725. His arrival had been anticipated by William Aikman, who had written to his cousin Sir John Clerk on 15 July 1725 about the decoration of his staircase at Mavisbank House, Midlothian:

> *at present I know nobody here (who) could perform it to your mind for Mr Kent is so busy about the staircase and gallery at Kensington that he can find no time to undertake it ... But in September next I expect my friend Mr Trench from Italy where he has been these two years past, studying colouring under the famous Solimena. He was master of design having studied ten or twelve years under Carlo Maratta and we expect he will do something in a right manner when he returns. So soon as he comes I will speak to him about our roof piece and doubt not he will undertake to do it at a reasonable rate.*[28]

There is no evidence of any contact between Sir John Clerk and Trench over this project. However, Mavisbank House was left unfinished due to the untimely death of the artist, which took place just over a year after his return. Unfortunately for the poor man, 'a whore beggar'd him, and he died of the pox'.[29] The Burial Register of St Mary's Paddington Green gives the date of death as 14 November 1726 and gives his entry as 'Henry Trench of St Giles in the Fields'.[30]

Trench spent over fifteen years in Italy and his work, in particular his choice of subject matter, demonstrates a thorough knowledge of the art of classical antiquity. No paintings by Trench have as yet come to light but his drawings, particularly those at the Accademia di S Luca, are important in their own right as rare examples of work carried out by an Irish artist in Italy in the early years of the eighteenth century.

Nicola Figgis

Nicola Figgis is Slide Curator in the History of Art Department, University College Dublin. She is writing a PhD thesis on Irish artists, patrons and dealers in Italy in the 18th century.

ACKNOWLEDGMENTS

I would like to thank the archivists of the Accademia Nazionale di S Luca, Dr Síghle Bhreathnach-Lynch, Prof Anne Crookshank, Sir Brinsley Ford, Dr Eileen Kane, Dr Edward McParland, Dr Sheila O'Connell and the Committee of the Association of Irish Art Historians for their kind assistance.

NOTES OVERLEAF

HENRY TRENCH (c.1685-1726) PAINTER AND ILLUSTRATOR

KNOWN WORKS

All his prize winning drawings, except that of 1713 (see below), are kept at the *Archivio Storico, Accademia Nazionale di S. Luca,* Rome including:

Cleopatra (37 x 53.5cm), *Apollo* (49 x 36cm) and *Bacchus* (49 x 38cm), with inscriptions *Enrico Trench Ibernese 1705* and details of prize on the *Cleopatra,* all red pencil on paper, cat. no. A184.

The Slaying of Tarpeia (51 x 71cm), inscribed on lower edge *1706 Pittura 2a Classe Primo Premio. Enrico Trench Ibernese,C44,* red pencil on two sheets of paper joined.

Accompanied by an exercise in black and red pencil, entitled *Hercules kills the Centaur* (32 x 22.5cm), inscribed *Provo d'Enrigo Trench,* cat. no. A194.

Furious Camillus and the Teacher (53 x 77.5 cm), inscribed on lower edge *1711, Pittura Prima Classe Secondo Premio Henrico Trench Ibernese – C128,* red pencil on two sheets of paper joined, cat. no. A258.

Preliminary drawings all dated 1712 for the second edition of Lord Shaftesbury's *Characteristicks,* mostly in pen and brown ink with grey wash, Department of Prints and Drawings, British Museum.

Draft for the Frontispiece to Vol II, (17.6 x 17.8 cm), Inv. 1880-2-14-263. (S O'Connell, 1988, cat. no. 38).

Draft for the upper border of the Frontispiece to Vol III, (6.1 x 18cm), Inv. 1880-2-14-262, (S O'Connell, 1988, cat. no. 42).

Draft for the central panel of the Frontispiece to Vol III, (18 x 36.7cm), Inv. 1880-2-14-276, (S O'Connell, 1988, cat. no. 44).

Draft for the lower border of the Frontispiece to Vol III, (6.3 x 19cm), Inv. 1880-2-14-268, (S O'Connell, 1988 cat. no. 46).

Detail study for the lower border of the Frontispiece to Vol III, (3.4 x 5.7 cm), Inv. 1880-2-14-265, (S O'Connell, 1988, cat. no. 47).

Draft for the upper border of the Frontispiece to Vol I, (7.7 x 19cm), Inv. 1880-2-14-267, (S O'Connell, 1988, cat. no. 50).

Draft for the central panel of the Frontispiece to Vol I, (19 x 37.3cm), Inv. 1880-2-14-277, (S O'Connell, 1988,, cat. no. 52).

Detail study for the central panel of the Frontispiece to Vol I, (4.2 x 5.6cm), Inv. 1880-2-14-266, (S O'Connell, 1988, cat. no. 53).

Draft for the lower border of the Frontispiece to Vol I, (7.1 x 19.6 cm), Inv. 1880-2-14-269, (S O'Connell, 1988, cat. no. 54).

Draft for the Headpiece of Treatise I, (8.4 x 20.6cm), Inv. 1880-2-14-270, (S O'Connell, 1988 cat. no. 57).

Draft for the Headpiece to Treatise II, (10 x 19.5cm), Inv. 1880-2-14-271, (S O'Connell, 1988 cat. no. 60).

Draft for the Headpiece to Treatise III, 9.3 x 21.4cm), Inv. 1880-2-14-272, (S O'Connell, 1988, cat. no. 63).

Draft for the Headpiece to Treatise IV, (10.3 x 21.6cm), Inv. 1880-2-14-272, (S O'Connell, 1988, cat no. 66).

Draft for the Headpiece to Treatise V, (10.2 x 21.6cm), Inv. 1880-2-14-274, (S O'Connell, 1988, cat. no. 69).

Draft for the Headpiece to Treatise VI, (9.5 x 21cm), Inv. 1880-2-14-275, (S O'Connell, 1988, cat no 72).

Reading an Omen, (57.5 x 46cm), Indian ink, wash and pen on grey paper, Department of Prints and Drawings, British Museum, Inv. 1874-8-8-135.

Etching of a figure with snake, after Raphael, inscribed *Raf. Ur. no./ Hen. Trench sculp. 1717,* Department of Prints and Drawings, British Museum, Inv. 1874-8-8-1025.

RECORDED WORKS

1. Drawing of statue of S Martina, 1713. (There is no record of this at the *Archivio Storico, Accademia Nazionale di S. Luca,* Rome.)
2. Drawing c. 1717 purchased by Thomas Coke, later 1st Earl of Leicester.[31]
3. Fernando Cortes after Titian, formerly in the collection of Hugh Howard.

NOTES

1. Anne Crookshank and The Knight of Glin, *The Painters of Ireland,* London 1978, p.34, based on George Vertue who recorded a ceiling decoration by Trench in a temple at Shireoaks Hall, Nottinghamshire. George Vertue, 'Notebooks', *Walpole Society,* vol. XX, 1931-2, (Vertue II), p.36.
2. The Brinsley Ford Archive (BFA), The Paul Mellon Centre for Studies in British Art, London. See biographical notes compiled by Georgina A Russell, 1970.
3. Sheila O'Connell, 'Lord Shaftesbury in Naples', *Walpole Society,* vol. LIV, London 1988, pp.149-219.
4. Russell, *loc. cit.,* p.1.
5. WG Strickland, *A Dictionary of Irish Artists,* Dublin 1913, Vol. II, p.453.
6. J Fleming, *Robert Adam and his circle in Edinburgh and Rome,* London 1962, p.39; Russell, *loc. cit.,* p.1.
7. The candidates were given very precise themes with specific details which had to be incorporated in their drawings: *Concorso Clementino 1706, Second Class:* The traitress Tarpeia has allowed the Sabines to enter the Citadel of the Capitol. The artists are required to represent the said Tarpeia on the threshold of the open entrance, thrown to the ground by the impact of the rushing soldiers. The soldiers, carrying out their promise to give her their golden armlets, hurl their heavy shields on her and as a result she is crushed and killed. Exercise: *Hercules kills the Centaur.* *Concorso Clementino 1711, First Class:* The Deed of Furious Camillus who has besieged Faleria and condemned the famous pedagogue to the public ignominy of being whipped naked by his own students. The teacher had treacherously led them to the camp in order to have them taken hostage. In exchange for the release of the students, the Falerii were to surrender their besieged city to the said Furious. To conform to the deed as recounted by Livy in the Fifth Book of the First Deca. Rome, *Archivio Storico Accademia Nazionale di S Luca, Concorsi Clementini.* (Note: the flavour of the Italian instructions is 18th century; the above is a rendition into modern English).
8. HMC Egmont Papers, London 1905-09, Vol. II, p.217. See also Russell, *loc cit.,* p.2.
9. O'Connell, *op. cit.,* pp.163-64.
10. *Ibid.*
11. *Ibid,* p.182.
12. *Ibid.,* p.150.
13. *Ibid.,* pp.184 and 193.
14. *Ibid.,* p.150. The first edition of the *Characteristicks,* published in London in 1711, comprised a collection of six treatises: *A Letter concerning Enthusiasm* (1708); *Sensus Communis: An Essay on the Freedom of Wit and Humour* (1709); *Soliloquy: or Advice to the Author* (1710); *An Inquiry concerning Virtue, or Merit* (1699); *The Moralists, A Philosophical Rhapsody* (1709) and *Miscellaneous Reflections* (1711).
15. O'Connell *op.cit.,* 151.
16. *Ibid.,* p.185.
17. *Ibid.,* p. 212.
18. *Ibid.,* p. 187.
19. *Ibid.,* p. 177.
20. *Stati dell'Anime,* parish records for S Lorenzo in Lucina. Archivio del Vicariato, S Giovanni in Laterano, Rome.
21. George Vertue, 'Notebooks', *Walpole Society,* vol. XXII, (1934), (Vertue III), p.36. There is no record of Trench winning a drawing in this competition. The first, second and third prizes were won by Domenico Frezza, Placido Romolo and Leonardo Siccardi respectively. Rome, *Archivio Storico, Accademia Nazionale di S. Luca, Concorsi Clementini di Pittura,* unpublished list of prizewinners, pp 27-28
22. George Vertue, 'Notebooks' *Walpole Society,* vol. XXIV (1935-36) (Vertue IV), p.163. William Kent's drawing: *S Andrea Avellino* (66 x 54.5cm), red pencil, cat. no. A276.
23. Russell, *loc. cit.,* p.3
24. George Vertue, 'Notebooks' *Walpole Society,* vol. XXIV (1935-36) (Vertue IV), p.163.
25. BFA, Wicklow MSS. transcripts.
26. Purchased at the Wicklow sale of August 1874.
27. BFA, Wicklow MSS. transcripts.
28. Fleming, *op. cit.,* pp. 39, 42.
29. British Library, Egmont Papers. Add 47025, f.80.
30. Russell, *loc. cit., p.5.*
31. *Ibid.,* p.3.

ALBRECHT DÜRER'S IRISH WARRIORS AND PEASANTS

'This is the attire of soldiers and peasants in Ireland, beyond England', wrote Albrecht Dürer on his 1521 drawing. **Jean Michel Massing** comments on the fascinating early representation of Hibernian costume.

Dürer's fascination with exotic costume became evident as early as his first trip to Italy (1494-95), when he recorded the dress of Venetians as well as of Orientals; it continued throughout his career.[1] He is, after all, the first artist to have represented an American Indian – or rather one of his own countrymen dressed in Tupinamba featherwork. He sketched him on fol. 41 of Emperor Maximilian's *Book of Hours* (1515) next to the accompanying passage from the Psalms: 'The Earth is the Lord's and the fulness thereof; the world and they that dwell therein for he hath founded it upon the seas, and established it upon the floods' (Psalms 31.1). Dürer's 'Indian' wears a feather cloak as though it were a skirt: Tupinambas, in fact, went more or less naked, but Dürer based his feather skirt on early German broadsheets which have no ethnographic basis. The cap worn by Dürer's Indian, however, seems to be a real Tupinamba bonnet of feathers fastened into the knots of a cotton net.

Most remarkable however is the ceremonial war club (*tacape*) of hardwood held by the Indian. With its long rounded handle decorated with feathers fastened in a similar way to those on the cap and with a flattened, round or slightly oval blade with sharp edges, it is quite similar to a specimen now in the Musée de l'Homme in Paris which may be the club of the Tupinamba chief Quoniambec brought back from Brazil by André Thevet in 1555 or 1556.[2] American Indians were also included by Hans Burgkmair in the Triumph of Maximilian (c. 1517-1518), among the people of Calicut. Still more remarkable, however, are two drawings by him in the British Museum (c.1519-1525) representing a black youth dressed in American artifacts. In the first of these, the youth holds in his left hand the famous Aztec mosaic shield now in the Museum für Völkerkunde in Vienna, which was recorded in the *Kunstkammer* in Schloss Ambras in 1596. It may be one of the shields given by Motecuhzoma to Hernàn Cortés and sent by him to Charles V.[3] This would mean that it would have been among the 'jewels, shields and clothing' which Dürer saw between 27 August and 2 September 1520 and described at length in his diary:

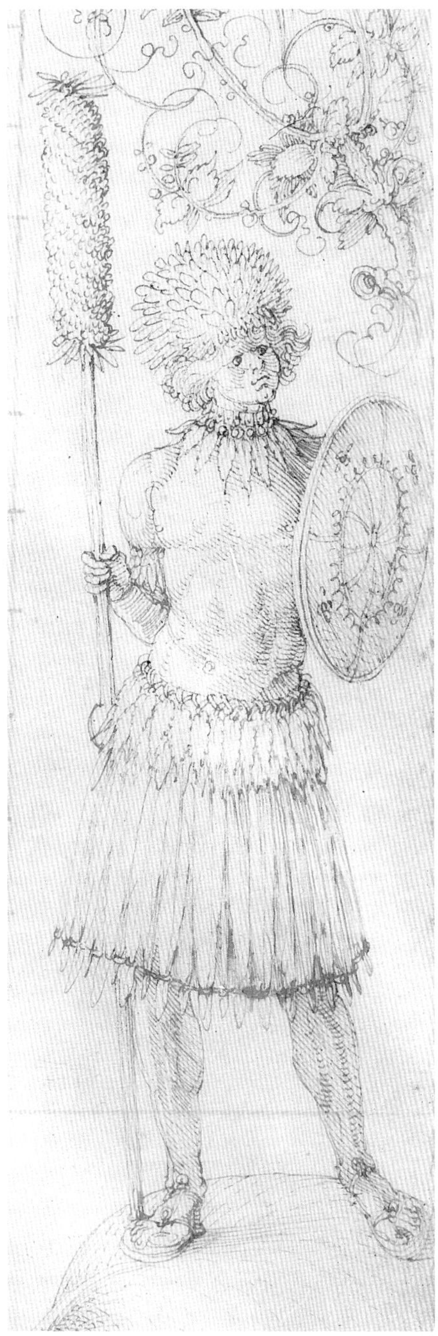

Albrecht Dürer, *Detail of Illustration of Psalm 24.1.* Book of Hours of Emperor Maximilian, *fol. 41r. Bayerische Staatsbibliothek, Munich.*

I saw the things which have been brought to the King from the new land of gold, a sun all of gold a whole fathom broad, and a moon all of silver of the same size, also two rooms full of armour of the people there, and all manner of wondrous weapons of theirs, harnesses and darts, very strange clothing, beds, and all kinds of wonderful objects of human use, much better worth seeing than prodigies. These things are all so precious that they are valued at a hundred thousand florins.
All the days of my life I have seen nothing that rejoiced my heart so much as these things, for I saw amongst them wonderful works of art, and I marvelled at the subtle Ingenia of people in foreign lands. Indeed I cannot express all that I thought there.[4]

Dürer was attracted by the monetary value, the craftsmanship and the sheer beauty of the objects, but also by their exotic character. During his trip to the Netherlands (1520-21), Dürer collected numerous *exotica*, including Afro-Portuguese ivories and Chinese porcelains. In Antwerp, his host, Jobst Plankfelt, gave him an old Turkish whip. From Dürer's Diary we also learn that he received, from a Herr Gilbert of whom we know nothing else, 'a small Calicut round shield made of fish skin, and two gloves with which the natives there fight'. Although Calicut is a city in India the name was generic, referring to all the newly discovered lands. The round shield and the gloves may even have been Eskimo artifacts.[5] The walrus which Dürer sketched in 1521 certainly came from the North Atlantic. In the left corner of the beautiful drawing in the British Museum the artist noted that the animal had been caught in the North Sea.

In Dürer's time walruses were found in Europe mainly on the northern coast of Norway and occasionally around Scotland and near the Shetland Isles. The animal recorded by Dürer may have strayed near the Netherlandish coast, but it is more probable that Dürer sketched a dead specimen, perhaps stuffed. It could well have been the walrus head preserved in salt that the Norwegian archbishop Erik Walkendorf sent to Pope Leo X in 1520; nothing much is known about the peregrinations of this object of wonder, but for the fact that it was exhibited in Strasbourg on its way to Rome.[6]

Quite extraordinary too are the costume studies made by Dürer in the Netherlands. In his Diary he noted that he 'drew a girl in her costume' at Goes; a few months later in Antwerp, he 'sketched in black and white on grey paper two Netherlandish costumes'.[7] The most splendid of his costume studies done in the Nether-

ALBRECHT DÜRER'S IRISH WARRIORS AND PEASANTS

lands are those of Irish warriors and peasants and those of Livonian women.[8] He may have first seen the latter in Antwerp during the great annual procession on the first Sunday after Assumption Day which he recorded at length in 1520: 'I saw the great Procession from the Church of Our Lady at Antwerp, when the whole town of every craft and rank was assembled, each dressed in his best according to his rank'. There were floats with various scenes, including 'the Three Holy Kings riding on great camels and on other rare beasts, very well arranged'. There could also be seen, in his own words, 'boys and maidens most finely and splendidly dressed in the costumes of many lands, representing various saints'.[9] The costume studies cannot have been executed on that occasion for they are clearly dated 1521. They could, however, have been done exactly one year later, when Dürer saw once more 'the great Procession at Antwerp on Holy Trinity day'.[10]

On his drawing of *Irish Warriors and Peasants* (Berlin, Staatliche Museen Preussischer Kulturbesitz, Kupferstichkabinett) Dürer wrote the following: 'This is the attire of soldiers in Ireland, beyond England,' and, 'This is the attire of peasants in Ireland'.[11] That the costumes are indeed Irish cannot be doubted.[12] The first soldier from the left has a helmet and wears a long quilted garment called in Gaelic *cotún*; he holds a lance, a weapon generally carried by horsemen, and has a knife at his side. The *cotún* is a coat of fence, like the English gambeson, which got its name from the fact that was quilted and padded with cotton. It was, in fact, vertically ridged and reached from the neck to below the knees.[13] The second soldier wears a helmet with a visored bassinet and a mail over a long tunic which falls almost to the ankle, but does not seem to be either padded or ridged. It appears to be a Gaelic *léin*. This soldier holds a large sword in his right hand, a bow in the left; he also has a dirk on his side and arrows under his arm, a rather heavy load for one person.

The sword, which is probably Irish, would have measured more than one and a half metres. The blade itself has a distinctive arrangement of grooves. The crossguard and the open ring of the hilt are clearly recorded, with the tang of the blade passing through the ring of the hilt. The sizes of the hilt and the blade would indicate that the sword was held with two

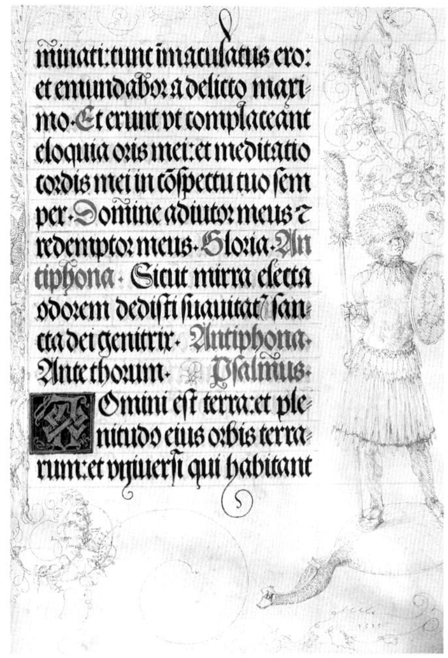

Albrecht Dürer, Illustration of Psalm 24.1. Book of Hours of Emperor Maximilian, *fol. 41r. Bayerische Staatsbibliothek, Munich.*

hands.[14] The bow is slightly recurved, with notches for the strings. The fletching of the arrows is not clearly defined but the metallic arrow-heads are varied: either pointed, tanged or with two points. The dirk (*scían*), finally, is a weapon commonly used at war as well as for domestic purposes.[15]

More traditionally dressed is the third soldier who, like his neighbours, holds a large sword also without scabbard but with a different hilt, crossguard and pommel. He wears over his tunic an Irish *brat*, a large woollen sleeveless cloak or cape with a shaggy lining which was wrapped around the body and, if necessary, covered the head of the wearer. Here it seems to be lined with fur: alternatively the curled fringes may have been achieved by sprinkling the drawn nap with honey. These mantles were heavy but less protective than mail.[16] The two 'peasants' armed with axes (the *tuagh*) are gallowglasses; they wear woollen tunics, and over them, at least one has a saffron coloured jacket probably also in wool tied at the waist. Such jackets are open at the front with a rolled collar and funnel-shaped sleeves.[17] One has a bag hanging from the belt, the other a horn. Unlike the soldiers – one of whom is wearing the traditional Irish single-soled brogues – they do not wear shoes.[18]

Dürer certainly based his drawing on Hibernian costumes; that the people wearing the costumes were actually Irish is, however, less probable, as they are without the characteristic trews (Gaelic *trius*), the close-fitting trousers reaching to the ankles.[19] The fact that the mail-clad warrior has a bow as well as a very large sword which he would have needed to hold with both hands confirms that Dürer did not sketch real soldiers.[20] Dürer's inscription on the drawing states that this is the way soldiers and peasants dress in Ireland. This does not have to imply, especially if one looks at the original German ('Also gand dy krigsman Jn Irlandia' and 'Allso gend dy pawern in Irlandyen'), that he saw real Irishmen in this garb. It has been suggested, in fact, that he copied someone else's drawings – the fact that when in Antwerp he lodged at Jobst Plankvelt's inn, in the Engelsche Straat, the street where the English merchants lived, could support such a hypothesis – but the almost archaeological exactitude of the drawing suggests that his discerning eye was at work. Dürer may simply have dressed local models – as he did for the American 'Indian' – in examples of Irish costume which may have featured, for example, in an Antwerp pageant. In the procession he witnessed in 1520 and 1521, Dürer saw youngsters 'most finely and splendidly dressed in the costumes of many lands, representing various saints'.[21] Irishmen may well have been included in the retinue of one or other of these saints, an illustration of the universality of Christian belief and, more specifically the antiquity of Irish Christianity.[22] Alternatively, the costumes could simply have been curiosities acquired by some collector.[23]

Jean Michel Massing

Jean Michel Massing, FSA, is a Lecturer in History of Art and a Fellow of King's College, Cambridge. He was one of the organisers of the Circa 1492: Art in the Age of Exploration *exhibition held at the National Gallery of Art, Washington in 1991-92. His publications include* Du texte à l'image. La Calomnie d'Apelle et son iconographie *(Strasbourg 1990).*

ACKNOWLEDGMENTS

Part of this note is based on my contribution to *Circa 1492: Art in the Age of Exploration*, the catalogue of an exhibition held at the National Gallery of Art in Washington in 1991-92. I would also like to thank Elizabeth McGrath and Mairead Dunlevy for their invaluable assistance.

NOTES OVERLEAF

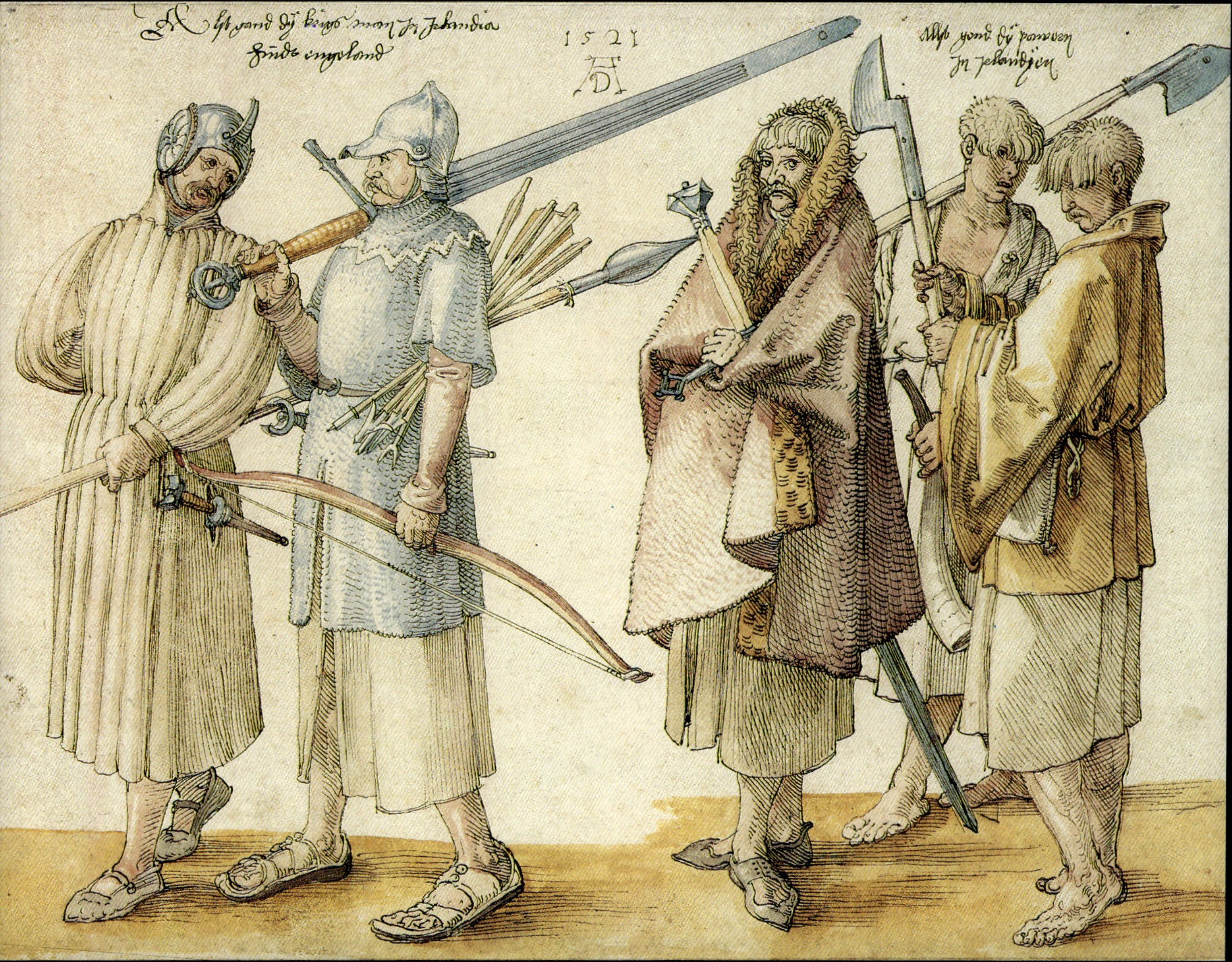

Albrecht Dürer, Irish Warriors and Peasants. *Pen, brown ink, watercolour. Signed and dated 1521. Inscribed. Staatliche Museen Preussischer Kulturbesitz, Kupferstichkabinett, Berlin.*

ALBRECHT DÜRER'S IRISH WARRIORS AND PEASANTS

NOTES

1. For Dürer's interest in Oriental costume, see J Raby, *Venice, Dürer and the Oriental Mode*, London 1982; more recently J Raby, 'Picturing the Levant', in *Circa 1492: Art in the Age of Exploration*. Ed. by JA Levenson, (Washington, National Gallery of Art, October 12, 1991-January 12, 1992) Washington 1991, pp. 77-81.
2. For a study of this page, see JM Massing, 'Early European Images of America: the Ethnographic Approach', in *Circa 1492 ...*, as in n.1, pp. 514-16, fig. 1.
3. Massing, in *Circa 1492 ...*, as in n. 1, p. 571, no 405, ill.
4. A Dürer *Schriftlicher Nachlass*, ed. H Rupprich, I, Berlin 1956, p. 155; for the English translation, see J-A Goris and G Marlier, *Albrecht Dürer. Diary of his Journey to the Netherlands, 1520-1521*, London 1971. p. 64.
5. For Dürer's interest in exotica, see Massing, in *Circa 1492 ...*, as in n. 1, pp. 117-18.
6. For Dürer's drawing of a walrus, see Massing, in *Circa 1492 ...*, as in n. 1, pp. 300-01, no 207, ill; also p. 116.
7. Dürer as in n. 4, I, pp. 162 and 173. For the English translation, see Goris and Marlier, as in n. 4, respectively pp. 77 and 94. For the study of a woman made by Dürer at Goes, see W L Strauss, *The Complete Drawings of Albrecht Dürer*, IV, New York 1974, p. 1966-67, no 1520032, ill.; for a drawing of a woman in Netherlandish dress done on a greyish-violet prepared paper, see ibidem, pp. 2040-41, no 1521/23, ill.
8. For Dürer's three drawings of Livonian Women, see Strauss, as in n. 7, IV, pp. 2066-71, nos 1521/37-39, ills; also U. Mende, 'Dürers Zeichnungen livländischer Frauentrachten und seine sogenannte Türkin', in *Kunstgeschichtliche Aufsätze von seinen Schülern und Freunden des KhIK Ladendorf zum 29. Juni 1969 gewidmet*, Cologne 1969, pp. 24-33.
9. Dürer, as in n. 4, p. 153: 'Auch ritten in dieser schaar, gar zierlich und auff das köstlichs beklaidet, knaben und mägdlein auff mancherleÿ land sitten zugericht, anstat mancherleÿ heiligen'; for the translation, Goris and Marlier, as in n. 4, pp. 60-61.
10. Dürer, as in n. 4, p. 172; Goris and Marlier, as in n. 4, p. 94.
11. For this drawing, see esp. Strauss, as in n. 7, IV, pp. 2064-65, no 1521/36; F Anzelewsky and H Mielke, *Albrecht Dürer: Kritischer Katalog der Zeichnungen (Staatliche Museen Preussischer Kulturbesitz)*, Berlin 1984, pp 111-12, no and fig. 108; Massing, in *Circa 1492 ...*, as in n. 1, p. 301, no 208, ill.
12. For early Irish costume, see H F McClintock, *Old Irish and Highland Dress*, Dundalk 1950 (for Dürer's drawing, pp. 30-31, fig. 17); also his *Handbook on the Traditional Old Irish Dress*, Dundalk 1958, esp. pp. 1-2; M Dunlevy, *Dress in Ireland*, London 1989. Information on dress is also found in John Hunt, *Irish Medieval Figure Sculpture, 1200-1600. A study of Irish tombs with notes on costume and armour*, I-II, Dublin and London 1974. In the course of my argument I have sometimes simply adopted *verbatim* the definitions of Irish garments and arms from the various authors I mention in notes.
13. For the *cotún*, see P Harbison, 'Native Irish Arms and Armour in Medieval Gaelic Literature, 1170-1600', *The Irish Sword*, XII, Dublin 1975-76, pp. 183-84; for the *léin*, pp. 182-82; for spears, see pp. 272-76. Hunt, as in n. 12, pp. 78 and 131, compares this soldier to the figures of the O'Cahan tomb in Cahan Abbey, Dungiven, Co Derry (see his pls 168 and 248-49).
14. For Irish swords, see Harbison, as in n. 13, pp. 270-72; also A Halpin, 'Irish Medieval Swords, c.1170-1600', *Proceedings of the Royal Irish Academy*, LXXXVI, Dublin 1986, pp. 183-230. Except in size the sword held by the soldier in Dürer's drawing is quite close to some Irish swords studied by Halpin. The hilt ending with a ring through which passes the tang of the blade is commonly found in Ireland; see McClintock 1950, as in n. 11, p. 30; Halpin (as above), pp. 207-213 (group 3). Most interesting is the helmet worn by the first soldier; Hunt, as in n. 12, p. 219, compares it to the head-pieces on the slab of Donat O Suibne and his wife at Sligo Abbey (pl. 171); they 'are of peculiar form, apparently bascinets with spreading crests and with horn-shaped projections upon the forehead as in the first soldier in Dürer's famous drawing'.
15. For the Irish *scian* see Harbison, as in n. 13, pp. 271-72. For bows and arrows, pp. 276-78.
16. For the *brat*, see McClintock 1958, as in n. 12, p. 1; also Dunlevy, as in n. 12, pp. 39-42.
17. For this garment, Dunlevy, as in n. 12, p. 59. For axes, see Harbison, as in n. 13, pp. 278-79: for him 'The axes shown in Dürer's picture are of a totally different nature [than those on a tomb-front at Roscommon Abbey for example], having in one case a neck only a little less wide than the blade, and in another a blade which is stepped at the top and has only a quarter-circle-shaped blade in front'.
18. For shoes, see Dunlevy, as in n. 12, p. 60.
19. For the *trius*, McClintock 1958, as in n. 12, p. 1; also McClintock, 'Some hitherto unpublished pictures of sixteenth century people and costumes appearing in them', *Journal of the Royal Society of Antiquities of Ireland*, LXXXIII, Dublin 1953, pp. 150-51. For archaeological material, Dunlevy, as in n. 12, pp. 57-58, fig. 41c-d.
20. See Harbison, as in n. 13, pp. 280-84, for the different kinds of Irish soldiers and their arms.
21. See above, n. 9. Such processions had many floats and included many scenes; see, for the Antwerp procession and others, H. Rupprich, 'Die Beschreibung niederländischer Prozessionsspiele durch Albrecht Dürer und Hieronymus Köler d. Ä', *Maske und Kothurn. Vierteljahrsschrift für Theaterwissenschaft*, I, Gras-Köln 1955, pp. 88-102. In the sixteenth century Irish characters became a standard feature of masques; see, for example, J Hennig, 'Notes on early representations of Irishmen in German books", *Journal of the Royal Society of Antiquaries of Ireland*, LXXX, Dublin 1950, p. 160.
22. For the dragon-infested Ireland-rock inhabited by St Patrick which was shown at a court festival in Stuttgart (1617), see E McGrath, 'Rubens's *Arch of the Mint*', *Journal of the Warburg and Courtauld Institutes*, XXXVII, London 1974, p. 208.
23. E Panofsky, *Albrecht Dürer*, I, Princeton 1943, p. 216, wrote that it was 'presumably based on ethnographical material which happened to come to Dürer's attention'; he supposes however (see II, p. 127 no 1293) that Dürer copied somebody else's drawing.

LEO WHELAN (1892-1956)

Wanda Ryan-Smolin
outlines the career of Leo Whelan (1892-1956), acclaimed for his distinctive portraits of Irish 20th century public figures and accomplished genre paintings.

Leo Whelan was primarily a portrait painter working within the confines of the academic tradition, and it is presumably for this reason that his work has received little critical attention since his death. Today he is remembered chiefly as one of the main portrait painters in Ireland in the first half of the twentieth century. His portraiture which chronicles the early political and social life of Independent Ireland, is of genuine historical significance. Equally important, if not more so, are the genre pictures and portrait interiors which make up a substantial body of his work and are in many cases quite outstanding in the context of Irish painting of the period.

Whelan was born in Dublin in 1892 of Irish parents from Co. Kerry. He was educated in Belvedere College, and studied art at the Dublin Metropolitan School of Art. He exhibited regularly from 1911 onwards at the Royal Hibernian Academy[1], and also at various other venues in Dublin and London (including the Royal Dublin Society, the Royal Academy, the Royal Society of Portrait Painters and the Royal Institute Gallery). He lived all his life at 65 Eccles Street where his parents and later his two sisters ran a small family hotel and he had studios at 64 Dawson Street and 7 Lower Baggot Street.

At the DMSA Whelan, from 1908, came under the influence and guidance of the Dublin-born artist Sir William Orpen (1876-1931). It is now fully recognised that Orpen's presence at the school had a major impact on the development of Irish art in the first half of the twentieth century. He taught there on a regular basis from 1905 until 1914, dividing his time between Dublin and London, where he was already established as a successful society portrait painter. As an artist of strong personality and considerable reputation, Orpen had a powerful influence on the artistic development of his students foremost of whom were Sean Keating, Patrick Tuohy, Margaret Clarke, James Sleator and Leo Whelan. Orpen is credited with rejuvenating and reorganising the teaching practices of the school. He placed particular emphasis on the benefits of drawing from the nude. Key elements in his teaching were precision of draughtsmanship and a sound understanding of colour and composition. Whelan was very receptive to Orpen's method of teaching which, while tending to have a dominating effect on those he favoured, was practically non-existent in the case of students whom he felt to be insufficiently talented.[2] Whelan, however, was among the chosen few[3] and soon proved himself worthy of Orpen's attention by producing a consistently high standard of work for which he received many prizes during the following decade.[4] The style which he adopted as his own in these early years was distinctive and competent and at the same time strongly reliant both technically and compositionally on that of Orpen.

Portraiture from the beginning was one of Whelan's main interests in painting, and from about 1911 onwards he began to receive regular commissions.[5] Apart from his commissioned work he also did portraits of his own family, many of which have a distinct genre quality. One of the finest of these is the portrait of his eldest sister Lena, painted in 1911. He exhibited it under the set title of *On the Moors* at the annual RDS Taylor Art Competition in 1912 and received a prize of £10 for it. For an early work this painting is extraordinarily assured and shows his strong adherence to the tenets of academic teaching – study from the model, good draughtsmanship and harmony of composition. The figure of the young woman and the red setter by her side are portrayed in superb detail against an evocative and remote landscape. The composition and a number of the accessories, in particular the feathered hat and leather gloves clearly show the artist's debt to Orpen and in particular to his 1909 portrait of *Gardenia*,[6] the daughter of his lover Mrs St George.

In the years immediately following, Whelan continued to show an interest in Orpenesque compositions. This is evident even in the titles of his exhibited paintings such as *Reflections* (1912), *The Mirror* (1913), and *The Girl in the Mirror* (1913).[7] But his greatest achievement of these early years in the field of genre was *The Doctor's Visit* (National Gallery of Ireland, cat. no. 4462). This earned Whelan the prestigious Taylor Art Scholarship prize of £50 in 1916. Despite the subject of the painting, which shows a girl sick in bed, it is a work which exudes a wonderful sense of calm and tranquillity. The title was again one set by the Taylor Art Scholarship Committee, and consequently the scene does not record an actual event. The setting is the artist's home in Eccles Street. His mother is seated at the foot of the bed, the bold stripe of her blouse just visible beneath a black shawl. In the middle distance the figure of Whelan's sister, in the uniform of a Mater Hospital nurse, holds open the door for the doctor who is about to enter. The girl in bed was Whelan's cousin. Essentially a carefully-studied composition of contrasting areas of dark and light, it is a piece which shows that Whelan had successfully mastered the polished technique of Orpen. It echoes in particular Orpen's *The Bedroom*[8] of 1900, the quiet self-absorption of the figures and the use of a canopied bed as a focal point are similar in both works. *The Doctor's Visit,* however, is painted in a more direct manner and with an air of restrained emotion which was to become the hallmark of Whelan's individual style.

While a significant proportion of Whelan's genre concerns the depiction of urban scenes, he also painted cottage interiors, the best known of which is the *Kerry Cobbler*.[9] Several of these are of old men or women seated by open fires in Kerry cabins with flagstone floors and rough plastered walls. Although Whelan was familiar with life in Kerry (his eldest sister was born in Tralee), he himself was a Dubliner whose main contact with the countryside was during his holidays in Ballybunion where he normally stayed in the relative comfort of the Central Hotel. Despite the authenticity of his Kerry pictures, they closely follow a formula used by Orpen and subsequently by many of his pupils.[10] Whelan's rural interiors are, however, distinctive in that they display a strong interest in the occupations and activities of the inhabitants. His portrait of *Mary O'Flaherty* (1920), which includes a cradle in the corner and kittens lapping milk in the foreground, is typical of the human interest common in much of his work of this kind.

Whelan was quite selective in his use and interpretation of Orpen's work and while his influence is evident in aspects of his portraiture and interiors, he chose not to follow Orpen's example in many other areas including the depiction of nudes or of female portraits of the more provoca-

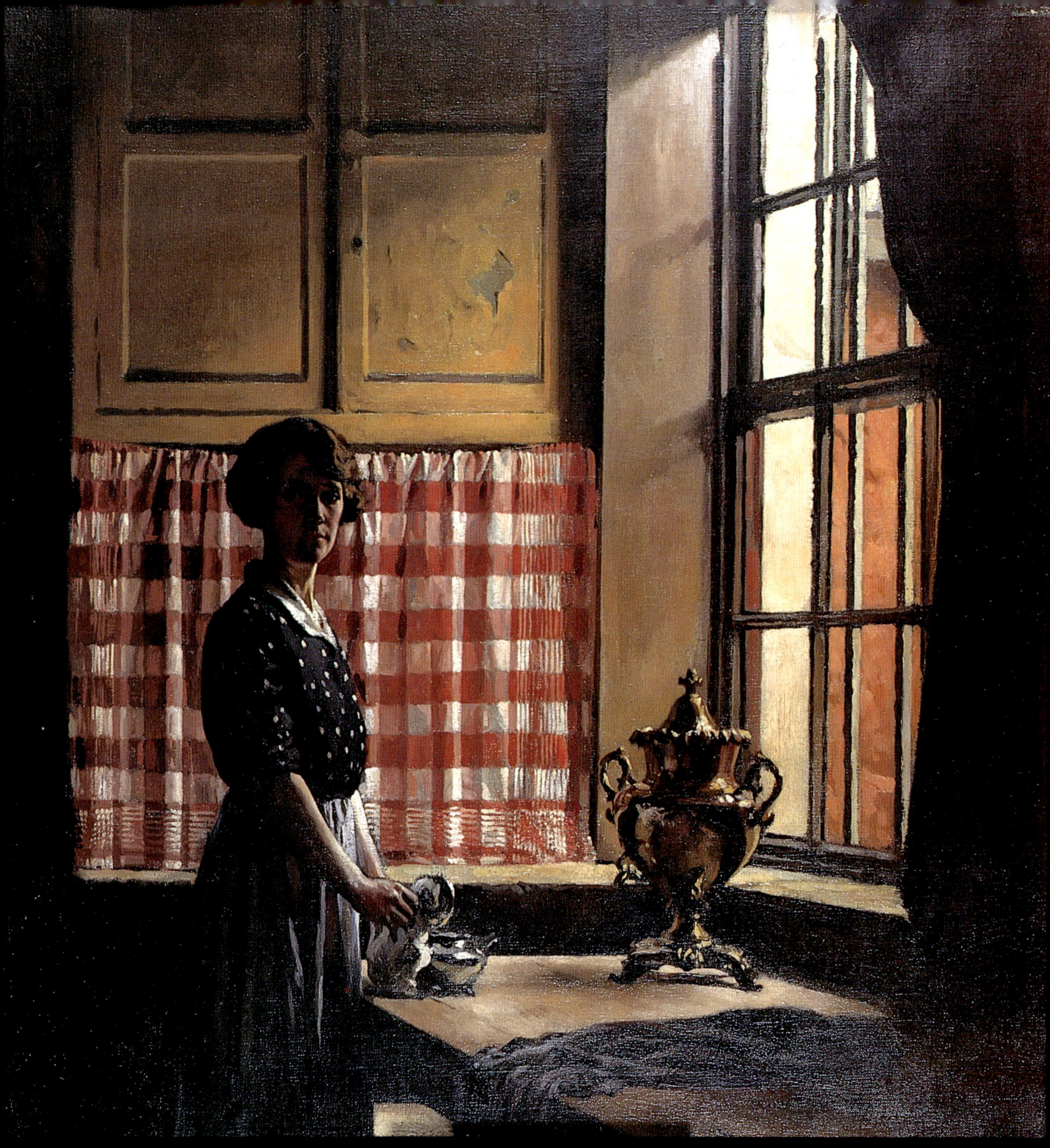

Leo Whelan, The Kitchen Window, *c.* 1927. *Oil on canvas,* 51.1 x 47.7 *cm. Crawford Municipal Art Gallery, Cork*

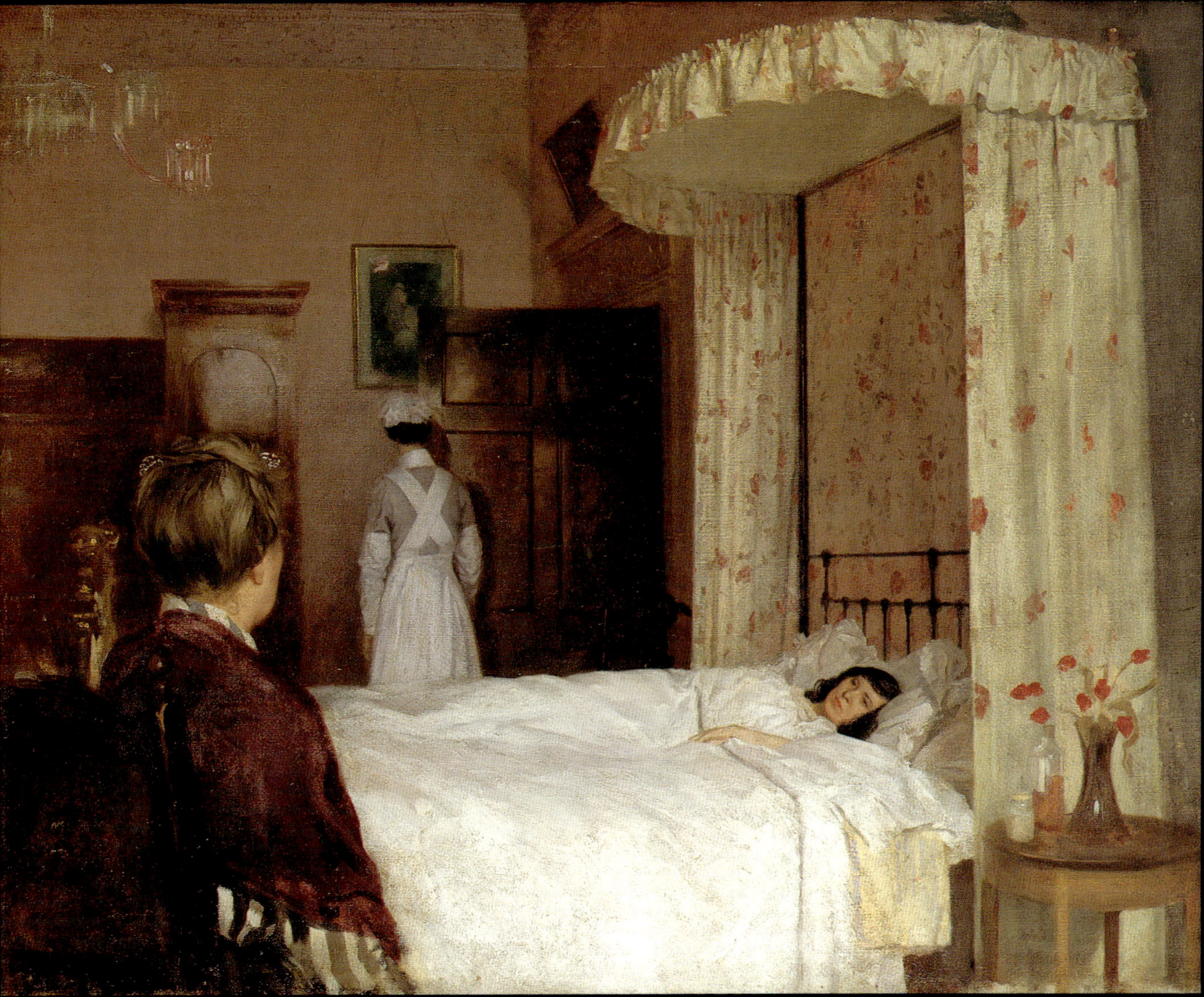

Leo Whelan, The Doctor's Visit c. 1916. Oil on canvas, 92 x 71 cm. National Gallery of Ireland.

LEO WHELAN (1892-1956)

tive, coquettish type. In general there is a certain prudishness and an absence of any overt sexual overtones in Whelan's work which sets it apart from Orpen and his world.

Perhaps the most interesting and individual of all Whelan's works were his kitchen interiors. Here we find a strong link with Dutch seventeenth-century painting and in particular with the work of Vermeer. In a sense, these technically brilliant works are twentieth-century versions of Vermeer's paintings. He painted these periodically throughout his career, and in 1926 one of them (*An Interior*) was highlighted in a review in *Studio* magazine which stated that 'It is as unaffected as it is accomplished and justifies those many admirers of his work who place him foremost in the ranks of Irish painters of genre'.[11] *The Kitchen Window* (Crawford Gallery, Cork)[12] painted in the following year, is an outstanding study of a light-filled interior. In it Whelan focuses on a corner of his basement kitchen in Eccles Street. Standing by the window is his sister Frances who modelled for the picture. While the whole arrangement of the composition is highly reminiscent of the Dutch school, Frances' firm pose and independent air is more representative of the spirit of the 1920s than it is of Vermeer's gentle world. The simplicity of the interior contrasts with the artist's meticulous rendering of all the material surfaces. The light falling in from the window serves to heighten our visual perception of a whole range of surface textures — the peeling paint on the cupboard door, the shining tea urn and the crumpled folds of the red gingham curtain. In *Interior of a Kitchen* (c.1935, Ulster Museum, Belfast[13]), painted some ten years later, we see the same woman, now older with a fuller figure and firmer face. The setting is the same Eccles Street basement but the view is to the centre of the kitchen with the table forming the focal point. Again Whelan demonstrates his great skill and dexterity in rendering a whole array of different shapes and textures; the clear glass bowl, polished apples, rough wicker basket and gleaming crockery. Another fine painting from this period is *A Dublin Kitchen* (1936)[14] which, with its tiled floor and window on the left, resembles the interiors of Vermeer so closely as to be uncanny. On the mantelpiece is a solitary tea caddie and above it a round mirror in which a reflection of the artist at work is clearly visible. The mirror

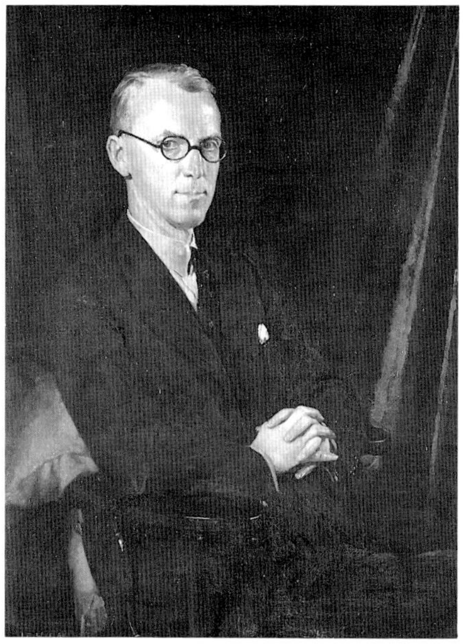

Leo Whelan, Cecil Lavery, 1939, Oil on canvas, 111 x 90 cm. Kings Inns, Dublin.

as a motif occurs in many of Whelan's works as it does in Orpen's. But while Whelan, like Orpen, greatly admired Velazquez's *Las Meninas*, the source that more readily comes to mind here is Jan van Eyck's *Arnolfini Marriage*.

By 1920 Whelan had exhibited an almost equal amount of genre subjects and portraits, and had even painted a number of very promising landscapes. Later, however, he began specialising in portraiture. After the death of his parents he became the main earner in a household which he shared with his two unmarried sisters (Frances and Lily), and it is reasonable to assume that it was this responsibility, together with prevailing market forces, which led Whelan to concentrate more and more on portraiture.

The 1920s saw Whelan emerge as one of the most successful portrait painters in Ireland. In a scathing review of the RHA exhibition of 1926[15] *The Irish Times* singled out Whelan's portrait of the Provost of Trinity College[16] as standing 'quite apart from the rest' though significantly added that in the field of figure pieces 'Mr. Whelan is again the bright exception with his Gypsy' and concluding that 'With his portraits, his Gypsy and his three or four landscapes Mr. Whelan has in this exhibition established his reputation firmly'. Also in that year he became an associate member of the RHA and only two years later a full member.[17] In 1926 he won a medal at the Tailteann Games for his portrait of another provost of Trinity College Dublin, Dr Claude L Purser (1926, TCD).[18]

In official portraiture Whelan's style was unpretentious, straightforward and realistic. Generally he favoured the restricted palette and dark tones characteristic of academic portraiture of the nineteenth century. Among the most memorable of these works are *Lord Dunraven* (1934),[19] *Herbert Dudgeon* (1937, Royal Irish Yacht Club),[20] *Cecil Lavery* (1939, King's Inns)[21] and *Ernest Henry Alton* (1942, TCD).[22] Whelan summed up his own style as portrait painter very well in an interview when he said that

> *present day portraiture is at a disadvantage because of the drabness of contemporary costume, no artist wishes continually to paint collar and tie. However this leads the artist to one of the greatest tests, the manner in which the monotonously-coloured clothes accentuate the hands. By the perfect placing of the hands one may be able to recognise the hint of genius in an artist, but failure to point this gesture will most certainly damn the picture, the portrait and the painter.*[23]

The portrayal of hands in Whelan's own work is often remarkable and indeed crucial to the whole composition.

Whelan's official portraits are well known to Dubliners as they hang in so many of our public institutions. His sitters included a wide range of eminent public figures from the political,[24] academic,[25] clerical, medical[26] and legal[27] worlds.

From the beginning of the 1920s appear his portraits of famous political figures. His family held strongly Republican views and he painted many of the key political figures of this turbulent historical period. His large unfinished group portrait of *GHQ Staff of the Pre-Treaty IRA* (on loan to McKee Barracks)[28] was painted in 1922 and was based on portrait sketches and studies made of individual members of the IRA during clandestine sittings at Whelan's Dawson Street Studio and at his home in Eccles Street (it includes Michael Collins, Richard Mulcahy, Gearóid O'Sullivan, Eamonn Price, Rory O'Connor, Eoin O'Duffy, Sean Russell, Sean McMahon, J J O'Connell, Emmet Dalton, Séamus Donovan, Liam Mellowes and Piaras Béaslaí). Artistically it is uninteresting, particularly because of its unfinished state; the individuals are clearly identifiable but stiff and unconvincing as a

LEO WHELAN (1892-1956)

group. His separate portraits of *Rory O'Connor* (1922, NGI, cat.no.967)and *General Richard Mulcahy* (McKee Barracks) are fairer examples of Whelan's work at this time. Possibly the best known of Whelan's political portraits is that of Michael Collins. Although he exhibited a portrait entitled *Michael Collins TD* in 1922 at the RHA, it is his posthumous portrait *The Late General Michael Collins* (Leinster House and replica in McKee Barracks) exhibited in 1943 (lent by Fine Gael) that is well known. The towering figure of Collins in uniform stands against a dark sky, the peak of his cap throwing his face into shadow. It is a strong and heroic image similar in style to much commemorative portraiture in Europe and America in the 1930s.

For the most part Whelan stuck to his own brand of direct and unromanticised realism for the political portraits of the 1930s and 1940s. Among the more notable of these are *Kevin O'Higgins* (Leinster House), *John F. Costello* (1948, King's Inns) and successive presidents *Douglas Hyde*, (c.1945, Arus an Uachtaran), *Séan T. Ó Ceallaigh* (c.1951, Arus an Uachtaran) and *Eamon de Valera* (1955, Leinster House). With the exception of the Kevin O'Higgins portrait, which has an animated and expressive quality with O'Higgins standing speaking in the Dail Chambers, the majority of these paintings serve to underline the desired permanency, solidity, and respectability of the new state rather than highlight any particular characteristics or personality traits of the individuals concerned.

In his interview of 1944, Whelan discussed what portrait painting meant to him and in doing so explained the criteria he set himself in attempting a portrait:

> *The essence of a good portrait lies in its likeness to the subject, because practical experience has shown that a sitter will never come to life unless the artist has caught those characteristics which delineate the mind. To talk of a good likeness suggests more than a copy of the outer shell. Similarly a painting which accentuates a certain feature of a man, an emphasis on one of his many facial expressions, will not be a portrait , it will be a caricature.*[29]

The majority of Whelan's portraits are characterised by a certain gravity and aloofness which seems to stress the independence and strength of his sitters' characters rather than bring them closer to us by means of highlighting specific personal attributes. This, it would seem, was Whelan's desired goal, he clearly wanted above all to be objective in his portraits and perhaps this accounts for the sense of detachment perceptible in many of his official portraits.

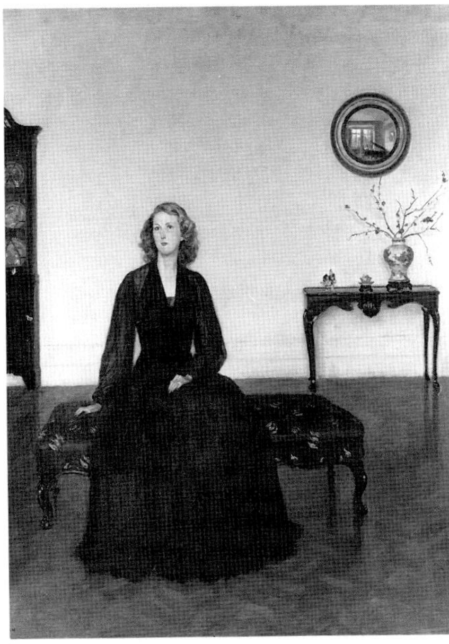

Leo Whelan, Gwladys McCabe in her drawing room c *1946. Oil on canvas 100 x 86.5 cm. National Gallery of Ireland.*

A similar feeling of detachment or distance is apparent in his more varied society portraits. It is interesting, however, to note that in nearly all other respects he kept these two streams of his art totally divorced. His society portraits predominately represent women or women and children. His treatment of women in general is different to that of male sitters whom he usually painted with the minimum of accessories against a monotone curtained background. There are a number of notable exceptions, such as the portraits of *SA Waters* (c.1927) in which the sitter, dressed in tweeds, relaxes in a drawing room interior with a dog by his side, and *Mine Host* in which Jack Nugent is set against the mirrored background of the Dolphin Bar. Also in this vein are the portraits of *The Hon W E Wylie* (both RDS) In one dated 1946 Wylie, who was chairman of the RDS for many years, is portrayed in an office interior with a variety of accessories, while in the other (1939) he is set in a wintry landscape dressed as master of the Ward Union Hunt complete with crop and horn.

Whelan's treatment of female portraits was akin to his treatment of genre figures in that the interior is invariably given equal importance to the sitters themselves. Indeed it is this very aspect that lends them a special significance today as detailed records of the 1920s and 1930s. As 'period pieces' they are excellent, and in many ways their appeal is similar to that of the Dutch interiors which Whelan so admired.

A good example of this type of work is his portrait of *Guendolen* (1925) which so perfectly captures the mood and ambience of the 1920s. Guendolen was the daughter of Sir Nevile Wilkinson, who was himself an accomplished artist and Royal Academy exhibitor. He commissioned the portrait at the time of his daughter's twenty-first birthday. The fashionably dressed figure, lit from behind, her face in half shadow, is portrayed in an appropriately elegant interior. The setting which is so faithfully reproduced is presumably the drawing room of the family's Dublin home. Here as, in many of Whelan's society portraits, the furnishings and decor are used to convey a sense of the sitter's life-style. A major feature in the composition is the carved Georgian mantelpiece with its interior surround of blue and white tiles and polished brass which forms a natural foil for the red and gold of Guendolen's dress. Equally prominent is the oval mirror with its reflection of a water-colour on the opposite wall. Whelan's meticulous attention to detail would not have been wasted on the Wilkinsons, who were themselves passionately involved in collecting miniature furnishings for the now famous dolls' house 'Titania's Palace' which Sir Nevile had completed in 1922 in response to Guendolen's enquires about the abodes of fairies.[30]

Painted with equal attention to surroundings and ambience in the 1930s are Whelan's interior portraits of *The Countess of Dunraven* (1934)[31] and *Aileen, Countess of Meath* (c.1935). In the latter the figure is enthroned in an empire style swan chair in the very grand setting of the marble columned drawing room at Kilruddery. Here too the stylish white satin dress of the sitter is picked up by, and echoed in, elements of the interior furnishings.

In comparison to *Guendolen* or the *Countess of Meath*, his portrait of *Gwladys McCabe* (National Gallery of Ireland, cat. no.4563) is more restrained and minimalist in approach. Painted over a long period of many sittings during the 1940s, this pic-

LEO WHELAN (1892-1956)

ture was not a commission but a gift for his friend and host of many years. Gwladys McCabe (1902-89) was a well-known Dublin socialite who was closely associated with theatrical, literary and artistic circles of the period. She was a lifelong member, and for some time President, of the United Arts Club. Unusually for Whelan, the interior is arranged, perhaps intentionally, somewhat like a stage setting. The Chippendale-style vitrine, Georgian side table, mirror and porcelain vase were not, however, stage props but were all part of the McCabe's interior. The sombre effect created by the black dress so typical of the war years is heightened by the bareness of the pictureless wall. Although an avid collector of Irish paintings, she was (according to her family) inclined to hang them in her study or in her husband's room, rather than in her drawing room.[32] Characteristically, Whelan has included the mirror in which a reflection of the window side of the room complete with grand piano, can be seen.

Throughout his career Whelan produced, alongside his interiors and society portraits, genre studies of individuals where the accessories and setting are as important as the figure. One of the most interesting examples of this sort of picture is his *Gypsy* (1923)[33] which is of a woman in a black felt hat and shawl, set against a west of Ireland type landscape with a caravan in the distance. This work, which echoes the work of Orpen, was, as we have seen, critically acclaimed and considered by both Thomas Bodkin[34] and AE[35] to have been one of the best pictures exhibited by anyone in 1924. Other subjects of this type are *Waiting* (c.1918), a portrait of Miss O'Sullivan seated in tiled hallway with a dog and *The Chinese Shawl* (c.1927), a portrait of his niece Lena wearing a white crepe de chine fringed shawl which is very probably the same shawl that Orpen used in his painting of the same title in 1912.[36] Whelan also used male figures for his subject-pieces, the most striking of which is *The Fiddler* (c.1932, Crawford Gallery, Cork) This naturalistic study is perhaps the best characterisation of a subject that he ever did. The utterly convincing figure of the fiddler with his balding head and wrinkled brow is painted with a subjectivity and sensitivity uncommon in Whelan's *oeuvre* and suggests a strong personal bond between artist and sitter. The model was not, despite appearances, a dedicated musician but a Dublin handyman noted for his fondness of the drink. He also appears in *The Cello Player* which together with *The Fiddler* and *The Whistler* comprise a series of musician subjects.

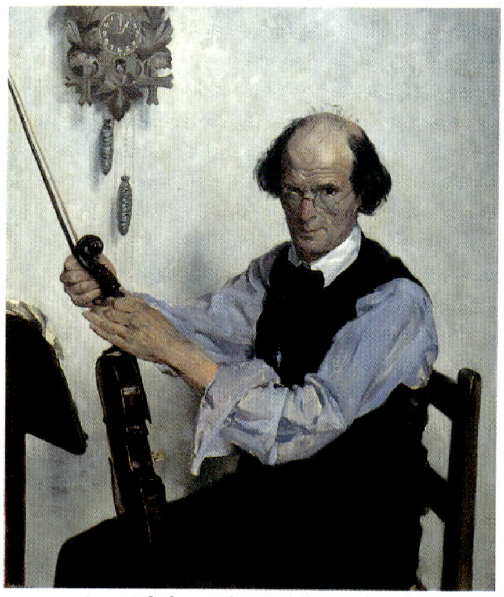

Leo Whelan, The Fiddler, *c 1935. Oil on canvas. 108 x 92.4 cm. Crawford Municipal Gallery, Cork.*

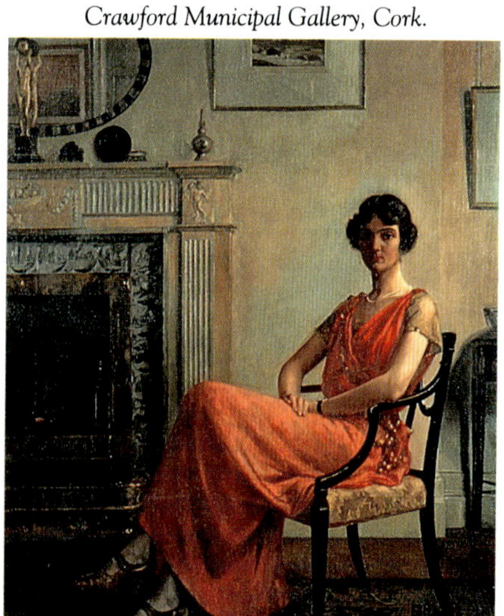

Leo Whelan, Guendolen Wilkinson, *1925. Oil on canvas, 51 x 40 cm. Private Collection.*

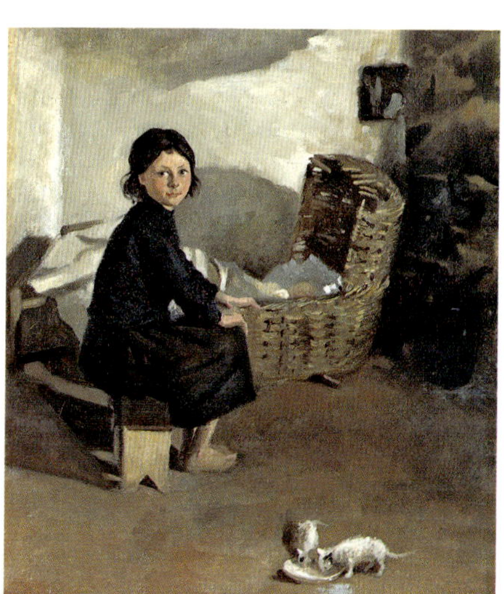

Leo Whelan, Mary O'Flaherty. *Oil on canvas, 37.5 x 29 cm. Private Collection.*

Finally, mention should be made of Whelan's religious pictures though admittedly these are very few in spite of his own religious convictions.

He exhibited only three religious pictures at the RHA and all of these were commissions. The most important was from the Haverty Trust, in 1931 to commemorate the Eucharistic Council of 1932. Thomas Bodkin, then Director of the National Gallery, proposed that Leo Whelan, Sean Keating and Margaret Clarke be commissioned to depict scenes of their own choice from the life of St Patrick.[37] These were exhibited at the time of the Congress and afterwards presented to public bodies. Clarke's *St Patrick Climbs Croagh Patrick* went to the Hugh Lane Municipal Gallery, Keating's *St Patrick Lights the Paschal Fire at Slane* to the Irish College, Rome and Whelan's *The Baptism by St Patrick of Ethna the Fair and Fedelmia the Ruddy, daughters of the Ard Rí Laoghaire* is also thought to have been presented to an Irish institution abroad.[38] Gills publishers commissioned *The Blessed Virgin Mary Mother of Ireland* in 1932 and *St Bridgit* in 1934 and made sets of two hundred prints from each. In the former, the Virgin and Child are set in a landscape and both the Virgin and the view are specifically Irish in feeling. The *St Bridgit* is interesting for the meticulous treatment of the white drapery of the saint's habit which is an important element of the composition.

One of Whelan's admirers and a patron was the famous Irish tenor Count John McCormack. McCormack is said to have repeatedly encouraged him to move to America where, with the right introductions, he felt sure Whelan would be successful. But Whelan was to resist all offers to move to either America or England where he had many contacts. He appears to have had no desire to live abroad, unlike his contemporaries and fellow portrait painters Sleator and Tuohy. His apparent lack of interest in travel may in his early years have been dictated by financial circumstances. George Russell's hope in 1924 'that some provision will be made so that artists of the calibre of Keating, Tuohy or Whelan could get scholarships which would enable them to study in London, in Madrid, in Rome',[39]

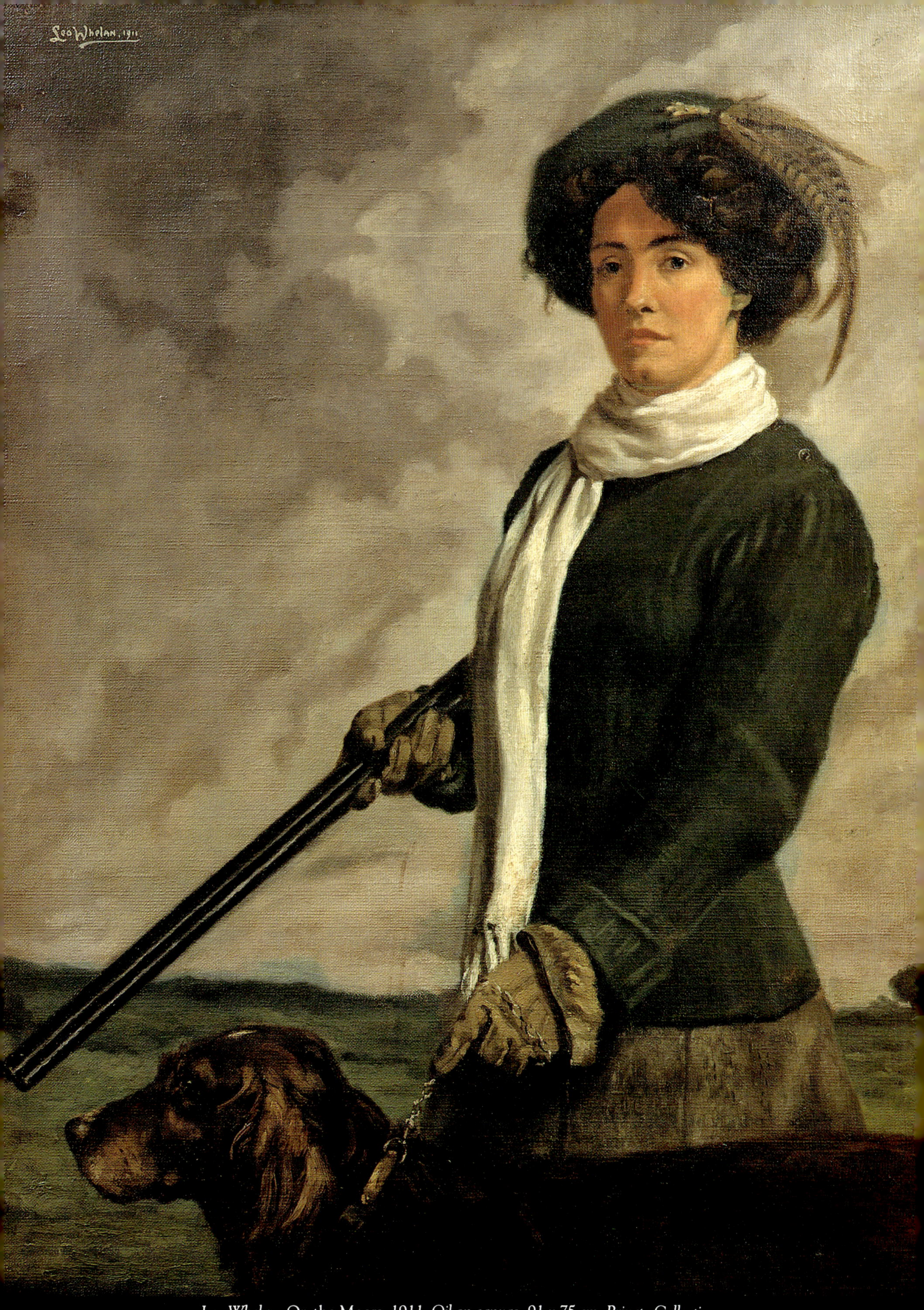

Leo Whelan, On the Moors, 1911, Oil on canvas, 91 x 75 cm, Private Collection

LEO WHELAN (1892-1956)

would certainly seem to suggest this.

Undoubtedly Whelan would have benefited by exposure to main stream European art. It would surely have encouraged him to experiment with a wider range of compositional forms and to have developed his personal style more fully. But because he limited himself to the artistic isolation which characterised Dublin in those years,[40] he was, it seems, ill-equipped initially to break away from Orpen's influence and later to achieve his full artistic potential.

As it was, he stayed in Ireland and built up one of the most successful portrait practices in the country. Not only was he adopted whole-heartedly, along with O'Sullivan, Keating and Sleator, as semi-offical state portraitist of the newly independent Ireland, but he also succeeded to Orpen's lucrative and fashionable Anglo-Irish portrait practice. By the time he died in 1956 from leukaemia he had become an established figure in the Dublin art world.[41]

Wanda Ryan-Smolin.

Wanda Ryan-Smolin has an MA degree in the History of Art from the Jagillonian University, Cracow. She was formerly on the staff of the National Gallery of Ireland (1981-89), and a lecturer in the National College of Art and Design (1988-91). She is the author of King's Inns Portraits *(Dublin, 1992).*

Note: All works are in private collections unless otherwise stated.

ACKNOWLEDGEMENTS:

I am most grateful to the artist's nieces, Eileen and Lena Murnaghan, for their invaluable assistance.

NOTES

1. He exhibited an average of about six paintings at the RHA every year between 1911 and 1956. See A.M. Stewart, *Royal Hibernian Academy of Arts index of exhibitors and their works 1826-1979*, (Dublin, 1986)
2. See John Turpin, 'William Orpen as Student and Teacher', *Studies*, LXVIII No.271-272, 1979 and 'The Dublin Metropolitan School of Art 1900-1923', *Dublin Historical Record*, XXXVII, No.2, March 1984; XXXVIII, No.2, March 1985 and XXXVIII, No.3, June 1985 and Bruce Arnold, *Orpen. Mirror to an Age*, (London, 1981), chapter 11 for a discussion of Orpen as a teacher at the DMSA.
3. William Orpen, *Stories of Old Ireland and Myself*, (London, 1924), p. 76
4. Between 1911 and 1916 Whelan won a total of five prizes at the Taylor Art Scholarship competitions in the RDS. From 1911 he entered as student of the DMSA and in 1916 as a student of the RHA, see the annual *Reports and Proceedings of the Royal Dublin Society*.
5. Dr. O'Connell-Redmond, JP, FRCSI. (exhibited RHA, 1911) and the Most Rev. Dr. Clare, Archbishop of Perth , Australia , c.1911-12 (All Hallows College).
6. Illustrated in Arnold, op. cit., p.240
7. A set piece, for which he was awarded a Taylor prize of £20.
8. Arnold, op. cit., plate 5.
9. Illustrated in Thomas Bodkin, *Twelve Irish Artists*, (Waddington 1940).
10. See Kenneth McConkey *A Free Spirit, Irish Art 1860-1960*, p. 132 for a discussion of Orpen's *Old John's Cottage, Connemara* (1908) and its influence on Irish painters of Whelan's generation.
11. Review of the New Irish Salon in the *Studio*, vol.91, 1926, p.357 (Ill.)
12. This was a Gibson Fund purchase from the artist for the Gallery in 1927.
13. Purchased by the Haverty Trust and presented to the Ulster Museum in 1941.
14. *The Dublin Kitchen* was exhibited three times at the RHA. in 1940, 1953 and 1957.
15. *Irish Times*,11 April, 1926, p.8
16. *John Henry Bernard*, Provost of Trinity College Dublin 1919-1927 and Archbishop of Dublin. This work is in TCD, see A. Crookshank and D. Webb, *The Paintings and Sculptures in Trinity College Dublin*, (Dublin, 1990), p.22 for details and illustration.
17. He was later to become a trustee of the RHA and a member of the council. He also taught for some time in the RHA schools and at the DMSA.
18. See Crookshank, op. cit., p.113
19. See S.B. Kennedy, *Irish Art and Modernism 1880-1960*, (The Institute of Irish Studies, The Queens University Belfast,1991), p.307
20. See Leo Whelan, 'What is a Portrait?', *Irish Art: A Volume of Articles and Illustrations* (Dublin, 1944), p.17
21. See Wanda Ryan-Smolin, *King's Inns Portraits* (Dublin, 1992), p.40
22. See Crookshank, op. cit., p.12
23. Whelan, op. cit., p.18
24. Three of these (Griffith, Collins and O'Higgins) are illustrated in *Memorial to the Founders of the State*, (Dublin, 1944).
25. See Crookshank, op.cit. for details and illustrations of the 8 Whelan portraits in Trinity College .
26. E. O'Brien, A. Crookshank and G.Wolstenholm, *A Portrait of Irish Medicine*, (Dublin, 1984) records 11 portraits by Whelan in various public institutions in Dublin.
27. See Ryan-Smolin, op.cit for details and illustrations of three portraits by Whelan in the King's Inns.
28. I am grateful to Thomas Ryan for his assistance in locating this work.
29. Whelan, op.cit. p.16
30. See Sir Nevile Wilkinson, *To All and Singular* (London, 1925).
31. Referred to in Kennedy, op. cit., p.168
32. Information supplied by A. Le Harivel, NGI.
33. Illustrated in S. B. Kennedy, *Irish Art and Modernism 1920-1949*. Unpublished Ph.D. dissertation, University of Dublin, 1987, vol.II, pl.155
34. *Studio*, vol.87, 1924, p.284
35. *Irish Statesman*, 17 May, 1924, p.296
36. Orpen's *The Chinese Shawl* (National Gallery of Victoria, Melbourne) is illustrated in Arnold, op. cit., p.284
37. *Irish Times*, 6 June, 1931, p.6
38. I am grateful to Gwen Woods for her assistance in trying to locate this work.
39. *Irish Statesman*, 17 May, 1924, p.296
40. For a relevant comment on the artistic climate of the period see Rosemarie Mulcahy, 'Patrick J. Tuohy 1894-1930', *Irish Arts Review Yearbook*, 1989-90, pp.114-15. For the political background see Brian P.Kennedy, *Dreams and Responsibilities. The State of the Arts in Independent Ireland*, (Dublin, Arts Council, 1990)
41. He was appointed to numerous committees including the RDS Irish National Art Committee, its Industries Art and General Purposes Committee and the selection committee of the Oireachtas Exhibition (1944). He was also a member of the Chelsea Arts Club, the Stephen's Green Club and the United Arts Club.

SIDNEY SMITH: PAINTER AND MURALIST (1912-1982)

The artistic career of Sidney Smith, painter and muralist, who left Belfast in 1948, is outlined by his daughter, writer **Paula Chabanais** and his nephew, artist, **David Goldberg.**

The revival of decorative mural painting in England was a project conceived and promoted by Henry Tonks during the early part of this century.[1] Tonks directed commissions to his chosen student, Rex Whistler, who painted his best-known mural, *The Pursuit of Rare Meats*, for the Tate Gallery Restaurant, London in 1926.

Whistler was killed in 1944 on active service, just when Sidney Smith was painting his first mural for the British Restaurant, Great Victoria Street, Belfast. During the next twenty years Smith was to pursue the art of mural painting, becoming a master of *trompe l'œil*, which he used in an ever more skilful and refined way. He established himself, first in Northern Ireland and later in London and Europe, as a muralist whose work was sought by nobility, bankers, commerce, hotels, and shipping lines. Smith estimated that during his career, he had painted 120,000 square feet in more than forty murals, totalling a minimum of seventy panels.

By the time he began mural painting in 1944, Smith was thirty-two. He had been married to Grace Hamilton for two years and their only child, Paula, had just been born. Though he continued to paint portraits and landscapes throughout his life, at this time he began the specialization in murals that would characterize the rest of his career. He had already taken his teaching diploma at the Belfast College of Art and was there engaged in part-time teaching. One of his close friends and an early admirer, John Hewitt, described him as one of the five outstanding Northern Irish painters, the others being Toogood, Luke, Carr, and Middleton.

Belfast: The Early Years (1912-1938)

Sidney Smith was born on 19 April, 1912, at 50, Landscape Terrace, a cul-de-sac adjoining Cliftonville Park in Belfast, a small Jewish enclave in the midst of the Protestant Shankill area of the Crumlin Road. He was the eldest of the three children of Alexander and Rachel Smith (née Cristol), both of whom were of Baltic Jewish origin. His father was born in Polonga, Latvia; his mother, of Lithuanian descent, was born in Cork.

The Smith family's house was a large, three-storey Victorian building at the top of Landscape Terrace. The ground floor had three large reception rooms. On the return of the first floor landing was the lumber room, which had a sloping, glass roof. It might have been custom-built as a studio, and indeed, became one.

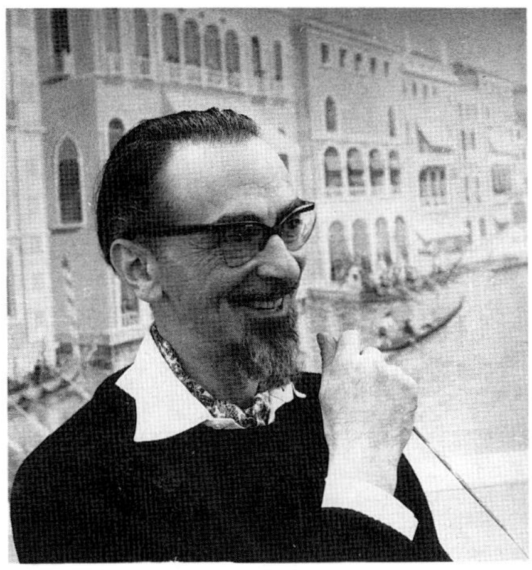

Sidney Smith with *The Rialto* mural for Transvaal Castle, 1962.

As a child Smith was frequently ill, and for much of his boyhood he was confined to bed, suffering from bouts of chronic bronchial pneumonia and pleurisy, not easily treated in those days. During those many hours in bed, he drew a great deal and was a voracious reader. On occasion he was attended by a resident nurse. The first drawing his sister, Sheila Goldberg, recalls was of the corner of the nurse's apron disappearing behind the door. As he said, 'the nurse was always rushing in and out.' What he saw and drew was the white of her apron flashing through the door.

It was his mother who supported and encouraged his appreciation and love of both art and music; (he became an enthusiastic guitarist, performing in public and for Northern Ireland BBC). Smith bought paints, took art classes and made good progress. When he was well enough to leave the house he could often be found painting for hours at the gates of Belfast Castle, which dominates a fabulous view of the city surrounded by greenery. John Hewitt, a friend, art critic, and writer, considered that Smith had most sympathy with cityscapes, especially gritty, suburban allotments, city streets under snow, or tall buses swaying in the rain.

Smith was in his early twenties when he met and became close friends with the eminent Belfast portrait painter and teacher, Boyd Morrison (1896-1969). Morrison had a fine reputation in England and was artist in residence to the late Lady Jersey. After his return to Belfast he took on some students, of whom Smith was one. Morrison was keen to teach the young man and often came to the lumber room, where they painted together.

This was to be a turning point. For the next few years Morrison taught Smith well, instilling a strong respect for drawing and colour. The lesson of Michelangelo to Antonio is one Smith learned and passed on to his own students, 'Draw, draw, draw.' He once recalled a lesson in tonality. When he had carefully worked out the tones and was just resolving the colour scheme, 'Boyd would come up behind you, like a shadow on your shoulder, and land a blob of lemon yellow into the middle of the canvas, and say, "pitch it to that." He'd wreck the whole bloody thing.'

In 1937, Smith painted a strong, full-scale portrait of a sailor in uniform, entitled *Marius*.[2] The pose resembles *Zouave* by Van Gogh, one of the artists Smith greatly admired. By 1938, Smith had made a painting trip to Brittany, possibly accompanied by Morrison. (A painting of *Cornfields*[3] exists from this trip.) In this year, Smith first exhibited at important society exhibitions in London at the Royal Society of British Artists and in Dublin at the Royal Hibernian Academy. Between 1940 and 1944, he exhibited annually at the Royal Hibernian Academy. Thereafter, he turned his attention more to murals and therefore ceased to exhibit much until the 1960s, when he exhibited again in such London Society exhibitions such as the Royal Society of British Artists and the New English Art Club. The exact details of dates and entries are not known.

Howard Street, Belfast: The War Years (1939—1947)

In 1940, Smith finally moved his studio from the lumber room of Landscape Terrace to two rooms on the top floor of 20, Howard Street. On the street level was an art shop that also sold paintings. At the time, there were only two galleries in Belfast, Rodman's and McGee's. He sold paintings through both dealers and is thought to have

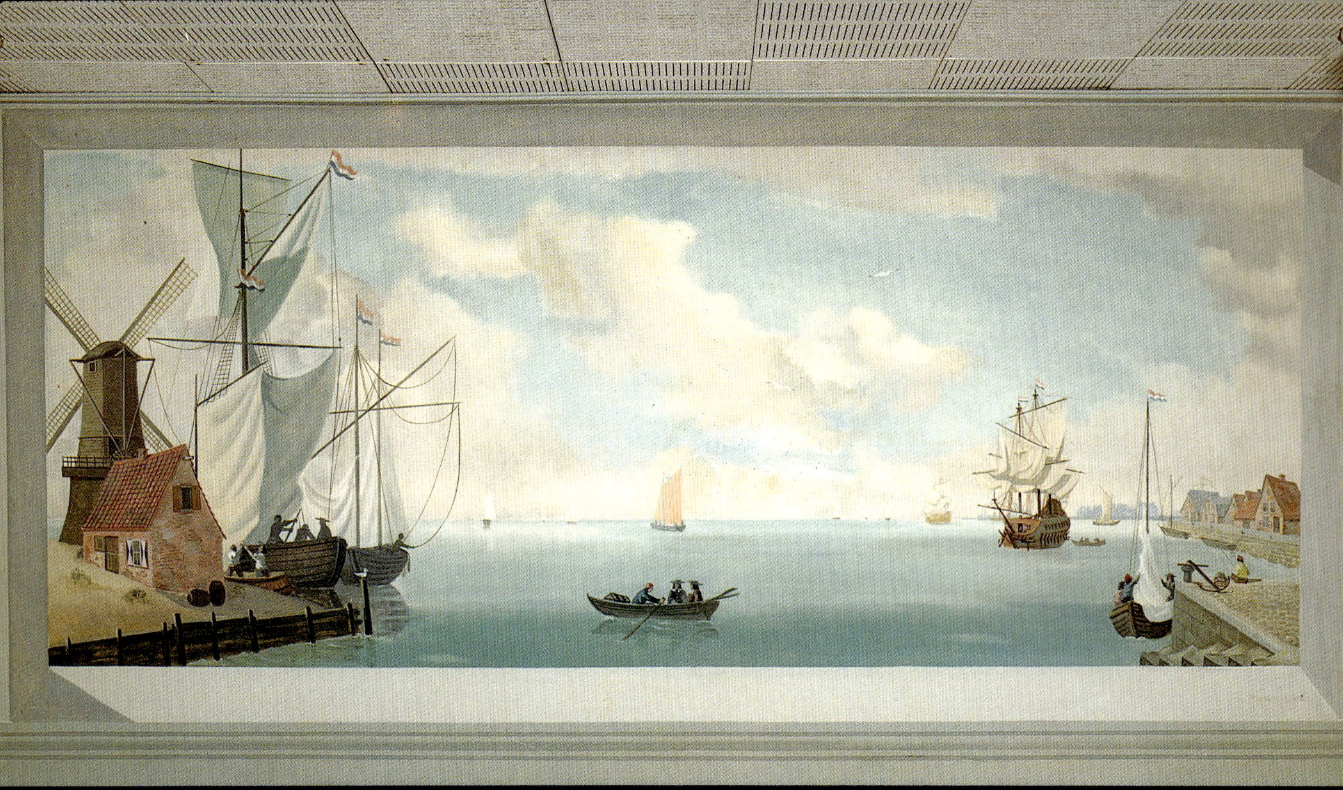

Sidney Smith, *Dutch Seascape*, c.1954, 8' x 4'. One of three panels for John Louden, Holland.

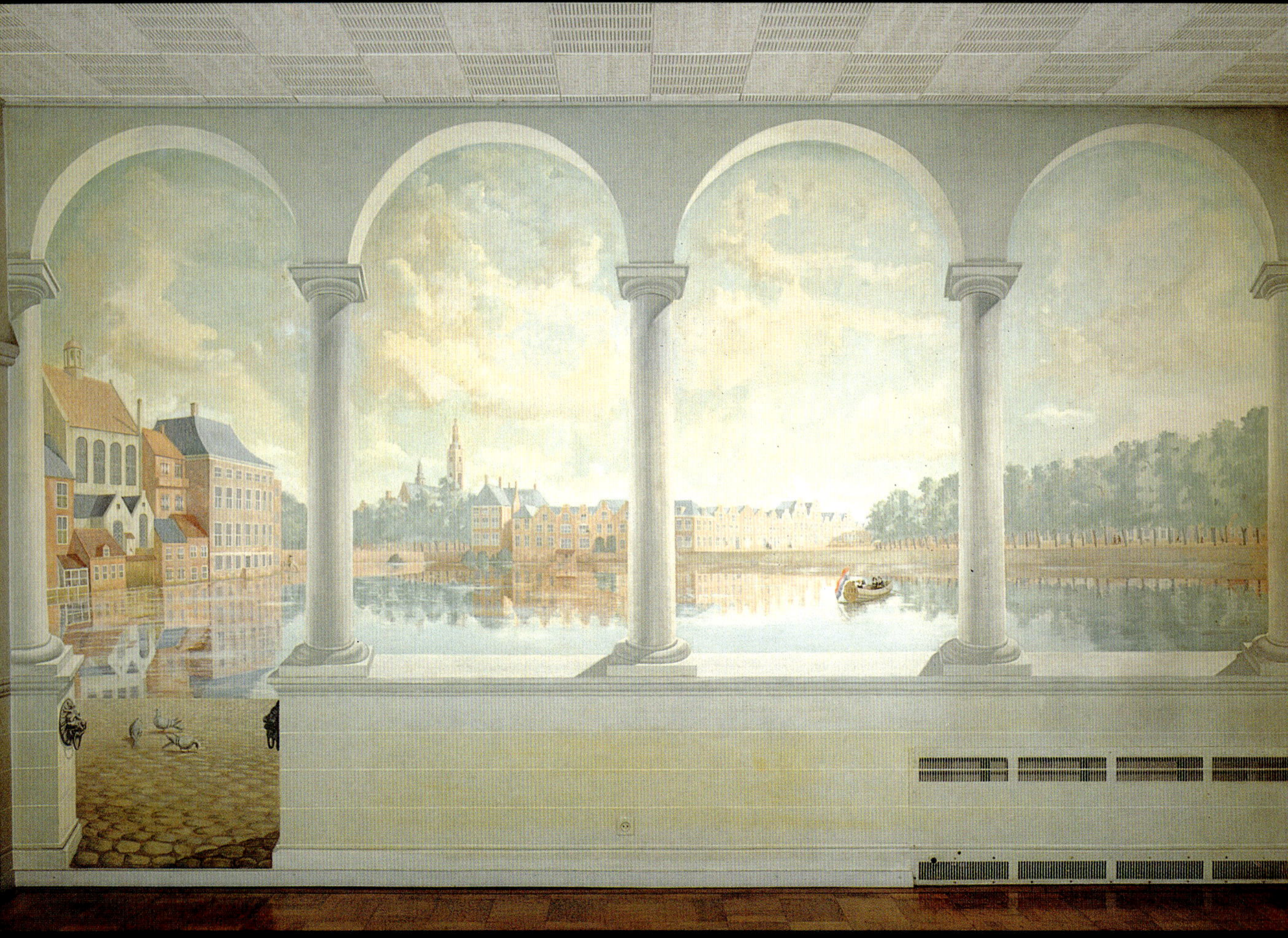

Sidney Smith, *The Old Hague*, c.1954, 22' x 11'. John Louden.

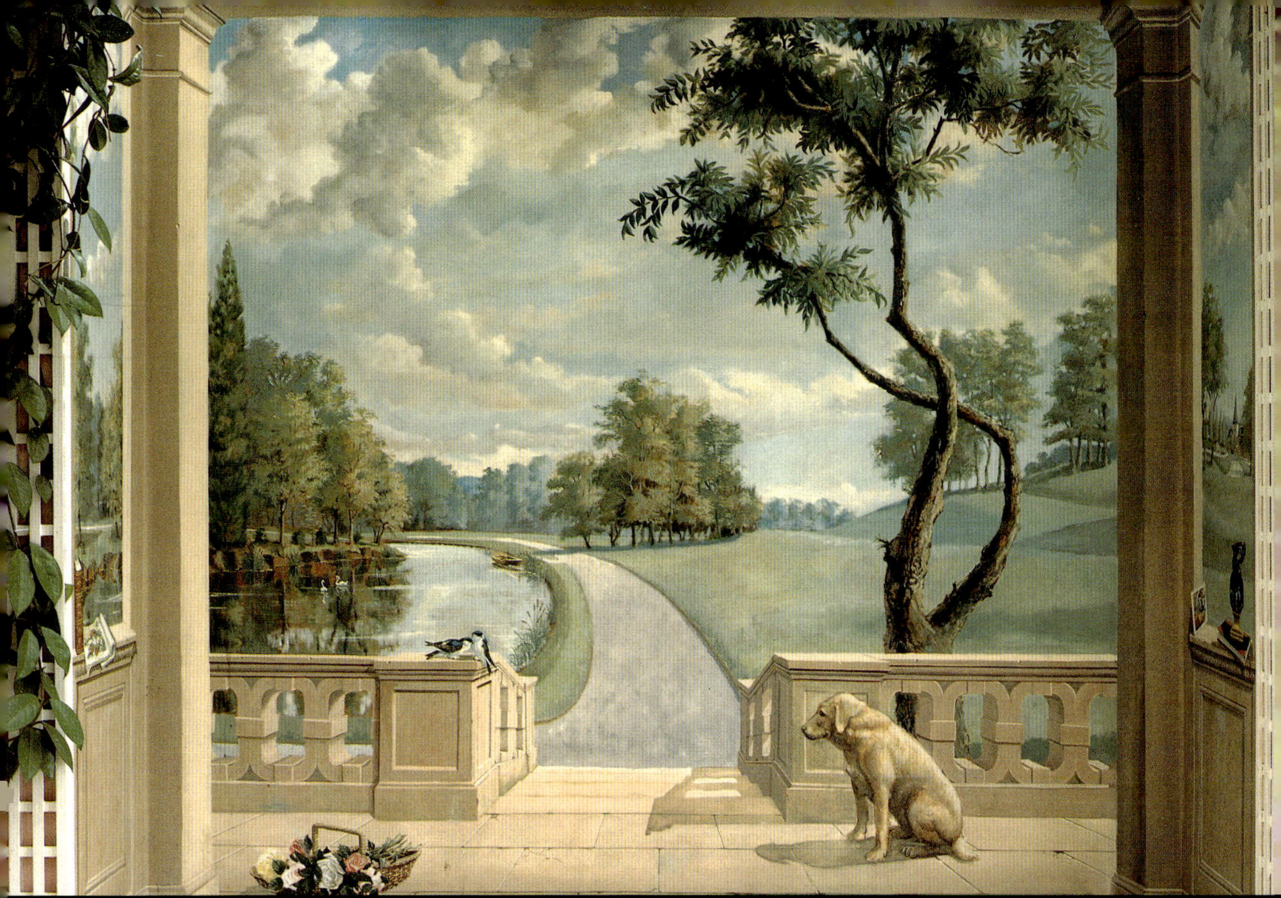

Sidney Smith, *Lockinge*, 1962, 15' x 9', Christopher Loyd, Wantage, Oxford.

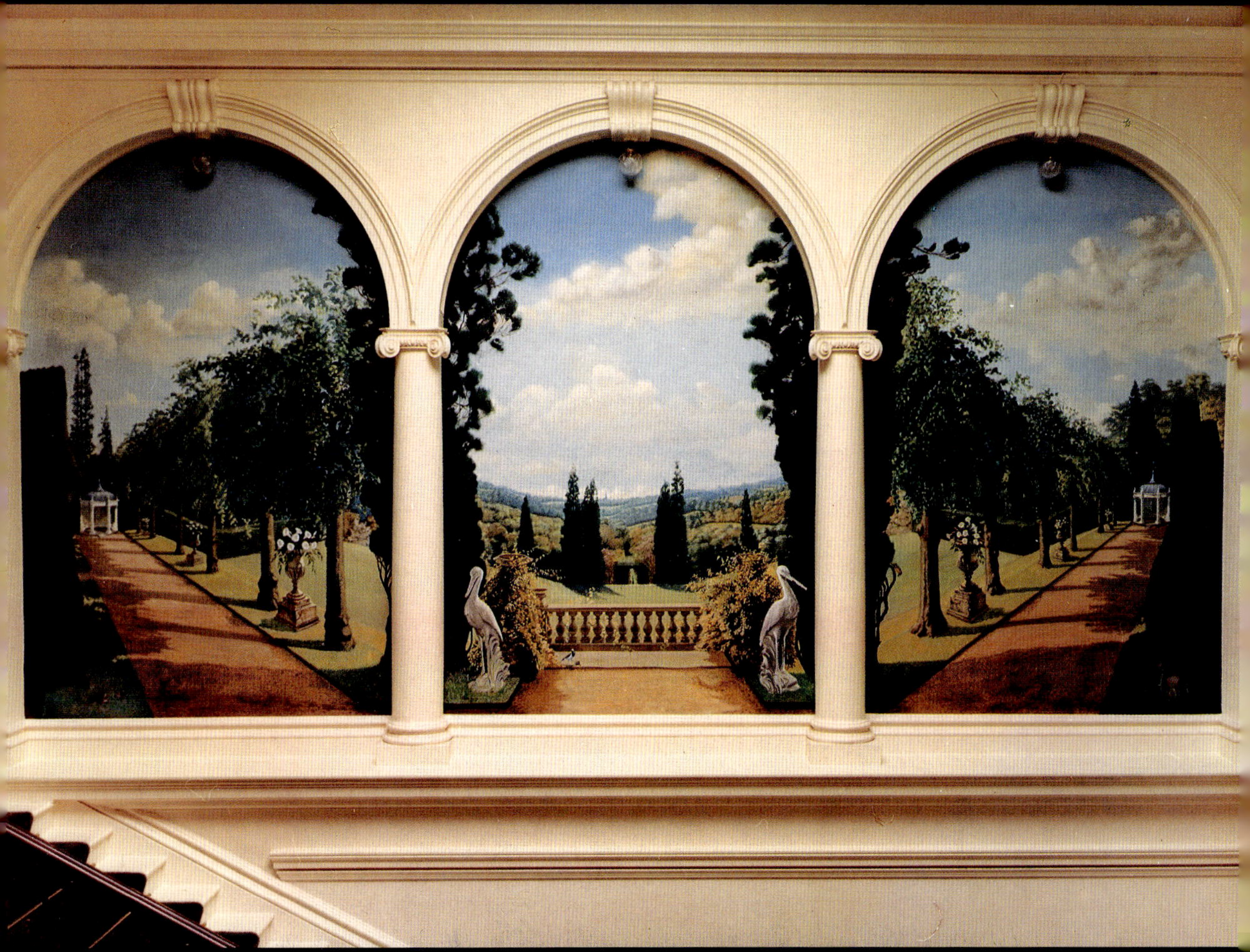

SIDNEY SMITH: PAINTER AND MURALIST (1912-1982)

consigned work to Victor Waddington, who had opened a gallery in South Anne Street, Dublin. By this time Smith was also receiving portrait commissions.

The Howard Street studio became a well-known meeting place for artists and writers. Tom Carr, one of his closest friends, remembers Smith as, 'a great personality and full of fun, he was someone one wanted to be with, who loved to enjoy himself, and was good at doing it. He was a great charmer and great at a party.' Carr can't recall exactly when they first met, but says:

> *...it was early in the war and probably in Campbell's Milk Bar, which I usually visited on trips to Belfast from Newcastle, where we lived. I was invited to his studio in Howard Street and offered the use of easel and paints and a shared model, a kindness which Sidney extended to other visiting artists, such as Daniel O'Neill (Smith's student) and Colin Middleton.*

Carr also recalls that clowns and acrobats from Dick Hunter's circus would sit for them on occasion. The Smiths also visited the Carrs in Newcastle. Carr remembers, '...here again we shared a circus theme when Duffy's came to town and set up tent and halted horse-drawn caravans for a week-end.' Smith also painted landscape and beach scenes but Carr's principal memory of him is as a portrait and mural painter.

Smith had the usual problems associated with his occupation, namely making a living from the sale of his work. It is thought that the studio in Howard Street must have been partially subsidised by his father. At one time, Smith tried working with his father, who was a money lender and a successful businessman, but business was not for Smith and it was a short-lived collaboration. Nonetheless, his father continued to help him both during the early years and during periods when illness rendered him incapable of working.

The recollections of Smith's contemporaries are contradictory. Some remember him as being quiet and rather introverted; while others remember a dapper, fun-loving young man, who was at the centre of a lively group of artists. James McIntyre remembers the frequent social evenings at the studio in the period from 1943 to 1948, though in all probability, they started at the beginning of Smith's tenure there, for Smith was gregarious. McIntyre recalls that, 'the studio was smashing. He had excellent equipment, and stacks of ready-primed canvases, and I remember pots and pots of brushes. No one else had anything like it. None of us had any money.'

At the outbreak of the war, both Smith and his brother volunteered for active service. Smith was rejected due to ill-health, but was not to be discouraged from making some contribution; together with Boyd Morrison he painted camouflage for the Army. He also gave talks on art in country towns and in Belfast factories, all under the auspices of CEMA (now the Arts Council of Northern Ireland). In 1942, Smith was assigned to the American Army in Northern Ireland as an unofficial war artist. As a result of this last role, he did many drawings of black soldiers and officers, and of balloon sites. John Hewitt wrote:[4]

> *He would respond vigorously to the romantic motifs of Breton matelots and coloured American soldiers, and once or twice he has achieved an Ardizzone gusto as in* Home Sweet Home, *a rowdy portrayal of an army billet, loud with song and instrument. Perhaps his best work is in the representation of balloon sites in which he has made arrangements of line and mass.*

In 1943, he was elected a member of the National Society of Painters, London and prepared a series of lectures for CEMA as well as a series of art review broadcasts for the BBC.

The Irish Murals (1944–1947)

Smith's career as a mural artist began around 1944, with a commission for the British Restaurant, Great Victoria Street, Belfast. Between 1944 and 1948 he was to paint no fewer than thirteen large murals on more than twenty panels. He painted for Wilson's factory canteen in Newforge and for the Derry and Lurgan war factories. The Derry mural was based on the famous siege of 1689, the longest in Irish history, lasting for one hundred and five days. The Irish army of James II laid siege to Derry and to ensure its efficacy laid a boom across the mouth of Lough Foyle. The siege ended when a ship broke through the boom and brought supplies to the city. The mural focused on the unloading of the ship. While he was painting it Smith had a visit from the Mayor of Derry, a man of temperance. Several barrels of rum that Smith had painted unloaded on the quayside caught the Mayor's eye. 'What's in them barrels?' he asked. Smith, aware that the a truthful answer would cost him the mural, replied, 'Them barrels are full of herring.'

For Narrow Water Castle on Carlingford Lough he painted three panels based on the legends of the lake. As well he created decorative panels at the Royal Ulster Agricultural Society, the Ideal Home exhibition, and the British Industries Fair .

Through his contact with the architect Henry Lynch-Robinson, he received six commissions to paint murals for lounge and cocktail bars as part of renovation undertaken to attract the 'custom of ladies.' Included among these were the LMS Lounge, the Fort Bar on the Springfield Road, and a thirty-foot-high ceiling for Kelly's Cellars. Kelly's was owned by JJ Tohill, who must have commissioned the mural. His son, also JJ Tohill, described the mural in his book *Pubs of Ulster*:

> *When the cocktail lounge was opened in 1948, the main talking-point was the inspired mural (Michelangelo style) on the ceiling, by the internationally-known local artist Sidney Smith. His unique mural, fully in keeping with the place, was classical mythology brought up to date. The entire ceiling was adorned with a playful decoration of Bacchus, God of Wine. Here were to be seen satyrs and centaurs romping through the Olympian skies bearing trays of wine in a mad sort of egg and spoon race.*

Twenty nine years later, Tohill wrote:

> *The Tudor lounge with the great rustic fireplace remains unchanged, but the cocktail lounge was just drab and dreary looking and drastically changed for the worse. I looked up at the ceiling expecting to see Sydney (sic) Smith's masterpiece, only to be aghast at what I saw: red paint! Somebody had committed a sacrilege by destroying an irreplaceable work of art. Sydney Smith's Vino Mythology cost the enormous sum of £600 way back in 1948. What would it be worth today? ...isn't it sad to think that one of his earliest and favourite creations is probably lost for ever?'*

This was not the only mural to be lost through deliberate action. In fact, destruction is almost a byword against the long list of Smith's creations, many of which disappeared well within his lifetime. Of the thirteen murals painted in Northern Ireland, only two exist and one is certainly at serious risk. One is in the Fort Bar, Belfast, where he also did a Bacchus mural, and the other in the side chapel of the British Sailor's Society where he might

SIDNEY SMITH: PAINTER AND MURALIST (1912-1982)

also have done a mural in the canteen. The Chapel mural was quite an early one. Leslie Owen Baxter, recalls that it was on the theme of 'I shall make ye fishers of men.' The mural depicted the figure of Christ in the centre with two figures on either side. In his hand he holds a huge black fishing net, which sweeps down and outwards, controlling the lower half of the mural. It is dark, olive-green and black; the face of Christ was modelled on Smith's own.

The three panels for Narrow Water Castle were done for the bar when the castle was a hotel. In recent years the panels were destroyed, ironically while the castle was being converted into an art gallery! Two murals that he painted for Leslie Brand's apartment have also vanished. And a mural he returned to Belfast to paint in 1963, in the Culloden Hotel, is, sadly, no longer extant.

During 1947, towards the end of his years in Belfast, Smith began an association with the Ballet Rambert. Marie Rambert was enthralled with his work and gave him *carte blanche* to sketch her dancers from back stage at all opportune moments. The bulk of this work has been dispersed among a large number of collectors.

The Move to London:1948

It was probably late in 1948 when, with his wife and small daughter, he left a burgeoning career in Belfast for the scope of opportunity afforded by London. The culture shock which must have ensued from leaving a small, tightly-knit community and arriving in post-war London can be imagined. London was then a city of depression and disbelief, desperately struggling to shake itself out of the ravages of war and the extensive damage inflicted during the blitz. Unexploded bombs were discovered daily and the city was just beginning its long and slow recovery. His daughter, Paula , then about four, dimly remembers the struggle of the early years in London:

> *We lived in a basement flat somewhere in Warwick Avenue, I remember interminable helpings of porridge, coupons, endless attendance in lengthy queues at the shops—every shop! and my father's concern and anxiety over where the next meal would come from.*

These early years were extremely difficult and the strains on the marriage, which many of their friends had considered ill-advised from the start, began to escalate. Smith struggled to make a living, and of necessity turned his hand to other skills, both old and new. He restored and applied new gold-leaf to the cornices of a number of eighteenth and early nineteenth-century ceilings. He worked with the recently developed technique of air-brushing for magazine illustration, and he was frequently commissioned to paint copies of the fruit and flower arrangements so beloved of the Victorians, a task he did not savour.

Gradually, portrait commissions came in and during the next few years he was to paint many and prominent figures in the arts and commerce. Domestic life continued strained and difficult, but fortunes improved slightly and the family moved to a larger flat in Randolph Crescent. In spite of the increasing animosity at home, nothing seemed to deter them from entering into an active social life. Paula recollects:

> *I remember my mother and father coming in to say good night to me before going out for the evening. He would be wearing a black wool, scarlet-silk-lined evening cape and be carrying a top hat and, I think, a silver-topped ebony cane. My mother had a very beautiful ball-gown of dove-grey chiffon, studded with small crystals on the smocked bodice, with a matching wrap. They looked*

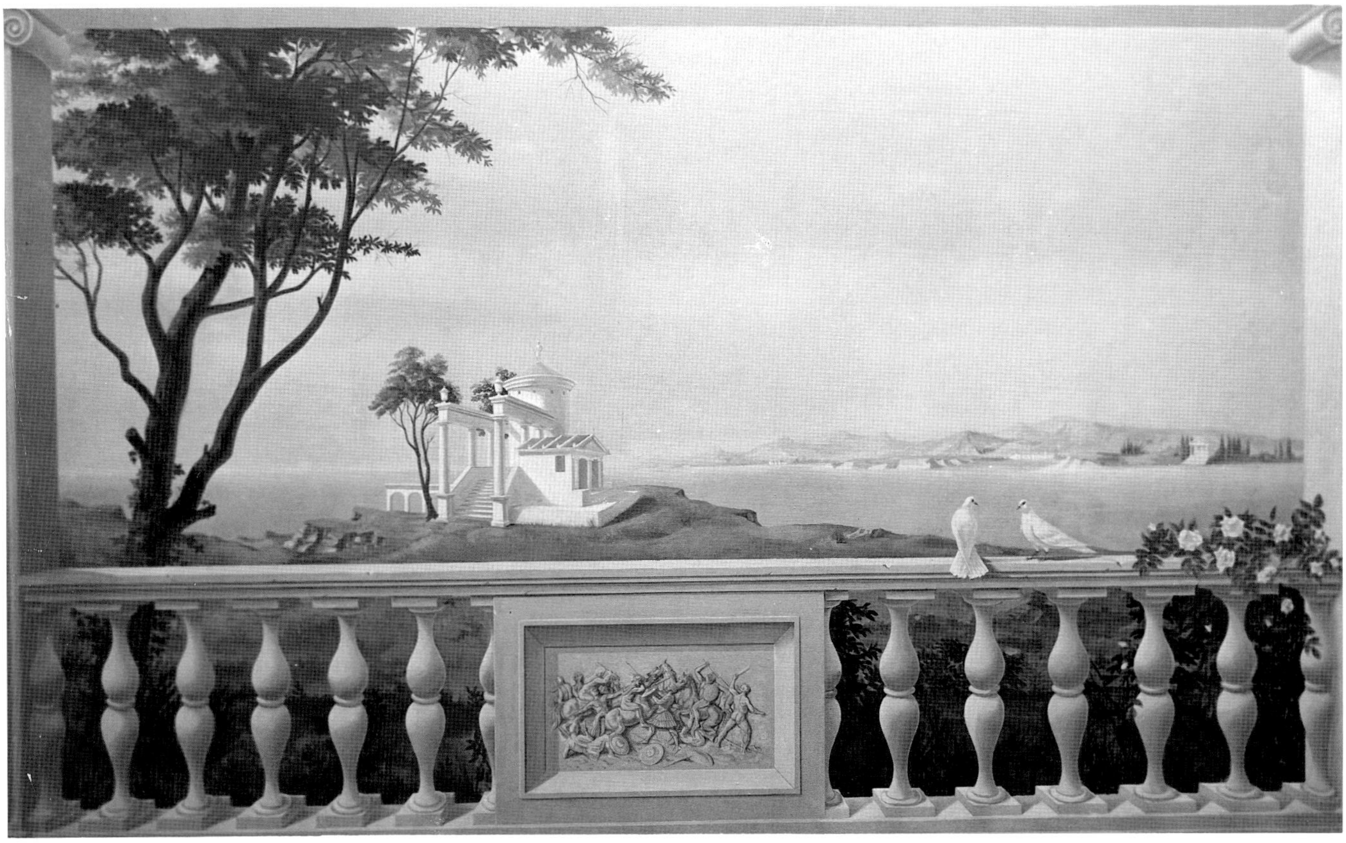

Sidney Smith, *Capriccio*, 20' x 11', entrance hall, Hon. DWR and Mrs Chubb.

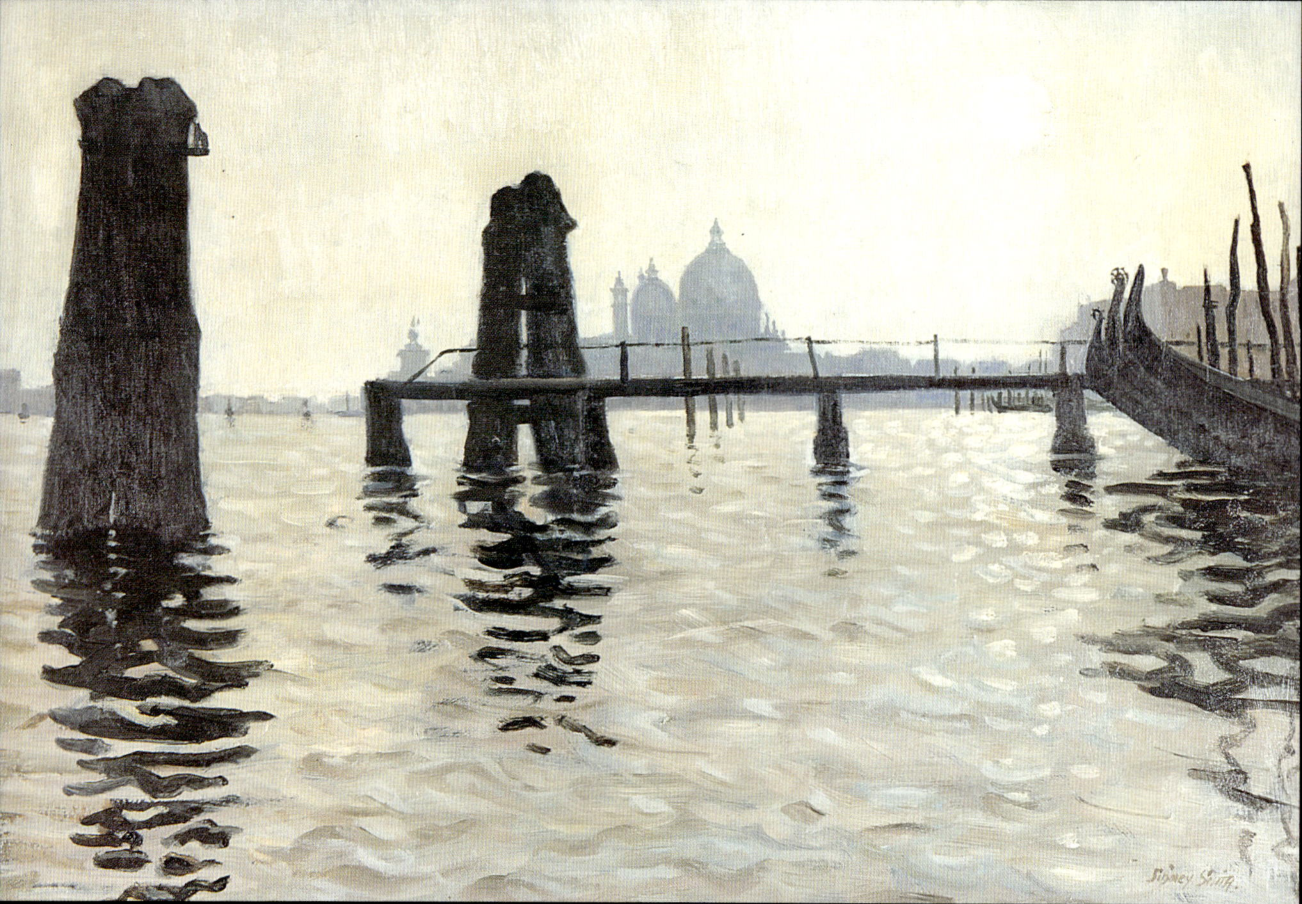

Sidney Smith, *Venice*, c.1970-74, oil, 76 x 53cm.

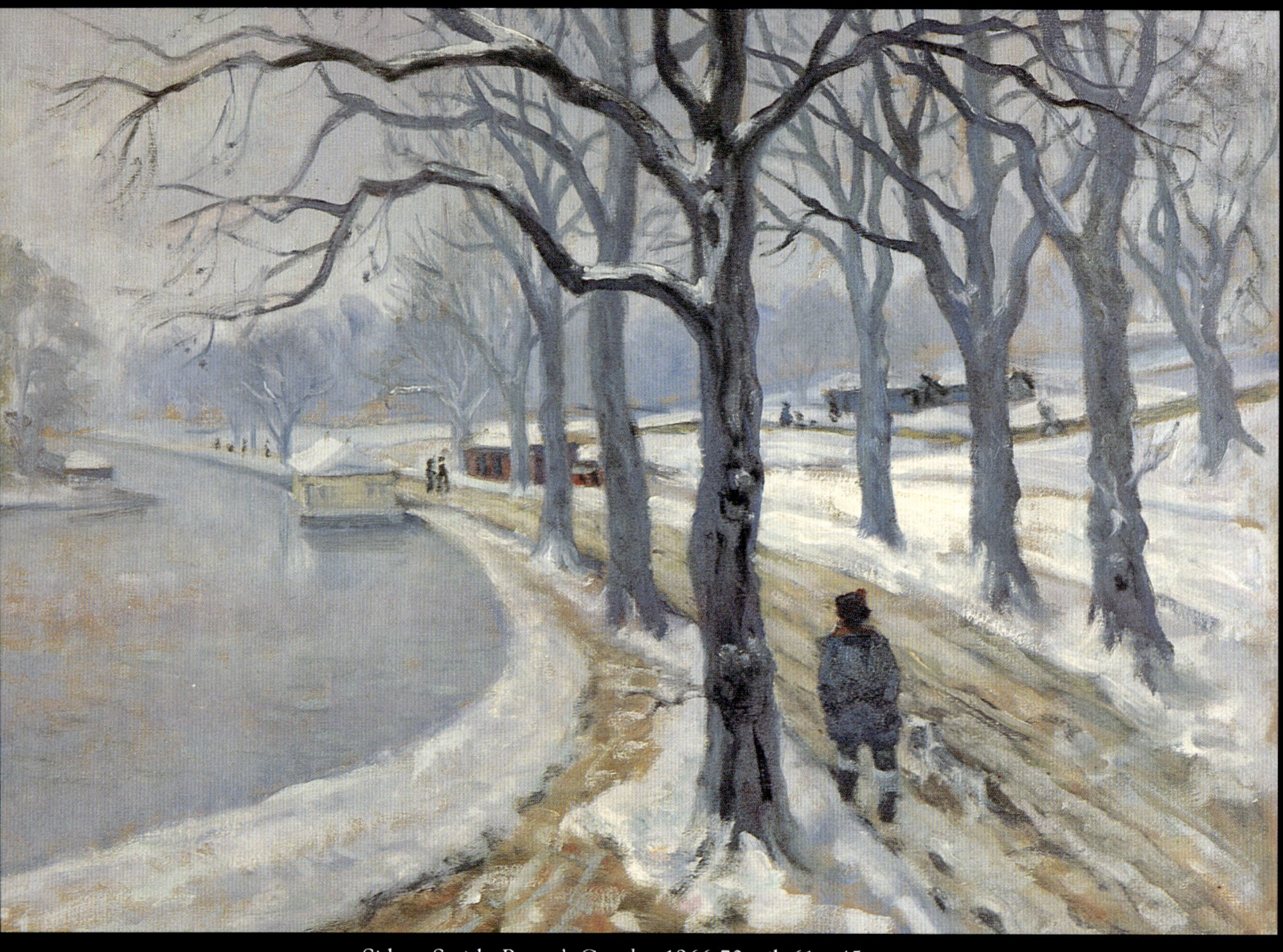

Sidney Smith, *Regent's Canal*, c.1966-70, oil, 61 x 45cm.

SIDNEY SMITH: PAINTER AND MURALIST (1912-1982)

wonderful. They had many friends, actors, writers, musicians, and artists who were constantly in one another's houses—many parties. I would be carted around and often left to my own devices, which once included raiding the prop box of a prominent London theatre and then waltzing out on an empty stage as a Spanish lady with full mantilla and shawl.

Little Venice, Regent's Canal: The Fifties

Smith's first proper studio in London was in Little Venice, on the Regent's Canal. It had a delightful view of adjoining small islands and the brightly painted, horse-drawn barges that travelled up and down the canal. He painted several pictures from this view. An adjacent studio was occupied by Felix Topolski, also a muralist and portrait painter.

Henry Lynch-Robinson, who moved between Belfast and London, had kept in touch, and it was through him that Smith received, in 1951, his first major commission in England. He was to paint *The Flight of the Huguenots* for the Festival of Britain. This is a strong, graphically detailed work of large-scale figures on the shore looking out to sea, sighting the ship that will take them to Ireland, where they were to found the linen industry.[5]

Smith was again struck by illness. A severe case of tuberculosis left him unable to work for at least two years. His daughter remembers visiting him in a convalescent home in Hastings:

> *There were groups of small, three-sided huts, all clustered in some large area near the sea. The huts could be revolved so that the permanently open side was positioned away from the prevailing winds. The theory behind this treatment was that the fresh air would either kill or cure you. Each hut held two patients and I remember my father's distress when he awoke one morning to find that his fellow patient had died in the night. All that was left was his friend's folded blanket on the bare springs of the bedframe and a small sparrow sitting on the bed post. I don't know how long he stayed there, but the next time I saw him he was in a more congenial environment, heavily involved in making paper sculptures. He made the most intricate sculptures for the ward—they seemed to be hung everywhere. If memory serves me, the treatment lasted for about two years.*

In 1952, the studios at Little Venice were scheduled for demolition, and the tenants decided to create an enormous mural to

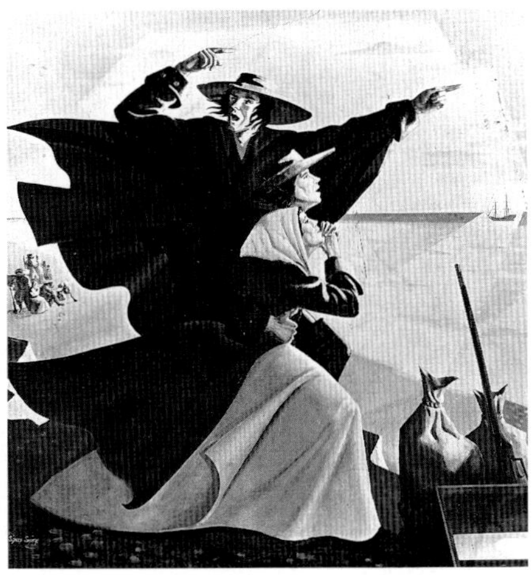

Sidney Smith, *Flight of the Huguenots*, 1952, 8' x 6', Bangor Heritage Centre.

run round all four walls. The mural was done in about three days and everyone took some part in its execution. The party went on through the night to the morning hours when, in a scene reminiscent of the film, *The Horse's Mouth*, the bulldozers moved in.

Shortly thereafter, Smith's marriage completely broke down and Smith moved out of the family home in Randolph Crescent into a small studio in Hay Hill. While this move was to herald an exciting period of growth and challenge in his professional life, sadly, it was also the start of a bitter divorce case that continued for the next thirteen years.

An important contact for Smith was Godfrey Bonzack, an interior designer who specialized in bathrooms and residential interiors. Bonzack, of Polish origin, had begun life as a painter and frequently worked with Smith on interiors. Through Bonzack Smith received numerous commissions: painting murals for the homes of London's elite; decorating their houses, including hallways, staircases, and even bathrooms. Among his clients were Lord and Lady Ednam, Paul Gallico, Lord Palumbo, and Lord and Lady Eliot.

Another significant association was with John H Loudon, managing director of The Royal Dutch Shell Company, for whose London flat he painted two small murals. Later Smith painted at Loudon's country house near Aerdenhout in Holland a mural consisting of three panels. The first of these panels shows The Hague on the lake and is especially brilliant in its design and execution. Here is *trompe-l'œil* at its most dazzling. The illusion is so total that one wonders if the dining room is really located on the quayside. There is the sense that one step through the arch on the left would find one walking along the old cobbled stones, inhaling the scent of the water and enjoying a tranquil view of the old town. To complete the illusion, Smith painted the pointing of the brick wall inside, right across the radiator, and then ingeniously affixed the lights to the pillars. One wonders if they are real or painted.

When Shell built its new office tower on the Thames embankment in 1962, John Loudon asked The Royal Dutch Shell Company to commission Smith to do a mural for the Upstream Restaurant on the rooftop terrace. Four panels were painted on the theme of London and Rotterdam, the capitals of the Shell empire. One panel depicts *The Arts of London*, represented by the buildings closely associated with those arts: the Tate Gallery; the National Gallery, the Athenaeum Club, the Theatre Royal, and the Albert Hall.

The second panel represents *Industry and Commerce* by grouping the Royal Exchange, the Bank of England, and the Monument around the newly completed Shell Centre. The two remaining panels treat the same themes set in Holland: the river and canal as lifelines that link the two. The entire scene is in a 'Venetian' setting and placed behind stone arches. In a newspaper interview, given in 1962, Smith was quoted as saying:

> *...my idea is to give people something to take their minds off business for awhile. I have taken representational buildings and painted them as if one was standing on a terrace and looking out at them through stone arches.*

The panels on the Arts and Culture also look back into each country's history and civilization, while in the panels on Industry and Commerce, the viewer looks forward to a future of new technology and science. What binds the four panels together is the gentle sense of colour, the feeling of peace and the serene atmosphere. The medium used was turpentine and wax on canvas. Regrettably, the mural was destroyed when the building underwent extensive renovation.

Bradbrook House: High Society & The Swinging Sixties

From the late 1950s, Smith lived in his last (and best) studio, Bradbrook House, Kinnerton Street, London. Ideally located in the heart of Knightsbridge just behind

SIDNEY SMITH: PAINTER AND MURALIST (1912-1982)

Harrods, it was a quiet and peaceful studio, spacious with a sloping glass roof. Smith had walls specially constructed so he could paint large murals. He had panels fitted under the roof so that he could control the light, and fitted good electric spot lights, enabling him to work in artificial light.

Upstairs lived and worked the fashion photographer, Ray Harwood. They became close friends and remained so for more than thirty years. They were frequently in and out of each other's studios, regularly dined out together, and could often be found at the Nag's Head pub, round the corner. This was London of the 'Sixties, Carnaby Street, King's Road, and mini-skirts (of which Sidney heartily approved). The whole city was alive with energy, new nightclubs, art galleries, restaurants, and discotheques were emerging all over the city. The studios of Harwood and Smith were not to be left out, there were numerous parties full of wine, women, and song.

In the first ten years at Bradbrook House Smith worked incredibly hard, painting the largest and most important murals of his career. Around this time he joined the prestigious gambling club, Crockford's, ostensibly to meet prospective clients. He looked then as he always had, dapper and affluent. With his magnificent olive-green and navy-blue mohair suits, his black hair and neatly trimmed, short, pointed beard, he was a striking figure. Whether he ever actually obtained a commission through his membership, is not known, but that he enjoyed it immensely is. He played the tables, usually blackjack and chemin de fer, even though he could ill afford to lose. It was at Crockford's, sometime during the middle of the decade, that he met Betty Asheton, with whom he lived until her death in 1978.

This was a busy time for Smith. He received several large and important commissions: The Grill Room, at the Ritz Hotel, Piccadilly; a large mural of Venice for MP Northcote, and another for Christopher Loyd's home 'Lockinge', near Oxford. This mural is situated on an end wall in the garden room at Betterton House, the original Lockinge House having been demolished after the war. It is a fine mural, with great sweeping skies, full of light and atmosphere depicting an imaginary view from the old Lockinge House to the lake, all in an eighteenth-century setting. On either side the walls return, and the pillars coincide with the corners. It is very convincing. On the right return is a view of nearby Ardington Church, while on the other the lake continues.

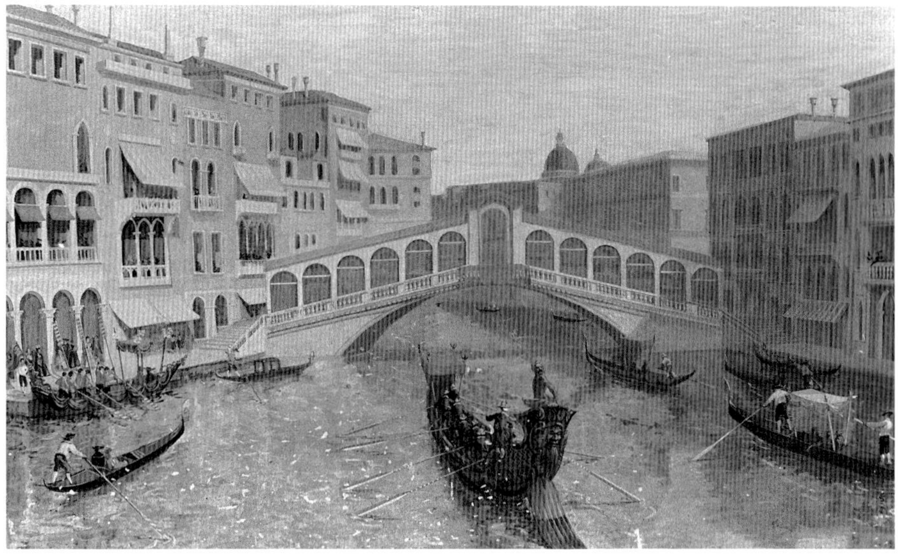

Sidney Smith, detail from *The Rialto*, 1962, 36' x 5', Transvaal Castle liner.

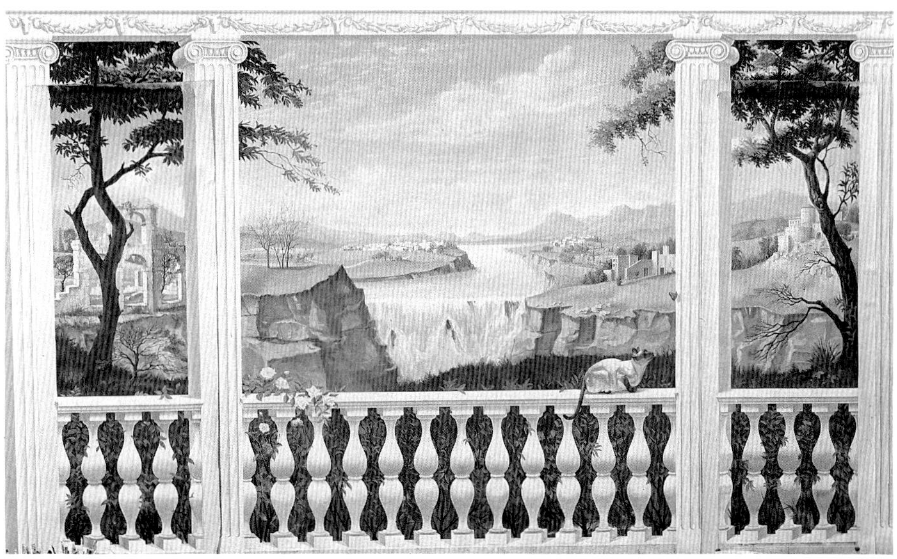

Sidney Smith, *The Falls of Tivoli during execution in the artist's studio*, 1962, 17' x 9', The Franconia liner.

Murals at Sea: 1956-1962

One of Smith's greatest achievements was as a ship's muralist. In all there were ten murals: five on board super liners, and five for cargo-passenger ships of the Clan Line. His first great liner commission came in 1956 from the Canadian Pacific Steamship Co Ltd for the new *Empress of Britain*. In 1964, the ship was sold to the Greek Line and became their flagship rechristened *Queen Anna Maria*.

The patron who gave him more work than anyone else during his career was Bernard Cayser, who was Chairman of the British and Commonwealth Lines, the company that owned the Clan Lines. Nothing is known about the murals painted on the Clan ships; all of them have been broken up. Smith also painted a mural for Bernard Cayser on the four walls of the ante-room to Cayser's office at British & Commonwealth House. *The World* depicted animals, plants, and fauna and it was apparently quite beautiful; but, like so many others, it was destroyed,

SIDNEY SMITH: PAINTER AND MURALIST (1912-1982)

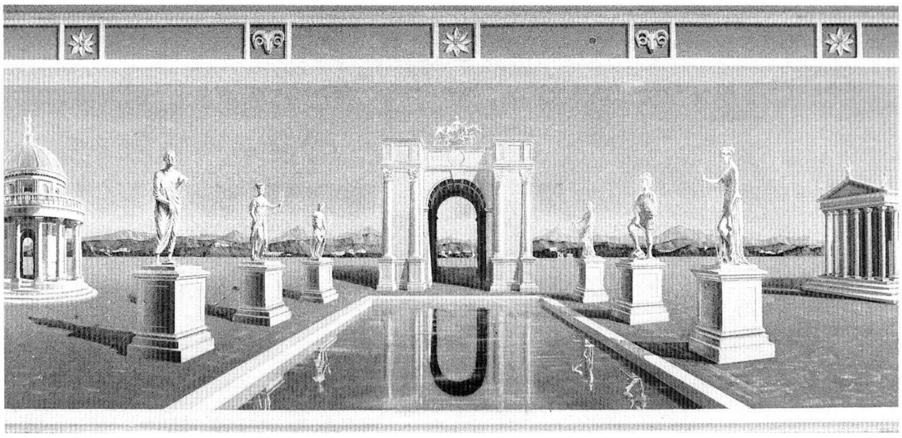

Sidney Smith, detail from *Etruscan Landscape*, 1960, 36' x 5', Windsor Castle liner.

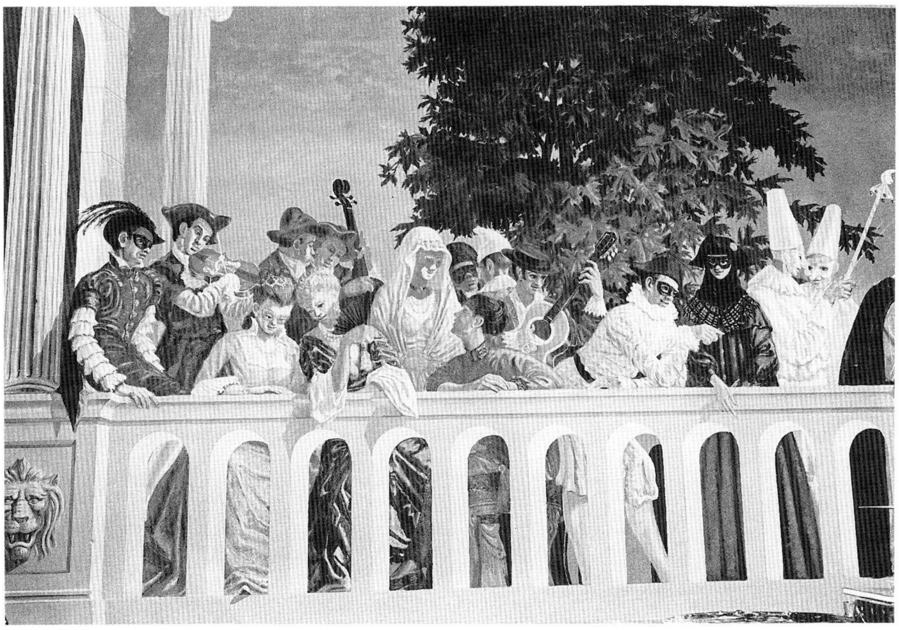

Sidney Smith, detail from *The Bal Masque*, 1964, 42' x 12', Beaverbrook Playhouse Theatre.

when the building was demolished. In 1957, Cayser Irvine Ltd. took over the Union Castle Line. Between 1958 and 1962 they built three new liners and Smith was again commissioned to paint murals for them.

The first of these was for *The Pendennis Castle*, built by Harland & Wolff, Belfast in 1958. Smith painted two panels, for the first-class dining-room and a private dining room. One panel was of columns and round arches in deep perspective, the other of musical instruments set in over the doorways. Above the fireplace was a romantic landscape in *trompe-l'oeil*. 'My assistant and I completed one of these (panels) in a week.' Smith reported to a journalist. 'It has staggered everyone including myself. I worked everything out in my London studio to the last detail. I got the commission about the middle of last year (1957) and have been working on the designs for some time.'

For *The Windsor Castle*, built at Cammel Laird, Liverpool in 1960, he created a mural based around a composite Roman/-Etruscan theme. It was designed, he said, on the vertical to give the room height and, with great emphasis on perspective, to give it depth. The murals were thirty feet wide and had to read perfectly from any view point. The motifs for the *Windsor* mural contain invented colonnades on the left and right. The Temple on the left is studied from Bramante's *Tempietto* in San Pietro in Montario, Rome, built in the sixteenth century. On the right is a classical Greek or Roman Temple with a very slight resemblance to the Maison Carré in Nîmes.

For *The Transvaal Castle*, built at the John Brown Shipyard, Glasgow in 1962, he painted a Venetian-inspired mural, which was situated amidships on the Promenade deck in a room with seating for three hundred passengers. The room had big windows that afforded a view of the decks; in the centre was a dance floor. At the far end of the room was the thirty-foot-wide mural that gave the viewer the impression of being on a bridge, looking up Venice's Grand Canal toward the Rialto.

The last great ship Smith painted for was the *Franconia*, which was being refitted for cruising by Cunard around 1961. The Franconia's mural incorporated on the left and right, two secret doors. Smith designed a waterfall in the foreground of an idyllic landscape, all viewed over a balustrade. In doing so he created a breath-taking vista, nine-feet high by seventeen-feet wide on a curved wall. The intention is that the viewer can lean over the balustrade and admire the spacious vista. Newspaper photographs taken in Smith's studio show him leaning on the balustrade, tickling the painted cat under the chin.

Smith's last great patrons were Lord and Lady Beaverbrook, for whom he painted his largest mural, *The Bal Masqué,* for Beaverbrook's Playhouse Theatre in Fredericton, New Brunswick, Canada. The enormous work, measuring forty -two feet wide and twelve-feet high, was painted on three panels in London during 1963/4. After a heart-stopping delay of ten days, when one of the panels was thought to have been lost at sea, the mural was successfully installed in 1964.

The composition is of larger-than-life size figures at a masked ball, sitting on a balcony looking over a balustrade. The mural covers three walls of the foyer some eight feet or more above the floor. Smith's intention was to make the theatregoers in the foyer below look up at the ball in progress in the 'minstrels' gallery. In turn, the masked merrymakers appear to lean over the balcony and stare down at the patrons. This is a remarkably executed work.

SIDNEY SMITH: PAINTER AND MURALIST (1912-1982)

The Beaverbrooks were so pleased with *The Bal Masqué* that they commissioned him do six panels (each eleven-feet wide by eight-feet high) for 'Cherkley', their country house in Leatherhead. The mural depicted their favourite views and walks in the beautiful grounds.

Addison Road, London: Painting & Travelling

These were to be Smith's last murals. Style in painting had changed dramatically. Easel painting of a figurative nature had been displaced by large-scale abstract painting, which held no interest for Smith. Perhaps there was no longer any demand for murals; certainly there was less appreciation of the gentle atmosphere of an idyllic scene, a formal garden, or something as detailed as a town behind arches. However, the truth may also be, that after more than twenty years of working Herculean hours, climbing up and down ladders in draughty, cold, and incompleted ships, constant travelling, frequent ill-health, and equally frequent socialising, he was completely exhausted.

Although there were always women in his life, he had, after his separation from his wife, only one permanent relationship, that with Betty Asheton, a wealthy American divorcée who, for tax purposes, left the UK for six months of every year. She was also an official of Amnesty International for whom she travelled as an ambassador at her own expense; Smith usually travelled with her. Smith moved into Betty's large and magnificent house on Addison Road, where they maintained a frantic social schedule and a demanding, albeit luxurious, lifestyle. Smith kept the Bradbrook House studio, but used it little and the lease was eventually surrendered.

During the latter half of the 1960s and the early 1970s, he and Betty Asheton travelled extensively. They took frequent trips to Europe (Smith's favourite places, and the theme for many of his landscapes, were Venice, Paris, and the south of France); and extended trips to India, the Republic of China, Mexico, and through Betty's work with Amnesty International, to Iran. In addition, both were members of an elite American art club that took its members on international tours of private art collections. During these travels Smith filled many sketch books and generated numerous paintings.

Although life had been good in the beginning of this relationship, it rapidly began to deteriorate. Betty had, for more than twenty years, required the on-going support of psychotherapy. As well, under the pressure of their demanding social life and frequent travelling, Smith's health broke down. Apart from the odd painting done from the windows of Addison Road and the occasional sketch of their dog, he ceased to paint or draw.

Smith's life was further devastated by Betty Asheton's tragic suicide in 1978. He became reclusive and depressed. Betty's will had left provision that he should enjoy all the material comforts of his life with her but this did not include maintaining the leasehold of the house on Addison Road. He dearly loved the garden there and its loss was a great blow to him. After encouragement and cajoling from friends, he finally moved to a flat on Royal Crescent. His daughter, who was by then living in Canada, remembers:

> *My father and I met for the last time in 1981, the Christmas before he died. He had by then, blossomed into the unapologetic curmudgeon he had always tried to conceal. His health was deteriorating, he could not walk without two canes and the help of a companion, and much of his earlier spirit was missing, yet he still enjoyed the occasional audience for his amusing recollections, raunchy jokes, and entertaining anecdotes. His principal pleasures were derived from his small garden, his loyal and magnificent dog, and a large record collection – all mixed with liberal shots of neat vodka.*

Smith died alone on 25 May, 1982. He was found by Betty Sparks, his housekeeper of more than thirty years, when she came that morning to clean. After his death, there was little left in his home other than a few pocket-size sketch books and several paintings. His once magnificent art library was, however, much depleted. The few remaining art books, were those of his first loves – Renoir, Degas, Turner, and Van Gogh. All his books on Roman and Greek mythology, which had provided inspiration for several murals, were gone.

David Goldberg and Paula Chabanais

ACKNOWLEDGMENTS

Armagh County Museum; Paul Barnes; Leslie Owen Baxter; Nelson Bell; Frank Capper; Tom Carr; Lord Cayzer; Brendan Corrigan, Carnival Cruise Lines, Miami; Maurice Craig; Anne Crookshank; Beverley Beetham Endersby; Annie Lewinter Frankl; Rowel Friers; Sophie Hurwitz; Gerald and Sheila Goldberg; Robert Greacen; Roger and Moira Hall;David Hammond; Ray Harwood; Lena Isacson; Christopher Loyd; John H Loudon; Roy McFadden; James McIntyre; Robert McKinstry; William Mc Quitty; Jane McQuitty; Jack Midgley; Marjorie Olley; Lord Palumbo; The Playhouse Theatre, Canada; The Ritz Hotel, London; Victoria Lynch-Robinson; Ray Rosenfield; The Shell Centre; Litzi Smith, Theo Snoddy; The Ulster Museum; Ulster Folk and Transport Museum; Helene Usiskin; Nicholas and Susan Usiskin; Charis Wahl; Gerald Whelan, RDS Library; Harland & Wolf.

NOTES

1. Lawrence Whistler. *The Laughter and the Urn: Rex Whistler*, London 1985
2. *Marius* was exhibited at the Ulster Academy in 1940 (No. 25).
3. *Market Day 1938*, No. 32. Price £31.10.0.
4. John Hewitt, ed. Robert Greacen, *Northern Harvest*. Belfast, 1944
5. The painting was later shown at the Ulster Farm and Factory Exhibition at Castlereagh, and now hangs in Bangor Heritage Centre, Bangor.

LIST OF WORKS

Murals at Sea: *Empress of Britain, Franconia; Pendennis Castle; Transvaal Castle; Windsor Castle*; 5 ships of the Clan Line.

Murals: Private Commissions: Lord & Lady Beaverbrook; Mrs Catherine Bray; Mr. Bernard Cayser; The Honourable D.W.R. & Mrs Chubb; Lord & Lady Ednam; Lord & Lady Elliot; Mr Paul Gallico; Mr & Mrs Charles Hambro; Mr & Mrs Christopher Loyd; Jonkeer J R & Mrs Loudon; Mr & Mrs Ralph Merton; Sir Brian and Lady Mountain; Mr & Mrs Speskin; Mr & Mrs Peter Palumbo; Sir Rowland and Lady Robinson; Mrs O Wigram; Mr & Mrs Charles Wolfson; Mr & Mrs Zamatt.

Murals in Public Buildings: 'Halcyon Days', London; American Air Force Officers' Club, London; Banco de Santandar, Barcelon, Spain; British Commonwealth Shippng Co. Ltd., London; Dorchester Hotel, London; Festival of Britain, 1951, London; Narrow Water Castle, N. Ireland; Ritz Hotel, London; The Playhouse Theatre, Fredricton, New Brunswick, Canada; Westbury Hotel, London.

Murals Northern Ireland: British Restaurant, Great Victoria Street; Wilson's Factory, Newforge; Derry and Lurgan war factories; Narrow Water Castle; Royal Ulster Agriculture Society; Ideal Home Exhibition; British Industries Fair; LMS Lounge; Fort Bar, Belfast; Kelly's Cellars; British Sailor's Society Chapel; Leslie Brand; Culloden Hotel.

Mixed Exhibitions: Leicester Galleries, London; Little Gallery, London; National Society of Painters, London; New English Art Club; Royal Hibernian Society, Dublin; Royal Society of British Artists, London; Royal Society of Portrait Painters, London; Ulster Academy, Belfast.

Paintings: Private Collections: Aardenhout, Holland; Antibes, France; Belfast, N. Ireland; Bermuda; Dublin and Cork, Eire; London, England; Malaga, Spain; New York, USA; Chicago, USA; Toronto, Canada.

Public Collections: Armagh County Museum; Ulster Museum; Arts Council N.I.

LETTERS FROM ST LOUIS

Ireland's exhibit at the St Louis World's Fair in 1904 was 'a brilliant and unqualified success'. The contributions of its generous and enlightened patrons, TP Gill and TW Rolleston, are outlined by **Homan Potterton**.

In the correspondence of John Quinn, now housed in New York Public Library[1] are a number of letters which shed light on the organisation of the Irish representation at the Louisiana Purchase Exposition – commonly called the St Louis World's Fair – in 1904.[2] Although Ireland had had a presence at the World's Columbian Exposition in Chicago in 1893,[3] – where that had been not just one, but two, Irish villages – the St Louis Exposition was the first occasion when Ireland had 'a separate national showing'[4] in such an important international arena.

Under the rules of the Exposition at St Louis, Ireland, being neither an independent country nor an autonomous State within the British Empire, was not allowed her own national pavilion.[5] And so a wealthy Irish-American entrepreneur, Thomas F Hanley of St Louis, obtained a concession to build an 'Irish Village' and formed a public company, The Irish Exhibit Company, for the purpose of organising the show.[6] This Company – which in the event proved to be more a philanthropic organisation than an actual business concern – defrayed all the costs of bringing the exhibits across the Atlantic although the Department of Agriculture and Technical Instruction for Ireland, whose co-operation Hanley had obtained in the early stages, also made some financial contribution.[7]

The Department, administered by Sir Horace Plunkett (as Vice President) and T P Gill (as Secretary), having come into being in 1900, brought its influence and enlightenment, both of which were substantial, to the planning of the exhibits.[8] In doing so they called upon the the assistance of other bodies[9]: the Congested Districts Board organised a 'Home, Cottage, and Art Industries' section and carpet weavers (from Donegal), lace-makers, embroiderers, damask weavers, and other workers were brought from Ireland to give demonstrations of their talents; and the Arts and Crafts Society of Ireland planned the Historic Loan Collections[10] (as they had done for the Cork Exhibition of 1902). Elaborate facsimiles of medieval metalwork, manuscripts, and sculpture as well as actual examples of eighteenth and nineteenth century furniture, silver, and glass were assembled in an impressive array. A further loan collection of engraved portraits and views of Ireland, arranged for the purpose by Walter Strickland of the National Gallery of Ireland, was also despatched.

In effect, what took place in St Louis amounted to a combination of an art exhibition and a trade show[11] where whiskey distillers, bacon curers, rope-makers and the like shared space with Donegal carpets, stained glass (exhibited by Sarah Purser), lace, homespuns, unbreakable doll-heads (the invention of an Irish lady), and Belleek. Samples of work from technical and art schools were exhibited alongside illustrations of farming and fisheries while the Historic Loan Collections completed a very creditable and comprehensive conspectus of Ireland.

From the point of view of the Irish Arts and Crafts Movement, the most interesting part of the show was the Industrial Section and, in particular, the exhibitors of 'Artistic Handicrafts'. There were several bog-oak carvers, the Killarney Furniture Industries, the Fivemiletown Metal Industry and J M Kavanagh, RHA was represented by 'repoussé work, silver, copper, bronze and aluminum plaques decorated in the celtic style'.[12] Oswald Reeves showed enamel work, the Naas Co-Operative, hand-tufted rugs while the Dun Emer Industries were the sole exhibitors in the fulsome category of 'Tapestry, Embroidery, Tufted Rugs, Handprinted and Hand Bound Books, Painted Fans, Etc.': Lily Yeats wrote to John Quinn in June 1904, '... my embroidery went to St Louis, it was only the pictures that failed. Dun Emer sent embroidery and rugs and vestments, not printing'.

Initially, Ireland's display was to include a collection of Irish paintings. Jack Yeats wrote to Quinn in January 1904, 'I thought I ought to send a few pictures to St Louis.'[13] His father, John Butler Yeats, also intended to contribute: 'Douglas Hyde & Russell & Hyde (I mean their portraits) are going over to the St Louis Exhibition ... Hugh Lane is going over with (them) ... I am sending about twelve or fifteen also Lavery & Sargent & many others – Sargent is partly Irish.'[14] In the event this plan failed and the pictures collected for the purpose were shown instead at Lane's historic Guildhall Exhibition in London.[15] Perhaps to fill the breach, it was decided to organise a collection of Irish-American 'relics' and a committee was formed in New York for this purpose. It is at this point that one of the key figures in the success of the Irish exhibit, TW Rolleston, enters the story. Rolleston had crossed to America on the *Etruria* with other members of the Irish delegation[16] and was staying at the Park Avenue Hotel in New York by 25 April 1904 when he dropped a note to Quinn:

> *Would it be possible for me to see you at your place of business, or anywhere else, tomorrow? I am in N.Y. (on my way to St Louis) for the purpose of making, if possible, definitive arrangements as regards the collection of Irish-American relics which it is proposed to incorporate in the Historic Loan Collection at St Louis. There are many points of detail to consider & settle before real work can begin & I hope we shall have your aid in the matter.*

Thomas William Hazen Rolleston (1857-1920)[17] is one of the more interesting lesser figures of the Irish Revival. Born in county Offaly, he had a brilliant career at Trinity (where he won the Vice Chancellor's Prize for English verse) and subsequently studied in Germany. He founded the *Dublin University Review* in 1885, was active in London in the Irish Literary Society, and became secretary of the Irish Industries Association in the early 1890s. While successfully pursuing a career as a lecturer and writer, he was, from 1900, employed as Organiser in the Department of Agriculture and Technical Instruction and it was in this capacity that he played such a vital role in the success of the St Louis World's Fair.

Quinn took to Rolleston immediately. (He) 'is a charming man and I like him very much' he wrote to AE on 2 May. He 'called me on Tuesday and good progress is being made in the formation of a committee here in New York to collect historical art relics representative of the work of Irishmen in America. The St Louis people will pay for the transportation of these goods to St Louis, insurance and re-shipment, and the New York committee will pay the money for the Secretary's work etc.' The President of the New York Committee – of which Quinn was Secretary – was Burke Cochran but the key figure was J D Crimmins. Rolleston dined with him in New York on 27 April 1904 when Crimmins suggested that Thomas Hamilton Murray might act as Executive Secretary of the Committee:

(Crimmins) spoke very strongly in favour of a man named Thomas Hamilton Murray who he says is thoroughly conversant with Irish and Irish-American history & who has been working with him for years in this branch of affairs – collecting relics etc. As C. is contributing enough things (some of which he showed me) to form a show in themselves & has practically guaranteed the finances I think we shall have to let him nominate the person who is to handle the things and carry out the details.

Within two weeks Rolleston had established himself at the University Club in St Louis and wrote Quinn a long letter (dated 14 May) describing his progress:

I am beginning to settle down a bit here now and understand the lie of the land. On the whole, things seem satisfactory, though there have been great delays & oversights. I found for instance that the show-cases for my collection about which I gave specifications in February, had not been touched yet! They are now in hands together with those required for the American-Irish collection & are promised, at least enough to do for the opening day, by the 27th inst. The formal opening or dedication is fixed for June 4th & Gill is coming over for it. Plunkett is invited.[18] *The 'Village' as everyone persists in calling it, although it is not on village lines at all, is quite a worthy and dignified representation of Ireland so far as buildings go, & having in view the limited space available. I send a set of prospectuses about it & also a plan of the Exposition where you will see its location marked at the end of the 'Pike'. It is close to the principal entrance & could not be better placed ...*

The 'Village' – to say the very least -was fantastic. The architect of the whole was FG Hicks of Dublin[19] and 'artists, sculptors and mechanics soon had reproductions of many famous Irish buildings, in most cases full size, rising up from the forests of Missouri'.[20] Constructed of metal and plaster,[21] the Dublin Parliament House (then and now the Bank of Ireland), Cormac's Chapel, Blarney Castle, the ruins of Muckross Abbey, St Lawrence's Gate, Drogheda, Kate Kearney's cottage and the ancestral homestead of President McKinley nestled comfortably together. Jaunting cars took visitors for a drive through a panorama of the Lakes of Killarney as well as along 'the famous rocky road to Dublin' while, in order to lend further authenticity of effect, soil and grass-sod were imported from Ireland to carpet the lawns.[22] When, by coincidence, the Swiss Pavilion (appropriately, life-size plaster peaks and precipices representative of the Alps) towered in an adjacent plot, the Irish organisers rechristened it the Macgillicuddy Reeks.[23] Also included in the Irish Village was a theatre (capacity 1800) and a bandstand where the 'Ireland's Own' brass and reed band played daily. The main Restaurant (tea was available in Kate Kearney's Cottage) was in the Houses of Parliament. With a full orchestra and seats for two thousand, it had the advantage of looking out on the main thoroughfare of the Exposition towards the Grand Court of Honor and the Cascade.

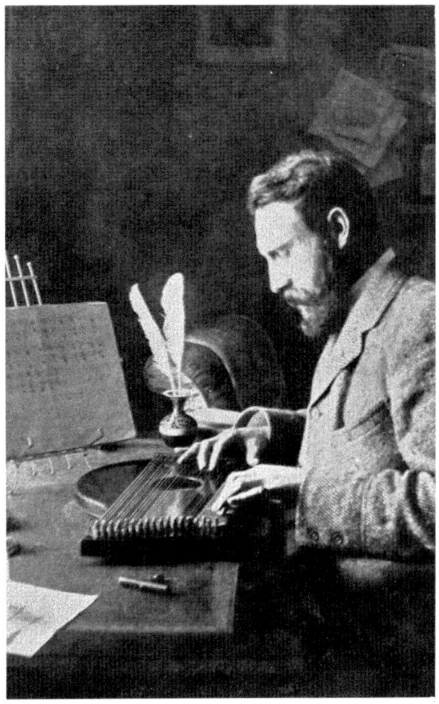

T W Rolleston who organised the Historic Loan Collection and the Arts and Crafts exhibit.

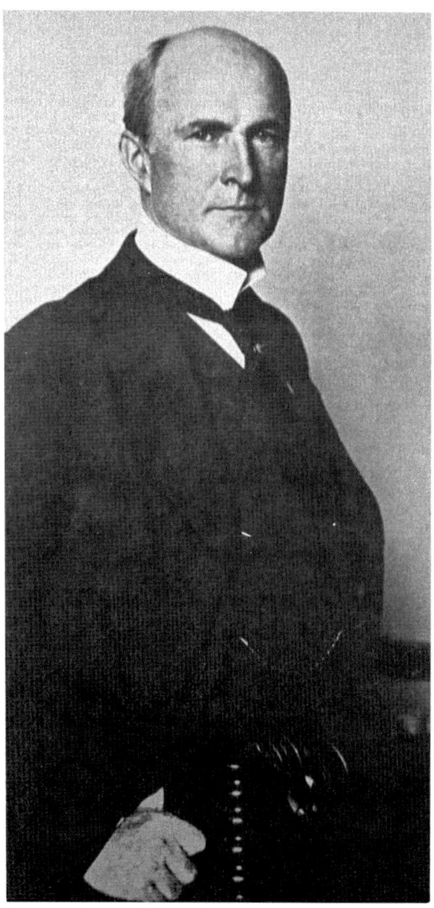

John Quinn, the American patron of Irish artists and writers who was Secretary of the American Irish exhibit at St Louis.

When the Irish exhibit opened 'with brilliant eclat'[24] on 11 June, Rolleston wrote to Quinn: 'Our opening day was a brilliant and unqualified success & we have prepared a pretty full report for the papers, which you will see.' The main speech was given by T P Gill who spoke of the origins of the exhibition, its arrangement, the work of his department, and Ireland's contribution of 'a precious asset ... her own population' to America. In conclusion he enunciated the real reason for Ireland's presence in St Louis when he issued an invitation to Americans 'the greatest commercial exploiters in the world...to give some thought to exploiting Ireland industrially with American capital and enterprise.'[25]

The Times (of London)[26] reported favourably on the display:

a very intelligent effort has been made to direct attention to the work of the Department. Altogether this exhibit, unique in its character, is one which reflects much credit upon its organisers ... it bids fair to become one of the most interesting and distinctive features of the grounds, and will probably attract a larger number of visitors than any other at which a separate charge for admission is made.

Retrospectively, the President of the Exposition wrote that the array of products was 'a revelation to the rest of the world'[27] while the Official History of the Fair[28] described the

twenty beautiful colleens accompanied by the most famous brass band in Ireland and numerous other natives of Ireland to the total number of 137 which made up the liv-

LETTERS FROM ST LOUIS

ing features of the Irish exhibit which had perhaps the choicest location on the Pike.

While it was generally agreed that the Irish Village was an outstanding success, both through the image of Ireland it portrayed and the crowds it attracted, the overall success of the venture was marred by a furore – which attracted enormous publicity both at home and in America – that centred on the theatre. 'The Disgraceful Stage Irishman Brought Out Three Times, Nothwithstanding Protests' screamed the headlines; 'Murphy and Hanley Think They Can Insult The Irish With Impunity' was the sub-text.

Initially, it was the intention to have WB Yeats' newly formed National Theatre Society perform but Yeats, on his visit to New York in January 1904, was advised against allowing his plays to be acted: 'it would be rather depressing for a theatre of art to compete in St Louis with pyramids of tin tomato cans and dromedaries and Egyptian beauties ...' Quinn reported to AE.[29] When, therefore, James Reardon as Director of Exhibits for the Irish Exhibit Company approached Yeats on the subject in Dublin, Yeats refused his permission;[30] but at the same time AE, while advising the actor Frank Fay against going to St Louis, consented for his play *Deirdre* to be performed.[31] George Moore and Edward Martyn also agreed that their plays might be acted.[32] Reardon was successful in engaging several actors in Dublin – Dudley Digges, Marie Quinn, Violet Mervyn, and PJ Kelley among them[33] – and arranging for them to come to St Louis. Some of these (Digges and Kelley) had acted with the Yeats company and their 'defection' to the St Louis players drove Yeats into 'a wild state of indignation.'[34] When they arrived in St Louis they were joined by about six American players and Quinn wrote to AE[35] describing their programme.

For the first two months they propose to give two performances a day ... each performance will be in two parts ... one part will be drama ... the second part will consist of music, harpists, bag-pipes and dancing and of 'moving pctures of Irish life.' They are going to play 'Kerry' an adaptation by Boucicault from the French, and a short version of 'The Jealous Wife,' a thing that I am not familiar with. Now that Murphy[36] has the Irish players on his hands he is extremely anxious to get permission to give Yeats' plays.

By now, Quinn was hopeful that Yeats' plays might be performed: 'Yeats' plays are best suited for the audiences which they will have at St Louis and are the right length,' he wrote.

If they don't get permission from Yeats then the bringing of the Irish actors over here will become a mere absurdity Murphy feels, for in the other plays which they will act American actors would do just as well. George Moore's plays and Martyn's plays are, so Murphy says, entirely too long for the kind of shows

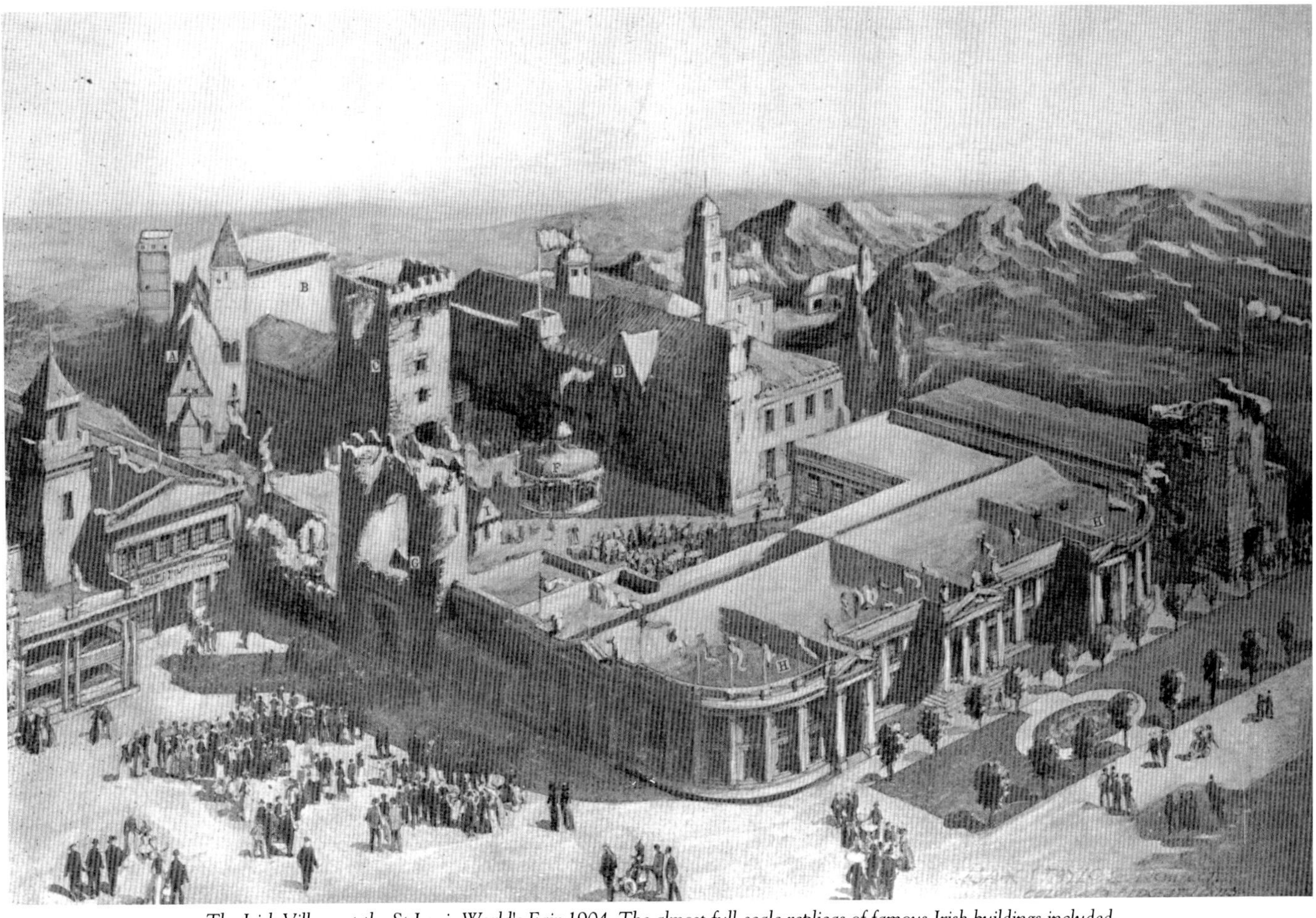

The Irish Village at the St Louis World's Fair 1904. The almost full-scale replicas of famous Irish buildings included A. Cormac's Chapel; C. Blarney Castle; E. Muckross Abbey; G. St Lawrence's Gate, Drogheda (with Kate Kearney's Cottage to the left); H. The Parliament House (Bank of Ireland); I. The ancestral cottage of President McKinley. The building marked 'B' was the theatre; 'D' was the main Exhibit Hall; and 'F' the Music Stand where the Ireland's Own band played each day. The mountain range in the background, intended as a replica of the Alps, is the Swiss Pavilion but the Irish delegation referred to them as the Macgillicuddy Reeks.

LETTERS FROM ST LOUIS

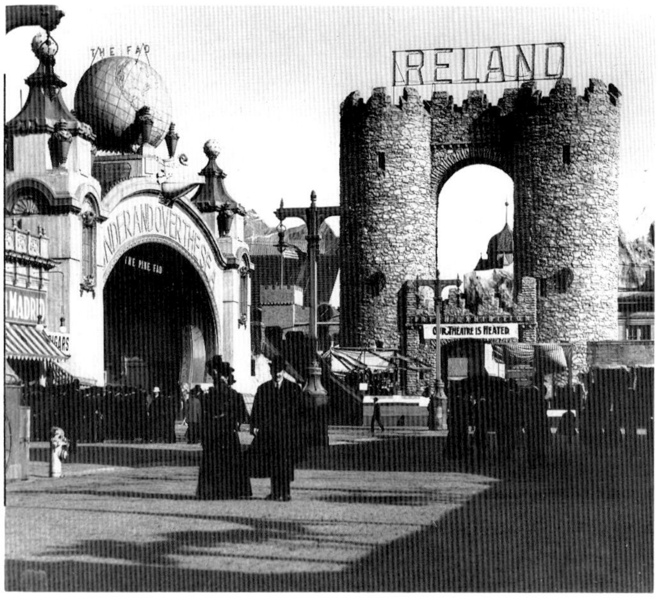

The Entrance to the Irish Village – a replica of the St Lawrence Gate, Drogheda.

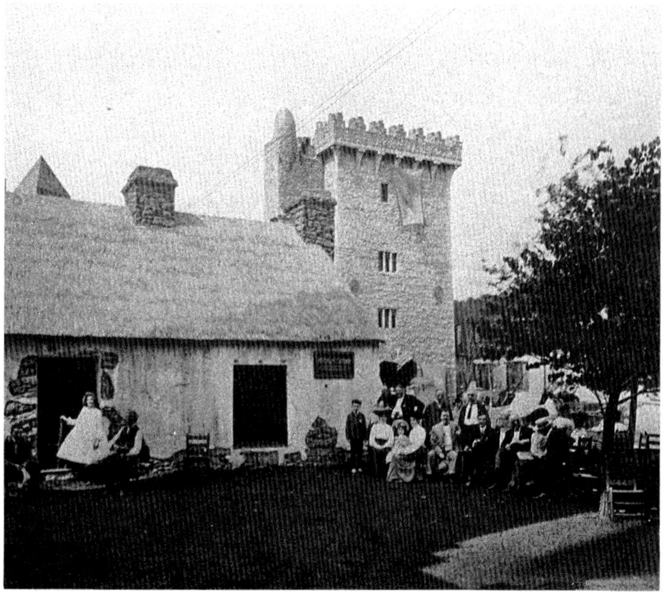

A replica of the ancestral home (in county Antrim) of President McKinley which was filled with relics and furnishings of his ancestors.

> *they propose giving ... I have written to Yeats and it is up to him now to decide what to do ...*

Yeats, however, remained resolute and in Rolleston's subsequent view 'was exceedingly wise in refusing to allow his plays to be performed to an Exposition audience. This is not the place for things of that kind.'[37]

As it happened, the theatre venture proved disastrous. Rolleston wrote to Quinn[38]:

> *The theatre folk are the great difficulty. Murphy says they are no good, except Miss Young & they won't leave. They performed* Deirdre *shortly after arriving. I was not there, but according to Murphy the performance was wretched – & what the miscellaneous crowd of Sioux, Cowboys, Demimondaines – pleasure seekers of all kinds who make up an average Pike audience thought of it would be an interesting study. They say M. should have special performances under patronage of literary societies, etc. and try to get the right kind of audiences together. Murphy says he would not put such a show before a cultivated audience, especially after Yeats – who had a great success here, had been leading them to think there was a serious dramatic movement on foot in Ireland. So there is kind of deadlock, & how it will all end I don't know.*

In the event, matters came to a head very soon. 'The company had nothing to act but *Deirdre*' Rolleston reported to Quinn[39] '... they could not act even that for they were no good ... & the termination of their engagement was only a question of time. This they must have perceived.' When one of the American actors, 'a Bowery Irishman' called Pat Tuohy, gave a performance which the Irish company perceived of as insultingly stage-Irish[40] they 'seized the golden opportunity of going out explosively as champions of Irish dignity & self-respect' and refused to go on stage 'thus causing a collapse of the performance before a large audience. This was quite inexcusable, & they have been properly sacked.'[41]

In taking this action the manager of the Village, Myles Murphy failed to appreciate 'the present sensitive – one might say morbid – condition of the Irish temper about the "stage Irishman". It has almost come to a point when an Irishman daren't be a comedian for fear of laughter being considered a "stage Irish" demonstration & an insult to the race!'[42] Accordingly, the Irish players – playing the nationalist card – circulated to all the Irish-American papers a lengthy account of the 'row' and in doing so cast aspersions on the whole Irish exhibit: 'For the information of Irish-Americans who are not acquainted with the correct state of affairs at the so-called Irish Village, it may be well to explain who and what are the representatives of the English Government department at present reigning there' and they described Gill ('a loyal and devoted servant of the English Crown'), Rolleston ('one-time Irish Revolutionist – now a devout loyalist'), and others in calculatedly unflattering terms.[43] TP Gill, still in St Louis at the time,[44] immediately issued a statement 'to squelch these absurd & vicious antagonisms that have arisen against us'.[45]

But the damage was done and Quinn, who was not alone in his disgust at the whole episode, described it to AE:

> *... The St Louis row has ended ... The Irish actors have done a great deal of damage to the very creditable Irish Exhibit by their hasty and exaggerated charges and by rushing into print. One would think that there were no self-respecting Irishmen in St Louis and that benighted America needed those 'champions' to tell her when to be indignant. I have seen so many Irish rows over nothing, that I think any Irishman or woman who makes no effort to overcome his seemingly innate desire for brawling, is unworthy of any consideration. For example, I've had it said to me at least ten times: 'Oh, I see as usual the Irish in St Louis have raised a row' and 'Why is it that not merely in politics but in everything else when you get a few Irish together there is a row...'*[46]

LETTERS FROM ST LOUIS

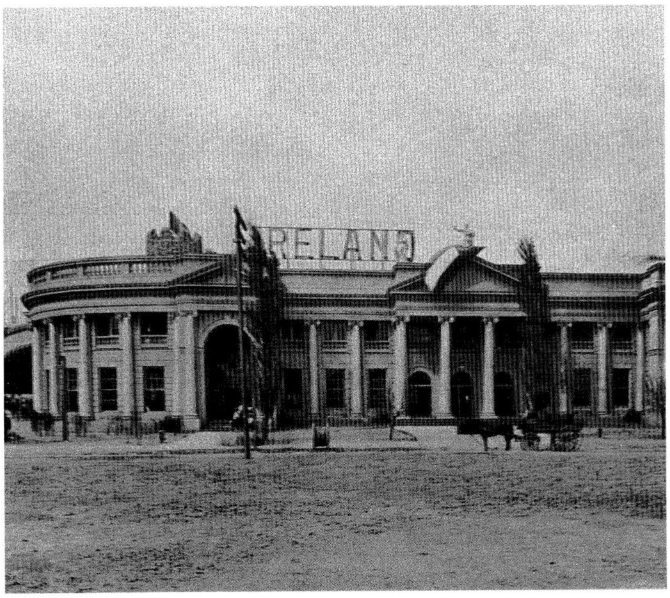

A replica of The Parliament House in Dublin which formed the main front of the Village. It contained a restaurant which could seat two thousand people and faced one of the principal thoroughfares of the Exposition – the Grand Court of Honor and the Cascade.

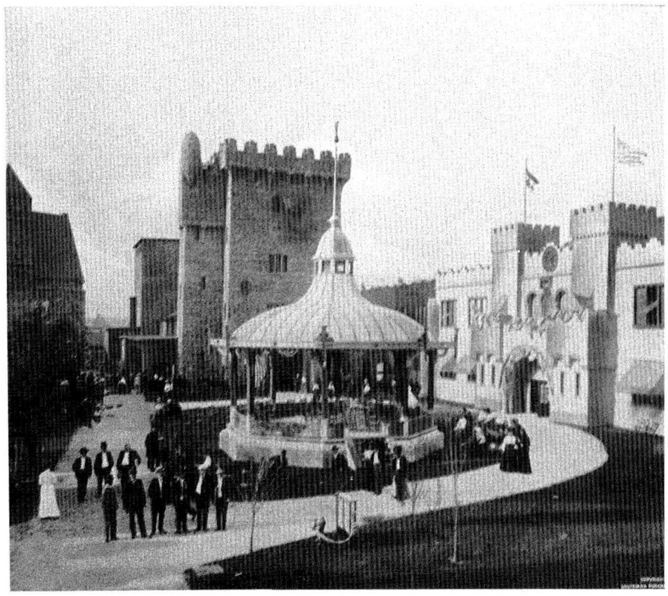

Inside the Village with a replica of Blarney Castle behind the bandstand.

AE replied: 'I am glad (the) row has subsided. I got innumerable letters about it but being wise in my generation, I answered none of them for which wisdom I feel nearer to heaven now.'[47]

Within weeks the theatre company was closed altogether when Murphy came to the conclusion that 'it is hopeless to try any legitimate drama at an Exposition'.[48]

Rolleston stayed on in St Louis after the Opening to complete his task. The American-Irish Collection did not arrive until the beginning of July: 'Murray arrived here yesterday and the (Irish American) collection too: it promises to be a most interesting adjunct to the show,' he wrote to Quinn on 1 July and continued 'we are getting good crowds now & all goes well. Weather perfect – warm and sunny without being sultry.' 'Everyone is delighted & surprised with the show' he wrote a few days later,

> *it is quite a reward for all the trouble to have some old farmer from Minnesota or somewhere come up & tell one his mind about it & to see his pride in the display we have made. It gives American or even Irish visitors quite a new conception of Ireland.*[49]

Gill, before leaving St Louis on 14 June, 'planned out a lot of work' for him[50] and Rolleston found himself very busy:

> *I've no time to read at present. My working hours are generally from 9 am to 1 am. The catalogue, press work, looking after photographs, putting finishing touches to the arrangements of exhibits, etc. fill up the days & night, & I am working to get everything that depends on myself into order before I leave...*[51] *I have sent the World's Fair Press bureau some 200 photographs & several stories about which they have written in complimentary terms and to which they will give great publicity.*

But, although T P Gill urged him to stay on in St Louis – 'Mr Gill told me that the longer you could stay in St Louis the better it would please him, as you were doing great work there' Quinn wrote to him[52] – Rolleston was anxious to return home. 'I can't delay my return longer ... I think my wife will have an action against Gill for compelling a husband to wife desertion if I put off my return longer'[53] and by 23 July he was in New York en route to Boston where he would embark the *Etruria* for Ireland.

Even after his return home, he continued to publicise the Exposition and sent articles to *Harper's Weekly*,[54] *Collier's*, and *The Evening Sun* about the Irish exhibit: 'I have done another article in a sketchy sort of style on the Limavady gold ornaments & the lawsuit about them in which gods and men & scientific persons were so greatly mixed up...'[55]

Encouraged by the success of the Irish Village and well before the Fair was due to end in November, Tom Hanley had ideas of bringing the exhibit to New York. 'Hanley came in to see me about two weeks ago' Quinn wrote to Rolleston[56]

> *and talked for an hour or so about bringing on the exhibits to New York for three or four weeks, substantially duplicating the St Louis exhibit except the amusement features ...*

Neither Quinn nor his friend Judge Byrne (who ultimately purchased the collection of prints shown as part of the Irish-American Loan in St Louis) did anything to encourage Hanley but, nevertheless, by November Rolleston was at work 'writing to all the exhibitors to tell them what is contemplated & to ask them whether if ... the transference of the exhibits to NY ... is decided on they will agree to let their exhibits remain for the New York show'.[57]

As it happened nothing came of these plans and Hanley – perhaps on account of his substantial financial loss at St Louis – seems to have soon abandoned the idea. The Irish Industrial Exhibition which took place the following year at Madison Square Gardens in New York was an entirely different affair. Quinn wrote to Lady Gregory[58]

> *There is an 'Irish Industrial Exposition' to be held at the Madison Square Garden the last*

LETTERS FROM ST LOUIS

week of September and the first two weeks of October. It was started by a small crowd of the 'patent leather' kind that Yeats and I used to have fun about but now that it is on we are all trying to make it a success …

Quinn 'lent all of (his) Irish paintings, including your father's (JB Yeats's) portraits …'[59] and

at (his) request Miss Lily Yeats and her sister sent over some rugs and tapestries and table covers and some church vestments to the Exhibition, I think about 150 pounds worth in all. The rugs are all without exception the most beautiful of the kind I have ever seen and the table covers are exquisite. Miss Elizabeth Yeats sent over two or three of her beautiful painted fans. This Dun Emer exhibit is by far and away the finest thing of the kind in the Garden.[60]

But, Quinn added, 'the lack of management of the whole exhibit has been exasperating' and in a letter to Lily he described how 'the whole thing was bungled and badly mismanaged.'[61]

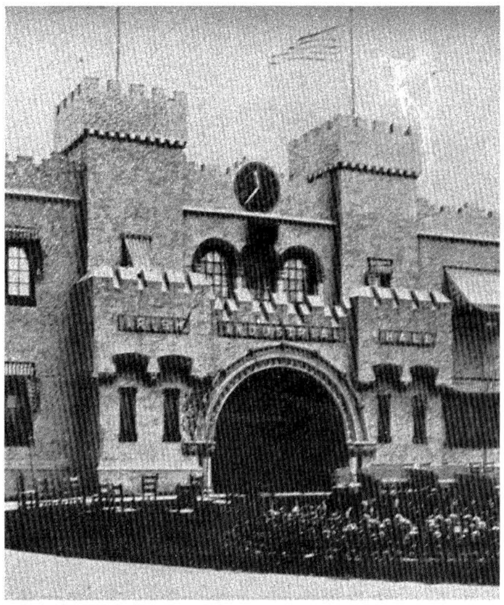

Industrial Hall, 260 feet long, was the site of the main exhibitions of Irish arts and industries.

Writing from Dublin,[62] Rolleston enquired anxiously,

I should be very glad to hear anything you can tell me or to have newspaper accounts, catalogue, etc. of the Madison Square Show. Of course it is being boomed here in certain quarters as the really fine and high toned show which is to redeem the St Louis 'fiasco'…

But , he added, and with ample justification, '*It seems hardly possible that it can come near the St Louis affair …*'

Homan Potterton

Homan Potterton is a former Director of the National Gallery of Ireland (1980-88).

NOTES

1. John Quinn Memorial Collection, Rare Books and Manuscripts Division of New York Public Library (Astor, Lenox and Tilden Foundations). Additional letters are among the Jeanne R.Foster-William M Murphy Collection in the same location. For Quinn see, B L Reid, *The Man from New York: John Quinn and his Friends* (New York, 1968); for Quinn as art-collector, see J Zilczer, *The Noble Buyer: John Quinn, Patron of the Avant-Garde*, exh. cat. Hirshhorn Museum (Washington, 1978).
2. The Louisiana Purchase Exposition, St Louis, Missouri, 1904. For the Irish exhibit see David R Francis, *The Universal Exposition of 1904* 2 vols. (St Louis 1913) vol. 1, pp.573-75 and 594; WB Stevens, *The Forest City; a portfolio of official photographic views of the Universal Exposition, St Louis 1904* (30 portfolios, published weekly between 14 April and 3 November 1904), see 16 and 30 June and 7 July (St Louis 1903); J W Hanson, *The Official History of the Fair, St Louis 1904* (1904), pp.437-38; T R MacMechen, *The Pike and its Attractions, World's Fair, St Louis* (St Louis 1904), pp.1-3; Jeanne Sheehy, *The Rediscovery of Ireland's Past: The Celtic Revival 1830-1930* (London 1980), pp.133-34; N Gordon Bowe, 'The Irish Arts and Crafts Movement (1886-1925)', *Irish Arts Review Yearbook 1990-1991*, p.180; Paul Larmour, *The Arts and Crafts Movement in Ireland* (Belfast 1992), pp.74, 114-15 and n.10, 11 p.223.
3. For a recent study of Ireland at the Chicago exhibition see the exhibition catalogue, *Imagining an Irish Past: the Celtic Revival 1840-1940*, Smart Museum, University of Chicago, (1992), *passim* (reviewed in this issue). For the two Irish villages see *ibid.* pp.89-105.
4. Hanson, *op.cit.*, p.437
5. See the address by T.P. Gill at the opening of the Irish Village published in *The Gaelic American*, 2 July 1904 (also published as a separate pamphlet); also TW Rolleston, 'Progress in Ireland as Shown at the Fair', *Harper's Weekly*, 5 November 1904; also Department of Agriculture and Technical Instruction for Ireland, *Fourth Annual General Report, 1903-04*, p.23.
6. For Hanley and the Irish Exhibit Company see 'Thomas F. Hanley, President and Organizer of the Irish Exhibition' in *The Gael* (October 1904) p.332: 'A syndicate of Jewish speculators had laid before the governing board of the Exposition an application for a site for an "Irish Village". Among the features which this syndicate proposed to install were a Donnybrook Fair and a free dancing platform. Camels were to be introduced as a special attraction. It was to be a mixture of the streets of Cairo and the slum beer garden. The national pride of Tom Hanley was aroused and he protested vigorously … the Hebrews lost the concession … and the suggestion was made that Mr Hanley himself should take the site and build an "Irish Village" that would be a credit to himself and his race.'
7. See 'The St.Louis Exhibition: IV. The Irish Exhibit', *The Times* (London) 15 September 1904. The Irish Exhibit Company expended $325,000 on the buildings and equipment; the Department spent an additional $60,000 in gathering, packing and installing the exhibits. *The Gael* (October 1904) p.332. It was later reported that 'Mr Hanley stands to lose $70,000 on the venture'. *The Gael* (November 1904) p.376.
8. See the Department's *Report* referred to in n.5 above. For the influence of the Department see N. Gordon Bowe, 'The Arts and Crafts Society of Ireland (1894-1925) with particular reference to Harry Clarke', *The Journal of the Decorative Arts Society 1850-The Present*, no.9 (1985), p.33; N. Gordon Bowe, 'Wilhelmina Geddes, Harry Clarke, and their part in the Arts and Crafts Movement in Ireland' *The Journal of Decorative and Propaganda Arts* (Spring 1988), p. 62; N.Gordon Bowe, 'Two Early Twentieth-Century Irish Arts and Crafts Workshops in Context: An Tur Gloine and the Dun Emer Guild and Industries', *Journal of Design History*, vol. 2, nos. 2 & 3 (1989), p.193; P. Larmour, *op.cit.* (1992), pp.73-74, 91, 96 and *passim*.
9. See TP Gill's address referred to in n.5 above. Also, 'The Irish Department at the St.Louis Exhibition', *The Gael* (May 1904), p.181-82.
10. See the *Journal and Proceedings of the Arts and Crafts Society of Ireland* (1906), pp.251-52.
11. See the official Catalogue of the Exhibition, *Irish Industrial Exhibition, World's Fair, St Louis, 1904* 3 Parts (Department of Agriculture and Technical Instruction for Ireland, 1904).
12. Joseph Malachy Kavanagh, RHA is best known as a painter and his metalwork is less familiar. Eithne Waldron, 'Joseph Malachy Kavanagh', *Capuchin Annual* (1968), p.326 notes that he produced bas-reliefs, bronzes, woodcuts, and porcelain work. He exhibited embossed silver plaques at the RHA in 1899 and 'Repousse work' in 1901. He also exhibited such work at the second Exhibition of the Arts and Crafts Society of Ireland in 1899: see Larmour, *op.cit.* (1992), p.72 where an example is illustrated.
13. Letter dated 10 January 1904. See further Homan Potterton, 'Jack B.Yeats and John Quinn', *Irish Arts Review Yearbook*, vol.9

LETTERS FROM ST LOUIS

(1993) pp.102-14.
14. Letter dated 25 January 1904.
15. See William M. Murphy, *Prodigal Father: the Life of John Butler Yeats (1839-1922)* (Ithaca & London, 1978), p.271.
16. Including the actors who were to perform at the Exhibition, see further below.
17. A useful summary of Rolleston's life is his obituary in *The Irish Book Lover*, vol. 12 (1921), pp.89-90. Also see C H Rolleston, *Portrait of an Irishman: a biographical sketch of T W Rolleston* (London 1939) where his work at St Louis is referred to on pp.2,8 and 69-71.
18. In fact Sir Horace Plunkett did not visit the Exposition until later in the year. Rolleston wrote to Quinn on 16 November 1904, 'Horace Plunkett goes out to St Louis by the "Baltic"...'
19. *Irish Builder*, 27 February 1904, p.108.
20. *The Gael*, (October 1904), p.332.
21. *Irish Builder*, 27 February 1904, p.108.
22. See the description by MJ Murphy, 'Ireland at the Fair', *The Gael* (April 1904), p.141; also T R MacMechen, *op cit.*, p.1.
23. Letter from TW Rolleston to John Quinn, 14 May 1904.
24. *The Gaelic American*, 2 July 1904.
25. *Ibid.*
26. 15 September 1904.
27. Francis, *op.cit.*, vol.1, pp.574-75.
28. Hanson, *op.cit.*
29. Letter dated 7 January 1904. Quinn had arranged for WB Yeats to meet in New York with 'Mr Augustus Thomas, a very successful playwright here who formerly lived in St Louis. Thomas thought that the company would not do well at St Louis. St Louis is very hot in the summer time, and as Mr Thomas phrased it, "A man from Dublin would not be happy there unless he had special facilities for perspiration."
30. WB Yeats wrote to Quinn: 'The Reardon dispute has been unpleasant. When he went away he and I were on personally good terms, though I was feeling pretty exasperated. I felt and feel the greatest suspicion but have no better reason for it than everybody's vagueness of mind about the project. I got an impression from Reardon that he would say one thing today and another thing tomorrow.' (Quoted by Quinn in a letter to AE dated 2 May 1904). Yeats proved correct in his suspicions and Quinn later described Reardon as 'neither intelligent nor wholly reliable' (letter to AE, 2 May 1904) while TW Rolleston was more frank: 'Reardon is an ass & is practically allowed to do nothing now' he wrote to Quinn, 14 May 1904. For Reardon's own account of his plans for the Village, see *The Gael* (February 1904), p.75.
31. AE to Quinn, 15 April 1904.
32. *Ibid.*
33. See William M. Murphy, *op.cit.*, n.110, pp.597-98.
34. AE to Quinn, 15 April 1904.
35. 2 May 1904.
36. Myles J Murphy who was General Manager of the Irish Exhibit Company and, therefore, effectively manager of the Irish Village, he is profiled in *The Gael* (April 1904), p. 137. Rolleston described him to Quinn (letter dated 14 May 1904) as by 'far the best man they have got, &...indeed a treasure. He is doing about three men's work, & if any good comes out of the show it will be very largely due to him.'
37. Rolleston to Quinn, 3 June 1904.
38. Letter dated 14 May 1904.
39. Letter dated 3 June 1904.
40. For the actors' own version of events see their statement issued to the press, 'Protest from the Irish Players', *The Gaelic American*, 9 July 1904.
41. Rolleston to Quinn, 3 June 1904.
42. Rolleston to Quinn, 4 July 1904.
43. The players also reported that when Rolleston presided at a concert aboard ship on the voyage to St Louis, he called on the Irish Band to play "God Save the King" which they refused to do. (*The Gaelic American*, 9 July 1904.) Rolleston refuted this in a letter to Quinn dated 3 June 1904: 'Have you come across an absurd myth to the effect that I called on the Irish band on the *Etruria* to play "God Save the King", as Chairman of the Seamans' Orphanage Concert? ...I hear it has found its way to the Dublin press now ! There is not a particle of truth in it...'
44. Rolleston to Quinn, 14 June 1904: 'Gill leaves us today for Chicago.'
45. *Ibid.*
46. Letter dated 1 July 1904.
47. Undated letter, August or September 1904.
48. *Ibid.*
49. Rolleston to Quinn, 4 July 1904.
50. Rolleston to Quinn, 15 June 1904.
51. Rolleston to Quinn, 4 July 1904.
52. Quinn to Rolleston, 9 July 1904.
53. Rolleston to Quinn, 11 July 1904.
54. 'Progress in Ireland as Shown at the Fair', *Harper's Weekly*, 5 November 1904. Rolleston completed this article while aboard ship on his way home.
55. Gill arranged for the *Collier's* article although it seems never to have been published; on 29 August 1904, Rolleston wrote to Quinn from Dublin that he had sent *The Evening Sun* a 1,000 word article about the Limavady Gold. This refers to a collection of objects in the National Museum of Ireland (replicas of which were shown at St Louis) which, after they were found in Limavady in 1896, were sold to the British Museum. The Royal Irish Academy, as statutory custodian of treasure trove found in Ireland, sued (successfully) for their return to Ireland.
56. Letter dated 16 September 1904.
57. Rolleston to Quinn, 16 November 1904.
58. Letter dated 30 August 1905.
59. Quinn to Jack Yeats, 13 October 1905.
60. Quinn to Mrs J F Byrne, 25 September 1905.
61. Quinn to Lily Yeats, 13 October 1905.
62. Rolleston to Quinn, 27 September 1905.

BOOK REVIEWS

RODERIC O'CONOR: A BIOGRAPHY, WITH A CATALOGUE OF HIS WORK.

JONATHAN BENINGTON
Dublin, Irish Academic Press, 1992, £29.95.

This book is a welcome addition to the growing bibliography of recent Irish art history. Roderic O'Conor was one of the foremost painters of his generation, but, since he spent the greater part of his career abroad, he had little influence on the art scene in Ireland. Moreover, he exhibited here on only three occasions during his lifetime, namely at the Royal Hibernian Academy in 1883 and again in 1885 and at the Royal Dublin Society in 1884, showing just seven pictures in all, so that his reputation has, until recent years, been one based on hearsay – even mystique – rather than on fact. His association with Gauguin, his alleged friendship with Van Gogh, his role as the model for the obstreperous painter Clutton in Somerset Maugham's novel *Of Human Bondage,* and his contact with Clive Bell, have been the sources of this mystique. Amongst collectors, on the other hand, he has enjoyed a small band of supporters who have fervently admired him and never doubted his worth as a painter.

Since O'Conor's death in 1940, his work has increasingly been seen in exhibitions in Ireland and elsewhere. Most notably the exhibition *Two Masters of Colour, Matthew Smith and Roderic O'Conor,* arranged at Roland Browse and Delbanco in London in 1956, did much to re-establish his name and reputation. Of more recent shows, perhaps, *Gauguin and the Pont Aven Group* (Tate Gallery, London, 1966) and *De Pont-Aven aux Nabis* (Grand Palais, Paris, 1971) have been the most notable. In Ireland he was included in *The Peasant in French 19th Century Art* (Douglas Hyde Gallery, Dublin, 1980), *The Irish Impressionists* (National Gallery of Ireland, Dublin, 1984) and, of course, Roy Johnston arranged the large and comprehensive O'Conor exhibition held in the National Gallery of Ireland and at the Ulster Museum in 1984. Thus his reputation has grown over the years since his death, although our knowledge of his career has lagged behind and his personality has remained elusive, the mystique largely intact. Benington's book in part rectifies the latter aspect of the artist's persona. Yet we are still left with an intangible personality who moved on the

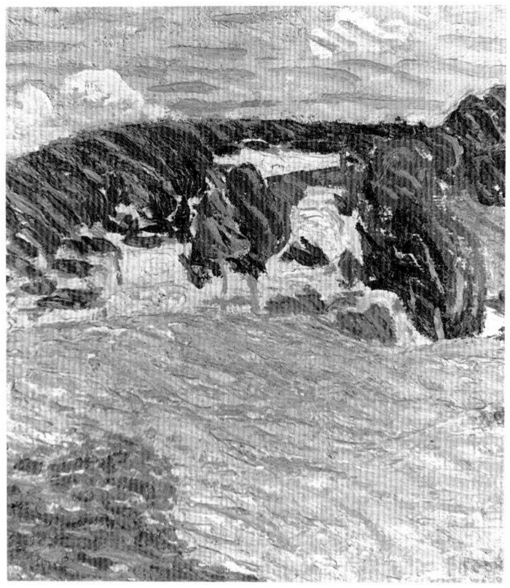

Roderic O'Conor, Field of Corn, *Ulster Museum, Belfast.*

periphery of events, watching and observing and, in private, often pontificated on things about which he remained either powerless or inert to influence. Despite the urging of his friends, he was loath to exhibit his pictures, especially in one-man shows which would have furthered his reputation, and only reluctantly submitted work to the larger group exhibitions. In a real sense O'Conor's elusiveness was a mark of personality and thus Benington has laid it as bare as it is probably possible to do.

Benington's book is excellent, his research being impressive and wide-ranging in scope. The difficulties for the art historian in exploring O'Conor's career are well stated – the lack of documentary evidence and general papers – the prime sources being his paintings themselves. But these, too, in their 'bewildering' (p.15) diversity of styles and subjects, combined with the uncertainty of parts of his chronology, bring their own problems. In the circumstances, Benington wisely chose not to attempt to categorise O'Conor as a Post-Impressionist, Expressionist, Fauvist, or whatever, but rather laid stress on his artistic temperament, identifying and evaluating the threads which run through his work.

O'Conor's career is described chronologically, the narrative being punctuated from time to time where appropriate to discuss developments in painting technique, subject-matter or other relevant issues. While occasionally Benington's prose is stiff, this is no more than the result of this being a first book and in the main he manages to combine a terse and scholarly style with ease of reading. The overall impression we get of O'Conor is of a man unsure of himself, lacking in self-confidence, both with regard to personal and artistic matters, and this no doubt coloured his pugnacity. Despite the fact that he generated widespread respect amongst his contemporaries, we see him constantly testing outside opinion of his work.

Benington has discerned three stylistic traits – animated handling of paint, heightened colours and simplified forms – as typifying O'Conor's *oeuvre,* and rightly considers the expressive impulse in his work to stem from the mildly revolutionary aspect of his personality. The most important phase of his career, and that for which he is principally remembered, is his early period in France. It was at this time that he met Gauguin and a number of others who greatly influenced him. It was Van Gogh, however, whom he probably never met, who had the most profound influence on him in terms of subject-matter, use of colour and handling of paint. In the early 1890s he developed a vocabulary through which he expressed ideas as avant-garde as any current at that time, and, indeed, one of Benington's achievements has been to demonstrate just how advanced O'Conor was in these years as, for example, his *Field of Corn, Pont Aven,* 1892 (Ulster Museum), with its stripes of contrasting complementary colours and agonised brushwork – the influence of Van Gogh is clearly apparent – illustrates. Here, too, as in many of his compositions of the time, the landscape is devoid of people, and this Benington suggests stems from his meditative trait of mind. To Benington, O'Conor was a 'reluctant' Romantic in the Baudelairean sense of one motivated by 'a way of feeling' (p.16). His approach to painting was spontaneous and sometimes erratic, and is well summarised by Somerset Maugham's description of Clutton (O'Conor) in *Of Human Bondage:*

> *The only reason that one paints is that one can't help it. It's a function like any of the other functions of the body … One paints for oneself … We paint from within outwards – if we force our vision on the world it calls us great painters; if we don't it ignores us; but we are the same … What happens to our work afterwards is unimportant; we have got all we could out of it while we were doing it (p.17).*

BOOK REVIEWS

O'Conor's pictures done during his time in Brittany in the 1890s are his most avant-garde works. There is an autobiographical quality to his landscapes in particular, and we share his sense of discovery when, for instance, he peers over precipices to paint the sea dashing against the rocks as, for example, in *The Foaming Sea* (1892). Here the whole composition is rendered Expressionistically in bold reds and greens and in a manner, as Benington points out, which preceded Fauvism by at least a decade. His figure studies of the same time, such as the *Breton Peasant Woman Knitting* (1893) or *Head of a Breton Boy with Cap* (c.1893) show the same advanced technique, and although his use of paint, which is laid on the canvas in stripes, often of complementary colours, recalls Van Gogh, nevertheless, O'Conor has brought his own personality and outlook to bear upon it.

By the first decade of the twentieth century O'Conor's painting had lost most of the fiery intensity of his earlier work and became more representational, although he retained a gestural approach, as is clear to be seen in *Evening, Montigny* (1902) and in a whole group of pictures painted on the river Loing. Yet even now, in his *Young Breton Girl* (1903) or *Boulevard Raspail* (c.1905, Hugh Lane Gallery, Dublin), for example, the influence of the earlier striped paintings can be detected. From about 1909 or so onwards, however, his approach became more gentle. The *Reclining Nude before a Mirror II* (1909) is a delightfully evocative work, full of pathos and atmosphere, while *Woman in White*, of about the same time (Ulster Museum) and *Still Life, Azaleas* (1911, Musée du Petit Palais, Geneva) show him in an unusually carefree mood, the latter being a riot of bright colours. His numerous studies of nudes, which seem to proliferate in his later career, often depict rather melancholic, isolated figures, as his *Seated Nude with Red Hair* and *Rest* (both c.1923), for example, demonstrate. Yet these pictures, taken along with his still lifes of the same time – *Still Life* (c.1917), *Red Roses in a Jug set on a Napkin* (c.1921-3) or *Tea-roses* (1923) – show him in a more relaxed mood which was probably a result of his by now settled, less nomadic way of life, a trend which continued after his marriage to Renée Honta. O'Conor's late works in general reflect his growing peace of mind. *The Bathers* (c.1925), for instance, depicts a sylvan scene of bathers by a river, while the mood in landscapes such as *Landscape with a Palm Tree* (c.1934-5) or *Torremolinos* (1935) is almost whimsical.

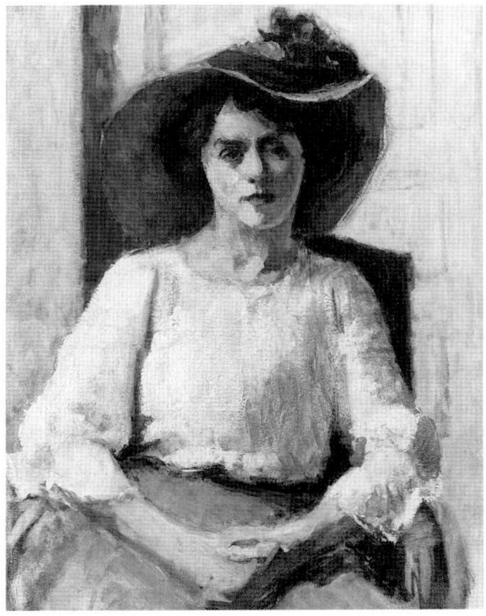

Roderic O'Conor, Woman in White, *Ulster Museum, Belfast.*

Overall, Benington gives a rounded view of O'Conor, matching his mood and circumstances to each twist of his style. By describing the influences upon him and by mentioning, for example, his literary inclinations (p.126), he helps to pin down the personality of his quarry. The illustrations throughout the book (80 colour, 79 black and white) are of excellent quality and amply represent the range – paintings, etchings and drawings – of O'Conor's art. The substantial catalogue of O'Conor's works which comes at the end of the book, and which lists the date of each work, its medium and measurements, provenance, exhibition and literary references and so on, is invaluable and must form the basis for any future research into the artist's career. There is, too, a complete list of all the exhibitions in which he participated during his lifetime, but it would have been useful to have brought this up to date. O'Conor was undeniably a painter of considerable merit, often ahead of 'mainstream' developments; yet it is a pity he didn't exhibit more in his lifetime for his achievement deserves to be better known. Alas, even now, too often he has to be defined through reference to others.

S B Kennedy

Dr S B Kennedy is Curator of twentieth century art in the Ulster Museum

ARTS AND CRAFTS CARPETS

MALCOLM HASLAM
David Black Oriental Carpets, London 1991.
200pp., 85 colour & 115 b/w illustrations.
Hardbound £45.00

Malcolm Haslam's well-researched and beautifully illustrated survey of Arts and Crafts carpets is a welcome addition to the literature on the movement. Carpets are only briefly touched upon in other studies of the textiles of the period, though carpet manufacture flourished in the last quarter of the nineteenth century, and designers and manufacturers associated with the Arts and Crafts movement were responsible for some of the finest carpets ever produced in the British Isles. Haslam's work brings together accounts of the various craft industrial ventures which produced them and considers the factors responsible for the renaissance in carpet design and manufacture.

Arts and Crafts architects generally considered floorboards to be both more aesthetic and hygienic than fully-carpeted rooms, and the use of rugs and carpets on wooden boards became a widely adopted practice in buildings designed by them. As carpet design is traditionally one of the most conservative areas in British furnishing textiles, architects and designers relied initially on the many splendid Oriental carpets which were being imported at the period, but a market clearly existed by 1880 for products more in keeping with the new impetus in design. One of the first to fill that gap was William Morris. Morris & Company sold a wide range of carpets that included both hand-knotted varieties made by Morris's own workforce and machine-woven carpeting made up to Morris's designs at factories in Yorkshire and Wilton. As with his printed and woven textiles, Morris's carpet designs successfully blend elements of Gothic, Renaissance and middle Eastern design with the contemporary, to produce patterns which looked startlingly fresh. Haslam's chapter on Morris covers fairly well-trodden ground but those on the Donegal venture and on the small, independent craft workshops such as the Dun Emer Guild (Paul Larmour, *Irish Arts Review*, vol2, no2, 1985, pp.18-22) usefully bring together much more scattered material.

The production of deep pile carpets in Donegal was started in 1898 by James Morton, younger son of Alexander Morton, an enlightened manufacturer of

BOOK REVIEWS

silk and woollen textiles whose main works were at Darvel in Ayrshire (Paul Larmour, *Irish Arts Review Yearbook* 1990-91,pp. 210-17). They quickly achieved renown for their quality and design, selling through Liberty's, Maple's and Story's in London and being widely exhibited. Early Donegals were closely modelled on Turkish and Persian examples, but in the wake of the Celtic Revival of the 1890s, which had made its influence felt on poetry, painting, architecture and design generally, from 1901 they were often made with Celtic designs, some adapted directly from the 'Book of Kells', others from new designs by Archibald Knox, a leading proponent of the Revival. Many Donegal carpet designs can also be attributed to CFA Voysey since they are adapted from textile and wallpaper patterns of his, with a border added. As the middle classes retreated after 1905 from the spectre of modernism engendered by the Arts and Crafts movement, Donegal carpets were increasingly designed in a more conservative neo-Georgian style.

Set up with the principal aim of encouraging light industry in what was an impoverished and over-populated district of Ireland, the Donegal manufactory was one of a large number of philanthropic ventures in the 1880s and 90s dotted throughout the British Isles. Together they constitute an interesting sub-text to the main body of work on the Arts and Crafts movement and, although known through scattered studies, would benefit from a closer and more focused analysis.

Though principally a survey of the designers and manufacturers involved in the production of Arts and Crafts carpets, Haslam's book also offers a brief but sound insight into the cultural and theoretical framework within which they were working. He traces the process of liberalisation which occurred between 1850 and 1900, by which time designers such as Walter Crane and Voysey felt confident enough to break most of the rules regarding propriety in carpet design that had been laid down by design reformers of the mid-century such as Pugin and Owen Jones. The book contains 85 specially commissioned colour photographs of the carpets and a large number of interesting documentary photographs in black and white, many taken from journals of the period.

Jennifer Harris

Jennifer Harris is Curator of Textiles and Deputy Director of The Whitworth Art Gallery, Manchester.

NATHANIEL HONE THE YOUNGER, 1831-1917

JULIAN CAMPBELL
National Gallery of Ireland, 1991. £19.95

Nathaniel Hone was one of the half-dozen major Irish painters working at the end of the nineteenth century, and it is high time a serious study such as this was devoted to him. There was no better person to do it than Dr Julian Campbell, who opened up the subject in his catalogue for *The Irish Impressionists* (1984), which included a section on Hone. The use of the word 'Impressionist' for that exhibition was misleading – there were no impressionists in Ireland, no artists who combined modern subject-matter, the use of the rainbow-palette, and a preoccupation with instantaneity. The description 'Impressionist' is particularly inappropriate for Hone, as Campbell establishes in this catalogue. We have been much too eager to fit late nineteenth-century Irish paintings into a teleological framework which sees Impressionism as a precursor of the modern movement, culminating in New York in the 1950s – the model set up by John Rewald in *The History of Impressionism.* The fact is that there were thousands of other painters in Europe in the period whose work is perfectly valid, who are not merely the troughs of waves whose peaks are Monet, Pissarro, Renoir and Sisley. Nor were the avant-garde as isolated as Rewald implies, but interlocked at all sorts of levels with the Parisian art world.

The Paris career of Nathaniel Hone is a very good example of the shifting character of French artistic life in the period. He arrived in Paris in 1853, when Realists like Courbet and Millet had managed to get a foothold in the art-world thanks to the revolution of 1848, but by which time there was already a reactionary backlash in favour of less disruptive art. He spent under a year in the studio of Adolf Yvon, famous for his documentary battle-pictures, then went on for three years to Thomas Couture. Couture's was one of the largest and most popular Parisian studios, full of an international crowd, including many Americans. Among Hone's friends at Couture's was Edouard Manet, soon to become the reluctant leader of the Parisian avant-garde.

Hone had the conventional Parisian training of a figure-painter, yet as soon as he left his pupillage behind he turned to landscape. It is entirely in keeping with this aim that he began to frequent the Forest of Fontainebleau, which had become a centre for Realist landscape artists, ancient, remote and mysterious, yet linked to the Parisian art market by the newly opened railway. Hone's allegiance to the Barbizon school is marked in two ways. It is evident in his manner of painting — for example *The Fairy Marsh*, painted in the forest in the late 1860s, low-key greens and browns and greys, laid on in vigorous strokes. Much later, when he had settled in Ireland, his works are often reminiscent of Barbizon — *Shepherd and Sheep on a Road, Glenmalure* with its rocks sticking out of scrubby ground, and its delicate stand of birches, for example. His allegiance to Barbizon is also evident in the fact that he lived in the Forest of Fontainebleau for many years. Having rejected figure-painting, he also rejected Parisian modernity, already being promot-

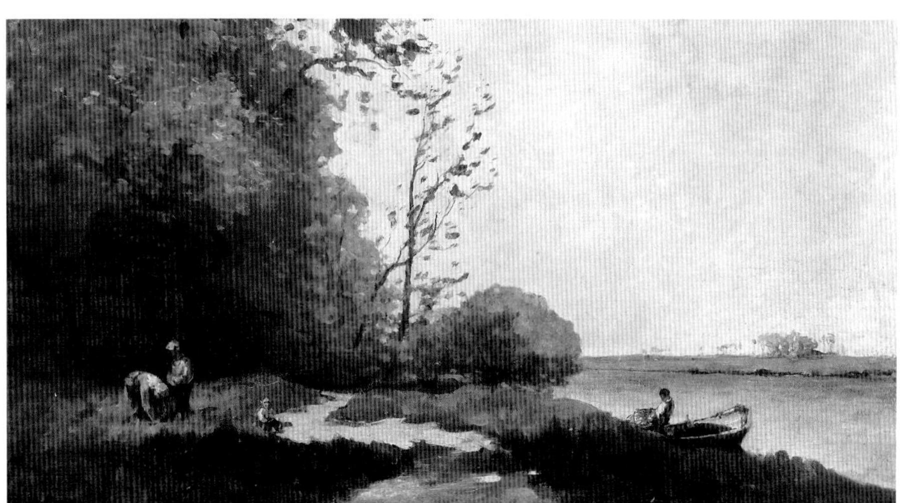

Nathaniel Hone the Younger, The Banks of the Seine. *Oil on canvas, 62 x 100 cm.*

BOOK REVIEWS

ed by Manet and Baudelaire, and chose the already fairly well-trodden path of Realist landscape.

One of the great revelations of this catalogue is the range of Hone's work. There was a story that the National Gallery of Ireland had so many cows-in-fields by him that they could not only paper a room, but match the pattern. This slur is entirely refuted by Campbell, who reveals the great richness of his output, landscapes, seascapes, portraits of buildings, not just in Ireland and France, but as far afield as Italy and Egypt. The freshness and vigour of the water-colours is a delight

This is a solid and scholarly catalogue, thoroughly documented, with a useful bibliography. It establishes Hone as a professional artist, in the European context to which he belongs. It provides an invaluable selection of his work, all reproduced in colour. My only quibble is that it could have done with more careful proof-reading – there are rather a lot of typographical errors.

Jeanne Sheehy

LATER FLEMISH PAINTINGS IN THE NATIONAL GALLERY OF IRELAND: THE SEVENTEENTH TO NINETEENTH CENTURIES

DAVID OLDFIELD

Dublin, The National Gallery of Ireland, 1992. 194pp. 147 ills. £30 (paperback).

A catalogue of a permanent collection formed over several generations, such as David Oldfield's praiseworthy volume, is a less glamorous undertaking than that of a temporary exhibition. The latter, because the works have been specially selected with an end in view, should have a coherence and thrust that compensates for the limited time-scale required for its production. In the case of a catalogue of a public collection, the deadline does not press – the works can be subject to long physical examination, provenances can be thoroughly researched – but still the compiler is confronted by the whims, mistakes even, of directors long past and by the vagaries of chance acquisitions through gifts and bequests.

Such considerations do not arise where a great collection is concerned, but in the case of the National Gallery of Ireland, this cannot be said so far as its holding of Flemish pictures goes. Oldfield can only present a mixed bag of eighty-one works by some forty-six artists of which about ten might be considered of a desirable, 'museum-quality' level. The majority was bought under the directorships of George Mulvany and Henry Doyle, which covered the first thirty years of the institution's existence. Histories of collections and catalogues of their constituent parts are distinct activities, but in this case, as a good few of the acquisitions appear so quixotic, they might usefully have been combined.

Oldfield catalogues nine copies after Van Dyck (although for one, no 672, no prototype is known and we may well here be dealing with the work of another artist – Soutman? – c.1635) and four after Rubens. It is to his credit that he treats them with the same degree of thoroughness as he does an original, while he erects critical constructs around works by such minor artists as de Gryeff or Lambrechts. This may be thought foolhardy especially when Oldfield's Muse is upstaged on occasions by a censorious spinster. 'Pubs' (surely an anachronism, like his use of the appellations 'upper middle class' and 'middle class', as for the 'tendency of seventeenth century patrons to upgrade their collections' the less said the better) allude to immoral behaviour. 'Smoking, like drinking [can lead] to inebriation [can it?] and idleness'. A young man's 'dubious character is underlined by his open-legged position' ... '[his] oafish manners are of a type normally associated with peasants'.

Influenced by the recent, but now-questioned, fashion of finding moralising themes in Dutch genre and landscape paintings, Oldfield's sense of proportion saves him from the absurd. Thus he realises that in a tavern scene by Teniers 'the tone ... is comical rather than overly moralistic'. He opines that a landscape with a young woman on a market cart by Siberechts has no erotic content in spite of (sic) 'the urinating horse, the watchful dog ... [and] the abundance of vegetables'.

The quality of Oldfield's entries increases *pari passu* with the quality of the pictures concerned, and on this higher level he has done a thorough job, useful both for scholars and the interested public alike.

He argues persuasively that the *Christ in the House of Martha and Mary* by Jan Brueghel II and Rubens has been cut to the left and right. A glance at the edges of the panel to see if they were bevelled or not could have confirmed this. The back of the support is noted as being 'heavily coated': this coating is probably a chalk ground occasionally applied at the time to the reverses of composite supports as a protection against atmospheric changes.

Quite rightly returned to Rubens, following the Gallery's aberration in 1981 when an attribution to Jordaens was advanced, is *The Tribute Money*. Oldfield has identified it as one of the pictures sold by Rubens to Carleton in 1618, but has not been able to detect which areas display Rubens' documented finishing touches. What is meant by such touches is not dwelt on: perhaps Rubens was using a courtly understatement, for there is evidence that the kneeling fishermen could have been introduced at this later stage. Rubens described the fishermen as 'cavati del naturale', and Oldfield, taking him at his word, omits to state that at least two of the faces depicted were the subject of earlier studies in oil.

An injustice may have been committed by his demotion of the *Annunciation* to a work of Rubens' studio. It is strange that, whereas Oldfield finds so many faults in its condition, Michael Jaffé recently has described the picture as 'perhaps the most beautiful of Rubens' treatment of the theme' [translation]. Oldfield enumerates numerous 'changes' without clarifying whether these are *pentimenti* or the result of later interventions. He is not alone in his negative view following, most recently, Julius Held, whose description of the picture as being on canvas leads one unusually to question this scholar's stance.

Oldfield writes at length on the two splendid Jordaens in the collection. The genesis of the *Veneration of the Eucharist* is well-argued from the drawing in the Pierpoint Morgan Library. St Jerome's lion in the drawing appears centre-stage in the painting and causes Oldfield some bewilderment. But does it not represent Belgium? It bears on its back a female personification, surely of the Catholic Church. So in fact the picture is much more than the veneration of the Eucharist. On that subject he writes intelligently in the context of the Counter Reformation. This makes the more surprising his reference to the Eucharist in the following entry (on the *Supper at Emmaüs*) as celebrated in remembrance of Christ's sacrifice. Bring on the Inquisition!

Gregory Martin

Gregory Martin is a Director of Christie's; previously he compiled the Catalogue of Flemish Paintings in the National Gallery, *(London, 1970, reprinted 1986).*

BOOK REVIEWS

ILLUSTRATED SUMMARY CATALOGUE OF THE CRAWFORD MUNICIPAL ART GALLERY

Incorporating a detailed chronology of art in nineteenth-century Cork and biographies of those Cork artists represented in the collection.
Compiled by Peter Murray
City of Cork Vocational Education Committee.
1992. pp 275. £45.00 (hardback) £29.50 (paperback)

Published in 1992, this is the first ever fully illustrated catalogue of the Crawford Gallery's entire collection. As with most catalogues of this scope, it is the result of many years work by a whole team of researchers. The main body of the publication is the summary catalogue which is divided into sections covering paintings, prints, sculpture, stained glass, decorative arts and ceramics. The paintings section which illustrates over 600 oils, watercolours and drawings (mainly nineteenth and early twentieth century Irish works) is the largest. The 'other media' collections are minimal but their inclusion in the catalogue perhaps serves to highlight areas like glass and ceramics which are worthy of development, particularly in a Cork context.

As its subtitle indicates, this is much more than a summary catalogue, it is also an invaluable work of reference. It includes in an interesting and informative history of the gallery building and of its founder's family, as well as an essay on the importance of the Gibson acquisitions fund. Both of these are by gallery director Peter Murray, as is an extensive documentary history of art and architecture in nineteenth-century Cork based to a large extent on contemporary newspaper reports. This thoroughly researched survey vividly portrays the art and artists of the period and will undoubtedly be of great use to art historians and others. Of more immediate use to the general reader is the fully annotated dictionary of Cork artists by Dr Julian Campbell. This incorporates much new research and includes Cork artists past and present, though only those that are represented in the Crawford itself.

In its entirety this work makes a major contribution to the study of art in Ireland.

Minor errors in details and typography are inevitable in a compilation of this type but it is surprising that in a collection so rich in portraiture no index of sitters was provided. Equally surprising is the omission of sitters' dates, which is bound to cause frustration and confusion for users of the summary catalogue.

On the whole, however, the catalogue admirably serves to record and present the gallery's collections, prepare the ground for further research and set the parameters for future acquisitions. It is a handsome volume, with a colour section illustrating over twenty paintings by various artists including Barry, Romney, Maclise, Lavery, Yeats, O'Malley and others, which makes it attractive to a wider public than would normally be the case with a summary catalogue. The design, layout and extremely high quality of the colour and black-and-white reproductions are very commendable, and add greatly to the overall enjoyment of this most welcome publication.

Wanda Ryan-Smolin

THE ARTS AND CRAFTS MOVEMENT IN IRELAND

PAUL LARMOUR
Friar's Bush Press, Belfast 1992, £19.95.

It is only fair to preface this review by stating that I too am preparing a book on the Irish Arts and Crafts Movement, scheduled for publication on the centenary of the Arts and Crafts Society of Ireland's first exhibition in 1895, and have long been working with much of the material that Paul Larmour includes in this book. But not all of it.

One of its most interesting (and hitherto unchronicled) aspects is its focus on Ulster, more specifically Belfast, not on the better-known graphics of John Vinycomb or Joseph Campbell, but on the School of Art (from 1901 the Municipal Technical Institute) under its progressive headmaster, Robert Dawson, himself a very competent designer, and on a generation of skilled teachers and students, several of whom went on to design successfully in industry (notably textiles), unlike their Southern peers. Among these, members of the Morrow and Ward families seem to have been particularly proficient, although William Douglas, chief stained-glass designer with Ward & Partners and also responsible for the second catalogue cover of the Arts and Crafts Society of Ireland, is rated highly by Dr Larmour along with the much more obviously talented and versatile Joseph Doran. While Charles Braithwaite, the Lethaby-trained illuminator from Lisburn, Co Antrim, and Rosamond Praeger, the sculptress from Holywood, Co Down, are given short descriptive passages, Praeger's younger friend and colleague Wilhelmina Geddes, and the Belfast-based Irish Decorative Arts Association are given chapters to themselves. The latter, hitherto only chronicled by a small but undocumented exhibition in the Belfast Linen Hall Library in 1990, represented mainly by Eva McKee, is difficult to assess from most of the pieces illustrated. Sometimes over-partisan but more often pertinent reports from the Ulster press also support the text throughout, although the two fascinating chapters in the first part of the book which refer to the two outstandingly enlightened and accomplished home art industry enterprises in the North of Ireland, Mrs Montgomery's Fivemiletown Art Metal-Work and Mrs Hart's Donegal Industrial Fund, were documented as much in England as in Ireland.

Given that the author is best known for his pioneering work on late nineteenth and early twentieth century Ulster architecture, and his 1981 booklet on Celtic Ornament, his exclusion of architecture and its corollaries in this book, except where it is immediately pertinent to his exposition on ornament and the applied arts, is unexpected and must count as an omission. Although an increasing number of general, contextual and subject-specific books, articles, papers and theses have been written over the past ten or so years (hardly any of which are listed in the plentiful and punctilious footnotes or in the surprisingly short post-1940 bibliography), this is the first full-length book to give an account of the Irish movement in any detail. This is not the first revelation or definition of the Irish contribution to the international Arts and Crafts movement, nor of the acknowledgment of Irish Arts and Crafts exponents to early Christian forms and eighteenth century skills as inspiration; nor is it the first time that the quality and variety of Irish Arts and Crafts work has been seen in any quantity (see *Irish Arts Review* Autumn 1985 for a review of the Dublin Arts and Crafts Exhibition held in Edinburgh where nearly 200 items were catalogued and displayed). But it is the first to brave a rounded historical survey, based on a detailed

BOOK REVIEWS

study of those items recorded as being exhibited between 1880 and 1930 and a thorough examination of valuable contemporary sources (mostly catalogues, ladies' magazines, newspapers and journals) published in Ireland and England. The author's welcomely prolific text references bear witness to his indefatigable search for clues as to the whereabouts of artwork made during a necessarily fairly broad definition of the Irish movement all over Ireland, and his success in piecing together a jigsaw of surprising complexity.

His chronological format emphasises the structure and development of the movement, serving as the most readily comprehensible way of introducing the subject. His text is clearly laid out (with a rather funereal cover design) and generously illustrated with forty-four colour plates of varying quality, and with monochrome illustrations, but these are neither listed nor referred to in the text, except where drawn from contemporary sources. When the latter were published, their sources are summarily given at the end of the book or beneath the illustration usually near its textual reference; but the present whereabouts of many of the pieces shown are not indicated even after a search through the abbreviated photographic sources. Perhaps this only emphasises the hidden nature of this informed exploration of a subject and an ethos undeservedly neglected in Ireland's cultural history.

A summary of the implications for Ireland's Home Art Industries of the nineteenth century William Morris-inspired craft revival in England precedes short, well-documented accounts of those amateur practitioners of the 1880s whom the author considers most important, prior to Lord Mayo's founding of the Arts and Crafts Society in 1894. Frederick Vodrey's Dublin art pottery, Margaret Stokes' exemplary illustrated volume on *Early Christian Art in Ireland* (1887), the Queen's Institute, subsequently the Irish Association for Promoting the Training and Employment of Women, and the Royal Irish School of Art Needlework (several inaccuracies here) paved the way for the profusion of trained and untrained groups of craft-workers of all classes. He steers his way ably through groups of philanthropically-charged needlewomen and woodcarvers (notably Everina Sinclair's Bonnyglen, Co Donegal class and the Ahane and Clonkeen classes in Co Limerick), selecting those whose work was singled out at the exhibitions which structure his chronological account. Sadly no illustrations of the much-praised Killarney School of Arts and Crafts or Furniture Industry, which he describes, are included among his interesting reproductions, mostly taken from primary and reference sources. The author's diligent and continual reference to illustrated reports is responsible for the remarkably few inaccuracies discernible. The insertion of an apostrophic, somewhat inconsequential chapter on 'Irish consciousness in art and patronage' at the end of Part Two would surely be better absorbed into his introduction; this ended by referring to Sir Edward Sullivan, antiquarian, designer and finisher of fine book bindings and George Coffey, who dabbled successfully in the same field before heading the National Museum's Antiquities Section in 1896, both key figures in the early years of the Irish Arts and Crafts Society. Since apposite allusions to national awareness, aspiration and syntheses of perceived periods of excellence in past periods of Irish visual history are analysed within the text, this chapter is an anomaly. He tantalisingly suspends until Part Two his conjecture of antiquarian links between the patron of the Celtic Revivalist gem of a church at Clane, Co Kildare and Lord Mayo (but not Lady Mayo?), imbued with Arts and Crafts zeal, seeking William Morris's advice, galvanising his influential friends in Ireland and formulating an Irish brand of the English Arts and Crafts Exhibition Society.

Here the varying stages, activities, hallmarks and notable exhibits of the emergent Society are comprehensively and concisely summarised until its demise in 1925. An illuminating chapter on the three main Schools of Art, Dublin, Belfast and Cork (very short) surveys the fundamental role each played in the Irish movement, principally in educating the key generation of individual art workers. Of these there is a valuable passage tracing the embossed metal- and leather-work of Mary Houston from Coleraine and a shorter one on her fellow Ulsterman and London *emigré*, Joseph Doran, both of whom worked successfully in what Dr Larmour calls an Art Nouveau-cum-Arts and Crafts vein; and Beatrice Elvery, likewise, with a purposely Irish dimension. He concludes by noting the most important Dublin, Belfast and regional early twentieth century exhibitions organised by supporting bodies like the Gaelic League, giving illustrated resumés of the Youghal Art Metal Workers, the Irish Art Companions, Ward and Partners of Belfast, the Kilkenny Woodworkers (only a carved Celtic interlace hall-seat illustrated) and what he sees as the more peripheral Donegal Carpets.

In Part Three, his chapters on Evelyn Gleeson's Dun Emer Guild, the Yeats family's Cuala Industries and Sarah Purser's Tower of Glass are clear synopses of existing research, well illustrated, with some interesting additional material. The following summary chapters on Harry Clarke and Wilhelmina Geddes, whom he deems the stars of the movement, refer to material recently published; that on Oswald Reeves documents his skill as an exceptional teacher, craftsman in enamels and metalwork and as champion of the later Irish Arts and Crafts Society. Part Four traces the increasingly popular but decadent movement in the 1920s and 1930s exemplified by selected Art Workers, notably Mia Cranwill, the Dublin 'Craftworkers' and Kathleen Cox; James Hicks and his patron and fellow craftsman, Sir Nevile Wilkinson, are given unwarrantedly short shrift here. While his main argument is convincing and his conclusion on the demise of the Irish movement sound, further contextual and analogous reference would have enriched this section.

This book is a succinct compendium of primary sources which attest to the motivation, range and skills of a discernible movement, whose output has been inadequately appreciated and rarely seen since it was made and recognised by contemporaries.

Nicola Gordon Bowe

BOOK REVIEWS

THE HIGH CROSSES OF IRELAND, AN ICONOGRAPHICAL AND PHOTOGRAPHIC SURVEY

with text by PETER HARBISON
Römisch – Germanisches Zentralmuseum
Forchunginstitut fur Vor- und Fruhgeschichte in Verbindung mit der Royal Irish Academy,
Bonn, 1992.
Three volumes, Ir£285, hardback

The carved stone crosses of Ireland, with their array of Christian iconography, are among the most impressive monuments of the so-called Dark Ages, a time when the art of stone carving was almost forgotten in continental Europe. More than a century has now passed since the first studies were made of these remarkable sculptures and, thanks to the efforts of scholars like Francoise Henry and Helen Roe,a great deal of progress has been made in understanding them. Fundamental questions, however, remain unsolved. It has always seemed strange that the carving of the better known crosses, as at Kells, Clonmacnois and Monasterboice, coincided with one of the most turbulent periods in Irish history, when the Viking raids were at their most intense. The precise purpose of the crosses also remains elusive, so too the role they played in Irish politics and society. We know very little about the way they were carved, and, despite the confident tone of the guide books, scholars are still baffled by many of the subjects depicted on the sculptured panels.

Since the late 1970s, Peter Harbison has been tackling some of these issues in a series of stimulating (and often provocative) articles. By 1985 he had completed the text of a major book but the scale of the work, and the costs of publication, delayed its appearance for a further seven years. Despite the problems, the book has now appeared in a most impressive format. It comes in three large volumes, two of them devoted exclusively to photographs. Almost half of the text volume is devoted to a catalogue of 235 crosses or cross fragments, accompanied by brief summaries of the iconography and decoration. The catalogue is linked to volume II, which contains a comprehensive photographic record of the sculptures. The remaining text is principally concerned with an analysis of the iconography, illustrated by detailed comparative photographs in volume III. It is a long time since the high crosses received such intensive study and their iconography has never been tackled with such thoroughness before. Potential readers be warned, however: the weighty tomes have to be studied simultaneously, so a fair amount of physical energy (plus a good sized table) is needed to grapple with them. A healthy bank balance is also a useful prerequisite for anyone anticipating purchase.

The catalogue includes many exciting discoveries and rediscoveries, the product of relentless fieldwork by Dr Harbison, who was determined to track down everything that might remotely resemble a high cross. He includes several pieces which came to light in the early 1980s and there is a remarkable reconstruction of a cross from Kilkieran (Kilkenny), cleverly assembled (by R Stapleton) from a variety of different fragments. In preparing his catalogue, the author clearly had some problems in deciding when to stop,and his definition of what constitutes a high cross (p.2) needs to be studied carefully. With a few exceptions, he excludes decorated cross slabs, as well as sculptured pillar stones like those at Kilnasaggart (Armagh) and Reask (Kerry). Despite these self imposed restrictions, the value of the catalogue is manifold. At a time when there is great concern about environmental damage, as well as theft and vandalism, it provides a permanent record of the crosses as they are today. By including plain or barely ornamented crosses, it also provides a far more balanced impression of the material than was hitherto available. Each entry contains a brief description of the figural panels, along with Dr Harbison's suggested identification and a note of how they have been identified in the past. There are also exhaustive bibliographies for each site (the value of which is slightly diminished for places with several monuments, where references to all crosses are lumped together). The accompanying photographs, many taken by the author himself, are of a such high quality that it is worth buying the book for the pictures alone. Raking light on some north faces suggests that Dr Harbison has been up at dawn to take his photographs. Only the top surfaces of the crosses seem to have eluded him! In fact the plates are so good that there is a danger that future visits to the monuments will become an anticlimax.

Dr Harbison is principally concerned with the question of iconographical identification. As he tackles each cross, the text reads like a sequence of detective stories. Even when erosion has rendered the sculpture well nigh invisible, as at Killamery (Kilkenny), he comes up with suggestions, albeit resorting to the 'eye of faith'. Nothing is regarded as sacrosanct and many long established interpretations are rejected. Among the victims are the Fall of Simon Magus (Monasterboice, west cross), Doubting Thomas (Monasterboice, south cross) and the well known panel at Clonmacnois, supposedly depicting King Diarmuid and St Ciaran founding the monastery (cross of the scriptures). He provides a completely new interpretation of the Broken cross at Kells and vastly extends the range of Christian subjects found elsewhere. He believes he can identify elements of a Joseph cycle (at Clonmacnois, Connor, and Clones), additional episodes from the story of David, scenes from the early life of the Virgin Mary (at Duleek) as well as previously unrecognised incidents from the life of John the Baptist. Most of these identifications concern panels which have been regarded as problematical in the past and Dr Harbison is well aware of the speculative character of some of his suggestions. While most scholars tend to be cautious by nature, Dr Harbison is not afraid of a good hypothesis. This at least has the merits of forcing others to confront the issue. His conclusions are heavily dependent on research carried out in the Princeton Index of Christian Art (and its copies in Utrecht and Rome), an archive which is arranged according to subject, rather than place or artist. The Index provides a quick way of finding comparable material and exploring the origin of a particular iconography. However, it is not quite a s valuable a tool as it sounds. Before using it, one has to identify a specific subject, and, with the Irish high crosses, that is where the problems begin. Moreover, confronted with the wealth of comparative iconography provided by the Index, it is always tempting to concentrate on the similarities, rather than differences.

The major difficulty in dealing with the iconography of the high crosses thus rests on the initial identification. Some of Dr Harbison's suggestions are immediately convincing. The recognition of the soldiers casting lots for Christ's robes on the cross of the scriptures at Clonmacnois, for example, is an inspired piece of observation. I am less sure, however, about his suggestions for other panels on this cross. It is difficult to believe the figure perched on the shoulders of a companion on the north side is the Egyptian hermit, St Paul. An evangelist supported on the shoulders

BOOK REVIEWS

of one of the four major prophets seems a more likely explanation, particularly as the upper figure is holding a book. Similar iconography is to be found in a stained glass window at Chartres Cathedral, illustrating the idea that, raised aloft by the prophets, the evangelists had a greater capacity to see the Truth.[1] Nor am I convinced that two scenes on the east face come from a Joseph cycle, for the comparisons offered do not look sufficiently close. Admittedly it is hard to come up with plausible alternatives, though it is just possible that the bottom panel depicts Moses and Aaron holding the brazen serpent, a subject often invoked by medieval commentators, as a 'type' for the crucifixion.

A similar situation arises with the Broken cross at Kells, which in its original form must have been one of the most powerful monuments in Early Christian Ireland. On the west fact Dr Harbison has ingeniously detected scenes from a Moses cycle, including the Lord appearing to the Israelites in the pillar of cloud (or the pillar of fire), with the crossing of the Red Sea in the panel above. The New Testament subjects on the east face are more elusive and here the identifications carry less conviction. For example, the fourth panel is said to show the washing of the Christ Child, with the infant Jesus standing in a basin flanked by the two midwives. But one of the flanking figures is semi-naked and carries a staff or spear, an unlikely attribute for Salome or Zelome at the birth of Christ. As the two figures to the left appear aggressive in intention, the composition looks more like a scene of arrest or imprisonment. Elsewhere in European art, the basin used for the washing is quite deliberately shown in the form of a chalice, which is certainly not the case at Kells. The scene below is equally puzzling and has produced a number of bizarre intepretations. One figure appears to be holding something that looks vaguely like a harp, which Arthur Kingsley Porter took to be the champion's portion of meat held up by CuChulainn at the feast of Bricriu. In his text Dr Harbison is unsure whether this shows the raising of Lazarus or Christ healing the lame man at the pool of Bethesda. Given the context, the scene almost certainly comes from the Gospels, and a clue may lie in the extraordinary contortions of the figure at the bottom left. In Romanesque art, such acrobatic displays are often associated with Salome dancing before Herod.[2] Does this scene in fact show the death of John the Baptist, with his head being brought into Herod on a charger?

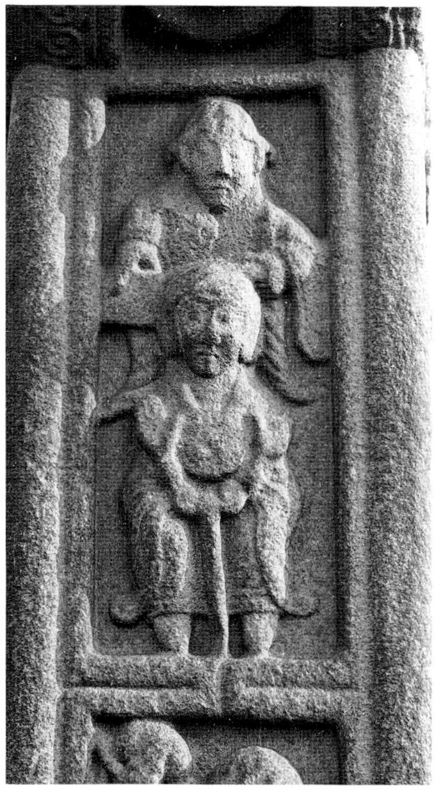

Panel on the north side of the cross of the scriptures at Clonmacnois, variously identified as St Patrick receiving the tonsure (Porter), St Matthew with his symbol (Henry), St Anthony and St Paul (Harbison) and an evangelist supported by one of the major prophets (Stalley).

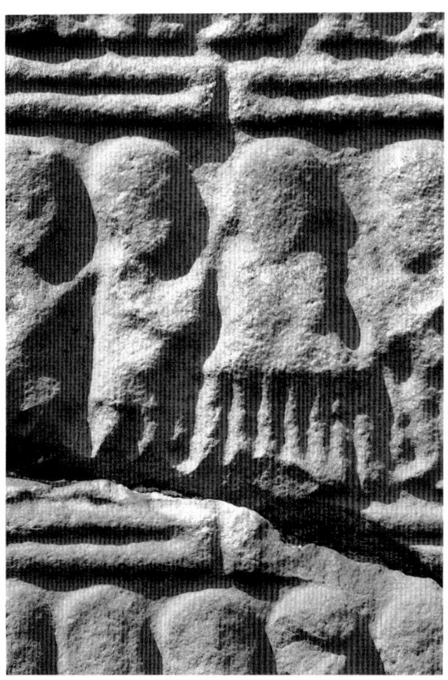

Problem panel on the broken cross of Kells. Harbison suggests that it depicts the washing of the infant Christ by the midwives.

In some cases the Irish sculptors employed universal images which could be applied to a variety of contexts. Thus the carving of two wrestlers on the Market Cross at Kells has often been interpreted as Jacob struggling with the angel. Dr Harbison prefers an alternative reading as Christ being embraced by Judas, though for an almost identical image at Durrow he opts for John the Baptist recognising Christ. If we could be sure of the context and the knowledge of the audience, both interpretations might have validity. When this same image appears in Romanesque art, however, as in the Rochester Priscian (Vatican Library, Rossiana Ms 500, fol. 158r) it does not appear to have any specific Biblican connotations. Furthermore, there is a hint that the figures in the sculpture at Kells and Durrow wear 'belts of strength', an attribute of giants in medieval art.[3] If this is the case, it is far from certain that the Irish carvings were intended to represent narrative scenes from the Bible.

The later chapters of the book deal with more general issues – the original of the iconography, the means by which it was transmitted to Ireland, as well as the date and function of the crosses. There is a useful account of all the inscriptions, plus a brilliant section showing how the ornament of the crosses frequently depended on models in metalwork. For iconography, however, Dr Harbison is convinced that the best parallels lie in the field of Carolingian wall paintings, particularly works executed during the reign of Louis the Pious (814-40). He argues that continental iconography was introduced to Ireland in the second quarter of the ninth century, appearing not on stone crosses, but on a group of 'prototype crosses', where the figural scenes were modelled in stucco. As these began to disintegrate, they were replaced later in the century by the stone crosses that we see today. He rejects Francoise Henry's opinion that Carolingian iconography was introduced through the medium of ivory carving, arguing instead that it was the arrival of continental stucco artists that was the critical factor in bringing Carolingian influence to Ireland.

Dr Harbison first presented his stucco hypothesis at the Cork conference in 1985,[4] but so far he has failed to convert

BOOK REVIEWS

fellow scholars to the idea. There is no archaeological or documentary support for the use of stucco in Ireland at this time, and the techniques involved are quite different from those employed in stone carving. While some of the comparisons with Carolingian art are indeed compelling, I believe there is a danger of exaggerating the extent of Carolingian influences.[5] Much of the iconography of the Irish crosses has older, Early Christian roots, and the numerous idiosyncrasies suggest it had been in Ireland for a long while. The enthroned Christ at Monasterboice, for example, has an animal head between the feet. As Françoise Henry pointed out, this must surely be a misunderstanding of the 'Cosmos' figure seen below Christ in an equivalent composition on the sarcophagus of Junius Bassus, dating from 359AD.[6] Moreover, if Carolingian art did exert a major influence on Irish cross carving, one would have expected it to have had an effect on sculptural style. There is very little sign of this.

It is important to remember that Ireland had its own traditions of Biblical exegesis, which need to be taken into account. During the sixth and seventh centuries the Irish church inherited the learning of the late Roman world, and its scholars acquired an impressive knowledge of the Early Christian Fathers. Dr Harbison pays little attention to this intellectual and religious background in Ireland, tending to treat the sculpture as if it was an autonomous development. As an aid to identifying scenes on the crosses, it would be worth knowing what subjects were uppermost in the minds of Irish ecclesiastics. The story of Simon Magus was well known to Irish audiences,[7] who would have no trouble identifying the tormentor of Peter and Paul in sculptures at Kells and Monasterboice, where a figure is shown catapulted to destruction.

The tribulations involved in the publication of *The High Crosses of Ireland* means that in some respects it has already been overtaken by events. For example the recent discovery of a 'Celtic' style cross, decorating a sixth century Coptic textile, has demonstrated that the concept of the ringed cross is far older than people once thought.[8] Liam de Paor has published important new evidence about the crosses at Tihilly and Kinnitty (Offaly), and within the last few years, new approaches to iconography have been introduced by scholars from other disciplines.[9] Nevertheless, this should not obscure Peter Harbison's Herculean achievement. Working almost alone, he has managed to organise a bewildering range of material, which at a stroke has set the study of high crosses on a new footing. Not everyone will agree with the author's conclusions. But then I am sure he never imagined that they would.

Roger Stalley

NOTES

1. Yves Delaporte, *Les Vitraux de la cathedrale de Chartres* (Chartres, 1926), pl. VIII. The evangelists are linked with the four major prophets on the colophon of the Book of Mulling, TCD Ms 60, fol. 94v. The background to this iconography is discussed by L Nees, 'The Colophon Drawing in the Book of Mulling', *Cambridge Medieval Celtic Studies*, 5 (1983), 76 and especially n. 33. I am grateful to Heather King, who first pointed out to me the possible relevance of the Chartres stained glass.
2. As for example in the Bury Gospels, for which see E Parker, 'A 12th century cycle of New Testament Drawings from Bury St Edmunds Abbey', *Proceedings of the Suffolk Institute of Archaeology*, 31 (1969), 263-302. Also Kauffmann.
3. G Zarnecki, *Studies in Romanesque Sculpture* (London, 1979), chapter VII. The theme of the wrestlers and its appearance in Romanesque and Gothic sculpture is discussed by Arthur Kingsley Porter, *The Crosses and Culture of Ireland* (New Haven, 1931), 125-8.
4. P Harbison, 'The Carolingian Contribution to Irish Sculpture' in *Irish and Insular Art AD 500-1200*, ed. M Ryan (Dublin, 1987), pp. 105-110.
5. Roger Stalley, 'European Art and the Irish High Crosses', *Proceedings of the Royal Irish Academy*, 90c (1990), 135-158.
6. F Henry, *Irish Art during the Viking Invasions, 800-1020 AD* (London, 1967), 185.
7. *Ibid.*, pp. 186-88.
8. M Werner, 'On the Origin of the Form of the Irish High Cross', *Gesta*, XXIX/1 (1990), 98-110.
9. L de Paor, 'The High Crosses of Tech Theille (Tihilly), Kinnitty, and related Sculpture, in *Figures from the Past, Studies on Figurative Art in Christian Ireland in honour of Helen M Roe*, ed E Rynne (Dublin, 1987), pp 131-158; E O Carragain, 'The meeting of St Paul and St Anthony: visual and literary uses of a eucharistic motif' in *Keimelia, Studies in medieval archaeology and history in memory of Tom Delany*, ed. G MacNiocaill and P Wallace (Galway, 1989) pp 1-58; E O Carragain, 'The Ruthwell Cross and the Irish High Crosses: some points of comparison and contrast', in *Ireland and Insular Art AD 500-1200*, ed. M Ryan (1987), pp.118-128.

COLLECTING IRISH IN THE NEW YORK SALESROOM

Homan Potterton
reviews the sales of Irish painting and antiques in New York last year.

It is hard to believe that the picture illustrated by Ricciardelli was actually painted in Dublin. Perhaps there is a distant – very distant – echo of the Sugarloaf mountains – both Little and Large – in county Wicklow but there is not another single feature about the painting – from the swaying fronds of the trees to the gothic campanile to the sphinx to the Corinthian columns – that reminds one of Ireland. Even the buck goat, silhouetted in the centre of the composition, has an aristocratic bearing – a *bella figura* – that would be quite unknown to an Irish Billy while the fact that the central fortified tower is based on the well-known antique remains of the Tomb of Cecilia Metella in the Roman Campagna tells us that, wherever the picture was painted, the scene is intended to be Italianate.

The artist was Gabrielle Ricciardelli who was born in Naples and the splendid work was painted in 1757. Gabrielle had arrived in Ireland some four years earlier, having been employed during the previous decade at the court of the King of Naples. Soon after his arrival in Dublin, he gave his address as 'at Mr Henderson's seed-shop, corner of Capel Street and the Quay' and he advertised that he was 'at liberty to paint for any gentlemen that think him deserving of their countenance'. During his time in Ireland he painted a number of views of Irish country estates – Dartry, county Monaghan and Stillorgan, for example – and these had a considerable influence on native landscape painters such as Thomas Roberts and George Mullins.

The *Capriccio* here illustrated, painted on canvas which is laid down on masonite (an unusual treatment for such a large picture), was included in a sale of Old Masters at Christie's, New York on 14 January 1993 (lot 103) when, against a pre-sale estimate of $25,000-$35,000, it fetched $26,400.

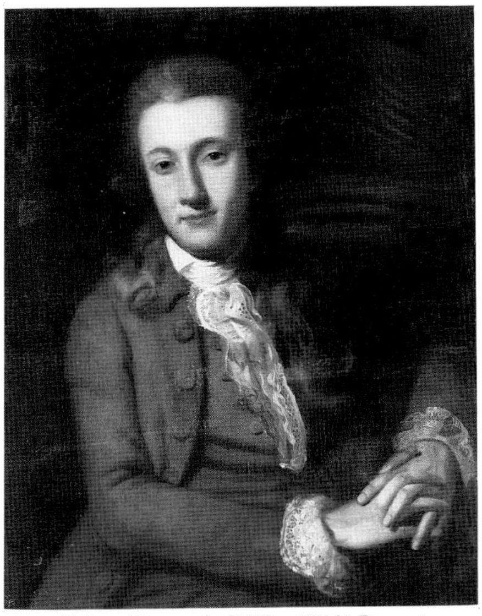

Robert Hunter (c.1720-c.1803) Portrait of a Gentleman. *Signed. (76.2 x 63.5 cm.) Sold at Sotheby's, New York, 22 January 1992 (lot 120) for $1,200.*

In quite a different vein – and unmistakably Irish, one might say – was a painting sold at Sotheby's, New York on 20 February 1992 (lot 264). This was by an unfamiliar artist, Robert Richard Scanlan, and it depicted Donnybrook Fair. Teeming with amusing detail, the attribution of this boisterous Victorian genre piece seemed to be based on tradition, as the painting was not signed. Scanlan, who exhibited portraits at the Royal Hibernian Academy in the 1820s (an engraved portrait of the Duke of Wellington after one of his drawings is in the National Gallery of Ireland) and later went to London, is described by Strickland as an animal and genre painter and indeed he was a regular exhibitor of such pictures at the Royal Academy. He was also, for a brief period of a year (1853-54), Master of the Cork School of Design. The picture at Sotheby's, which sold for $10,450 (estimate $5,000-$7,000), may have been the same as the *Donnybrook Fair* exhibited by Scanlan at the Belfast Fine Art Society in 1859.

The accomplished eighteenth-century Irish portrait painter, Robert Hunter, is now very well documented (see Anne Crookshank's catalogue of his portraits in IAR 1989-90, pp. 169-85). A modest addition to his *oeuvre*, although a signed example, was a half-length kit-kat size portrait of a gentleman sold at Sotheby's, New York on 22 January 1992 (lot 120) for a very reasonable $1,200 against a pre-sale estimate of $2,000-$3,000. As the picture was neither dated nor inscribed with the name of the sitter, it is unlikely that it can be identified from the records of pictures which Hunter exhibited during his lifetime.

George Russell (AE) was such a prolific artist that it is inevitable that his paintings should appear from time to time on the market abroad. Apart from that, he was patronised in the early part of the century by the American collector, John Quinn, who owned a considerable number of his works. Quite an ordinary canvas by Russell of figures in a landscape, painted in even more ethereal colours than usual, was included in a Sotheby's sale on 28 February 1992 (lot 55) with an ambitious presale estimate of $6,000-$8,000. It was no sur-

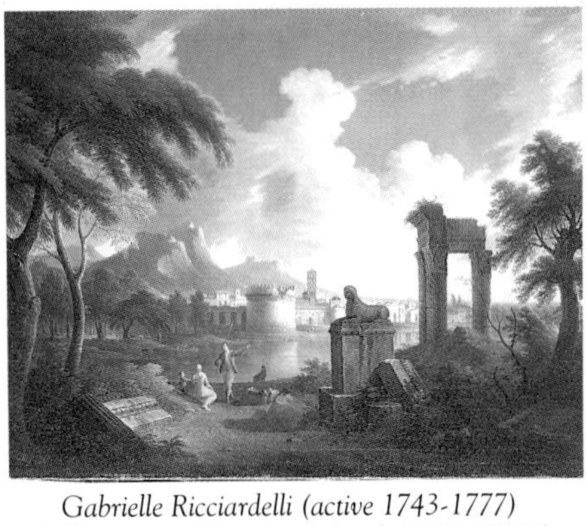

Gabrielle Ricciardelli (active 1743-1777) A Capriccio. *Signed and dated, 1757. (38.75 x 52.25 ins.). Sold at Christie's, New York, 14 January 1993 (lot 103) for $26,400.*

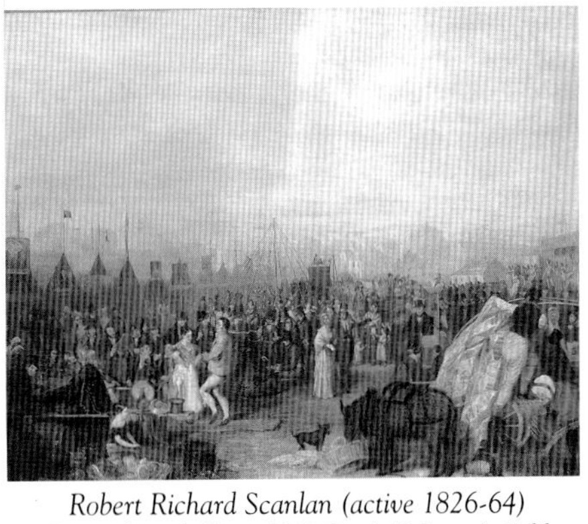

Robert Richard Scanlan (active 1826-64) Donnybrook Fair. *(102.9 x 142.2 cm.). Sold at Sotheby's, New York, 20 February 1992 (lot 264) for $10,450.*

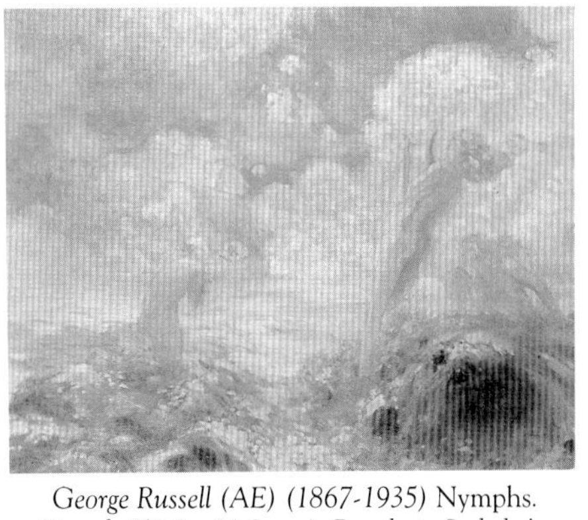

George Russell (AE) (1867-1935) Nymphs. *Signed. (53.3 x 81.3 cm.) Bought in Sotheby's, New York, 28 February 1992 (lot 55) at $2,500.*

COLLECTING IRISH IN THE NEW YORK SALESROOM

prise when it was bought in at $2,500.

Good Irish furniture, particularly of the robust eighteenth-century variety, turns up in New York auctions with a fair degree of regularity. The style, similar to much New England furniture of the same period, has always appealed to American collectors who find its showy excess particularly desirable. Side-tables are often among the best examples and some typically exuberant pieces have passed through the New York saleroom in the past year. At Sotheby's on 23 January 1993 (lot 285) a handsome table – catalogued as George II – with carving that was relatively refined and a typical green marble top went for $21,800 (estimate $15,000-$18,000) while at Christie's on 17 October 1992 (lot 239) a beautiful serving table of the same period sold well above its estimate of $12,000-$14,000 for $24,200. By contrast with these exceptional prices, a more restrained table with a low-relief frieze sold at Christie's on 30 January 1993 (lot 266) for $8,800 against a presale estimate of $10,000-$15,000.

A pair of very elaborate tables of this type, although dating from the nineteenth century, appeared at Sotheby's on 23 January 1993 (lot 178). Although extravagantly estimated at $30,000-$40,000, they failed to find a buyer. In somewhat similar vein was a pair of mahogany side-chairs which probably also dated from the nineteenth century (although in an eighteenth century style) which sold at Sotheby's on 24 October 1992 (lot 230) for $6,000 (estimate $8,000-$12,000).

A more exceptional piece of furniture came under the hammer at a Christie's sale on 17 October 1992 (lot 314). This was a painted white table in the Victorian Gothic style which originated from Birr Castle and indeed it was probably made on the Birr estate at about the time of the Gothicisation of the Castle in the early nineteenth century. Rather large and sturdy, the table went for $10,450 (estimate $8,000-$10,000). In the same sale (lot 317) was another painted table, said to date from the third quarter of the eighteenth century and based on a design by Chippendale. This too came from an Irish house, Luttrellstown, county Dublin, from where it was sold at the time of the house sale in 1983. But in spite of its provenance – or perhaps because of it – it fetched only a modest $5,500 in New York.

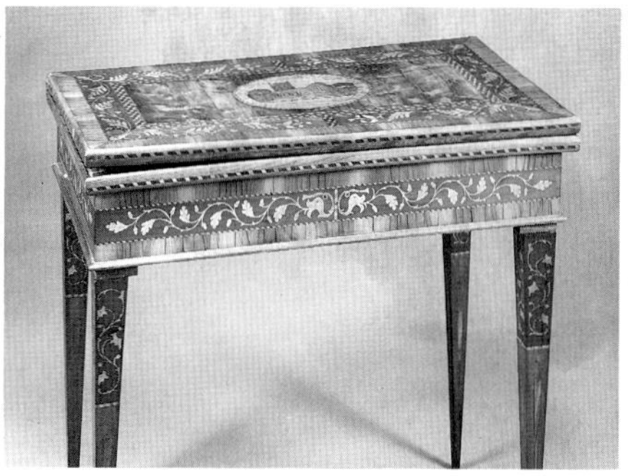

Killarney fruitwood games table (81.3 cm. wide) sold at Christie's, New York, 23rd January 1993 (lot 251A) for $4,312.

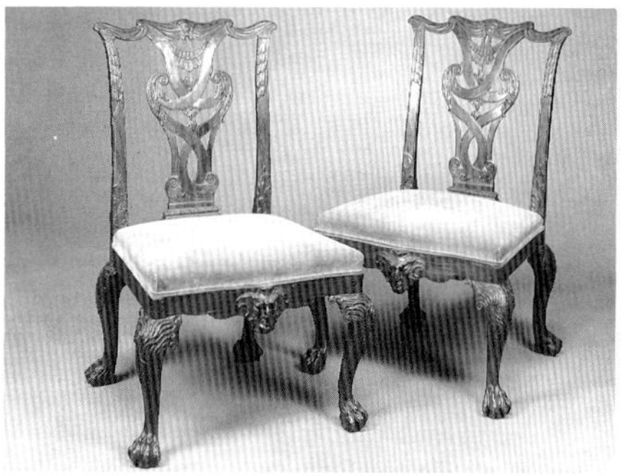

Pair of Side Chairs, probably early 19th Century sold at Sotheby's, New York, 24th October 1992 (lot 230) for $6,000.

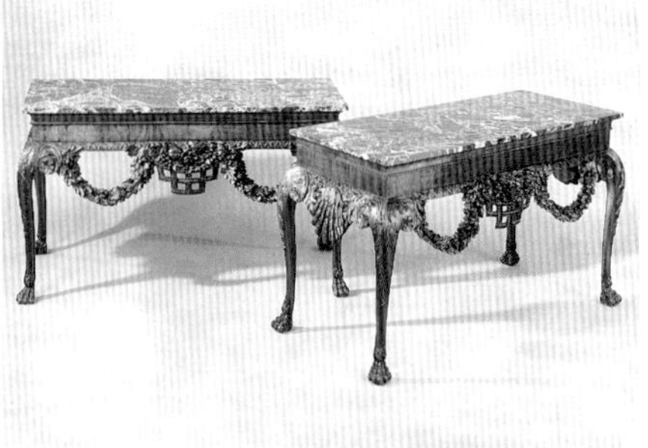

Pair of 19th Century Mahogany and Walnut side tables (135 cm. wide) bought in at Sotheby's, New York on 23 January 1993 (lot 178).

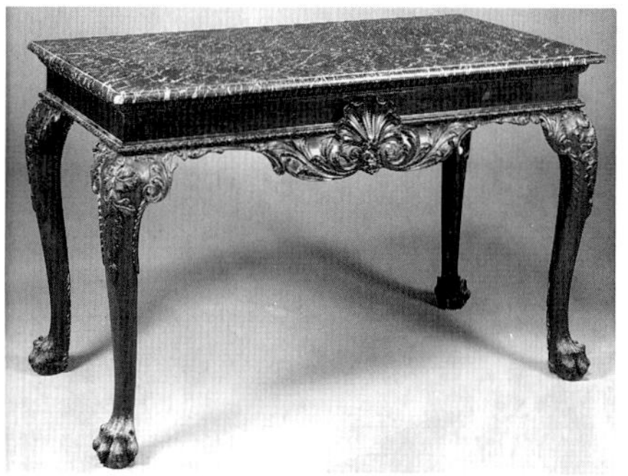

George II Mahogany Side Table, (138 cm. wide), sold at Sotheby's, New York, 23 January 1993 (lot 285) for $21,850.

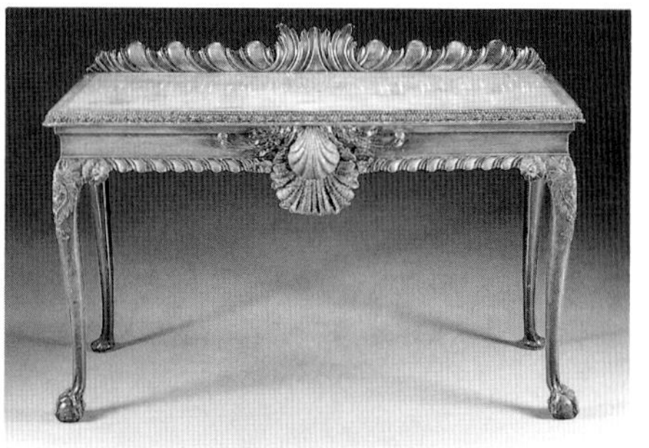

George II Mahogany Serving Table, (155 cm. wide), sold at Christie's, New York, 17 October 1992 (lot 239) for $24,200.

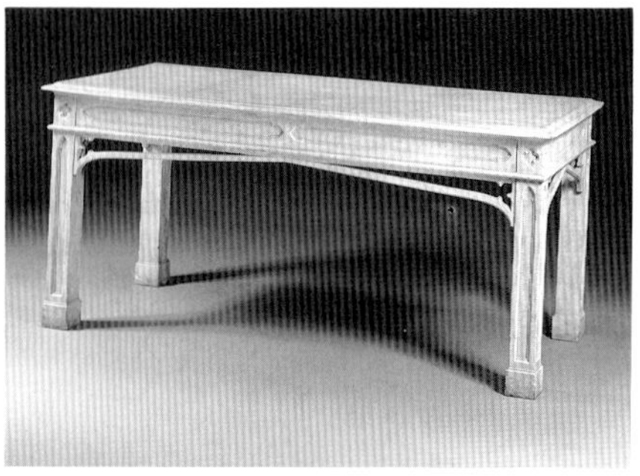

Early Victorian white-painted side table (181 cm. wide) sold at Christie's, New York, 17 October 1992 (lot 314) for $10,450.

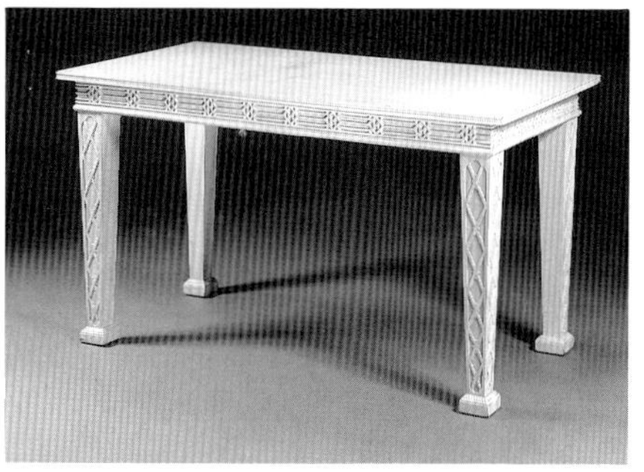

White-painted side table (152 cm. wide) sold at Christie's, New York, 17 October 1992 (lot 317) for $5,500.

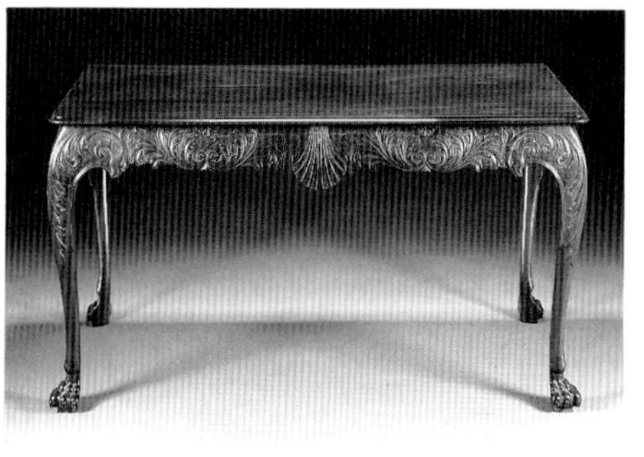

George II Mahogany Side Table, (149 cm. wide), sold at Christie's, New York, 30th January 1993 (lot 266) for $8,800.

COLLECTING IRISH IN THE NEW YORK SALESROOM

Killarney furniture, dating from the nineteenth century, is rather an acquired taste but a quite special item sold at Christie's New York saleroom recently. (23 January 1993, lot 251A). This was a fruitwood games-table with the usual intricate inlaid decoration. The hinged top featured a depiction of the ruins of Muckross Abbey on the outside and opened to a games-board surrounded by foliage and other appropriate ruins. The table, accustomed to the dampness of Ireland, had suffered considerably on being exported to the New World: it was very badly warped and, probably as a result sold at the low end of its $4,000-$6,000 estimate for $4,312.

Signed furniture by Irish makers is very much of a rarity with the result that an assortment of pieces bearing the stamp of 'J. Nolan' included in a Christie's sale on 24 January 1992 (lots 179-183) was of particular interest. Additionally, all the items were miniature pieces and were, therefore, probably cabinetmaker's samples. 'J.Nolan' was probably James Nolan who reputedly was a late nineteenth century Dublin carriage-maker and cabinetmaker who continued a family tradition from the eighteenth century. The examples at Christie's included a longcase clock, a bureau, a linen press, and bookcases and with estimates varying between $1,000 and $6,000 a piece, prices realised ranged from $1,800-$4,400.

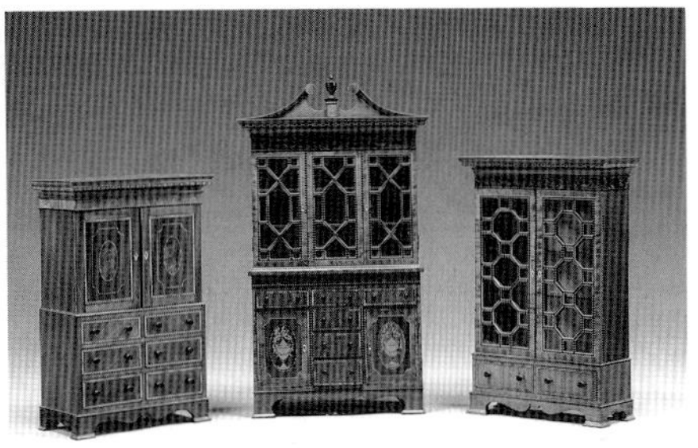

Miniature inlaid mahogany linen press and bookcases by Joseph Nolan of Dublin, late 19th century. (All about 60 cm. high). Sold at Christie's, New York, 24 January 1992 (lots 181, 182 & 183) for $0000 respectively.

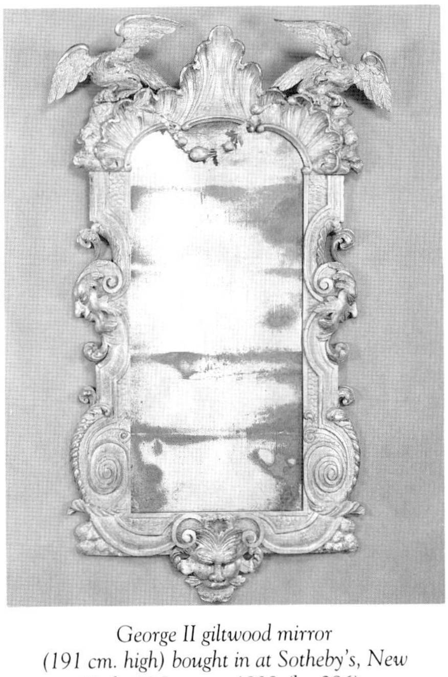

George II giltwood mirror (191 cm. high) bought in at Sotheby's, New York, 23 January 1993 (lot 286).

The richly-inventive carving that is the hallmark of much eighteenth century Irish furniture is often seen at its most elaborate on the gilded frames of mirrors which were produced in relative profusion in Ireland. An example, with winged eagles somewhat in the manner of the plasterwork of Robert West and grotesque masks, came up for sale at Sotheby's, New York on 23 January 1993. There were certain awkwardnesses in the design of the piece – it may indeed at some stage have been actually altered by being cut down – and, with an estimate of $25,000-$35,000, it failed to sell.

Good Irish silver featured prominently as usual in the New York saleroom during the year and (on 27 October 1992) Christie's, in particular, offered a number of choice Irish items from the Elizabeth McMahon Donaghue collection. The top price of $24,200 was achieved for a set of four candlesticks in the rococco style (c.1760) by Robert Calderwood but an unusual wax jack (c.1770) by John West went well above its estimate of $1,500-$2,500 to sell at $5,750. Other prices were more modest: an early (1739) dish-ring by William Walshe went for $2,640 (estimate $3-$5,000); a dressing-glass (c.1740) possibly by John Laughlin, $7,150 (estimate $5-$8,000); an attractive Cork coffee-pot by John Nicolson (c.1770) fetched $4,400 (estimate $4-$5,000); and a Dublin dish-ring by Francis Jones (1762) went for $7,150 against an estimate of $3-$5,000.

At Sotheby's silver sale the same week (28 October 1992) there were a number of Irish pieces the most exceptional of which was a very fine pair of quatrefoil salvers, dated 1736, by John Hamilton of Dublin. These were engraved with the arms of William Palliser of Rathfarnham and Mary Pennefather of Cashel. Against a pre-sale estimate of $50-$60,000, they sold for $50,000.

Homan Potterton

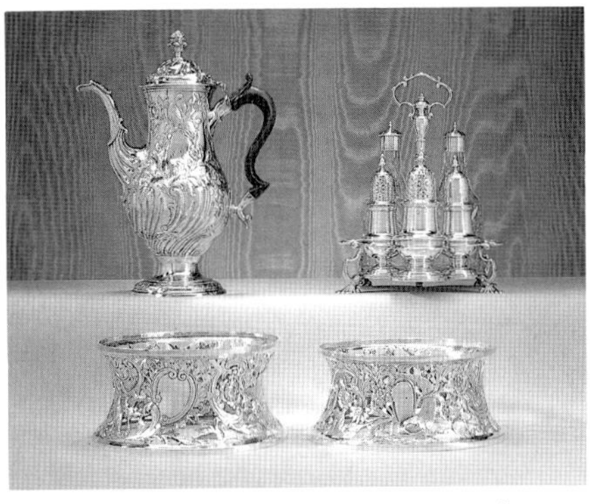

Irish silver sold at Christie's, New York 27 October 1992: Silver coffee-pot, 1772, by Matthew West of Dublin – $2,750; Cruet-stand, c.1770, maker unidentified – $4,620; Dish-ring, 1762, by Francis Jones – $7,150; Dish-ring, c.1760, maker unidentified – $1,650.

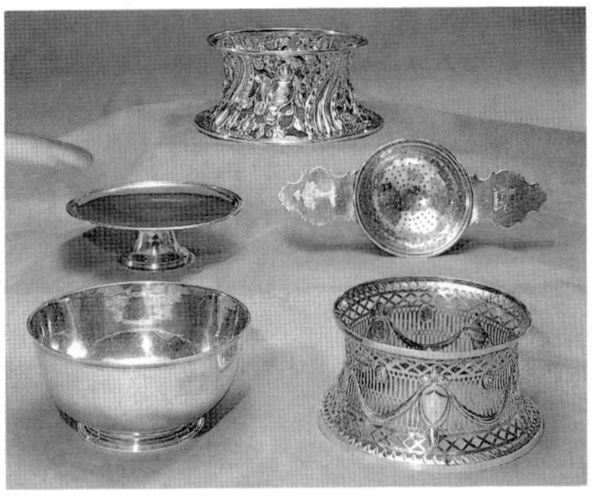

Irish silver sold at Sotheby's, New York 28 October 1992: Dish-ring, c.1765, by John Nicolson of Cork – $3,700; Salver, c.1715-25, probably by Joseph Wall of Kinsale – $2,750; Punch-strainer, c.1740, maker unidentified – $2,250; Bowl, c.1745, by Christopher Locker – $4,250; Dish-ring, c.1780, by Rober Wyke – $4,750.

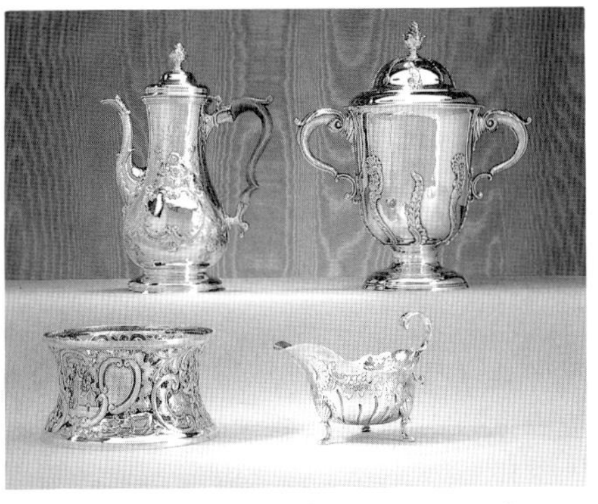

Irish silver sold at Christie's, New York 27 October 1992: Silver coffee-pot, c.1770, by John Nicolson of Cork – $4,400; Two-handled cup, c.1750, by Robert Calderwood – $2,420; Dish-ring, 1739, by William Walshe – $2,640; Sauceboat, c.1770, by William Townsend – $1,320.

IRISH ART IN THE LONDON SALEROOMS

Gertrude Prescott Nuding looks back at the major London sales of Irish art and analyses reassuring trends.

Question: When are the lack of headlines and camera crews jostling in for one painting good news? Answer: When a market is stabilising. A certain reassurance can be drawn from the lack of sensationalist coverage of the Irish art market over the 1992 and early 1993 season. For while good prices continued to be paid for good paintings, the field was not beset by the boom/bust syndrome which hit other 'national' markets, such as that for Scandinavian paintings. Speculators, private and commercial, kept their heads well down (indeed some preferred simply to disappear altogether) and let the long-term participants, both private and trade, manoeuvre for winning bid position. Major private buyers seem to have retained confidence in the field, helped by their growing knowledge, access to recently-published scholarly publications, and through seeking advice from specialists before wielding paddles to the coaching of pre-sale departmental estimates.

As always, so much is dependent on the relationship between the supply and the demand. In the booming later 1980s, speculative involvement in the market drove up the middling price range of Irish paintings in particular: the more routine McKelveys, Craigs, and Wilks seemed to appeal to newish buyers through their easily-read depiction of the Irish scene. During the boom such paintings appeared with regularity in the major London sales, with their prices unrealistically pulled upwards by the momentum of the appreciating top-quality lots, press headlines and gullible speculators' buying. Over the past year few routine landscapes have appeared in the major London sales, reflecting both a drying up of supply and demand, as well as indicating a return to a more rational market.

During the late 1980s frenzy, the three period aspect of Yeats' work and the uneven quality of paintings within O'Conor's *oeuvre*, had presented more of a challenge to inexperienced buyers both in terms of aesthetic discernment and art historical evaluation. These artists appealed (and continue to appeal) to more sophisticated buyers. As a result their price structure makes more 'sense' in the long term. (Collectors of O'Conor will be further aided now by the recent publication of Jonathan Benington's monograph).

Again analysis of supply is more revealing than a simple reeling off of annual prices realised. Crucially, no major large-scale paintings by Yeats turned up in the 1992-early 1993 London saleroom season. It would seem that major Yeats paintings from collections formed in the period from 1940s through to the early 1960s came onto the market in the mid-to-late 1980s. These appear to have entered collections which are dormant, in immediate market terms. The most significant of Yeats' works this year was offered at Christie's 12 March 1993 sale. Pyms Gallery paid the low estimate (£60,000-80,000) for *The Amateur Ventriloquist Driving Sheep over Westminster Bridge,* (1945) which depicted an audience watching actors on a stage; a painting from Yeats' late *oeuvre*, it continued all the Yeatsian bravura plus the evocative attraction of a particularised scene. From Yeats' middle period was the 1930 *Between Cork and Kerry* sold to a telephone bidder for £13,000 at Christie's 6 November sale (estimate £10-15,000). Showing how crazy estimates can be, an unfinished, indifferent but nonetheless highly-estimated (£18-24,000) painting, *Quiet Men,* flopped at £12,000 immediately preceding the *Between Cork and Kerry.* The National Gallery of Ireland revealed itself a perceptive buyer in the London market by its purchase of Yeats' *Four Scenes in Search of Characters,* stage scenes probably painted in the late 1920s. Offered at Sotheby's 4 November 1992 sale with an estimate of £60-80,000, the winning bid was placed at the low estimate. (The National Gallery had also astutely purchased, by private treaty in February 1992, Yeats' *That Grand Conversation was under the Rose,* 1943). Of more academic and personal appeal, as well as an object of aesthetic beauty, was the pencil and black-chalk *Self-portrait* dated 1921 by Yeats' father, John Butler Yeats, which came up at Sotheby's 10 March 1992 sale; a study for a large self-portrait which remains in the artist's family collection, the drawing proved a good buy for the Pyms Gallery at £900 against an estimate of £1,500-2,000.

A certain pattern emerges from these Yeats painting prices. Rather than concluding that the market has fallen because purchases were made generally at the

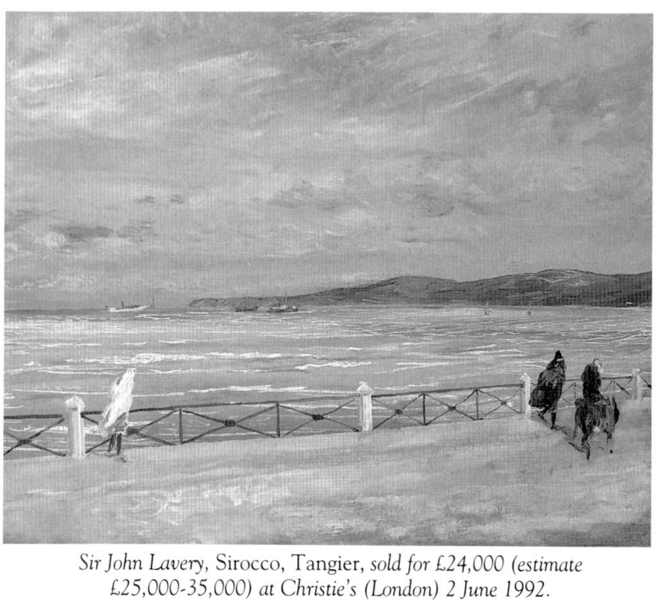

Sir John Lavery, Sirocco, Tangier, *sold for £24,000 (estimate £25,000-35,000) at Christie's (London) 2 June 1992.*

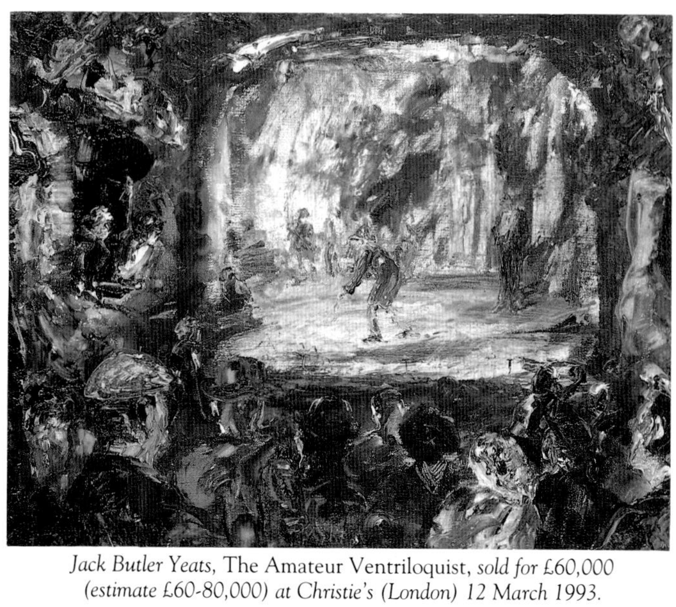

Jack Butler Yeats, The Amateur Ventriloquist, *sold for £60,000 (estimate £60-80,000) at Christie's (London) 12 March 1993.*

IRISH ART IN THE LONDON SALEROOMS

lower end of the estimates, the estimates should be regarded as too optimistic given the general market and the settling of this specialised field. (Perhaps there is a certain truth to be found in the frequently-voiced trade complaint that auction house estimates are used as a means of securing consignments). The price achieved should be regarded as good and reassuring. Further, they reflect a growing tendency amongst serious collectors to cross over from collecting only Irish paintings to considering European paintings of the period as well. Such comparison-shopping by seasoned, increasingly knowledgeable collectors serves to help keep a specialist field in line with the greater art market (which was not the case in the Scandinavian market for instance).

In contrast, trade or well-advised bidding was noticeably absent when Yeats' *Winter in Galway* came up at Sotheby's on 30 September 1992; catalogued as 'painted from Lady Gregory's house at Coole Park' and estimated at £7-9,000, it sold for £8,200 despite unsubstantiated trade rumours that it 'wasn't right'. Knowledgeable buyers also stayed away from a peculiar 'Yeats' whose authenticity 'was guaranteed by the vendor (a Mr Boyle) and not by the auction house' (a most unusual disclaimer, even given the more usual time-honoured jargon of auction houses). Offered by Wealdon Auction Galleries of Cranbrook (Kent) on 5 October 1992 and entitled *The Last Supper,* the catalogue entry dwelt lengthily on the provenance, which included the 'Duke de Stackpole' and film directors Henry de Vere Clifton and Brian Desmond Hurst. The catalogue entry also included the price figures for four major Yeats paintings sold at auctions in 1989 and 1990. 'Mr Boyle' did not return this art historian's post-sale call, placed with the auction house, and the painting, which was offered without an estimate, failed to meet its reserve.

Irish artists whose works traditionally have fit snugly within the Modern British market also continued to perform well, given considerations of quality, condition and period within the artist's *oeuvre*. Sir William Orpen's *A Woman in Grey* (a portrait of the artist's wife Grace) was consigned to Christie's by The Art Institute of Chicago, which had bought the painting directly from the artist in 1912. Revealing the influence of Velazquez, its sombre setting provided a foil for a shimmering full-length portrayal. The painting was esti-

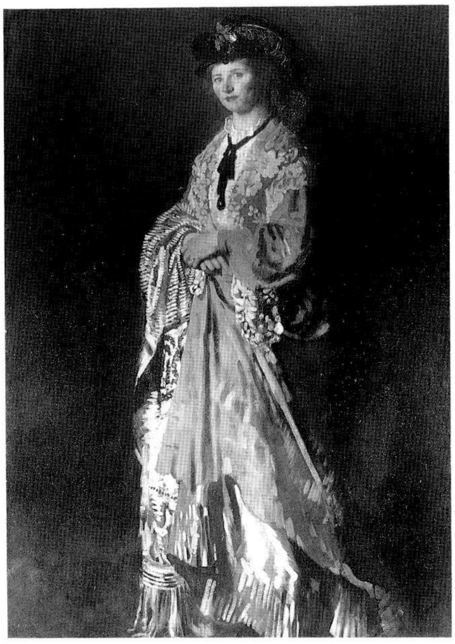

Sir William Orpen, A Woman in Grey, *sold for £108,000 (estimate £120-160,000) at Christie's (London) 12 March 1993.*

mated for the 12 March 1993 sale at £120-160,000 and sold to the Pyms Gallery for £108,000; given the lack of other activity in the room, this price must have been the reserve. Undoubtedly, enthusiasm was dampened by Christie's pre-sale cleaning of the painting, which evidently did not solve the problem of a damaged area in the background to the right of the figure; at some stage, the painting had suffered from damp and the damage apparently extended beyond the varnish. Perhaps buyers would have preferred to have done their own research and have chosen the restorer of their choice to work on the area. Some viewers also objected to the 'cling film', characterless varnish that had been applied and, to be sure, the painting, as an object, lacked the pull that one suspects it might have had, given a more sympathetic period varnish. Another Orpen, *Girl in a Blue Hat* (the American Vera Brewster who married the Irish writer Joseph Hone) was offered by Christie's on 6 November 1992 (estimated £80-120,000), only to be greeted by a silent room. The painting, previously offered in the early 1980s and one of several versions of the portrait, failed to sell, with 'bidding' supposedly advancing to £75,000.

Sir John Lavery's works seem also to be holding their own. At Christie's 5 June 1992 sale, *Sirocco, Tangier* (1921) (where spectacular Mediterranean light and an activated sea and sky were depicted with skilled suggestive strokes) sold for £24,000 (estimate £24-35,000). *Rain in the Distance, North Berwick* (1919) offered at Christie's 12 March 1993, sold for £18,000 (estimate £20-30,000). A sketchily-pointed, high-horizoned composition, *From the Royal Albion, Brighton* (1936) was bought-in at £18,000 (estimate £20-30,000) at Sotheby's 4 November 1992 sale; while the artist exploited the angled advance of the pier out into the sea, the flat, unresolved foreground lacked the attraction and lustre of the brushstrokes of other Laverys. A lovely, small *San Giorgio Maggiore from the Riva dei Schiavoni, Venice* elicited bids from various places in the room and over the telephone at Christie's 12 March 1993 sale. Among the later bidders were the London dealer James Kirkman and the Pyms Gallery, with the telephone winning at the fall of the hammer on £18,000 (estimate £8-12,000). With the exception of the Venetian scene, which appeals to a broad sector of buyers, prices for the other Laverys tended, as with the Yeats' paintings, to be at the low estimate.

The market for eighteenth-century Irish paintings continues to develop. A portrait by Robert Fagan (1761-1816), an artist only very rarely available, sold at Sotheby's British Paintings sale of 15 July 1992 for £28,000 against an estimate of £4-6,000. Purchased by the Pyms Gallery, it has since found a home in an English private collection.

Perhaps the surprise of the year was the announcement by Christie's that it would be holding a Dublin sale of Fine Irish Paintings and Drawing in May 1993; these sales had seemed to be a thing of the past (as with other 'national' paintings sales). With so many auction houses already competing in Ireland for the same goods, one wonders whether enough prior lessons have been learnt. While, according to trade rumours, consignments were still being sought in late March, news of this event will have to wait until next year's *Review*.

Gertrude Prescott Nuding

Dr. Gertrude Prescott Nuding has written regularly on art market issues for various publications, including The Art Newspaper, Art & Auction, Apollo *and* The Art Book Review, *since 1988. Her exhibition review of the Tate Gallery's* The Swagger Portrait *appeared in* The Wall Street Journal Europe *in 1992 and her chapter on* Britishness and Portraiture *appeared in Roy Porter's* Myths of the English *in 1992.*

ART SALES IN IRELAND

Robert O'Byrne reviews Irish art and antiques prices in Dublin and around the country.

May 1992 opened with one of those country house auctions which continue to attract large numbers of buyers even though the properties now rarely yield up any real bargains. Doneen House, outside Patrickswell, Co Limerick has been owned by one of the Earl of Harrington's sons, the Hon Steven Stanhope, in recent years. Conducted by Mealys of Kilkenny, the auction drew such crowds on viewing days that admission had to be restricted for fear that the house floors might not be able to withstand the assault. A total of more than £450,000 was realised on the actual day of sale, with the top price of £10,000 being made by both a pair of demi-lune satinwood sidetables and a George III-style mahogany dining table on three stems. A pair of Irish George III brass-bound peat buckets fetched £7,000, a set of eight Chinese Chippendale-style dining chairs £4,000 and a small walnut chest £4,200. Amongst the paintings,a somewhat unusual Lavery portrait of a poodle (which seemingly was called Kita) sold for £7,000 and a picture of deer in a forest by Rosa Bonheur went for £500 more, while a moorland scene by Douglas Anderson made £5,000. Later that same month, Mealys held a two-day sale on its own premises, with all mixed bag of over 1,000 lots. Amongst all this, an Irish eighteenth-century mahogany fold-over table made the top price of £4,500, followed by £4,000 for a nine-piece French painted and parcel gilt suite. A Regency period mahogany drop-leaf sofa table lived up to its pre-sale expectations by reaching £3,500, while an early nineteenth-century Irish carved mahogany and parcel gilt architectural mirror surpassed its £1,200-1,800 estimate to fetch £2,800.

At Mullen of Bray, Co Dublin, an Irish Georgian longcase clock sold for £1,400, with a boulle credenza making the top price of £4,600. Meanwhile, Town and Country auctioned the residue of contents from 3 Windsor Terrace in Dun Laoghaire, former home of Teddy Jacobs (once owner of the Scotsman's Inn). At this sale, the best price as expected, was made by a late nineteenth century satinwood display cabinet which went over its top estimate of £3,000 by a further £800, unlike the French secretaire *abattant*, estimated to fetch £2,200, which was eventually sold for £1,550 and a George II serpentine side table, which went for £2,100 (top estimate £3,000). Across the city in Sutton, Denis Drum auctioned the residue of another home, that formerly belonging to the late Gerald FitzGibbon, whose grandfather of the same name had been Lord Justice of Appeal in Ireland at the turn of the century. A railway and tram enthusiast, Mr FitzGibbon's house contained evidence of his hobby in the form of electric and clockwork railway engines and rolling stock, but amongst the furniture, the best price made at the sale was £1,350 for an Adam-pattern inlaid mahogany sideboard. Around the same time, Taylor de Vere's Spring auction paintings was held in the National Concert Hall, a relatively low-key affair which nonetheless managed to sell some 70 per cent of the work offered. Highest price was achieved by a small Walter Osborne called *Near St Patrick's Close* which went for £9,700, despite expectations that it could go up to £15,000; perhaps the modest dimensions and dark tone were a deterrent for potential buyers. Similarly, a charming Leech, *The Apple Orchard*, depicting the artist's Devon home during the Second World War, which carried a pre-sale estimate of £6,500-9,000, in the end went for just £5,700 and a Roderic O'Conor watercolour of *Sweet Peas in a Glass Bowl with a Green Vase* was only sold after the auction for £5,250. On the other hand, Mainie Jellett's gouache *Descent from the Cross* – a study for the painting of the same name which is now in the Hugh Lane Gallery – realised £3,200 which was close to its upper estimate, and two Tony O'Malley oils, *The Patio* and *Summerscape* made £2,000 and £2,200 respectively.

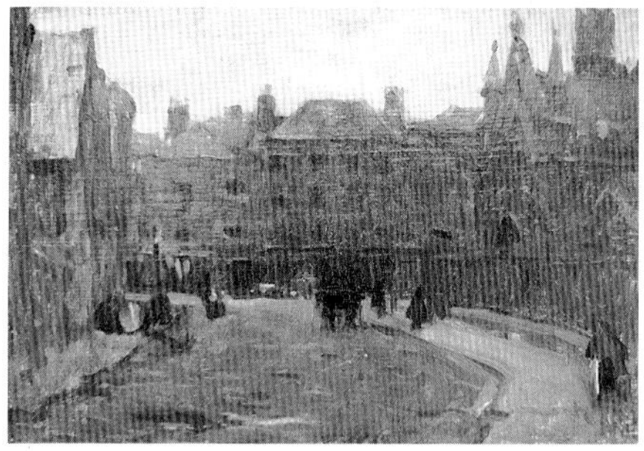

Walter Osborne, Near St Patrick's Close. *£9,700. Taylor de Vere.*

In Belfast, Ross's returned to business after a three-week closure due to fire damage on the premises, with a furniture auction in which a carved mahogany D-end table with two extra leaves sold for £1,800 and a set of twelve Regency-style dining chairs made £1,100. Early the following month, the same auctioneers achieved £1,200 for an Edwardian display cabinet and £800 for a set of eight mahogany balloon-back dining chairs. A curiosity at Temple Auctions around the same time was a portrait of Sir Stanley Spencer by Stephen Ward,one of the principal protagonists in the Profumo Affair thirty years earlier. This fetched £420.

Another portrait, that of Bridget Moynan by her father Richard Thomas Moynan, was included in the mid-June auction of Irish art at James Adam; its obvious appeal explained why this picture made £12,000 which was its upper estimate, whilst another by the same painter, *Study of a Young Boy,* went for £4,000 (estimate £3,000-5,000). Two years earlier, Moynan's *The Flower Seller* had been sold at James Adam for £11,000; now it turned up again, at Thomas Adams of Blackrock, and made an astonishing £18,000. This was, however, one of the few highs in a generally desultory market, with many pictures in both sales doing well to reach their lowest estimates. At James Adam work which fell into this category included Yeats' *The Poetic Morning,* which went for £20,000, Paul Henry's *Reflections* (£8,000) and George Russell's *Mountain landscape at Dusk with Sheep* (£1,250), although Harry Kernoff's study of itinerant caravans at Dolphins' Barn, Dublin surpassed pre-sale expectations to reach £2,500 and James Sleator's *Corner of Studio* also did well, fetching £7,000.

A sudden outbreak of house auctions occurred in the early summer, beginning with Ross's sale of the contents of a house in the Malone district of Belfast. A Victorian walnut piano-top davenport desk here reached £3,500 while a Regency rosewood turnover-leaf games table made £2,200, and a Victorian mahogany chiffonier sold for £1,350. Down in Dublin, Mealys of Castlecomer, in association with Town and Country, held a clearance sale of work belonging to the well-known antique dealer Gerald Kenyon on the latter's premises at Lower Ormond Quay. The high reputation which Kenyon and his wife Pat enjoyed amongst the trade and private buyers alike, ensured that there was a substantial turn-out for this sale, with more than 750 lots of the finest quality, including the dealer's col-

ART SALES IN IRELAND

lection of old Treen and early Dutch tobacco boxes. One of the most magnificent items, a Georgian 15-feet long campaign dining table, once in the possession of the Earls of Mayo, went over its £13,000-16,000 estimate to reach the day's best price of £18,500. Only £500 less secured an equally superb Georgian double breakfront bookcase, inlaid with Gothic moulded pediment, which again went well over its £12,000-16,000 estimate. The Kenyons' own Hepplewhite-period carved mahogany patent campaign four-poster bed, with the label of Morgan and Saunders of London fetched £6,500, whilst an eighteenth century demi-lune mahogany side-table, attributed to Gillows, went for £4,500.

Shortly afterwards came the house contents sale of Humewood, Co Wicklow, home of the late Catherine Marie-Madeleine Hume-Weygand, whose family had owned the estate for almost three centuries. Mme Hume-Weygand, who died the previous November, left the proceeds of the sale of the house and its contents to her local friends and employees, with any balance to go to the village and the Roman Catholic diocese of Kildare and Leighlin. The building and surrounding estate were bought by Mrs Renata Coleman, who also acquired some of the house contents when these were auctioned in mid-July. But such was the interest that the sale aroused, with some 7,000 viewers and more than 1,000 bidders over the two-day event, that prices were often very high, the total reaching around £1 million. Two lots shared top price, one being a pair of satinwood, mahogany and marquetry side-tables by James Hicks of Dublin, which were not part of Humewood's original contents, but brought in for the sale; they went way past their pre-sale estimate of £15,000-20,000 as did an early nineteenth-century English mahogany bookcase with a slight breakfront and brass-inlaid doors which also reached £28,000 (estimate £8,000-12,000). An Italian neoclassical walnut, rosewood and marquetry commode fetched £20,000 (£8,000-12,000), as did a portrait of Charlotte Cotton, by John Michael Wright. Not all lots did so well, however, with one notable failure being the painting of Thames Ditton in Surrey (a former Hume family home) once attributed to Constable, but here merely catalogued as being from the circle of John Linnell, which, despite exciting considerable interest before the auction, did not subsequently find a buyer.

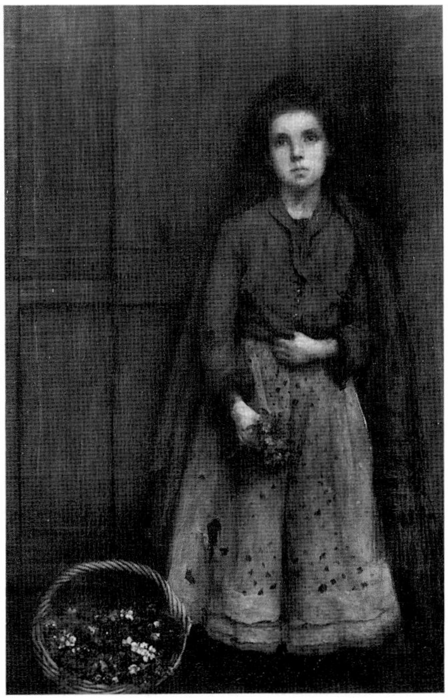

Richard Thomas Moynan, The Flower Seller, *£18,000. Thomas Adams, Blackrock.*

Inevitably, after the allure of Humewood, any other sale during July seemed slightly anti-climactic. Still, James Adam's auction on its own premises of silver and furniture did secure £7,000 for an Irish George III oval double-dropleaf hunting table which showed all the signs of having been exceedingly well-used, and a George IV inlaid mahogany serpentine-front sideboard made £1,700. Amongst the silver, a George III urn-shaped wine cooler, dated 1810, fetched £1,900, a two-handled cup of 1748 by Charles Townsend of Dublin went for £900 and a set of six bright-cut taper-handled tablespoons by John Pillar of Dublin, dated 1773, made £350.

At Thomas Adams of Blackrock, another 15-feet long D-end dining table, this time mid-Victorian with six leaves and in need of some attention, made £3,000, while a set of twelve mahogany balloon-back dining chairs which would have made an appropriate match, went for £1,000 less. Meanwhile, at Allen & Townsend, a set of eight mahogany Chippendale-design dining chairs with two carvers fetched £1,500 and a William IV drum table £950.

Around this time, Dublin stamp dealer Ian Whyte held an auction in Buswell's Hotel, which was most notable for the dispersal of the Rev Edwin Davey's collection, particularly rich in Irish postal markings of the eighteenth and nineteenth centuries. A set of letters concerning the infamous burning of Wild Goose Lodge in Co Louth in 1815 fetched £280, somewhat below its estimate, and a 1823 entire printed letter with a handstuck 'Charity Letter' mark made £1,000, despite hope that it could go as high as £1,500.

The 27th Irish Antiques Dealers' Fair opened in early August, as always at the Mansion House but this time separated by a number of weeks from the Dublin Horse Show with which it traditionally coincided. Despite complaints within the trade that business was worse than ever, there were the same number of dealers present, thirty in all, as previous years, with both Gerald Kenyon, whose premises had been totally cleared at auction a month earlier, and Paul Cooke, whose Francis Street building was badly damaged by a fire around the same time, being amongst those taking stands. There was no one outstanding item in the fair, but the curiosities included a pair of pre-nineteenth century paintings documenting the Florentine frescoes painted by Andrea del Sarto on the walls of the garden of SS Annunziata in 1519, which were almost totally destroyed in a subsequent fire. These were being offered by Mike McGlynn of Bunratty, Co Clare, whilst James Weldon's display included a rare piece of Galway silver: a tankard made specially by Richard Joyce for the wedding of Patrick and Mary Kirwan in 1703. Fortland Antiques from Charleville, Co Cork had a Carlton House satinwood desk in impeccable order and George Stackpoole of Adare, Co Limerick produced a delightful study by the writer/poet Aubrey de Vere of the grounds of his ancestral home, Curragh Chase, in Co Limerick. Overall, attendances during the week were judged to be only slightly down on the previous year's fair, with best sales achieved by pieces priced below £1,000; evidence, if any were needed, that the continuing recession has had an effect on buying patterns.

Still, the continuing popularity of an artist like Frank McKelvey was shown when his oil, *Mixed Herd* came up for sale at Andersons in Belfast around this time and made £6,500, with a marquetry-cased Georgian grandfather clock in the same auction going for £2,500.

After a subdued few weeks of late summer, the autumn season began promisingly in early September with a sale of house contents conducted by Hamilton Osborne

ART SALES IN IRELAND

King at Summerhill near Thomastown, Co Kilkenny, the building and eighty-eight acres having already been sold for £270,000. A Regency rosewood and boxwood inlaid sofa table, after the manner of John Maclean went up to its top estimate of £6,000, whilst a mid-eighteenth century Irish mahogany side table fetched £4,000. On the other hand, an hexagonal cellarette, brass-banded and with brass handles, dating from around 1790, having been expected to sell for between £2,500 and £4,000, only made £1,400. Amongst the pictures, a scene with gundogs and game signed *E Armfield*, fetched £4,000 and a coastal scene by Charles Bonchez £3,000, well over its pre-sale estimate of £1,500 to £2,000.

There were similar successes in Dublin, where James Adam held a furniture sale, with the day's best price of £8,000 being made by a William IV mahogany rectangular dining table (estimate £5,000-£7,000). Other good prices were achieved by a large blue-and-white eighteenth century octagonal serving dish made by Henry Delamain of Dublin, which fetched £1,500, an Edwardian repeat carriage clock expected to make £2,000-3,000 eventually went to a telephone bidder for £4,600, a pair of Regency mahogany hall chairs went for £4,500 and a George III inlaid mahogany rectangular side-cabinet £4,200.

The first of the autumn season's big picture sales was held by Christie's in Belfast towards the middle of September making a total of almost £200,000. Although almost all the lots found a buyer, usually around their estimates, the day's expected star proved something of a disappointment. This was a very large canvas by William Conor, a symbolist painting called *Children of Ulster* which carried an estimate of £20-£30,000 but in the end did well to make £16,500 – the top price of the sale but still far short of what had been hoped. By comparison, a fine Gerard Dillon, *Boy with Net,* surpassed its £7-10,000 estimate to reach £11,500, after which came Colin Middleton's *Tree with Wren* which went for £7,480 and Maurice MacGonigal's *The Islander – An Fear Fiadáin* which fetched £7,000. Amongst the watercolours, Mildred Anne Butler's pleasant-enough *Spring Garden* also went beyond its top estimate of £6,000 though only by £380 and Rose Barton's *St Patrick's Cathedral, Dublin* made £4,950.

Meanwhile, Sheppard of Durrow was the first of the regional auction houses to hold an autumn sale, as always with such

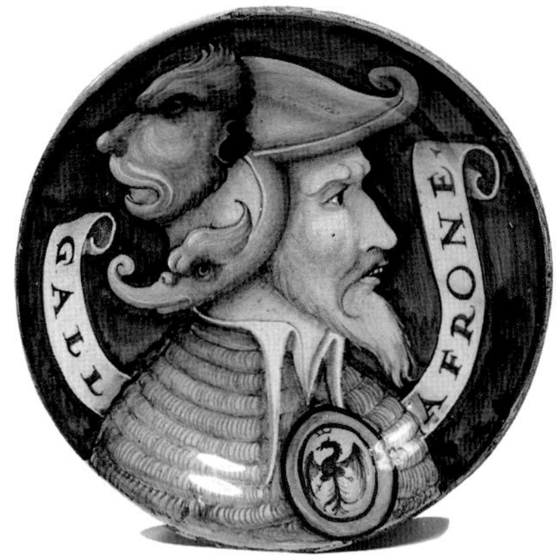

Castel Durante majolica dish, £28,000 (est £700-£1,000). Christie's/Hamilton Osborne King sale at Stackallen, Co Meath.

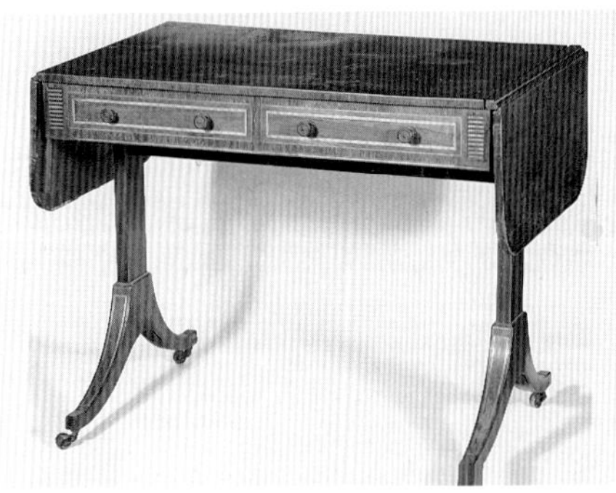

Regency rosewood and boxwood inlaid sofa table, £6,000. Hamilton Osborne King sale at Summerhill, Co Kilkenny.

events, an occasion offering a wide variety of items, including a set of ten nineteenth century Chippendale-style mahogany dining chairs, which made the best price of £5,000 – their lower estimate. A fine nineteenth-century mahogany and marquetry bureau bookcase achieved a respectable £3,000, but an equally handsome mahogany longcase clock with a brass and silver dial from the same period went for £2,800; some what less than its £3,-4,000, reflecting the continued uncertainty of the market.

There were three more longcase clocks on offer at Mealys of Castlecomer's two-day sale in late September with one of the trio, an early nineteenth-century German example, fetching £600 more than its £4,000 estimate. Other furniture fetching good prices included a drop-leaf Irish mahogany hunting-table and an Irish Georgian glass wine urn, both of which made £4,000, along with a heavily decorated French satinwood and kingwood display cabinet, which fetched £4,400 (pre-sale estimate £2-3,000). In an auction of approximately 1,300 lots which made a total of almost £300,000, the best price of all – £9,500 – was fetched by two paintings: Joseph Peacock's *The Patronal Festival of St Kevin at Glendalough* and a continental school picture *The Broken Sleigh.*

Not all the paintings in James Adam's sale of the end of the month fared as well, with pictures by Moynan, Sleator, Carey and Le Brocquy failing to find buyers.

An early Le Brocquy from 1944, *Tennis Courts in April, Kenilworth Square, Dublin* went for £5,000, well below its £6-8,000 estimate, while Sadler's view of the Four Courts just made its lower estimate of £5,000 and Daniel O'Neill's *Early Morning* fetched only £4,500 (estimate £6-8,000). Similarly, Nathaniel Hone's *St Doulough's Church, Raheny* sold for £1,700 (£2-4,000) and even a popular painter like Frank McKelvey could only command £5,800 for his *Feeding Chickens* despite a pre-sale estimate of £6,800. A somewhat similar story was told at Fleury's of Cahir, where a one-day auction was held in early October. Almost 600 lots were offered, many of them the kind of heavily ornamented nineteenth-century pieces which have rather fallen out of favour today and this may account for the relatively low prices paid. There was, for example, a French nineteenth-century carved giltwood mirror signed by the Gueret brothers, which went for just £2,200 and a fine Louis XV period carved giltwood console table sold for the day's best price, a modest-enough £3,400. There was also an Italian early nineteenth-century giltwood centretable which commanded £2,600 and a nineteenth-century carved giltwood and gesso overmantel at £2,400.

In Belfast during the same period, more furniture bargains were to be found, such as yet another of those Victorian mahogany D-end dining tables which seem to have been produced in such profusion; this one sold for £1,800 at Ross's, whilst a set of eight carved mahogany chairs from the period went for £1,000. And at Anderson's, a Victorian mahogany-framed double-end sofa sold for £900. There was plenty of furniture on offer at the biggest of the autumn's house sales, that organised by Christie's in association with Hamilton Osborne King at Stackallan, Co Meath, home for many years of bloodstock breeder Mrs Elizabeth Burke, who had decided to move into a smaller rectory in the same county. Naturally, as at Humewood earlier in the year, the event attracted considerable publicity and an equally substantial number of viewers in the days before the auction. The total spent during the day

ART SALES IN IRELAND

itself was around £760,000 with the highest price of £28,000 being paid for a Castel Durante majolica dish slightly under nine inches in diameter, which had been estimated in the catalogue to fetch between £700 and £1,000. Similarly, a bronze statue of Mercury, after Giambologna, on a marble pedestal, though estimated to sell for £4-6,000, was eventually sold to an Italian dealer for £26,000. By contrast, an early George III Irish mahogany and parcel gilt display cabinet, originally from Bracklyn Castle in Co Westmeath only made £25,000, well short of its pre-sale estimate of £30-50,000, and a group portrait of the artist's children by Sir Francis Grant, which had excited considerable interest, in the end went for the same price as the cabinet. An Irish George II walnut secretaire cabinet doubled its estimate to reach £24,000, whilst two earlier eighteenth-century Brussels tapestries depicting mythological scenes fetched £14,000 and £13,000 respectively.

The success of Stackallan's sale did much to restore confidence after a rather shaky start to the season. It was followed by a charity auction organised by accountant and noted art collector Fergus Ahern of Boyle, Co Roscommon to raise funds for Somalia. Hundreds of artists and other collectors donated work for the event which eventually made more than £50,000 with best prices being paid for a Louis Le Brocquy oil (£10,000) a William Crozier canvas (£3,200) and a Hilda van Stockum oil (£1,300).

The demand for furniture of good quality which had been demonstrated at Stackallan could be seen again at Mullen's of Bray where a Regency sideboard fetched £3,300 and a marble fireplace of the same period £2,300, the same price being paid for a pair of silver sauce boats. Meanwhile, at Sheppard's of Durrow, a Regency mahogany Pembroke table commanded a price of £1,800, a three-place Louis XV-style giltwood drawing room suite £2,200 and a pair of Adam alcove bookcases £3,000.

Another pair of bookcases, this time part of a 800-lot one-day sale, made £8,000 at Mealy's; understandably, the auction's best price, as they were in fine condition, made of mahogany and from the William IV period. Only three other items, in a sale which took in a total of approximately £200,000, individually made more than £2,000. These were a Kerman carpet (£2,500), a late Regency rosewood sofa table (£2,200) and a near pair of writing tables in the style of Gillows (£2,000).

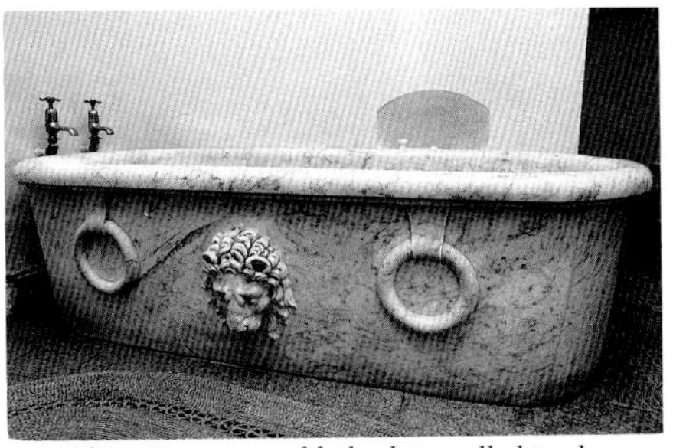

White Roman marble bath installed in the 1820s for Lord Robert Tottenham, Bishop of Clogher, £7,200. Hamilton Osborne King sale at Woodstock, Co Wicklow.

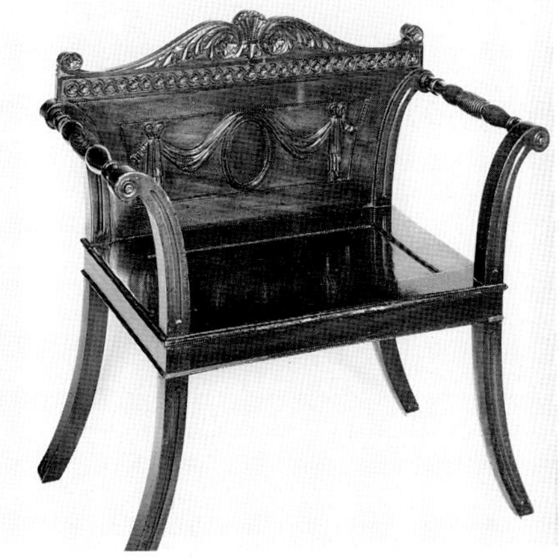

Irish mahogany hall bench by Walsh of Bachelors' Walk, £11,000. Hamilton Osborne King sale at Woodstock, Co Kilkenny.

Naturally, there was plenty more furniture on offer at the house contents sale of Woodstock, near Newtownmountkennedy in Co Wicklow, conducted by Hamilton Osborne King. Some pieces had been brought in for the event from Quinville Abbey, Co Clare but one item which was certainly original to the house and still *in situ* was the white Roman marble bath installed in the 1820s for a previous occupant, Lord Robert Tottenham, Bishop of Clogher; this eventually fetched £7,200, respectably above its estimate of £5,000 in a sale which made over £400,000 altogether, despite appalling weather conditions and far less publicity than that attending the Stackallan auction. The highest price, £28,000, was achieved by a handsome Irish mahogany architect's cabinet, whilst second-best at £11,000 was made by another Irish piece, a mahogany hall bench bearing the trade label of Walsh of Bachelor's Walk. Other good prices included £7,000 for a giltwood pier mirror, £6,800 for a mahogany serving table with Kilkenny marble top, £6,500 for a giltwood compartmented overmantel mirror and £6,200 for a set of fourteen mahogany dining chairs.

Up in Northern Ireland at Moylan's, a pair of 8ft high cast iron urns were auctioned for £8,500, whilst an equally large piece of statuary, a group entitled *Mother and Three Children*, signed *Berthe Girardet* and dated 1910, made £5,000. Prices, if not dimensions, were even larger at the sale held by Adams of Blackrock on the company's premises, where a Roderic O'Conor – subject of a newly-published and somewhat controversial catalogue raisonné by Jonathan Benington – made its lower estimate of £14,000. Something of a bargain, but not as great as the set of seven stained glass windows by Harry Clarke, each of them some 12ft high, removed from a Dublin church, which sold together for just £4,000.

Christie's were called in to disperse the collection of Jack Chambers, former head of Lennox Chemicals who over the years prior to his death early in 1922 had managed to cram his one-bedroomed flat in Fitzwilliam Square with over 500 choice pieces which were put on display in the RHA Gallagher Gallery prior to auction. Again, this was a highly social occasion, testimony to Chambers' popularity as much as to his taste, with the day's best price, £13,000, being made by a small Walter Osborne *A Seaside Promenade*, whilst amongst the furniture, the most expensive piece (£9,000) was an Irish George III mahogany serving table. An Irish artist's table from the same period made £5,000 and a kneehole desk the same. Since Jack Chambers was a well-known collector of glassware, this also performed well, with £2,000 being paid for an oval-shaped salad bowl.

Taylor de Vere held its annual picture sale at the National Concert Hall in early December, when over 80 per cent of the 130-odd lots were bought for a total of just under £200,000. The major disappointment here was that a Jack B Yeats painting *The Last Voyage*, carrying an estimate of £40-60,000, failed to secure a buyer, although it was rumoured to have been sold subsequently. On the day itself, Nathaniel Hone's big *Gathering Seaweed* did best, surpassing its £13-£16,000 estimate to reach £19,500. Similarly, Walter Osborne's *Workers in the Field* went up to £11,200 (estimate £6-9,000), and Lilian Davidson's charming *The Flax Pullers* £10,000 (£5-8,000). Just as delightful, Paul Henry's *Whitewashing the Cottage* was sold for £8,500 (£6,500-8,000) and Sarah

ART SALES IN IRELAND

Purser's *Summer Flowers* almost made its upper estimate when fetching £9,500.

The total of £100,000 made by James Adam at its picture sale a week later was more modest than that achieved by Taylor de Vere, but still included some respectable figures such as the £10,000 paid for a small Yeats oil *Grand Canal*, estimated to reach only £8,000. A collection of eleven of Flora Mitchell's well-known Dublin watercolours all sold for prices between £600 and £1,200, a Le Brocquy painting of St Stephens Green made £7,000 and a Mary Swanzy *Village Landscape* £4,000. Up in Belfast, the year concluded with a picture sale at Ross's where a painting by Northern artist Lilian Davidson did best at £10,000 in an auction which altogether realised more than £100,000. After that price, it was a long drop to £4,500 for a William Conor, followed by £4,000 for one of Lavery's Tangiers scenes.

Early January 1993 was spent by most of the houses reviewing the previous year, with James Adam's annual report settling for comfort in the knowledge that 'the market survived in 1992' although 'while caution remains the keyword, we have an optimistic outlook on 1993.' Silver, porcelain and good quality period furniture were considered to have done well during the previous twelve months, but problems arose in the picture market, not least because of 'caution on the part of both vendors and auctioneers in consigning paintings for sale.' A similar point was made by Taylor de Vere, which commented that 'our problem stemmed from a lack of stock ... quality pictures were rarely available to bring out serious money.'

James Adam of Dublin held its first auction of the year in late January, a mixed collection of some 450 lots which included paintings as well as furniture, silver, china and glassware. Amongst the silver, a pair of plain George I square salvers from London and dated 1719 made £1,400, while a George III teapot made by John Williams of Cork in 1795 went for £760. A George IV mahogany secretaire bookcase, also believed to be from Cork, sold for £3,600, an Edwardian Sheraton revival inlaid mahogany semi-circular fold-top card table £1,250 and an eighteenth century octagonal bronze sundial by Lynch of Dublin £600.

Even better prices were achieved in early February by Mullens of Bray, which made its best-ever house record for an auction totalling more than £110,000 worth of sales. The individual highest item was a nineteenth-century painted satinwood Pembroke table, sold for £3,000, just £100 more than what was paid for a nineteenth century Georgian-style mahogany breakfront bookcase, with the next best price being £2,400 for a Regency period statuary marble fireplace; again this was £100 more than the sum fetched by a nineteenth-century French kingwood bureauplat. At Thomas Adams of Blackrock, meanwhile, £3,500 was paid for a George III satinwood and tulipwood oval Pembroke table and £1,650 for a set of six Chippendale-style mahogany dining chairs. The contents sale conducted by Cork auctioneers Marsh's at Mount Verdon on the city's Wellington Road attracted an exceptional degree of interest with well over 1,500 people turning up for the two-day viewing and so many prospective bidders arriving for the auction itself that not everyone could be accommodated in the rooms. Top price of £6,000 was paid for a Sheraton inlaid bowfronted sideboard estimated to fetch £4-5,000. Unfortunately, a Georgian secretaire bookcase expected to go as high as £7,000 ended by only making £3,400, just as an eighteenth-century mahogany D-end design table (estimate £8,000) mustered only £3,600. Still, a Georgian mahogany linen press with brass drop handles did go for a reasonable £2,000, with a French painted Pembroke table fetching £100 less. At the other end of the island, there was more furniture being sold through Ross's auction house, where a Regency sideboard on barley-sugar legs went for £2,400 and a Georgian rosewood sofa table £2,100. And at Bloomfield Auctions, a number of pictures by Northern Ireland artist William Conor made excellent prices such as the £1,420 paid for a crayon drawing *Passing Time* with another *The Scene Shifters* going for £1,200.

Sheppards of Durrow held a 400-odd lot auction in mid-February where the best price was made by an elegant nineteenth century mahogany and inlaid breakfront bookcase, surpassing its upper estimate of £3,500 by a further £100. Just making its lower estimate of £2,500, a nineteenth century George II-style mahogany cabinet bureau came next with a Louis XV ormolu-mounted kingwood and parquetry tallboy fetching £1,700.

Plenty of furniture was offered by Fleury's of Cahir at the sale held on the premises in early March, but the item which aroused the most interest was a pair of pistols, still with their original fittings and case. The 15-bore flintlocks had been made for by McDermott of Dublin around 1795 for a Major Lombard, second in command of the North Cork Militia, which was stationed in Wexford during the 1798 uprising; Major Lombard was killed at the Battle of Oulart near Gorey, Co Wexford. His pistols were bought by an Irish businessman for £28,000, somewhat less than the £30-40,000 which had been hoped for. In the same sale, a fine Regency mahogany sideboard made for the diningroom of Doneraile Court, Co Cork fetched £10,000 and a pair of Regency tea tables £3,400. In Clonakilty, Co Cork, local auctioneers Con O'Neill & Sons were brought in to sell the 400 or so lots collected by the late Robert Burgess, a London antique dealer who had retired to west Cork. A Louis XVI white carved marble chimney piece initially drew a single bid of £500 when it was offered in the morning, but eventually fetched £1,700 before the end of the day. A pair of Adam marquetry side tables in need of restoration went for £2,900, the best price, with £2,200 being paid for a pair of Regency mahogany pedestals with brass inlay and ormolu mounts, and £1,600 for a mahogany Chippendale carved card table.

Another collection was dispersed at the RUAS showgrounds by Comber auctioneer Tim Martin, who secured £2,000 for nine Victorian mahogany dining chairs on fluted tapering legs, £1,750 for a Victorian walnut and ormolu mounted credenza and £1,050 for a mahogany half-tested bedstead and mattress of the same period. At Ross's, a giltwood Victorian drawingroom suite fetched £2,200 and a set of eight Chinese Chippendale chairs £1,200.

Meanwhile, James Adam of Dublin realised £4,000 for a set of eight nineteenth century mahogany Hepplewhite-style dining chairs, with £3,000 being paid for a pair of rosewood rectangular folding-top card tables, the same price also being paid for both a pair of Louis XV inlaid walnut rectangular glazed cabinets and a pair of George IV D-end rosewood sewing tables.

Mealys of Castlecomer offered more than 700 lots in mid-March, as always with plenty of variety in the stock which made a total of over £160,000. The highest figure achieved was £5,000 for an elaborately carved Georgian giltwood overmantel reflecting the mid-eighteenth century fondness of chinoiserie. A William IV yewwood cheval mirror, made by Henry Norman of Rathkeale, Co Limerick for a

ART SALES IN IRELAND

John Southwell-Brown in 1835 greatly exceeded its pre-sale estimate of £700 to make £2,000, the same paid for a 58-piece English Imari-pattern porcelain dinner service and for a pair of William IV mahogany bookcases, as well as a painting *Repentant Saint with hands clasped* signed 'S Ricci.'

In Ulster, Anderson's secured £2,250 for a D-end table, and £1,700 for another, as well as £1,250 for a pair of cabriole-leg specimen cabinets. Ross's in Belfast held a big sale of Irish paintings which made a total of more than £125,000, with over three-quarters of the lots sold. As expected, the best price was made by Erskine Nicol's *Waiting for the Praties* which went for £7,000, followed by £6,000 for William Conor's *The Flute Player*. A record price at auction for the work of Kieran McGowan was made by his *Children on the Pier* whilst another picture by the same artist, *Botanic Gardens,* sold for £3,500 and Frank McKelvey's *Atlantic Drive* found a buyer at £4,700.

Plenty of pictures were on offer in Taylor de Vere's first auction of 1993 held towards mid-March in the National Concert Hall, but overall prices here were rather disappointing, such as the £3,800 paid for a highly unusual Paul Henry; not one of his landscapes but a gloomy deathbed scene called *A Prayer for the Departed.* George Campbell's *Women at the Well* went for £4,400 but Louis Le Brocquy's *Fantail* failed to find a buyer, as did a landscape by Emer O'Rorke Dickey, a Northern Irish artist whose work rarely comes to auction.

A double-sided eighteenth century mahogany writing table, expected to make £2,500-£3,500, actually sold for £4,000 at the auction held a few days later by Mullen of Woodbrook, Co Dublin. However, a Regency rosewood and inlaid chiffonier did well to fetch its lowest estimate of £3,000 here, the same price being achieved by a Georgian mahogany secretaire china cabinet with £2,800 paid for an Edwardian mahogany double corner cupboard and £2,600 for a French gilt overmantel.

At James Adam, an exceptionally handsome pair of Edwardian Sheraton inlaid mahogany display cabinets sold for £9,000, with eight Edwardian Sheraton inlaid mahogany dining chairs making £2,100 and a George III mahogany longcase clock by Thomas Sanderson of Dublin £2,200. Amongst the silver in this sale, a pair of Irish Georgian cast table candlesticks were sold for £1,400, a Victorian four-piece tea and coffee service £1,200 and a George III Irish boat-shaped sugar bowl made in Dublin around 1790, £470.

James Adam was the venue again for one of the Spring's most important painting sales held in early April. The outcome here was decidedly mixed, with a small Jack Yeats *The Canoe* making the best price at what must be considered, for this artist, a relatively modest £20,000. That was the upper estimate for a bold Roderic O'Conor, *Reclining Nude,* but even when even the bottom estimate of £15,000 failed to be reached, the painting was withdrawn and went unsold. Yet another of Lavery's Tangiers views fetched £6,800; a Maurice MacGonigal called *Shanty Man* a respectable £6,700; *Trees in January, Kilmurry* by Mildred Anne Butler commanded £5,200; Maurice Wilks' *Evening on the Moss* £4,600 and James Humbert Craig's *West of Ireland Mountain River Landscape* £4,400, suggesting that the market at the moment preferred to play safe, with landscape a particular favourite.

A new fine art auction house was opened in Limerick during late March by John Dunphy, who proceeded to hold his first sale in the appropriately-named The Auction Rooms, where a Sheraton revival display cabinet did best at £2,500, with a Victorian mahogany dining table fetching £2,200 and a William IV library table £1,400. Ross's conducted a house auction at Jordanstown during April with a Frank McKelvey street scene going for £6,000, followed by an Edgar Burdy canvas called *Cavaliers* which made £5,500. At the same sale, a set of twelve William IV mahogany dining chairs fetched £3,000, a Victorian inlaid mahogany display cabinet £2,100 and a walnut Davenport desk of the same period £1,800. Around the same time, Anderson's sold the contents of Kieran McGowan's studio, with £1,000 being paid for *Rainy Day at the Races*, £900 for *Studying the Form* and £850 for *Donegall Square.*

There were two further house sales in April, the first of them conducted by Mealys of Castlecomer at Cregg House near Carrick-on-Suir in Co Tipperary which realised a total of almost £300,000. An eighteenth-century Irish mahogany sidetable, heavily carved, had carried a pre-sale estimate of £12,000 but eventually went for considerably more: £18,000. Next, at £9,500, came a set of ten Chippendale-style mahogany dining chairs by James Hicks, who was also attributed as responsible for the pair of George III-style mahogany demi-lune sidetables which sold for £3,400. A pair of Georgian demi-lune card tables fetched the much higher figure of £8,250, a set of ten nineteenth-century decorated dining chairs £7,000 and an Irish Georgian mahogany breakfront library bookcases £4,200.

Next came the house sale at Somerville, near Balrath in Co Meath, although in this case, little of what was on offer could claim to be original to the property. Nonetheless, Hamilton Osborne King realised an impressive total of over £350,000 for the day; two Irish mask tables from the mid-eighteenth century, one slightly more ornate than the other, went over their estimates to fetch £17,000 and £16,000 respectively and the other three lots to fetch more than £10,000 were a large, early nineteenth century rectangular dining table on three pillars (£15,000), a pair of Empire bronze and ormolu candelabra (£13,000) and a rosewood sidecabinet (£12,000). Among the rest, a mahogany breakfront bookcase went for £4,000, a pair of Canton baluster vases £5,600, a rosewood crossbanded and brass inlaid sofa table £4,500 and an Irish mahogany serving table £5,500. Clearly, these results show that a successful house sale can still be conducted even when the contents have only recently arrived.

Somerville's sale did not seem to affect prices at the auction held by Sheppard's of Durrow a few days later, when a pair of Edwards & Roberts nineteenth-century mahogany and inlaid display cabinets, estimated to reach £6-7,000 actually made £600 more than the upper figure. Next came a nineteenth-century mahogany breakfront bookcase at £4,000 with a handsome Carlton House desk from the same period sold for £3,400. A Vernis Martin cylinder bureau went for £2,400, a Victorian card table £2,600 and a William IV library table £2,600. And there were more good prices paid two days later at the James Adam salesroom, where a nineteenth-century Dutch marquetry display cabinet sold for £4,400, while a set of four late Victorian Louis XV-style three-light wall scones in gilt plaster and gesso went for £3,600. A Victorian mahogany oval extending diningtable with four extra leaves sold for £2,500 and a set of eight mahogany dining chairs £1,400. These results were sufficiently encouraging to leave salesrooms facing into the Spring with a much greater sense of optimism than had been left for quite a long time.

Robert O'Byrne

INDEX

PICTURE CREDITS

The numbers are those of the pages on which the photographs appear.

(100, 101, 102) Peter Cook; **(108A)** David Davison; **(108B)** Warburg Institute; **(113)** Sally Kerr Davis; **(117, 118B, 119)** Denis Mortell; **(127, 128)** David Davison; **(138)** Figs 9 & 10, courtesy of Christie's; Fig 11 and **(139)** Fig. 12, Pawsey & Payne Ltd., Fine Art Dealers, London; **(146, 148, 149)** John Kellett; **(147A)** The Leger Galleries, London; **(147B)** Michael Dudley; **(151A)** Cynthia O'Connor Gallery; **(160A)** Reproduced by kind permission of the Trustees of the Lady Waterford Hall, Ford, Northumberland; **(160B)** The Royal Library, Windsor Castle. Reproduced by kind permission of Her Majesty the Queen. **(195)** copyright G. A Duncan Photo Archives; **(197 B, C, D, 199)** Reproduced from Charles de Tolnay *Michelangelo, Sculptor, Painter, Architect,* (Princeton and London 1975); **(203)** Denis Mortell; **(205)** Irish Architectural Archive; **(209)** National Library of Ireland; **(211, 212)** Niall Moore; **(220, 221)** British Museum; **(248A)** Missouri Historical Society; **(261)** Christie's, New York.

ACKNOWLEDGEMENTS

For permission to quote from unpublished correspondence on pp. 245-51, we are grateful to the Rare Books and Manuscripts Division of the New York Public Library, Astor, Lenox and Tilden Foundations, for material from the John Quinn Memorial Collection and Jeanne R Foster-William M Murphy Collection.